Knight's Treasury
of 2,000
Illustrations

Knight's
TREASURY
of 2,000
Illustrations

Walter B. Knight

Author and Compiler of
3,000 Illustrations for Christian Service
and *Knight's Master Book of 4,000 New Illustrations*

William B. Eerdmans Publishing Company
Grand Rapids, Michigan

Copyright © 1963 by Wm. B. Eerdmans Publishing Co.
255 Jefferson Ave. SE, Grand Rapids, Mich. 49503

Printed in the United States of America

00 99 98 97 96 95   21 20 19 18 17 16 15

ISBN 0-8028-4067-1

DEDICATION

With love and affection,
I gratefully dedicate this book to my
grandchildren.
May they be Christlike Christians in word and in deed,
always emulating the example of the One who said,
"Suffer little children, and forbid them not, to come unto me:
for of such is the kingdom of heaven" (Matthew 19:14).

PREFACE

In writing and editing this book, *Knight's Treasury of Quotations and Illustrations*, it has been my undeviating effort to make it the most helpful book of its kind for pastors and Christian workers. I personally know their needs, having been a pastor and writer for many years.

I have endeavored to exclude any items which are in my other books — 3,000 *Illustrations for Christian Service* and *Knight's Master Book of New Illustrations* — and include up-to-date items, bereft of archaism, circumlocution and redundancy.

I gratefully acknowledge the help of my wife, Alice M. Knight, whose painstaking effort is reflected throughout the book.

—WALTER B. KNIGHT

Contents

Contents

Knight's Treasury
of 2,000
Illustrations

ASSURANCE

Short Quotes

Said George Gallup, world-famed statistician, "I could prove God statistically! Take the human body alone. The chance that all the functions of the individual would just happen is a statistical monstrosity!"

* * *

I have treated many hundreds of patients. Among those over thirty-five, there has not been one whose problem, in the last resort, was not that of finding a religious outlook on life. —Dr. Carl Jung, psychiatrist, in *Time*

* * *

I lay me down to sleep
　　With little care
Whether my waking find
　　Me here or there!
　　　　　—G. Campbell Morgan

* * *

I believe the promises of God enough to venture an eternity on them.
　　　　　—Isaac Watts

* * *

If you have any certainties, give them to me. I have doubts enough of my own.
　　　　　—Goethe

* * *

God's children do not know what the future holds, but they know the One who holds the future, and in whose hands reposes all power in heaven and in earth: "He is able to subdue all things unto himself" (Phil. 3:21).

* * *

As Adoniram Judson lay in a foul Burmese jail with thirty-two pounds of chains on his ankles, and his feet tied to a bamboo pole, one sneeringly asked, "What about the prospects of converting the heathen?" Instantly Judson replied, "The prospects are just as bright as the unfailing promises of the never-failing God!" —W. B. K.

Who can forget the sad farewells, weepingly spoken by fathers, mothers, wives, and sweethearts as loved ones at railway stations entrained for army camps and the field of battle? Alas, so many of them never returned! Just before a train with hundreds of inductees aboard left a station, one of the inductees, in a clear, full voice, began to sing the quieting, assuring hymn:

What have I to dread, what have I
　　to fear,
Leaning on the everlasting arms;
I have blessed peace with my Lord
　　so near,
Leaning on the everlasting arms!

Are not the lives of God's children "hid with Christ in God"? Is not the encamping angel of the Lord round about them? Are not the unslumbering eyes of God over them? What, then, have we to fear?
　　　　　—Rev. Ralph W. Neighbour

* * *

God cannot be explained, but He can be experienced: "I know whom I have believed."

* * *

"She's sinking!" said a friend at the bedside of a dying Christian who heard what was said. "Not so!" she said. "How can one sink through a Rock? He only is my rock and my salvation!" (Ps. 62:2).

* * *

God makes a promise. Faith believes it. Hope anticipates it. Patience awaits it.

* * *

"Where are you going?" asked an unbeliever of a boy. "I'm going to Sunday school," replied the boy cheerily. "Why are you going to Sunday school?" "To learn about God," said the boy. "How do you know there is a God?" questioned the unbeliever. "Why, Sir,

1

my Sunday-school teacher *knows* Him!"
Do you so present God to others that
they know that He is a living reality
to you? —W. B. K.

• • •

Heaven above is softer blue,
  Earth around is sweeter green,
Something lives in every hue,
  Christless eyes have never seen!
Birds with gladder songs o'erflow,
  Flowers with deeper beauties shine,
Since I know, as now I know,
  I am His and He is mine!
          —Wade Robinson

• • •

The phrase, "Able to save to the uttermost," does not refer to the depths
of sin from which Christ has lifted us,
but rather to the extremity of time to
which Christ can carry us. There is, of
course, no limit either way, but this
verse has to do only with the "completion" of our salvation. It tells us that
Christ is able to carry us through all
temptation, trials, tests and victories,
until He presents us faultless before
the throne at the end of life.
          —*Moody Monthly*

• • •

I know not where His islands lift
  Their fronded palms in air;
I only know I cannot drift
  Beyond His love and care!
          —Whittier

• • •

The more I study science the more I
am impressed with the thought that this
world and universe have a definite design, and a design suggests a designer.
      —Paul Amos Moody, Professor
    of Zoology, University of Vermont

• • •

I don't know about tomorrow,
  I just live from day to day,

I don't borrow from its sunshine,
  For its skies may turn to gray.

Many things about tomorrow
  I don't seem to understand,
But I know Who holds tomorrow,
  And I know Who holds my hand!

• • •

Sir Walter Raleigh went to his unjust sentence of death unafraid, for
he knew that his soul would live on after
the death of his body. So he wrote in
his great poem, "The Soul's Errand":
    Yet stab at thee who will,
    No stab the soul can kill!

• • •

If we live, Christ will be with us: "Lo,
I am with you alway" (Matt. 28:20).
If we die, we will be with Christ: "I
. . . desire to depart, and be with Christ"
(Phil. 1:23). Triumphantly we exclaim, "Whether we live, or die, we are
the Lord's" (Rom. 14:8). —W. B. K.

• • •

Servant of God, well done,
  Thy glorious warfare is past,
The battle is fought, the race is run,
  And thou art crowned at last!

• • •

He is no fool who gives what he cannot keep [his life] for that which he
cannot lose [eternal life]. —Jim Elliot,
    one of five missionaries who were
    martyred by Auca Indians

• • •

To be assured of our salvation is no
arrogant stoutness. It is faith. It is
devotion. It is not presumption. It is
God's promise. —Augustine

• • •

Whichever way the wind doth blow,
Some soul is glad to have it so;
Then blow it east, or blow it west,
The wind that blows, that wind is best.

Illustrations

I Know Whom I Have Believed!

One day as I visited the patients in
the Chicago Home for the Incurables, I
came alongside the bed of an aged Methodist minister. He was totally blind.
Before leaving him, I prayed. In my
prayer I thanked God that we could

confidently say, "I know whom I have
believed." At the close of the prayer,
the aged minister said, "I'm glad that
you didn't use the preposition 'in' in
the verse you quoted. Many do. Isn't
it wonderful to know that nothing comes
between us and Him, 'whom I have believed'!" —W. B. K.

This Will Be Enough!

Isadore Sofer is the son of a Hebrew Christian. Little Isadore was given a part to recite on a children's program — the twenty-third Psalm. As he faced a large congregation, he got frightened. He was a courageous boy, however, and he began to recite: "The Lord is my shepherd; I shall not want." Here he stopped. He tried to recall the next verse, but couldn't. After an embarrassing moment, he said, "This will be enough!"

What a precious spiritual lesson! When the Lord is our Shepherd, what else could we want?

—Rev. Moses Gitlin

* * *

I Know Him Personally

One summer I spent some time at Mount Robson, British Columbia, where I camped and climbed with fellow mountaineers of the Alpine Club of Canada. On a rainy day a group of us were drinking tea in a tent, when a discussion arose about religion. A young scientist turned to me with a patronizing air and said, "But you don't really believe, do you, that Jesus is the Son of God?" I replied, "Yes, I do." "But how can you prove it?" he said. "How do you know it is true?" I shall never forget what followed. I simply did what any other convinced man would have done: I looked him straight in the eye and said: "How do I know that Jesus is the Son of God? I know it, *because I know Him personally.*" For at least a half minute our eyes locked. Then he turned away. The argument was over. When Christ is really our life, we know Him with an immediacy of personal knowledge that is unmistakable.

—*Christianity Today*

* * *

My Times Are in His Hands

My times are in that mighty Hand
    That formed the earth, the moon
        and stars;
That measured oceans, heaven spanned,
    And for the sea set doors and bars.

Why should I fear what man can do,
    When in that Hand I rest secure?
In life, or death, 'twill bear me through
    There I have shelter, safe and sure.

My times are in my Father's Hand
    How could I wish or ask for more?
For He who has my pathway planned,
    Will guide me till my journey's o'er.

My times are in my Saviour's Hand,
    Nail-pierced upon the cross for me,
And He will lead me to that land,
    Where I with Him shall ever be.

—Margaret K. Fraser

* * *

Hitherto

Hitherto Thy hand hath led me —
    Oh, how sweet to feel Thy care;
When the way is dark and dreary,
    Love's enduring strength is there.

Hitherto Thy love hath blest me —
    Oh, what changeless love divine!
When my heart was weak and faithless,
    Thou didst bind it fast to Thine.

Hitherto Thy Word hath fed me —
    And my soul is satisfied;
Thou wilt be forever with me,
    Daily manna to provide.

—*Selected*

* * *

Get on with the Operation!

A Scottish soldier was badly wounded. A Christian surgeon said to him, "I must operate right away. I think I ought to tell you that you have one chance in a hundred to come through the operation. Have you anything to say?" The brave lad said, "No, doctor, get on with the operation! All is well with my soul. Whichever side I come out on, there will be a welcome for me. If I come through the operation, Mother will welcome me. If I don't, Jesus will welcome me!" —W. B. K.

* * *

Kept!

A man whose heart had been deeply touched by the death of a friend, expressed a desire to begin the Christian life, and he told the minister so.

"There's just one thing makes me hesitate," he added. "I'm afraid I can't hold out. You know, where I work there are some pretty rough fellows. I don't believe there's a real Christian in the crowd."

For answer the minister reached down

and lifted a flower from the vase on the table.

"Do you see this flower, Arthur?" he asked. "It grew right in the mud and slime of a marsh. Yet see how clean and spotless it is. That's because God kept it. And He can keep you, too!"

—*Prairie Overcomer*

* * *

God Manifested in His Works

(Romans 1:20)

Is there a God? Yon rising sun
In answer meet replies,
Writes it in flame upon the earth,
Proclaims it round the skies.

Is there a God? Hark! from on high
His thunder shakes the poles;
I hear His voice in every wind,
In every wave that rolls.

Is there a God? With sacred fear
I upward turn my eyes;
"There is," each glitt'ring lamp of
light —
"There is," my soul replies.

If such convictions to my mind
His works aloud impart,
Oh, let the wisdom of His Word
Inscribe them on my heart.

—*Selected*

* * *

I Will Go to God's Village

A missionary visited a Pygmy village in Africa. The missionary recognized a man to whom he had previously given the gospel. "Have you received God's Word into your heart?" asked the missionary. "Yes I have, and my people, too, have received it. Every night we meet for prayer. We sing our songs, 'Jesus Loves Me,' and 'What Can Wash Away My Sins?' Then we ask God to protect us through the night!"

"That's fine," the missionary said, then asked, "If you should suddenly die, would you go to heaven?" The Pygmy stood at attention. He saluted smartly and replied, "When I die, I will go to God's village. I will salute Him and say, 'Greetings, God, I am come to my house in Your village!' When God asks me what right I have to enter, I will tell Him that His Son, Jesus Christ, died for me and washed my heart clean

in His blood. Then He will say to me, 'Enter, your house is waiting for you!' "

—W. B. K.

* * *

The Mystic Union

A dear old saint whom I knew in former years bore the name of Peter. Everyone called him Pete. One day, talking with me, he said: "If God should take me to the very mouth of hell and say to me, 'In you go, Pete; here's where you belong,' I should say to Him, 'That is true, Lord. I do belong here. But if You make me go to hell, Your dear Son Jesus Christ must go with me. He and I are one, and You cannot separate us any more.' " This is called in theology by the not very clear title, "the mystic union." It is of first importance, both to the Atonement and to the new moral life of the Christian. —*Moody Monthly*

* * *

That's Enough!

A pastor in Norfolk, Virginia, phoned the editor of religious news for a paper and gave him the topic for his Sunday morning's sermon, "The Lord Is My Shepherd." The editor asked, "Is that all?" The pastor replied, "That's enough." The editor, thinking that the words were a part of his subject, announced the pastor's topic as follows: "The Lord Is My Shepherd. That's Enough." To know the Lord as our protector and provider is enough to allay all fears and assuage all our sorrows. —W. B. K.

* * *

God's Unchanging Word

For feelings come and feelings go,
And feelings are deceiving;
My warrant is the Word of God,
Naught else is worth believing.

Though all my heart should feel con
demned
For want of some sweet token,
There is One greater than my heart
Whose Word cannot be broken.

I'll trust in God's unchanging Word
Till soul and body sever;
For, though all things shall pass away,
His Word shall stand forever.

—Martin Luther

I Die Without Hatred!

"In a little while, at five o'clock, it is going to happen; and that is not so terrible. On the contrary, it is beautiful to be in God's strength. God has told us that He will not forsake us if only we pray to Him for support. I feel so strongly my nearness to God that I am fully prepared to die. I have confessed all my sins to Him and have become very quiet. Therefore do not mourn, but trust in God and pray for strength. . . . Give me a firm handshake. God's will be done. . . . Greet everybody for the four of us. . . . We are courageous. They can take only our bodies. Our souls are in God's hands. . . . May God bless you all. . . . Have no hate. I die without hatred. God rules everything. Kees."

> —Written by a Dutch patriot just before his execution by a Nazi firing squad.

* * *

There Is No Hell Where Jesus Is!

A bright Negro lad attended a Sunday school conducted by a missionary. The lad heard the wondrous story of Jesus and His love for all mankind. "How wonderful are the words I hear!" said the boy to himself. He trusted in Jesus as his own personal Saviour. How happy he was!

Later, he became ill. When the missionary came to see him, he said, "I am very happy! I hope I shall not get well again!" "Why not?" asked the missionary in astonishment. The boy replied, "Because I would like to go to heaven where I shall see Jesus and be with Him always!" To test the reality of the boy's faith the missionary asked, "What would you do if Jesus were not in heaven?" "Then I would follow Him," said the boy. "What if Jesus went to hell? What would you do then?" With an intelligent look and happy smile on his face the boy said, "Ah, Missionary, there is no hell where Jesus is!"

—W. B. K.

* * *

I'll See You All Again!

Three Doolittle flyers were shot down over Japan during World War II. They were captured and sentenced to death. Before his death, one of them wrote a letter to his loved ones. It said in part: "Don't let this get you down. Just remember God will make everything right. I'll see you all again in the hereafter. My faith in God is complete. I am unafraid!" —W. B. K.

* * *

The Upward Tug and Pull

A boy was flying a kite. It flew so high that it could not be seen. Yet the boy knew it was aloft by the tug and pull of the string.

"How do you know your kite is still up, my boy?" asked a passerby. "I can't see it." Said the boy, "Hold this string! You'll know it is up yonder by the tug and the pull of the string!"

How do we know that God is over all and above all, and that His children are the objects of His tender care and unfailing mercy? By the upward tug and pull of our heart strings we are enabled to endure "as seeing him who is invisible," the affirmation of our hearts being, "Whom having not seen, [we] love: in whom, though now [we] see him not, yet believing, [we] rejoice with joy unspeakable and full of glory" (I Peter 1:8).

—Told by Rev. Gordon E. Markey

ATHEISM

Short Quotes

If God did not exist, it would be necessary to invent Him. —Voltaire

* * *

The world embarrasses me, and I cannot think that this watch exists and has no watchmaker. —Voltaire

In the evolutionary pattern of thought there is no longer need or room for supernatural beings capable of affecting the course of events.

—Sir Julian Huxley,
British Biologist

Atheism has never founded empires, established principles, or changed the world's heart. The great doers in history have always been men of faith.
—E. H. Chapin

* * *

Said the famed criminal lawyer and confessed atheist, Clarence Darrow, "My colleagues say that I'm a success. Many honors have come my way, but in the Bible is a sentence which expresses the way I feel about my life. That sentence is this: 'We have toiled all night, and have taken nothing.'"
—W. B. K.

* * *

The task of Christianity is not to argue with Islam, Hinduism, or Buddhism, but with materialism, secularism, naturalism. It is no longer which prophet, book revelation, rite, or church is to be trusted. This is why we must trade the word "missionary" and accept 'fraternal worker" in its stead!
—Dr. W. E. Hocking

* * *

An associate pastor of a large eastern church brazenly asked: "Since when does orthodoxy, church membership, or anything else require that we believe in the virgin birth, bodily resurrection, the — of all things — substitutionary atonement of Jesus Christ?"
—*Christianity Today*

* * *

The modernistic movement, adjusting itself to a man-centered culture, has

. . . watered down the thought of the Divine, and, may we be forgiven for this, left souls standing like the ancient Athenians — before an altar to an unknown god. —Harry Emerson Fosdick

* * *

I believe you will find in all histories that no nation that did not contemplate this wonderful universe with an awe-stricken and reverential belief that there was a great unknown, omnipotent, and all-wise and all-just Being superintending all men in it and all interest in it, ever came to very much, nor did any man either who forgot that.
—Thomas Carlyle

* * *

The Oxford Dictionary defines secularism thus: "The doctrine that morality should be based solely on regard to the well-being of mankind in the present life, to the exclusion of all considerations drawn from belief in God or in a future state."

* * *

I fear God, and next to God I chiefly fear him who fears Him not.
—Saadi, Persian Poet

* * *

Let us not deceive ourselves. Man is governed by nothing but his conception of the future. Any nation which *en masse* gives up all faith in what lies beyond the grave will become utterly degraded. —Renan, French Historian, in *The History of the People of Israel*

Illustrations

No Atheists in Foxholes

His name was Kees Jonker, a Dutch entomologist who was an outspoken atheist. One night he got caught in quicksand in the Ogowe River area of the Cameroons and lay spread-eagled on his back for half an hour while I worked to get him out. One of the essentials in such situations is that the victim lie quietly, not even speaking, until the rescuer can get support under him. Even the effort of whispering causes the shoulders to sink more rapidly.

Jonker mumbled and talked during most of the half hour. I finally dragged

him to safety after a struggle so strenuous that my ears and nose bled. After my pounding heart had quieted so I could speak, I said to him:

"If you had not talked so much, Jonker, I would have had an easier time."

"Sorry," he said, "I wasn't talking, I *was praying*." —Alexander Lake, in *You Need Never Walk Alone*

* * *

Going, But Not Together

The Rev. Dr. Witherspoon, formerly president of Princeton College, was once on board a packet ship where, among other passengers, was a professed atheist who said he did not believe in a God and a future state, not he! By-and-by there came a terrible storm; and the prospect was that all would go to the bottom. There was much fear and consternation on board; but no one was so horribly frightened as the atheist. In his extremity he sought out the clergyman. He found him in the cabin, calm and collected; and thus he addressed him: "Oh, Mr. Witherspoon! We're all going down! Don't you think we are, Doctor?" Dr. Witherspoon turned on him a look of most provoking coolness, and replied in broad Scotch: "Nae doot, nae doot, mon, we're a ganging; but you and I dinna gang the same way."

—*Christian Digest*

. . .

Whence the Cloud?

A professor at a large university made no secret of the fact that he was an agnostic. Moreover, he boasted of his philosophy whenever opportunity to do so came his way.

He would tell his students, "If you don't throw aside your faith in God, and act in your own knowledge and strength, you'll not get very far in this world."

One day, during a class, the matter of "rain-making" entered the discussion, so the professor inquired hypothetically: "What help was faith in God during the recent drought? A lot of farmers got down on their knees and asked God for rain. What did they get in answer to their prayers? The Dust Bowl! Do you know what they should have done? They should have sought help from science. Send a man up in a plane, drop some chemicals on a cloud, and you get rain. No need of God there! Any questions?"

"Yes, I have a question," replied one of the students. "Who furnishes the cloud, if not God?" —*The Pilgrim*

. . .

Your Argument Is Unanswerable!

An atheistic scientist was incurably ill. A Christian friend visited him and said, "You realize that you will not recover, don't you?" Anticipating that the question was designed to elicit a discussion of religion, the scientist said, "But I don't believe in God, or a hereafter."

"You haven't long to live," continued the friend, "and you want life above everything else, don't you, Bill?" "Above everything else," quietly replied the scientist.

Then the Christian spoke of a physiological law in God's creation. "You are a biologist, Bill, and as you know the lion was made to eat flesh, not straw. The cow was made to eat hay, not flesh. The fins of fish indicate that water is the medium of its being. The wings of the birds indicate that the air is its predetermined element. Do you think that the Creator has capriciously implanted in man, who stands at the acme of His creation, soul-yearnings for which He has made no satisfying provision? Your insatiable yearning for life is indicative of the fact that God has given to you an immortal soul which can know no rest until it rests in Him, finding satisfaction in the eternal God."

The scientist, who through the years had sought for biological truth, said, "You have got me! I confess that your argument is unanswerable."

It is hoped that the newly enlightened scientist turned in faith to the One who said, "I am come that they might have life, and that they might have it more abundantly" (John 10:10b); "And this is life eternal, that they might know thee the only true God, and Jesus Christ, whom thou hast sent" (John 17:3).

—Told by Dr. Merrill C. Tenney

. . .

What About the Fragments?

A teacher was telling her class of the time when the Lord Jesus fed the multitude with five loaves and two fishes. She said, "And of course you will understand, children, that it does not mean that Jesus actually fed all those thousands with a few loaves and fishes. That would have been impossible. It just means that He so fed the people with His teaching that they lost all sense of bodily hunger, and went home satisfied."

But an inquiring girl put this question, "But, Miss —, what was it that filled the twelve baskets of fragments left over?" —*Christian Herald*

Atheist Speaks at Own Funeral

A Denver atheist, O. O. Whitenack, made a recording of the things he wanted said at his funeral. He died recently, and the record was played. His voice was heard to say, "This is my funeral. I have the utmost contempt for this theological nonsense. The Bible and religion have done nothing but spread ignorance and impede the progress of the human race." He continued his attack on religion, the Bible, and Christians. He closed with the simple words, "That's all."

But that wasn't all: "It is appointed unto men once to die, but after this the judgment" (Heb. 9:27).

—*Gospel Herald*

God's Footprints

Many years ago an atheistic French scientist was crossing the Sahara Desert with an Arab guide. The Arab believed in God and prayer. When he was uncertain of the way, he would kneel and ask God for guidance. This annoyed the scientist. Contemptuously he asked, "How do you know there is a God?" Solemnly the Arab asked, "How do I know that a man and not a camel passed by our tent last night in the darkness?" "Why, by his footprints in the sand," said the atheist. "I see God's footprints in the things He has created — the sun, moon and stars. They proclaim His power and greatness! These things just didn't happen!" said the Arab. —W. B. K.

Turning in Fright to God

Usually those who call on God only because of extreme danger turn from God when the danger is past, despite fervid promises made to God during the danger.

A blatant, blasphemous unbeliever was drifting rapidly in a boat down a river in the Canadian backwoods toward his destruction in the rapids. In despair he cried, "O God, save me and I will serve You!"

A missionary, who was an excellent swimmer, heard his frantic cry. He plunged into the turgid waters, swam out to the boat, and brought it and its occupant to shore.

Some days later the missionary saw a group of people gathered around the man whom he had rescued. He was ridiculing the Bible, blaspheming God, and denying that there is either a heaven or a hell. —W. B. K.

Spiritually Blind

A minister faithfully proclaimed the gospel in an open-air meeting in Glasgow. At the conclusion of his message, an unbeliever stepped from the crowd and said: "I don't believe what the minister said. I don't believe in heaven or hell. I don't believe in God or Christ. I haven't seen them."

Then a man, wearing dark glasses, came forward and said: "You say there is a river near this place — the River Clyde. There is no such thing. You say there are people standing here, but it cannot be true. I haven't seen them — I was born blind! Only a blind man could say what I have said. You are spiritually blind and cannot see. The Bible says of you, 'But the natural man receiveth not the things of the Spirit of God: for they are foolishness unto him: neither can he know them, because they are spiritually discerned'" (I Cor. 2:14). —W. B. K.

Man Is Incurably Religious

In reality, there is no such thing as an atheist. Let some sudden danger overtake the so-called atheist, and almost invariably he ejaculates, "O God!" Robert Ingersoll professed to be an atheist. He heaped ridicule upon the Bible and the God of the Bible. When he came down to death, however, his soul began to freeze with terror. In his fright he cried out, "O God, if there be a God, have mercy on my soul, if I have a soul!" In the clutches of the grim reaper, death, he seemed to realize that when man ceases to breathe, he does not cease to exist. The supremest tragedy of life is to enter death without God, and go into a Christless hereafter. —W. B. K.

As Old As Adam

"After 250,000 years of evolving by trial and error, man now has the unprecedented power to begin consciously and willfully directing the course of his own future evolution. He can with scientific tools available to some extent take over the reigns of his own destiny and make himself what he wants to be through artificial selection rather than leave it to natural selection and chance," said Arthur J. Snider, *Daily News* science writer.

This highfaluting assertion may sound up-to-date. It is as old as Adam, however. Did not Satan say to our first parents: "Ye shall be as gods"?
—*The Watchman-Examiner*

* * *

Have You Ever Seen a Pain?

An unbelieving doctor said to a minister, "I believe only in what my five senses reveal to me. I have never seen,

heard, tasted, smelled or felt a soul. That's why I don't believe in the existence of a soul."

Said the minister, "You have never seen, heard, tasted, or smelled a pain, but you have felt a pain."

"That is true," said the doctor. "I have felt a pain and I have treated thousands of people who have."

Then the minister continued: "I have not seen, heard, tasted, or smelled a soul, but there have been times without count that I have *felt* a soul, as I have listened to the music of the masters, and looked upon a setting sun or an autumnal forest, and thought upon the deeds of heroism of patriots, or the fortitude and sacrifice of some mother or father, or of the flawless, selfless life and vicarious death of the Saviour for the sin of the world!" —W. B. K.

BIBLE

Short Quotes

A minister visited a poor woman in a hospital in Surrey, England. It was during World War II. She had been bombed out of her home and was badly injured. She said, "I've lost everything — husband, home and earthly possessions!" After a moment's pause, she said, "I've lied! I have the Lord and His Word to begin my new home with. These are treasures beyond compare!"
—W. B. K.

* * *

Every American military plane that flies over water carries a collapsible boat which contains food rations and a copy of the Bible in a waterproof package. "We know that spiritual equipment can be as important as food and drink in saving lives," say Army officers.
—*Treasures*

* * *

There's a big difference between the books that men make and the Book that makes men. —*In a Nutshell*

* * *

You who like to play at Bible,
Dip and dabble here and there

Just before you kneel, aweary,
And yawn through a hurried prayer;
You who treat the Crown of Writings
As you treat no other book —
Just a paragraph disjointed,
Just a crude, important look, —
Try a worthier procedure,
Try a broad and steady view.
You will kneel in very rapture
When you read the Bible through.
—Amos R. Wells

* * *

Is it too late to bring the old-time Bible stand down from the attic or up from the cellar? Is it too late to give it the choice spot it once enjoyed in many homes? While 4/5ths of adult Americans said they believed the Bible to be the revealed Word of God, only 53 per cent could identify the four gospels! —Dan W. Dodson, in *The Wesleyan Methodist*

* * *

In five years from now there will not be a Bible in America. I have gone through the Bible with an axe and cut down all its trees. —Tom Paine

The Bible is always a new book to those best acquainted with it.

* * *

Other books were given for our information. The Bible was given for our transformation. —W. B. K.

* * *

Men do not reject the Bible because it contradicts itself, but because it contradicts them.

* * *

The King James Version outsells the Revised Standard Version by about eight to one, a NCC check revealed.

—*Christianity Today*

* * *

There is only one great issue and that is to get the truths of the Bible into the hearts of the people.

—William Gladstone

* * *

Every time a little boy went to a playmate's house, he found the friend's grandmother deeply engrossed in reading her Bible. Finally his curiosity got the better of him. "Why do you suppose your grandmother reads the Bible so much?" he asked. "I'm not sure," said his friend, "but I think it's because she's cramming for her finals."

—Carl T. Schuneman

* * *

The best repository for the Bible is a warm, glowing, grateful heart: "His word was in mine heart as a burning fire shut up in my bones" (Jer. 20:9).

—W. B. K.

* * *

Of the hundreds of thousands of artifacts found by the archaeologists, not one has ever been discovered that contradicts or denies one word, phrase, clause, or sentence of the Bible, but always confirms and verifies the facts of the Biblical record.

—Dr. J. O. Kinnaman

* * *

Many things in the Bible I cannot understand; many things in the Bible I only think I understand; but there are many things in the Bible I cannot *mis*understand. —*Moody Monthly*

All I have written, whatever greatness there has been in any thought of mine, whatever I have done in my life, has simply been due to the fact that, when I was a child, my mother daily read with me a part of the Bible, and daily made me learn a part of it by heart. —John Ruskin

* * *

He who wrests the Scriptures will never find rest in them.

* * *

One evidence of the value of the Bible is the character of those who oppose it.

* * *

It is impossible mentally and socially to enslave a Bible-reading people. The principles of the Bible are the groundwork of human freedom.

—Horace Greeley

* * *

It is my confident hope that my subjects may never cease to cherish their noble inheritance in the English Bible which is the first of national treasures. Its spiritual significance is the most valuable thing the world affords.

—King George V

* * *

The weakest and unworthiest of human instrumentalities can sow the seed, God's Word. The life is not in the sower, but in the seed. —W. B. K.

* * *

The New Testament is *concealed* in the Old; the Old Testament is *revealed* in the New. —W. B. K.

* * *

Take a text out of its context and you often have a pretext. —W. B. K.

* * *

When the Bible says, "Thou shalt," or, "Thou shalt not," it is only saying, "Do thyself no harm." —W. B. K.

* * *

An old lady glowingly said in a testimony meeting, "I always got a lot of help out of the Bible verse which says, 'Grin and bear it'!"

* * *

John Wesley read and reread the Bible through many times. In his old age he said, "I am a *homo unius libri*" — a man of one book.

Defend the Bible? I would as soon defend a lion! —Spurgeon

* * *

What glory gilds the sacred page,
Majestic like the sun!
It gives a light to ev'ry age,
It gives, but borrows none.

—Cowper

* * *

I thoroughly believe in a university course for both men and women, but I believe a knowledge of the Bible without a college course is more valuable than a college course without the Bible.
—Dr. Wm. Lyon Phelps,
Professor, Yale University

* * *

Misquotes are sometimes m o r e searching than accurate quotes. "Re-Bible us again," prayed a native Indian as he pleaded for a spiritual awakening. Must we not be "re-Bibled" before we can be revived? —W. B. K.

* * *

"Beware of that man!" exclaimed one Moslem to another. "He distributes the Scriptures. He is far worse than the preacher who speaks and walks away. That man leaves a Book that can convert you to Christianity!"

* * *

Believe God's Word more than you believe your own feelings and experiences. Your Rock is Christ, and it is not the Rock which ebbs and flows, but your sea. —Samuel Rutherford

* * *

Wherever the spade has dug; wherever it has turned over an ancient civilization; wherever it has brought to light some ancient monument; wherever it has unearthed anything that has to do with a name, an event, or a place of the Bible, it has vindicated the Bible.
—Dr. Harold John Ockenga

* * *

An African woman was asked if she enjoyed reading her new Bible. She replied, "Sir, I am not reading this Book. The Book is reading me!"
—*Bible Society Record*

* * *

When Edward VI was crowned King of England, three swords were placed before him as tokens of his power. Said the king: "Bring another sword — 'the sword of the Spirit, which is the Word of God!' I need this sword more than any other to overcome evil!"

* * *

The Bible contains many thousands of promises. It is God's book of signed checks. —F. B. Meyer

* * *

The Bible has been the Magna Charta of the poor and oppressed. Down to modern times no state has had a constitution in which the interests of the people are so largely taken into account as in the Bible —Thomas Henry Huxley,
English scientist

* * *

The same 14 chemical elements which go to make up the body of man are those which compose the dust of the earth.
"And the Lord God formed man of the dust of the earth" (Gen. 2:7).
—Dr. E. E. Slossen, Chemist

* * *

I know nothing about the origin of man except what I am told in the Scriptures that God created him. I do not know anything more than that and I do not know anybody who does.
—Sir William Dawson,
Canadian geologist

* * *

The Book, the Bible, more than any other single piece of literature in the history of mankind, is an everlasting wellspring of inspiration, a source of hope and a promise of reward in the hereafter for faith and charity exercised during mortal existence," said Freeman Gosden and Charles Correll, known to millions as Amos 'n Andy.

* * *

There are four things that we ought to do with the Word of God — admit it as the Word of God, commit it to our hearts and minds, submit to it, and transmit it to the world.
—Bishop Wilberforce

* * *

Most people are bothered by those passages in Scripture which they cannot understand. The Scripture which troubles me most is the Scripture I do understand. —Mark Twain

* * *

Spurred by reason and fear of today's headlines, large numbers of Americans are rediscovering an old truth — that man cannot live by bread alone. —*Life*

* * *

A colporteur entered a village in Ceylon. There he sold a copy of the book of Proverbs to a notoriously dishonest man who took bribes and bore false witness in the courts. The next day, the man returned it to the colporteur and said, "Take back this book. It tells against me, and reproves everyone who is in the wrong path. Take it, and give me back my money!" —W. B. K.

* * *

There is nothing in the Bible that benefits you unless it is transmuted into life, unless it becomes a part of yourself, just like your food. Unless you assimilate it and it becomes body, bone and muscle, it does you no good.
—Henry G. Weston

* * *

It was the Bible that gave fire and nobleness to England's language; it was the Bible that turned a dead oppression into a living church; it was the Bible that put to flight the nightmare of ignorance before the rosy dawn of progress. . . . You might as well quench the sun, and suppose that the world can get along without light, as to think that men or that nations can do without God. . . . The world has no other trumpet of peace save Holy Scripture for souls at war; no other weapon to slay terrible passions; no other teachings to quench the heart's raging fires. —F. W. Farrar

* * *

An unbeliever said to a minister: "It is quite impossible nowadays to believe in the teaching of any book by an author whose authority is unknown." Asked the minister: "Is the author of the multiplication table known?" "No," answered the skeptic. "I assume logically then that you do not believe in the multiplication table. Right?" "Of course, I believe in it. It works well." Said the minister: "So does the Bible."
—Told by Dr. Pentecost

The Bible's almost incredibly correct historical memory has been validated many times by archaeological discoveries. No discovery has ever controverted a Biblical reference.
—Dr. Nelson Glueck, Jewish archaeologist, in his book *Rivers in the Desert*

* * *

My experience as a teacher in the Bible department of a denominational college is leading me to believe that we have on our hands a generation of Biblical illiterates. This is shocking in itself. But more shocking is the fact that most of these illiterates have been regular attendants at Sunday school for the major part of their lives.
—Joseph M. Hopkins, Professor of Bible and Philosophy, Westminster College, New Wilmington, Pa.

* * *

A missionary worked among some backward tribes in the jungles of Brazil. The natives often watched him read his mail. They stared at the pieces of paper from which he read. They had never seen paper or writing before. One day he showed them his Bible. "When I read this Book, I receive news from God, my heavenly Father," he said. From that time on, the natives would ask him: "What news is there today from the heavenly Father?" The Bible is God's letter to us. —W. B. K.

* * *

Out of the Cold Harbor slaughter emerged Carter E. Prince of the 4th Maine Volunteers. A bullet hit his suspender buckle and carried it through the New Testament in the pocket of his blouse. Pushed by the bullet, the buckle went through all the chapters between Revelation and St. Mark and came to rest at Mark 12:36, where is recorded the saying of the Lord: "Sit thou on my right hand, till I make thine enemies thy footstool."
—Carl Sandburg, in *Guideposts*

* * *

"Every plowboy should know the Scriptures," said William Tyndale who printed the first English New Testament in 1525, and with the help of friends smuggled thousands of copies of it into England. Later he was arrested and held in solitary confinement in a cold, dark prison in Vilvorde, Belgium. He was finally choked to death and his body burned.

William Tyndale gave his life to give us our Bible. His last words were: "O Lord, open Thou the King of England's eyes!"

At what price has this wondrous treasure come to us! —K. B. K.

* * *

A little boy saw his father use a square to see if the board he was planing was straight. "Why are you so careful, Daddy?" asked the boy. "We can't guess in carpenter work," his dad said. "You have to be just right. People guess at too many things. God does not like that way of living." "I guess there are no squares for living by," said the boy. "Yes, there are squares to live by, and you will find them in the Bible. Test all that you do by them, and you will go straight in life, my boy."
—W. B. K.

* * *

A liberal minister, with great show of learning, exerted himself in explaining away certain passages of the Bible, saying with finality that God didn't mean what the passages obviously said. An aged saint asked him at the close of his lecture, "If God didn't mean what He said, why didn't He say what He meant?" The unbeliever had no answer to that. —W. B. K.

* * *

Scatter the Bible without stint. Strew the sacred pages "thick as the leaves of Vallombrosa." Put it in the hand of prince and peasant. Give it to the skeptical philosopher and to the unsophisticated child: "In the morning sow thy seed, and in the evening withhold not thy hand." Spread the Scriptures till they are as universal as the light; as all-pervading as the air; as all-refreshing as the dew! —Spurgeon

* * *

Modernism has failed, because the world has forgotten the Bible, and has thereby lost a treasure.
—Dr. S. Parks Cadman

Today we face this challenge: the whole Bible is available in the languages of 90 per cent of the world's population. Another 5 per cent has some portion of the Bible. The task we face now is supplying the necessary Bible study helps as quickly as possible. The world is gradually becoming more and more literate. It is said that 100 people learn to read every minute, a million a week, and 52 million a year.
—Dr. Eugere Nida, Secretary for Translations, American Bible Society

* * *

Sir Monier Williams, possibly the greatest authority on the so-called sacred books of the East — the Koran, the Hindu Vedas, the Buddhist Tripitaka, and the Zend Avesta — said: "They all begin with some flashes of true light, and end in utter darkness. . . . There is a gulf between the Bible and the so-called sacred books of the East which severs the one from the other utterly, hopelessly and forever, a veritable gulf which cannot be bridged over by any science of religious thought!"

* * *

The real influence of the Bible cannot be measured. It is reckoned only in terms of hearts that have been lifted up, decisions that have been changed, and men and women who, in response to its impervious demands, have done justice and loved kindness and walked humbly with God. —J. Carter Swaim

* * *

A brilliant young man, who was working for his doctorate, said to me, "I have taught in Sunday school. I consider myself a person of average intelligence, but I would flunk on a simple Bible examination!"
—Dr. Henrietta Mears

* * *

Some years ago, British and American archaeologists came upon a ten-foot layer of mud far beneath the surface of the earth. Underneath the layer they discovered artifacts from the Stone Age. Excitedly the scientists flashed a message to the world: "We have found evidences of the Flood!" Tests in surrounding areas showed that the layer of clay was the residue of a vast, catastrophic deluge that had, circa 4000 B.C., covered the river plains of southern Mesopotamia, the center of the known world at that time. —W. B. K.

* * *

The Bible is immensely popular. Last year, 1960, the various members of the United Bible Societies distributed more than 29,500,000 copies of Scripture. To this figure must be added the undisclosed circulation from all the great commercial publishing houses.
—Rev. Laton E. Holmgren, D.D.

* * *

There is nothing in science that reached the origin of anything at all. We must accept the words of the Bible: "In the beginning, God created the heaven and the earth."
—Lord Kelvin, noted British scientist

* * *

When you're gathering up material
For that sermon you will preach;
Don't you know you really have it
All combined within your reach?
Where in clippings, books or papers,
Commentaries, could you look,
And find answers for life's problems?
Why not just "stay in the Book"?

Wherever the Bible has gone, civilization has taken root, and dehumanizing, degrading customs have disappeared. Two sailors swam from their wrecked ship to a cannibal island in the South Pacific. "We will probably end in the pot!" said one. Going inland in search for food, the two men cautiously entered a hut whose occupant was out. Seeing a Bible on a table, one exclaimed: "We're all right! We are safe!" —W. B. K.

* * *

Some insects subsist on the nectar of flowers. The bee and the butterfly are among them. The latter darts down here and there, and sips only the external nectar. Then off it flies to other readily available sap. How different it is with the bee. If the flower has depth, the bee goes to its bottom. If the flower is closed, the bee exerts itself and explores its innermost recesses. Ere long, winter comes. The butterfly dies in October. The bee is safe in its hive, "midst the fragrant nectar it acquired with diligence."

In reference to God's Word, do not skim over it superficially, but go to its depths. —W. B. K.

Illustrations

Proving that Luke Was Right

Some years ago a little group of freethinkers in Scotland decided on a plan whereby they might show up the inaccuracies of Scripture and so cause the people to realize, as they put it, that the Bible was not really the Word of God. One member was given the task of going to Asia Minor and southern Europe and the islands of the Mediterranean, and visiting all the places mentioned by Luke in connection with Paul's journeys. It was hoped that he would be able to unearth so much information as would make evident the falsity of Luke's record, that many who had pinned their faith to the book of Acts as a part of God's inspired Word would have to give it up. The young man chosen was Sir William Ramsay.

He investigated very carefully, and after the most minute examinations concluded that Luke was absolutely accurate in every particular; and he himself, once a freethinker, became a Christian, and has written some splendid books in defense of the Word of God.
—Dr. H. A. Ironside

* * *

Quick and Powerful!

A man who had been a pickpocket stood up in a meeting and said, "I was a pickpocket. One day, on a busy street, I saw a man whose hip pocket bulged. I said, 'There is a fat purse in that pocket!' I slipped out the purse. I didn't look at it until I got home. When I took it from my pocket, I saw that it was a New Testament. In disgust, I threw it on the floor. After a while, however, I picked it up. I began to read it. It told me that I was a sinner. It told me of Jesus, the sinner's Friend. I asked Jesus to come into my heart, and clean up my life. He did that. Now I find my greatest joy in telling others about Him!" —W. B. K.

* * *

The Greatest Missionary

There are still 2,000 dialects spoken by native peoples in all parts of the world that do not have a written language. We have translated the Bible into 132 new dialects, and have trained more than 3,000 persons to do this kind of work. Today we could use at least 7,000 more persons to work on the languages that still remain. *The greatest missionary is one that never gets sick, never needs a furlough, is never considered a foreigner, lives constantly with the people, and is the means of making other missionaries unnecessary — the Bible in the language of the people!"*

　　　　　—Dr. W. Cameron Townsend,
　　　　　Director of the Wycliffe Bible
　　　　　Translators

* * *

Bible Saves Life!

"I bought a rifle today," said a boy to a missionary in the Kentucky mountains, "and I am going to kill the man who killed my father. I swore I would do it on the day of my father's funeral!" Pleaded the missionary, "But, my boy, if you do that terrible thing, you will have to flee from home. When caught, you will go to prison or be hanged! Do you know what God's Word says about it?" The boy answered, "We ain't got no Bible at our house." The missionary talked earnestly to the boy about the Lord Jesus, and forgiveness. The boy began to weep. The missionary took a Bible from his bag, wrote his name in it and gave it to him. The boy began to read the Bible. Shortly thereafter, he made a public confession of his faith in Christ. That little Bible saved an old man's life, and a boy from becoming a murderer!

　　　　　—W. W. Bradshak, missionary of
　　　　　American Sunday Schools Union

How Could God Tell You?

A girl was happily converted. Immediately she began to read God's Word. One who disbelieved the Bible and took delight in ridiculing it asked the girl, "Why do you spend so much time reading a book like that?" "Because, Sir, it is the Word of God," said the girl. "Nonsense! Who told you it is the Word of God?" scornfully asked the unbeliever. After a moment's silence the girl asked, "Who told you that there is a sun in the sky?" "Nobody," quickly replied the scoffer. "I don't need anybody to tell me. The sun tells me." "Yes," said the girl in triumph, "and that is the way God tells me about His Word. I feel His warmth, and sense His presence as I read His wonderful Word!" —W. B. K.

* * *

Converting the Soul!

An English merchant, on leaving India on a business trip, left with the Hindu overseer a New Testament.

A year passed. The Englishman returned on a Saturday. Around ten o'clock on Sunday morning, he heard a bell ringing. He saw a number of natives wending their way into the schoolhouse. Then he heard them singing. He called a servant and asked what the people were doing there. The servant said they had church every Sunday. "Has any missionary been here since I left here?" "No, Sir," replied the servant. "Then who started this church, and who conducts it?" The servant replied, "The sahib you left in charge when you went away, and to whom you gave a New Testament." "And what do they do in church?" asked the Englishman. "They sing, and pray, and then the sahib talks to them about Jesus!" —W. B. K.

* * *

More Than 500,000,000

More than 500,000,000 volumes of the Bible have been distributed by the American Bible Society since it was founded in 1816. At that time, the Bible had been translated into 73 languages. Today that number has risen to 1130 languages and dialects. The goal of the society is the distribution of

as many copies of the Bible, and portions of the Bible, during the next twenty-five years as have been distributed during the last 140 years.
—Wilbur M. Smith, D.D.

* * *

Priceless and Precious

A man inherited an antique desk. One day by accident he touched a secret spring. A hitherto unopened drawer opened. In it lay a great sum of money! The antique desk was valuable, but the treasure it contained was much more valuable. God's Word is priceless and precious. Unknown spiritual riches await those who will search therein for them: "More to be desired are they than gold, yea, than much fine gold: sweeter also than honey and the honeycomb" (Ps. 19:10). —W. B. K.

* * *

Beholding His Face in a Glass

It is good for us to see ourselves as others see us.

A police magistrate in Philadelphia has a novel way of sobering some of the daily stream of drunks brought into the station. They are lined up before a large mirror on the wall. They see themselves as they are — bleary-eyed, filthy, and ragged! Some are humiliated and are ready to sign the pledge.

The Bible is God's looking glass. It is the only Book which shows man as he really is — "dead in trespasses and sins," with a deceitful and desperately wicked heart. —W. B. K.

* * *

Why Are Pagan Religions Strong?

The devotees of the great pagan religions of the world put Christians to shame in this regard: They memorize their sacred writings! Their minds and hearts are "saturated" with them. No one can teach in a Mohammedan mosque until he has memorized the Koran! For twenty-one hours, some Buddhist priests, and others adhering to Buddhism, quoted from memory their sacred scriptures, making no mistakes and not repeating anything!

The Christians who are most effective in soul-winning are those who hide

away much of God's Word in heart and in head.
—Rev. Hubert Mitchell, a former missionary to Sumatra and India

* * *

Goat Done Et Up Where He's Gwine!

The Bible is the *only* book which tells man his origin and his destiny, whether heaven or hell. It is of utmost importance for man to know his eternal destiny before he closes his eyes in death.

A crated goat was picked up at a railway station. A Negro was in charge of the baggage car. A tag, indicating the goat's destination, was attached to the crate. As the train moved swiftly along, the Negro looked for the tag, and saw that it was gone. Only the string, to which the tag had been attached, remained. With a look of puzzlement on his face, the Negro exclaimed in his unique dialect, "Dis 'ere goat has done et up where he's gwine!"

That goat reminds us of those who reject the Word of God which tells man of his eternal destination, and warns him to flee from the wrath to come! Said an outspoken champion of modernism toward the close of his earthly life, "Modernism has taken the Bible away from the people and has given them nothing to take its place! The situation is serious!" Nothing can take the place of God's eternal, inerrant Word! Of it we say:

A sacred halo gilds its page,
Eternal like the sun,
It gives to every age a light,
It gives but borrows none!
—Rev. R. E. Neighbour, D.D.

* * *

The Healing Word

During World War II, a fine Christian girl was engaged to a serviceman who was overseas. One morning she received a telegram from the War Department, whose opening words ominously said: "We regret to inform you. . . ." Something snapped in the girl's mind. She lapsed into unconsciousness which lasted for days. A faithful pastor co-operated with doctors and stood faithfully by, doing his best to bring the girl out of her dazed condition. As he prayed, this thought came to him: "I'm going to read the Word of God to her whether she can hear me or not." He began to read comforting, reassuring verses and chapters. Suddenly the pent-up sorrow and emotions of the girl burst forth into a profusion of tears. Her tears presently ceased. She said to her mother, "It's all right now!"

In relating what occurred when the pastor began to read God's healing Word, she said, "At first his voice sounded far away and unreal. Then, as I listened to the familiar passages, the words came closer and closer. Finally they seemed to reach my heart!"

"He sent his word, and healed them, and delivered them from their destructions" (Ps. 107:20). —W. B. K.

* * *

I Will Be Waiting for Her Up Yonder!

A soldier had been mortally wounded when Pearl Harbor was attacked. He lingered for a few days in a hospital. There a chaplain gave him a New Testament. Before the soldier died, the chaplain visited him again. Said he to the chaplain:

"Just as I was leaving home my mother put her arms on my shoulders and said, 'Son, if anything should happen that you do not return, I have comfort in knowing that I'll see you up yonder in glory.' I bowed my head and said, 'Mother, I am not a Christian, and I cannot tell you that I will see you again, if anything should happen.' I left my mother weeping with a heavy heart. Mother is a very devout Christian. I have called you to do me a favor. After I am gone write mother telling her I found the Lord by reading this little Testament, and that I will be waiting for her up yonder."

* * *

Why She Hid the Bible

Some Christian women met in a home in Hollywood for their weekly Bible study. The leader, standing before the group, said, "O my, I came away without my Bible!" The hostess hurried away to get her Bible. She looked where she usually kept it, but it wasn't there! She searched for it, but couldn't find it. "What will those ladies think of me?" she thought. Running downstairs, she said to the newly employed cleaning woman, "Mattie, have you seen my Bible?" Mattie exclaimed, "Praise the Lord! Praise the Lord!" "Why, what do you mean, Mattie?" Beamingly, Mattie said, "The first thing I do when I go to work at a new place is to hide the Bible." "But why?" asked her employer in astonishment. Mattie said, "Just to find out how long it takes the people to miss it. You'll find your Bible in the linen closet under the sheets!" —W. B. K.

* * *

In the Morning, Sow Thy Seed!

Years ago, in the city of Toronto, Canada, a young man passed a street meeting. He heard only one verse from the Bible: "Son, give me thine heart." At the time, the verse apparently went in one ear and out the other. More than fifty years later, the verse, which had lain dormant in his heart, became accusingly and convictingly alive. Then he fell on his knees, crying to God for His mercy and forgiveness.

Let us be alert and aggressive in obeying the command, "In the morning sow thy seed, and in the evening withhold not thine hand: for thou knowest not whether shall prosper, either this or that, or whether they both shall be alike good" (Eccl. 11:6).

Even the weakest and unworthiest ones may sow the seed, remembering that the life lies not in the *sower*, but in the *seed!* —W. B. K.

* * *

Tumbling Walls!

At the turn of tne century, a German-Austrian expedition uncovered ancient Jericho, and by 1936, explorations had proceeded far enough for a British expedition to determine that the walls of Jericho had indeed fallen with great violence. Reported Expedition Leader John Garstang: "The space between the two walls is filled with fragments and rubble. There are clear traces of a tremendous fire." Says the Bible: "When the priests blew with the trumpets . . . and the people shouted with a great shout . . . the wall fell down flat

. . . and they burnt the city with fire, and all that was therein." Scientists conclude that an earthquake may have tumbled the walls. —*Time*, Oct. 29, '56

. . .

Tower of Babel Discovered!

From 1899 to 1917, a team of Germans worked to excavate Babylon. In the process, they unearthed the remains of the Tower of Babel. The scientists were able to calculate that it had been 295 feet high, or about as high as the Statue of Liberty. The Queen of Sheba's visit to King Solomon with "spices, and gold in abundance, and precious stones" had often been thought a pious tale until archaeologists uncovered the ruins of Sheba in Yemen in 1951, found indication that the kingdom's chief trade route ran through Israel. This threw new light on the Queen's visit: it was probably a high-level business conference. —*Time*, Oct. 29, '56

. . .

Science and the Bible

In general . . . science's discoveries have proved the Bible startlingly accurate in many checkable details. Take the case of a Bible-reading British major who surprised and decimated a Turkish force in Palestine in World War I by attacking through the same narrow mountain pass which Saul and Jonathan had used to fall upon the Philistines centuries earlier. The Bible told just where to find it: "And between the passages . . . there was a sharp rock on the one side, and a sharp rock on the other side . . . the forefront of the one was situated northward over against Michmash, and the other southward over against Gibeah." A few years ago Israeli Businessman Xiel Federmann began to brood over the account of the destruction of Sodom and Gomorrah ("and, lo, the smoke of the country went up as the smoke of a furnace"), guessed such conflagrations might indicate underground gas — and underground gas meant oil. He was right. In 1953 Israel's first oil well went into operation near the ancient site of Sodom and Gomorrah. —*Time*, Oct. 29, '56

Distorted Mirrors

The governor of Leeds Prison, in England, was formerly the aide-de-camp to King Abdullah of Jordan. He told how the King had two mirrors which he used in rooms where he entertained guests. One, which made people look thin, was put in the room where guests assembled before dinner. The other, which made people look fat, was put in the salon to which guests moved after eating.

We live in rooms of distorted mirrors and must never be taken in by things as they seem to be. There is great folly in outward appearances. There are those who look small to the world who are great for God. There are people who seem to be fruitful in activity who are barren in fruit. The only safe place to look is in the Word of God, which reflects all things as they are. —*Eternity*

. . .

This Will Destroy the Bible!

After writing some fine pamphlets on freedom, including *The Rights of Man*, Thomas Paine wrote *The Age of Reason*. "This will destroy the Bible. Within 100 years Bibles will be found only in museums or in musty corners of second-hand bookstores," he said. His book became the scourge that tormented him until his death. "I would give worlds, if I had them, had *The Age of Reason* never been written," he remorsefully lamented. His prophecy concerning God's Word failed. The Bible has become the best-seller of all books. It is the guide of millions of God's children who daily experience its comforting and sustaining power! —W. B. K.

. . .

In Heart and Head

To me the memorizing of Scripture has been an unfailing help in doubt, anxiety, sorrow, and all the countless vicissitudes and problems of life.

I believe in it enough to have devoted many, many hours of stowing away passages where I can neither leave them behind me or be unable to get to them.

The Word of God is the Christian's best weapon and must be with him always.

Facing death alone on a floating piece of ice on a frozen ocean, the comradeship it afforded me supplied all I needed. It stood by me like the truest of true friends that it is.

With my whole soul I commend to others the giving of some time each day to secure the immense returns that memorizing the Word of God offers and insures. —Wilfred T. Grenfell, M.D.

* * *

What Ruskin Valued Highest

When Ruskin was a small boy, his mother insisted on his memorizing, "every syllable accurately," seventeen chapters of the Bible, in addition to eight Psalms. Of the six chapters of the Old Testament which he memorized, two were from the Book of Exodus, Chapters 15 and 20. Looking back upon those days when fifty-five years old, Ruskin said that his mother's insistence that he memorize these chapters "established my soul in life. Truly, though I have picked up the elements of a little further knowledge — in mathematics, meteorology, and the like — in after life and owe not a little to the teaching of many people, this material installation of my mind in that property of chapters I count very confidently the most precious and on the whole the one essential part of all my education. —*Moody Monthly*

* * *

If God Said It, It's True!

One time Hudson Taylor became deeply depressed. As he read his Bible, these words gripped his soul: "My cup runneth over." He said: "Yes, Lord, if Thou dost say so, it is true! My cup, however, is very far from running over, for there is not enough money for the missionaries and there is dissention among some of them. But, Lord, Thou art eternal, and Thy Word is eternally true. So, in spite of feelings and circumstances I do now believe it and count it true and thank Thee for it!"

Our feelings are as variable as the weather vane atop the barn. God's Word is changeless: "For ever, O Lord, thy word is settled in heaven" (Ps. 119:89). —W. B. K.

Assorted Remedies

Once the clumsy camel driver of a medical missionary caused a lot of tabloid medicines to be thrown from the camel's back and scattered over the sands. They were all mixed up, could not be separated, and so were left lying on the ground. But one of the quack native doctors gathered them up, and, some years later, the medical missionary called on him and found on a shelf a large bottle labeled "Assorted Pills." "These," said he, "are more sought-after than any of my drugs. I give them only to patients whose cases I do not understand." This is a parable of Bible study. Too often we go to our Bibles as that native doctor went to his bottle of "Assorted Pills." What wonder that the Bible, used in that way, has no healing virtue for our souls! The Bible is a complete pharmacopoeia. It contains a cure for every ill. But it is not to be treated as a book of necromancy.

—*Christian Herald*

* * *

An Undiscovered Treasure

A Christian worker entered a wretched, poverty-stricken home. Beneath a rickety table, he saw a dust-covered Bible. As he left, he said, "There's a treasure in this house which if discovered and believed would make you all rich!" A diligent search was made for the hidden treasure. "Could it be a jewel or a pot of gold left by the former occupants of the home?" asked the searchers one of another. Their search was in vain. No treasure was found.

Not long thereafter, the mother picked up the old Bible. She began to shift the pages of the unread Bible. On the flyleaf were written these words, "Thy testimonies are better to me than thousands of gold and silver!" "Ah!" she exclaimed, "can this be the treasure the stranger spoke of?" She and the other members of the family began to read the Bible. A change came into their lives. A change came into the home. Love, joy and peace came into hearts which were formerly filled with sin and discontentment.

When the Christian worker returned to the home, the grateful family exclaimed, "We have found the treasure, and in reading it and receiving it into our hearts, we have also found the Saviour!" —W. B. K.

* * *

Catenati — Chained!

In the early centuries of the middle ages, there were very few Bibles. The Bibles in existence were bestowed as rare gifts by bishops and princes. The skillful pens of copyists and brushes of artists made those early Bibles things of artistic beauty. Their covers were sometimes made of silver or gold. Some of them were studded with rare gems! They were chained to pulpits, or desks. They were called, *Catenati*, which means "chained."

In England these chained Bibles were the only ones known to the people. Wycliffe, Tyndale, and other translators worked faithfully to give the Bible to the people in their native tongue, so that every plowboy in England could have his own copy of the Scriptures. In their work they encountered much opposition and suffered persecution. However, their labors were crowned with success. In the year 1611, the King James Version of the Bible appeared!
—W. B. K.

* * *

Science Catches Up with Bible!

How up-to-date is the Bible! Though not a book of science, its pronouncements on scientific subjects are true to the known facts of science. Two quotes are most interesting:

"A new method of artificial respiration, designed for parents to use in resuscitating babies and children who have stopped breathing, has been developed and is being taught by the American Red Cross. It's an adaptation of the ancient mouth-to-mouth technique used in Bible times!"

Said Dr. Paul D. White, famed heart specialist and consultant to President Eisenhower: "It is conceivable that a few years from now we medical men may repeat . . . the advice that Moses was asked by God to present to the children of Israel 3000 years ago: 'Ye shall eat no manner of fat, of ox, or of goat . . . ye shall in no wise eat it!' "
—W. B. K.

* * *

Bible in School or Penitentiary?

"The Bible was the chart and compass of the fathers of this Republic, and was the guiding star of the framers of our Constitution," editorialized the *Chicago Daily News*. "It never entered their minds to prohibit the reading of the Bible in schools. Yet the Supreme Court of Illinois, by a vote of five to two, has prohibited the reading of the Bible in the public schools in Illinois."

How paradoxical is this prohibition in reference to a provision of an Illinois prison law which stipulates: "It shall be the duty of chaplains to perform religious services in the penitentiaries; to attend to the spiritual wants of the convicts; to visit the convicts in their cells for the purpose of giving them moral and religious instruction and to furnish, at the expense of the State, a Bible to each convict"!

Would it not be sounder economy to furnish the schoolboy with a Bible *before* he reaches the penitentiary, rather than *after* he arrives there? Isn't it better to build safeguards at the top of the precipice rather than hospitals at its base? —W. B. K.

GOD'S CARE

Short Quotes

An English exchange tells of an old custom still in use at a certain east-coast town of England. When a ship is about to sail, the captain asks his men, "Are we all here?" They reply, "Yes, Sir, and in God's care." Then the captain asks, "Is there anything then to fear?" "No, Sir, nothing," they answer. Then they set sail, unafraid of the many dangers which, even in peace time, are the lot of those who go down to the sea in ships. —*The Watchman-Examiner*

Undress your soul at night by shedding, as you do your garments, the daily sins of omission or commission.

—Dr. Wm. Osler's recipe for restful sleep

* * *

Consider the ravens,
  Their trust in their Maker!
They sow not, they reap not,
  They store not away;
And yet they are nourished
And fed by your Father:
Are ye not, His children,
  Far better than they?

—W. M. Czamanske

* * *

He knows, He loves, He cares,
  Nothing this truth can dim,
He does the very best for those,
  Who leave the choice with Him.

* * *

Everything is needful that He sends,
Nothing is needful that He withholds.

—John Newton

* * *

I do not know, I cannot see,
What God's kind hand prepares for me,
Nor can my glance pierce through the haze,
Which covers all my future ways,
But yet I know that o'er it all,
Rules He who notes the sparrow's fall!

God's might to direct me,
God's power to protect me,
God's wisdom for learning,
God's eye for discerning,
God's ear for my hearing,
God's Word for my clearing.

—St. Patrick

* * *

I have nothing to do with tomorrow,
  My Saviour will make that His care,
Should He fill it with trouble and sorrow,
  He'll help me to suffer and bear.
I have nothing to do with tomorrow,
  Its burdens then why should I share?
Its grace and its faith I can't borrow
  Then why should I borrow its care?

—Selected

* * *

A well-known missionary who has gone to his heavenly Father, told how on one occasion he had to make all possible haste to a certain place on the mission field. A deep stream which had to be crossed was all in flood, no boat was available, and humanly speaking it was an impossibility to cross at that time. He and his party camped, and prayed. His heavenly Father knew all. As they prayed a loud crashing noise was heard. A tall tree which had stood the storms of years had fallen, and it fell clear across the stream. Truly He knows how to deliver the godly.

—Sword of the Lord

Illustrations

Let Him Bear Your Burden

As a farmer was jogging along over a country road in his buckboard, he overtook a fellow who was trudging along with a heavy bundle on his shoulder. "Hop in, neighbor," said the farmer cheerily, "I'll give you a ride!"

The traveler clambered into the buckboard, sat down wearily, and placed his burden in his lap.

"I am carrying you," said the farmer with a puzzled look on his face, "but you are still carrying your burden!"

How like many of God's children was he. Our burden bearer, the Lord Jesus, has bid us cast all our cares upon Him. Yet we often fail to do this to our own spiritual and physical detriment.

It is His will that I should cast
  My care on Him each day;
He also bids me not to cast
  My confidence away.

But oh! how foolishly I act
  When taken unaware,
I cast away my confidence
  And carry all my care!

—Told by Rev. James Seward

* * *

He Carries Our Burden

A preacher was busy in his study, while his little boy looked at a book of pictures by the fireside. He suddenly wanted a large book he had left upstairs, and asked his boy to go for it. He was away a long time, and after a while the father thought he heard the sound of sobbing on the stairs. He went out, and at the top of the staircase he saw his son crying bitterly, with the large book he had tried to lift and carry, lying at his feet. "Oh, Daddy," he cried, "I can't carry it. It's too heavy for me." Then, in a moment, the father was up the stairs, and stooping down, took up both the book and the little fellow in his strong arms, and carried them both to the room below. "And that," he found himself thinking later, "is how God deals with His children when they cry to Him in their need. He carries both them and their burdens, and there is no longer need for tears."

—*Methodist Recorder*

* * *

My Father Knows
So often in a time of stress,
In hours of trial and unrest,
This thought comes like a sweet caress,
   "My Father knows."

And often in a time of pain,
When I am tempted to complain,
This tender thought comes back again,
   "My Father knows."

And then in times of fear and doubt,
Of storms within and clouds without,
This thought has turned me face about,
   "My Father knows."

My Father knows and cares for me,
His Word can still the troubled sea,
This thought brings peace and victory,
   "My Father knows."

My Father knows what perfect bliss,
How real, how sweet a love like this,
No greater cure for all my woes, than
   simply this,
   "My Father knows."
            —*Selected*

* * *

God Doesn't Forget
   A young woman arrived in a strange city where she was supposed to be met by the man she expected to marry. She waited at the station from early morning until noon. She began to despair as she had little money and knew no one in that city. The woman in the Travelers Aid office had noticed her and knew by the look on the girl's face that there was something wrong. She offered help, and the girl told her her circumstances. When the Travelers Aid inquired about the man, they found he had left the city. The woman got the girl a good meal, then took her to a Christian home where she stayed until she found work. One day as she tried to thank the woman for her great kindness the girl said: "I haven't been a Christian very long, and that day at the station I felt God had forgotten me, but I know now that He has people like you to help those in despair. It has made me want to be the best kind of Christian, and by God's help I'll pass on your kindness to someone else."

—*The Sunday School Times*

* * *

Hitherto
When the soul is much discouraged
   By the roughness of the way,
And the cross we have to carry
   Seems heavier every day;
When some cloud that overshadows
   Hides our Father's face from view,
Oh, 'tis well then to remember,
   He has blessed us hitherto!

Looking back the long year over
   With a varied path — and yet,
All the way His hand has led us
   Past each hindrance we have met;
Giv'n to us the pleasant places —
   Cheered us all the journey through;
Passing through the deepest waters,
   He has blessed us hitherto!

Surely, then, our souls should trust Him,
   Tho' the clouds be dark o'erhead;
We've a Friend that draweth closer
   When our other friends have fled;
When our pilgrimage is over,
   And the Gates we're sweeping through,
We shall see, with clearer vision,
   How He blessed us hitherto!
            —*Selected*

If God Forgot

If God forgot the world,
Forgot for just one day —
Forgot to send the sunshine,
And change the night to day;
Forgot to make the flowers grow,
Forgot the birds and bees,
Forgot to send the sweetness
Of the south wind in the trees;
Forgot to give us friendships,
Forgot to send us rain,
Forgot to give the children play,
Forgot to soften pain;
What would happen to this world and us?
Would we still be gay?
If God should forget —
Forget for just one day?

—George M. Anderson
in *Pentecostal Testimony*

* * *

When God Let It Alone

Someone remarked to a farmer who was very proud of his growing oats, "That is a fine field of oats!" "Yes," said the farmer, "if God Almighty lets it alone, it ought to be a bumper crop." The crop immediately stopped growing. God withdrew the rain and elements that would have made it a luxuriant crop, and it withered and died. Something like this can happen to us unless we have a greater sense of dependence upon God. Too many feel they can get along better without God than with Him, and so God, the Bible, the church, and religion are discarded. But if God lets us alone, like the oats, we will perish. —*Day by Day With Jesus*

* * *

What God Does

Everything I ever see
Tells me God is good to me;
All the flowers seem to say
He takes care of them each day.

Rivers flowing calm and still
Show us that they do His will;
Birdies in the tops of trees
Praise Him with the greatest ease.

Skies above so bright and blue
Show us what our God can do;

Oh, a million wonders He
Does which none of us can see!

—*Selected*

* * *

He Careth for You

What can it mean? Is it aught to Him
That the nights are long, and the days are dim?
Can He be touched by the griefs I bear
That sadden the heart and whiten the hair?
About His throne are eternal calms,
And strong, glad music, and happy psalms,
And bliss unruffled by any strife —
How can *He* care for *my* little life?

And yet, I want Him to care for me,
While I live in this life where sorrows be!
When the lights die down from the path I take,
When my strength is feeble, and friends forsake;
When love and music, that once did bless,
Have left me to silence and loneliness,
And my life-song changes to silent prayers,
Then my heart cries out to the God who cares.

O wonderful story of deathless love!
Each child is dear to the Heart above!
He fights for me when I cannot fight,
He comforts me in the gloom of night,
He lifts my burden, for He is strong,
He stills the sigh and awakes the song;
The sorrow that brought me down, He bears,
And loves and pardons, because He cares!

So, all who are sad, take heart again —
We are not alone in our hours of pain;
Our Father stoops from His throne above,
To soothe and quiet us with His love;
He leaves us not, when the storm is high,
And we have safety, for He is nigh.
All of our troubles He truly doth share;
Oh, rest in peace, for the Lord doth care!

—Marianne Farmingham

CHILDREN

Short Quotes

A child of five, if properly instructed, can as truly believe and be regenerated as an adult. —Spurgeon

* * *

Matthew Henry was converted when 11 years old; Dr. Watts, 9; Polycarp, 9; Spurgeon began to awaken spiritually at 12. Count Zinzendorf, leader of the Moravians, when 4, signed his name to this covenant: "Dear Saviour, do Thou be mine and I will be Thine!" Lady Dobby, wife of the Defender of Malta, said, "As far back as I can recall, I cannot remember any time when I did not believe in Christ as my Saviour!" —W. B. K.

* * *

It is almost the easiest thing in the world to lead a child from 5 to 10 years of age to a definite acceptance of Christ. —Dr. R. A. Torrey

* * *

A large part of nervous and mental disorders, according to psychiatrists, are due to a smoldering sense of guilt incurred in childhood, arousing fear, worry, despondence. Why not efface them from the scroll of memory by bringing them to Christ in childhood? —W. B. K.

* * *

"Whom shall he teach knowledge? and whom shall he make to understand doctrine? them that are weaned from the milk, and drawn from the breast." —Isaiah 28:9

* * *

A teen-age tough was picked up by the police in an eastern city. The officer sought for the ruffian's mother. They found her at a woman's club lecturing to the group on the subject, "How to Bring Up Children!" —W. B. K.

* * *

The parents of America can strike a telling blow against the forces which contribute to our juvenile delinquency if our fathers and mothers will take their children to Sunday school and church regularly. —J. Edgar Hoover

There was a crooked man,
  Who had a crooked smile,
Who made a crooked fortune,
  In a very crooked style!

He lived a crooked life,
  As crooked people do,
And wondered why it turned out,
  His sons were crooked, too!

* * *

Some parents say, "We will not influence our children in making choices and decisions in the matter of religion!" Why not? TV and radio will! The press will! The movies will! Their neighbors will! The politicians will! We use our influence over flowers, vegetables and cattle. Shall we ignore our children? —*Church Herald*

* * *

Said an English mother to her son: "Charles, your father and I have trained you in righteousness. We have taught you the Word of God. We have lived a godly life before you. If you do not live a godly life, we will stand before God in the day of judgment and bear witness against you!" That son became one of the world's greatest preachers — Charles H. Spurgeon! —W. B. K.

* * *

A mother asked a psychologist, "When should I start training my child?" "How old is he?" she was asked. "Five." The psychologist said, "Madam, hurry home! You have already lost five years!" —W. B. K.

* * *

Fifty per cent of the children of India die before they are ten years of age. The life expectancy of the people of India is twenty-six years. In the United States it is sixty-seven years. —Bishop Fulton J. Sheen

* * *

Juvenile delinquency is proving that some parents are just not getting at the *seat* of the problem. —Kenneth Shively

Higher than every painter, higher than every sculptor and than all artists do I regard him who is skilled in the art of forming the soul of children.

—Chrysostom

* * *

Little boy, so earnest, sweet,
Kneel right now, your Saviour meet;
Pray, "Dear God, I come to Thee,
Thine I'll always, ever be!"

Jesus died for you to save,
Rose again up from the grave;
Now in heaven, He watches you,
Cares for you the whole year through!

—Evelyn Miriam Adams
in *God's Revivalist*

* * *

We need love's tender lessons taught,
As only weakness can;
God hath His small interpreters,
The child must teach the man!

—John Greenleaf Whittier

* * *

Gentle Jesus, meek and mild,
Look upon a little child,
Pity my simplicity,
Suffer me to come to Thee.
Fain would I to Thee be brought,
Gracious Lord, forbid it not;
In the kingdom of Thy grace,
Make a little child a place.

* * *

Standing forth in life's rough way,
Father, guide them;
Oh, we know not what of harm
May betide them;
'Neath the shadow of Thy wing,
Father, hide them;
Walking, sleeping, Lord, we pray,
Go beside them.

—Selected

* * *

They pass so soon, the days of youth;
The children change so fast:
Quickly they harden in the mould,
And the plastic years are past.

Then shape their lives while they are young;
This be our prayer, our aim —
That every child we meet shall bear
The imprint of His name!

—Martha Snell Nicholson

Someone has given this definition of a baby: "A baby is a small member of the animal kingdom that makes love stronger, days shorter, nights longer, the bank roll smaller, the home happier, clothes shabbier, the past forgotten, and the future worth living for."

* * *

In a little mountain church in North Carolina, a revival meeting closed with only one convert, a little boy. That boy grew to be one of the world's greatest Greek scholars — Dr. A. T. Robertson. —W. B. K.

* * *

There are 22 million children under 5 years of age in America. There are 4 million babies being born in America every year. At the rate of present absorption in Sunday school and cradle rolls, we are going to leave one-half of them pagan! —*The Christian Herald*

* * *

There are more than 700,000 mothers in the United States who mourn the fact that their boys and girls, all under voting age, either are or have been in jail, in reformatories, in prisons, or have met death in the electric chair or by the hangman's rope! —J. Edgar Hoover

* * *

A four-year-old girl was spending the night away from home. At bedtime she knelt at her hostess' knee to say her prayers, expecting the usual prompting. Finding her hostess unable to help her, she concluded thus: "Please, Lord, 'scuse me! I can't remember my prayers, and I'm staying with a lady who don't know any!"

* * *

The priceless treasure of boyhood is his endless enthusiasm, his high store of idealism, his affection and his hopes. When we preserve these, we have made men, we have made citizens, and we have made Americans. —Herbert Hoover

* * *

A boy is a complete self-starter, and therefore wisdom in dealing with him consists most in what to do with him next. —Herbert Hoover

I have seed to raise and I plough the
field
And I plant my crops with care,
And I thank the Lord for the rain He
sends
As I watch them growing there.
But I don't sit down with a book by day,
And let my crops run wild,
For crops won't grow by themselves, I
know;
Is it different with a child?
　　　　　　—Edgar A. Guest

* * *

Every means by which a child is
guided in the right direction is a means
of discipline. —Jan Waterink, in *Basic
Concepts in Christian Pedagogy*

* * *

The race moves upward or downward
on the feet of the children.
　　　　　　—Phillips Brooks

* * *

If we do not reach their hearts today
they may break our hearts tomorrow.

* * *

When Lowell was asked, "When should
the training of a child begin?" he said,
"One hundred years before the child
is born!"

Dear Lord, please make all the bad
people good, and all the good people
nice! —A little girl's prayer

* * *

Look for me in the nurseries of
heaven!

* * *

God's kingdom goes forward on the
feet of little children.

* * *

It is a statistical fact that 18 per cent
of our converts come from our Sunday
schools.

* * *

"An inch of boy is worth a thousand
yards of carpet," said a pastor to some
who complained that the boys were
wearing down the new carpeting in their
meeting place. —W.B.K.

* * *

The day after the great earthquake
and fire in San Francisco, a newsboy
assisted a dazed man through the scene
of desolation and destruction. Said the
boy, "It took men a long time to put
all this stuff up, but God tumbled it
over in a minute! Say, Mister, it's no
use for a fellow to think he can lick
God!"

Illustrations

Twenty-nine out of 4,800 Cases

Judge Sam David Tatum of the
Juvenile Domestic Relations Court of
Nashville, Tennessee, said: "The Juvenile Court over which I preside has
jurisdiction over children under seventeen years of age, who have violated the
law. I have tried approximately 4,800
cases. Of this number only twenty-nine
have a regular Sunday-school or church
record. So far, I have not had a child
in Juvenile Court whose father or mother
attended either Sunday school or church
regularly."

* * *

Love Child — Hate Dirt!

A fashionably dressed young woman,
sight-seeing in the slums of New York
City, shuddered over a dirty, unkempt
ragamuffin playing in the filth of the
gutter. "Just look at that child!" she
cried. "Why doesn't someone clean him
up? Where is his mother?"

"Well, it's this way, Miss," explained
her guide, "the child's mother loves her
child, but she doesn't hate the dirt.
You hate the dirt but you don't love
the child. Until love for the child and
hate for the dirt get into the same
heart, the poor child remains just about
as he is." —*Gospel Banner*

* * *

That Boy Was Dwight L. Moody!

A man stepped up to us one day at
the close of a meeting, and said, "I want
to tell you a story. Years ago I was
teaching a class of boys in a certain
city. There were eight boys in the class.
It was in the days before the lesson
helps were so plentiful as now, and we
were confined to the use of the Bible
alone. There was but one Bible for
the whole class. This was passed from
hand to hand in due order. I noticed
especially how the second boy in the
class acted when the book reached him

in turn. He fumbled at the leaves. He hesitated and halted at words of but ordinary difficulty. The big words he skipped entirely. Yet he was most faithful and persistent in it all. My brother," said the speaker, "that boy was Dwight L. Moody."

—James McConkey

* * *

When to Begin Influencing a Child

A mother's meeting was discussing the question, "How early in a child's life ought one to seek to influence that life to accept Jesus as Saviour and Lord?" Many views, variant but vital, were expressed. The presiding mother, observing that a visiting gray-haired grandmother, though evidently much interested, did not share in the discussion, invited her viewpoint. The aged visitor rose and made this arresting reply: "I'll tell you when I began to influence my daughter Christward. I began twenty years before she was born, by giving myself to the saving and keeping power of Jesus Christ."

—From a convention address by Mrs. Mary Foster Bryner

* * *

When Is a Child Too Young?

I was admitted into the church at the early age of eight. I loved Christ and felt a strong desire to be identified with His people. When I mentioned the fact to some of the deacons, they looked askance and expressed grave doubts whether I should be allowed to sit at the Lord's table. Among them, however, there were wiser men. Their counsels prevailed, and after some months of probation I was admitted. From that day until now, I have never ceased to thank God that I was induced to take the important step at the time I did. Had I not done so I doubt whether I should have been a missionary — if a member of the Christian church at all.

—Griffith John in *Dawn*

* * *

My Child and Sunday School

Shall I make my child go to Sunday school and church? Yes! And with no further discussion about the matter. Startled? Why? How do you answer Junior when he comes to breakfast on

Monday morning and announces to you that he is not going to school any more? You know! Junior goes. How do you answer when Junior comes in very much besmudged and says, "I'm not going to take a bath." Junior bathes, doesn't he?

Why all this timidity then, in the realm of his spiritual guidance and growth? Going to let him wait and decide what church he'll go to when he's old enough? Quit your kidding! You didn't wait until you were old enough! You don't wait until he's old enough to decide whether he wants to go to school or not — to start his education. You don't wait until he's old enough to decide whether he wishes to be clean or dirty do you? Do you wait until he's old enough to decide if he wants to take his medicine when he is sick? Do you?

What shall we say when Junior announces he doesn't like to go to Sunday school and church? That's an easy one to answer. Just be consistent. Tell him, "Junior, in our house we all go to church and Sunday school, and that includes you." Your firmness and example will furnish a bridge over which youthful rebellion may travel into rich and satisfying experience in personal religious living.

The parents of America can strike a telling blow against the forces which contribute to our juvenile delinquency, if our fathers and mothers will take their children to Sunday school and church regularly. —J. Edgar Hoover

* * *

Armfuls of Affection

Little Mary Nell was rapidly eating fistfulls of chocolate candy when suddenly her father appeared, coming up the walk. Cramming the last piece of chocolate in her mouth, she squealed with delight as she dashed toward her father. She threw herself into his outstretched arms, joyously exclaiming: "Daddy! Daddy! You're home! You're home!"

Father saw Mary Nell's chocolate-smeared hands, mouth, and dress too late! His white shirt was a mess! His first impulse was to reprimand her. He put her down, however, and laughed heartily! How could he react differently to the spontaneous outburst of love, joy and armfuls of affection, when he thought, "Did I not come to the heavenly Father soiled by years of sinful living? Did He not enfold me in His arms of love?" —W. B. K.

* * *

That Shabby Lad

Sometimes the lad who'll make a man
Is quite unpromising to scan;
He saunters up and down the street
With dirty hands and dirty feet;
With grimy cheeks and tousled hair
For whom nobody seems to care;
And yet beneath the dirt and grime
Perhaps there beats a heart sublime.

His clothes are grimy like his face
And all he does seems out of place;
He's just a shabby-looking lad,
A little fellow rude and bad;
And yet perhaps he's far from mean,
With intellect that's bright and keen;
A boy that people say is "tough,"
Perchance a diamond in the rough.

He romps about from day to day,
Quite fond of frolic and of play;
He climbs the fence and jumps the rills,
And swims the streams and scales the hills
He keeps the neighbors ill at ease,
And so they turn on him the keys,
Lest he should "call" when they are gone
And cannot lay the hickory on.

But give this little lad a chance
And see some day how he'll advance;
He'll master books and make a name
That many others cannot claim;
He'll make success and rise somehow
With godly laurels on his brow,
Till men may say, "How could this be
From such a shabby lad as he?"
—Walter E. Isenhour

* * *

Send Them to Bed With a Kiss!

O mothers, so weary, discouraged,
Worn out with the cares of the day,
You often grow cross and impatient,
Complain of the noise and the play;
For the day brings so many vexations,
So many things go amiss;
But mothers, whatever may vex you,
Send the children to bed with a kiss!

The dear little feet wander often,
Perhaps from the pathway of right,
The dear little hands find new mischief
To try you from morning till night;
But think of the desolate mothers
Who'd give all the world for your bliss,
And, as thanks for your infinite blessings,
Send the children to bed with a kiss!

For some day their noise will not vex you,
The silence will hurt you far more;
You will long for their sweet, childish voices,
For a sweet, childish face at the door;
And to press a child's face to your bosom,
You'd give all the world for just this!
For the comfort 'twill bring you in sorrow,
Send the children to bed with a kiss!
—*New Orleans Picayune*

* * *

Two Hands Reaching Heavenward

Often God teaches us precious and profound lessons through little children.

A father took his little twenty-month-old son with him to a special prayer meeting in which God's presence and power were felt. In indicating his desire for a closer walk with God, the father responded to the leader's appeal and raised his hand. Two little watchful eyes saw what Daddy did. Instantly the little boy raised both hands!

Who is so undiscerning as to say that the One who received and blessed the little ones long ago didn't look with favor and acceptance upon those little lifted hands? —W. B. K.

* * *

What Is a Boy?

Between the innocence of babyhood and the dignity of manhood we find a delightful creature called a boy. Boys come in assorted sizes, weights, and colors, but all boys have the same creed: to enjoy every second of every minute of every hour of every day and to protest with noise (their only weapon) when their last minute is finished and the adult males pack them off to bed.

Boys are found everywhere — on top of, underneath, inside of, climbing on, swinging from, running around, or jumping to. Mothers love them, little girls hate them, older sisters and brothers tolerate them, adults ignore them, and heaven protects them. A boy is truth with dirt on its face, beauty with a cut on its finger, wisdom with bubble gum in its hair, and the hope of the future with a frog in its pocket.

When you are busy, a boy is an inconsiderate, bothersome, intruding jangle of noise. When you want him to make a good impression, his brain turns to jelly or else he becomes a savage, sadistic jungle creature bent on destroying the world and himself with it.

A boy is a composite: he has the appetite of a horse, the digestion of a sword swallower, the energy of a pocket-size atomic bomb, the curiosity of a cat, the lungs of a dictator, the imagination of a Paul Bunyan, the shyness of a violet, the audacity of a steel trap, the enthusiasm of a firecracker and, when he makes something, he has five thumbs on each hand.

He likes ice cream, knives, saws, Christmas, comic books, the boy across the street, woods, water (in its natural habitat), large animals, Dad, trains, Saturday mornings, and fire engines. He is not much for Sunday school, company, schools, books without pictures, music lessons, neckties, barbers, girls, overcoats, adults, or bedtime.

Nobody else is so early to rise, or so late to supper. Nobody else gets so much fun out of trees, dogs, and breezes. Nobody else can cram into one pocket a rusty knife, a half-eaten apple, three feet of string, an empty Bull Durham sack, two gumdrops, six cents, a slingshot, a chunk of unknown substance, and a genuine supersonic code ring with a secret compartment.

A boy is a magical creature. You can lock him out of your workshop, but you can't lock him out of your heart. You can get him out of your study, but you can't get him out of your mind. Might as well give up — he is your captor, your jailor, your boss, and your master — a freckled, pint-sized, cat-chasing bundle of noise. But when you come home at night with only the shattered pieces of your hopes and dreams, he can mend them like new with two magic words: "Hi, Dad!"

—Alan Beck in *Reader's Choice*. Written for the New England Mutual Life Insurance Company

* * *

Babies versus Battalions

A century ago men were following with bated breath the march of Napoleon, and waiting with feverish impatience for news of the wars. All the while, babies were being born in their own homes. But who could think about babies? Everybody was thinking about battles.

In one year, 1809, midway between Trafalgar and Waterloo, there came into the world some babies who were destined to be stars of greatest magnitude — Gladstone, Oliver Wendell Holmes, Tennyson, and Felix Mendelsohn. But nobody thought of babies, only battles. Yet which of the battles of 1809 mattered more than the babies of 1809? We fancy that God can manage His world only with big battalions when all the while He is doing it by babies. When a wrong wants righting, or a truth wants preaching, or a continent wants opening, God sends a baby into the world to do it!

—Frank W. Borehan

* * *

I Am a Baby!

One has represented a baby as saying: "I am a baby. All the world waits for my coming. All the world watches with interest to see what I shall become. Civilization hangs in the balance, for what I am, the world of tomorrow will be. I have come into your world, about which I know nothing. Why I came I know not. How I came I know not. I am curious, and am interested. You hold in your hand my destiny. You determine largely whether I shall succeed or fail. Give me, I pray, those things that make for happiness. Train me, I beg you, that I may be a blessing to the world!" —*Selected*

* * *

DEAR TEACHER:

Please find attached to this note one five-year-old boy, much cleaner and quieter than usual and with new haircut and dungarees. With him go the prayers of his mother and father.

He's good at creating airplanes and chaos, very adept at tying knots and attracting stray dogs. He especially likes peanut butter, horses, TV westerns, empty boxes and his shirttail out.

He is allergic to baths, bedtime, taking out trash and coming the first time he's called.

He needs to be taught and spanked, loved and spanked, and reminded to blow his nose and come straight home from school.

After having him in your class and on your nerves, you may not be the same, but I believe you'll be glad to know him because, while he strews books, toys and clothes, he has a special way of scattering happiness!

Written, I'm afraid, with prejudice.
His mother.
—Mildred B. Duncan in *Guideposts*

* * *

Pictures Preach

Childhood impressions are lasting impressions. As a boy, I attended Sunday school in a little Methodist church in which there was a beautiful stained-glass window, depicting Christ leading a flock of sheep, and holding in His arm a lamb. As the rays of the sun shone through that window, it became a thing of dazzling beauty. How helpless and trustful were the sheep and the lamb! Most impressive of all was the look of tenderness on the face of the Good Shepherd — Jesus. At the bottom of the picture were these words: "He shall feed his flock like a shepherd: he shall gather the lambs with his arm, and carry them in his bosom, and shall gently lead those that are with young."

What a mighty though silent sermon that picture preached to my childish heart! —W. B. K.

* * *

Wait!

I recall an incident that happened in 1921. The distraught father of a diabetic child asked, "Should we prolong this child's misery? Since he can never grow up to be a healthy man, mightn't it be better to let him die?" On the following day the discovery of insulin was announced. Today that diabetic child is a splendid physician, the father of four children!

—Dr. I. S. Ravdin, Professor of Surgery, University of Pennsylvania School of Medicine

CHOOSING

Illustrations

Emphasis on the Wrong World

When David Livingstone's body was brought back from Africa to England, great throngs along the streets watched the funeral procession. An elderly man in the crowd burst into sobs. Lamented he, "I knew Livingstone when I was a young man. We went together. We were friends. When he told me of God's call to him to go to Africa, I ridiculed him. I was ambitious. I chose a life of self-ease. I cared only for my own selfish interests. Now, with a misspent life behind me, I acknowledge that Livingstone made a wise choice when he answered and obeyed God's call. I put the emphasis on the wrong world!"

—W. B. K.

Darkness or Light?

Once to every man and nation,
   Comes the moment to decide,
In the strife of truth with falsehood,
   For the good or evil side,
Some great cause, God's new Messiah,
Offering each the bloom or blight,
And the choice goes by forever,
   'Twixt that darkness and that light.
         —James Russell Lowell

* * *

What Made the Difference?

Dr. Pierce Harris, pastor of the First Methodist Church, Atlanta, Ga., spoke to some prisoners. The prisoner in introducing him said, "Several years ago, two boys lived in a town in north

Georgia. They went to the same school, played together and attended the same Sunday school. One dropped out of Sunday school and said that it was 'sissy stuff.' The other boy kept going. One rejected Christ; the other accepted Him. The boy who rejected Christ is making the introduction today. The boy who accepted Christ is the honored preacher who will speak to us today!" —*Power*

* * *

What Would I Have Done?

What would I have done had I been
    there?
Would I have helped His cross to bear?
Would I have cried, "Oh, set Him free!
Release this man and take thou me!"

What would I have done had I been
    there?
Would I offer comfort, aid, or care
To Him who left His heavenly throne
To bear His rugged cross alone?

What would I have done had I been
    there?
Would I of His affliction share?
Would I have stood before the crowd
To save the Saviour from His shroud?

What would I have done had I been
    there?
Would I have stood to scoff and stare?
What would I have done? I cannot say.
What matters is what I do today!
    —Paul Lightle

* * *

For or Against Me?

I stood alone at the bar of God
    In the hush of the twilight dim
And faced the question which pierced
    my heart:
What will you do with Him?
Crowned or crucified? Which shall it be?
No other choice was offered to me.

I looked on the face still freshly marred
    By Gethsemane's agony.
The look in His kind eyes broke my
    heart,
    'Twas full of love for me.
"The crown or the cross," it seemed to
    say,
    "For or against Me — Choose thou
    today."

He held out His loving hands to me
    While He pleadingly said, "Obey:
Make Me thy choice, for I love thee so";
    And I could not say Him nay.
Crowned, not crucified, thus it must be;
    No other way was open to me.

I knelt in tears at the feet of Christ
    In the hush of the twilight dim,
And all that I was, or hoped or sought,
    Surrendered unto Him.
Crowned, not crucified; my heart shall
    know
    No king but Christ who loveth me so.
    —*Selected*

* * *

A Way and a Way

To every man there openeth
    A Way, and Ways, and a Way,
The High Soul climbs the High Way,
    The Low Soul gropes the Low,
And in between, on the misty flats,
The rest drift to and fro.
But to every man there openeth
A High Way, and a Low,
And every man decideth
The Way his soul shall go.
    —John Oxenham

* * *

That's the Way He Wanted It!

The body of a suicide floated in the icy waters of the Chicago River. The bridge above became jam-packed with onlookers as policemen roughly dragged the body at the end of a rope. "Poor soul," said one feelingly. "That's the way he wanted it," said another.

It is certain that the suicide chose death. How like myriads of others. The Saviour came that all might have eternal life, but many choose spiritual death. How tragic it is that so many, like the prodigal son in the far country, are starving spiritually when Jesus, the Bread of life, might be had for the asking! —W. B. K.

* * *

Whose Side Are You On?

During one of the Italian wars, some recruiting officers came to a small town. Men and boys of all ages were recruited and joined in a parade, armed with swords, guns and sticks. An old lady was so stirred by the spectacle that she shouldered her broom and fell in line.

Proudly she marched along, keeping perfect step with the others. Onlookers jeered at the old lady. They asked, "What good can you do in a battle?" She replied, "Not much, but I want everybody to know whose side I am on!"

"How long halt ye between two opinions? If the Lord be God, follow him: but if Baal, then follow him" (I Kings 18:21). —Rev. William McCarrell, D.D.

* * *

A Deliberate Choice to Go to Hell

A man regularly attended a Bible class. Then he suddenly stopped coming. The teacher visited him. "Why did you drop out of the class?" he asked. Said the man, "I cannot come to the class, hear the kind of teaching given here, and go on living the way I live." Then the teacher asked, "Do you deliberately choose to continue in sin, reject the Saviour, and go to hell?" The man's reply was startling. "Yes, I choose hell, not heaven!" Later, the man died and went out into a lost eternity. —W. B. K.

* * *

Knowingly Rejecting Christ

A St. Bernard dog, high in the Alps, found and rescued his sixty-ninth man and dug the fallen, freezing man out of the snow. The effort to help the man cost the dog his life. After digging him from the snow, the dog stretched himself over the body of the man, as he had been trained to do to impart warmth and revive the flickering spark of life. When the man began to thaw out, he saw the huge dog hovering over him. In his dazed, drowsy condition, he mistook the dog for a wolf, intent on devouring him. Quickly he plunged a dagger into the animal's side! Without a whimper, the noble dog crept away to his master's cabin where he bled to death at the doorsteps.

How like that are imperiled men who "crucify anew the Son of God," and spurn His offer of eternal life! There is this difference, however — the freezing man was in a semi-conscious condition when he rejected his would-be rescuer. Man deliberately and knowingly rejects the Saviour. —W. B. K.

Gooseberries or Evergreens?

In our pine grove some branches were turning brown. A tree expert diagnosed the trouble as "pine blister." You must deal with it at once and drastically, he advised, or your whole stand of pine will be ruined. Pull up all the gooseberry and currant plants within a radius of a thousand feet, and the pine infection will spread no further.

His prescription seemed absurd to us. Those bushes had always seemed harmless and their fruit had supplied us with tasty jelly. Why should we root them out? The expert explained, "These gooseberry and currant growths act as host for the pine blister. Only as it incubates in them will it spread and infect your trees."

The choice was not an agreeable one. But we could not hesitate long between gooseberry tarts and our tall, spreading evergreens! —Arthur Gordon in *The Sunday School Times*

* * *

Our Can't's and Can's

If you would have some worthwhile plans
You've got to watch your can't's and can's;
You can't aim low and then rise high;
You can't succeed if you don't try;
You can't go wrong and come out right;
You can't love sin and walk in light;
You can't throw time and means away;
And live sublime from day to day.

—*Selected*

* * *

The Big Pearl

The choice before us, as Christian people, is not a choice between what is bad and what is good, but rather between what is good and what is better. You will recall our Lord's story about the pearl merchant: "Again, the kingdom of heaven is like unto a merchant man seeking goodly pearls who, when he had found one pearl of great price, went and sold all that he had and bought it." Never forget that the things he sold were not sticks and stones and rubbish. He sold pearls! He did one of the hardest things a man ever does — he parted with something good for something better. —Harold Cook Phillips

The Only Signal

The town in which I live has an elevated railway. One of the stations is near a great burying ground, Calvary Cemetery. For many years, because in that part of the town there were many more dead than living folk, the trains did not stop at the cemetery except on request. Just after leaving the nearest station, the guard would open the door and say, "Next station is Calvary. Train stops on signal only. Anybody for Calvary?"

It is a parable of life's train. At all the other stations every train stops. At Market Street, at School Street, at University Avenue, at Main Street, at Vanity Fair, at Broadway, at Church Street, at Home Avenue. No special notice is needed, but to get off at Calvary — that means a choice and an expressed desire. —*Christian Digest*

* * *

The God Who Is Enough

'Tis far, far better to let Him choose
The way that we should take;
If only we leave our life to Him
He will guide without mistake.
We, in our blindness, would never choose
A pathway dark and rough,
And so we should never find in Him,
"The God Who Is Enough." —*Selected*

* * *

Two Brothers — Two Ways

The session of the Church Bible School was just closing. Two brothers, both of teen age, came down the steps of the house of God. Suddenly one turned and, looking his brother squarely in the eye, announced his decision: "Well, I am through. This is my last day of attendance at this place." His brother, with equal firmness, answered, "This is not my last day here. I intend to learn more of God and His will concerning my life."

Years later there was a great reception given at the Pan-American Exposition to the President of the United States. The Chief Executive was standing in line to greet the surging crowds that presented themselves. Among them was a man with his hand covered with a handkerchief. Instead of grasping the President's extended hand he pulled the trigger of a concealed revolver, and

the great William McKinley dropped mortally wounded.

The assassin was Leon F. Czolgosz, the boy who years before had turned away from the Church School —*Eternity*

* * *

Where the Choice Was Made

Far up in one of the secret places of the Alps there lies, hidden away, a tiny lake. The path by which it is reached does not permit a sight of it until one is but a stone's throw away. There is a small stream which starts at this tiny lake, and as it takes its downward course for a few yards it is confronted with a large, imposing boulder. The small stream seems to hesitate here, then divides into two, one of which flows into the Rhone River and the other into the Rhine. Now these two streams which part company and flow, one into the warm, sunny southern part of Europe, and the other into cold northern climates, represent the two streams of life as they flow in diametrically different directions. Together they rise in the hills of Birth, but soon they reach the boulder, representing the Cross of Christ, and it is here that the choice must be made. —*Good News Broadcaster*

* * *

Daddy, Did They Let Him In?

A little girl stood with her father before the great painting of *Christ Knocking at the Door*. Reverently and silently, they looked upon the tender, beseeching face of the Saviour. Presently, the little girl turned to her father and asked, "Daddy, did they let Him in?"

When we stand in the presence of God, our eternal destinies will be determined by whether or not we invited Him to come into our lives and transform them by grace divine.

What will you do with Jesus?
Neutral you cannot be;
One day your heart will be asking,
"What will He do with me?"
—W. B. K.

* * *

A Wasted Life!

One night, Canon Hay Aitken preached to a large audience in Bristol, England, from the text, "Ye must be born again." Horatio Bottomley, a fine, brilliant young fellow, listened with rapt attention. He was deeply moved. At the close of the message an invitation was given to the unsaved publicly to confess Christ and seek His mercy. Bottomley thought: "Not I. This is not for me. I'll run my own life."

He did run his own life. He made a fortune. He became the people's hero. He was a champion of the rights of the common man. He exposed swindlers and vigorously prosecuted them.

When sixty-three years old, Bottomley, who had exposed the crimes of others, was himself found guilty of crime and sentenced to seven years in prison.

Captain Prayer of the Church Army visited him in prison. He told Bottomley the story of his conversion. Said he: "Years ago I was in Colston Hall in Bristol. Canon Hay Aitken preached on the text, 'Ye must be born again.' I was convicted of sin and of my need of the Saviour. I accepted Christ and since that memorable time, Christ has been all and in all to me!"

Bottomley thought deeply. Then he said, "I, too, heard that searching message. I felt my great need of the Saviour, but I rejected Him." Then he said remorsefully, "*A life without God is a wasted life!*" —W. B. K.

CHRISTIAN EXAMPLE—INFLUENCE

Short Quotes

A man's Sunday self and his weekday self are like two halves of a round trip ticket: *not good if detached.*
—Lee H. Bristol, Jr.

* * *

The devil is willing for a person to confess Christianity as long as he does not practice it.

* * *

A Hindu student said to Billy Graham in Madras, "I would become a Christian if I could *see* one!" Said Graham, "And when he said that, he was looking at me! That was one of the greatest sermons ever preached to *me!*"

* * *

If Christ is the center of our lives, the circumference will take care of itself.

* * *

So let our lives and lips express
The holy gospel we profess;
So let our words and actions shine.
To show the doctrine all divine.

* * *

"O God, when I am wrong, make me easy to change, and when I am right, make me easy to live with!"
—Peter Marshall

* * *

Four ministers were discussing the merits of the various translations of the Bible. One liked the King James Version best because of its simple, beautiful English. Another liked the American Standard Version best because it is more literal and comes nearer the original Hebrew and Greek. The third liked Moffatt's translation best because of its up-to-date vocabulary. The fourth minister was silent. When asked to express his opinion, he replied, "I like my mother's translation best." The other three expressed surprise. They wondered what he was driving at. "Yes," he replied, "Mother translated the Bible into everyday life, and it was the most convincing translation I ever saw."
—*Emergency Post*

* * *

Read thou, but first thyself prepare
To read with zeal and mark with care;
And when thou read'st what here is writ,
Let thy best practice second it;
So twice each precept writ shall be
First in the Book and then in thee.

* * *

Christianity is either relevant all the time or useless any time. It is not just a phase of life — it is life itself.
—Richard C. Halverson

* * *

A new book on Islam, *The Call of the Minaret*, says that Mohammedanism "developed in an environment of imperfect Christianity." Christian failure, says the author, made Islam possible — a failure in love, in purity, in fervor, and a failure of the spirit. —W. B. K.

* * *

Holiness vanishes when you talk about it, but becomes conspicuous when you live it.

* * *

A Jew was given a New Testament which he read for the first time. Said he to a friend, "Parts of it are most beautiful, but I do not see what these people around here called Christians have in common with this book!"

—Earnest Worker

* * *

The Christian is the world's Bible, and in many cases a revision is necessary. —D. L. Moody

* * *

I don't care how loud a brother shouts and how high he jumps just so he walks straight when he comes down.

—Bud Robinson

* * *

First, plant five rows of peas: Preparedness, Promptness, Perseverance, Politeness, and Prayer. Next to them plant three rows of squash: Squash Gossip, Squash Criticism, and Squash Indifference. Then five rows of lettuce: Let us be Faithful, Let us be Unselfish, Let us be Loyal, Let us be Truthful, Let us Love One Another. And no garden is complete without turnips: Turn up for Church, Turn up with a Smile, Turn up with Determination.

—Moody Monthly

* * *

Walk in newness of life (Rom. 6:4).
Walk honestly (Rom. 13:13).
Walk in the Spirit (Gal. 5:16).
Walk worthy of the vocation (Eph. 4:1).
Walk in love (Eph. 5:2).
Walk as children of light (Eph. 5:8).
Walk circumspectly (Eph. 5:15).
Walk worthy of the Lord (Col. 1:10).
Walk in wisdom (Col. 4:5).
Walk worthy of God (I Thess. 2:12).
Walk pleasing to God (I Thess. 4:1).
Walk as He walked (I John 2:6).

A well-known restaurant hired some men to carry signs advertising the splendid meals it served. These men, however, were shabby looking and hungry in appearance. What poor advertisements they were of a high-class restaurant! Their counterparts can be seen in most churches. How repellent they are, especially to the youths. —W. B. K.

* * *

A well-known owner of a chain of hotels endeavors to render the best of service to the guests in his hotels. He often says to his employees, "Remember, my reputation is in your hands!"

In a sense, Christ's reputation is in our hands. Others will judge Him by those who profess to know Him and serve Him.

* * *

While a missionary was speaking to a group of Hindu women, one of them silently walked away. Soon she returned and listened more intently than before. "Why did you leave in the midst of my message?" asked the missionary. "I was so interested in the wonderful things you were saying that I went to ask your servant if you live like you teach. He said you do. So I came back to hear more about Jesus," said the woman. —W. B. K.

* * *

The Duke of Wellington asked an officer in uniform, "Why do you stand so slouchily, in a nonmilitary posture?" The officer answered, "Sir, I am off duty!" Flashed Wellington: "A British officer is never off duty! Always maintain your military bearing!"

Christians are never off duty either. Watch your Christian bearing!

—W. B. K.

* * *

"They say she got religion," said Aunt Dinah doubtfully of an acquaintance, "but if she did, she took it mighty light. It don't hinder her none from carrying on like she always did, and no one needn't be afraid of catching it from her!" —Alice M. Knight

* * *

Soon Woo Lee was from Korea. He lived in a Christian home in America. He had a keen mind. He sought to know the truths of God's Word. In speaking of the father in the home, Soon said, "I know in my heart I'll always try to be like him. The father does not say, 'Do these things,' or 'Must not do those.' He just shows us *by the way he lives*. Long time I know God to be honored and worshiped, but never before do I know God to love. Now, I know and feel His love!" —W. B. K.

Illustrations

The Golden Rule

In your daily round of duties,
  As you make your way through life;
As you gaze upon its beauties,
  And you look upon its strife,
There's a rule of conduct given,
  Which I will commend to you:
Always do unto another
  What you'd have him do to you.

If, perchance, along life's highways,
  You should meet a man that's down,
Or you meet him on the byways,
  Where he meets with many a frown,
Won't you try to help him, brother,
  Ere he passes from your view?
Won't you do unto another
  What you'd have him do to you?

Once upon a time the Saviour
  Came into this world of sin,
Came into this world to suffer,
  Precious souls that He might win.
And He gave to us a precept
  Did this Saviour, kind and true:
Always do unto another
  What you'd have him do to you.
          —James Wells in
          The Church of God

* * *

Definition of a Christian

He has a mind and knows it;
He has a will and shows it;
He sees his way, and goes it;
He draws a line and toes it;
He has a charge and takes it,
A friendly hand and shakes it,
A rule and never breaks it;
If there's no time, he makes it.

He loves the truth, stands by it,
Nor never tries to shy it,
Whoever may defy it,
Or openly deny it.
He hears a lie and slays it;
And as I've heard him praise it,

He knows the game and plays it;
He sees the path Christ trod,
And grips the hand of God.
          —Christian Digest

* * *

Why, We Know Him!

A missionary who had been in Africa for many years was assigned to a new tribe. Immediately he began to preach Jesus. As he spoke of Jesus' healing, helpful ministry, the natives said, "Why, we know Him! He used to live here!" "Oh, no," said the missionary, "He never lived here. He died some two thousand years ago. But He arose again and is now in heaven!" The natives, however, insisted that they knew Him. Here's why: years before, a missionary had lived in this tribe. He lived so like Christ among them that when the second missionary came preaching Christ, the natives thought he was talking about the missionary who had lived among them. —W. B. K.

* * *

A Most Christlike Person

A Christian storekeeper in a small town was thoroughly honest in his business, as Christians should be. A family came to the town and moved into a home across the street from the store. Almost daily the father, who was not a Christian, entered the store. After a year he went to a minister and said, "The storekeeper is one of the most honorable and Christlike persons I have ever known. I want what he has. Will you help me?" The minister told him of Jesus and of His power to change our lives. The man accepted Christ. His home became a Christian home. Two of his daughters became missionaries. How did these wonderful things come to pass? Simply because a storekeeper lived as Christians should live. —W. B. K.

His Ambassadors

Innuendoes and insults were heaped upon one of our ambassadors by an ambassador of an enemy country. Our ambassador stood unruffled, unperturbed, unangered! At the close of the tirade, he said, "Sir, it makes little difference to me what you think of me. All that matters to me is what the world thinks about the nation I represent!"

When we are privileged to suffer shame for Christ's sake, let this be our only concern, that our reactions be such as to cause others to think highly of Him, whose ambassadors we are!

"Now then we are ambassadors for Christ, as though God did beseech you by us: we pray you in Christ's stead, be ye reconciled to God" (II Cor. 5:20).

—W. B. K.

* * *

If I Could See a Christian, I would Like to Be One!

Many years a missionary employed a great Chinese scholar to translate the New Testament into the Chinese language. The scholar was a Confucianist and had never heard of Christianity until this missionary had engaged him. The scholar was a painstaking person and wanted to produce a splendid translation. As he completed his work, the missionary recalled that he had not said one word to him about his soul and his need of the Saviour. Engaging the scholar in conversation, the missionary said, "You have been a great help to me. As you translated the New Testament, has not the beauty of Christianity appealed to you? Would you not like to be a Christian?" "Yes," replied the scholar, "it does appeal to me. It is a wonderful system of ethics. I think that if I could see a Christian, I might become interested." "But," said the missionary, "I am a Christian!" "You," said the scholar, "are you a Christian? Oh, no, pardon me, I don't want to offend you, but I have observed you. You are not a Christian. If I understand aright, a Christian is a follower of Jesus, and Jesus said, 'A new commandment give I unto you, that you love one another.' But I have listened to you talk about others who were not present, say-

ing unkind things about them. I have watched you closely in other things, and I have had to conclude that you are not a Christian. I think that if I could see a Christian, I would like to be one!" concluded the Chinese scholar.

—W. B. K.

* * *

I Am Dore!

A great artist wandered into the mountains of Switzerland. An official asked for his passport. The artist searched for it. "My!" he exclaimed, "I do not seem to have it with me." "Who are you?" asked the official. "I am Dore," said the artist. The official knew about Dore, but didn't know him personally, so he said, "Prove to me that you are Dore." Taking a piece of paper, the artist hastily sketched a group of peasants standing nearby. He did it so skillfully and with such ease that the official exclaimed, "Enough! You are Dore!"

An unbelieving world is unimpressed by empty religious profession. It cannot gainsay, however, God's children who *practice* what they profess.

—W. B. K.

* * *

True Education

Education does not mean teaching people what they do not know. It means teaching them to behave as they do not behave. It is not teaching youth the shape of letters and the tricks of numbers and then leaving them to turn their arithmetic to roguery and their literature to lust. It is a painful, continual, and difficult work to be done by kindness, by watching, by warning, by precept, and by praise, but above all — by example. —John Ruskin

* * *

What Is Christianity?

In the Home it is kindness.
In business it is honesty.
In society it is courtesy.
In work it is fairness.
Toward the unfortunate it is pity.
Toward the weak it is help.
Toward the wicked it is resistance.
Toward the strong it is trust.
Toward the fortunate it is congratulations.

Toward the penitent it is forgiveness.
Toward God it is reverence and love.
—*Christian Digest*

* * *

Christian Principles in Business

We need to define, much more clearly
and implicitly than we have yet defined
it, the intimate relationship between a
man's religious faith and what he does
in his business. Our need to demonstrate
that religion is just as relevant to the
individual in his office as in his home
or church. Especially do we need to
establish explicitly-understood Christian
principles for the conduct of business
affairs. The decisions they are required
to make often require courage that can
come only from conscious adherence to
eternal verities, not the shifting sands
of expediency.   —James C. Worthy,
Vice-president, Sears,
Roebuck and Company

* * *

Measure of a Man

Not, how did he die?
But, how did he live?
Not, what did he gain?
But, what did he give?

These are the merits
To measure the worth
Of a man as a man,
Regardless of birth.

Not, what was his station?
But, had he a heart?
And how did he play
His God-given part?

Was he ever ready
With word of good cheer
To bring a smile,
To banish a tear?

Not, what was his church?
Nor, what was his creed?
But had he befriended
Those really in need?

Not, what did the sketch
In the newspaper say?
But, how many were sorry
When he passed away?
—*Selected*

A Christian

Could I be called a Christian
If everybody knew
My secret thoughts and feelings
And everything I do?
Oh, could they see the likeness
Of Christ in me each day,
Oh, could they hear Him speaking
In every word I say?

Could I be called a Christian
If everyone could know
That I am found in places
Where Jesus would not go?
Oh, could they hear His echo
In every song I sing
In eating, drinking, dressing
Could they see Christ in me?

Could I be called a Christian
If judged by what I read,
By all my recreation,
And every thought and deed?
Could I be counted Christlike
As I now work and pray,
Unselfish, kind, forgiving
To others everyday?
—*Selected*

Why Are You Different?

The man was not a preacher. He
could not sing or speak in public. He
worked in a factory with men who
swore and cursed. There he lived a
quiet, Christian life, and spoke for
Jesus when there was an opportunity.
One day as he ate his lunch, one of the
men asked him, "May I sit by you, Bob?
There is a question I have wanted to
ask you for some time, but I was
ashamed to do it. I want to know what
makes you different from the rest of
us. You never get angry, no matter
what we rough fellows do or say to
you. What do you have that we don't
have?" Bob replied, "I am no better
than others, but Christ is in my heart.
He enables me to live differently from
others. To Him be the glory!"
—W. B. K.

* * *

We Would See Jesus!

Adelina Patti, the great singer, instructed her home post office to forward
her mail to a post office in a small
French village. There she planned to

pick it up. "Any mail for Adelina Patti?" she inquired of the postmaster to whom she was a stranger. "Yes," replied the postmaster, "but have you anything to identify you?" She presented a visiting card which the postmaster said was insufficient evidence. "What can I do?" she mused. Then a brilliant idea came to her. She began to sing! In a few moments, the post office was filled with people, listening in wonderment to the rapturous voice! As she concluded her song, she asked the postmaster, "Are you satisfied now that I am Adelina Patti?" "Abundantly satisfied!" said he apologetically. Only Adelina Patti could sing as you have sung," he exclaimed as he gave her a bundle of mail.

A disillusioned, desponding world is saying to you and me, "We would see Jesus!" We can convince others of the reality of Jesus only by having a sustained melody of peace and joy in our hearts, and by living a radiant, victorious life! —W. B. K.

A Monkey Salvationist

Evangeline Booth, when a little girl, had a pet monkey. One day she dressed the monkey in a specially made uniform of the Salvation Army. Mrs. Booth was displeased. She hastily undressed the monkey. Little Evangeline couldn't understand. "Why did you undress the monkey?" she asked. "Because the monkey can't live the life," she said.

Christians can live the life through the power of God. Some of them don't, however, because the inward man does not reflect the outward appearance.

—W. B. K.

CHRISTMAS

Christmas Meditation

Suppose that Christ had not been born
That far-away Judean morn.

Suppose that God, whose mighty hand
Created worlds, had never planned
A way for man to be redeemed.
Suppose the Wise Men only dreamed
That guiding star whose light still glows
Down through the centuries. Suppose
Christ never walked here in men's sight
Our blessed Way, and Truth, and Light.

Suppose He counted all the cost,
And never cared that we were lost,
And never died for you and me,
Nor shed His blood on Calvary
Upon a shameful cross. Suppose
That having died He never rose,
And there was none with power to save
Our souls from death beyond the grave!

As far as piteous heathen know,
These things that I've "supposed" —
    are so.
                —Martha Snell Nicholson

Heaven Proclaimed His Birth!

An hour after Queen Elizabeth's third child was born, 128 cables were sent to all parts of the world! Lights in Buckingham Palace, the Home Office, Foreign Office, Colonial Office, and Commonwealth Relations Office had burned all night. The palace's big switchboard was manned all night. The personnel on night duty was doubled in the ministries.

How different was the birth of Jesus, "The Prince of Peace!" No earthly potentates proclaimed His coming. Atrocious, bloodthirsty Herod concerned himself with the event because he thought some rival ruler had appeared.

God, however, signalized the birth of Jesus by dispatching angelic hosts to proclaim the good news and by placing in the heavens the guiding star to direct seekers to the lowly place in Jesus' birth. —W. B. K.

The Unspeakable Gift

Long ago, there ruled in Persia a wise and good king. He loved his people. He wanted to know how they lived. He wanted to know about the hardships they suffered. Often he dressed in the clothes of a workingman or a beggar, and went to the homes of the poor. No one whom he visited thought that he was their ruler.

One time he visited a very poor man who lived in a cellar. He ate the coarse food the poor man ate. He spoke cheerful, kind words to him. Then he left. Later he visited the poor man again and disclosed his identity by saying, "I'm your king!" How surprised the poor man was! The king thought the man would surely ask for some gift or favor, but he didn't. Instead he said, "You left your palace and your glory to visit me in this dark, dreary place. You ate the coarse food I ate. You brought gladness to my heart! To others you have given your rich gifts. *To me you have given yourself!*"

The King of glory, the Lord Jesus, gave Himself to you and me! The Bible calls Him, "the unspeakable gift!"

—W. B. K.

* * *

The Stable

I am so glad He was not born
In some rich palace bed.
I am so glad to know it was
A lowly place, instead,
A place where soft-eyed cows and sheep
Were sheltered and were fed.

For to the country-born of earth
A stable will ever be
A wholesome place, where night comes down
With its tranquillity,
A place of heart's ease and content
For all who choose to see.

And so I like to think of Him,
First opening His eyes
In that good elemental place
Beneath the friendly skies,
That the men of fields could find Him there,
As well as the great and wise.

—Grace Noll Crowell

* * *

Fear Not

Not to the priest in the temple of old,
Not to the king in his palace of gold,
Not to the famous — the men of the hour,
Not to the great with their might and their power;
But to the shepherds alone in the night

God sent His glorious angels of light,
Bearing their tidings, so blessed and true,
"Fear not! a Saviour is born unto you."

Not to the men who in arrogant pride
March ever on over life's surging tide;
Not to the boastful who make their life's aim
Only to seek after worldly acclaim;
But to the humble, the meek, and the low,
When in the night of great trial and woe,
God sends His Spirit to whisper anew,
"Fear not! Your Saviour abideth with you!"

—James A. Dillon

* * *

In a Stable

A London city missionary went into a stable and began to talk to a jockey about the salvation of his soul.

"This is no place to talk religion, so there's an end of it!" exclaimed the jockey.

"Oh, no, that's not the end of it; it's only the beginning," said the missionary. "Christianity began in a stable. Jesus Christ was born in a stable, and you can be born again in one."

—*God's Revivalist*

* * *

The Shepherd's Tale

Silver moon, and a starry night;
Over the hills we sped.
Walls of Bethlehem gleaming white,
Villagers long abed.
"Open the gate, O watchman grim,
Open, the dawn is nigh,
Christ has been born, and we hasten to Him,
Reuben, and Judah and I."

Swift we passed through the silent street
On to the stable rude;
Flutter of wings beneath our feet —
Hen, with her startled brood;
Stepping softly, with bated breath,
What do you think we saw?
Joseph and Mary of Nazareth,
And a babe on a bed of straw!

Dear little dimpled babe we saw,
Cozy and warm and sweet,

Lying asleep in a bed of straw
Strewn where the oxen eat.
Tender toes, and a tiny face
Fair as the morning sky —
That's what we found in that stable place,
Judah, and Reuben and I.
> —Frederick H. Sterne, in
> *The Watchman-Examiner*

* * *

Born in You

'Tis not enough that Christ was born
Beneath the star that shone,
And earth was set that holy morn
Within a golden zone.
He must be born within the heart
Before He finds a throne,
And brings the day of love and good,
The reign of Christlike brotherhood.
> —*Selected*

* * *

A Newborn Babe Gives Sight to Others

An obstetrician approached an anxious father in a waiting room of a New York City hospital and said, "I am sorry to inform you, but your baby lived but two hours after its birth, though we did everything we could to save its life." As the sympathetic doctor was about to leave, the quick thinking father said, "I read only recently that human eyes are needed in corneal operations. Could my baby's eyes be used to enable someone to see again?" The next day the Red Cross carried an eye each to two different hospitals. In one, a corneal graft restored the sight of a working man with a large family. In the other, sight was given to a mother. A babe, who lived only two hours, gave physical sight to a grateful father and a mother. Some 2,000 years ago a Babe came into our sin-darkened world to give spiritual sight to all who will receive it without money and without price. At His coming, "the people that walked in darkness [saw] a great light." —W. B. K.

* * *

I Pity You Palefaces!

An aged Indian woman spoke in her native tongue at a Christmas service for the benefit of the Indians who were present. Then she turned to the English-speaking people and said in English, "I have told my people the story of the birth of Christ. It is a wonderful story! Do you know, I pity you palefaces. You never knew the astonishment and wonderment that I felt when I heard this story for the first time! You have always been familiar with it. It says nothing special to you. My best Christmas wish for you is that you may be moved again by the glory of the gospel, as if you were hearing it for the first time, so that Christ may really be born in your hearts as in mine!"
> —W. B. K.

* * *

Christmas — That Magic Carpet!

Christmas — that magic carpet that wraps itself about us, that something so intangible that it is like a fragrance. It may weave a spell of nostalgia. Christmas may be a day of feasting, or of prayer, but always it will be a day of remembrance — a day in which we think of everything we have ever loved. Then we realize that He who has led us down through the labyrinth of years, born two thousand years ago, showed us the way, saying that we would have peace on earth if we love one another.

There was a gift for each of us left under the tree of life two thousand years ago by Him whose birthday we celebrate today. The gift was withheld from no man. Some have left the packages unclaimed. Some have accepted the gift and carry it around, but have failed to remove the wrappings and look inside to discover the hidden splendour. The packages are all alike: in each is a scroll on which is written, "All that the Father hath is thine." Take and live! —Arnold Westcott in
> First Baptist Church
> Bulletin, Syracuse, N. Y.

* * *

God in a Frame

"I will manifest myself to him."
(John 14:21)

A little boy, whose father was away from home most of the time, looked at his dad's picture on the wall and said to his mother: "Mother, I wish father would come out of that frame."

Is God real to you, a Person near at hand? Or is He more like a picture on the wall, a motto, a doctrine, something wonderful to look at and think about, but still in a frame? Have you wished He might come out of the frame, become a glorious living Reality? Have you cried, "Oh, that I knew where I might find Him"? —Rev. Vance Havner, D.D.

* * *

Star of the East

Star of the East, that long ago
Brought wise men on their way
Where, angels singing to and fro,
The Child of Bethlehem lay —
Above the Syrian hill afar
Thou shinest out tonight, O Star!

Star of the East! Show us the way
In wisdom undefiled
To seek that manger out and lay
Our gifts before the Child —
To bring our hearts and offer them
Unto our King in Bethlehem!
—Eugene Field

* * *

I Am the Christmas Spirit

I sweep across oceans, through dark continents, into cities, into the country, into rich homes, into poor homes, into the hearts of those far away from home — into everyone's life all over the world. I go with a speed that is so well timed that I am in all parts of the world in one week's time.

People know I am coming long before I actually arrive, and big, little, old and young, black, white, brown and yellow plan for my arrival. I am the most contagious thing on the face of the earth, and if it were in the mind of anyone to try to stop me, no power, no vaccine, no order from any government could check me. When I come I touch all lives and everyone is inoculated so that he, too, breaks out with a thorough case of me. There is no way to immunize the soul against me.

But the strange part of it is that no one wants to fight against my ravages of human hearts anywhere in all the world. Instead, people plan for me long weeks before I arrive. All kinds of plans are laid for my coming; homes, schools, churches, business houses, governments talk of my coming and lay plans for my reception. They well know that I will cost them dearly in money, in time, in strain — in many ways, and yet old and young alike plan for my

coming with an eagerness and a quickened heart pulse. However much of a Scrooge anyone tries to be, I come and I inject my spirit into his heart where it immediately begins to grow.

Over and above all the things and the wonderful spirit which I bring into existence, I bring to every human being the greatest hope of the world — Jesus.
—*Cumberland Presbyterian*

* * *

What a Night!

That night when in the Judean skies
The mystic star dispensed its light,
A blind man moved in his sleep
And dreamed that he had sight.

That night when shepherds heard
The song of hosts angelic choiring near.
A deaf man stirred in slumber's spell
And dreamed that he could hear.

That night when o'er the new-born babe
The tender Mary rose to lean,
A loathsome leper smiled in sleep,
And dreamed that he was clean.

That night when in the manger lay
The Sanctified who came to save,
A man moved in the sleep of death,
And dreamed there was no grave.
—*Selected*

* * *

Where Is the Child?

A five-year-old refugee was being shown the wonders of a large toy department by his foster parents. His eyes grew wide with wonderment but gradually an expression of disappointment clouded his face. He began to search up and down the aisles and under the tables and counters. At last he burst out, "But where is the child?"

After an embarrassed silence, a store official ordered a Christmas crib to be found at once and set up in a prominent place in the toy department. At this the little boy smiled with delight. Young as he was, he had given a lesson in the real significance of Christmas.
—"Living Tissue"

* * *

Music Hath Power

Lieutenant Gitz Rice was a member of a famous Canadian regiment which went to France in World War I. The regiment fought in Flanders' Fields. It fought across the desolate "No Man's Land" under cover of a fearsome barrage — sometimes even without the sheltering shells.

Rice's company carried a strange implement of war — a piano. On that piano in France, Gitz Rice composed one of the famous songs of the soldiers, "Mademoiselle from Armentieres."

The afternoon before Christmas Eve it was decided that the piano should be taken up to the front-line trenches. It was hoisted into an army truck and finally deposited at its destination.

Peace had settled over "No Man's Land" that night. But the barbed wire remained and a morning attack threatened each side. The hostile troops were so close that one could hear them conversing.

Shortly before the hour of midnight Rice began playing Christmas carols in the British trench. First he played, "Silent Night, Holy Night." This was followed by "Hark, the Herald Angels Sing" and other beloved carols familiar to all the Christian world.

The Canadian soldiers sang lustily, then they paused. From across the shallow field they heard the German troops singing with them. It was Christmas Eve!

Rice then played an aria from Wagner's "Tannhäuser." As he began the opening chords, a Canadian soldier mounted the rim of the parapet and sang the words.

"More! More!" shouted the Germans. Then one of their own singers, a rich baritone, repeated the song to Rice's accompaniment, standing as a target for British rifles.

Such incidents bring to light the seeds of good will which are hidden in the hard soil of our embittered world. If we look for them, we can find them.

—*Gospel Banner*

* * *

Feeding and Clothing Jesus

Martin was a poor, obscure shoemaker. He worked long hours every day in his little shoeshop. He made a meager living. Yet he was a joyous, friendly man, who gave a helping hand to all those in need.

One night, after a frugal meal, Martin went to bed. As he slept, he dreamed that he was visited by a most wonderful Person. He had never before seen such a kind, gentle face! "Martin," said the Visitor, "tomorrow I am going to visit you in your shop!" Martin was sure the Visitor was Jesus!

In his dream, the morrow came swiftly. How happy Martin was as he tidied up his little shop! Soon all was shipshape for the joyously anticipated Visitor. But no one came, except an old man, who had been shoveling snow. How cold and hungry-looking he was! Martin served him hot tea and bread. How grateful the man was as he left! Then a strange woman, with a scared, careworn look on her face entered. She was poorly dressed. She held close to her heart a sickly-looking little baby. Martin gave her warm, nourishing food, and as she left, he removed his jacket, and spread it over the little baby. Though there was deep satisfaction in Martin's heart because he had helped the needy ones, he felt a twinge of disappointment that the expected Visitor had not come.

Then, just before Martin awoke from his dream, he heard a soothing, tender voice which said, "Martin, didn't you recognize Me? Twice I visited you today. I knew you wanted to do kind, helpful things for Me, and this you did when you helped others in My name!" Then Martin understood the meaning of these words, "Verily I say unto you, Inasmuch as ye have done it unto one of the least of these . . . ye have done it unto me!" —W. B. K.

* * *

God's Children Didn't Fail!

Childish impressions are lasting impressions. My father died when I was nine years old. My mother was left penniless with five half-orphaned children. Sorrows came thick and fast! We all came down with typhoid fever. An older and a younger brother died. When Christmas approached there were no toys or other things which rejoice the heart of childhood. It was then that I got an early and lasting impression of the great love and unselfishness of true Christian people. On Christmas Eve, they came with arms filled with toys, candy, nuts and fruits! How dismal Christmas would have been for my sisters and me but for the kindness and thoughtfulness of God's children.

—W. B. K.

* * *

Forgive Us Our Christmases!

The day before Christmas had been full of incidents, some of them unpleasant. Father seemed to be burdened with worries as well as bundles. Mother's anxiety had reached the breaking point on many occasions throughout the day. Wherever the little girl went, she seemed to be in the way.

Finally she was hustled to bed. The feverish excitement of the Christmas planning had completely unnerved her. As she knelt by her bed to pray the Lord's Prayer, she got all mixed up and prayed, *"Forgive us our Christmases,* as we forgive those who Christmas against us."

As we watch the tense, nervous shoppers this season, we feel like praying as the little girl did, "Forgive us our Christmases." —*Gospel Herald*

CHURCH

Short Quotes

A room of quiet,
  a temple of peace;
A home of faith —
  where doubtings cease.
A house of comfort,
  where hope is given;
A source of strength
  to help us to heaven;
A place of worship,
  a place to pray —
I found all this
  in my Church today.

—The Reverend Owen W. Glassburn

* * *

The typical American has developed a remarkable capacity for being serious about religion without taking religion seriously.

* * *

The most critical need of the church at this moment is men, the right kind of men, bold men, free men. The church must seek, in prayer and much humility, the coming again of men made of the stuff of which prophets and martyrs are made. —The Rev. A. W. Tozer, D.D.

* * *

Lost or strayed (I hope not stolen) a few hundred of the Lord's sheep. Not seen for several weeks. Please return tomorrow morning — Sunday — to the green pastures of St. Mary's Church where a table will be prepared and the cup will be running over! No questions will be asked. —Put in Lost and Found section of a local paper by the Rev. Joseph Witkofski, rector of St. Mary's Episcopal Church, who reported, "Fine Results!"

* * *

A boy brought up in Sunday school is seldom brought up in court.

—Dr. Clay Risley

* * *

The world needs terribly the solid glories of our faith: creation, incarnation, atonement, resurrection, ascension. We can almost hear stricken humanity sighing for good news. The church has it!

—Rev. Massey Mott Heltzel

* * *

If a church has too little influence over a community, it is because the community has too much influence over that church.

—Rev. George McDaniel, D.D.

* * *

Our people do not so much need to have their heads stirred as to have their hearts touched. —Jonathan Edwards

* * *

Religion today is not transforming the people — it is being transformed by the people. It is not raising the moral level of society — it is descending to society's own level and congratulating itself that it has scored a victory because society is smilingly accepting its surrender. —The Rev. A. W. Tozer, D.D.

* * *

We can't spell Sunday without U,
We can't spell church without U,
We can't spell success without U —
Our church needs U to help:
We are counting on U!

* * *

There are three kinds of church members: effective, ineffective and defective. —Dr. Lloyd Doughtery

* * *

In essentials — unity,
In nonessentials — liberty,
In all things — charity.
　　　　　　　　—Augustine

* * *

Many churches are fundamentally sound — *asleep!* "Awake thou that sleepest . . . Christ shall give thee light" (Eph. 5:14). —Barnhouse

* * *

The church in America is faced with an amazing paradox. On the one hand more people are attending church than at any time in our history. Our budgets are larger than ever before. Yet never has the church lacked spiritual power so greatly as now in the face of a staggering opportunity and the most accelerated moral decline of any nation in world history. —Billy Graham

* * *

In this world, a churchless community, where men have abandoned and scoffed at or ignored their religious needs, is a community on the rapid downgrade. Church work and church attendance mean the cultivation of the habit of feeling some responsibility for others. There are enough holidays for most of us. Sundays differ from other holidays in the fact that there are fifty-two of them every year — therefore, on Sundays go to church. Yes, I know all the excuses. I know that one can worship the Creator in a grove of trees or in a man's own home. But I know, as a matter of cold fact, the average man does not thus worship.
　　　　　　　—Theodore Roosevelt

There are 41,197,313 persons enrolled in the Sunday schools of America, and today the total number of churches of all kinds is 309,449. In 1959, 5393 new churches were built in this nation. There are approximately 70 million eligible non-churchgoers in America.
　　　　　　—Rev. Horace F. Dean, D.D.

* * *

The phone rang in the office of the church where President Franklin D. Roosevelt usually attended. "Are you expecting the President in church Sunday?" "That I cannot promise," replied the rector, "but we expect God to be there, and that should be incentive enough for you to be there!" —W. B. K.

* * *

There are 69,000,000 persons in our country who have no church affiliation; 19,000,000 of these are youths twelve to twenty-three years of age; 31,000,000 persons move every year; crime is growing four times as fast as population; population is increasing at the rate of 2,500,000 per year. —Harry Denman, Executive Secretary of the General Board of Evangelism (Methodist)

* * *

"Why is not God already real to Americans who are among the most churchgoing people in the world?" asked the editor of *Life.* "Partly because of the blight of secularism in the churches which have become just another valued *branch* of American democratic culture instead of its center. What used to be the minister's study is now his office, and as a busy agent of the social gospel he is less a spokesman of God than a useful citizen, making East Overshoe a better place to live," commented the editor. —*Gospel Banner*

* * *

Wake up, sing up, pray up, stay up, and never give up nor shut up until the cause of Christ in this church and in this world is built up!
　　　　　—A motto in a Negro church
　　　　　　　　in Kansas City, Mo.

* * *

The church is filled with willing people — some willing to work and others willing to let them.

Wanted: Men, women and children to sit in slightly used pews Sunday morning — Saratoga Congregational Church.
—In *"Wanted"* section of
St. Charles Minnesota Press

* * *

How spiritually poor is that church which venerates the crucifix, but is not vitalized by the Crucified!
—Dr. Herbert Lockyer, Sr.

* * *

Laymen make up more than ninety-nine per cent of the membership of the church, and ministers only about three-tenths of one per cent. The first leaders of the church were laymen.
—Paul W. Milhouse

* * *

Statistics kept by pastors show that the number of people "ill" on Sunday is greater than the total number of ill on the other six days.

* * *

Don't go to church in the morning if you plan to go to the devil in the evening. —Rev. Rex Humbard

* * *

The world sleeps in darkness. The church sleeps in the light. The world is not waiting for a new definition of the gospel, but for a new demonstration of its power. The hour is too late for another denomination to be born. God is now preparing His last great offensive against militant godlessness, a great last outpouring of revival that will be as new wine bursting the skins of dried-up sectarianism.
—Evangelist Leonard Ravenhill

* * *

"I'll join a church when I find a perfect church," said a self-righteous young man to a wise old pastor. Quipped the pastor, "Should you find a perfect church, I advise you, young man, not to join it, for if you do, it would cease to be a perfect church!" —W. B. K.

* * *

Conversion is but the first step in divine life. As long as we live we should more and more be turning from all that is evil, and to all that is good.
—Tryon Edwards

There are 72,800,000 in America who never go to any church.
—Dr. Henrietta Mears

* * *

There is increasing piety along the Potomac by our government's leaders, but danger lies in the temptation to use religion as a promotional gimmick or to view all religion, whether true or false, as good. —Dr. Carl F. H. Henry, editor
Christianity Today

* * *

Two-thirds of the membership of the churches know little or nothing about conversion as a personal, experiential fact. —Dr. E. Stanley Jones

* * *

I have observed that over 85 per cent of the criminals were non-churchgoers.
—Judge Julius H. Miner

* * *

Out of 8,000 delinquent children, only 42 attended Sunday school regularly.
—J. Edgar Hoover

* * *

Love for God holds the family steadfast. A home built on religious concepts is a fortress against crime. We go into church wavering. We go out strengthened and inspired. Home training, though indispensable, can never offer an adequate substitute in the religious education of a child for the planned instruction of the Sunday school and church. —Judge Julius H. Miner
Circuit Court, Chicago

* * *

The world is being inoculated with a mild form of Christianity which is making us immune to the real thing.
—Dr. James DeForest Murch

* * *

The holiest moment of the church service is the moment when God's people — strengthened by preaching and sacrament — go out of the church door into the world *to be the church*. We don't go to church; we *are* the church.
—Canon Ernest Southcott

* * *

The church was built to disturb the peace of man, but often it does not perform its duty for fear of disturbing the

peace of the church. What kind of artillery practice would that be which declined to fire for fear of kicking over the gun carriages, or waking up the sentries asleep at their posts?
—Henry Ward Beecher

* * *

The spiritual thrust, it seems to me, has been almost *numerical*. There is this great influx into the churches, and this great interest, but so much of it is *superficial!* —Billy Graham

* * *

If absence makes the heart grow fonder, some people ought to love their church greatly. —W. B. K.

* * *

It is better to have no godliness at all than a mere form of godliness. What is deader than a dead orthodoxy? "Thou hast a name that thou livest, and art dead" (Rev. 3:1).
—Rev. William McCarrell

* * *

It is more essential to ring door bells than church bells when there are 72,-800,000 in America who never go to church. —Roger Babson

* * *

The danger with our generation is that we are becoming church conscious rather than Christ conscious.
–The Rev. R. R. Brown, D.D.

* * *

Rarely do the parents of delinquent children attend church, and even small-er is the number of them who are active church members. Less than 10 per cent of our delinquent children attend Sunday school, and only a few of these could be listed as regular in their attendance. —Judge Allen Ardell

* * *

Man, at long last, has come to know that the security and safety of mankind — in fact, his very existence — now depend upon wisdom far greater than humans possess. Many are turning to God and the church to seek a way out of the labyrinth of disasters that seem to threaten them. —Rep. Russell V. Mack, in an address to the House of Representatives

* * *

In the time of the early Church, Peter said, "Silver and gold have I none; but such as I have give I thee" (Acts 3:6). Some churches today, reveling in riches can only say, "Silver and gold have we in abundance, but such as you need, we have not." —W. B. K

* * *

The church which is not a missionary church will be a missing church when Jesus comes. —Dr. F. B. Meyers

* * *

"I can never hope to destroy Christianity until I first destroy the Christian Sabbath," said Voltaire. Many, to their own spiritual impoverishment, have made Sunday a fun-day. The holy day has become a holiday.
—W. B. K.

Illustrations

Where the Cross Must Be Raised

I simply argue that the cross must be raised again at the center of the marketplace as well as on the steeple of the church. I am recovering the claim that Christ was not crucified in a cathedral between two candles, but on a cross between two thieves; on the town garbage-heap; at a cross-road so cosmopolitan that they had to write His title in Hebrew and in Latin and in Greek . . .; at the kind of place where cynics talk smut, and thieves curse, and soldiers gamble. Because that is where he died. And that is what he died about. And that is where churchmen should be and what churchmanship should be about.
—George MacLeod in
Only One Way Left

* * *

Emotion in Religion

A crudely emotional approach to religion is preferable to religious formalism which is purely aesthetic and orderly and lacking in dynamic power. One of our serious troubles in the church today is that it has become legitimate

to be emotional in anything but religion. The need is for something that will summon one's whole enthusiasm. The moment the church becomes completely programized and depersonalized, it becomes a monument to God's memory and not an instrument of His loving power.
—Dr. John A. Mackay in
Christianity Today

* * *

Which Kind Are You?
A lot of Christians are like wheelbarrows — not good unless pushed.
Some are like canoes — they need to be paddled.
Some are like kites — if you don't keep a string on them, they fly away.
Some are like kittens — they are more contented when petted.
Some are like a football — you can't tell what way they will bounce next.
Some are like balloons — full of wind and ready to blow up.
Some are like trailers — they have to be pulled.
Some are like lights — they keep going on and off.
And there are those who always seek to let the Holy Spirit lead them.
—*Christian Index*

* * *

The Heavy Flea
A flea and an elephant walked side by side over a bridge. Said the flea to the elephant after they had crossed, "Boy, we sure did shake that bridge!" This is like some church members. They ride the wagon while others push, criticize while others try, are light as a feather when weighed in the balances, and then cry, "Boy, look what *we* did!" Are we fleas or elephants when it comes to our working in this congregation?
—*Baptist Standard*

* * *

What Theodore Roosevelt Said
A man at church may not hear a good sermon, but he will hear a sermon by a good man who, with his good wife, is engaged all the week in making hard lives a little easier. He will listen to and take part in reading some beautiful passages from the Bible, and if he is not familiar with the Bible he has suffered a loss. He will take part in singing some good hymns. He will meet and nod or speak to good, quiet neighbors. He will come away feeling a little more charitable toward all the world, even toward those excessively foolish young men who regard church going as a soft performance. I advocate a man's joining in church work for the sake of showing his faith by his works. —*Wesleyan Methodist*

* * *

Protestant
This word does not mean, as so many people think, "To protest against." It is not a negation. "A Protestant is always against something," we say. This is incorrect. Our word "protest" comes from two Latin words, "pro" and "testare," which mean "to testify for." As applied to members of the original movement — the Reformation — it meant, "one who testifies that he has had an inner spiritual experience." "Protest" is an active, positive affirmation. Protestantism began not so much in the mood of condemnation as in the spirit of affirming great truth which has been neglected or forgotten. This is the true meaning of "Protestantism." 'Tis well to remember this. —Bulletin of the First Baptist Church, New Bedford, Mass.

* * *

The Empty Pew
"Thou shalt be missed, because thy seat will be empty." —I Sam. 20:18.
The empty pew has an eloquent tongue. Though its message is unpleasant, it is one that all may hear.
To the preacher, the empty pew says, "Your sermon is not worth while."
To the visitor it whispers, "You see we are not holding our own."
To the treasurer it shouts, "Look out for a deficit."
To the stranger who is looking for a home church it suggests, "You had better wait a while."
To the members who are present it asks, "Why don't you go visiting next Sunday, too?"
The empty pew speaks against the service. It kills inspiration, it smothers hope, and it dulls the fine edge of zeal. The empty pew is a weight; the occupied pew is a wing. —*Gospel Banner*

God Builds No Churches

God builds no churches. By His plan
That labor has been left to man.
  No spires miraculously arise;
  No little mission from the skies
Falls on the bleak and barren place
To be a source of strength and grace.
  The humblest church demands its price
  In human toil and sacrifice.

Men call the Church the House of God
Toward which the toil-stained pilgrims
    trod
  In search of strength and rest and
    hope,
  As blindly through life's mists they
    grope.
And there God dwells, but it is man
Who builds that House, and draws its
    plan;
  Pays for mortar and the stone
  That none need seek for God alone.

The humblest spire to mortal ken
Where God abides was built by men.
  And if the Church is still to grow,
  Is still the light of hope to throw
Across the valley of despair
Men still must build God's House of
    Prayer.
  God sends no churches from the skies.
  Out of our hearts they must arise.

                    —Edgar A. Guest

* * *

An Old Question

Question: Can I be a Christian without joining the church?

Answer: Yes, it is possible. It is something like being:

A student who will not go to school.
A soldier who will not join an army.
A citizen who does not pay taxes or vote.
A salesman with no customers.
An explorer with no base camp.
A seaman on a ship without a crew.
A business man on a deserted island.
An author without readers.
A tuba player without an orchestra.
A parent without a family.
A football player without a team.
A politician who is a hermit.
A scientist who does not share his findings.
A bee without a hive.

                    —*Wesleyan Christian Advocate*

Church Member Beatitudes

Blessed is he who will not strain at a drizzle and swallow a downpour.

Blessed is he who tries a little harder when all around say, "It can't be done."

Blessed is he whose program contains time for regular Bible reading.

Blessed is he who serves faithfully on a committee.

Blessed is the church official who is not pessimistic.

Blessed is he who loves his church before his business.

Blessed is he who can walk as fast to a religious service as to town.

                    —*Religious Telescope*

* * *

They Won't Miss Me!

"They won't miss me!" said the mother as she repeatedly left her children for rounds of teas and parties. The devil did not "miss" the children either.

"They won't miss me!" said the soldier as he went AWOL. But he spent 30 days in the guard house after that.

"They won't miss me!" said the man on the assembly line, as he slipped away without permission. But that airplane crashed and killed his brother for lack of a single part.

"They won't miss me!" said the sentry as he slipped away from duty. But the enemy surprised and massacred his comrades that very night.

"They won't miss me!" said the church member as he shed his responsibilities in a day of crisis, and then wondered why his country gave way to softness and demoralization.

"They won't miss me!" said the church member as he omitted worship one Sunday, and then another, for trivial reasons, and then wondered why he no longer enjoyed a victorious Christian life. —*The Christian Herald*

* * *

Denominationalism — Good or Bad?

Charles V of Spain spent the long and uneventful years of his reign in a futile effort to bring about a unanimity of religious belief among his subjects. He gave up the hopeless task and abdicated his throne. At Yuste, where he lived in retirement, he collected many clocks and watches, and tried to make them all keep the same time. He gave up the task as hopeless. Dejectedly he confessed: "How foolish I have been in trying to make men believe alike religiously when I cannot make two timepieces keep the same time!"

Is denominational division among God's children a good or a bad thing? Does this division engender strength and spiritual freedom in Christ? It is certain that God has used and is now accomplishing His purposes through different denominations. God has His children among the different denominations. People are different emotionally and temperamentally. Is it not a good thing for the individual to go with that group whose ways of expressing themselves religiously corresponds to his? The writer's grandfather, John W. Knight, was an old-fashioned Methodist circuit rider. When his cup of joy overflowed, he would shout. His grandson is totally different. The more joyous he becomes in the Lord, the quieter he becomes before the Lord and others. Differences in church polity, without disagreement as relates to the central truths of God's Word, could bespeak strength, not weakness.

—W. B. K.

* * *

A Hindu's Impressions

A Hindu student from India, a Ph.D., attended the morning service at "one of the leading evangelical churches in California." He was much impressed with the beautiful building, remarking, "This is a magnificent building that you have here . . . much finer than our temples in India." But he was greatly astonished to learn that the building was used mainly on the Sunday morning, a much smaller number of people attending the evening service also, and a handful turning up for the midweek prayer meeting. His comment:

"Do you mean to tell me you have this elaborate, expensive building, and you use it only two or three times a week? In India we go to prayer in our Hindu temples every morning at sunrise and every night at sunset. The Moslems go to prayer five times daily. How can you expect us to accept Christianity when we pray more to our gods than you do to yours?"

—*International Student*

* * *

All Necessary and Needed

The carpenter's tools were having a conference. Brother Hammer was acting as chairman, but the group soon informed him that he must leave, for he was too noisy. Brother Hammer said, "If I leave the carpenter shop, Brother Gimlet must go, too. He is so insignificant that he makes little impression." Little Brother Gimlet rose and said, "All right, I will go, but if I go, Brother Screw must go, also. You have to turn him around and around before you can get him to go anywhere." "If you wish, I will go," said Brother Screw, "but then Brother Plane must leave. All his work is on the surface — there is no depth to him." To this Brother Plane replied, "Well, Brother Rule, you will have to withdraw, too, for you are always measuring folks as though you were the only person who is right." Brother Rule complained against Brother Sandpaper and said, "He should leave because he is rougher than he ought to be. He is always rubbing people the wrong way." In the midst of the heated discussion, the carpenter walked in. He put on his apron and walked to the bench. He employed the hammer, the gimlet, the screw, the plane, the rule, the sandpaper, and all the other tools. When the day's work was over, he had completed a pulpit from which the Gospel would be preached. —*Baptist Leader*

* * *

After a Week of Perplexing Problems

After a week of perplexing problems and heated contests, it does so rest my soul to come into the house of the Lord and worship, and to sing, and mean it, "Holy, Holy, Holy, Lord God Almighty," and to know that He is my Father and takes me up into His life and plans, and to commune personally with Christ. I am sure I get a wisdom not my own, and a superhuman strength for fighting the moral evils I am called to confront.

—Theodore Roosevelt

The Parable of the Mudites and the Anti-mudites

Two men met, a great many years ago, at a church convention. They were mutually surprised, as they became better acquainted, to discover that both had formerly been completely blind, and that Jesus had opened their eyes and given them sight.

"Isn't it marvelous," said the one, "How the Master makes clay, puts it into your eyes, and tells you to go and wash? Then when you wash, your eyes are opened, and you can see!"

"Mud? Jesus doesn't use mud. He just speaks a word, and you can see!"

"Jesus does use mud!" "He doesn't!" "Does!"

"He does not! I ought to know. I was blind, and He opened my eyes, and now I see!"

"He does use mud! If He didn't use mud, He didn't open your eyes. You can't see. You just think you can. You are still blind, and I'll have nothing more to do with you. You have denied one of the fundamentals of our faith!"

And presently those whose blind eyes Jesus had opened with mud came together in an exclusive group, and excluded all others. And those whose eyes Jesus had opened without mud joined together also, and the two groups spent their time in rivalry between themselves, while the blind all about them groped through life, unaware that there is One who came to bring Light to all who walk in darkness. —*Selected*

* * *

A Believe-as-You Like Church!

Glenview Community Church has no simple pastor with assistants but a "team ministry" of four clergymen, all equal in authority. Their church is a believe-as-you-like, worship-as-you-please fellowship of searchers, and the ministers' language often sounds less religious than sociological. "Christians should develop a relationship with God," enabling them "to live out their potential"; an eye must be kept on "fringe individuals"; the church is "developmental-task-oriented" and its beliefs are "anchored but open-ended."
—*Time*

Anemic Liberalism, Bickering Fundamentalism

Laymen are sick and tired of anemic liberalism on the one hand and fighting, bickering fundamentalism on the other. Both fail to *live* what they so loudly proclaim. . . . The dominant force in many churches is Phariseeism and worldliness. Laymen are beginning to wake up to the fact that many churches are more interested in statistics and meeting the budget than they are in spiritual power. —Billy Graham

* * *

Staying Home from Church

Some stay home because it's cold,
And some, because it's hot;
And some, because they're getting old,
And some, because they're not!

Some stay home because their hat
The milliner's not finished;
And some because their liking for
The minister has diminished.

Some declare they don't enjoy
The singing of the choir;
And others, because their fellow saint
Aroused their wrathful ire.

Alas! alas! our excuses grow
To drive our thoughts from God,
And turn us from the House of Prayer,
The place our fathers trod.
—*Simpson Summons*

* * *

Temples Not Made with Hands

We, the Church, are the temple of the living God, and every chapel and cathedral is but a symbol. God the Holy Spirit calls, gathers, enlightens, sanctifies and preserves a *people* upon the earth. They are the Church! They defy the boundaries of race and color, culture and creed, and become *one* in their common Lord and Saviour.

They are not held together primarily by their registered membership in a congregation, nor by the sameness of their denominational label. All these may be only external marks of their oneness.

They are one in Christ, if Christ dwells in them and they in Christ. They are a new creation through a new birth brought about by the work of the Holy Spirit in their hearts. Together, like stones interlocked and fitted, they become a holy temple for the Living God.

—Selected

. . .

Jaunty Saints

Today dark-browed Pessimism has gone out of vogue and her happy and irresponsible sister Optimism has come on to take her place. Christianity is now conceived as fun and the only cross is the one on which Jesus died several hundred years ago. Christ's yoke is not only easy; it is downright thrilling; His burden is not only light, it is jaunty. The church goes along with everything and stands against nothing — until she is convinced that it is the safe and popular thing to do; then she passes her courageous resolutions and issues her world-shaking manifestoes — all in accord with the world's newest social venture, whatever it may be.

—The Alliance Witness

. . .

Does Your Church Need a Diet?

Is your church program overweight? Are there some non-essentials which a strict diet would lop off and thus restore your church to robust, vigorous health?

A church leader in the East said some weeks ago, "Churches must drop many of their 'social activities' in favor of more urgent tasks. If the church today suffers from any one ailment above others, it is from triviality. . . . The more urgent tasks that must be conserved are the teaching of the youth the truth of the Christian message and the preaching of judgment and mercy of God to a world which is desperately in need of the redeeming power of the Gospel."

—The Evangelical Witness

. . .

A Great History

What a history the Church of Christ, in spite of its failings, has had! How filled with heroism, romance, indomitable perseverance, and promise of ultimate and unselfish success! No continuous organized movement has ever had a mission, a life history, a conquest over difficulties, and an idealism comparable to that of the Christian Church. No organization has ever done so much in molding human society and individual character.

The Church bears in her body the stigmata of Christ. She has been baptized with the blood of martyrs and glorified by deeds of supreme devotion and sacrifice. She has been the mother of saints and sages and heroes, builder of cathedrals and shrines and institutions of sacred learning, inspirer of art and poetry, upholder of morality and social order, and pioneer of new and daring enterprises. She has met with indifference and opposition, but the gates of hell have not prevailed against her.

—John Wright Buckham

. . .

Quaint Rules for Church Decorum

I
Thou shalt not come to service late,
Nor for the Amen refuse to wait.

II
Thy noisy tongue thou shalt restrain
When speaks the organ its refrain.

III
But when the hymns are sounded out,
Thou shalt lift up thy voice and shout.

IV
The endmost seat thou shalt leave free,
For more must share the pew with thee.

V
The offering plate thou shalt not fear,
But give thine uttermost with cheer.

VI
Thou shalt this calendar peruse,
And look here for the church's news.

VII
Thou shalt the minister give heed,
Nor blame him when thou'rt disagreed.

VIII
Unto thy neighbor thou shalt bend,
And if a stranger, make a friend.

IX
Thou shalt in every way be kind,
Compassionate, of tender mind.

X
And so, by all thy spirit's grace,
Thou shalt show God within this place.

—Selected

Putting God First

Dr. Lyman Abbott was traveling through a district that had been devastated by fire. It was a district largely populated by sincere Puritans. There were many temporary log houses and rough shanties in view; in these crude dwellings the people were sheltering themselves. But Dr. Abbott was surprised to see one fine, large brick building that stood out obviously above the rest. In reply to his question he was informed that the brick building was the church. "Oh," he said, "then the church was not damaged by fire!" "Oh, yes," he was told, "it was completely destroyed. That is the new church. We have rebuilt that before we have rebuilt our own houses."

—*Sunday School Times*

* * *

Something You Should Know

5% of reported church members do not exist;
10% cannot be found;
20% never pray;
25% never read the Bible;
30% never attend church;
40% never give to any cause;
50% never go to Sunday school;
60% never go to church Sunday nights;
70% never give to Missions;
75% never engage in any church activity;
80% never go to prayer meeting;
90% never have family worship;
95% never win a soul to Christ.

Let us determine to dedicate ourselves for His service, so that the whole world may hear the whole Gospel.

—*Crusade Contact*
Child For Christ Crusade

* * *

Church Gypsies

There are religious grasshoppers and church gypsies who never can find a pastor or church good enough for them; who chase favorite preachers and live on samples brought back from Canaan instead of crossing Jordan and living in the Promised Land themselves, packing their note books with epigrams, but not hiding the Word in their hearts. Some of them have the impression that one

is not living the Christian life unless he is in a state of ecstasy at a high pressure meeting. They want to fly all the time and have found no grace for running without weariness or walking without fainting. They go up like rockets and come down like rocks.

—Rev. Vance Havner

* * *

Judge Advises Prayer

A New Jersey judge advised prayer as a solution to a church property dispute. "It is hard to understand," he told members of both factions in the courtroom, "how professed Christians could become so bitter as to bring a matter involving only dollars and cents into court.

"This controversy should be resolved by members of both groups on their knees in prayer to demonstrate your right to be called Christians. I hope in that way the Holy Spirit will enter your hearts and reunite your parish." Well spoken! —*The Gospel Banner*

* * *

Christ Better Seen Inside

A woman, who was a non-going church member, met her minister in front of the church. "Don't you miss the church and the friendly fellowship of other Christians?" the minister asked. The woman said, "I don't have to go to church to have faith." "That's right," said the minister as he glanced at the beautiful stained glass window. "You don't have to go to church to see that beautiful window either, do you?" She shook her head. "Let's go inside for a moment," said the minister. On the inside the window was beautified by rays of light coming from the afternoon sun. The figure of Christ, only faintly visible on the outside, stood out boldly. The tender look of pity and love on the Saviour's face greatly impressed the non-churchgoing member. "It's wonderful," she said. "The most remarkable thing about it is that you see Him much more clearly on the inside!" said the minister. "That's right," confessed the woman, "and I'll be more faithful in coming to the services in God's house." —W. B. K.

He Needed Only to Be Asked

A businessman, on his way to prayer meeting, saw a stranger looking in the window of the church. He invited him to go in with him. "All right," said the stranger. That was the beginning of a Christian life for him and his family. He afterward told the friend: "I lived in this city for seven years before I met you. No one had ever asked me to go to church. I wasn't here three days before the grocer, the dairy man, the insurance man and the ward politician called on me. You are the first one to invite me to church!" —W. B. K.

* * *

Good-bye, Dear God! Good-bye!

A farmer finished moving the last load of furniture to a home some distance from where he and his family had lived for years. When he returned for his wife and children, his little girl asked, "Is there a church where we are moving to, Daddy?" "No, there isn't," said the father sadly. "Is there a Sunday school there?" "I don't believe there is," said the father. "Well, Daddy, is God there?" asked the little girl sadly. The father didn't reply. The little girl went to her room. She knelt and prayed, "Dear God, we are going to a new home. There is no church there. There is no Sunday school there, and I am afraid there is no God there! Good-bye, dear God! Good-bye!"

—W. B. K.

* * *

The Perfect Church

I think that I shall never see
A Church that's all it ought to be:
A Church whose members never stray
Beyond the Strait and Narrow Way;
A Church that has no empty pews,
Whose Pastor never has the blues,
A Church whose Deacons always deak,
And none is proud, and all are meek;
Where gossips never peddle lies,
Or make complaints or criticize;
Where all are always sweet and kind,
And all to others' faults are blind.
Such perfect Churches there may be,
But none of them are known to me.
But still, we'll work, and pray and plan
To make our own the best we can.
—*Selected*

We Cleaned Our Church!

We cleaned our little church today,
  Wiped all the dust and dirt away,
We straightened papers, washed the floors,
  Wiped off the lights and painted doors.

We brushed the dirt stains from the books,
  And whisked the cobwebs from the nooks,
We polished windows so we'd see,
  The newly greening shrub and tree.

The menfolks, too, raked up the yard,
  They laughed and said it wasn't hard,
And, oh, it felt so very good,
  To have the place look as it should.

We said, "How wonderful 'twould be,
  If we cleaned out what we can't see,"
Such things as grudges, hates, and lies,
  And musty thought much worse than flies.

If all would let God's Spirit in,
  To cleanse each heart from soiling sin,
Ah, then, our church would really shine,
  Our fellowship would be divine!
—*Selected*

* * *

The Board of Absentees

1. The Board of Absentees will meet each time the services of the church meet. At this meeting, we will discuss ways of keeping the attendance as low as possible. We will see that there is no enthusiasm for increased attendance.

2. The Board of Absentees will discuss ways of decreasing the offerings, and will seek ways to weaken the preaching of the Word.

3. The Board of Absentees will discuss ways of decreasing any revival efforts of the church.

4. Your Board of Absentees is composed of the following members:
Mr. Real Unconcern
Mrs. Sleep Late
Mr. U. R. Lazy
Mr. Don't Come At All
Mr. and Mrs. Don't Like the Preacher
Mrs. At Ease
Mr. and Mrs. Take It Easy

Mr. Do Little
Mrs. Every Other Sunday

It is our deepest desire to close the door of this church as quickly as pos-

sible. If you ever want an excuse for being absent, please contact us immediately — we have all the answers.

—Board of Absentees

CIGARETTES — TOBACCO

Short Quotes

It has been proved beyond doubt that excessive cigarette smoking is not only the major contributory factor of lung cancer but also plays a role in a variety of other ills, including coronary artery disease and peptic ulcer.
　　—Dr. E. Cuyler Hammond, in
　　　Cleveland Plain Dealer,
　　　　　　　March 23, 1961

* * *

Statistical association between smoking and lung cancer is so strong that scientists believe that the annual cancer toll can be reduced from 40,000 to 4,000 if everybody stops smoking.
　　—Earl Ubell, HTNS., in
　　　Chronicle-Telegraph,
　　　　　　　Mar. 25, 1961

* * *

"I'm disturbed in reading so much about the link between cigarettes and lung cancer," said a heavy smoker to a friend. "I've decided to do something about it!" Inquired the friend, "Giving up cigarettes?" "No, I'm giving up reading!"

* * *

Smoking is the chief cause of the sharp rise in lung cancer. What is more, no filter tip or tobacco treatment yet devised is effective in cutting out the tars suspected of causing cancer.
　　—U.S. Surgeon General Leroy
　　　Burney, in *U. S. News and*
　　　　　　　World Report

* * *

The enormous weight of statistical evidence linking lung cancer with heavy smoking can no longer be refuted. A majority of manufacturers either oppose or ignore the problem.
　　—Patrick O'Neil-Dunne, technical
　　　director of Rothmans of Pall
　　　Mall, British cigarette maker,
　　　as quoted in *Time*, Aug. 11, '58

Of the 30,000 men and women who will die of lung cancer the next year, death in 95 per cent of the cases will be traceable to smoking!
　　—Dr. Alton Ochsner, famed
　　　　　　　chest surgeon

* * *

More than a million American schoolchildren are presently doomed to die of lung cancer according to The American Public Health Association which body urged a campaign to discourage them from smoking cigarettes.
　　—*Associated Press* dispatch

* * *

Some 95 per cent of the lung cancer victims are smokers. Prevention means no smoking, absolutely none. Children should be warned not to start smoking. Even heavy smokers can reduce the chance of getting a lung cancer if they stop smoking. —Hugo Hecht, M.D., in
　　　Cleveland Plain Dealer

* * *

After forty-four months study of 188,-000 men between the ages of fifty and seventy, Drs. D. Hammond and D. Horn reported: "Lung cancer deaths rate over one thousand per cent higher among regular cigarette smokers than among non-smokers."

* * *

We found cigarette smokers had so much higher death rates that we didn't think we could withhold the information another year. We are thinking of saving lives. —Dr. E. Cuyler Hammond,
　　　Yale University statistician
　　　　　　　and biologist

* * *

There is not only very strong evidence of a causal relationship between heavy cigarette smoking and lung cancer, but we have the additional evi-

dence that cigarette smoke contains a factor that will produce cancer in experimental animals of unrelated species.
—Dr. Evarts A. Graham, noted chest surgeon and cancer researcher

* * *

Cigarette smoking is indeed a major cause of lung cancer. The risk increases with the amount smoked. The evidence of a cause-effect relationship with lung cancer is adequate for considering the initiation of public health measures.
—Frank M. Strong, biochemist, University of Wisconsin

* * *

Among chest surgeons 63 per cent said heavy smoking may lead to lung cancer. Among pathologists 50 per cent agreed. Among researchers 52 per cent agreed. Asked if they would advise patients to reduce smoking or give it up 90 per cent of the chest surgeons said yes; 83 per cent of pathologists said yes and 57 per cent of cancer researchers said yes. From the Sloan-Kettering Institute, New York, came another study showing heavy smoking alone or in combination with heavy drinking greatly increases the risk of developing cancer of the larynx, or voice box. —Dr. Charles S. Cameron, medical and scientific director in a report to the AMA

* * *

Lung cancer is almost nonexistent in those born into the Seventh-day Adventists Church. The church forbids smoking. —Arthur J. Snider, *Chicago Daily News* science writer

* * *

Smoking is more of a menace to health than radioactive fall-out. Long use of tobacco knocks as much as eight or nine years off the average life-span. Medical men, as guardians of the health, should be ashamed of themselves for not setting an example.
—A Boston chest surgeon, in *The Church Herald*

* * *

The threat of lung cancer in this country is almost as great as the risk of death in a traffic accident. Lung fatalities are increasing at the rate of 2,000 a year. —Dr. Overholt, professor of surgery, Tufts College, Boston

* * *

A new kind of prohibition — on cigarettes — would save at least 20,000 lives a year in the United States. Such a ban would be difficult to invoke because tobacco is considered neither a food nor a drug and is immune from all regulations except taxation. Besides many people subscribe to the theory that it is a constitutional right to choose one's poison. As a result, the government can do more to protect the population from chemically contaminated cranberries whose dangers for man are at most theoretical than from the hazards of tobacco.
—Dr. Michael Shimkin, in *The Cleveland Press*

* * *

A tobacco company sent packages of cigarettes to some high-school boys with this explanation: "We are sending you a package of our cigarettes. We hope you will use them to your satisfaction and want more." One of the boys used the cigarettes, and wrote the tobacco concern: "I received the package of cigarettes and put them in a quart of water. With it I sprayed our bug-infested rose bushes. Every bug died! The cigarettes are surely a good poison! I want more to use next spring if any bugs survive!" —*Christian Advocate*

* * *

Said Jack Dempsey to a manufacturer of cigarettes who sought his endorsement of his brand of cigarettes: "You could not get me to sign that for ten times what you offer. I do not smoke cigarettes and never did. Do you think I am going to ask the thousands of boys who have read about me to take up cigarette smoking?"

* * *

For non-smoking men between the ages of 55 through 59, there is one chance in 8197 of dying from lung cancer; light smokers, one chance in 2075; moderate smokers, one chance in 867; heavy smokers, one chance in 573. For non-smokers between the ages of 60 through 64, there is one chance in 7092 of dying from lung cancer; light smokers, one in 1081; moderate smokers, one in 552; heavy smokers, one in 371. For non-smokers over 65 years of age, there is one chance in 3165 of dying from lung cancer; light smokers, one in 412; moderate smokers, one in 393; heavy smokers, one in 296.

—*Scripps-Howard Bureau*

* * *

Smoking cigarettes weakens and unnerves the youth. It destroys the victim's memory, impairs his reasoning faculties, robs him of his power of attention, saps his will power and deprives him of his initiative.

—Judge de Lacy, Juvenile Court, Washington, D. C.

* * *

One cigarette has nineteen different poisons which get into the blood stream, making heart action difficult. One to three cigarettes when smoked will contract the small arteries and cause the heart to beat faster, and raise blood pressure from one to twenty-five points.

—Dr. John Kellog

* * *

"I'm not much of a mathematician," said the cigarette, "but I can add to a boy's nervous trouble. I can subtract from his physical energy. I can multiply his aches and pains. I can divide his mental power. I can take interest from his work and discount his chances of success!" —*The Bible Friend*

* * *

In spite of the overwhelming evidence of the causal relationship of cigarette smoking and cancer, the tobacco industry has refused to admit the evidence, and has tried to confuse the issue by blaming other possible factors, such as air pollution. It seems to me that they would be on much firmer ground if they would admit that there is a calculated risk in smoking and inform the public of this risk so that the responsibility of smoking is entirely the individual's.

—Dr. Alton Ochsner, famed lung surgeon

* * *

Every heavy smoker will develop lung cancer unless heart disease or some other sickness claims him first.

—Dr. Alton Ochsner

* * *

Roman Catholic Bishop Cornelius Lucey of Cork, Ireland, has coined a new word for cigarettes — *cancerettes!* "The heavier a smoker you are, the more likely you are to be a victim of lung cancer," said the Bishop.

COMMUNION WITH GOD

Short Quotes

For real communion with His Father, Jesus went to lonely hilltops and seaside silences. —Daniel Heitmeyer

* * *

A moment in the morning,
Ere the cares of day begin,
Ere the heart's wide door is open,
For the world to enter in,
Oh, then alone with Jesus,
In the silence of the morn,
In heavenly, sweet communion,
Let your joyful day be born,
In the quietude that blesses,
With a prelude of repose,
Let your soul be soothed and softened,
As the dew revives the rose!

—*Selected*

"What do you do during the day?" a friend asked an elderly Scotch woman who lived alone. "Well," she said, "I get my hymnbook and sing. Then I get the Bible and let the Lord speak to me. When I get tired of reading and cannot sing anymore, *I just sit still* and let the Lord love me!" —W. B. K.

* * *

In the silences I make in the midst of the turmoil of life I have appointments with God. From these silences I come forth with spirit refreshed, and with a renewed sense of power. I hear a voice in the silences, and become increasingly aware that it is the voice of God.

—David Brainerd

If you are too busy for God, you're too busy.

* * *

Slow me down, Lord, I'se a-going too
    fast
I can't see my brother when he's walkin'
    past
I miss a lot o' good things, day by day,
I don't know a blessin' when it comes
    my way.

* * *

Only the quiescent ones can know God in profundity: "Be still and know that I am God" (Ps. 46:10). Rush and unrest are foreign to Him. The frenzied and disturbed ones are out of tune with the Infinite. God is quiet. The silence of eternity enwraps Him. When He speaks, He seldom shouts — He whispers. As He marches through the ages, He doesn't use brass bands or advertising ballyhoo to announce His coming or going. In creation, there was no fuss or friction. The universe was born as silently as a new day dawns: "For he spake, and it was done; he commanded, and it stood fast" (Ps. 33:9).
         —Will R. Johnson
         in *Moody Monthly*

* * *

We mutter and sputter
   We fume and we spurt;
We mumble and grumble,
   Our feelings get hurt;
We can't understand things,
   Our vision grows dim,
When all that we need is
   A moment with Him!
         —Mary Helen Anderson

Illustrations

A Necessity

As a statesman I often feel, beyond and beneath that ever-flowing stream of letters, interviews, deputations, committees, speeches and despatch-boxes, a still small voice that challenges all my efforts, searches out my motives, questions the meaning of everything that I do, and forces me to stand, as it were, in the full glare of the white light of eternity. And it is necessary for us that we should withdraw ourselves, if it be for only five minutes or ten minutes, that we may heed that voice and that we may think. —Stanley Baldwin,
         former Prime Minister
         of Great Britain

* * *

Unwise Haste

A gallant officer was pursued by an overwhelming force, and his followers were urging him to a greater speed when he discovered that his saddle girth was becoming loose. He coolly dismounted, repaired the girth by tightening the buckle, and then dashed away. The broken buckle would have left him on the field a prisoner. The wise delay to repair damages sent him on in safety amid the huzzas of his comrades. The Christian who is in such haste to get about his business in the morning that he neglects his Bible and his season of prayer and quiet waiting before God, rides with a broken buckle!
         —C. Cook in *Christian Life*

* * *

O, For a Closer Walk With God!

One of God's servants had walked so blessedly and so long in the King's highway that the glow and glory of the Yonderland shone on his face. Having held converse with his Saviour during the long span of years, he was on the friendliest of terms with his Lord. As he closed his eyes in sleep, he would serenely say, "Good night, dear Jesus!" Awakening in the morning, he would joyously exclaim, "Good morning, dear Jesus!"

Oh, that more of us knew Him so intimately that we, too, thus enjoyed the preciousness of a friendly and familiar, though not irreverent, relationship to Him! —Rev. Harold Walker

* * *

The Time Is Short

That was a grand action by Jerome, one of the church fathers. He laid aside all pressing engagements and went to fulfill the call God gave him to translate the Holy Scriptures. His congregations were larger than that of many preachers of today, but he said to his people, "Now it is necessary that the Scriptures be translated. You must find another minister. I am bound for the wilderness, and shall not return until my task is finished." He went away, and labored and prayed until he produced the Latin Vulgate.

So we must say to our friends: "I must away and have time for prayer and solitude." And though we do not write Latin Vulgates, yet our work for God will be immortal. —Spurgeon

* * *

Sweet Communion

When you awoke from sleep this morning,
  Though the hour was rather late,
Did you stop to speak with Jesus,
  And His benediction wait?
Did you thank Him for His mercy,
  For His care through all the night,
That no evil had befallen,
  That no tears now dim your sight?

Did you ask Him for the blessing
  Of His presence through the day,
For His leading safely onward,
  For His guiding, lest you stray?
Did you tell Him that you'd gladly
  Go wherever He would lead;
That you'd try to do His bidding,
  Helping every soul in need?

If you go without these blessings
  As you start another day,
Be assured your strength will fail you,
  And you'll faint along the way.
Oh, live closer to the Master;
  For unless you're very near,
Words of love He whispers to you
  Will not reach your listening ear.
                              —*Selected*

* * *

Tell Jesus

When thou wakest in the morning,
  Ere thou tread the untried way
Of the lot that lies before thee
  Through the coming busy day;
Whether sunbeams promise brightness,
  Whether dim forebodings fall,
Be thy dawning glad or gloomy,
  Go to Jesus — tell Him all.

In the calm of sweet communion
  Let thy daily work be done;
In the peace of soul outpouring
  Care be banished, patience won;
And if earth with its enchantments
  Seek thy spirit to enthral,
Ere thou listen — ere thou answer —
  Turn to Jesus — tell Him all!

Then as hour and hour glide by thee,
  Thou wilt blessed guidance know,
All thy burdens being lightened,
  Thou canst help the weak ones go,
And as thou count thy gain but loss,
  Thou canst raise them up that fall;
But remember, whilst thou servest,
  Still tell Jesus — tell Him all!

And if weariness creep o'er thee
  As the day draws to its close,
Or if sudden fierce temptation
  Bring thee face to face with foes.
In thy weakness, in thy peril,
  Raise to heaven a truthful call;
Strength and calm for every crisis
  Come — in telling Jesus all!
                    —*The Christian Witness*

* * *

Fellowship With Him!

What has stripped the seeming beauty
  From these idols of the earth?
Not the sense of right or duty,
  But the sight of nobler worth.

Not the crashing of those idols,
  With its bitter pain and smart,
But the beaming of His beauty,
  The unveiling of His heart.

'Tis the look that melted Peter,
  'Tis the face that Stephen saw,
'Tis the heart that wept with Mary,
  Can alone from idols draw.

Draw and win and fill completely,
  Till the cup o'erflow the brim;
What have we to do with idols
  Who have companied with Him?
                              —*Selected*

* * *

Alone With God!

Dr. Alexander Maclaren was one of the clearest Bible expositors of the age. How he became such a Bible scholar is worthy of note. One who in his early ministry was an assistant to the great

Baptist preacher, once asked him what had contributed most of all to his success. Doctor Maclaren, after deprecating the idea that he had attained "success," said that he owed all that was in himself and his ministry to the habit, never broken, of spending one hour a day "alone with the Eternal." The hour which he took was from nine to ten in the morning. His assistant says that he was sometimes allowed to be in the room with the pastor; "but no word passed between us. In his well-worn armchair he sat, with his big Bible on his knees, sometimes reading its pages, more frequently his hand over his face. During that hour he did not allow himself to read even the Bible for texts, or as a student. It was read as a child would read a letter from an absent father; as a loving heart would drink in again the message from a loved one far away."

"As newborn babes, desire the sincere milk of the Word, that ye may grow thereby."

—*Pittsburgh Christian Advocate*

* * *

Walk Quietly

Walk quietly —
And know that He is God.
When the dawn on winged steed, comes riding high,
To blazon painted banners on the morning sky,
And the Holy Spirit seemeth nigh —
Walk quietly.

Walk quietly —
And know that He is God.
When the blaring trumpets roar a thrilling beat
Life is lived in storm and strife and noon-day heat —
With the mighty tread of tramping feet
Walk quietly.

Walk quietly —
When evening shadows lie against the hill —
In the hush of twilight, when the world is still,
And the balm of peace soothes every ill —
Walk quietly.

Walk quietly —
And know that He is God.
Let your life be governed by His guiding hand
E'en though it varies from the way you planned,
Bow your head in quiet submission and
Walk quietly.

—*Selected*

* * *

Listening In

God has a wireless to everywhere:
We call it the Word of God and prayer.
And every one may daily win
God's choicest gifts by "listening in."

First you must shut out every sound
From the heedless world that throngs around.
Vanity fair makes a deafening din
On purpose to hinder "listening in."

The devil will use his utmost power
To keep you from having this quiet hour.
He knows that you can be freed from sin
Always and only by "listening in."

But when you prayerfully read God's Word,
The still small voice is clearly heard.
And wondrous peace and power within
Daily results from "listening in."

God longs to give His best to you
To keep you loyal and strong and true.
If you haven't begun, today begin
To prove the joy of "listening in."

—*Selected*

* * *

Unbroken Fellowship

J. Wilbur Chapman once came to F. B. Meyer with the question, "What is the matter with me? So many times I seem half empty, and so many times utterly powerless; what is the matter?"

He put his hand on Chapman's shoulder and answered, "Have you ever tried to breathe out three times without breathing in once?" Thinking it might be some new breathing exercise, Chapman answered, "I do not think I have." "Well," said Meyer, "try it." So he breathed out once, and then he had to breathe in again.

"Don't you know," said Dr. Meyer, "that you must always breathe in before you breathe out, and that your breathing out is in proportion to your breathing in?"

We must fill the reservoir by prayer and a meditative study of the Word before we can draw out for service.

—*The Evangelist*

* * *

Learning Quietness

The leader of a missionary prayer group tells this experience: "I used to have much difficulty getting our group meeting started. One member in particular always had some 'experience' she felt she must tell. But something happened, and one night this lady said: 'I'm only learning now certain truths from God's Word I should have grasped years ago. I'm learning when we go on with Christ in simplicity, and keep in the path, the narrow path of obedience to Him, a true quietness comes upon us, and we know there are experiences we

must keep close. I'm ashamed now, on looking back, to note how talkative I was. When we truly sit at the feet of the Lord Jesus, a lot of 'gush' and 'froth' go from our hearts. I want to learn more about this."

—*The Sunday School Times*

* * *

God's Voice in the Morning

"My voice shalt Thou hear in the morning, O Lord; in the morning will I direct my prayer unto thee, and will look up" (Ps. 5:3).

If we felt more the majesty of life we should be more careful of its mornings. He who rushes from his bed to his business and waiteth not to worship is foolish as though he had not put on his clothes or cleansed his face, and as unwise as though he dashed into battle without arms or armor. Be it ours to bathe in the softly flowing river of communion with God before the heat of the wilderness and the burden of the way begins to oppress us. —C. H. Spurgeon

COMMUNISM

Short Quotes

In the past four decades, we have seen the forces of international communism reach out from the Kremlin to threaten all nations of the world. Today, the communists control approximately one-fourth of the earth's land surface — an area inhabited by nearly one billion people. And the ultimate goal of communism is to dominate the entire earth. —J. Edgar Hoover

* * *

We must work until religion is synonymous with insanity. We must work until the officials of city, county and state governments will pounce on religious groups as public enemies!

—A secret manual on communism

* * *

In 1925, a handful of Communists met to culminate plans for the conquest of the world by 1971. According to their far-reaching plans, America would be the last nation to fall. It is said that

the Communists are far ahead of their schedule! —Dr. Clate Risley, Executive Secretary, National Sunday School Association

* * *

If anyone believes our smiles involve abandonment of the teachings of Marx, Engels and Lenin, he deceives himself poorly. Those who wait for that must wait until a shrimp learns to whistle!

—Nikita S. Khrushchev

* * *

The Russian dictator, Lenin, predicted that the United States would eventually spend itself into bankruptcy. Karl Marx, patron saint of communism, said: "The surest way to overturn the social order is to debauch the currency." Lenin said: "Taxation, with its offspring — inflation — is the vital weapon to displace the system of free enterprise." Free enterprise is the system on which our nation was founded. It is the sys-

tem which has made us the most prosperous people of all history.
—General Douglas MacArthur

* * *

We shall never forego our ideological principles. We are waging and shall wage an implacable struggle for the Marxist-Leninist ideology for the triumph of the ideals of Communism.
—Soviet Premier Nikita Khruschev

* * *

America is facing an emergency, a crisis which threatens the very existence of our nation. —J. Edgar Hoover

* * *

Communism is a disease. It is a disease of the body. It has killed millions of people, and purposes to kill millions more. More tragically, it is a disease of the mind, because it is associated with systematized delusions, not susceptible to rational argument. Terrifyingly, it is a disease of the spirit, because it denies God, robs man of spirit and soul and reduces him to the level of a baseless creature!
—Dr. Fred C. Schwarz

* * *

Dr. Harry Schwartz, author of *Russia's Soviet Economy*, said in an address to the Overseas Press Club: "I often feel that the most important thing one can say in the present situation is that we need a lot of Paul Reveres telling America to *wake up!* We're in a fight and if we don't wake up we can be licked!" —W. B. K.

* * *

Communism is a false ideology. But it is an ideology and can only be met with moral and spiritual weapons. We are in an ideological battle. Therein lies the decisive task. It may last decades, but it must be won. A nation with an ideology is always on the offensive. A nation without an ideology is self-satisfied and dead.
—Chancellor Adenauer

* * *

We have to use any ruse, dodges, tricks, cunning, unlawful method, concealment and veiling of the truth. The basic rule is to exploit conflicting inter-

ests of the capitalist states and systems. As long as capitalism remains we cannot live in peace. —Lenin

* * *

Sincere diplomacy is no more possible than dry water or wooden iron. —Stalin

* * *

We do not accept into membership anyone with reservations whatsoever. We will not accept into our membership anyone unless he is an active, disciplined, working member in one of our organizations! —Lenin

* * *

It is not a struggle merely of economic theories or forms of government or military power. The issue is the true nature of man. Either man is the creature whom the Psalmist describes as a "little lower than the angels, crowned with glory and honor," holding "dominion over the works" of his Creator, or man is a soulless animated machine to be enslaved, used, and consumed by the state for its own glorification.
—General Dwight D. Eisenhower

* * *

We must remember that one of Karl Marx's cardinal proposals for the destruction of capitalism was debauchery of the currency, with subsequent loss of confidence, contentment, and security on the part of the people. Unless economic sanity is restored to our Federal Government, it needs no flight of the imagination to say that the day may come when Wheaton College sophomores may spend a thousand-dollar bill for a raspberry soda at the Stupe!
—Dr. V. Raymond Edman, President Wheaton College

* * *

The Communists disdain to conceal their views and aims. They openly declare that their aims can be attained only by the forcible overthrow of all the existing social conditions. Let the ruling class tremble at a Communist revolution. The proletarians have nothing to lose but their chains. They have a world to win!
—*Communist Manifesto*, by Marx

First, we shall take Eastern Europe, then the masses of Asia. After that, we shall surround and undermine the United States which will fall into our hands without a struggle — like an overripe fruit!

—Lenin (In an address in 1922)

* * *

The twentieth century has witnessed the intrusion into its body fabric of a highly malignant cancer — a cancer which threatens to destroy Judaic-Christian civilization. One-fourth of the world's land surface has been seared and blackened by this cancer, while one out of every three human beings is caught in its tentacles! At this very hour, some are wondering whether we, as a free nation, can survive the frontal and underground assaults of this tumorous growth of Communism!

—J. Edgar Hoover

* * *

"Religion is the opium of the people," said Karl Marx, the atheist. "Atheism is an integral part of Marxism," said Lenin. "Marxism is materialism. We must combat religion. This is the ABC of all materialism, and consequently of Marxism. Down with religion. Long live atheism," said Lenin. "Lenin is God," said Stalin.

* * *

We make war against all prevailing ideas of religion, of the state, of country, of patriotism. The idea of God is the keynote of a perverted civilization. It must be destroyed. The true root of liberty, of equality, of culture, is atheism. —Karl Marx

* * *

We can have no confidence in any treaty to which Communists are a party except where such a treaty provides within itself for self-enforcing mechanisms. Indeed, the demonstrated disregard of the Communists of their own pledges is one of the greatest obstacles to success in substituting the rule of law for the rule of force.

—President Eisenhower

Words must have no relation to action. Otherwise what kind of diplomacy is it? Words are one thing, actions another. Good words are a mask for concealment of bad deeds. —Stalin

* * *

Panmunjon will ever stand as a monument to the unblushing falsifying and hypocrisy of the Communists. When will we learn that one can never trust the word of an atheist?

—Dr. V. Raymond Edman

* * *

Negotiators with Soviet Russia have to remember that lies, betrayals and infringements of treaties are part of the Red creed to which Khrushchev and Bulganin subscribe as completely as Stalin did. The present Red rulers have never renounced Lenin's golden rule: "It is necessary to use any ruse, cunning, unlawful method, evasion, concealment of the truth." Or one of his favorite maxims: "Promises are like piecrust, made to be broken." —Eugene Lyons

* * *

A University of Atheism has been opened in the Soviet Union at Ashkabab in the Moslem section of the USSR. Courses consist of sixty lectures, including one on "Marxism and Leninism on Religion, and Ways of Overcoming It."

—*Gospel Banner*

* * *

Life is short, and I want to see the red flag float over the whole planet in my lifetime.

—Premier Nikita S. Khrushchev in speech in Austria, July, 1960

* * *

We remain atheists and we will do all we can to liberate a certain people from the charm of the religious opium that still exists.

—Premier Nikita S. Khrushchev

* * *

Italy, the home of Catholicism, has the largest percentage of Communists in its population of any country in the world — larger than Russia, larger than China. —Frederick G. Schwarz in *Christianity Today*

Illustrations

Marx or Mark's Gospel?

A soldier came to a chaplain one day, "I have little use or time for this dope called religion."

"That's a bit strong," replied the chaplain. "You sound as though you are an atheist."

"I certainly am. Not only that, I am a communist. I know how hollow this religious stuff is."

The chaplain soon discovered that the man was well read and commented on his knowledge.

"I read as much as I can and I have read everything that Karl Marx ever wrote," boasted the soldier.

"Have you ever read Mark's gospel?" ask the chaplain.

"I have read everything Marx ever wrote."

The chaplain took a copy of Mark's Gospel from his pocket. "Since you enjoy reading, take this little book. It won't take long."

A week later the soldier came back to the chaplain. "Padre, I am not going to apologize for what I said last week because I believed it was true. But I would like to thank you for letting me read this little book. It has Karl Marx whacked to a frazzle. Have you any other?" —Walter McCleary in *Sunday*

* * *

Lord, to Whom Do I Belong?

Colonel LaCraw, a devout, soul-winning Christian, was a top adviser to General Eisenhower in planning the Normandy Beach landing. Later he sat opposite the Russian representative at a conference table in Vienna. He was deeply concerned about the soul's welfare of the brilliant Communist and yearned to win him to Christ. Observing the direction in which Colonel La Craw's conversation was going, the Communist interrupted him, saying: "Colonel LaCraw, you are trying to make me a religious man. I am a Communist. I belong to the Party. With me the Party comes *first*. I am an atheist. I had to declare myself one to become a member of the Party. Now, if I were commanded by the Party to

kill you, I'd do it! It is the same with my wife and my children. The Party comes *first* because I belong to the Party. Now, stop your trying to make me religious!"

Colonel LaCraw went to his room with a heavy heart. There, on his knees, he prayed: "O Lord, to whom do I belong? For whom would I be so obedient?" —W. B. K.

* * *

We Shall Grapple with the Lord God!

In 37 short years Communism has taken over life-and-death control of 822 millions of the world's population. Much of this conquest has been accomplished through murder and bloody revolution. But more dangerous than war, more to be dreaded than battle, is the "according to plan" peace offensive. In this the Communists have not changed their objective to "banish God from the skies, freedom from the earth, and to establish a world Soviet State." Zinonieff said, "We shall grapple with the Lord God. In due time we shall vanquish Him from the highest heaven, and where He seeks refuge, we shall subdue Him forever."
—*Oriental Crusades*

* * *

The Peace of the Cemetery

In 1930 the head of the Communist International issued this statement: "War to the hilt between Communism and Capitalism is inevitable. Today, of course, we are not strong enough to attack. Our time will come in 20 or 30 years (1960). To win, we will need the element of surprise. The bourgeoisie will have to be put to sleep. So we shall launch the most spectacular peace movement on record. There will be electrifying *overtures* and *unheard-of concessions*. The capitalist countries, stupid and decadent, will rejoice to co-operate to their own destruction. *They will leap at another chance to be friends.* As soon as their guard is down, we shall smash them with our clenched fist." This thing is taking place before our very eyes. The "peace" that Communism offers is the peace of doom and enslavement — the peace of the cemetery —

the "peace" of the canary that has been swallowed by the cat.

     —*Oriental Crusades*

* * *

A Fruit of Atheism — Hatred

"We hate Christians," said a commissioner of education of the Soviet Republic, "We hate Christians, even the best of them must be regarded as our worst enemies. They preach love to one's neighbor and pity. This is contrary to our principles. Christian love is a hindrance to the development of the revolution. Down with love for one's neighbor. What we want is hatred. We must know how to hate, for only at this price can we conquer the universe!" —*Christian Victory*

* * *

Lenin Is God

Red Square, Moscow, is the Mecca of atheistic Russia. There, thousands of subservient Russians daily worship the mummies of Lenin and Stalin. Their remains are perfectly preserved in glass showcases in a red-marble mausoleum. They are immaculately dressed, the only well-dressed people in Moscow — all dressed up and nowhere to go!

In his lifetime, Stalin said repeatedly, "Lenin is God. The party cannot be neutral toward religion. Antireligious propaganda is a means by which the complete liquidation of the reactionary clergy must be brought about."

Lenin stated, "Religion is a kind of spiritual gin in which the slaves of capital drown their human shape and their claims to any decent human life. Marxism is materialism. The materialist relegates God and all the philosophical rabble who believe in Him to the sewer and manure heap. Down with religion! Long live atheism!"

     —W. B. K.

* * *

Our Father, Stalin!

When the atheistic program was being introduced in the Russian schools, the Communists employed subtle, satanic methods in teaching the children unbelief in God. The instructor would say, "Now, children, let's imagine we have no bread and are starving. Let's ask God to give us bread. Let's say the prayer, 'Our Father which art in heaven. . . . Give us this day our daily bread.'" Having thus prayed, the teacher would say with a sardonic, scornful grin, "See, children, nothing has happened. We are still hungry and without bread. Now let's change our prayer, and say, 'Our Father, Stalin, who art in Moscow, give us this day our daily bread!'" As the children said these words, a trapdoor in the ceiling of the room sprang open and loaves of bread fell in abundance upon the children, the desks, and the floor!

How long will God let arrogant, blatantly-defiant man go on insulting Him?

     —W. B. K.

CONFESSION OF CHRIST

Illustrations

A Nine-Day Journey to Learn More

Secretary Twentyman was visiting a coastal village in Peru. During one of his meetings several Indians came in and sat quietly. When he spoke to them, he found they had come eight or nine days' journey from the high Andes because several months previously they had bought a Bible from a colporteur. They had read it every evening among themselves, and at length decided to make the long trip to the

coast in order to make public profession of their faith and to learn more.

     —*Bible Society Record*

* * *

Father and Mother More Than Me

Testuju Tsuchiyama was born in a devout Buddhist home. When a young man, he came to America. Before leaving home, he vowed to his parents that he would never become a Christian. "It would be an act of disloyalty to your

parents, ancestors and national gods if
you did," they said. His mother gave
him a bag of amulets. In America he
became ill and lonely. He suffered many
hardships. He could no longer find
any satisfaction in the pantheistic gods
of Buddhism, nor in the moral teachings of Confucius. He began to study
the Bible. He found it to be "sweeter
also than honey in the honeycomb" to
his hungry soul. He wanted to become
a Christian. Yet he remembered the
vow he had made to his parents. One
night he read these words: "He that
loveth father or mother more than me
is not worthy of me . . . he that taketh
not his cross, and followeth after me,
is not worthy of me . . . he that loseth
his life for my sake shall find it" (Matt.
10:37-39). He decided to confess
Christ publicly.

After completing his education in
America, he returned to his native land.
There Dr. Tsuchiyama taught in the
Osaka Theological Seminary for many
years. —W. B. K.

* * *

It Was for You!

A contractor, examining a building
under construction, fell from a high
scaffold. One of the workingmen below
saw his body plummeting down. He
knew that death was certain. Quickly
he leaped to the place where his body
would strike the pavement, and caught
him as he fell! The weight of the falling man drove his arms into their sock-
ets, crushed his shoulders, twisted his
spine, and made him walk the streets
ever after an object of pity. One day,
someone asked him about the man he
had saved. His face lit up, and he said,
"Oh, my, he gave me half of his fortune. He gives me half of his income,
and he never lets me want for a thing."
We know how to appreciate that. But
sometimes we seem to forget that there
was One who was crushed and broken,
there was One who was wounded for
our transgressions and bruised for our
iniquity, and yet we have never publicly
declared ourselves for Him.

—Rev. John F. MacArthur in
Confessing Him

66

I'm So Glad I Confessed Christ!

'Twas a foggy Monday morning in the
small Floridian town, Crescent City.
The aged driver of the school bus had
but two more children to pick up before
going on to school with his load of
carefree, happy children. As he was
halfway across a railway track, an unseen and unheard fruit train came
through the fog and crashed through
the middle of the school bus! Instantly
the railway track was bestrewn with
horribly mangled bodies and fragments
of bodies. Four children, in one family, were decapitated. The seriously injured ones were placed first in ambu-
lances and rushed to nearby hospitals.
As the writer placed one of the older
girls in an ambulance, it was evident
that her life was rapidly ebbing away.
Said she to him, "I'm so glad I confessed Christ as my Saviour last night
in the little church!" How glad I was,
too, that she had confessed Him, though
neither of us knew at the time that death
was so near.

Have you ever known anyone standing at death's door who regretted having confessed Christ, or having lived for
Him?

* * *

Chained to the Seat!

"It takes real courage to confess
Christ," said Dr. Wilfred T. Grenfell,
medical missionary to Labrador. "Let
me tell you how I came to my decision
to receive and serve Christ. I was in a
meeting in which the minister urged
those who had made a decision for Christ
to stand up. There were a number of
my friends in the meeting, and also
about a hundred sailors who were from
a training ship in the harbor. I felt
chained through fear to the seat. Suddenly one of the sailors stood. I knew
he would be ridiculed when he got back
to his ship. His standing gave me the
nerve also to stand up and confess
Christ as my Saviour. How thankful
I am that I did! That act gave new
meaning of life to me!"

Suppose that sailor had not bravely
stood and confessed Christ. Would Grenfell have ever become a Christian and
a medical missionary to Labrador?
—W. B. K.

I All Break Down! I'll Take Jesus!

Some of us will never forget . . . an instance a number of years ago in Sacramento, California, when an unconverted Japanese was present. We had barely replaced the bread and cup upon the table, before this heathen man rose to his feet in great emotion, and burst out in prayer, about as follows: "O God, I all broke up to pieces. I, a poor sinner. For long time, for one whole year, I fight You hard — but here I see Your people eat the bread, drink the wine, that show how Jesus He die for sinners. O God, I can fight no more — I all break down. I take Jesus; He be my Saviour now!" And that very day, at his earnest request, he was baptized as owning his personal faith in Christ.

—Dr. H. A. Ironside in
Sailing with Paul

* * *

Keep Not Silence

A chaplain spoke to some English soldiers in a seaport. He asked: "Soldiers, are you ashamed of your uniform?" "There was an emphatic and a unanimous, "No!" "Are you ashamed of our country?" Again there was a thunderous, "No!" Then the chaplain asked: "Are you ashamed of your Queen?" Again their answer was an emphatic, "No!" Then he asked: "Are you ashamed of the Lord Jesus?" A dead silence followed. Then one stood and said: "Sir, I am not ashamed of my Saviour!"

It is remotely possible that there were others who at some time confessed faith in Christ, but now they were cowardly silent about Him.

If we are silent about Him, He will be silent about us. If we confess Him, He will confess us. —W. B. K.

* * *

Scared Stiff!

A Christian man gave two hitchhikers a ride in his car. They were paratroopers, and on their way to join their outfit which was soon to be shipped overseas. The Christian, ever on the alert to bring unsaved ones to Christ, veered the conversation toward spiritual things. At the proper moment, he asked the soldiers, "What is your relationship to God through Christ?" The soldiers were courteous and honest. They replied, "We are not Christians, but we know that we ought to be." Then one of them said this significant thing: "It takes a lot of courage to take the first jump out of an airplane. You are *scared stiff!* It seems to take an eternity to get the chute open. It would take even more courage, however, for me to walk down the aisle of a church and confess my faith in Christ!"

It does take courage to confess Christ, not only in a church, but anywhere. If we deny Him, He will deny us. If we are genuinely saved we will confess Him: "For the scripture saith, Whosoever believeth on him shall not be ashamed" (Rom. 10:11). —W. B. K.

* * *

Ashamed of God?

A Hindu asked his American hostess, "What do you think of Jesus Christ?" Replied the hostess, "We don't talk about that at the dinner table." The next day, the Hindu asked a businessman, "What do you think of Jesus Christ?" Said the businessman, "Let's go out on the balcony and talk about this." In commenting upon the two incidents, the Hindu said, "This is the first nation I've been in where people are ashamed of their God!"

—Dr. Louis H. Evans, minister-at-large for the Presbyterian Church, U. S. A.

* * *

He Counted the Cost

Before the Communists took over China, an influential Chinese, who held a high office in the educational life of China, accepted Christ. He had magnificent prospects before him — position, influence, opportunity, all were his. The study of the New Testament brought him the conviction that Christ was the Saviour of men, and his Saviour. After a period of struggle, and of counting the cost, he determined upon his confession before men. His dearest friend pleaded with him earnestly, agonizingly. He pleaded in vain. Then he urged him to secret discipleship. "Bow to the tablet of Confucius; it is only an empty form, and you can believe what you like in your heart!" It was a struggle, but he replied: "A few days ago One came to dwell within my heart; He has changed all life for me forever. I dare not bow to any other, lest He depart."

—Nelson Briton in
The Regeneration of China

CONFESSION OF SIN

Illustrations

I Know Some People Who Do!

A Sunday-school teacher of a class of small boys was emphasizing the necessity of our *personally* confessing our sins to God. As he closed the lesson, and wanting to see if he had put across to the boys the emphasis he had made, he asked, "Now boys, how many of you have sins you would like to confess to God?" The boys sat as still as a mouse. Finally, one little fellow raised his hand and said, "Teacher, I don't have any sins to confess for myself, but I know some people who do!"

—Told by W. Woodward Henry

* * *

I Was Wrong

There may be virtue in the man
Who's always sure he's right,
Who'll never hear another's plan
And seek no further light;
But I like more the chap who sings
A somewhat different song;
Who says, when he has messed up things,
"I'm sorry; I was wrong."

It's hard for anyone to say
That failure's due to him —
That he has lost the fight or way
Because his lights burned dim.
It takes a man aside to throw
The vanity that's strong,
Confessing, " 'Twas my fault, I know;
"I'm sorry; I was wrong."

And so, I figure, those who use
This honest, manly phrase,
Hate it too much their way to lose
On many future days.
They'll keep the path and make the fight,
Because they do not long
To have to say — when they're not right —
"I'm sorry; I was wrong."

—*Herald of Light*

A Troubled Conscience

A young man, with a worried look on his face, came to a pastor. He worked in a bank. He began to gamble. He stole money from the bank. He juggled certain accounts, and for a while covered up the shortages. The young man knew that, sooner or later, his sin would be detected. The faithful pastor said, "Go immediately to the bank president. Tell him what you have done and promise to pay back every cent with interest." Some days later, the young man again visited the pastor. His countenance was bright and cheerful. He said, "I went to the president of the bank and confessed my sins. I have squared my life with both my employer and God!" —W. B. K.

* * *

I Was Not in Thy Pasture

An old shepherd offered prayer in a Welsh revival meeting. He put it exactly right when he lamented his backslidings in these words: "Lord, I got among the thorns and briers, and was scratched and torn and bleeding. But, Lord, it is only fair to say that it was not in Thy pasture!" —W. B. K.

* * *

You Wicked Wretch!

A governor visited incognito a large penitentiary. It was his secret plan to pardon a prisoner who met a certain condition known only to himself. He entered into conversation with a large number of inmates. All of them said that they were victims of injustice, and had been wrongly treated and were innocent of any crime. Finally one inmate said, "I have no reason to complain. I have been a wicked, desperate wretch. I believe it is a great mercy I am here, for I deserved to be hanged!"

The governor, disclosing his identity to the honest prisoner, said, "It is a pity you should be here among so many 'innocent, honest' men! According to your own confession, you are bad enough to corrupt them all! You shall not stay with them a day longer!" The governor pardoned him and ordered his immediate release.

The most difficult words for arrogant man to say are: "I have sinned!"
—W. B. K.

* * *

I Am a Poor and Needy Sinner!

It is said that Vanderbilt, multimillionaire, asked as he neared death a faithful Negro servant, to come to his bedside and sing the old gospel hymn, *Come Ye Sinners, Poor and Needy.* The Negro put much feeling and pleading pathos into the hymn.

"Come ye sinners, poor and needy,
  Weak and wounded, sick and sore,
Jesus, ready, stands to save you,
  Full of mercy love and pow'r!

"Let not conscience make you linger,
  Nor of fitness findly dream,
All the fitness He requireth,
  Is to feel your need of Him!"

At the conclusion of the hymn, Vanderbilt said, "I'm a poor and needy sinner!" Such are *all* of us in God's sight whether we be penniless paupers or multimillionaires! The *only* prayer for the unsaved ones to pray is this prayer, "God be merciful to me a sinner!"
—W. B. K.

* * *

Like a Festering Sore for Forty Years!

Things were at a standstill in a revival meeting in the First Baptist Church in Clinton, Mississippi. It was difficult for the evangelist to preach. Souls were not being saved. Then, on the fourth night of the meeting, a prominent businessman went forward as the evangelist pleaded for Christians to get right with God. Said he, "Forty years ago, I stole money from my employer! Over the years, the Holy Spirit convicted me of the sin. But I was *too proud* to go to the one from whom I had stolen the money, and repay it with interest. God has shown me tonight that I can get right with Him *only* by confessing this long-standing sin, and making the crooked path straight!" Others followed the example of the businessman and got right with God and with others.
—W. B. K.

CONSCIENCE

Short Quotes

What your conscience knows about you is more important than what your neighbors say about you.

* * *

You can no more keep thought from returning to past transgression than you can keep the sea from returning to the shore after it has gone out. In the sea we call it the tide, but the guilty man calls it conscience. Conscience heaves the soul as the tide does the ocean.
—Victor Hugo, in *Toilers of the Sea*

* * *

The internal revenue collector of Minneapolis received a check for $765 from the Billy Graham Evangelistic Association. An accompanying letter stated: "This has come to our office from the people whose consciences would not let them keep money that they had wrongly held back from the government." One who sent $145 to the Association wrote, "Since I have given myself to Christ, I want to make this right. I do not want this money in my possession any longer." —W. B. K.

* * *

A boy had stolen a watermelon. He stood before the judge to be sentenced. Asked the judge, "Have you anything you wish to say before I pass sentence upon you?" The boy thought for a moment, and then said, "Judge, have you ever stolen a watermelon?" Subdued laughter was heard throughout the court room, until the judge pounded the gavel for order. Then he said to the boy, "No cross-examination allowed! Case dismissed!"

Let all thy converse be sincere,
Thy conscience as the noonday clear,
For God's all-seeing eye surveys,
Thy secret thoughts, and words, and ways.

—Bishop Thomas Ken

Illustrations

When His Conscience Found Him

Once a gypsy boy found a nest of hen eggs in a ditch far from a farmyard. He argued to himself that as long as he did not have to go into the farmyard after them and since he had found them, they were his. He filled his trouser pockets with them. His next difficulty was to get out of the ditch without breaking them, but he managed. Next he took his way across a plowed field where the walking was difficult. He heard a man shout, and thought that he wanted him, but did not desire to give him an interview. So he ran, and, as he ran, he fell, and when he fell the eggs all cracked. He got up, and looking around, saw nobody. The man whom he thought was pursuing him was only shouting to a man in another field. It is truly written, "The wicked flee when no man pursueth." He thought he had found the eggs, but his conscience found him. —From the late Gypsy Smith's Autobiography

* * *

The Fierce, Unutterable Pain

Confession of murder by a former Illinois policeman opened the door to freedom for a South Carolina house painter who twice had heard himself sentenced to death for the crime. The confessed murderer said: "My conscience has been bothering me. I have read the Bible and prayed. When I woke up last night, I could see the wife of the condemned, innocent man. This has been constantly on my mind and conscience!" —W. B. K.

* * *

Stolen!

A postal clerk had long been suspected of stealing stamps. Postal detectives wrote on some sheets of stamps with invisible ink and placed them where he worked. Later, they were found upon the person of the clerk. He insisted that he had bought them. "What! These?" exclaimed the detectives as they passed a moist brush over one of the sheets from which the words "Stolen from the general postoffice" glowed in red! Conscience-stricken, the guilty clerk confessed.

God knows all about our secret sins. He can make the conscience yield up its secrets. —W. B. K.

* * *

Now My Conscience Is Clear!

An elderly man walked into a Canadian National Railways station. "What is the price of a railway tie?" he asked the clerk. How puzzled was the clerk at the odd question! Finally, however, he dug up the information asked for. "Four dollars and twenty-four cents," he said. The old man plopped down the money on the counter, and, with smiles wreathing his face, he said to the startled clerk, "I stole a railway tie in 1931. It has been bothering me ever since I became a Christian. Now my conscience is clear!"

* * *

Tortured for Twenty Years!

A breath-taking incident occurred at a commencement service sometime ago at Vanderbilt University. After living for years with a tortured conscience which at times bordered on terror, a graduate of the University returned his diploma. The undersigned commencement speaker told the following impressive story:

"The most impressive scene I ever witnessed there was when the venerable

Chancellor Garland one Wednesday morning announced from the platform that a certain graduate, whose name he withheld, had sent back his diploma. It had been returned with the confession that in a single examination the student had used forbidden help, and though he had never been suspected and years had passed, he had never had any peace of mind. He, therefore, returned his diploma and asked that his name be stricken from the roll of alumni and announcement made of his confession, preferring public disgrace rather than to bear longer the intolerable memory of a single secret sinful act. The Chancellor said that he had after much consideration decided that the young man's repentance and suffering had been a sufficient atonement for his error, and insisted on his retaining his diploma. But the young man would not consent. 'And here is the diploma,' said Dr. Garland, holding out the mutilated parchment, but I have cut out the name, and the secret will die with me.' The hall was as still as death."

—Dr. Charles F. Smith

* * *

Confesses Murder After Thirty Years

In a town in Maine a century ago, a carpenter went on trial for stabbing his sweetheart to death in the park one night. Although the evidence against him was only circumstantial, it appeared to be an open-and-shut case. Everything fitted the pattern of guilt.

Murder weapon? The defendant admitted that the knife belonged to him.

Motive? That very afternoon, the girl had said she would never marry him.

Opportunity? He had no provable alibi for the time of his crime. He claimed he had been very upset and had walked aimlessly for hours along the bank of the river. But no one had seen him.

The attorneys, prosecution and defense, summed up; the judge charged the 12 good men and true, and they retired to the jury room. Eleven of them, it turned out, were ready to bring in a guilty verdict at once.

But to their surprise, Juror No. 12 demurred.

Was it right, he asked gently, to condemn a man to death on circumstantial evidence? After all, no one had actually seen him plunge the knife into the victim's body. Wasn't there a possibility of error, a shadow of doubt?

Hour after hour after hour, the others hurled arguments at Juror No. 12, but he wouldn't budge. For five long days he kept up his dogged fight to save the defendant from the gallows. And so persistently did he sow the seeds of uncertainty that at last the 11 yielded to the one. When they filed back into the courtroom, they brought a unanimous verdict of not guilty.

The judge, the lawyers, even the spectators, were thunderstruck when the result was announced. But there is no questioning a verdict.

Reluctantly the judge ordered that the accused man be given his freedom.

Thirty-three years later, when Juror No. 12 lay on his death bed, he called for pencil and paper. In a trembling hand, he scrawled these words — as if in answer to the unspoken "Why?" that had hung over his life: "Because I killed her myself." —Will Bernard, in *Coronet*

* * *

The Memory of Your Deed!

Years ago a father, in a fit of anger, swung an ax and killed his son. He was imprisoned, and during his incarceration, pending his trial, he had much time to sorrow and suffer because of his terrible deed. After hearing his case, the judge said, "We have known you in this community as an honorable, law-abiding citizen. Your horrible deed was unpremeditated. Your sentence will be the memory of your deed!"

Could there have been a severer punishment? We think not. Shakespeare says, "To be alone with my conscience is hell enough for me!"

"Trust me, no torture that the poets feign
Can match the fierce, unutterable pain,
He feels who, night and day, devoid of rest,
Carries his own accuser in his breast!"

—Told by Dr. R. E. Neighbour

CONSECRATION

Short Quotes

A Christian is a mind through which Christ thinks; a heart through which Christ loves; a voice through which Christ speaks; a hand through which Christ helps.

* * *

When quite young, Gounod said, "I make music." Later, he said, "I and Mozart make music." Still later, he said, "Mozart and I make music." Years later, he said, "Mozart makes music!" Not until we reach the place of utter dedication, saying, "Not I, but Christ," are we fully blessed —W. B. K.

* * *

I knelt in tears at the feet of Christ,
In the hush of the twilight dim;
And all that I was, or hoped, or sought,
I surrendered unto Him.

* * *

Since the first day that God put the poor of London, England, upon my heart, God has had all there was of William Booth. —William Booth

* * *

Lay any burden upon me, dear Lord; only sustain me. Send me anywhere, only go with me. Sever any tie, but that which binds me to Thy service and to thy heart! —A prayer

* * *

Who answers Christ's insistent call
Must give himself, his life, his all,
Without one backward look,
Who sets his hand unto the plow;
And glances back with anxious brow,
His calling hath mistook.
Christ claims him wholly as His own;
He must be Christ's and Christ's alone.

* * *

I will place no value on anything I have or may possess except in relation to the Kingdom of Christ. If anything will advance the interest of that Kingdom, it shall be given away or kept only as by the giving or keeping of it shall most promote the glory of Him to whom I owe all my hopes in time and eternity.
—David Livingston

Those who see God's hand in everything should leave everything in God's hands.

* * *

Consecration begins when self-interest ceases, and ends when self-interest begins.

* * *

"Come to Paris and make me a statue of Venus for the Louvre," commanded Napoleon of the German sculptor of Stuttgart, Johann Von Dannecker. "I cannot do it, Your Excellency. A man who has made a statue of the Saviour would commit sacrilege if he should employ his art in carving a pagan goddess. My art is a consecrated thing!" replied Von Dannecker.

* * *

As a missionary died, she whispered: "Bring!" One asked: "What shall we bring?" She said: "Bring forth the royal diadem and crown Him Lord of all!"

* * *

On the night of his graduation from medical college, Dr. Howard A. Kelly, world-famed surgeon and gynocologist, wrote in his diary: "I dedicate myself, my time, my capabilities, my ambition, *everything* to Him. Blessed Lord, sanctify me to Thy uses. Give me no worldly success which may not lead me nearer to my Saviour!" —Orville S. Walters, in *Christianity Today*

* * *

O grant, Lord Jesus, mine may be
A life surrendered unto Thee;
A vessel need not be of gold,
Need not be strong, or wise or bold,
It must be clean, for Thee to use,
So fill my heart, till all shall see,
A living, reigning Christ in me!

* * *

Recall the 21 years of my service; give me back its shipwrecks; give me back its standings in the face of death; give me it surrounded by fierce savages with spears and clubs; give it back to me with arrows flying around me; give it back to me with clubs knocking me

down; give all this back to me, and
I will be your missionary still!
—*Gospel Banner*

* * *

'Tis the look that melted Peter,
  'Tis that face that Stephen saw,
'Tis that heart that wept with Mary,
  Can alone from idols draw,
Draw and win and fill completely,
  Till the cup o'erflow the brim,
What have we to do with idols,
  Who have companied with Him?

* * *

Florence Nightingale at thirty wrote
in her diary, "I am thirty years of age,
the age at which Christ began His mission. Now no more childish things, no
more vain things. Now, Lord, let me
think only of Thy will." Years later,
near the end of her illustrious, heroic
life she was asked for her life secret,

and she replied, "Well, I can only give
one explanation. That is, I have kept
nothing back from God."
—Rev. Paul Rees, D.D.

* * *

Years ago a young man began a small
cheese business in Chicago. He failed.
He was deeply in debt. "You didn't
take God into your business. You have
not worked with Him," said a Christian
friend to him. Then the young man
thought, "If God wants to run the
cheese business, He can do it, and I'll
work for Him and with Him!" From
that moment, God became the senior
partner in his business. The business
grew and prospered and became the
largest cheese concern in the world!
You ask the name of that young man?
J. L. Kraft who became president of
the Kraft Cheese Company! —W. B. K.

Illustrations

Take All the Keys, Lord!

Dr. F. B. Meyer came to a crucial,
transitional time in his ministry. He
sat dejectedly in his study. "My ministry is unfruitful, and I lack spiritual
power," he said to himself.
Suddenly Christ seemed to stand beside him. "Let me have the keys to your
life," Christ said. The experience was
so realistic that he reached into his
pocket and took out a bunch of keys!
"Are all the keys here?" "Yes, Lord,
all except the key to one small room in
my life." "If you cannot trust Me in
all the rooms of your life, I cannot accept any of the keys." Dr. Meyer was
so overwhelmed with the feeling that
Christ was moving out of his life because he was excluding Him from one
interest in his life that he cried out,
"Come back, Lord, and take the keys to
all the rooms of my life!" —W. B. K.

* * *

The Same Loveth Much

A young African woman was saved
from a horrible life of sin and savagery.
One Christmas day, she came to the
house of God to give her sacrificial offering of praise! The native Africans

are very poor. At best they can give
only a handful of vegetables, or a bunch
of flowers to show their love for their
Lord. The new convert handed to the
missionary a silver coin, worth about
one dollar. The missionary was amazed.
At first she refused to accept it, but
finally she did. At the close of the service she asked the girl, "Where did you
get such a fortune?" Smilingly, the
girl said, "I went to a neighboring planter and sold myself to him as a slave for
the rest of my life for that coin. I
wanted to give to Jesus an offering
which satisfies my heart."
She had brought the financial equivalent of her life and laid it down, in a
single gift, at the feet of her Lord!
—W. B. K.

* * *

Away With These Empty Vanities

Baron von Wely renounced his title
and wealth and went as a missionary to
Dutch Guiana. There he rendered sacrificial and loving service to God. In
speaking of his forsaking all to follow
Christ, he said, "The title 'wellborn'
means nothing to me since I have been
born again in Christ. The title 'lord'
means nothing to me since I desire only

to be the servant of the Lord Jesus. What is it to me to be called 'Your Grace' when I have need of God's grace? Away with all these empty vanities! I will stay at the feet of Jesus, learn of Him and have no hindrance in serving Him aright." —W. B. K.

* * *

Take! Break! Make!
Lord, TAKE me,
  Me, with all my selfishness, with
  All my pride and jealousy,
  All my willful disobedience,
  All my lack of love to Thee,
  Me, with all my faults and frailties,
  All my secret, hidden sins.

And BREAK me!
  Break my stiff and stubborn will, Lord.
  Break my self with all its pride;
  All its dearest dreams, ambitions. . . .
  Break my heart, its idols smash, —
  Till in splintered, shattered fragments
  I lie helpless at Thy feet.

And MAKE me!
  With Thy tender, skillful hands, Lord,
  Make me like Thyself to be,
  Moulded in Thy glorious image,
  Sweet and loving, humble, kind,
  Faithful, gentle, finding pleasure
  Only in my Father's will.
                                          —*Selected*

* * *

Myself
One day I looked at myself,
  At the self that Christ can see;
I saw the person I am today
  And the one I ought to be.

I saw how little I really pray,
  How little I really do;
I saw the influence of my life —
  How little of it was true!

I saw the bundle of faults and fears
  I ought to lay on the shelf;
I had given a little bit to God,
  But I hadn't given myself.

I came from seeing myself,
  With the mind made up to be
The sort of person that Christ can use
  With a heart He may always see.
                                          —*Selected*

The Corpse Began to Stir!
John Sung came to America in 1920 to work on his doctorate in chemistry. He excelled in his studies. Attractive offers of jobs came to him. Also Christ's call came to him. After a period of great spiritual struggle, he dedicated himself utterly to God. Soon afterwards, he had a most unusual dream in which he saw himself in a casket. God seemed to say to him, "John Sung is dead — dead to self, but alive to Christ!" Then it seemed that the corpse began to stir. Angels began to weep! "Don't weep, angels," said John. "I will remain dead to the world and live only for Christ!" He became a mighty preacher of the gospel. For 15 years, he was "a burning and shining light" in China and southeast Asia. He was acclaimed China's greatest evangelist.
                                          —W. B. K.

* * *

Unused!
An unused harp had stood for years in the front room of a home in the mountains of Kentucky. Being a family relic, it was kept bright and clean. One day, a stranger stopped at the home and asked for lodging for the night. After the evening meal all gathered in the front room. The stranger looked at the harp intently. He asked if he could play it. After tuning it, he swept his hands across the strings. The loveliest music filled the room. How enchanting were the sweet, rapturous strains! The instrument had been muted for years. Now, in the hands of a master, the most exquisite of music came from it.

Hearts long muted by sin and unbelief, in the hands of the Master, Jesus, can give forth sweet music and joyous praise! —W. B. K.

* * *

All Given to the Government
When Hitler's planes were raining death and destruction on London, and when invasion of England by the foe was imminent, an Englishman wrote to an American friend: "As one man, the whole nation has handed over *all* its resources to the Government. We have invested the Cabinet with the right to conscript any of us for any task, to take

our goods, our money, our *all!* Never have rich men set so little store by their wealth. Never have we been so ready to lay down life itself if only our cause may triumph!"

What tidal waves of blessings would sweep over our churches if God's children would say: "As one man, we give ourselves unreservedly to Thee. Take our goods, our money, our *all,* and use them as seemeth good in Thy sight!"

—W. B. K.

* * *

What Is Consecration?

A young lady came to me near the close of the summer. Her face was wreathed with smiles. Exclaimed she joyfully, "This summer, at conference, I consecrated myself to God!" I expressed my deep joy, for her spiritual unconcern and worldliness had pressed heavily upon my soul during the wakeful, prayerful hours of many nights. To test the girl's sincerity, I said, "It is wonderful that you have dedicated your life to God. Does this mean that you will stand with us, working to win souls, out on the street corner in the open-air meeting? Does it mean that you will come and pray with us on prayer meeting nights? Does it mean that you are forsaking questionable, worldly pleasures, and saying in your heart:

'Jesus, I my cross have taken,
All to leave to follow Thee'?"

The smile faded from her face. The joy seemed to vanish from her heart. She went silently away.

With solicitous, prayerful concern, I observed the girl's life thereafter. She continued to be what I had known her to be — only a nominal church member.

How serious it is to sing, "Now I belong to Jesus," when we are living a divided, Christ-dishonoring life. Was not this what Jesus spoke against when He said, "This people draweth nigh unto me with their mouth, and honoureth me with their lips; but their heart is far from me" (Matt. 15:8)? Oh, that those who plead for Christians to dedicate their lives to God would fully disclose what it means — dying to self, dying to the world, dying to the praise, or censure, of others, and possibly dying a physical death! —W. B. K.

Our Every Gift

Our every gift, O God, is Thine
To help achieve Thy great design.
Our earthly treasures, time and skill
We dedicate to do Thy will.

Our length of days from early youth
We offer Thee to spread Thy truth.
Our work in office, mart or mill
We dedicate to do Thy will.

Our strength of arm and skill of hand
To run a lathe or till the land,
To make a home or nurse the ill,
We dedicate to do Thy will.

The art of leadership or speech,
Our aptitude to sing or teach —
Our powers in any place we fill —
We dedicate to do Thy will.

—Perry L. Stone

* * *

Life's Glory Dead

Dr. Tauler of Strasbourg was a great preacher. He did much to prepare the way for Luther and the Reformation. One day Nicholas of Basel said to him, "Dr. Tauler, you must die to yourself, your gifts, your popularity, your own goodness before you can do your greatest work for God, and before you can know the full meaning of the cross!"

At first, Dr. Tauler resented the words, lovingly and searchingly spoken. Later, however, he left "life's glory dead" at the foot of the cross. A new power came upon him and God used him mightily as a fearless champion of righteousness. —W. B. K.

* * *

Why He Couldn't Work

Standard Oil Company wanted two extra men, as recounted in *China's Millions*. A Mr. Li was one of the two chosen. He was housemaster in a boys' boarding school of the China Inland Mission. His wages were to be double what he earned in the school; but when he found he would have to work on Sundays, he gave up the new job. He was then offered three times his former wages and excused from Sunday work. He returned to the job, but soon became very unhappy in it. Finally, after much prayer, he wrote this letter:

"I am sorry I cannot work for your company. I have decided to work for God and win the boys to Jesus Christ." The manager said to one of his friends, "I thought I did well to hire a Christian, but I see they put Jesus first and business second." Do we?

　　　　　　　　　　—*Sunday School Times*

. . .

Owning His Ownership

When I was fourteen, I heard Lyman Beecher preach on the Lordship of Jesus Christ. I went to my room, locked the door, then threw myself on the floor of my room. This was what I said: "O God, I belong to Thee. Take what is Thine own. I gladly recognize Thy ownership on me. I now take Thee as my Lord and Master!" From that time to this I have never known a thing to be wrong without having an aversion to it. I have never seen anything to be right without having an attraction to it!" —Wendell Phillips

. . .

My Voice Belongs to God!

A dedicated Christian girl sang at a formal church wedding. In the audience sat a man who was on the lookout for talented young men and women to sing and play in night clubs and other places of worldly amusement. At the close of the wedding ceremony he approached the soloist and said, "Name your price! I am sure I can meet it!" The consecrated young woman courteously replied: "Sir, my voice isn't mine. It belongs to God. I will use it only to sing His praises, hoping and praying thereby to bring glory only to Him and souls to the Saviour!"

(The one who refused the offer is the writer's daughter, Alice, who is now a Wycliffe Bible Translator in Guatemala.) —W. B. K.

. . .

Daddy Has All There Is of Me!

In returning from Bible conferences, I usually bring little gifts to my girls. One night I came home after they were asleep. Next morning, as I sat in my study, I could hear overhead the patter of little feet. In a moment the oldest girl bounced into the study and entwined

her little arms around my legs. Just then I heard the pitter-patter of little feet on the stair steps. In a moment, the youngest little girl came and stood in the door. Tears pearled in her eyes and trickled down her face. She was sad because she had failed to greet me first. The older sister said to her, "See, I have all there is of Daddy!" I reached down and took the tearful one in my arms, and folded her to my heart. Looking down at her sister, she said, "You may have all there is of Daddy, but Daddy has all there is of me!"

　　　　　　　—Told by Rev. Alan Redpath

. . .

If

IF
God can hang the stars on high,
Can paint the clouds that drift on by;
Can send the sun across the sky,
　　What could He do through you?

IF
He can send a storm through space,
And dot with trees the mountain's face;
If He, the sparrow's way can trace
　　What could He do through you?

IF
God can do such little things
As count our hairs, or birds that sing,
Control the universe that swings,
　　What could He do through you?

　　　　　　　　　　—G. E. Wagoner

. . .

A Contradiction Corrected

Said a young woman to her pastor, "I really would like to surrender my life to the Lord Jesus Christ; but you know that I am an accomplished pianist and have had the privilege of playing on the concert stage here in Edinburgh. I am afraid that if I surrender to the Lord, He will ask me to give this up. Then if I yield my life to the Lord I am afraid He will tell me I am needed in India as a foreign missionary; and I do not want to go." The pastor turned to the "Not so, Lord" of Peter. He explained that this was a contradiction in terms. If Christ was Peter's Lord, then Peter had no right to say, "Not so"; and if Peter had the right to say, "Not so," then Christ was not his Lord. The girl saw this. The pastor then wrote the three words on a piece of paper and asked her to make her choice. Either "not so" must be crossed out, or "Lord" must be deleted. The pastor left the

room. In a few minutes he came back. The woman's head was on her arm, and she was sobbing softly. The pastor glanced over her shoulder. "Not so" was crossed out.

—*Good News Broadcaster*

CONVERSION

Illustrations

Only Existing

"If you are not a Christian, you are only existing and not living," said one of God's servants in his radio broadcast. A young banker and his wife were listening to the minister's earnest message. "That describes us perfectly, doesn't it?" asked the young man of his wife. Before she answered, he continued: "Our lives are empty. We go out on Saturday nights and have our good times. On Sunday mornings, we sleep with little thought of God and of our spiritual destinies. Yes, we are only existing, not living!" They resolved to go to God's house the following Sunday. There they heard the glorious gospel of Christ. They believed it. They invited Christ to come into their hearts. Today they are joyous Christians!

—*W. B. K.*

* * *

Changed

The foreman in a factory was a slave driver. Men worked in terror of his furious outbursts of temper. At such times he would hurl anything at hand or strike the object of his wrath. No man would continue long in his employ if he could find work elsewhere.

Then the foreman was converted to a new way of life. He called the men together for a conference and said to them, "I've been a brute to you; but now I've found my Saviour. Henceforth I'll treat you like brothers. If you have any complaint to make, come and see me. I'll listen. Help me, boys, to make this factory a good place to work in."

It was a change that caused comment all over the factory, but it was not long until the men knew that he was sincere

and in earnest. They responded to this overture of good will and Christian brotherhood. Labor troubles vanished. The factory output increased. Men were changed and worked with a will.

—*Bible Study Monthly*

* * *

Toplady's Conversion

It happened in his sixteenth year when he was attending a meeting at Codymain, Ireland. An illiterate layman, James Morris, preached from the text: "But now in Christ Jesus ye who were sometimes far off are made nigh by the blood of Christ" (Eph. 2:13). In after years Toplady said, "By the grace of God under the ministry of that dear messenger and under that sermon, I was, I trust, brought nigh by the blood of Christ in August, 1756. Strange that I, who had so long sat under the means of grace in England, should be brought near to God in an obscure part of Ireland amidst a handful of God's people met together in a barn, and under the ministry of one who could hardly spell his name. The excellency of such power must be of God, and can not be of man."

—*Gospel Herald*

* * *

Kamikaze

"Kamikaze" was a word often heard during World War II. The word designated the pilot of an explosive-laden Japanese plane whose sole mission was a suicidal dive upon a target, especially a ship!

Sakae Kobayashi was appointed to be a Japanese suicide pilot. He is now a minister of the Gospel. Through the reading of Christian literature, and the prayerful efforts of a Christian girl, Kobayashi became a Christian.

One day, in 1945, he was sitting in the cockpit of his plane in Tokyo waiting to take off on a mission from which he knew he would not return. While the engines were warming up, a ground crewman ran to tell him that Japan had surrendered. "I went home despondent and bitter," said Kobayashi. "My home had been burned, and my mother and grandmother killed. There was no food and no work."

Later, Kobayashi found work in an old refinery. There he met a Christian girl who showed him the New Testament she was reading. She persuaded him to go to church with her. Out of curiosity he went. The sermon he heard dealt with loving one's enemies. His interest was aroused. He went to the church again. He was blessedly saved! "I discovered newness of life which only Christ can bring," he glowingly testified.

Kobayashi entered a theological seminary the following year. He married the girl whom God used to bring him to Christ. —W. B. K.

* * *

This I Did for Thee!

Years ago, in a little chapel in a European village, a young nobleman knelt. As the rays of the sun cast its shafts of light through the beautiful stained glass windows onto pews and pulpits, the kneeling figure poured out his heart to God. At the front of the chapel stood a statue of the Saviour on His cruel cross, dying for the sin of the world. The statue was subscribed: "All this I did for thee — what hast thou done for Me?" With fixed gaze, the young nobleman looked upon the crucified One. He repeated over and over the words. "All this I did for thee — what hast thou done for Me?" Then and there, a young nobleman, Count Zinzendorf, gave his all to the Saviour, renouncing a vast fortune amassed by others in the brewery business. By his action, he said:

Take my life and let it be,
Consecrated, Lord, to Thee!
—W. B. K.

All Saved Except DeWitt

A soul-winning pastor visited the home of DeWitt Talmage. "Are all your children Christians?" asked he of DeWitt's father. The father replied, "Yes, all of them are saved, except DeWitt." Then the faithful pastor looked intently into the fireplace and vividly told a story: "It was a dark and stormy night. The wind swept the rain over the mountainside. A shepherd counted the sheep of his fold. All were safe within the fold except one lamb which was out in the storm and imperiled!" Said DeWitt Talmage later, "Had that man of God looked me straight in the eyes instead of looking into the fireplace, he could not have spoken so probingly to my slumbering soul. I never found any peace until I was *sure* I was inside the fold where the other sheep were!"
—W. B. K.

* * *

The Black Samaritan — Chaplain Lilly!

One of the greatest and most unselfish Christians I have ever known was Chaplain Raymond Lilly, "The Black Samaritan." For years he lived and preached Christ to the sick and dying thousands in the largest charity hospital in the world, the Cook County Hospital, Chicago, Illinois. The story of his conversion is most thrilling. It occurred in a church in Evanston, Illinois. As he entered the church, he carried in his hands a package containing a large brick, used in paving streets. In Lilly's heart burned an intense hatred for the minister. He had vowed that he was going to use the brick to batter out the brains of the minister. But, miracle of miracles, a *power* greater than Satan's pervaded the meeting as the minister exalted Christ, the Almighty Saviour. Raymond Lilly listened as if in a trance. The hardened features of his face softened into tenderness. Presently tears of heartbroken sorrow glistened on his black face. Because of grace Divine, instead of the minister's head being broken, Lilly's heart was broken! Shortly after Lilly's death, a brick was displayed in a memorial service for the "Black Samaritan." Subdued sobs were heard, as all listeners silently extolled the "name which is above every name," and thanked God for His heart-transforming power. —W. B. K.

* * *

For Rich and Poor Alike

A gentleman in London was invited to dinner at the home of a wealthy friend. After the meal was over the host asked his guest where he would like to go for the evening. The guest suggested Drury Theater where Moody and Sankey were holding meetings. With poor grace the host accompanied him.

When they arrived, the theater was filled. The guest, determined not to lose his prey, sent a note to an usher, "Come to door 10 and get us in. I have a wealthy sporting gentleman with me, but I will never get him here again if we do not get seats." He ushered them across the stage and seated them almost under Moody's nose.

The host never took his eyes off Moody. "I will come and hear this man again," he said afterwards. He kept his word, and went again until he was soundly converted.

His name was Edward Studd, father of C. T. Studd, who led his famous son to the Lord. —*Sunday Magazine*

* * *

Judson's Conversion

Although the son of a devout Congregational parson, Adoniram Judson, during his days at Brown University, chose as his best friend a product of "New Thinking," who was an ardent atheist. Judson soon became as strong a scoffer and unbeliever as his friend.

Determining to enter upon a stage career, Judson after graduation joined a theatrical party. One night he found himself just out of New York City in a country inn. In the room next to his a man was dying and Judson was forced to listen to the man's dying groans.

Inquiring the next morning, he was told that the man had died. Dazed, Judson learned that the man was his infidel college chum. Suddenly overwhelmed with the futility of life without God, Judson surrendered his life to Christ. —Ken Anderson in *Sunday*

CO-OPERATION

Illustrations

Only By Working Together

All have a share in the beauty,
    All have a part in the plan.
What does it matter what duty
    Falls to the lot of man?

Someone has blended the plaster,
    And someone has carried the stone;
Neither the man nor the master
    Ever has builded alone.

Making a roof from the weather,
    Or building a house for the King,
Only by working together
    Have men accomplished a thing.
                        —*Selected*

* * *

Keeping the Hands in Their Place

Rodin had just finished the statue of Honore de Balzac. The figure wore a long robe with loose sleeves. The hands were folded in front. Exhausted but triumphant the sculptor eyed his work with satisfaction.

Although it was four in the morning, Rodin hastened to awaken one of his students. The student's eyes slowly focused upon the hands.

"Wonderful!" he cried. "What hands . . . Master, I've never seen such marvelous hands before!"

Rodin's face darkened. A moment later he returned with another student. This one, too, remarked upon the hands. And a third was likewise overpowered by the beauty of this single feature.

Something appeared to snap in Rodin. With a dismayed cry he ran to a corner of the studio and grabbed an axe. Horror-stricken, his students threw themselves upon him, but in his madness he shook them from him. Then, with a well-aimed blow he chopped off the mag-

nificent hands, and turned to his stupe-
fied pupils.

"Fools!" he cried. "I was forced to
destroy these hands because they had a
life of their own. They didn't belong
to the rest of the composition. Remember this, and remember it well: No part
is more important than the whole!"

Thus the statue of Balzac stands in
Paris, without hands. The long, loose
sleeves of the robe appear to cover the
hands, but in reality Rodin broke them
off because they seemed more important
than the whole figure.   —Lajos Egri,
"The Art of Dramatic Writing."

* * *

Working at Cross-Purposes

A well-groomed man stood for several
minutes watching a muscular drayman
heaving at a heavy box. It was almost
as wide as the doorway through which
he was trying to move it. The onlooker
asked, "Would you like to have me help
you?" "Sure thing," said the drayman.
For two minutes the two men, on opposite ends of the box lifted, pulled and
perspired. The box didn't move an inch.
Finally, the volunteer helper straightened up and said, "I don't believe we
can ever get it out!" "Get it out?" the
drayman roared. "Why, you fool, I'm
trying to get it *in!*" —W. B. K.

* * *

God and You

Antonio Stradivari was the greatest
violin maker of all times. It is estimated that he made more than a thousand violins, all after he was sixty years
old. He died when he was ninety-three.
He spoke poetically of the teamwork between himself and God:

When a master holds
'Twixt chin and hand a violin of mine,
He will be glad that Stradivari lived,
Made violins, and made them of the best!
For while God gives them skill,
I give them instruments to play upon,
God choosing me to help Him.
If my hand slacked,
I should rob God, since He is fullest
    good,
Leaving a blank instead of violins,
    He could not make
Antonio Stradivari's violins without
    Antonio!

—W. B. K.

COURAGE

Short Quotes

Have courage for the great sorrows
of life and patience for the small ones,
and when you have accomplished your
daily task, go to sleep in peace. God is
awake. —Victor Hugo

* * *

Human strength and human greatness,
    Spring not from life's sunny side,
Heroes must be more than driftwood,
    Floating on a waveless tide!

* * *

A missionary society was deeply impressed by the courageous devotion of
David Livingstone who worked single-
handedly for God in Africa. The society
wrote to Livingstone: "Have you found
a good road to where you are? If so, we
want to send other men to join you."
Livingstone replied: "If you have men
who will come only if there is a good
road, I don't want them. I want men
who will come if there is no road at all."
—W. B. K.

* * *

A frenzied mob stormed a building
where John Wesley was preaching in
Falmouth, England. Wesley went out
and fearlessly confronted the mob, saying, "Here I am. Which one of you has
anything to say against me?" So impressed were they by the quiet courage
of the little man that, without knowing
what they did, they made way, and Wesley quietly walked through into the
street, where he began to preach. As
he spoke, the crowd became anxious to
hear, and presently the very leaders of
the mob — the "captains" of it, as he
called them — gathered around him and
shouted, "Not a man shall touch him;
let him speak!" Later he wrote in his

Journal, "I never saw before the hand of God so plainly shown as here."
—Dr. R. F. Horton in *Christian World Pulpit*

* * *

Forward, the Light Brigade!
Was there a man dismayed?
Not though the soldier knew
Someone had blundered.
Theirs not to make reply,
Theirs not to reason why —
Theirs but to do or die!
—Tennyson

* * *

Oh, do not pray for easy lives. Pray to be stronger men. Do not pray for tasks equal to your powers. Pray for powers equal to your tasks.

* * *

The bravest are the tenderest;
The loving are the daring.

* * *

A man is a hero, not because he is braver than anyone else, but because he is brave for ten minutes longer.
—Emerson

* * *

John Foster Dulles asked Charles de Gaulle, "What are your plans for solving the Algerian problem?" Replied de Gaulle, "One doesn't solve problems. One learns to live with them."

* * *

O God, give us serenity to accept what cannot be changed, and courage to change what should be changed and wisdom to distinguish the one from the other. —Dr. Reinhold Niebuhr

* * *

Chaplain Clarke Poling, son of Dr. Daniel Poling, was one of four chaplains who went down with the *Dorchester* during World War II. They gave their lifeboats to others. Shortly after Chaplain Poling entered the service, he wrote to his loved ones: "I know

I shall have your prayers. But please don't pray simply that God will keep me safe. War is a dangerous business. Pray that God will make me adequate."
—Rev. Paul Rees, D.D.

* * *

Segments of his battle line were falling back in disorder and defeat. "Beat a *retreat!*" shouted Napoleon to a drummer boy. Saluting smartly, the heroic drummer boy said, "Sir, you never taught me to beat a retreat. I can only beat a charge!" The lad's reply kindled new courage in Napoleon, who instantly gave the command, "Then beat a charge, drummer boy!" He did, and seeming defeat was turned into victory.

The Captain of our salvation, the Lord Jesus, commands, "Forward!"
—W. B. K.

* * *

Set us afire, Lord
Stir us, we pray!
While the world perishes
We go our way,
Purposeless, passionless,
Day after day.
Set us afire, Lord,
Stir us, we pray!
—Cushman

* * *

In Edinburgh, Alexander Duff spoke for two and one-half hours before a great convention. Then he fainted. He was carried out. When he revived, he pleaded, "Take me back! I must finish my message!" "You will die if you go back," he was told. Said he, "I'll die if I don't go back!" He went back and pleaded earnestly for volunteers to go to India. "If there is no one who will volunteer, I'll go back to India, and let them know that there is one Scotsman who is willing to die for those who grope in heathen darkness!"
—Paul W. Rood in *The Alliance Witness*

Illustrations

I Know Where to Draw the Line!

At an office party liquor was being served. A dissenting member of the office staff was coaxed to drink. She refused. Then she was ridiculed, but she stood fast. Sneeringly, one said, "Surely, you are strong enough to know when to stop!" She replied, "Where liquor is concerned, I am taking no chances. My life was spoiled by a drunken husband. He used to say to me, 'I know where to draw the line.' He didn't, however. It took a terrible illness to make him slow down, and then he didn't actually stop drinking. You sneer at me for not joining with others in drinking. I am not sneering at you for taking it, but I, as a Christian, would like to tell you that, if you want deliverance from this evil destroyer, there is One who'll make you strong and give you victory over it, and over every sin. Try Jesus Christ!"

—W. B. K.

* * *

Discipleship, a Risky Business

At the entrance of a driveway to a church is a sign which reads: ENTER AT YOUR OWN RISK.

How intriguing is the sign! Though placed there for a different purpose, it proclaims the fact that church affiliation, if it means what it ought to mean — separation from sin and utter dedication to God — could be risky and dangerous. Discipleship costs something. Many have hazarded their lives to follow Christ: "Men that have hazarded their lives for the name of our Lord Jesus Christ" (Acts 15:26). Some have forfeited their lives to follow Him: "And they loved not their lives unto the death" (Rev. 12:11). —W. B. K.

* * *

I Am Personally Opposed!

Pat Boone is a popular young singer. He signed a contract with the American Broadcasting Company. The *TV Guide* said he had previously turned down offers from three networks to put on his show. Two of these were to be sponsored by cigarette companies, the third by a brewery. Said Boone: "I realized these people wanted me because of my influence with teenagers. I am personally opposed to both smoking and drinking. I do not want to be responsible for influencing anyone else in taking them up!" —W. B. K.

* * *

Himself He Could Not Save!

During World War II on a Pacific island a platoon of U. S. Marines took shelter in a rocky cave. Believing that they were safe from the enemy, the lieutenant planned for their next attack, unaware that a Japanese sniper had crept close enough to hurl a grenade directly in their midst. One of them, Jim, a fine lad from Louisiana, saw the peril of his buddies. He threw his body on the grenade and was instantly blown to pieces! His buddies escaped with their lives. —W. B. K.

* * *

No Retreat

I sought a shelter from the storms
Of life, and as they beat
Upon my craft's frail, trembling sides,
God whispered, "No retreat,
But rather strength to face the task,
To make your work complete."

"But Lord," I cried, "it is too great
A job for me to do."
And He agreed it was too much
For one, but not for two.
"Have faith," He cried. "Have I not said
That I will see you through?"

—John W. Little

* * *

I Have No Fear of Death!

During World War II, a captain, who was an unbeliever, noticed a private near him in a trench, who was reading a New Testament. The captain sneeringly said, "What are you doing with that book? It will make you as cowardly as an old woman!" "Not at all, Sir," replied the private. "Since I came to read, love and understand this Book, I have no fear of death!" Just then a shell fell in the trench. The private was blown to bits. How ashamed the captain was! The New Testament lay nearby — unharmed. Reverently he put it in his pocket. In his dugout, he read it. Light came to his sin-darkened heart. He called upon the Saviour to save him. God answered his cry. He began immediately to tell others about Jesus. He secured from a chaplain a large number of New Testaments. "I want my men to be brave. I know that if they will read this Book and hide it in their hearts, they will know no fear, even in times of danger."

—W. B. K.

Abandon Ship!

Some six miles above the panhandle of Texas, a jet bomber on S.A.S. patrol was fatally disabled when No. 6 engine exploded and the wing was enveloped in flames. The chief pilot gave the word to abandon ship and the necessary apparatus went into effect blowing off the canopy and ejecting the seats. Lieutenant J. E. Obenauf, however, had trouble bailing out. His ejection seat failed. As he went stumbling through the ship trying to find an escape hatch, he stumbled over the body of Major Joseph Maxwell. What would he do? To hesitate would mean certain death. Why not jump and leave the unconscious body where it lay? Without hesitation, Obenauf deliberately turned around and got into the pilot's seat. In spite of intense heat and imminent danger, he performed a superhuman task. Alone he took the ship down through a storm and fog and landed in safety! It was a miracle but Maxwell, the man who lay unconscious in the belly of that cabin, was saved and given a second chance in life. If jet-age evangelism is going to be effective, our language and service must equal the jet age's demands for fidelity and sacrifice.

—The Watchman-Examiner

Christ Shall Be Magnified

A brilliant Chinese student was offered a fine position with the government. When Bishop Wilson S. Lewis asked the young man why he refused the splendid offer and volunteered to preach the Gospel for a mere pittance, he said:

"During the Boxer Uprising I lived in an inland village where there was a temple for devil worship. The Christians were led by the soldiers to that temple and ordered to renounce their religion and bow before the devil image or they would be executed. I saw one hundred and sixty-three of my townsmen walk by the devil god with heads erect, when a little bow would have saved their lives — then out to a great beam over which they placed their heads for the swift stroke of the executioner's sword that sent their heads rolling in the dust. My father was one of that

number. It was the unshaken integrity of their faith that thrilled me and gave me a longing for the new life. I must go back and tell my fellow townsmen of Christ who loves them, and of His power to save." —*The Upper Room*

General Jackson Is Here!

As Peter Cartwright preached in a little Southern church, he denounced sin. Someone near him whispered, "General Jackson is here!" Said the fearless preacher, "And who is General Jackson? If he doesn't repent of his sins, he will be forever lost!" Many feared that General Jackson would become angry. He didn't however. The sincerity and courage of the minister deeply impressed him. He said to the preacher at the close of the service, "If I had an army of such fearless men, I could be victorious in every attack!"

—W. B. K.

I My Cross Have Taken!

Some splendid young people volunteered as foreign missionaries. One of them was the only daughter of a multimillionaire. She was socially prominent, wealthy and worldly. Her parents were not Christians.

One evening, out of curiosity, the young lady entered a little Presbyterian church. There she heard the gospel for the first time. She was converted, and later she heard God's call to go as a missionary to China. She told her parents of her decision. Sneeringly they said, "You are mad. This is only a passing whim. We'll put a stop to it!"

The volunteer was engaged to a successful businessman. He was not a Christian. She appealed to him to surrender to Christ. He, too, laughed at her. He said to himself, "I'll dissuade her from this fantastic idea!"

Sometime later, the parents gave a gala social function to which they invited their socially prominent and wealthy friends. The parents told these friends of their problem, and enlisted their efforts to change the mind of their daughter. That evening, the daughter listened in silence to the discouraging pleas. She stood firm, however. Going to the piano, she began to play and sing:

Jesus, I my cross have taken,
   All to leave and follow Thee,
Destitute, despised, forsaken,
   Thou from hence my all shall be!

Her fiance was deeply touched. Going to her, he said, "I did not know Jesus Christ could mean so much to any person. If He means this to you, pray for me that I, too, may be saved and become His devoted follower!" Her prayer was answered! They were happily married, and *both* went to China where they labored for God for many years. —Told by Dr. M. E. Dodd

* * *

They May Hurt You!

Some years ago a native woman in Brazil heard a missionary preach Jesus. Soon she opened her heart to the Saviour. Then she wanted to be baptized to show that she believed in Jesus. The missionary said, "The people in this village are angry because I have been preaching the gospel here. If you are baptized they may hurt you!" She replied, "I believe in Jesus, and I want to be baptized to show that I am now His follower. I am not afraid to suffer for Him!" The missionary arranged for the baptismal service on the following Sunday. The news about the service spread rapidly. A large crowd gathered on the bank of the river to watch the baptizing. When the missionary and the woman went into the water, angry mutterings were heard. The missionary proceeded with the baptism. How happy the woman was as she obeyed the command of her Lord. As they came out of the water, rocks began to fly! The woman was hit on the forehead. Blood began to trickle down her face. Instead of weeping, she shouted, "Praise God! I am now suffering for Jesus my Saviour!" —W. B. K.

* * *

Latimer, Consider Well!

Bishop Latimer once preached a sermon before King Henry VIII which greatly offended him. The king ordered him to preach again next Sabbath and to make public apology for his offense. The bishop ascended the pulpit and read his text, and thus began his sermon: "Hugh Latimer, dost thou know before whom thou art this day to speak? To the high and mighty monarch, the king's most excellent majesty, who can take away thy life if thou offendest; therefore take heed that thou speakest not a word that may displease. But then, Hugh, consider well! Dost thou not know from whom thou comest — upon whose message thou art sent? Even the great and mighty God, who is all-present and able to cast thy soul into hell! Therefore take care that thou deliverest thy message faithfully." And with increased energy, he preached the self-same sermon as the week before. The fear of God delivered him from the fear of man. —*The Watchman-Examiner*

* * *

Or Else

A Communist teacher in East Germany said to a class of children: "Stand and say, 'There is no God.'" A little eight-year-old girl from a Christian home refused. She was threatened, but she wouldn't say the words. Finally the teacher angrily said, "Go home and write fifty times, 'There is no God,' and give me the paper tomorrow!" That night she sat down and wrote fifty times, "Es gibt doch ein Gott" — "There *is* a God!" The teacher was angry. "When you go home write five hundred times, 'There is no God,' or else!" The "or else" meant terrible punishment. The next day, the father and the little girl went to the superintendent of the school and told him what had happened. "Don't worry," he said to the little girl. "Your teacher was killed in a motorcycle accident last night. The matter is settled. Go to your class!" —W. B. K.

* * *

Ike, Get Me Out of This!

At the close of World War II, the Russians held a reception for Field Marshall Sir Bernard L. Montgomery. At the reception, he was awarded the Soviet Union's Order of Victory. Vodka flowed freely at the function. Montgomery was surrounded by a score of imbibing, high-ranking Russian officers. Being a total abstainer, he was "on the spot." He was embarrassed. Just then, General Dwight D. Eisenhower came near. In an undertone, Montgomery said: "Ike, get me out of this!" Ike came promptly to his aid. He explained that the British Marshal did not drink. —W. B. K.

* * *

All for One — One for All

A Chinese heard the gospel and became a Christian. At new year, he refused to perform the religious rites of burning paper and incense to the ancestors. The head of his clan gave him fifteen days to change his mind and decreed that he would be beaten with a thousand stripes if he failed to do so. Toward the end of the fifteen days, a native Christian said to the head of the clan: "You don't understand this Christian religion. When a man believes in the Lord Jesus Christ, God is his Father, and every other believer is his brother or sister. We are one family. I could not see my brother beaten and stand idly by. What all we Christians propose to do is this: If you insist on carrying out your sentence, all of us who are brothers and sisters in Christ

are going to come and share those stripes with him!"

The decree was rescinded. Christian unity and mutual love had triumphed over the heathen powers of darkness.
—W. B. K.

* * *

Safe Return, Doubtful!

The following ad occurred in a London newspaper: "Men wanted for hazardous journey, small wages, bitter cold, long months of complete darkness, constant danger, safe return doubtful. Honor and recognition in case of success." The ad was signed by Sir Ernest Shackleton, Antarctic explorer. Thousands responded instantly to the call. They were ready to sacrifice all for the elation of adventure and uncertain honor. Should God's children do less for the One who paid the supreme sacrifice for the sin of the world and who said: "If any man will come after me, let him deny himself, and take up his cross and follow me. For whosoever will save his life shall lose it: and whosoever will lose his life for my sake shall find it" (Matt. 16:24, 25)?
—W. B. K.

COVETOUSNESS

Short Quotes

He always said he would retire,
  When he had made a million clear,
And so he toiled into the dusk,
  From day to day, from year to year!

At last he put his ledgers up,
  And laid his stock reports aside,
And when he started out to live,
  He found he had already died!
—*Selected*

* * *

What They Left in Death

Lewis Struber, eighty-eight years old, was a retired shoe merchant. He lived alone. He was eccentric. In death, he left $82,000 in an unlocked safe in his barn, deposits in banks of more than $53,000 and securities of an undetermined value.

Mrs. Carrie Wherritt, eighty-six years of age, lived, during the last four years of her life, in a ramshackle brick dwelling in a neighborhood in Detroit that was undergoing demolition to make way for an expressway. From her bed in a charity ward, she said to police officers: "All I have is in the safe at home." It was unlocked. There the officers found $291,000 in currency which the owner was soon to leave.

* * *

Oscar Hastings, eighty-four years old, lived a frugal life. Everyone thought he was a pauper. It was revealed in his death, however, that he was a rich man — he left an estate of $100,000.

Chelestino Chiesa, seventy-three years old, lived in a seven-by-four-foot cubicle in a flophouse at 809 South State Street, Chicago. He paid twenty-five cents per day for the cubicle in which he slept, and which was enclosed by chicken wire. He lived in squalor and loneliness. He lived only to amass money which brought no joy or comfort to him or others. Those who knew him said he never treated himself to a full and enjoyable meal. He died in a charity ward in Cook County Hospital. He left a fortune of $250,000.

* * *

Here lies a miser, who lived for himself,
And cared for nothing but gathering pelf,
Now where he is, or how he fares,
Nobody knows, and nobody cares!
    —An epitaph on a tomb in
    an English churchyard

* * *

Some years ago Mrs. Reva Andelman fell unconscious on a street in Chicago. She was taken to the Cook County Hospital. Astonished nurses found nearly $15,000 sewed in the lining of her shabby, dirty coat! For years she had begged for meals on the streets of Chicago and had lived in an $11-a-month room! —W. B. K.

* * *

Is covetousness a disease? Yes! It is a disease of the soul! With the passing of the years, passions burn low. Not so of the soul-shriveling, character-tarnishing, personality-dwarfing sin of covetousness. This sin tightens its grasp upon its wretched victims as they grow older.
That man may breathe, but never live,
  Who much receives, but nothing gives;
Whom none can love, whom none can thank,
Creation's blot, creation's blank!
     —W. B. K.

In death, the Christian goes to his riches: "But lay up for yourselves treasures in heaven" (Matt. 6:20). In death, the unsaved leave their riches: "For we brought nothing into this world, and it is certain we can carry nothing out" (I Tim. 6:7). —W. B. K.

* * *

A classic literary representative of grasping greed is Père Grande. Illustrating how covetousness tightens its grasp upon its victims to the close of life, Balzac tells of a priest administering the last rites of the Roman Catholic Church. He dangled a golden crucifix before the glazed eyes of Père Grande. At the sight of the golden object, ghoulish delight lit up his pallid face! With great effort, he reached for the glittering crucifix, and then fell back — dead! —W. B. K.

* * *

Two men called on a well-known miser for a gift for an orphanage. "They mean nothing to me," countered the miser to the persuasive pleas of the men. Finally they left. "And to think that old scoundrel has money to burn," said one of the men. Said the other, "Yes, and that's just what would happen to it if he could take it with him!"
"Nor thieves, nor covetous, nor drunkards . . . shall inherit the kingdom of God" (I Cor. 6:10).

* * *

Some time ago Laura and Margaret Moroselli, sixty-nine and seventy years old respectively, were found starving to death in their New York City apartment. Only a blackened pan of potatoes and a partially used can of spaghetti were found in the apartment. Neither weighed over ninety pounds. Assets valued at $100,000 were found in the apartment where they lived as recluses for sixteen years. They never admitted anyone and only Margaret went out occasionally. —W. B. K.

Illustrations

A Bombshell in Deacons' Meeting!

A young lady indulged in a worldly pleasure against which her church covenant spoke, and upon which many Christians look with disfavor. In time, the matter came to the attention of the deacons' board. One of the deacons, who was notoriously close-fisted, giving little for the support of the church or for missions, wanted the name of the young woman to be dropped from the church roll. Others urged a conciliatory attitude. Finally, the pastor was asked to express himself. Said he, seriously, "Since this unpleasant situation has been brought to our attention, I am requesting that you not make an example solely of this young woman. I request that the treasurer of the church be summoned to appear before this body, and that we go over the record of each member, and that all those guilty of the sin of covetousness be forthrightly turned out of the church!"

What a bombshell did the pastor throw into the midst of that meeting! All got on their knees and prayed earnestly for the offending young woman. Later she was visited by the pastor and won to a life of utter dedication to God.

—Told by Dr. George W. Truett

* * *

High Cost of Covetousness

An eminent physician had cured a little child of a dangerous illness. Full of gratitude, the mother went to the home of the physician, and said to him: "Doctor, there are some services that cannot be repaid. I really don't know how to express my gratitude. I thought you would accept this purse, embroidered by my own hands." "Madam," said the doctor coldly, "medicine is not a trivial affair. Small presents serve to sustain friendship, but they do not sustain our families." "But, doctor," said the lady, "what is your fee?" "Forty pounds, Madam." The lady opened the embroidered purse, took out five bank notes of twenty pounds each, gave two to the doctor, put back the remaining three, bowed coldly, and took her leave. Covetousness had cost much and lost more. —*Gospel Gleaners*

* * *

She Starved with $274,000 in Her Closet!

The above headline, with the subhead, "Find $200,000 More in Banks," lured millions of readers of daily newspapers over the nation to read one of the queerest stories about a frail little widow who starved to death in her dreary fire-charred Staten Island, New York, flat!

Eloquently and convincingly her life and death showed that covetousness is a disease of the soul which stifles and extinguishes the nobler aspirations, and which renders its victims powerless to grasp the true meaning of existence.

The frail little widow's name was Mrs. Emma Buhl DeHart. Besides the money discovered in the flat and in banks, she owned hundreds of shares of stock. Her total assets came to about half a million dollars. Her wealth had been largely untouched during her lifetime. She ate skimpily. She saved boxes and wrappings for her stove. It was her habit, in later years, to arise about noon and go to a nearby dime store for a hotdog or hamburger.

She died intestate, without a will. A court fight was precipitated by nephews and nieces, claimants of the estate of the decedent!

"Take heed and beware of covetousness!" —W. B. K.

* * *

What They Lost in Becoming Christians!

An aged couple was solicited for a contribution for a worthy Christian cause. The wife, though a Christian, had not been delivered from the sin of covetousness. She lamented to her husband, "We have lost a lot of money by becoming Christians, and contributing to Christian work!" The husband, who had made more progress in the Christian life than his wife, replied, "Yes, Mary, we have lost a great deal by our religion. I lost an old slouch hat, a patched coat, and unsightly shoes. I lost the habit of getting drunk and quarreling with you. I lost a burdened conscience, a wicked heart, and many guilty feelings and fears! All my sins are lost, completely lost, like a millstone, cast into the depth of the sea! They will never be remembered against me! Daily my soul feeds upon the living Bread! You, too, Mary, have been a loser, though not as great a loser as I. Before we were saved, you washed clothes to help with our expenses. Your clothes were worn and shabby. You lost an aching heart, filled with concern for me. You lost them joyously! How spiritually rich we are, Mary! God has imparted blessings which money cannot buy. So let us continually show our gratitude to Him by supporting His cause." —W. B. K.

* * *

Wesley Has Spoiled It All!

A miserly farmer of some means went to hear Wesley preach on stewardship. Wesley began his message by saying: "Get all you can!" The farmer whispered to the one beside him, "This is strange preaching. I never heard the like before, but I like it." After Wesley had praised the diligent ones, he passed on to his second point: "Save all you can!" Thought the farmer: "This is one grand sermon!" Wesley spoke contemptuously of thriftlessness and waste, and then took up the third point of his message: *"Give all you can!"* The covetous farmer winced as if dodging from a missile hurled at him. Low-

ering his head in displeasure, he mumbled: "Oh, dear! Wesley has spoiled it all!" —W. B. K.

* * *

The Dying Pickpocket

Years ago, during the early morning hours, a minister was called to see a notorious pickpocket who was dying. The minister told the man of the Saviour, and of His willingness to save him if he would only look to Him for mercy. Then the minister knelt and prayed. When he arose from his knees, the man was dead! His rapidly-stiffening fingers were clutching the minister's gold watch chain. The sight of the glittering chain and the urge to steal it from the preoccupied minister was too much for the dying pickpocket to resist.

Covetousness, a disease of the soul, tightens its grasp upon its victims right up to death's door! —W. B. K.

CRIME

Illustrations

Rules for Tragedy

The police department of Houston, Texas, issued a leaflet giving rules for raising delinquent children: (1) Begin with infancy to give the child everything he wants. In this way he will grow up to believe the world owes him a living. (2) When he picks up bad words, laugh at him. This will make him think he's cute. It will also encourage him to pick up "cuter" phrases that will blow off the top of your head later. (3) Never give him any spiritual training. Wait until he is 21 and then let him "decide for himself." (4) Avoid use of the word "wrong." It may develop a guilt complex. This will condition him to believe later, when he is arrested for stealing a car, that society is against him and he is being persecuted. (5) Pick up everything he leaves lying around — books, shoes, and clothes. Do everything for him so that he will be experienced in throwing all responsibility on others. (6) Let him read any printed matter he can get his hands on. Be careful that the silverware and drinking glasses

are sterilized, but let his mind feast on garbage. (7) Quarrel frequently in the presence of your children. In this way they will not be too shocked when the home is broken up later. (8) Give a child all the spending money he wants. Never let him earn his own. Why should he have things as tough as you had them? —*Wesleyan Methodist*

* * *

As a Man Thinketh

Amazing, but true! Psychologists have proven that if a person thinks often enough and long enough about committing a crime he will commit the crime, or at least try. They say, "What you believe is what you are."

Behind every wicked act is a process of wicked thinking. Murder is preceded by murderous thoughts; immorality is preceded by unclean thinking. It is impossible to think wickedly and do righteously. "As he [a man] thinketh in his heart, so is he." Outward actions and words are just the expressions of inner thoughts. —*Revelation*

I Reared a Criminal

In the August, 1960, issue of the *Ladies' Home Journal* is an article entitled, "I Reared a Criminal." It is the true story of a heartbroken mother. We quote:

We loved him, but —

His father was too busy to be with him when he was young.

I couldn't bring myself to punish him for misbehavior.

We sided against his teachers when they complained about his work (and conduct) in school.

As he grew up he would hardly discuss the time of day with us.

He was expelled from school.

We gave him money so he wouldn't steal again.

I wept when the police called and I had to turn my boy over to them. . . . As I watched them search him my life seemed to end.

—*Allegheny Conference Messenger*

* * *

Nothing Like This!

"We have murders in Lebanon, but nothing like this," said Colonel Chahine J. Azzi of Beirut, Lebanon, who for twenty-nine years has been a member of the police force in Lebanon. He was commenting upon the slaying and dismemberment of the body of a fifteen-year-old Chicago girl. "If we want to fight crime we must avoid suggesting or encouraging criminal acts. I think we should never show a film in which a man who is carrying a gun is the hero. In Lebanon we do not look with favor on American gangster movies, or even on cowboy movies if they play up shooting and violence, or have as the hero a gun-toting man." —W. B. K.

* * *

Germs of Future Crimes

Society contains in itself the germs of all future crimes . . . the criminal is only the instrument which carries them out. Every social order, therefore, preconditions a certain number and assortment of crimes which result as a necessary consequence from its organization.

—Quetelet, Belgian mathematician

$1 for Church — $12 for Crime!

For every one dollar spent for churches and their work, twelve dollars are spent on crime. America's annual crime bill is twenty billion dollars.

—Attorney General of United States

* * *

No Juvenile Delinquency Among Chinese-Americans

P. H. Chang, Chinese consul-general in New York City was asked to comment on the fact that there are no juvenile delinquents among Chinese-American youths. He said: "A Chinese child, no matter where he lives, is brought up to recognize that he cannot shame his parents. Before a Chinese child makes a move, he stops to think what the reaction on his parents will be. Will they be proud or will they be ashamed? That is the sole question he asks himself."

—W. B. K.

* * *

Criminals Are Not Born

Criminals are not born. They are reared in an era which has discarded morality. They are victims of spiritual starvation. Irreligion has obviously become the major contributing factor to our national juvenile crisis.

—Judge Julius H. Miner,
Circuit Court, Chicago

* * *

Guilty As Charged!

More and more children are being led toward crime as parents throw away responsibility. Selfishness is often the keynote of the day and materialism the inspiration for living. God, in many instances, is not accepted in the home, and concepts of morality have been relegated to the junk heap.

—J. Edgar Hoover

* * *

As a Russian Sees It

American television, saturated with killings, knifings, stabbings and shootings, is the reason American children are delinquent says the wife of the Soviet ambassador, Mrs. Mikhail Menshikov. Recently she spent six hours in a New York City hotel room watching TV.

"It was terrible. Men shooting each other, fighting, throwing furniture around. Little boys and girls should not see such things. No wonder they grow up bad," she said.

—Doris O'Donnell

* * *

Read and Weep!

"The most sobering single aspect of my fourteen years on the bench," remarked Kings County Judge Sam Leibowitz, "is the downward trend in the age of criminals. Once when burglars were brought before me they were hardened men in their forties, fifties and sixties, usually with a long prison history behind them. Today," the judge said, "the burglar I must sentence is very likely to be a boy in his teens, every bit as hard as the confirmed criminal of years gone by, and sometimes even harder."

—*Selected*

* * *

Spanked Boy, 11, Slays Three Kin!

The above caption topped the front page of a great metropolitan daily newspaper. The terrible happening screamingly points an accusing finger at the decaying society which man has created apart from God. "The world we have created is too much for us," said Dr. Robert Maynard Hutchins, former chancelor of the University of Chicago. He is right. Our forgetfulness of God is exacting an alarming toll, and has unorbed and unanchored ever increasing numbers of children and youths. Society has eaten the proverbial "sour grapes," and the youths' teeth are set on edge! Now let us go back to the "spanked boy," who, with cold-blooded deliberation, took the lives of his mother, father, and older brother: "I'm going to kill you," the boy said to his older brother as he felled him with a rifle bullet. Seeing his mother through a bedroom window, he sent a bullet scudding through her heart. Going around to the front of the house, he saw his father rushing out. "Hi, Dad," said the boy as he fired at him. "He fell to his knees and I fired again. He was still after the second shot, but I fired a third to make sure!"

We relate these gruesome and heartbreaking facts solely for one purpose: That all who read may weep, and cry

to God to look in pity and mercy upon a world floundering in a veritable morass of immorality, drunkenness, and the sin diseases which brought about the downfall and disintegration of the nations of the yesteryears! Since man's extremity is God's opportunity, we weepingly and pleadingly cry to God, "It is time for thee, Lord, to work: for they have made *void* thy Law" (Ps. 119:126). Let this be our ceaseless heart-cry, "O Lord, revive thy work in the midst of the years, in the midst of the years make known: in *wrath* remember *mercy*" (Hab. 3:2). —W. B. K.

* * *

Youth Insensitive to Death and Pain

The predominance of brutality in television is making our nation's youth insensitive to human suffering. They are becoming so accustomed to an overwhelming amount of crime and violence, that death and pain are becoming meaningless. —The Senate subcommittee investigating juvenile delinquency

* * *

Does This Startle You?

In two years Judge B. E. Johnson, of Pierce County Juvenile Court, Tacoma, Wash., had over 2,000 young people ten to eighteen years old appear before him. All but one listed a denominational preference. However, at the time of their arrest less than 2 per cent were in regular contact with a church or Sunday school. The judge asked each of these youngsters if, when they dropped out of Sunday school, anyone contacted them to get them back. During the two years only two youngsters said such a contact was made. Does this startle you? What about your Sunday school?

—Dr. Clate A. Risley, executive secretary National Sunday School Association

* * *

Found Out!

A young man and woman robbed a loan company. They got away with several thousand dollars. "This is a perfect crime. How smoothly everything went," they mused. But was it a perfect crime? It was a total flop, for in the office of the loan company were several hidden cameras which photographed every move of the robbers, and the pictures taken revealed their identity and led to their immediate arrest.

Evildoers at times are unapprehended and undetected by man, but not by God: "Thou God seest me!" —W. B. K.

* * *

Society Is to Blame

A little six-year-old girl was horribly killed by some depraved, possibly dope- or liquor-drugged sadistic sex deviate. A brokenhearted father gave a true explanation of the reason for this unspeakably sad occurrence: "I wouldn't blame the man as much as the *society* which produces such men. It is a society that measures Hollywood stars by their bosoms, and a society where the telling of dirty stories and the use of foul language is commonplace. It is a society that allows sex magazines on newsstands for kids to read. These things make sex perverts of people who have the slightest abnormal tendencies. They are encouraged by everything around them. Until the day society changes its fundamental moral principles and reasserts a belief in God, we will have sex perverts!"

Long ago, the world's Saviour indicated unregenerated, depraved man's basic need when He said: "Ye must be born again." Until the "desperately wicked" heart of man is changed by the grace of God, man will continue in crime and nameless vice. —W. B. K.

* * *

Why He Became a Bum

Some years ago, in a St. Louis murder trial, a young criminal said: "My father always said I was no good. Mother said I'd never amount to anything. The school teachers told me I was no account. Even my own home town never expected me to be anything but a criminal. I always wondered why, for, as far as I could see, I was just like other boys, only a bit more independent. The only creature that ever really seemed to understand or believe in me was my dog. When he died, I became a bum!"
—*Moody Monthly*

CRITICISM

Short Quotes

There is something wrong with a man, as with a motor, when he knocks continually.

* * *

Criticizing others is a dangerous thing, not so much because you may make mistakes about them, but because you may be revealing the truth about yourself. —Judge Harold Medina

* * *

The moon could not go on shining if it paid any attention to the little dogs that bark at it.

* * *

There has been only one faultless person in this world, and He has promised to present all believers "faultless before the presence of his glory with exceeding joy" (Jude 1:24).
—*Clarion Call*

You may go through the world,
But 'twill be very slow,
If you listen to all
That is said as you go.;
You'll be worried and fretted,
And kept in a stew,
For critical tongues
Must find something to do,
For people will talk.

* * *

Don't mind criticism. If it is untrue, disregard it. If it is unfair, keep from irritation. If it is ignorant, smile. If it is justified, learn from it.

* * *

The human race is divided into two classes — those who go ahead and do something and those who sit still and inquire, "Why wasn't it done the other way?" —Oliver Wendell Holmes

Before criticizing another's faults, take time to count ten *of your own.*

* * *

Scrutinizing an owl, a man said: "That owl is not stuffed right! Its head is not on right! The body is not poised right! The feathers are not fixed right! If I could not stuff an owl better than that, I would go out of the taxidermist business!" Just then the owl moved. The man had criticized a *live* owl! —*The Sunday School Times*

Said a fault-finding minister to Bishop Ryle as they sat in one of Moody's meetings in England, "Do you hear that young Yankee smashing the Queen's English?" Replied Bishop Ryle, "Yes, but do you see him breaking sinners' hearts in the gallery?" —W. B. K.

* * *

Until we know all, we should not pass judgment at all.

—*The Watchman-Examiner*

Illustrations

No Answer

While contending with the manifold problems of geography and climate in the building of the Panama Canal, Colonel George Washington Goethals had to endure the carping criticism of countless busybodies back home who freely predicted that he would never complete his great task. But the resolute builder pressed steadily forward in his work, and said nothing.

"Aren't you going to answer your critics?" a subordinate inquired.

"In time," Goethals replied.

"How?"

The great engineer smiled. "With the canal," he replied. —Adrian Anderson

* * *

Church Cannibals

With regularity, a Christian father and mother attended church with their children. After the services, around the dinner table, the pastor, the choir, the church officials were served "a la carte" as the family roundly and unjustly criticized. In time the hearts and minds of the children became hardened against the pastor and the church, thus making it impossible for the pastor to reach them for Christ. They became "gospel hardened," a fatal spiritual malady. They fell completely away from the church. They went recklessly into sin and worldliness. How overcome with grief were the mother and father over the way their children had gone! But now it was too late!

How different it might have been had the father and mother directed the conversation aright around the dinner table,

and instead of "picking to pieces" the pastor, the church, and its officials, had poured out their hearts in prayer for them, and for the unsaved ones, including the children about the dinner table! —Told by a pastor

* * *

A Little Walk Around Yourself

When you're criticizing others and are finding here and there
A fault or two to speak of, or a weakness you can tear;
When you're blaming someone's meanness or accusing one of pelf —
It's time that you went out to take a walk around yourself.

There's lots of human failures in the average of us all,
And lots of grave shortcomings in the short ones and the tall;
But when we think of evils men should lay upon the shelves,
It's time we all went out to take a walk around ourselves.

We need so often in this life this balancing of scales,
This seeing how much in us wins and how much in us fails;
Before you judge another — just to lay him on the shelf —
It would be a splendid plan to take a walk around yourself.

—Helen Welshimer

* * *

Me and Thou

An aged man said to his aged wife, "Honey, I think everybody is peculiar excepting me and thou, and sometimes

I think that thou art a little peculiar!"

How human it is to see the faults of others and be blind to our own faults. The Saviour asks this question of chronic critics: "And why beholdest thou the mote that is in thy brother's eye, but considerest not the beam that is in thine own eye?" (Matt. 7:3).

—W. B. K.

* * *

What Can You Expect for a Dime?

A grouchy father attended church with his little boy. There was nothing in the service which the faultfinding father liked. As he walked home with his boy, he criticized the minister and his sermon. He found fault with the choir, and with everything in general. The boy had noticed that when the offering was taken, his father had put a dime into the collection plate. So he asked his father, "Well, Dad, what can you expect for a dime?" —W. B. K.

The Wrecking Crew

I stood on the streets of a busy town,
Watching men tearing a building down:
With a "Ho, heave, ho," and a lusty yell,
They swung a beam and a sidewall fell.

I asked the foreman of the crew,
"Are those men as skilled as those you'd
    hire if you wanted to build?"
"Ah, no," he said, "no indeed.
Just common labor is all I need.
I can tear down as much in a day or two,
As would take skilled men a year to do."

And then I thought as I went on my way,
Just which of these two roles am I try-
    ing to play?
Have I walked life's road with care,
Measuring each deed with rule and
    square?
Or am I one of those who roam the town,
Content with the labor of tearing down?
—*Selected*

THE CROSS

Short Quotes

It has been a strange trial, our Lord's accusers and His judges have been the same persons. An officer, during the proceedings, has been allowed to strike Jesus. Messengers, scurrying from home to home in the darkness, have got the Sanhedrinists into a night session, contrary to their rules, and that body has made its decision against Jesus when a sleeping populace could not become aroused. —*Christianity Today*

* * *

An intimate friend of Handel called on him just as he was composing the music for the words, "He was despised," and found him sobbing, so greatly had this passage of the shame and suffering of Christ affected him. —W. B. K.

* * *

The cross of Christ is the sweetest burden I ever bore.
—Samuel Rutherford

* * *

Christ has no velvet crosses.
—Samuel Rutherford

In vision, Martin Luther seemed to see Satan approaching him with a large book under his arm. "This book," said Satan, "contains the record of the sins of your life!" As Satan began to read, Luther said, "Stop! Here is another Book — the Word of God. It says, 'The blood of Jesus Christ . . . cleanseth us from all sin'" (I John 1:7). —W. B. K.

* * *

A missionary was asked, "Give us proof of the transforming power of the cross." He replied, "When I arrived in the Fiji group, my first duty was to bury the hands, arms, feet, and hearts of eighty victims whose bodies had been roasted and eaten at a cannibal feast. I lived to see those very cannibals, who had taken part in such horrible feasts, gathered about the Lord's table!"
—W. B. K.

* * *

"Jesus died for me," said Charles Haddon Spurgeon, "are four words I have lived by, and they are the words I am going to die by!"

None ever came as far as He,
None ever bore such agony,
None ever gave as liberally,
  As Christ who died for me!

No love so great has e'er been known,
No grace so vast was ever shown,
No blood for sin could e'er atone,
  But Christ's who died for me!

* * *

The transformation of the blood-stained wooden cross of Calvary to the diamond-studded gold cross of a ca-thedral may well signify man's attempt to remove the offense of the cross.
  —Carl F. H. Henry, in
    Christianity Today

* * *

Christ's vicarious death was deficient for none; sufficient for all; efficient only for those who believe. —W. B. K.

* * *

Morality may keep you out of jail, but it takes the blood of Jesus Christ to keep you out of hell. —Spurgeon

Illustrations

'Twas for You

Be still, and know that I am God,
Where you now tread, I too have trod —
I know your griefs — I have a part,
I know the anguish of your heart.
Did I not walk the toilsome road,
A wanderer, without abode?
Did I not stand in Pilate's Hall,
Though innocent, hear judgment fall?
Did I not hang on yonder Tree
At Golgotha, to die for thee?
Did I not break the bars away,
On that first Resurrection Day?

Ah, yes, my friend, I've journeyed far,
To break the might of death's cold bar —
'Twas all for you I paid the price,
For you, I made such sacrifice,
In Me, you'll find your source of power,
To gird you in this trying hour —
Let not your heart then troubled be,
Believe in God, and so in Me,
Where you now tread, I too have trod,
Be still, and know that I am God.
  —Selected

* * *

Trampled Under Foot

A Scottish botanist lay flat on his stomach in a meadow. He was looking through his microscope at a common heather bell. He seemed to be oblivious of the shepherd near him until his shadow announced his presence. Looking up, the botanist said to the shepherd, "Take this and look into it!" The rugged shepherd, for the first time, saw the heather bell magnified in all of its intricate beauty and marvelous design. As he continued to look, tears began to trickle down his weather-beaten face. Regaining his composure, he said to the botanist, "And just to think I have been trampling these beneath my rough feet all these years!"

There is a greater act of sacrilege, or wanton desecration of which *we* can be guilty. We may trample "the Rose of Sharon," the Lord Jesus Christ, beneath our feet. God's Word says, "He that despised Moses' law died without mercy under two or three witnesses: of how much *sorer* punishment, suppose ye, shall he be thought worthy, who hath trodden under foot the Son of God, and hath counted the blood of the covenant . . . an unholy thing. . .?" (Heb. 10:28, 29). —W. B. K.

* * *

Where's the Lamb?

Several years ago I was teaching in a city in the United States and had the opportunity to speak at a businessmen's lunch. I had preached on the necessity of the new birth, and at the close a man came to speak to me, who, I was warned, was a Jewish millionaire who owned a big department store in the city, and who always tried to put the ministers on the spot. He handed me a card and said, "I am a Jew, and I want you to answer me 'yes' or 'no.' Do you think that if I do not believe in Jesus, I will go to hell?" I replied, "I cannot answer you 'yes' or 'no.'" He said, "I want you to." I said, "You have heard the old story about the lawyer who wanted a 'yes' or 'no' answer on the witness stand, and the witness said you cannot answer all questions by 'yes' or 'no,' and the lawyer said, 'Yes, you can.' 'Well,' said the witness, 'have you stopped beating your wife? If you say yes, people think you don't do it any more, and if you say no, they say you are still doing it.' " Then the little man said to me, "Do the best you can." I said, "Do you believe there is a hell and a heaven?" "Oh, yes," said he. I replied, "If you are going to be in heaven you have to get there the same way that Moses got there." He said, "I am glad you are broad-minded; Moses got there by keeping the law." I said, "I will collect and give five thousand dollars to the Red Cross or any other charity if you can show me one verse in the Bible which says that Moses got to heaven by keeping the law." He said, "How did Moses get there?" and I said, "By having his brother Aaron kill a lamb and shedding its blood for the remission of his sins. Without the shedding of blood there is no remission. You must have a Saviour. You must either go to Jerusalem and find Moses' brother Aaron killing a lamb, or you must take God's Lamb," and he went away.

—Rev. Donald Grey Barnhouse, D.D.

* * *

Three Crosses

Three crosses on a lonely hill,
  A thief on either side,
And, in between, the Son of God . . .
  How wide the gulf — how wide!

Yet one thief spanned it with the words,
  "Oh, Lord, remember me";
The other scoffed and turned aside
  To lost eternity.

Forsaken is the hilltop now,
  And all the crosses gone,
But in believing hearts of men
  The center cross lives on.

And still, as when these sentinels
  First met earth's wondering view,
The presence of the Lord divides —
  Upon which side are you?

—Helen Franzee Bower in
The Sunday School Times

The Convincing Fifty-third Chapter

I was traveling some years ago with one of the most eminent Jews of our time, the late Dr. Cappadose of Amsterdam. He said to me, "Would you like to know how I became a Christian?" "I should, very much," I replied. He said, "I was reading my Hebrew Old Testament, and I came to the fifty-third chapter of Isaiah. I had read it before, but this time my eyes seemed opened. I began to think it was the New Testament I had gotten hold of by mistake. I turned the back of it toward me to make sure it was my own Bible. As I read it again and again, I saw what I had never seen before — sin laid on another. And who could it be but the Lord Jesus? The end of that was that I became a Christian without the New Testament at all!"   —Dr. J. H. Wilson in
The Illustrator

* * *

He Became Sin for Us

O the mystery of His mercy!
  Unguessed depths of matchless grace,
Christ became that which He hated,
  While God turned away His face.

Turned in wrath from His Beloved,
  Hanging there upon the tree,
Strangely changed, and strangely bearing
  All the sins of you and me.

Angels dared not look upon Him,
  But averted stricken eyes,
Seeing, not the Lord of glory,
  But a bleeding Sacrifice.

Through the circling, endless ages
  Such a sight had never been;
He, the spotless Lamb of Heaven,
  Christ the Lord, becoming sin!

—Martha Snell Nicholson

* * *

Then Jesus Came!

There is an estuary of the sea on the Scottish coast which is two miles across. To reach the other side of the inlet involved a long journey by land. The estuary divided the populations on each side until it was spanned by the great Firth Bridge which united the two shores.

Until Jesus came, there was an unbridged gulf between man's need and lostness, and the mercy and forgiveness of God. Now, "Ye who . . . were far off are made nigh by the blood of Christ" (Eph. 2:13).
Oh, the love that drew salvation's plan!
Oh, the grace that bro't it down to man!
Oh, the mighty gulf that God did span
  At Calvary!
—W. B. K.

* * *

I Helped to Crucify Jesus

Rembrandt, the famous Dutch artist, painted a picture of the crucifixion. Vividly he portrayed Christ writhing in nameless agony on the cruel cross. Vividly he depicted the various attitudes of those about the cross toward the suffering Saviour by their facial expressions. Apart from the Saviour's death, the most significant thing about the painting is the artist's painting of himself, standing in the shadows on the edge of the onlookers. This was Rembrandt's way of saying, "I was there, too! I helped to crucify Jesus!" We, too, were there, standing with Rembrandt in the shadows!
  'Twas I that shed the sacred blood,
  I nailed Him to the tree;
  I crucified the Christ of God,
  I joined the mockery!
—W. B. K.

* * *

Transfusion Refused

A young man was seriously injured in a two-car collision. He had a ruptured spleen, rib fractures, and a contused kidney. The surgeons said, "We must operate immediately." The young man and his wife said, "Go ahead." "You have lost a great amount of blood, and we cannot operate without replacing the lost blood. Without it you would probably die on the operating table!" The patient and his wife refused to allow blood transfusions because their religion forbids blood transfusions.
So far as I know, the Bible says nothing regarding blood transfusions. The Bible, however, does say much about the precious blood of Jesus which He gave on the cross for the sin of the world. All who refuse Christ will die in their sin, and be eternally lost.

"Of how much sorer punishment . . . shall he be thought worthy, who hath trodden under foot the Son of God, and hath counted the blood of the covenant . . . an unholy thing" (Heb. 10:29).
—W. B. K.

* * *

The Rattlesnake!

A little Indian girl was playing near her mud hut. She approached a large stone. Beside it there lay a large rattlesnake. The snake coiled and then struck the girl, burying its fangs deep in the flesh of the girl's leg. She screamed. Her brother rushed to her aid. He killed the snake, and then began to suck the deadly venom from the girl's leg. But he had a sore in his mouth, and the poison entered it. Soon he was dead! It cost him his life to save his sister's!
It cost Jesus His life to save you and me: "For Christ also hath once suffered for sins . . . that he might bring us to God" (I Peter 3:18). —W. B. K.

* * *

He Suffered There for Me!

My mother-in-law, a schoolteacher, had constant difficulty with one of the boys. She tried every method she knew — reasoning, kindness, sternness. Not knowing what else to do, she applied a ruler to the palm of his hand.
One day when she was about to raise the ruler to strike, the thought flashed to her mind, "I'll reverse this. I'll let him strike the palm of my hand." Surprised, the boy gave his teacher a smart blow. Never again did she have the slightest trouble with him.
Who can count the multitudes who, knowing of Christ's suffering on the cross, have repented of their sins saying, "He suffered there for me"?
God's divine power saves us when we repent of our sins and realize that Jesus cared enough to be bruised in our stead for our sins. —Sven S. Olafsson

* * *

No Double Jeopardy

There is in human jurisprudence that which is known as double jeopardy. We heard a great deal about double jeopardy during the time that the 18th Amendment was in effect. We have a rule that a man cannot be held twice for the same transgression. The State, for instance, cannot ask of him a penalty, and the Federal Government ask another for the same transgression. This same principle is in effect in divine jurisprudence. God can never hold us in double jeopardy. He cannot ask for a second payment for the same transgression. The Bible declares that He placed all of our sins upon Christ and Christ paid the penalty for all of them. Therefore, there is offered to us forgiveness for *all* of our sins. To those that receive forgiveness there can be no further penalty for sin. —Erling C. Olsen

* * *

Accepted

'Tis not for works which I have wrought,
'Tis not for gifts which I have brought,
Nor yet for blessings that I sought,
    That I have been accepted.

'Tis not for tears that I have shed,
'Tis not for prayers that I have said,
Nor yet for slavish fear or dread,
    That I have been accepted.

'Tis not for these, however right,
That God has formed intense delight,
Nor is it these that have made white
    The robes of those accepted.

From these I turn my eyes to Him,
Who bore the judgment due to sin,
And by Christ's blood I enter in
    And share in His acceptance.
                —*Selected*

* * *

Would Go Anywhere with Story of Cross

Said a bishop of the Methodist church, when that church was noted for its evangelistic fervor, "I wouldn't cross the street to make a Methodist, or a Baptist, or a Presbyterian of a man. I wouldn't lift my finger to make a mere church member of anyone. But if it pleased God, I would go around the world again and yet again to tell perishing sinners everywhere:
There is a fountain filled with Blood,
    Drawn from Immanuel's veins;
And sinners plunged beneath that flood,
    Lose all their guilty stains!
                —W. B. K.

Just One Remedy

A well-known firm of drug manufacturers, Parke-Davis, is authority for the statement that ninety per cent of all prescription medicines used today were unknown seventeen years ago. This is one of the most astounding truths of our generation, and has its tremendous effect in the population rises of the emergent nations, and in the history of the human race.

But it is more important to remember that the *only* prescription for misery, unrest, sadness, sorrow, tears and all the other by-products of sin, has not changed since God, in the Garden of Eden, shed the first blood that was ever spilled upon this earth to provide a covering for a man and a woman who had just believed His simple word about the coming of the Lord Jesus Christ to put His heel upon the head of Satan. Christ is still the *only* answer to the world's need.   —Clayton Presbyterian
                      Church Bulletin

* * *

Wounded for Our Transgressions

An Associated Press dispatch told of a fifteen-year-old girl in Formosa who appealed to the supreme court of that land for permission to be executed in the place of her father, a widower, so he could support her young brothers. The father, Chia Ling-Shu, was one of three men sentenced to death for robbing and murdering a bank cashier. Her appeal was rejected by the court.

Centuries ago, in China the emperor, moved by the filial devotion of children, sometimes spared their parents from death, allowing children to die in their stead.

As we read of the self-sacrificing spirit of the Formosan girl, we think of the One who died on a cruel cross in our stead. Of His vicarious death the Bible says, "But he was wounded for our transgressions, he was bruised for our iniquities" (Is. 53:5). —W. B. K.

* * *

The Way of the Cross

The geographical heart of London is Charing Cross. All distances are measured from it. This spot is referred to simply as "the cross." A lost child was one day picked up by a London "bobby." The child was unable to tell where he lived. Finally, in response to the repeated questions of the bobby, and amid his sobs and tears, the little fellow said, "If you will take me to the cross I think I can find my way from there."

The Cross is the point where men become reconciled to God. If we find our way to God and home we must first come to the Cross.

I must needs go home by the way of
    the cross,
There's no other way but this;
I shall ne'er get sight of the gates of
    light,
If the way of the cross I miss.
        —Jessie Brown Pounds

* * *

I'll Pay the Fine for You!

Two young men were university friends and graduated together. They went into the world to make their names. One became an eminent judge. The other became a businessman and amassed a fortune. He had constant dealings on the stock exchange. Unfortunately, a black day came and he lost everything. Then, in an effort to regain his old position of influence, he embezzled a large sum of money. At his trial, he pleaded guilty, hoping for clemency from the judge. The judge was the embezzler's old friend of university days. Court attaches speculated as to how far the friendship would influence the judge's verdict.

The judge clearly summed up the case, making no attempt to minimize the seriousness of the offense. When he pronounced the sentence, an audible gasp was heard throughout the court. It was the heaviest fine the law could impose! Then something happened. As the prisoner was about to be led away, the judge, removing his robe, went to the prisoner's side. Extending his hand to his old friend, the judge said, "I'll pay the fine for you!" Then the judge left before the prisoner could say a word.

In paying his friend's fine, the judge was reduced to serious financial straits!

How like Jesus, our Saviour-Substitute! In our lost condition, we stood judged and condemned before God. Then Jesus "interposed His precious blood!"

Jesus paid it all,
All to Him I owe;
Sin had left a crimson stain,
He washed it white as snow!
        —Adapted from *His*

* * *

The Cross Was His Own

They borrowed a bed to lay His head
When Christ the Lord came down;
They borrowed the ass in the mountain
    pass
For Him to ride to town;
    But the crown He wore
    And the cross He bore
    Were His own.

He borrowed the bread when the crowd
    He fed
On the grassy mountain side;
He borrowed the dish of broken fish
With which He satisfied;
    But the crown He wore
    And the cross He bore
    Were His own.

He borrowed the ship in which to sit
To teach the multitude;
He borrowed the nest in which to rest,
He had never a home so rude;
    But the crown He wore
    And the cross He bore
    Were His own.

He borrowed a room on the way to the
    tomb
The passover lamb to eat;
They borrowed the cave; for Him a
    grave;
They borrowed the winding sheet.
    But the crown He wore
    And the cross He bore
    Were His own.

The thorns on His head were worn in
    my stead,
For me the Saviour died.
For guilt of my sin the nails drove in
When Him they crucified;
    Though the crown He wore
    And the cross He bore
    Were His own
    They rightly were mine.
        —*Selected*

Divinely Unnatural

Mary Baker Eddy says, "One sacrifice, however great, is insufficient to pay the debt of sin. The atonement for sin requires constant self-immolation on the sinner's part. That God's wrath should be vented upon His beloved Son is divinely unnatural. Such a theory is man-made!"

The eternal Word of God says, "But now once in the end of the world hath he appeared to put away sin by the sacrifice of himself" (Heb. 9:26); "But this man, after he had offered one sacrifice for sins for ever, sat down on the right hand of God" (Heb. 10:12).

Which will you believe — the Bible, or Mrs. Eddy? —W. B. K.

* * *

The Unlighted Cross

Six lives were snuffed out when a plane crashed into a mountain in Pennsylvania, near a sixty-eight-foot stainless-steel cross which served as a marker for a Methodist training center. The Associated Press dispatch, reporting the tragedy, said, "The cross has electric lights, but they were not turned on at the time."

From this incidental reference to the unlighted cross, one might conclude that perhaps this terrible tragedy might have been averted if the cross had been lighted.

The message of the Cross, the only hope of eternal life, has ceased to be the theme of some pulpits, and souls are groping in spiritual and moral darkness.

Christ crucified is still the power of God unto salvation. "For I am not ashamed of the gospel of Christ: for it is the power of God unto salvation to every one that believeth" (Rom. 1:16). —W. B. K.

* * *

A Necessary Contrast

An unimaginative editor of Beethoven's Fifth Symphony once proposed to make a correction in the Andante where a high note, held through several measures, is sharply discordant. But the editor was wrong, for the discord is resolved into a haunting harmony, the beauty of which is all the greater because of the contrast. Were we to fix the character of God we might be tempted to leave out the Cross, and be as mistaken as the editor who would leave out the crux of the great master's symphony. —W. E. Schramm in *The Sunday School Times*

* * *

General, Here's Your Hill!

It was a day of terrific loss for both the Northern and Southern Armies. The battle, throughout the long day, ebbed and flowed, at times favorable to the South, at times favorable to the North. When the conflict was joined at the beginning of the fateful day, General Forrest committed the keeping of a strategic hill to one hundred Confederate soldiers, under the command of his younger brother, who was an officer in the Southern Army. The General's orders were brief: "Keep this hill against every attack. It must be retained!" Late that afternoon, the General recalled the hill and the brother stationed there to defend it. Riding swiftly to the eminence, he beheld a sight most gruesome. Some ninety-five bodies covered the field of carnage. The General's brother was mortally wounded. With his remaining strength, he drew himself up erectly, saluted, and said, "General, here's your hill!"

The Captain of our salvation, the Lord Jesus, has committed to us a hill to hold — a hill of shame, sorrow, and death. It is the hill whereon transpired an event which bridged the chasm between man's guilt and lostness, and God's mercy and forgiveness.

On a hill far away stood an old rugged Cross,
The emblem of suff'ring and shame;
And I love that old Cross where the dearest and best
For a world of lost sinners was slain. —W. B. K.

* * *

Not the World's Sin, but Mine, Yours!

A saintly African Christian told a congregation that, as he was climbing the hill to the meeting, he heard steps behind him. He turned and saw a man carrying a very heavy load up the hill on his back. He was full of sympathy for the Man and spoke to Him. Then he noticed that His hands were scarred, and he realized that it was Jesus! He said to Him, "Lord, are You carrying the world's sins up the hill?" "No," said the Lord Jesus, "not the world's sins, just *yours*!" As the African told simply the vision God had given him, the hearts of the listeners and the narrator were broken because they saw *their* sins on Jesus at the Cross!

—W. B. K.

* * *

Second Crucifixion

They crushed the thorns into His brow
  And struck harsh blows that day.
O Lord, I would not treat Thee so —
  I only walked away.

They drove the nails into His hands
  And raised the cross on high.
O Lord, that men could be so vile —
  I only passed Thee by.

But blinded eyes and heart of stone
  Will spurn a love like Thine.
O Lord, I struck the cruelest blows;
  The sharpest thorns were mine.

—Victoria Beaudin Johnson

* * *

The Cross and the Tomb

"He died," saith the Cross; "my very name
Was a hated thing and a word of shame;
But since Christ hung on my arms outspread,
With nails in His hands and thorns on His head,
They do not measure — set high, flung wide —
The measureless love of the Crucified."

"He rose," saith the Tomb; "I was dark and drear
And the sound of my name gave a spell of fear;
But the Lord of Life in my depths has lain
To break Death's power and rend his chain;
And a light streams forth from my open door,
For the Lord is risen; He dies no more."

—Annie Johnson Flint

Your Cross Is Heavy

An American tourist had just seen the Passion Play at Oberammergau. Approaching Mr. Lang, who played the part of Christ, he asked, "May I be photographed with you, lifting your cross?" "You may," said Mr. Lang. The tourist stooped to lift the cross, but he couldn't. He exerted more energy, but still could not lift it. Looking at Mr. Lang, he said, "Your cross is surely heavy!" Said Mr. Lang, "Sir, I cannot represent Christ with a light cross!"

—W. B. K.

* * *

Argument ad Hominem

When Robert Hall first went to Cambridge to preach, the Cambridge folk were nearly all Unitarians. So he preached on the doctrine of the finished work of Christ.

Some of them came to him in the vestry and said, "Mr. Hall, this will never do."

"Why not?" said he.

"Why, your sermon was only fit for old women."

"And why only fit for old women?" said Mr. Hall.

"Because," said they, "they are tottering on the borders of the grave, and they want comfort, and, therefore, it will suit them, but it will not do for us."

"Very well," said Mr. Hall, "you have unconsciously paid me all the compliment that I could ask for; if this is good for old women on the borders of the grave, it must be good for you if you are in your right senses, for the borders of the grave are where we all stand."

—C. H. Spurgeon

* * *

Spoiling a Finished Work

"But I can't see it," said a certain cabinetmaker to a friend who was trying to show him how the death of Christ completed the work of atonement. At last an inspiration struck his friend, who, lifting a plane, made as though he would plane the top of a beautifully French-polished table that stood near.

"Stop!" cried the cabinetmaker; "don't you see that's finished? You'll simply ruin it if you use that plane on it."

"Why," replied his friend, "that's just

what I have been trying to show you about Christ's work of redemption. It was finished when He gave His life for you; and if you try to add to that finished work you can only spoil it. Just accept it as it stands — His life for yours, and you go free."

Like a flash he saw it, and received Jesus Christ into his life as his Saviour. Will you?

—*Sunday School Times*

* * *

Did the Jews Crucify Jesus?

A Jewish lady in a large Jewish hospital in Chicago was given a gospel tract by my daughter, Alice. The title of the tract was, "Knowing Christ as Saviour, Lord and Friend." The Jewess received the tract graciously. Seeing the title of the tract, she asked, "Do you believe, like some people believe, that the Jews crucified Jesus?" Alice prayed silently for a moment, asking God to give her the right answer to the question. Then she said, "It was my sins and your sins which put Christ on the cross." Then she quoted a verse from the Old Testament — "But he was wounded for our transgressions, he was bruised for our iniquities" (Isa. 53:5).

—W. B. K.

* * *

The Cross on the Wall

An expert swimmer taught college men how to swim and dive. One night he couldn't sleep. He decided to go to the swimming pool and have a swim, hoping that the exercise would induce sleep. Said he, "I didn't put the lights on. I knew every inch of the place, and the roof was made of glass. The moon shone through, throwing the shadow of my body on the wall at the other end of the pool. I started to dive. My body and arms made a perfect sign of the cross! I cannot explain why I did not dive at that moment. I had no premonition of danger of any kind. As I stood looking at the shadow of the cross, I began to think of the cross of Christ and its meaning. I was not a Christian. I found myself repeating the words of a hymn I had learned as a boy: 'He died that I might be forgiven.' I cannot tell you how long I stood poised on the diving board, or

why I did not dive. I came down from the diving board and walked along the pool to the steps that I knew led to the bottom of the pool and began to descend. I reached the bottom and my feet touched the cold, smooth bottom of the pool! The night before the caretaker had drained the pool dry and I knew nothing about it. I realized then that had I dived, I would have dived to my death! The cross on the wall saved me that night. I was so thankful to God for His mercy in sparing my life I knelt on the cold bricks and asked the Christ of the cross to save my soul. I experienced a twofold deliverance that night!" —*The Listening Post*

* * *

Continuous Cleansing

The deepest mines in the world are in Africa. There the natives work endlessly in their quest for the vast mineral wealth God placed there. As they work, clouds of dust arise. But for a sprinkling system, the dust, being of such cohesive nature, would seal the sweat glands of the natives. Thus the cooling and cleansing systems of the body would be decommissioned, and death would ensue in a short time.

Peter speaks of the "sprinkling of the blood of Jesus" (I Peter 1:2) which incessantly cleanses the believer from sin's defilements. John said, "The blood of Jesus Christ his Son cleanseth (keeps on cleansing) us from all sin" (I John 1:7). —Told by a missionary

* * *

Because of What He Did

A young soldier had been condemned to death for treason. Just before the court-martial pronounced the sentence, an older brother stepped forward. In fighting his country's battles, he had lost both arms. He made an earnest plea for his brother's life, basing his plea, not on anything his brother had done, but on what he had done. "My brother is guilty and is worthy of death," he said. The sight of the stumps of his arms spoke eloquently and convincingly of the sacrifice he had made for his country. For his sake, the judges pardoned the guilty brother.

We are guilty before God: "For all

have sinned" (Rom. 3:23). We deserved to die: "For the wages of sin is death" (6:23). Another paid the penalty for our sins: "But he was wounded for our transgressions" (Isa. 53:5). God freely forgives us, not because of anything we have done but because of what Christ did. —W. B. K.

DEATH

Short Quotes

The Bible gives the record of one "deathbed" repentance that none need despair; but only one that none may presume. —W. B. K.

* * *

He who provides for this life, but takes no care for eternity, is wise for a moment, but a fool forever. —Tillotson

* * *

How hopeless and starless the night of death would be but for the gloom-dispelling words of the triumphant One: "I am he that liveth, and was dead" (Rev. 1:18). —W. B. K.

* * *

There is no flock, howsoever tended,
But one dead lamb is there;
There is no fireside, howsoever defended,
But has its vacant chair.
                        —Longfellow

* * *

As Saul came down to death's door, he remorsefully said: "I have played the fool" (I Sam. 26:21). Paul said at life's setting sun: "I have kept the faith" (II Tim. 4:7). Which will you say when you stand at the gates of death? —W. B. K.

* * *

Join thyself to the eternal God, and thou shalt be eternal. —Augustine

* * *

More than two and a quarter billion people live on the earth; 50,000,000 die every year; 136,986 die every day; 5,707 die every hour; 95 die every minute; 2 die every second. —*The Gideon*

* * *

The mournful dirge of the pulse, reverberating through the human system, is — "nearer death, nearer death, nearer death." —Rev. Paris W. Reidhead
        in *The Alliance Witness*

He who passed through the horror of darkness of Calvary, with the cry of forsakenness, is ready to bear you company through the valley of the shadow of death until you see the sun shining upon its further side.
                        —F. B. Meyer

* * *

Annually, 85,000 Americans die needlessly of cancer, according to the American Cancer Society. Only God knows how many needlessly die spiritually. "Why will ye die?" (Ezek. 18:31). There is but one reason why people die spiritually — "And ye will not come unto me, that ye might have life" (John 5:40). —W. B. K.

* * *

For a child of God, death is simply the angel waiting on the threshold of the unseen to disrobe the soul of its earthly garments, preparatory to its passing into the presence of the King.

* * *

Death will never take me by surprise. I feel strong in Christ. He has not led me so tenderly thus far to forsake me at the very gate of heaven.
                        —Adoniram Judson

* * *

When William Sidney Porter, whose *nom de plume* was O. Henry, was dying, he said: "Turn up the lights! I don't want to go home in the dark!"
Goethe, while fading away, whispered his famous last words: "Mehr Licht! Mehr Licht! Mehr Licht!" — "More light! More light! More light!"

* * *

The gates of death cannot swing open for any of God's children unless the One who holds the key unlocks them: "I am alive for evermore . . . and have the keys of death" (Rev. 1:18). —W. B. K.

When the sainted Frances Havergal neared death, she asked that the following verse be read: "I the Lord have called thee in righteousness, and will hold thine hand, and will keep thee" (Isa. 42:6). With a smile on her face, she said: "Called, held, kept! I can go to heaven on that!"

* * *

Out, out brief candle! Life's but a walking shadow, a poor player that struts and frets his hour upon the stage, and then is heard no more. It is a tale told by an idiot, full of sound and fury, signifying nothing.
—Shakespeare

"For what is your life? It is even a vapour, that appeareth for a little time, and then vanisheth away" (James 4:14).

* * *

When we die, we leave behind us all we have, and take with us all we are.

* * *

Death is not a period but a comma in the story of life. —Dr. Amos J. Tarver, in *Christian Herald*

* * *

Ah, what a sign it is of evil life, when death's approach is seen so terrible!
—Shakespeare

* * *

I have never known anyone who, on his deathbed, repented of being a Christian. —W. B. K.

* * *

"Is Jesus with you in the dark valley?" tenderly asked a mother of her dying boy. "Dark valley!" he whispered. "Why, Mother, it's not dark! It's get-ting brighter and brighter. Oh, it's so bright now, that I have to shut my eyes!" —W. B. K.

* * *

When I go down to the grave I can say, like so many others: I have finished my work, but I cannot say I have finished my life. My day's work will begin the next morning. My tomb is not a blind alley. It is a thoroughfare. It closes in the twilight to open in the dawn. —Victor Hugo

* * *

Suicide as a cause of death ranks tenth in the United States. There are over 16,000 cases each year, while men outnumber women four to one.
—*Gospel Banner*

* * *

The boast of heraldry, the pomp of
    power,
And all that beauty, all that wealth
    e'er gave,
Await alike the inevitable hour:
The paths of glory lead but to the
    grave!
—Thomas Gray

* * *

One night, a somnambulist or sleep walker got out of his bed, walked down the stairs, onto the porch and into the street. On he walked on his bare feet until he started across a stream of water. As his feet touched the cold water, he suddenly awakened.

What a picture of myriads of lost souls who do not awaken to their lost condition until they come up to the chilly waters of death; when it is too late!
—W. B. K.

Illustrations

Arrived!

"Absent from the body . . . present with the Lord" (II Cor. 5:8). "For I am in a strait betwixt two, having a desire to depart, and to be with Christ; which is far better" (Phil. 1:23).

Oh, say, "She has arrived!"
    And not that, "she is gone!"
May ev'ry thought of her
    Be in the land of morn!

Arrived to hear Jesus' voice,
    And see His welcoming smile,
And then to greet again
    Those she has "lost a while!"

Arrived to tread no more
    The weary path of pain,
Nor feel the waning strength
    The body feels, again.

—*Selected*

One-sided Preparation

Two years before his death, Mike Hanzas, who lived alone, began to make preparation for his demise. He bought a lot in the cemetery. Weekly, he visited the site where his mortal remains would be interred. He planted grass there and mowed it regularly. On Memorial Day, he placed flowers on the grave site, for he said, "I want to see flowers there now. I will not be able to see them when I'm gone!"

A while later Mike went into a funeral home. "I want to buy the casket which will be my new home," he said. Whenever he passed the funeral home he would go in. Standing beside the casket he would say, "That's where I'm going to live someday!"

One day Mike invited a nephew and the rest of his family to come to see him. After a hearty meal, Mike began to dispense some canned goods and personal effects among his visitors. Then he handed his nephew his will. As he did this, he dropped dead of heart failure!

So far as we know, Mike Hanzas had made every provision for his body but none for his soul. In the midst of this meticulous preparation he failed to reckon with the fact that God would sometime say to him, "This night thy soul shall be required of thee!"

God's Word says, "It is appointed unto men once to die, but after this the judgment" (Heb. 9:27). —W. B. K.

* * *

The Casket on the Front Porch

In the city of Cleveland, Ohio, on the front porch of a home in a thickly populated residential section is a neatly wrapped, full-sized casket. It has been there for years. It has become an object of sight-seeing. It is of such macabre interest, and of such an unbelievable nature, that Ripley included a reference to it in his, "Believe It or Not" column.

An aged cabinetmaker, who lives alone, made the casket and placed it on the front porch of his home. There it awaits the time of the oldster's demise.

Apart from its being queer, we must confess that this is preparation for the body carried to its ultimate degree!

One wonders if the man has made preparation for his undying soul and the hereafter. My friend, who pointed out the conspicuous object to me, couldn't say.

This we know — that anyone who makes preparation only for his brief sojourn here and not for the unending hereafter is guilty of unpardonable folly. Of such, God says, "Thou fool!"

—W. B. K.

* * *

God's Appointed Time

At the entrance of a large cemetery in Chicago are two mammoth, treelike marble columns, chiseled at the top irregularly and jaggedly, to appear as if violently broken off. They convey the thought of unrealized purposes and an unfinished course. They are the sculptor's representation of death. They do not, however, represent the Christian's conception of death. God's children pass through death's door at God's appointed time. Triumphantly they can say: "I have finished my course." Standing at the gates of death is death's Conqueror, the Lord Jesus who holds the "keys of hell and death." It is He who swings heaven's gates ajar! —W. B. K.

* * *

Can Anyone Tell Us How to Die?

During World War II a group of soldiers spent a few hours in London on the eve of their being returned to the front. A church sought to fill those hours with entertainment and companionship. At the close of the evening, one of the soldiers stood up to express their appreciation to the leaders of the church. For a moment he spoke in a light vein, endeavoring to keep up the frantic false gaiety of the evening. But in spite of himself he became grave and serious. He said, "We are returning to the front to face battle. Some of us will die! Can anyone tell us how to die?" There was silence for a moment. Then a woman stood and quoted the hope-bringing words of the Saviour: "I am the resurrection, and the life: he that believeth in me, though he were dead, yet shall he live" (John 11:25). She went to the piano and began to sing and play the hymn "Leaning on the

Everlasting Arms." Heads were bowed in reverence. Many felt that the question had been answered. —W. B. K.

* * *

A Wreck Must Mark the End

How dark and dismal were Colonel Robert Ingersoll's thoughts on death. He was an atheist. To him, death was an irreparable calamity. "It may be best in the happiest moments of the voyage, when eager winds are kissing every sail, to dash against the unseen rock, and in an instant hear the billows roar above the sunken ship. For whether in mid-sea or among the breakers of the farther shore, a wreck must mark the end of each and all. Every life . . . will, at its close, become a tragedy as sad and deep and dark as can be woven of the warp and woof of mystery and death!" —W. B. K.

Protects Insured After Death!

"Are you a new life insurance salesman?" asked the party who answered a visitor's call. "No, I'm your new Lutheran pastor," he replied. When the pastor returned to his car, he began to think. "Why, I am a life insurance salesman. I sell *real* life insurance. My organization offers the *only* policy which takes care of the holder's life *after* death, and it promises Christian consolation to survivors. Of course, there are premiums — fearless faith, sainted service, deliberate discipline, conscientious consecration. But the dividends are the largest and finest in all the world! Next time, I shall be prepared. I'll answer, 'Yes, I am the new-life insurance salesman!'"
—Rev. Leslie Conrad, Jr.,
in *The Lutheran*

DEVIL

Illustrations

More Than Conquerors

Dr. Carl Armerding watched an attendant enter the cage of a wildcat at a zoo. While shivers went down his spine, Dr. Armerding said to the attendant, "You certainly are a brave man!" "No, I ain't brave." "Well, then that cat must be tame," said Dr. Armerding. "No, Mister, he ain't tame; but he's old, and ain't got no teeth," answered the man while he chuckled.

Satan is not old, but he is a defeated foe. Satan's conqueror, Jesus, is with us, and in Him we are more than conquerors.
*Did we in our own strength confide,
Our striving would be losing.*
—W. B. K.

* * *

The Weakest Saint

Every night little Mary knelt at her bedside and prayed while Mother stood nearby. One night Mary prayed longer than usual. When she finally arose, Mother asked, "Why did you pray so long tonight?" Said little Mary, "Today in church we sang a song that said,

'Satan trembles when he sees the weakest saint upon his knees.' I wanted to make him tremble longer!" —W. B. K.

* * *

Velvet Slippers

Satan is never more dangerous than when he walks in velvet slippers: "Satan . . . is transformed into an angel of light" (II Cor. 11:14).
—J. K. Van Baalen

* * *

My Soul, Be on Thy Guard

During World War II a most subtle, disalerting and dangerous nuisance became prevalent in England — "the Optimist Nuisance." The false impression was created that the war was all but won because England was triumphant at the time on land, sea and in the air. But the nation was still confronted by an implacable foe. Recruiting fell off, and many became lax. The Department of State had to issue grave warnings to checkmate the erroneous impression that the war was drawing to its victorious end.

God's children are engaged in an incessant warfare. Our adversary, the devil, is an implacable foe. In our warfare no armistice can be declared. Some are lulled to sleep by the suavity and graciousness of false religionists who deny the existence of our adversary. It is hazardous for God's children to cease to be watchful and wakeful.

> O watch, and fight, and pray,
> The battle ne'er give o'er;
> Renew it boldly every day,
> And help divine implore.
> —W. B. K.

* * *

Be Vigilant!

In the earlier days of our country, vast numbers of wild horses grazed on the prairies in the West. Sometimes, as they grazed, wolves would gather in the distance. Detecting the presence of the wolves by their keen sense of smell, the wild horses would become instantly alerted and alarmed. As long as they continued so, they were safe. Their swiftness of movement could put a safe distance between them and their enemies. The wolves, however, had a clever way of attacking their victims. Leisurely, and seemingly unconcernedly, they came closer and closer to the horses. Two or three of the older wolves would stroll about listlessly, and then retreat in like manner. While doing so, they would frolic and caper about. Observing the seeming friendliness of the wolf pack, the horses would become disalerted. Then the fatal moment would come. With unerring accuracy the wolves would pounce upon an unwary victim! A peaceful scene changed instantly into a scene of carnage and death!

Let us take seriously the warning: "Be . . . vigilant; because your adversary the devil . . . walketh about, seeking whom he may devour" (I Peter 5:8). —W. B. K.

* * *

Trapped!

The sundew grows in bogs and is an insectivorous herb. It has sticky glands on its leaves. Woe to unsuspecting insects that alight on its harmless looking leaves!

A botanist, lying lazily on a grassy plot, saw a sundew growing nearby. Presently, a fly lighted upon it. It tasted one of the tempting glands. Suddenly three crimson-tipped, fingerlike hairs bent over and touched the fly's wings, imparting a sticky substance which held it fast. The fly made every effort to free itself, but its struggle was in vain. The more the fly struggled, the more hopelessly it became enmeshed in the sticky hairs. But while the hapless creature struggled, it would protrude its tongue and feast on the gluey substance. When the fly became so feeble that it could no longer struggle, the edges of the leaf folded inward like a clenched fist and devoured the fly. Later, the leaf unfolded, ready for another hapless victim!

How like the sundew is the enemy of souls, Satan! He lures and enmeshes unwary ones by seemingly harmless devices, the glitter and glamor of which blind the eyes of undiscerning victims.

Satan does not always appear as "a roaring lion." Frequently he appears as "an angel of light." May God give us the vision to discern his presence in things that often seem harmless, "lest [he] should get an advantage of us: for we are not ignorant of his devices" (II Cor. 2:11). —W. B. K.

* * *

Satan — An Angel of Light

Some years ago, a radio announcer presented one of America's well-known liberal ministers for a broadcast. The announcer wanted to give the minister a good buildup. He said, "Today I have the pleasure of presenting to you America's outstanding prince of the power of the air," meaning of course, that the minister was a prince among the radio clergy. He obviously did not know that the words he used referred to Satan (cf. Eph. 2:2).

—Told by W. Woodward Henry

* * *

Orphaned

"Have you heard the good news?" asked two bantering, sinful youths of one of God's servants. "No, what is it?" asked the minister. "It is great news indeed," said one youth, "and if it is true, your business is done!" Then in unison, the youths said, "The devil is dead." The minister, looking with solemn concern upon the youths, replied, "Oh, poor, fatherless children. What will become of you?" —W. B. K.

* * *

Judas, the Goat

Years ago, when slaughtering methods were different from those of the present day, a large goat was used in a slaughtering house to lure unsuspecting sheep to their slaughter. The goat was appropriately named *Judas*. He seemed to take delight in what he had been trained to do. Capering and prancing, he would lure the innocent sheep to the point where their throats were slit. Then he would leap to one side while the sheep died.

The devil is like that deceptive goat. How many, going in his seemingly attractive pathway, have done so to their own destruction and eternal sorrow! Let us not be ignorant of his subtle stratagems, or we may find ourselves the victims of his wiles! —W. B. K.

* * *

Death on Leathery Wings

Many horror stories have been told about vampire bats. These fearful stories do not seem fictional in Latin America where vampire bats attack human beings and animals whose blood they drink. Lately the vampire menace has increased in the Latin Americas, according to *Time*. In Trinidad eighty-nine people have died of bat rabies in recent years. In the Brazilian state of Rio Grande del Sue, vampire bats killed 50,000 cattle in 1956. Since rabies is common among vampires, their bloodletting often brings agonizing death.

These blood-drinking creatures carry rabies from animals to human beings. They usually attack people by biting them in their toes! The blood of sleeping animals, however, is their staple diet. After they bite their victims, they retreat slightly, hover in the air, and observe whether the victim has awakened. If it continues to sleep, several bats may flutter down to drink from the same trickle of blood. The gentle fluttering of their wings with the resulting gentle movement of the air lulls their prey into deeper sleep.

Man has a far deadlier enemy than the blood-sucking vampire — Satan, the enemy of souls! Many under his sway are sleeping the sleep of deadly unconcern and indifference, heedless of the warnings: "Flee from the wrath to come" (Luke 3:7b); "Awake, thou that sleepest, and arise from the dead, and Christ shall give thee light" (Eph. 5:14). —W. B. K.

* * *

The Point of No Return

Spurgeon told of a wicked king who wished to impoverish and destroy one of his subjects, a blacksmith. He ordered him to make a chain of a certain length. When it was finished, he ordered him to make it longer, and after that still longer. Finally, the blacksmith had no more money to buy metal. Then the wicked king commanded that he be bound with the chain.

If you are not a Christian, your master, the devil, is telling you to make a chain. Possibly you have been many years in welding it. Still your master commands, "Go, and make it still longer." Each new low depth to which you descend into sin adds another link. On and on you go until you get to the point of no return. There, the enemy of your soul says, "Take him and bind him hand and foot and cast him into outer darkness!" —W. B. K.

* * *

When Wounded by Satan

There is a small, weasellike animal called the ichneumon. It can overcome and destroy a venomous snake of over a yard long. It is said that the ichneumon attacks a snake only when it is near a certain plant whose leaves contain an antidote for snake bite. When bitten, the little creature immediately retreats to the life-saving plant and nibbles its leaves. It is restored and ready to renew the attack. Each time it is bitten, it goes to the plant and then returns to fight the enemy.

When attacked and sorely wounded by our merciless enemy, Satan, there is One to whom we may go for healing and renewal of strength. Of this ever present Helper, we can experientially say: "He giveth power to the faint; and to them that have no might he increaseth strength" (Isa. 40:29). —W. B. K.

ENCOURAGEMENT

Illustrations

That's All Right — You Tried!

In a meeting in the poor section of a southern city, a boy stood to play a violin solo. After beginning three or four times, he gave up and sat down. How discouraged and embarrassed he was. Some snickered. The boy's father stood up. The pastor thought that he was going to scold the people for their rudeness. He didn't, however. He walked to where his boy sat. He put his arm around his shoulders and encouragingly said, "That's all right, Son. You tried!" —*Baptist Adults*

* * *

Courage, My Boy!

A cheerful, encouraging word, spoken by an English naval officer, saved a youthful sailor from disgrace and dishonorable discharge. The sailor was only fourteen years old. During a fierce engagement with an enemy ship, the volleys from a number of firearms so frightened the sailor that he trembled and almost fainted. The officer, seeing him, came close beside him and said, "Courage, my boy! You will recover in a minute or two. I was just like you when I went into my first battle!" Afterward the yong man said, "It was as if an angel had come to me and given me new strength!"

Only a word of kindness,
But it lightened one heart of its grief;
Only a word of sympathy,
But it brought one soul relief!
Only a word of gentle cheer,
But it flooded with radiant light
The pathway that seemed so dark before,
And it made the day more bright!"
—W. B. K.

* * *

You'll Be a Great Singer, My Boy!

As a boy, he worked long hours in a factory in Naples. He yearned to be a singer. When ten years old, he took his first lesson in voice. "You can't sing. You haven't any voice at all. Your voice sounds like the wind in the shutters," said his teacher. The boy's mother, however, had visions of greatness for her son. She believed that he had a talent to sing. She was very poor. Putting her arms around him, she encouragingly said, "My boy, I'm going to make every sacrifice to pay for your voice lessons."

Her confidence in him and constant encouragement paid off! That boy became one of the world's greatest singers — Enrico Caruso! —W. B. K.

* * *

Say It Now

If you have a tender message,
Or a loving word to say,
Don't wait till you forget it,
But whisper it today!

The tender words unspoken,
The letter never sent,
The long-forgotten messages,
The wealth of love unspent.

For these some hearts are breaking,
For these some loved ones wait,
Then give them what they're needing,
Before it is *too late!*

* * *

No One Had Any Faith in Me

A kleptomaniac is one who has a seemingly inborn and irresistible urge to steal. One such a person, after serving part of a sentence in a penitentiary, was paroled to a businessman who gave him a position of trust. He apparently believed in the parolee and trusted him. The confidence imposed in him was a great incentive to the parolee to go straight. He did go straight for a long time. "How can I lapse into the old ways of thievery when my employer believes in me and has given me an opportunity to go straight?" he reasoned with himself.

108

One day, however, he made the discovery that his employer was spying on him, thereby proving that he did not trust him. When he made this discovery, the old urge to steal became alive again. Lamented he afterwards, "I just couldn't go straight when no one had any faith in me!" —W. B. K.

* * *

Rubinstein Praised Him!

A red-haired, talented Polish lad wanted to be a pianist. However, teachers at the conservatory gave no encouragement. He was told that his fingers were too short and thick for the piano. Later he bought a cornet. The same answer was given to him with the statement that he should try another instrument. Passed around like a hot potato, he went back to the piano.

Embittered, discouraged . . . he chanced to meet the famous composer and pianist, Anton Rubinstein. The young Pole played for him. Rubinstein praised and encouraged him. The lad promised to practice seven hours a day. Words of praise changed the entire world for Jan Paderewski.

—Loy C. Laney

* * *

It Isn't Enough!

It isn't enough to say in our hearts
  That we like a man for his ways,
It isn't enough that we fill our minds
  With paeans of silent praise;
Nor is it enough that we honor a man,
  As our confidence upward mounts,
It's going right up to the man himself,
  And telling him so, that counts!

If a man does a work you really admire,
  Don't leave a kind word unsaid
In fear that to do so might make him
    vain
  And cause him to "lose his head."
But reach out your hand and tell him,
  "Well done," and see how his gratitude
    swells;
It isn't the flowers we strew on the
    grave,
  It's the word to the living that tells.

—Selected

It's a Shame!

A Christian young man left his home in the country and got a job in a city office. "By God's help, I'll live a clean, consistent life before the people with whom I work," he resolved. Some professing Christians made sarcastic remarks about him. "He's narrow," they said.

A man in the office, who did not profess to be a Christian, greatly admired the young man for his courage. He said, "Stick to what you believe, sonny. Keep it up!"

The young man thought much about those encouraging words. "It is a shame," he thought, "that Christians often gossip about one another instead of trying to help one another in the Christian walk. Here is a man of the world giving me encouragement to continue in the Christian life at all costs. How much better and brighter the world would be if more Christians were using their tongues to help others and not hinder them." —W. B. K.

* * *

Never Mind!

Sometimes, when nothing goes just right,
  And worry reigns supreme,
When heartache fills the eyes with mist,
  And all things useless seem,
There's just one thing can drive away
  The tears that scald and blind —
Someone to slip a strong arm 'round
  And whisper, "Never mind."

No one has ever told just why
  Those words such comfort bring;
Nor why that whisper makes our cares
  Depart on hurried wing.
Yet troubles say a quick "Good-day,"
  We leave them far behind
When someone slips an arm around
  And whispers, "Never mind."

But love must prompt that soft caress —
  That love must, aye, be true
Or at that tender, clinging touch
  No heart ease come to you,
But if the arm be moved by love,
  Sweet comfort you will find
When someone slips an arm around,
  And whispers, "Never mind!"

—Evangelical Visitor

You Will Win!

Daniel Webster left his country home and went to Boston to study law. He entered, without invitation, the office of Christopher Gore, then head of the Massachusetts bar. There he was looked upon as an intruder, and nobody paid any attention to him. One day Rufus King saw the lonely, solitary student. He warmly shook his hand and said, "I know your father well. Be studious and you will win. If you need any assistance or advice, come to me." Years later, after he had achieved greatness, Webster said: "I can still feel the warm pressure of that hand, and hear those challenging words of encouragement!" —*God's Revivalist*

* * *

A Little Push and Pull

A little push when the road is steep
  May take one up the hill;
A little prayer when the clouds hang low
  May bring the soul a thrill;
A little lift when the load bears down
  May help one to succeed;
A little pull when the will slows down
  May help one gain his speed.

A little clasp from a hand that's kind
  May lift from crushing care;
A little word from a voice that's sweet
  May save one from despair;
A little smile when the heart is sad
  May bring a sunbeam in;
A loving word when the spirit droops
  May help one rise and win.

A little love for a soul that's lost
  May help him seek God's grace;
A little tear and a "God bless you"
  May brighten someone's face;
A little deed from a Christian's heart
  May bless a weary soul;
A little boost when the battle's hard
  May take one to his goal.
    —Walter E. Isenhour

* * *

Many Are Waiting!

The writer was visiting among the sick in the great Presbyterian Hospital in Chicago. Going from bed to bed, he spoke for his Master, Jesus. Nightfall was just coming. The lights in the great ward had not yet been turned on. Coming to the bed of an aged child of God, he introduced himself and spoke kindly to the sufferer. Tears of gratitude welled in her eyes as she exclaimed, "Oh, I was just lying here, praying that God would send someone to speak some words of cheer and encouragement!" Her prayer is typical of the prayers of multiplied thousands in the streets, in the homes, in the hospitals — *everywhere!*

Oh, that my tongue might so possess
The accent of Christ's tenderness
That every word I breathe should bless!
For those who mourn a word of cheer,
A word of hope for those who fear,
And love to all men, far and near.
Oh, that it might be said of me,
"Surely thy speech betrayeth thee,
A friend of Christ of Galilee!"
    —W. B. K.

* * *

God's "Large Place" for You

When a famous preacher arises, swaying the crowds, one by-product is that some of his contemporaries begin to imagine that they must be out of God's will or not filled with the Spirit, because they are not achieving similar results. But God is sovereign. He chooses men for special tasks, and if one hits the headlines, that is no reflection on the host of little-known ones. The Spirit divideth severally as He will. A country preacher ministering to two hundred people may be as Spirit-filled to his capacity as was Moody. Moody had around him many lesser lights who helped him in his work, who filled their orbits as well as he filled his. And what would the "big" preacher do without the help of the "small fry"? Seek neither more nor less than God's will for you. Do not compare yourself with men above or below you in station, lest you become depressed or exalted. Simply find His place for you and happily serve Him there. Anywhere He puts you is a "large place"!
    —Rev. Vance Havner in *Day by Day*

TREATMENT OF ENEMIES

Illustrations

Forgive Us as We Forgive

The little Belgian children suffered much during World War I. Many of them had been taught to pray the Lord's Prayer. As some children prayed one day in an orphanage, "And forgive us our debts as we . . ." they suddenly stopped. They could not say, "As we forgive our debtors" — those who had treated them so cruelly, by destroying their homes and killing their loved ones. King Albert had been standing near the door, listening. As the children hesitated, the king continued the prayer, saying, "as we forgive our debtors!" How surprised the children were! How much like Christ King Albert was! Christ prayed for His enemies, "Father, forgive them; for they know not what they do" (Luke 23:34). —W. B. K.

*   *   *

Son Shot in Presence of His Father

During the Korean War a Christian was arrested by the Communists and ordered to be shot. Before the sentence was carried out, the Communist leader learned that the prisoner ran an orphanage which cared for small children. He decided to spare him and kill his son instead. The son was shot in the presence of his father. Later, the young Communist leader was captured. He was condemned to death. Before the sentence was carried out, the Christian father whose boy had been killed pleaded for the life of the killer. "Give him to me," he begged, "and I'll train him!" His request was granted. He took him into his home and cared for him. Today that young erstwhile Communist is a Christian pastor!

—Adapted from *Moody Monthly*

*   *   *

Magnanimous General Lee

Jefferson Davis, President of the Southern Confederacy, asked General Lee's opinion of a certain officer. General Lee commended him very highly. "I am greatly surprised at your commendation of that officer," said an aide-de-camp to General Lee. "Why, that officer habitually says unkind things about you!" To which General Lee replied, "I understand that the President wanted to know my opinion of this officer, and not that man's opinion of me!" —W. B. K.

*   *   *

No Hatred in the Hearts of Children

At the close of World War II some children gathered in a little chapel in Guam. They were all old enough to remember how the Japanese had come and killed their fathers and mothers. They remembered, too, how many of their playmates had perished as the battles raged. Children, however, do not allow hatred to rankle in their hearts. These children were happy. They talked excitedly. They had brought their pennies, nickels, dimes and quarters, which they had earned by selling coconuts and bananas to the American soldiers, for an offering to be used *for the little children of Japan!* One boy brought a silver dollar. He had seen his mother and father killed by enemy soldiers. His silver dollar looked to him much larger than a wagon wheel. His gift and the gifts of the other poor, ragged children of Guam represented not only good will toward a former enemy, but also the greatest of sacrifice. —W. B. K.

*   *   *

I'll Do Anything to Get Right!

A young minister felt that he had been mistreated by another minister. Whether he had been or not was no reason for him to allow a "root of bitterness" to rankle in his heart. With the passing of time, he became most unChristlike in his attitude toward the other minister. How miserable and joyless he became! It is always the case when a Christian has a wrong attitude toward anyone. The Holy Spirit was grieved. Although God is "slow to anger," and does not "afflict willingly," He will not "keep his anger for ever!" Finally His chastening rod fell. One

Lord's day morning, the hate-harboring young minister was told to go immediately to the emergency room of a hospital. There he saw rigid in death a little boy dear to his heart who had been tragically killed! His soul was overwhelmed by sorrow. God's voice seemed to say to him, "Are you now willing to go to that brother minister and confess *your* wrong attitude toward him and ask his forgiveness?" His soul was so chastened that he weepingly sobbed out, "Yes, Lord! I'll do anything to get right with You and my brother minister!" —W. B. K.

* * *

Now He Belongs to the Ages!

When Abraham Lincoln was a young, struggling lawyer, he was employed on an important case. The fee was large. He journeyed to a distant city for consultation with other lawyers on the case. One of the lawyers got a glimpse of Lincoln as he sat in the reception room. "What's he doing here? Get rid of him! I will not be associated with such a gawky ape as that!" Lincoln pretended that he did not hear him, though he knew that the insult was deliberate. In spite of his mortification, he went downstairs where he met with the group of lawyers. Then all went into the courthouse.

As the trial got under way, Lincoln was ignored. He did not sit with the other lawyers. The lawyer who had so cruelly insulted him brilliantly defended his client. His logic was masterful. His handling of the case held Lincoln spellbound. He won the case. That night Lincoln said, "His argument was a revelation to me. I have never heard anything so finished and so carefully prepared. I can't hold a candle to him. I'm going home to study law all over again!"

Time passed. Lincoln became President of the United States. Among his most outspoken critics was the lawyer who had insulted him and so sorely wounded him. But Lincoln never forgot that the lawyer of the brutal words was also the lawyer of the brilliant mind. When he selected a man for the vital post of Secretary of War, he chose *Edwin M. Stanton,* the one who had wounded and insulted him! Only a man of Lincoln's character and forgiving spirit could have risen above Stanton's insult!

Later, Lincoln lay dying — the victim of an assassin's bullet. When Lincoln's eyes finally closed in death, Stanton, filled with inconsolable grief, said, *"Now he belongs to the ages!"*
—W. B. K.

* * *

Overcome Evil with Good

A traveling salesman was rudely treated by a member of a business concern. He related the humiliating experience to a friend. "And you did nothing about it afterward? A fellow like that should be taught a lesson!" "Yes," said the salesman, "but I'm not here to avenge personal wrongs. I'm on business for my employer."

We are on business for the One of whom it is written: "Who, when he was reviled, reviled not again; when he suffered, he threatened not" (I Peter 2:23). —W. B. K.

* * *

Special Treatment

"I did it," said a badly wounded soldier to a Christian doctor in a mission hospital, "but for God's sake save my life!" The doctor walked silently away. He said to himself, "He's the one who killed my loved ones. The time has come to avenge their death! Some slight inattention by me, and he will be gone. But I'm a Christian. Jesus loved His enemies and He taught us to love ours."

The doctor returned to the wounded soldier. He went beyond the call of duty in an all-out effort to save the life of the one who had taken the lives of his loved ones. —W. B. K.

* * *

It Hurts Me

He who holds a grudge injures himself more than the one against whom he cherishes the spirit of spite. Hatred and malice, like anger and worry, are injurious to the body, since they poison the blood. More serious is the injury which they bring to personality. A bad spirit paralyzes the powers which should help to refine our natures and make for finer character. And this spirit of ill will has a strange way of increasing, for "a grudge is the only thing that does not get better when it is nursed."

—*The Watchman-Examiner*

* * *

You Have No Hatred!

A highly trained Christian Chinese leader was falsely accused by the Japanese. He was imprisoned and severely beaten at each round of questioning. But no confession could be forced from him. He was innocent of any wrong, and had nothing to confess. Before setting him free, a Japanese officer said, "I can't understand what kind of a man you are! You have suffered much, and you have no hatred toward those who tormented you!" Among the first things he did upon being set free was to buy a New Testament and send it to the Japanese officer who couldn't understand why he hated no one. On the flyleaf he wrote, "I trust you will read this Book, for you will find in it the explanation of what kind of man I am, and why!"

—W. B. K.

* * *

How to Destroy an Enemy

A Quaker had a quarrelsome, disagreeable neighbor whose cow often got into the Quaker's well-cultivated garden. One morning the Quaker drove the cow to his neighbor's home. Said he, "Neighbor, I have driven thy cow home once more. If I find her in my garden again —." Before the Quaker could finish the sentence, the neighbor said angrily, "Suppose you do? What will you do?" "Why," said the Quaker softly, "I'll drive her home to thee again!" The cow didn't give the Quaker any more trouble. —W. B. K.

Did She Press Thorns on Your Brow?

In one of my churches in Macon, Ga., two women became estranged from each other. With the passing of time, the ill will hardened into hatred of the bitterest kind. I visited one day in the home of one of the embittered women. She began to talk severely against the other woman. I listened silently. Then I asked, "Did she press cruel thorns onto your brow? Did she spit in your face?" "Why, indeed, she didn't," replied the wrathful woman. "Did she drive cruel spikes through your hands and feet?" Silence ensued. Eyes which formerly flashed hatred became suffused with penitent tears. "Oh," she exclaimed, "I see what you are driving at! How wicked I have been in allowing a root of bitterness to rankle in my heart. How could I have been so unlike my Master?" In a short while, the two women confessed their sins, asked each other's forgiveness and God's forgiveness. —Rev. T. W. Callaway, D.D.

* * *

Christ Made the Difference

Even in war, with its brutalizing cruelties, there are shining incidents of Christian love and good will. A Japanese soldier came upon an American soldier in a jungle. The American was reading the New Testament. He was utterly at the mercy of the Japanese. The latter approached and asked, "You Christian? Me, too, Christian. Me love that Book!" Hatred and ill will vanished as two Christian soldiers entered into fellowship around the Word of God. After a fond farewell, the Japanese withdrew with no thought of taking the American as a prisoner of war.

—W. B. K.

FAITH

Short Quotes

Did you ever wonder about the Trinity? John Wesley said: "Bring me a worm that can comprehend a man, and then I will show you a man that can comprehend the triune God!"

Never try to arouse faith from within. You cannot stir up faith from the depths of your heart. Leave your heart, and look into the face of Christ.

—Andrew Murray

I said to the man at the gate of the year, "Give me a light that I may tread safely into the unknown." He replied, "Go out into the darkness and put your hand into the hand of God. That shall be to you better than light and safer than a known way." —M. L. Haskins

* * *

Be conscientious about the fundamentals but not contentious over incidentals.

* * *

Faith is to believe what we do not see, and the reward of this faith is to see what we believe. —Augustine

* * *

Why is it that we *believe* so much and *experience* so little? Why is it that our *heads* are so full and our *hearts* so empty? —Alan Redpath

* * *

Our faith doesn't save us. It only links us to the One of whom the Bible says: "Neither is there salvation in any other: for there is none other name under heaven given among men whereby we must be saved" (Acts 4:12)
—W. B. K.

* * *

A physician who walks into a sick-room is not alone. He can only minister to the ailing person with the material tools of scientific medicine. His faith in a higher power does the rest. Show me the doctor who denies the existence of the Supreme being, and I will say that he has no right to practice the healing art.   —Dr. Elmer Hess, President American Medical Association

* * *

In the realm of the natural, seeing is believing. In the realm of the spiritual, believing is seeing. Jesus said: "If thou wouldest believe, thou shouldest see the glory of God" (John 11:40). —W. B. K.

* * *

Believe God's love and power more than you believe your own feelings and experiences. Your Rock is Christ, and it is not the *rock* that ebbs and flows but the sea. —Samuel Rutherford

* * *

I can't understand a religious truth until I first believe it. —Anselm

Religious attitudes of mind help keep men's bodies healthy. Attitudes such as love, faith, hope, unselfishness, forgiveness, tolerance, and a desire for justice and truth set the body at rest and strengthen it physically. Anti-religious attitudes such as hate, envy, jealousy, guilt, vanity, malice, vindictiveness and selfishness put a strain on the body and are conducive to the development of disease. —Andrew C. Ivy, M.D.

* * *

Satan tried to satisfy all the external religious cravings of unregenerate man while suppressing the one thing upon which man's eternal destiny depends — simple faith in the One who said, "He that believeth on the Son hath everlasting life" (John 3:36). —W. B. K.

* * *

When Sir Harry Lauder's only son was killed in World War I, he said to a friend: "When a man comes to a thing like this, there are just three ways out of it — there is drink; there is despair, and there is God. By His grace, the last is for me!"

* * *

Three boys gave their definition of faith. One said, "Faith is taking hold of God." The second said, "Faith is holding on to God." A third said, "Faith is not letting go!" Each boy was right.
—W. B. K.

* * *

Doubt sees the obstacles,
  Faith sees the way!
Doubt sees the darkest night,
  Faith sees the day!
Doubt dreads to take a step,
  Faith soars on high!
Doubt questions, "Who believes?"
  Faith answers, "I!"
—*Gospel Banner*

* * *

Faith forms the axles of the universe.
—Robert L. Stevenson

* * *

The waves may be defeated,
  But the tide is sure to win,
Your griefs may be repeated,
  But your joys are coming in,
The Christ has ne'er retreated,
  And to doubt Him would be sin.
—*Christian Beacon*

Believe your beliefs that are founded on the Word of God, and doubt your doubts that come from disease, despair, disappointment, or disobedience. Doubt paralyzes — faith vitalizes.
—Dr. V. Raymond Edman

* * *

So on I go, not knowing,
    I would not, if I might;
I'd rather walk in the dark with God
    Than go alone in the light;
I'd rather walk by faith with Him,
    Than go alone by sight!

* * *

Let me not lose faith in my fellow men. Keep me sweet and sound of heart, in spite of ingratitude, treachery, and meanness. Preserve me from giving little stings, or resenting them.
—Phillips Brooks

* * *

A cab driver in Ireland was reading his New Testament. "What are you reading?" a fare asked as he entered the cab. "The New Testament, Sir." "Why do you read it?" "I love it, Sir, and the Saviour of whom it tells." "What is your creed?" "It is very simple, Sir: Believe all that God has said; obey all that Christ has commanded; expect all that Christ has promised!" —W. B. K.

* * *

In England, inscribed on the statue of Sir William Rathbone are these words: "Because he had faith in God, he could not despair of man."

* * *

Faith sees the invisible, believes the incredible, and receives the impossible.

* * *

Faith is the outstretched hand of the soul taking what Christ offers.
—Dr. Samuel Zwemer

* * *

Said Thomas A. Edison: "We do not know one-millionth part of one per cent about anything. We do not know what water is. We don't know what light is. We do not know what electricity is. We do not know what gravity is. We don't know anything about magnetism. We have a lot of hypotheses, but that is all."
"Through faith we understand" (Heb. 11:3).

Faith never stands around with its hands in its pockets.

* * *

Saint Theresa wanted to build a great orphanage. She had only three shillings. She said to those who ridiculed her, "With three shillings Theresa can do nothing, but with God and three shillings there is nothing that Theresa cannot do!" —W. B. K.

* * *

The steps of faith fall on the seeming void, but find the rock beneath.
—John Greenleaf Whittier

* * *

Never put a question mark where God has put a period.

* * *

Christ never failed to distinguish between doubt and unbelief. Doubt is *can't believe.* Unbelief is *won't believe.* Doubt is honesty. Unbelief is obstinacy. Doubt is looking for light. Unbelief is content with darkness.
—Henry Drummond

* * *

When fear knocks at the door of the heart, send faith to open it, and you will find that there is no one there.

* * *

A traveler crossed a frozen stream
    In trembling fear one day,
Later a teamster drove across,
    And whistled all the way.
Great faith and little faith alike,
    Were granted safe convoy,
But one had pangs of needless fear,
    The other all the joy!

* * *

Faith is dead to doubts, dumb to discouragements, blind to impossibilities, knows nothing but success. Faith lifts its hands up through the threatening clouds, lays hold of Him who has all power in heaven and on earth. Faith makes the uplook good, the outlook bright, the inlook favorable, and the future glorious.
—Dr. V. Raymond Edman

* * *

"Dreadfully tarnished," exclaimed a woman as she showed a massive piece of family silver to a friend. "I cannot keep it bright unless I use it!" To which the friend replied, "That is just

the way with faith. You cannot keep faith bright unless you use it!"
—W. B. K.

* * *

Augustine was once walking by the sea shore. He was greatly perplexed about the doctrine of the Trinity. He observed a little boy with a sea shell running to the water, filling it and then pouring it into a hole which he had made in the sand. "What are you doing, my little man?" asked Augustine. "Oh," said he, "I am trying to put the ocean in this hole!" Augustine learned his lesson, and as he walked away, he said, "That is what I am trying to do. I see it now. Standing on the shores of time I am trying to get into this little finite mind of mine things which are infinite." Let us be content to let God know some things which we cannot know. —*Moody Church News*

* * *

When Cardinal Manning was experiencing great depression of soul and a darkening of his faith, he went into the shop of a well-known book concern. There he saw one of his own books entitled, *Faith in God*. As he waited for a copy of his book to be sent up from the storeroom, he heard a clerk calling up from the elevator shaft, "Manning's *Faith in God* all gone!" He took the words to heart. —W. B. K.

* * *

A minister was crossing the Atlantic on a freighter. The captain called his attention to two compasses. The lower compass was affected by the steel in the framework of the ship. "The pilot steers by the higher compass," said the captain.
"That's the way it should be as we steer our ship through life's stormy sea. The compass of feeling is affected by the changing winds of time and circumstances, and may dash us upon the rocks. The compass higher up — the compass of faith — points steadily to the changeless One — Jesus," answered the minister. —W. B. K.

* * *

I believe Jesus Christ to be the Son of God. The miracles which He wrought establish in my mind His personal authority, and render it proper for me to believe whatever He asserts. I believe, therefore, all His declarations, as well when He declares Himself to be the Son of God as when He declares any other proposition. And I believe there is no other way of salvation than through the merits of His atonement.
—Daniel Webster

* * *

I once stood in Arlington National Cemetery at the grave of William Jennings Bryan. Out of reverence for the memory of the great Christian statesman, I removed my hat. Then I read the inscription carved on the simple headstone: "Lord, I believe. Help Thou my unbelief!" I left that hallowed spot breathing the same prayer, "Lord, I believe! Help Thou my unbelief!"
—W. B. K.

* * *

He took the loaves and fishes few
  And fed the hungry throng.
He saw the mite of faith he had
  And made the cripple strong.

He took the lumps of clay and gave
  The blind man precious sight.
He, seeing Mary's trust in Him,
  Brought Lazarus back to light.

He takes my whispered, silent prayer,
  My faith like mustard seed
And makes what once was vague and dim
  Reality indeed!
—Chorsten Christensen in
The Sunday School Times

Illustrations

Faith Resting on God's Word

"I don't have faith in revivals," said a pastor to an evangelist. "However, I see from the Bible that the Holy Spirit gave to the Church evangelists, and because I see this in the Bible, and apart from my personal feelings, or inclinations, I'm going to have revival meetings in my church as a regular thing."
That's real faith. One's feelings or inclinations are frequently wrong. When one acts apart from feelings, or per-

sonal preferences, upon a matter which has the sanction of God's Word, one cannot go wrong. —W. B. K.

* * *

Little Faith

O Thou of little faith,
  God hath not failed thee yet!
When all looks dark and gloomy,
  Thou dost so soon forget!

Forget that He has led thee,
  And gently cleared thy way;
On clouds has poured His sunshine,
  And turned thy night to day!

And if He's helped thee hitherto,
  He will not fail thee now;
How it must wound His loving heart
  To see thy anxious brow!

Oh! doubt not any longer,
  To Him commit thy way;
Whom in the past thou trusted,
  And is the same today!
                —*Selected*

* * *

O For a Faith

O for a faith that will not shrink,
  Tho' pressed by every foe
That will not tremble on the brink
  Of any earthly woe!

That will not murmur nor complain
  Beneath the chastening rod
But in the hour of grief and pain
  Will lean upon its God;

A faith that shines more bright and clear
  When tempests rage without,
That when in danger knows no fear,
  In darkness feels no doubt.
             —William Bathurst

* * *

Get Into the Wheelbarrow!

Years ago a strong wire was stretched across Niagara River, just above the roaring falls. It was announced that a tightrope walker would walk on that suspended wire from the American to the Canadian side. The thrilling moment for the death-defying fete arrived. Great crowds watched with wide-eyed wonderment as the man performed, with calm deliberateness, the awesome stunt. The people cheered wildly! Then the performer did an even more daring thing. He began to push a wheelbarrow with a grooved wheel across the suspended wire. At the conclusion of this breath-taking performance, thunderous applause went up. The performer observed a boy whose wonderment was clearly discernible on his bright face. Asked the man, "My boy, do you believe that I could put you in this wheelbarrow and push you over the falls?" "Oh, yes," said the boy quickly. "Then, get in the wheelbarrow," said the man. Instantly the boy dashed away! In reality he did not believe that the tightrope walker could take him safely across the falls.

How like many of God's children was the boy! We say we believe in the power of Christ to pilot us safely "o'er life's tempestuous sea," yet we fail, at times, to utterly commit ourselves into His pierced hands. —W. B. K.

* * *

Through Faith

Through faith we understand
  The things we cannot know —
The hidden pattern God has planned,
  And why each threat is so;
We trace life's vast design
  And lose His golden strand,
But when our wills with His entwine
Through faith we understand.

Through faith we understand
  What to our sight is dim,
And still Love's sweet, all-knowing hand
  Leads those who trust in Him.
Ours not to know the way,
  But bow to His command;
And when our childlike hearts obey,
  Through faith we understand.
           —E. Margaret Clarkson

* * *

Only One Took an Umbrella

The writer's grandfather, John W. Knight, was a Methodist circuit rider. Before his conversion, he was a notorious, blatant atheist. When God saved him his life was totally changed. It is said that, wherever he went, a revival of "the old-time religion" broke out. Bishop Pierce, in his biography of "Uncle Knight," tells some interesting stories of him. The following incident shows the old circuit rider's faith. A destroying drought had cast its sear mantle over the countryside. Crops were withering and lying in the parched fields. "Uncle Knight" and others wended their way to the little Crawford Church in Putnam County, Georgia, to pray for rain. "Uncle Knight," however, was the *only* one who took an umbrella with him to the prayer meeting. On bended knees the old man began to pray as follows: "O, Lord, we need rain. O, Lord, we need much rain. O, Lord, we don't want any drizzly-drazzly rain. We want a gully-washer!" God as He always does, honored the simple faith of the old circuit rider, and the people soon knew the answer to the ancient question, "Where is the Lord God of Elijah?" —W. B. K.

* * *

Autumn Leaves

Upon the breeze, the autumn leaves
   Are carried thither, yon;
They rest at last, upon the grass,
   One moment, then they're gone.
They're tossed about, and in and out,
   They fly across the way;
And up and down, they sail around —
   The wind they must obey.

Now, if you please, the autumn leaves
   Are much like most of us;
We're tossed about, by fear and doubt,
   And things we rare discuss.
This need not be, for you or me —
   There is a surer way;
The solid Rock, will bear the shock,
   No matter what the fray.

He who believes, is not like leaves,
   That drift with every wind;
His faith is fixed in God, unmixed
   With doubts that Satan sends.
He walks with God, while earth he
      trods —
   He's led by pow'r Divine;
When life is through, beyond the blue,
   He'll dwell in lands sublime.
                            —C. Carl Williams

* * *

Because the Master Said It

A schoolmaster gave three of his pupils a difficult problem. "You will find it very hard to solve," he said, "but there is a way." After repeated at-

tempts, one of them gave up in despair. "There is no way!" he declared. The second pupil had not succeeded, yet he was smiling and unconcerned. "I know it can be explained, because I have seen it done." The third worked on, long after the rest had given up. His head ached and his brain was in a whirl. Yet as he went over it again and again, he said without faltering, "I know there is a way, because the master has said it." Here is faith — that confidence that rests not upon what it has seen, but upon the promises of God.
                            —*Moody Monthly*

* * *

Boy, Drop! I'll Catch You!

Your condition is like that of a lad in a burning house, who escaped to the edge of the window, and hung on to the windowsill. The flames were pouring out of the window. The lad would soon be burned, or, falling, would be dashed to pieces. He therefore held on with a deathlike clutch. A strong man below said, "Boy, drop! I'll catch you!" Now it was no saving faith for the boy to believe that the man below was strong. He might have known that and perished. It was saving faith when the boy let go and dropped down into the big man's arms. You are a sinner, clinging to your own sins or to your good works. The Saviour pleads, "Drop! Drop into My arms!" It is not working that will save you. It is trusting in that work which Jesus has already done. Trust, and the moment you trust you are saved! —Spurgeon

* * *

Salvation by Character?

A minister was sitting in a railway coach beside an unbeliever who said to him, "I differ with you. I don't believe that anyone is admitted into heaven because of his faith. I believe that when God receives anyone into heaven, He inspects his character and good works rather than his faith." Presently the conductor came along and looked carefully at every ticket the passengers gave him. After he passed, the minister said, "Did you notice that the conductor looked carefully at every ticket the passengers gave him, and took no pains to inspect the passengers? A railway ticket entitled them to transportation. So faith in Christ brings saving grace. It also produces Christian character which is pleasing to God. The Bible says, 'For by grace are ye saved through faith; and that not of yourselves: it is the gift of God. Not of works, lest any man should boast.'" —W. B. K.

* * *

Handel's Severest Test

Handel lost his health. His right side was paralyzed. His money was gone. His creditors threatened to imprison him. Handel was so disheartened by his tragic experiences that he almost lost faith and despaired. He came through the ordeal, however, and composed his greatest work, "The Hallelujah Chorus," which is the climactic part of his great *Messiah.*

John wrote, "This is the victory that overcometh the world, even our faith." —W. B. K.

* * *

Faith That Saves

Some years ago, two men, a bargeman and a collier, were in a boat above the rapids of a cataract, and found themselves unable to manage it, being carried so swiftly down the current that they must both inevitably be borne down and dashed to pieces. One was saved by grasping a rope that was thrown to him. The same instant that the rope came into his hand, a log floated by the other man. The thoughtless and confused bargeman, instead of seizing the rope, laid hold on the log. It was a fatal mistake; they were both in imminent peril; but the one was drawn to shore, because he had a connection with the people on the land, while the other, clinging to the loose, floating log, was borne irresistibly along, and never heard of afterwards. Faith has a saving connection with Christ. Faith is on the shore, holding the rope, and, as we lay hold of it with the hand of our confidence, He pulls us to the shore; but our good works, having no connection with Christ, are drifted along down to the gulf of fell despair.

—Charles Haddon Spurgeon

* * *

He Is Able

Canst thou take the barren soil
And with all thy pains and toil
  Make lilies grow?
Thou canst not. O helpless man,
Have faith in God — He can.

Canst thou paint the clouds at eve?
And all the sunset colors weave
  Into the sky?
Thou canst not. O powerless man,
Have faith in God — He can.

Canst thou still thy troubled heart
And make all cares and doubts depart
  From out thy soul?
Thou canst not. O faithless man,
Have faith in God — He can.

—From *Traveling Toward Sunrise,*
by Mrs. Charles E. Cowman

FAITHFULNESS

Illustrations

Evangelism in Prison

A very earnest preacher of the Gospel was caught and put into prison in the south of Spain, and expected to die. There were Anarchists and Communists in the prison; they were desperate, and began to write curses on the wall against their captors, so the evangelist wrote on the wall, "Fear not them which kill the body, but are not able to kill the soul; but rather fear him which is able to destroy both soul and body in hell." Underneath he wrote John 3:16 in full. That attracted attention. One of the prisoners was a young schoolmaster, and the evangelist had the joy of leading him to Christ. One day the schoolmaster said to him, "My name is on the list today to be shot; I am so glad you wrote that text on the wall. Before,

I should have been desperate, but now, although I do not want to die, I am not desperate because I know I am going to be with Jesus, and I shall see you again one day." —P. J. Buffard

* * *

Consider His Ways — Mend Your Ways

The cheetah is the swiftest of all animals. It has been clocked running at a speed of seventy miles an hour. One of the most interesting things about the cheetah is this. At mealtime, the cheetah singles out one animal among the grazing herd. Then the chase begins! Along the chase may be other animals which the cheetah could easily seize. Nothing, however, can detract or turn the cheetah aside from his one fixed purpose — the catching of the unfortunate victim he singled out for his meal.

Go to the cheetah, ye quitters, consider *his* ways, and mend *your* ways!
—W. B. K.

* * *

I'll Never Go Back!

A girl from a godless home began to attend a Bible class. She was genuinely converted. Her parents ridiculed her, and did their best to get her to renounce her faith in Christ. "It is not natural for a young girl like you to be religious," they said. The girl, however, was steadfast. She said, "The change of heart I have had is not natural. It is supernatural. It is altogether from God. Only God could do what He has done in my life. By His grace I'll never go back to the old life!"

Time passed. Her father, observing the change which had taken place in her life, said, "I guess it must be real, Mary, because now you get up at six o'clock every morning to study the Bible. Before that you were so lazy we had trouble getting you out of bed!"
—W. B. K.

* * *

What Saved a Judge's Life

Judge Shepherd, Circuit Court Judge of Nashville, Tennessee, was a deacon in his church. It was his unvarying custom to attend the services of his church on every Lord's day. One Sunday his pastor, Dr. Norman W. Cox, noticed that the judge was not sitting in his accustomed place. Inquiry was made. "Where is Judge Shepherd today?"

Later Dr. Cox said, "Suddenly I became worried. When there was no answer to the phone call at his home where he lived alone, I went there and found the house locked. I convinced the police that it was unlike the judge not to be at church, and he must be in his home. The officers forced a door open. They found him unconscious from gas fumes caused by a faulty heater. Another half hour would have been too late. The judge's fixed custom to go to God's house on the Lord's day saved his life!" —W. B. K.

* * *

That's Why I Love Old Shep!

Old Shep was a fat, lazy mongrel. Yet her master, a young law student, was deeply attached to her. Daily they walked together on the street. "Why do you love that worthless cur so much?" asked one who had observed the mutual attachment of dog and master. "Here's why," said the young man. "One day I was riding horseback. Twelve miles away from home, the horse threw me. I fell over a bluff, breaking and mangling my right arm. I lay unconscious. Old Shep ran back home — twelve miles. Looking into my father's face, she whined and howled beseechingly. Father said, 'Something is wrong! Something has happened to Robert!' Horses were saddled. Father and others dashed down the road, old Shep leading them. Coming to the bluff, old Shep began to whine and howl. Rescuers descended for me. I was rushed to a hospital, still unconscious. There my arm was amputated. That's why I love old Shep. Money couldn't buy her!" —W. B. K.

* * *

You Did Not Deny Me!

Years ago, a young university student worked with a godless gang of surveyors during the summer vacation to help with his college expenses. The student was a devout Christian. In fact, he was the *only* Christian in that gang of surveyors. When the evening meal was over, the men would gamble and drink and, oftentimes, the atmosphere of the large room where they stayed would

become "blue" with profanity. On his first night with the gang, before the Christian student retired, he read his Bible and then knelt to pray. Pillows and shoes began to fly about the kneeling form. The praying student was ridiculed and mocked. The foreman of the gang allowed the mockery to go unabated for a moment, but then something noble asserted itself in his heart. Leaping to his feet, he said, "The next man who throws a pillow or a shoe, or says anything in ridicule of that Christian boy will get one of the soundest thrashings anyone ever got! That boy is genuine. He is more of a man than the whole shebang of us!" The Christian finished praying. Then he got into his cot. That night God seemed to say to him, "Eddie, I want you to preach My Gospel. You did not deny Me, and I will honor and greatly use you as My messenger!" Thus Dr. R. E. Neighbour got *his call* to the Christian ministry.
—W. B. K.

* * *

Faithful to the End

John Eliot, on the day of his death, in his eightieth year, was found teaching the alphabet to an Indian child at his bedside. "Why not rest from your labors?" said a friend. "Because," said the venerable man, "I have prayed to God to make me useful in my sphere, and He has heard my prayer, for now that I can no longer preach, He leaves me strength enough to teach this poor child his alphabet." Eighty years of age, and bedridden, yet still at work for others! And shall the young find nothing to do for those about them?
—*Grace and Hope Evangel*

* * *

Faithful Dog Saves Family

Each one of us can be, and ought to be, trustworthy and faithful. These virtues, sometimes lacking among God's children, are often exemplified by God's animal creatures. Take Shep, the faithful collie who saved the lives of Mrs. D'Angelo and her six sleeping children one night.

During the small hours of the early morning, their home caught fire. Shep's furious barks and scratching at bedroom doors aroused the family. Then Shep

streaked out of the burning house and rushed to the factory where Mr. D'Angelo was working. Trotting to him, Shep whined and pulled repeatedly at his trousers. "Something is wrong," he said, and he and Shep dashed out of the factory, Shep leading the way. The glare of the burning home lit up the darkened sky. The man arrived at his home just as the last member of his family ran from the burning structure.

Oh, that more of us were just as faithful in warning impenitent sinners to flee from the wrath to come! —W. B. K.

* * *

Dog Lay on Master's Grave Twelve Years

Years ago, a shepherd came in from the country district to the city of Edinburgh, Scotland. He brought with him a little dog. The man died while he was in the city, and was buried in Grey Friars' Churchyard. The little dog made its way in through the iron gates and lay down upon the grave of its master. It didn't lie there merely for a day or a week or a month — it lay there *twelve years!*

Every day, at one o'clock, they fire the gun in the castle in Edinburgh. Then everyone looks at his watch to check the time. The little dog would run from the churchyard as soon as it heard the shot to a local baker who gave it a pie and some water. Then the dog would go back to the grave again. There it lay until he died.

What fidelity! What faithfulness that little dog displayed!

"Be *thou* faithful unto death."
—W. B. K.

* * *

I'll Not Deny Him

A Hindu in India became a Christian. Other Hindus said, "Give up the religion of the foreigners." "No," he replied, "I love Jesus Christ because He loves me, and I must obey Him. Even if I knew that heaven was full, and there was no room for me, I would still love Christ and live for His honor and glory!" His friends argued with him. His relatives wept over him. Some threatened to take his life if he didn't give up Jesus. Still he remained faithful to the One who had saved him. He

said, "Threats I can bear. Arguments can't shake me. The hardest thing to bear is the weeping of my loved ones. It almost breaks my heart. But not even this can make me deny my Lord!"
—W. B. K.

* * *

Greater Love Hath No Man

For thirteen years a faithful missionary worked in Urfa, Mesopotamia, without seeing anyone confessing Christ. Humanly speaking, the situation was hopeless. Then a destroying scourge came to the people — an epidemic of cholera! The fear-shaken natives fled like stampeding cattle, abandoning the sick and dying to sure death. The missionary faithfully stood by the sufferers. How grateful they were! Finally he succumbed to the dreadful disease and died. His body was interred outside the city walls. Had all his labors been in vain? No! Another missionary was appointed, and now many turned to Christ. A church was built and dedicated to the memory of the fallen missionary whom the natives endearingly spoke of as "the man who died for us!"

If we forget ourselves for others, others will never forget us. —W. B. K.

* * *

Faithful in Well-doing

Those who are faithful in well-doing need not fear those that are spiteful in evil-doing, for they have a God to trust who has well-doers under the hand of His protection, and evil-doers under the hand of His restraint.

—Matthew Henry

* * *

I Will Not Deny My Lord!

A Baptist pastor from Latvia spoke in Chicago. When his country was taken over by the Communists, many were put to death, and many others were sent to a *living death* in slave-labor camps. The pastor spoke of the horrible persecution which Christians there have suffered. He related the story of a brave boy to whom the *Communists* had said, "If you will deny Christianity and Christ, we will let you live!" The brave boy had answered, "I will not deny my Lord Jesus Christ!" Thinking

that they might change his steadfastness, the Communists then said, "We will give you two hours to think over your fate and change your mind!" Bravely the boy replied, "I don't need two hours. I know what I will do. I will not deny my Lord Jesus Christ!" He was put to death. —W. B. K.

* * *

Only One Visibly Present

A church in a small community decided to discontinue the midweek prayer service. There was little protest about the decision. One woman, however, never failed to attend the midweek service unless ill or away. She said, "I am going to be present at the usual time for the midweek prayer meeting." The following Wednesday night she was present in the prayer room of the little church. Next day, someone jestingly asked her, "Did you have a prayer meeting last night?" "Yes," she replied cheerfully. "Ah, that we did!" "How many were present?" "*Four*," she said. "Why, I heard that you were there all alone!" "No, no!" she protested. "I was the only one *visibly* present, but the Father, the Son, and the Holy Spirit were there, and we were all agreed in prayer!" —W. B. K.

* * *

Give Up Your Faith, or Else!

There was a clamorous knock at the African pastor's door and in came a murderous group of Mau Mau! The leader said, "It's simple. Give up your faith in Christ, subscribe to our oath, or die!" The brave pastor replied, "I will not give up my faith in Christ, and I will not sign your oath!" He was dragged from his humble home. A noose was placed about his neck and the rope was thrown across an overhanging limb. His hands were tied behind his back. The rope was drawn sufficiently taut to suspend his body so that his toes barely touched the ground. Agonizing hours passed. As the day began to break, his persecutors again said: "It's simple. Give up your faith in Christ, subscribe to our oath, or die!" Resolutely the pastor replied, "I will not give up my faith in Christ, and I will not sign your oath!" "Then die!" said the leader. —W. B. K.

I Leave the Results with God!

An explorer was going through the wilds of Alaska. It was bitter cold. He came to a little church and mission school where a lone missionary preached and taught. "What are you doing here in this cold, dreary, out-of-the-way place? How can you waste your life in a place like this?" asked the explorer. The missionary smiled and answered, "God sent me here. Here I shall remain until I die, or until God gives me further orders!" The explorer said, "But the task here is hopeless! You have made so few converts in all these years; the results have been so small!" The missionary said, "Results are not my business. I leave the results with God. I must be faithful and do my best for God. Some day results will come!"

—W. B. K.

FATHERS

Short Quotes

It was Sunday morning. A father sat in his easy chair reading the Sunday newspaper. Then he said to his boy, "Put down that funny paper. Get ready for Sunday school. "Daddy, aren't you going with me?" "No, I'm not going with you, but I want you to hurry up and get ready." "Daddy, did you go to Sunday school when you were a little boy like me?" "Certainly I did. I went every Sunday," said the father. Said the little fellow as he walked sadly away, "I bet it won't do me any good, either!" —*Baptist Standard*

* * *

For years a devout Christian father prayed for the conversion of a wayward son. The burden for the son's salvation rested heavily upon his heart. Even on his deathbed the father continued to cry to God for the conversion of his son. Faintly he prayed: "O God, save my boy! O God, save my boy! O God, —!" Then death stilled his lips with the prayer unended. I believe that the prayer was concluded in heaven!

—W. B. K.

* * *

"What will you have?" asked a waiter of a man who had taken his seat at a table in a restaurant. "A glass of beer," said the man. "And what shall I get for the little boy?" asked the waiter of the boy sitting beside his father. "Same as Dad," said the boy. Instantly, the father said, "Give me something else!" —W. B. K.

If I had a son, I'd do one thing. I'd tell the truth. I'd never let him catch me in a lie. In return, I'd insist that he tell the truth. When children go astray, it isn't the fault of the children but of their parents. A spoiled boy grows into a spoiled man. I'd try to be a pal to my boy. I'd have my son go to church. What's more, *I'd go with him.* —J. Edgar Hoover

* * *

His little arms crept 'round my neck,
   And then I heard him say,
Four simple words I can't forget,
   Four words that made me pray.

They turned a mirror on my soul,
   On secrets no one knew,
They startled me, I hear them yet,
   He said, "I'll be like you!"

—Herbert Parker

* * *

A wayward son brought shame and disgrace to his father who was a good and law-abiding citizen. A friend inquired, "How is the son doing nowadays?" "Very badly," said the sorrowing father, "worse than ever." "I wonder how you can put up with him," said the friend. "'If he were my son, I would turn him out and have nothing more to do with him!" "Yes," said the father, "and so would I if he were *your* son. But, you see, he is *my* son and not *your* son. I will hold on to him. I will continue to love him, hoping and praying that someday he will come to his senses!" —W. B. K.

Some time ago, Ruth Graham, wife of the evangelist, asked me, "Prexy, if you had it to do over again, what would you do differently for your children?"

My reply was immediate: "There are many things I would do differently. Especially, I would deliberately, even doggedly, take more time to be with my children. Our four boys realized that there were many demands on my time, and were very understanding. However, if I had it to do over again, we would have more time for reading and playing together, for picnics and trips. Reading and praying together add love and security to young hearts."

    —Dr. V. Raymond Edman

* * *

Some years ago at a fair in Dallas, Texas, an interesting and yet tragic exhibition attracted many: a sallow-faced, emaciated boy was displaying a prize-winning hog. The boy seemed intent on seeing how many cigarettes he could smoke in the shortest period of time. The owner of the prize-winning hog was the father of the boy. He was a *success* at raising hogs, but a dismal *failure* at raising a son!

    —Told by Dr. George W. Truett

* * *

A father had a splendid crop of grain. A terrible hail- and wind-storm destroyed it a few days before it was ready for harvest. The man and his little boy looked over the field of destroyed grain. The lad expected to hear words of despair from his father. Instead he began to sing softly, "Rock of ages, cleft for me, let me hide myself in Thee!" Years later that boy, grown to manhood, said, "That was the greatest sermon I ever heard!" The father lost a fine crop of grain, but that was possibly the turning point in that little boy's life. He saw the faith of a godly father in *practice*.

    —*The Sunday School Guide*

* * *

One snowy day, General Robert E. Lee was out walking with his son Custis. Soon General Lee saw that his son was doing his best to walk in his tracks in the snow. Said General Lee to some friends later: "When I saw this I said to myself that it behooves me to walk very straight when this fellow is already following in my tracks!" —W. B. K.

* * *

Last night my little boy confessed to me
Some childish wrong;
And kneeling at my knee
He prayed with tears —
"Dear God, make me a man
Like Daddy — wise and strong,
I know You can."
Then while he slept
I knelt beside his bed,
Confessed my sins,
And prayed with low-bowed head,
"O God, make me a child
Like my child here —
Pure, guileless,
Trusting Thee with faith sincere."

Illustrations

Too Late!

A little girl with shining eyes,
  Her little face aglow,
Said, "Daddy, it is almost time
  For Sunday School, let's go!

They teach us there of Jesus' love,
  Of how He died for all,
Upon the cruel Cross, to save
  All those who on Him call."

"Oh, no," said Daddy, "not today,
  I've worked hard all this week,
And I must have one day of rest,
  I'm going to the creek."

Months and years have passed away,
  But Daddy hears that plea no more,
"Let's go to Sunday School."
  Those childhood days are o'er.

She says, "O, Daddy, not today —
  I stayed up most all night,
I've got to have some sleep —
  Besides, I look a fright!"

And how he'd love that shining face,
  Again, with eyes aglow —
And go with her to Sunday School,
  If only she would go!

    —*Selected*

To My Dad

Somehow a fellow can't express
   The feelings he has had
While through the years he's walked and
   talked
   And laughed and played with Dad.
He cannot put in words the love —
   The pride that wells within,
The admiration in his heart,
   Whene'er Dad looks at him.

Dad is the hero of his dreams,
   The king upon the throne,
The pattern for that ideal life
   Which he would make his own.
He knows that Dad well understands
   The conflicts in his breast,
And shared the problems he must face,
   Though often unexpressed.

How could a fellow go astray,
   Who with his Dad has stood
Within the secret place of prayer
   Before a holy God!
And this my constant prayer shall be,
   That until life is done,
My conduct here shall honor him,
   Who proudly calls me "Son."
          —Alvis B. Christiansen in
          The United Evangelical

* * *

Give Bouquets Now!

Some stalwart Christian men gave a dinner in honor of their aged father. The father sat at the head of the table and beamed with joy as he looked upon his fine sons. After the sumptuous dinner, the eldest son quietly went to his father and said, "Dad, you've been a wonderful father to me. Your Christian character has deeply influenced my life and caused me to love and serve our great Saviour. I owe everything to you, Dad!" Then each of the other sons went to their father and placed a kiss of affection on his cheeks and spoke endearing words of love and esteem.

Toward the midnight hour that night, the phone of Dr. R. E. Neighbour rang. The oldest of the brothers was calling. Said he midst subdued sobs, "Brother Neighbour, Dad just passed quietly to be forever with the Lord. How glad I am that I told him earlier tonight of my love and affection for him!" —W. B. K.

Except Henry

In the home of a devout Christian father hung this motto: "But as for me and my house, we will serve the Lord" (Josh. 24:15). The motto was most meaningful to the father. He prayed daily that each one of his children would be saved. In time, each child was genuinely converted except the oldest son. He persistently refused to come to Christ. As the father and son sat alone one day in the room where the motto was displayed, the father said, "I cannot and will not be a liar any longer. You are a member of my household. You reject Christ, and will not serve Him. I must add the following words to the motto: 'Except Henry!' It hurts me to do this, my boy, for I dearly love you and yearn for your conversion!" The tender concern of the father so touched the son that he knelt and prayed the salvation-bringing prayer: "God be merciful to me a sinner!" Then the home was unanimously Christian! —W. B. K.

* * *

Little Eyes Upon You

There are little eyes upon you,
   and they're watching night and day;
There are little ears that quickly
   take in everything you say;
There are little hands all eager
   to do everything you do.
And a little boy who's dreaming
   of the day he'll be like you.

You're the little fellow's idol,
   you're the wisest of the wise;
In his little mind about you
   no suspicions ever rise;
He believes in you devoutly,
   holds that all you say and do
He will say and do in your way
   when he's grown up just like you.

There's a wide-eyed little fellow
   who believes you're always right,
And his ears are always open,
   and he watches day and night.
You are setting an example
   every day in all you do
For the little boy who's waiting
   to grow up to be like you.
          —*Selected*

Not Afraid!

Upon a rocky trail one day
I met a friendly pair,
A father and his little lad —
A storm was in the air.
The precipice was dangerous,
The wind was coming on,
But on that child's trusting face
Was joyfulness and calm.
My own heart quaked a bit with fear
Of what might lie ahead,
But when I said, "Aren't you afraid?"
The laddie shook his head,
Astonished at my ignorance,
"Oh, you don't understand,
Why, Mister, I can't be afraid
When Daddy holds my hand."

               —Alice Mortenson

* * *

I Understand Now

Used to wonder just why Father,
Never had much time to play;
Used to wonder why he'd rather
Work each minute of the day.

Boys are blind to much that's going
On about them every day,
And I had no way of knowing
What became of Father's pay.

All I knew was when I needed
Shoes I got 'em on the spot;
Everything for which I pleaded,
Somehow Father always got.

Wondered season after season
Why he never took a rest,
And that I might be the reason
That I never even guessed.

Rest has come — his task is ended,
Calm is written on his brow,
Father's life was big and splendid,
And I understand it now.

               —Edgar A. Guest

* * *

An Untarnished Name — My Request

To you, O son of mine, I cannot give
   A vast estate of wide and fertile lands;
But I can keep for you, the whilst I live,
   Unstained hands.

I have no blazoned scutcheon that insures
   Your path to eminence and worldly
      fame;
Longer than empty heraldry endures
   A blameless name.

I have no treasure chest of gold refined,
   No hoarded wealth of clinking, glitter-
      ing pelf;
I give to you my hand, and heart, and
      mind —
   All of myself.

I can exert no mighty influence
   To make a place for you in men's
      affairs;
But lift to God in secret audience
   Unceasing prayers.

I cannot, though I would, be always near
   To guard your steps with the parental
      rod;
I trust your soul to Him who holds you
      dear,
   Your father's God.

            —Dr. Merrill C. Tenney

FELLOWSHIP

Illustrations

One in Christ

While I was conducting a meeting in Chicago near the close of World War I, I attended a fellowship dinner. There were representatives from several nations present. A Christian Jew presided over the meeting. Next to him sat a German. I, an Englishman, sat next to an Irishman. An Italian sat next to an Austrian. A Japanese sat next to a Chinese, and so on around the table. Were they fighting? Not at all! They were having the most blessed fellowship that believers can have on earth. They were united by one Spirit in Christ! At the close of the dinner, we stood and joined hands — our hearts were already united in Christian love — and sang, "Blest be the tie that binds!"

            —Dr. Louis T. Talbot

They Are Getting Something We're Missing!

A family was driving along the highway one Sunday in a comfortable car, listening to a good sermon on the radio. They passed by a small country church where cars were parked and they could tell that a service was going on. Someone in the car said, "I'm sure they are not hearing as fine a sermon as we are."

"No," said the father, "but they are getting something which we are not. They are in the Lord's house. They are having fellowship together and they may be remembering Jesus as He asked them to do. We hope they are doing as the early Christians did (Acts 2:42). We are not." —*Golden Moments*

* * *

Brothers in Christ

When in London I was walking home from a meeting. Part of the way I was accompanied by the Marquis of Aberdeen and the Lord Bishop of Norwich. Being an American, and unaccustomed to titles, I felt embarrassed as to how I should address men of their rank. I expressed my perplexity, and the Marquis replied, "My dear brother, just address us as your *brethren in Christ*. We have no higher honor than that." —Dr. Harry A. Ironside

* * *

Only Christ Could Have Done It

Left Hand, a war chief of the Southern Arapaho, was converted late in life. At a convention in Oklahoma City, he gave a touching testimony. As he sat down, a gray-headed minister stood and said: "Years ago I lived in Denver. I enlisted in the army to fight the Indians, then on the warpath. At the battle of Big Sandy, Left Hand led the Arapahos. I sought his blood that day, but today I am his brother in Jesus Christ, our Lord!"

The convention was profoundly moved. The presiding officer asked that Left Hand and the aged minister come to the platform. The former enemies on the field of battle joyously embraced each other as Christian brothers!

—W. B. K.

* * *

I Yearned for Christian Fellowship!

One of God's children was hospitalized a distance from home. It was the eve before surgery. Without, the shades of night were falling. "Within my heart there was a sense of loneliness, though I knew the ever-present Friend and Saviour was with me," she said. "I yearned for Christian fellowship. The unfailing One knew of the longing of my heart. Just then, I heard someone humming the hymn, 'Safe in the Arms of Jesus.' Going in the direction from whence the tune came, I met a Russian lady, one of God's dear children. I could speak no Russian, and she could speak no English. We prayed together. I didn't know what she prayed. However, the Holy Spirit, who indwells all of God's children, caused me to know that we had an audience with God, and in the joy of that knowledge, all loneliness vanished from my heart, and the peace of God flooded my soul!"

Blest be the tie that binds
Our hearts in Christian love,
The fellowship of kindred minds
Is like to that above!

—W. B. K.

FORGETTING GOD

Short Quotes

A bookseller wired a book concern in Philadelphia for a copy of the book *Seeking After God* by Harrer. He received the following reply: "No seekers after God in Philadelphia, or New York. Try Boston."

—*News Sheet*, Minneapolis

Said Henry Drummond, the modern apostle of theistic evolution, toward the close of his life: "I am going way back to the Book, the Bible, to believe and to receive it as I did at the first. My soul can no longer rest on uncertainties!" —W. B. K.

Just on the verge of danger, not before,
God and the doctor we adore;
When danger is past,
And all things are righted,
God is forgotten,
And the doctor is slighted.

* * *

France, in former years, officially abolished God. The experiment worked so disastrously that Robespierre, in addressing the States-General, said, "Gentlemen, it is extremely necessary to restore God to France!" —W. B. K.

* * *

Turn back to where you left Him,
And you will find Him there.
He is waiting by the bedside
Where you used to kneel in prayer.
He is standing in the chapel
By that long-abandoned pew.
He stands by your forsaken swath
Where laborers are few.
You are older, sorer — broken.
You are tired of self — 'tis true.
But return to where you left Him;
He is waiting there for you.
              —Raymond C. Hoag in
              The Watchman-Examiner

While wondering what the world is coming to, we forget Him who has come to the world. —Vance Havner

* * *

Some Christians seem to think of God as a kind of "spare tire." A spare tire is forgotten for months until suddenly, on the road, we have a flat. Many forget God when things go well with them. When sorrow, sickness and troubles come, then they remember God and want Him to help them. He wants us to call on Him when we are in trouble. He also wants us to remember and serve Him when we are not in trouble. —W. B. K.

* * *

Dale Evans Rogers attended an 8 o'clock communion service in an old cathedral in London. There were seven present! She asked an English friend why so few were present. "Well, it's like this — we English people are a nation of crisis. We are at our best in a crisis. Then we get on our knees and ask God to help us. After the crisis is over, and everything is all right again, we thank Him for His help and go our own way again!" —W. B. K.

Illustrations

A World in Torment!

We stand today at one of those decisive moments in history when we begin to see what the late H. G. Wells called "The Shape of Things to Come." The clouds thin, the mist rises, and we see heaven or hell — we cannot yet know which.

As we look at the civilized world in the morning's news we can scarcely put a finger on any point that is not somehow troubled. Within the past few days conflict and uncertainty have revealed themselves, first in one spot, then in another. Poland, Hungary, Egypt — there the spotlight has concentrated and moved. We do not know what the next day's news may be from the Far East or the heart of Africa.

This is not alone a political crisis. It is also, above all and beyond all, a philosophical crisis. By what and for what do men live? Shall they move

toward freedom or away from it? Where is the boundary, where is the truce line, between anarchy and tyranny? We hunt for words to describe what is going on. . . . Out of chaos and torment there is arising a new world, a world unplanned, perhaps not even desired.
              —*The New York Times*

* * *

Mother, I've Lost God!

Henry W. Grady was one of Georgia's greatest statesmen and journalists. After the Civil War, he, with his pen and tongue, did much to restore good will between the North and the South. His book, *The New South*, did as much to heal the wounds of a mutually destructive war as *Uncle Tom's Cabin* did to precipitate it. One day, as he sat at the editor's desk, he lapsed into heart-searching meditativeness. He soliloquized, "Though fame and honor have overtaken me, I feel that I have lost much of the joy of God's presence which I knew in my earlier years under the influence of my godly mother and a Christian home!" Then he said to his secretary, "I will be away from my desk for a day or two. Tell no one where I am." Returning to his country home, he said to his mother, "Mother, I have won fame, but I have lost God! I have come back to you to help me to rediscover God. Let me kneel at your knees again, and let me feel again the caressing touch of your gentle hand on my head. Then, Mother, when bedtime comes, let me see you at my bedside, tucking the covers about me, and smiling at me just as you did when I was a boy!" Later, Grady returned to his editor's desk, renewed spiritually, and ready to carry forward the work of bringing unity and understanding to a nation smoldering in the ashes of a recent fratricidal war. —W. B. K.

* * *

David Ben-Gurion's Question

David Ben-Gurion, Prime Minister of Israel, said to William L. Hull, a missionary, "The New Testament teaching and standards are wonderful but where are those who live up to them? Are there any in the world? Are there any living the Christian life? Can this book really produce what it sets forth?"

Mr. Hull told the Prime Minister of the transforming power of God's Word and that he was a new creature in Christ Jesus.

"Are there others like you?" asked Ben-Gurion. "Yes, there are millions of Christians throughout the world," replied the missionary.

"Why do they let conditions that are in the world today exist?" seriously asked the Jewish leader who closed the conversation with the question which

many are asking — "Why do the nations act as they do at the present time?"

Our answer to the question is this. The nations have forgotten God. God's indictment of His ancient people, Israel, is applicable to the nations today: "For my people have committed two evils, they have forsaken me the fountain of living waters, and hewed them out cisterns, broken cisterns, that can hold no water" (Jer. 2:13). —W. B. K.

* * *

Has Science Left Us Without God?

Some years ago, before the atomic bomb was a dread reality, Dr. Iago Galdston, executive secretary of the New York Academy of Medicine, made an attack on the "conceits of science." He said: "Science has given mankind immense control over his environment and over the material world. Yet science has not only failed to solve the essential problems of human relations, but has compounded and aggravated them immensely. I go further and charge that science has dissipated, laid ruthlessly waste, if not maliciously, at least ignorantly, the cultural and moral heritage of mankind and has left it spiritually bankrupt!

"Science has given us power over lightning, waterfalls and coal fields, but no power over ourselves. Science has shown us how to make the inside of a pest house habitable, but it has not shown us how to have a regenerated spiritual interior in our bosoms. Science has added years to the span of life, but why live longer if we are not living gloriously for God? Why live longer if we are living selfishly? The selfish man bestows a benefit on the community when he dies."
—Dr. Robert G. Lee

GOD'S FORGIVENESS

Illustrations

God's Offer to Fugitives

A man serving a life sentence for murder escaped from the Oklahoma State Penitentiary. The warden, Jerome J. Waters, offered the fugitive

$1,500 if he presented himself at the gate of the prison. There was a catch to the offer, however. The reward was to be earned and saved by the escapee by his working in the prison. "If he

comes, we will see that he doesn't get
out again. Justice must prevail," said
the warden. How different, by contrast, is the offer God makes to all
fugitives from divine justice! There
is no catch to His offer: "Let the wicked
forsake his way . . . and let him return
unto the Lord, and he will have mercy
upon him; and to our God, for he will
abundantly pardon" (Isa. 55:7). God's
justice has been satisfied by the vicarious death of the Saviour. All who present themselves to God in faith and
repentance will be received, not as fugitives, but as sons of God, "justified from
all things" (Acts 13:39). —W. B. K.

* * *

Gone!

One day a Christian visited a minister in his home. As he sat in the
minister's study, he began to read one
of the minister's books. While reading, he suddenly cried, "Glory! Praise
the Lord!" The minister ran into the
study, asking, "What's the matter,
man?" The visitor replied, "This book
says that the sea is five miles deep!"
"Well, what of that?" asked the minister. "Why, the Bible says my sins
have been cast into the depth of the
sea, and if it is that deep, I'm not afraid
of their coming up again!" exclaimed
the radiant Christian. —W. B. K.

* * *

It's Mercy I Need!

An aged Negro was arraigned. In
court, charges of a serious nature were
placed against him. As court prelimi-
naries were getting under way, it was
very evident to the young lawyer that
his client was ill at ease and under great
tension. In his effort to impart comfort
to the man and allay his fears, the
young lawyer said, "Charlie, you need
not have any fear. I'm going to see that
you get *justice* in this court today!" A
meditative look displaced the hitherto
look of fright on the man's face. In
measured words, he said, "White man,
it isn't justice that I want in this court
today. *It's mercy!*"

Only the merciful ones obtain mercy:
"For he shall have judgment without
mercy, that hath shewed no mercy"
(James 2:13).

—Rev. T. F. Callaway, D.D.

Only Thy Forgiveness I Ask!

Copernicus was a great mathematician. His studies and calculations rev-
olutionized the thinking of mankind
about the universe. When he lay dying, *The Revolution of the Heavenly
Body* was placed in his hands. It had
just been printed. At death's door, he
saw himself, not as a great scholar, or
astronomer, but only as a *sinner* in
need of the Saviour. On the tombstone
at his grave at Frauenberg are carved
the following words which he chose for
his epitaph: "I do not seek a kindness
equal to that given Paul. Nor do I ask
the grace granted to Peter. But that
forgiveness which Thou didst grant to
the robber — that, earnestly I crave!"
—W. B. K.

* * *

When God Forgives, He Forgets!

A man was deeply convicted of sin
and of his need of the Saviour. Rest-
lessly he wandered one night along a
country road, seeking relief for his misery. Wearily he sat down beside a
hedge. After sitting there for a while,
he heard two girls talking on the other
side of the hedge. They were discussing
a sermon one of them had heard. "I
will never forget the thing the minister
said in the sermon. It gave me hope
and encouragement," one girl said.
"What was it?" eagerly inquired the
other girl. "The world always says that
you make your own bed, and you must
lie in it, but One greater than the world
has said, 'Take up thy bed, and walk.
Thy sins be forgiven!'" When the distressed man heard those wondrous
words, he called upon the sinner's
Friend, Jesus, and felt his burden taken
away. —W. B. K.

* * *

For Years I Have Gone Straight

"I have had a very unsavory past,"
admitted a woman to the authorities in
San Francisco, "but for years I have
gone straight." With tears in her eyes,
she lamented, "How can people get away
from their yesterdays if others shove
their past into their todays? I've tried
to let the dead past bury the dead. But
the State of California wants to make
my past my present." How differently
does God deal with those who penitently

seek His mercy and forgiveness: "For I will be merciful to their unrighteousness, and their sins and their iniquities will I remember no more" (Heb. 8:12).
—W. B. K.

* * *

Cast Into the Depth of the Sea

How dark it is in the depth of the sea! The pressure of the water is so great there that if the largest battleship could be sunk to that depth, it would be crushed like an egg shell. Nothing can live down there. The Bible says, God "will have compassion upon us . . . and thou wilt cast all [our] sins into the depths of the sea" (Micah 7:19). This means that they will never be brought up before us again!

I will cast in the depths of the sea,
All thy sins whatever they be,
Though they mount up to heaven,
Though they sink down to hell,
They shall sink in the depths,
And above them shall swell,
All the waves of God's mercy,
So mighty and free!
—W. B. K.

* * *

Blessed Alternative!

A priest censured a young woman for not coming to confessional for a long time. When finally she came, he asked her to confess her sins of yesterday, last week, last month and last year, to which she replied, "I have none!" Said the priest, "You are either a great saint, or an awful liar!"

A friend, hearing of the incident, said, "But there is another alternative. She may have confessed her sins to the Lord Jesus Himself and found full forgiveness in keeping with the sure promise of God's Word: 'If we confess our sins, he is faithful and just to forgive us our sins, and to cleanse us from all

unrighteousness,' 'and the blood of Jesus Christ his Son cleanseth us from all sin.'" —W. B. K.

* * *

Make It Plain, Father!

After the Battle of Gettysburg, a young man lay seriously wounded in a hospital. His father was sent for. The doctor said to him, "Your son cannot last long." With heavy heart the father said to his son, "You may go at any time!" "But," pleaded the son, "I cannot die; I must not die. I am not ready to die. Father, make it plain to me now how I can die right with God, and have all my sins forgiven," implored the son.

At once, an incident in the school life of the son came to the grief-stricken father. "Son, do you remember when you were expelled from school, how I rebuked you for the wrong you had done, and how you abused me with harsh words? Do you recall how, later, you came in great sorrow and begged my forgiveness? Do you recall how freely I forgave you?" "Yes," replied the son. "Son, did you doubt that I would freely and fully forgive you?" "No, Father, I *knew* that you forgave me from your great heart of love!" Then the father said, "My son, just as freely and as fully as I forgave you so also will God forgive you your sins, blotting them out, never to remember them against you!"

Later, the son said, "Father, Jesus has forgiven me! I *know* He has. I have asked Him to blot out my sinful past. I believed that He would do it, just as I believed, in the long ago, that you would forgive the wrong I had done against you, and the sorrow I had brought to you." —Told by Rev. Louis Albert Banks, D.D.

OUR FORGIVENESS

Short Quotes

President McKinley was shot by an anarchist. Instantly the assassin was apprehended. In a moment he lay, helpless and bloody, beneath the blows of the officers. McKinley, raising his hand which was smeared with his own blood, said, "Let no one hurt him!"
—W. B. K.

No man is able to force me so low as to make me hate him.
—Booker T. Washington

* * *

Never let me put up a fence against anyone, God, and keep me from putting a fence around myself. —Dale Evans

* * *

He who does not forgive others burns before him the bridge to God's forgiveness. —W. B. K.

* * *

There is no faculty of the human soul so persistent as that of hatred. There are hatreds of race, sect and social and personal hatreds. If thoughts of hatred were thunder and lightning, there would be a storm over the whole earth all the year round. —Beecher

* * *

Let no dog-in-the-manger attitude make you snappy, snarly, or sullen. Be a Christian — not a cur.
—Dr. V. Raymond Edman

* * *

I once rebuked a Christian worker for manifesting an unforgiving spirit toward another. At length she said, "Well, I will forgive her, but I never want to have anything more to do with her!" I said to her, "Is that the way you want God to forgive you? Do you want Him to say He will forgive you, but He will have nothing more to do with you?" —Rev. G. L. Hamilton

A Zulu chief savagely beat his wife because she attended a gospel meeting where she heard and responded to the call of Jesus. He left her as dead. Later he returned to the place where he had left her. She was not dead. The chief leered at her and asked, "And what can your Jesus Christ do for you now?" Gently she replied, "He helps me to forgive you!" —W. B. K.

* * *

Mercy, like the regions of space, has no limit, and as these stretch away before the traveler who looks out from the farthest star, so the loftiest intellect and the largest heart can discover no bounds to mercy. Like our Father in heaven, we are to forgive without stint, forgiving as we expect to be forgiven.
—Guthrie

* * *

I stood at the bedside of a noble Christian mother just before she underwent a serious operation. Like many other Christians, she had allowed a "root of bitterness" to rankle in her heart against one who had wronged her. Now, as she realized that she might not survive the operation, she said to me, "Do please tell him that I forgive all; that I have nothing in my heart against him, and that I ask his forgiveness for the ugly, un-Christian attitude I have so often shown."
How differently do we see things when we stand on the borderline of eternity! —W. B. K.

Illustrations

Become a Worm and Be Squashed!

In a church in the south I spoke on "The Life of Selfless Love." I emphasized the fact that the Lord could not use a Christian who had ill will in his heart against anyone. "I must have a heart-to-heart talk with you," said the pastor's wife. "I would do anything if we could be united in this church!" We knelt and prayed. After tearful prayer, she confessed that she had resentment in her heart against a prominent lady of the church. I said to her, "Are you willing to become a worm and be squashed? Go to her immedi-

ately. Don't try to justify or excuse yourself. Tell her that you have had unkind thoughts about her. Be humble and ask her forgiveness!" At first she said, "I can't!" After a moment of tense silence, she submissively said, "I am willing to be a crushed worm for Jesus' sake!"

The next morning she went to the lady and confessed her un-Christian attitude toward her and asked her forgiveness. The one whose forgiveness she sought burst into tears. She said, "You came to confess sin against me. I should be confessing the wrong attitude I've had against you and asking your forgiveness!"

The reconciliation of those two women became the talk of the church. Others got right with each other and with God. God began to work mightily in that church because one of God's children was willing to be a crushed worm for Christ's sake! —Dr. E. L. Langston, Keswick leader of England

* * *

I Used to Be So Happy!

A man came to me and said, "I cannot understand it, Sir, but it seems as if God is blotted out of my life. I used to be so happy."

I asked, "How is it?"

Said he, "I think it has to do with my treatment of my brother. He served me cruelly over my father's will, and I said I would never forgive him. I am sorry I said it, but he has been going from bad to worse. He has lost his wife and child, and is now on his deathbed, and I cannot go to him because I said I never would."

I said, "My friend, it is better to break a bad vow than keep it. Go."

He went, and the smile of God met him just there. —Dr. F. B. Meyer

* * *

How Queen Victoria Began Her Reign

Shortly after Queen Victoria succeeded to the throne of England, the Lord Chamberlain presented to her several documents that required her signature. Among them was a paper pertaining to a man who had committed a crime, and who had been sentenced to death. The queen's signature was needed for his execution to be carried out. "And must I become a party to his death?" asked the eighteen-year-old queen. "I fear it is so, unless Your Majesty desires to exercise her royal prerogative of mercy!" To her delight, she was informed that she had the power to pardon the condemned man. "As an expression of the spirit in which I desire to rule, I will exercise my royal prerogative!" she said. She wrote the word pardoned on the document and the prisoner was set free. —W. B. K.

Gladstone's Forgiveness

When William E. Gladstone was Chancellor of the Exchequer, one of his statisticians made a serious mistake. The House of Commons was stirred with excitement. Newspapers picked up the stories and revealed the glaring inaccuracies. Gladstone went to his office, sent for the statistician, and said to him: "I know how much you must be disturbed by what has happened, and I have sent for you to put you at your ease. For a long time you have been engaged in handling the intricacies of the national accounts and this is the first mistake you have made. I want to congratulate you and to express my appreciation." The quality of forgiveness is lacking in many of our human relationships. And yet Jesus said we must forgive one another if we hope to receive divine pardon. This constructive quality of forgiveness will serve to make us both humble and loving, and will ease the tension in many situations. —*The Sunday School Times*

* * *

I Forgive You!

A white settler in South Africa found a native of the Kaffir tribe near his stable, and accused him of trying to steal a horse. The native declared that he was simply taking a short cut home, but the white man was not a Christian, he had no faith in Kaffirs, and decided he would make them afraid of him. So he tied the poor native to a tree and cut off his right hand. Months afterward the white man was overtaken by darkness and storm far from his cabin. Seeking shelter in a Kaffir hut he was given food and a place to sleep. When he awoke a tall Kaffir was standing over him. As their eyes met the native held up his arm without a hand. The white man felt his time had come. He knew the Kaffirs were cruel and revengeful. He waited, expecting each moment to be his last. Slowly the right arm dropped, and the Kaffir said: "This is my cabin and you are in my power. You have maimed me for life, and revenge is sweet; but I am a Christian, and I forgive you." —As told by a missionary

Love That Rights the Wrong

One of God's servants had preached a searching sermon on forgiveness. He urged God's children to get right with God and with one another. He emphasized the fact that God's children cannot be right with God, and at the same time wrong with one another, if it is within their power to right the wrong. He quoted the verse, "If it be possible, as much as lieth in you, live peaceably with all men" (Rom. 12:18). "Oh, that more of us had the 'love which rights the wrong!' Then more hearts would be 'filled with cheer and song!'"

At the close of the service, a lady, who had harbored hatred in her heart for the pastor, openly confessed to him the wretchedness of her heart, saying, "Your reference to the 'love that rights the wrong' went like an arrow to my heart. Do forgive me for the wrong I have done you, as I feel that God has forgiven me!" —W. B. K.

. . .

I'm Going to Love Every One!

Little Jackie was enjoying playing "elevator boy" while his grandfather made some purchases in the large department store. Jackie would say to those entering the elevator, "Up or down?" The operator of the elevator beamed with joy because Jackie was having such a fine time. A sour-faced woman approached the elevator. Little Jackie called out to her, "Up or down?" "Neither one," barked out the woman to Jackie, adding, "Get out of here, you little pest!" Jackie was sorely wounded. With heavy heart and dragging feet, and with tears trickling down his little face, he went and fell into the waiting arms of his grandfather, who saw and heard what occurred. "Why did she call me a little pest?" asked little Jackie. Grandpa tried to explain to Jackie that sometime in the past the rough-speaking woman must have been hurt, and the hurt had left scars on her soul. "She feels that, by hurting others, the scars on her soul will heal, but that isn't true, Jackie, for when she hurts others, her scars become worse," said Grandpa.

When little Jackie prayed that night he asked God's blessings upon many whom he mentioned by name. "But, dear Lord," he prayed, "don't bless the woman with scars on her soul, because she has put scars on my soul!" Grandpa heard what little Jackie prayed, and he said, "Jackie, if we want to be truly loved by Jesus, and forgiven by Jesus, we must love and forgive others!"

Some weeks passed. Grandpa thought little Jackie had forgotten all about the unpleasant experience. But it was not so. One day he came and said, "Grandpa, I am going to love everyone that has scars on his soul. And I am going to love everyone who has put scars on my soul!" —W. B. K.

. . .

As I Hope to Be Forgiven

Maskepetoon was a powerful Indian chief. He engaged in savage warfare with his enemies. One night he heard a missionary speak on the dying Lord's prayer for His enemies, "Father, forgive them." The next day Maskepetoon saw the Indian who had murdered his son. Coming face to face with him, Maskepetoon said in a tremulous voice, "You have murdered my son. You deserve to die. You have done me and my tribe the greatest injury that is possible for a man to do. You have broken my heart and destroyed him who was to have succeeded me. But for what I heard from the missionary at the campfire last night, I would now bury this tomahawk in your heart. But the missionary told us that if we want God, the great Spirit, to forgive us, we must forgive our enemies." With deep emotion he continued: "As I hope the great Spirit will forgive me, I forgive you!" Then, pulling his war bonnet over his face, Maskepetoon bowed down over his horse's neck and gave way to his agony in tears! —D. M. Panton

. . .

What Would You Have Done?

Not long after the beginning of his new pastorate, a member of the official board of the young pastor's church fell into disgrace. The inexperienced pastor was greatly troubled. He called a meeting of the board. As they sat before him, he asked the first one, "If you had been tempted as was our sinning brother, what would have been your reaction? Would you have sinned as grievously as he did?" "O, no, pastor, I am sure I would not have fallen as disgracefully as he did!" All, excepting one, gave a similar answer. "And what would have been your reaction to the temptation which caused our brother to fall?" asked the pastor of him. The man replied with difficulty and with tears in his

eyes, "I feel that if I had been in the place of our erring brother, I would have fallen even lower than he fell!"

Then the pastor said, "My brother, let's you and I go immediately and obey God's command which says, 'Brethren, if a man be overtaken in a fault, ye which are spiritual, restore such an one in the spirit of meekness; considering thyself, lest thou also be tempted.'"

—Told by Dr. George W. Truett

FREEDOM

Short Quotes

Freedom — no word was ever spoken that has held out greater hope, demanded greater sacrifice, needed more to be nurtured, blessed more the giver, or came closer to being God's will on earth.
—General Omar N. Bradley

* * *

We find freedom when we find God. We lose it when we lose Him.
—Paul Scherer

* * *

Mr. Khrushchev said to me that my grandchildren would live under Communism. I said, "Your grandchildren and my grandchildren shall live under freedom!" —Richard Nixon

* * *

Liberty has never come from government. Liberty has always come from the subjects of it. The history of liberty is a history of resistance. The history of liberty is a history of limitations of governmental power, not the increase of it. —Woodrow Wilson

* * *

Liberty was infinitely precious to our fathers, because it bore the marks of sacrifice. It was crimsoned with the red stain of their own blood. We are inclined to hold our liberties cheaply because they cost us nothing. —Jowett

* * *

Those who give up essential liberty to purchase a little temporary safety deserve neither liberty nor safety.
—Benjamin Franklin

Make us to see that our liberty is not the right to do as we please, but the opportunity to please to do right.
—Peter Marshall, in a prayer for the U. S. Senate

* * *

Religious liberty in America is being slowly and surely taken away. There seems to be a code of platitudes that certain people have prepared who, in many cases, make no profession of true Christianity. You either use these platitudes or you are silenced or, if permitted to be heard, smeared as a bigot or fanatic. —Dr. Albert J. Lindsey, in an address before the National Association of Evangelicals

* * *

Of the brave Pilgrims who fled Old World tyrannies for freedom in the New World, Felicia D. Hemans has written:
What sought they thus afar?
Bright jewels of the mine?
The wealth of seas, the spoils of war?
They sought a faith's pure shrine!
Aye, call it holy ground,
The soil where first they trod!
They have left unstained what there they found:
Freedom to worship God!
—W. B. K.

* * *

Contemporary world peace propagandists encourage us to sacrifice something precious — even facets of our freedom, if necessary — for the sake of human survival. But peace bought in the bond-age-mart, and flying the flag of justice only at half-mast, is surely a prelude to totalitarianism or to tyranny. Such peace is no triumph for human dignity and destiny. The surest way for the West to seal up the era between the Protestant Reformation and the Russian Revolution is to purchase peace from dictators who whittle away our liberties.   —Carl F. H. Henry in *Christianity Today*

Illustrations

Things to Bury

On the night when the slaves were set free in Jamaica, in 1838, a large mahogany coffin was made and a grave was dug. Into that coffin the liberated slaves threw the reminders of their former life of slavery — whips, torture irons, branding irons, coarse frocks and shirts, large hats, fragments of a tread-mill, and handcuffs. Then the lid of the coffin was screwed down. At the stroke of midnight the coffin was low-ered into the grave and buried. Then the liberated natives sang the doxology:
Praise God, from whom all blessings flow,
Praise Him, all creatures here below,
Praise Him above, ye heavenly host,
Praise Father, Son, and Holy Ghost!

When Christ comes into our lives, He sets us free from the bondage of sin. There are many things of our former life which we throw away, discard, bury! Paul enumerates some of them: "Uncleanness, inordinate affection . . . and covetousness, which is idolatry" (Col. 3:5). Peter also mentions some of them: "Wherefore laying aside all malice, and all guile, and hypocrisies, and envies, and all evil speakings" (I Peter 2:1). —W. B. K.

* * *

A Chink in a Soviet Tank!

There is in the human spirit a driving force toward freedom, absent only in the imbecile and in the primitive savage, subjected for generations to a soul-de-stroying regression. We see a little Hungarian, carrying a rifle too cumber-some for his twelve-year-old limbs, try-ing to find a chink in the armor of a Soviet tank, to fire just one shot, in a remote hope of stopping it. And when the churning wheels of the iron be-hemoth knock him down and reduce his muscles to bleeding flesh, his mother, who has been watching him from the sidewalk, clasps his mangled figure in her arms, and moans, "*He died for free-dom!*" The boy had felt the drive for freedom, and so had his mother. Such an example . . . cannot be in vain as long as there are any left with freedom enough to learn of it and tell it!
—Frank H. Yost, Editor of *Liberty* magazine

* * *

A Privilege, Not a Burden

An elder entered the tailor shop of a Polish Jew. He complained about high taxes. But the Polish Jew pro-tested, "Don't say one word about taxes. I for one am glad to pay them. In the country from which I came, unless one had property on which to pay taxes, he had no rights at all. He had no voice in the government. He had no freedom. He was denied all the rights that even non-taxpayers have in the United States. Being a Jew, I was not allowed to at-tend public school. We were not allowed to worship in our homes. Often we were forced to unite with the established church before we were permitted to carry on our business. Ah, don't com-plain about paying taxes. Be glad and thankful that you live in a country like America with all its liberties that are granted to everybody regardless of his race, or his ownership of property. I gladly pay taxes because of the many benefits I enjoy!" —W. B. K.

* * *

Helping "Miss Liberty!"

An eight-year-old girl was taken to New York City to see the sights. Among other things she was taken to see was the Statue of Liberty. She was fasci-nated with the statue, which has stood for many years at the entrance to New York harbor, lifting aloft her torch of liberty to enlighten the world. She

could not get the scene out of her mind. After the excitement of the day, sleep did not come easily that night. "Daddy," she said, "I am thinking of that beautiful lady out there all by herself, with nobody to help her hold up her lamp. It is dark out there. Shouldn't we be helping Miss Liberty hold up her lamp?" Yes, it is dark out there and it is grow-ing darker all the time. Miss Liberty *does* need our help if she is to hold up her lamp in this darkness. How can we help? By keeping the Bible available to all the peoples of the world. If the Bible falls into disuse the beautiful lady's light will go out. "Where the Spirit of the Lord is, there is liberty."
—*Bible Expositor and Illuminator*

FRIENDSHIP

Short Quotes

Dear Lord, my friends have been to me
 Interpreters of love divine,
And in their kindness I have seen
 Thine everlasting mercy shine!

And so I pray on this Thy day,
 That Thou wilt search through gifts
 of Thine,
And choose Thy rarest, fairest ones,
 To shower upon these friends of mine!
   —Martha Shell Nicholson

* * *

Some friends are like an umbrella — Johnny-on-the-spot when the sun shines, but they cannot be found when it rains.

* * *

I went out to *find* a friend,
 But could not find one there,
I went out to *be* a friend,
 And friends were everywhere!

* * *

A rich man, feeling that he was without friends in the world, said that he would divide his fortune among his friends if only he knew who they were. Years passed. Then the rich man died. His death occurred during a midwinter blizzard. His last request was that the funeral be held at four o'clock in the morning. During his lifetime, many had boasted of being his intimate friends. Only three men and one poor woman turned out to lament his passing, and to show their last respects at the graveside. When the rich man's will was read, it directed that his vast fortune be equally divided among those who attended his funeral! —W. B. K.

* * *

It is my joy in life to find,
 At every turn of the road,
The strong arm of a comrade kind,
 To help me on with my load.

And since I have no gold to give,
 And love alone must make amends,
My only prayer is while I live,
 "God make me worthy of my friends!"

* * *

You can make more friends in two months by becoming interested in other people than you can in two years by trying to get other people interested in you. —Dale Carnegie

* * *

I think that God will never send,
A gift so precious as a friend,
A friend who always understands,
And fills each need as it demands,
Whose loyalty will stand the test,
When skies are bright or overcast,
Who sees the faults that merit blame,
But keeps on loving just the same,
Who does far more than creeds could do,
To make us good, to make us true,
Earth's gifts a sweet contentment lend,
But only God can give a friend!
   —Rosalie Carter

* * *

A soldier was telling of a frightful wound received in battle. "Did you fall?" someone asked. "No," he replied, "my buddies saw I was hurt and gathered so closely about me I couldn't fall!" —*Christian Standard*

. . .

Friendship is like a garden,
  Of flowers fine and rare,
It cannot reach perfection,
  Except through loving care,
Then, new and lovely blossoms
  With each new day appear,
For friendship, like a garden
  Grows in beauty year by year.
—Anna Holden King, in *Guideposts*

. . .

A friend steps in when others step out. A friend never gets in our way except when we are on the way down.
—W. B. K.

. . .

A young man said to Dwight L. Moody, "My friends are not Christians. They cannot understand the standards I wish to set for myself. How can I give them up? They have been my companions for years." Mr. Moody answered, "That's not difficult. Live a true, consistent life and undesirable companions will give you up!"

Friendship is a chain of gold,
Shaped in God's all-perfect mold,
Each link a smile, a laugh, a tear,
A grip of the hand, a word of cheer,
As steadfast as the ages roll,
Binding closer, soul to soul,
No matter how far, or heavy the load,
Sweet is the journey on Friendship's
  Road.

—*Gospel Gleaner*

. . .

We all too seldom put in words
  Our thoughts from day to day
About how much we value friends
  Who brighten up life's way.

So this is just to let you know
  What's now and always true:
All the best that friendship means
  Is centered right in *you*.

Illustrations

The House by the Side of the Road

A stranger was walking along a dusty road in New England. He was weary and worn. He stopped to rest beneath a tree. Nearby was a sign which read, "Here is a spring. If thirsty, drink!" When he walked further, he saw a bench on which were painted the words: "If weary, rest on this bench!" Still further on he saw a basket of delicious apples and a sign which read, "If hungry, help yourself!" "I must find out who does these nice things for strangers and passers-by!" the stranger thought. Soon he came to an old hut. There sat an aged man whose face beamed kindness. "The blessings of the day to you," said the old man. "I have enjoyed the blessings placed by you along the dusty road. Why are you so kind and generous?" asked the traveler. The old man replied, "There are shade trees, benches, water and fruit aplenty. So why not share them with strangers and weary travelers? God gives me great joy as I share what I have with others!"

The weary traveler on that dusty road was *Sam Walter Foss*. The old man's unselfishness and kindness to strangers inspired him to write the famous poem, "The House by the Side of the Road."
—W. B. K.

. . .

The Love of a Friend

Like music heard on still waters,
Like pines when the wind passeth by,
Like pearls in the deep of the ocean,
Like stars which enamel the sky,
Like June and the odor of roses,
Like dew and the freshness of morn,
Like sunshine which kisses the clover,
Like tassels of silk on the corn,
Like notes of thrush in the woodland,
Like brooks where violets grow,
Like rainbows that arch the blue heaven,
Like clouds when the sun dippeth low,
Like dreams of Arcadian pleasure,
Like colors which gracefully blend,
Like everything breathing of pureness,
Like these is the love of a friend.

—*Selected*

GIVING

Short Quotes

Give as you would if an angel
  Awaited your gift at the door;
Give as you would if tomorrow
  Found you where giving was o'er.

Give as you would to the Master
  If you met His loving look;
Give as you would of your substance
  If His hand the offering took.

* * *

The windows of heaven hinge on the tithe: "Bring ye all the tithes. . . . I will open you the windows of heaven, and pour you out a blessing" (Mal. 3:10). If we withhold the Lord's tithe, have we a right to pray for open windows and outpoured blessings?
—W. B. K.

* * *

Some folks give their mite,
Others give with their might,
And some don't give who might.
—Rev. Walter B. Keffries

* * *

A special offering was being taken for missions. A man was approached with the question, "How much will you give, brother?" "Oh," was the answer, "I guess I can give ten dollars and not feel it." Then the advice was given, "Make it twenty and *feel it!* The blessing comes, you know, when you feel it!"
—W. B. K.

* * *

Unless a man cultivates a habit of systematic giving when he has not much to give, he will give little when he is rich. —Samuel Chadwick

* * *

Not what we give, but what we share,
For the gift without the giver is bare.
—Lowell

* * *

God judges what we give by what we keep. —George Muller

* * *

If you want to be rich, give;
If you want to be poor, grasp;
If you want abundance, scatter;
If you want to be needy, hoard.

Two men were engaged in conversation. One said, "You give far too much to God's work. I have decided to wait until I amass a large amount of money, and then I will give." "No," said the other, "I give as God prospers me, and according to His plan — 'Upon the first day of the week let every one of you lay by him in store' (I Cor. 16:2)."

The first speaker failed in business. The other became a prosperous businessman.

If we give willingly and cheerfully to God, we are insured for time and eternity. The greatest earthly bank is a weak institution compared with the bank of heaven upon which the God-honoring Christian may draw!
—Rev. Ralph W. Neighbour

* * *

Is thy cruse of comfort failing?
  Rise and share it with a friend!
And through all the years of famine
  It shall serve thee to the end.
Love divine will fill thy storehouse,
  Or thy handful still renew;
Scanty fare for one will often
  Make a royal feast for two.

For the heart grows rich in giving:
  All its wealth is living grain;
Seeds — which mildew in the garner —
  Scattered, fill with gold the plain.
Is the burden hard and heavy?
  Do thy steps drag wearily?
Help to lift thy brother's burden —
  God will bear both it and thee.

* * *

"I'll give my mite," said a prosperous merchant to one who asked for a contribution for a charitable cause. "Do you mean the widow's mite?" the other asked. "Certainly!" said the merchant. "I will be satisfied with half that much!" was the reply. "Just how much are you worth?" "Seventy thousand dollars," said the merchant. "Then give me your check for $35,000. That will be half as much as the widow gave, for she gave 'all that she had, even all her living!'" —*Christian Victory*

He said he wouldn't make a pledge
Unto the church at all,
That he would give just when he felt
The urgency — the call.

But still he bought a car and pledged
To pay it off some day.
And then a house in which to live
And each month he would pay.

He pledged to pay his telephone,
Electric and his gas;
He pledged to pay his water bill —
He never let it pass.

He pledged to pay his taxes, too,
Upon his house and sod,
But not *one cent* he'd ever pledge
To the house of God.

—*Selected*

* * *

A little girl was given ten bright new pennies. Instantly she began to part with them. "This one is for Jesus. This one is for you, Mommie. This one is for you, Daddy," — and so on until she had only one penny left. "And this one is for Jesus," she said again. "But you have already given one to Jesus," said the mother. "Yes, Mommie, but that one *belonged* to Jesus. This one is a *present!*" —*A Threefold Cord*

* * *

Andrew Fuller asked an old friend for money for foreign missions. The friend said, "I will give you five pounds, Andrew, since it is for you." Fuller refused the money. "I cannot take it since it is for me, as you said." Then the friend said, "I see the point, Andrew. You're right! Here are ten pounds, since it is for the Lord Jesus!"

—Rev. Paul Rees, D.D.

* * *

One of greed's victims read the verse: "It is more blessed to give than to receive." How revealing of his sordid, shriveled soul was his comment: "Well, perhaps so, but receiving is good enough for me." Is receiving good enough for you? Would you rather be a beggar than a benefactor? a panhandler than a philanthropist? a blight than a blessing? a parasite than a producer? a getter than a giver?

—Rev. Herschel H. Hobbs, D.D.

Not what I get, but what I give
This be the gauge by which I live.
Not merely joys that come my way,
But the help I give to those astray.
Not the rewards of money and fame,
But the loads I lift in Jesus' name.
This be the pay at the end of the day,
Not what I keep, but give away.

—*Selected*

* * *

God gives the soil: Psalm 24:1. God gives the seed: Genesis 1:11. God gives the rain: Job 5:10. God gives you life: Acts 17:28. God gives you health: Jeremiah 30:17. God gives you strength: Psalm 144:1. God gives "riches and honour": I Chronicles 29:12. God gives grace: II Corinthians 12:9. God gives eternal life: Romans 6:23. "What hast thou that thou didst not receive?" (I Cor. 4:7). —W. B. K.

* * *

Said an English nobleman just before death: "What I spent, I had; what I kept, I lost; what I gave, I have!"

* * *

Moody was a very practical man. A group of businessmen, all of average and above-average means, were praying that God would send a needed $1,500 to meet a pressing church obligation. Moody, listening at the door of the room where the men were praying, went in and said, "Men, stop asking God to give you the needed money. Any one of you could write a check for this amount right now. Write the check and begin praising God!" —W. B. K.

* * *

What can I give Him?
As poor as I am,
If I were a shepherd,
I would give Him a lamb.

If I were a wise man,
I would do my part,
But what can I give Him?
I will give Him my heart!

—Christina Rossetti

* * *

What a wealth of divine giving lies between the first and the last words of the Bible on giving: "God said, Behold, I have given you every herb" (Gen. 1:29); "I will give unto him that is

athirst of the fountain of the water of life freely" (Rev. 21:6).
—*Trusting and Toiling*

* * *

What we are is God's gift to us. What we become is our gift to God. —Nizer

* * *

It's not what you'd do with a million,
If riches should e'er be your lot,
But what you are doing at present,
    With the dollar and quarter you've got.

A woman in India stood by a Buddhist temple that was in process of construction. "What is the cost of the temple?" asked a missionary. "Cost?" asked she of the questioner, "why we don't know. It is for our god. We don't count the cost!" —*Pilgrim Holiness Advocate*

* * *

Who gives himself with his alms feeds three:
Himself, his hungering neighbor, and Me.   —Lowell

Illustrations

I Give Myself in the Offering!

There was a missionary meeting in a church in Scotland. The people were greatly moved. They gave generously to send missionaries into God's worldwide vineyard. Little Alexander Duff, just ten years old, sat in a pew. His heart was strangely moved. But he had nothing to give. After the offering was taken, the ushers returned to the rear of the church. Little Alexander followed them. Looking into the face of one of the collectors, the lad said, "Please, Sir, put the basket low!" The usher, catering to what he thought was a childish whim, put the basket on the floor. "There you are, my boy," he said, smiling. How surprised all were when the boy stepped into the basket and said, "O God, I have no money to give, but I give myself in the offering!"
—W. B. K.

* * *

Think It Over

God made the sun — it gives.
God made the moon — it gives.
God made the stars — they give.
God made the air — it gives.
God made the clouds — they give.
God made the earth — it gives.
God made the sea — it gives.
God made the trees — they give.
God made the flowers — they give.
God made the fowls — they give.
God made the beasts — they give.
God made the *plan* — He gives.
God made man — he . . .

—*Selected*

Here's a Nickel!

Bishop McCabe, who was trying to raise a million dollars for missions, received in his mail one day many discouraging letters, excepting one from a little boy. When the bishop opened it, out tumbled a badly battered nickel. In the letter the boy had written: "I'm so glad you are going to get a million dollars for missions. I'm going to help you get it, too. Here's a nickel towards it! It's all I've got now, but when you want any more, call on me!"

When God is in it, little is much!
—W. B. K.

* * *

The Art of Giving Self

One of my favorite stories is about a missionary teaching in Africa. Before Christmas he had been telling his native students how Christians, as an expression of their joy, gave each other presents on Christ's birthday.

On Christmas morning one of the natives brought the missionary a seashell of lustrous beauty. When asked where he had discovered such an extraordinary shell, the native said he had walked many miles to a certain bay, the only spot where such shells could be found.

"I think it was wonderful of you to travel so far to get this lovely gift for me." the teacher exclaimed.

His eyes brightening, the native answered, "Long walk, part of gift."

Not what we give, but what we share,
For the gift without the giver is bare!
—Gerald Horton Bath, in
Guideposts

Earning More for Christ

Some of God's children are divinely enabled to make money and use it for God's work. The Bible says: "It is he [God] that giveth thee power to get wealth" (Deut. 8:18).

A Christian layman had an extensive business. The death of relatives brought great riches to him. "Shall I retire from business?" was the question he pondered seriously. He decided to continue in business, not for himself but for Christ, saying, "I will trust Him to give me strength to earn money for Him." Later he testified, "I never knew before what real joy was. Formerly I worked to earn a living for myself. Now I am carrying on the same business as diligently as if for myself, even more so. It is now for Christ and all profits of the business go into the treasury of the Lord!" —W. B. K.

* * *

One of the Least

A poor Christian woman was told about another poor woman who greatly needed a warm house coat. "I can give her mine. She possibly needs it worse than I do. I can do without it. But I want to wash and mend it as neatly as I can. I'll have it ready for her tomorrow." It was prepared with loving care. A handkerchief was tucked in one of the pockets. In the other, a fifty-cent piece and a little booklet of promises from God's Word. As she gave the coat to a friend to deliver, she said, "As it's for one of His 'least of these,' I wanted it to be as nice as I could afford to make it!" —W. B. K.

* * *

How Much I Owe Him!

A man of means gave weekly a sizable sum of money to his church. A poor widow was a member of the same church. She worked hard to support herself and her six children. Her income was small. She also gave regularly out of her scant earnings. One day the man said to the pastor: "The poor widow ought not to give anything to the church. What she gives represents great sacrifice. I will increase my weekly contributions, adding the amount the widow has been giving on every Lord's day." The minister told the widow what the wealthy member had said he would do. Tears came to her eyes. She said, "Does he want to take from me the comfort I experience in giving to the Lord's work? Think how much I owe Him! My health is good. My children keep well. I receive so many blessings that I feel I couldn't live if I did not give my offering to Jesus each week!" —W. B. K.

* * *

Take Dese Six Eggs!

When Booker T. Washington was raising five hundred dollars to buy a farm on which Tuskegee Institute now stands, an aged colored woman hobbled into the room where Washington sat. She was leaning on a cane. She was clothed in rags, but they were clean. She said, "Mr. Washin'ton, God knows I spent de bes days of my life in slavery. God knows I's ignorant and poor. I knows you is tryin' to make better men an' women for de colored race. I ain't got no money, but I wants you to take dese six eggs, what I's been savin' up, an' I wants you to put dese six eggs into de eddication of dese boys an' gals!"

Booker T. Washington said later, "Since the work at Tuskegee started, I have received many gifts for the institution, but never any, I think, that touched me so deeply as the sacrificial gift of that noble woman." —W. B. K.

* * *

Amens From the Heart

Fervid *amens* can be a great boost to the pastor. The amens must be from the heart, however, and never mechanical.

A stranger began to attend the services of one of my churches. At the conclusion of a song, and during my sermon, he would thunder a loud amen! I had a little difficulty for a while in determining whether the brother's amens were from his heart, or merely mechanical. Then, one night, he came to me, expressing deep concern for the lost ones and the effort of the church to reach them in street meetings. Then he placed in my hand two hundred dollars to help carry on the work of the church. He backed up his amens in a most practical way. "Go, and do thou likewise!" —W. B. K.

Covetousness and Its Cure

A neighbor of a converted miser sustained a great loss. He and his family were in need of the necessities of life. "I'll go to the smokehouse and get a ham for my needy neighbor," he said. As he walked toward the smokehouse, the tempter, Satan, seemed to say to him, "Give him half a ham!" The struggle was terrific, for covetousness is a foul sin whose shackling hold upon its victims is not easily broken. However, the new convert resolved, by God's help, to get the victory over the sin of avarice. As Satan persisted in his suggestions for half a ham, the man said, "If you don't pipe down, Satan, I'll give him every ham in the smokehouse!"

—W. B. K.

• • •

The Calf Has Not Yet Been Sold!

How contradictory are the words: a *stingy Christian.* We might as well speak of an honest thief, or a truthful liar. How can one help but be openhearted and open-handed if he has been saved by God's wondrous and free grace? The true Christian delights in spending and being spent in the service of God.

A stingy member of a rural church was asked to make a contribution to the church. The miser owned, among other animals, a calf which he said he was trying to sell. He said, "I'll give something when the calf is sold." On a Sunday night, while the miser was feeding his animals in his barn, some joyous Christians were returning from the church service. As they walked along they sang the hymn, "The Half Has Never Yet Been Told!" The stingy owner of the calf misunderstood the words of the song. He thought they sang, "The calf has never yet been sold!" Conscience-stricken, he sold the calf and gave the money to the church.

—W. B. K.

GOD, NO RESPECTER OF PERSONS

Illustrations

None So Blind

Too often concrete facts have not availed against preconceived notions and prejudices. When Galileo was summoned before the Inquisition to be tried for the "heresy" of affirming the revolution of the earth, he said to the judges: "I can convince you. Here is my telescope, look through it, and you shall see the moons of Jupiter." They refused to look. They were certain that the earth did not revolve around the sun, and no evidence could convince them otherwise! —*Earnest Worker*

• • •

Courteous to All People

A Sunday-school teacher was endeavoring to impress upon his class of teenagers to have right attitudes toward everybody. He said, "If we let the Bible criticize our thoughts, we will have the right attitude toward everybody. It will help us to act as Christians should act in all their relationships with others. Now tell me if you understand the truth I am trying to put across to you." "I think I do," said a seventeen-year-old girl. "Before I knew the Lord Jesus as my personal Saviour, I used to single out certain people to be nice to. In my thoughts certain people were more important than others, but now I know that, as a Christian, God expects me to be courteous to everybody."

—W. B. K.

• • •

The Lord Looketh on the Heart

Some missionaries in Landaur, India, hired a young Hindu as a handy man about the home. His name was Burean, meaning "evil one." His mother had given him that name in the hope of warding off evil spirits. Burean attended family worship each morning. It was evident that light was coming to his darkened soul as the missionaries prayed and read from God's Word. One morning Burean said, "What wonderful things you read out of that Book! I never heard such things before!" The missionaries asked, "Do you believe them, Burean?" Burean said, "They are wonderful, sahib, but they are not for me. They are for you. They are for the King's children. You have white skin! I am only a poor, dark-skinned Hindu mountain lad!" "Yes, I am a child of the King, but it is because I believe in Jesus, not because of my white skin. The words I read from the Bible belong to everyone who believes. Where you live, what you possess, or the color of your skin makes no difference!"

The color of one's skin does not commend one to God, though around the world there seems to be the deep-seated belief that God is more favorable to races of fair complexion. —W. B. K.

* * *

Everyone a Prime Minister!

Dr. Bouden, an eminent surgeon, was one day sent for by the Cardinal du Bois, prime minister of France, to perform a very serious operation upon him. The Cardinal on seeing him enter the room said to him, "You must not expect to treat me in the same rough manner that you treat your poor miserable wretches at your hospital of the Hotel Dieu." "My Lord," replied the surgeon, with great dignity, "everyone of those miserable wretches, as Your Eminence is pleased to call them, is a prime minister in my eyes."
—*Biblical Illustrator*

* * *

In Christ

In Christ there is no East nor West,
In Him no South nor North,
But one great fellowship of love
Throughout the whole wide earth.

In Him shall true hearts everywhere
Their high communion find;
His service is the golden cord
Close binding all mankind.
—*Harvest Field*

GOSPEL

Short Quotes

I would like to make myself quite clear: I intend to go anywhere, sponsored by anybody, to preach the gospel of Christ, *if there are no strings attached to my message.* —Billy Graham

* * *

The secret of John Wesley's power was his kingly neglect of trifles as he mastered the important thing — the preaching of the gospel.
—Bishop Gerald Kenedy

* * *

Christ did not attack the dark evils of the ancient world as such. He did something infinitely better — He injected into human society an ameliorating, character-transforming gospel which produces in those receiving it an inward transformation which outward restraints are powerless to accomplish. —W. B. K.

* * *

As Tennyson passed the cottage of an aged lady, he asked, "What news this morning?" Replied the old lady,

"Lord Tennyson, I know only one piece of news — that Jesus Christ died for all mankind!" "Madam," said Tennyson, "that is old news and new news and good news!" —Howard A. Banks in *The Sunday School Times*

* * *

With tears in his eyes, a man from the savage Auca tribe, deep in the jungles of Ecuador, told Wycliffe translator Rachel Saint, "I did not do well before I knew God. I have killed for the last time. We did not understand that the outside men wanted to help us. I killed the first one!" —W. B. K.

* * *

A young minister asked the Duke of Wellington: "Does not your grace think it almost useless and absurd to preach the gospel to the Hindus in view of their obstinacy?" The Duke instantly replied, "Look, Sir, to your marching orders — 'Preach the gospel to every creature'!" —*Trench*

It is dangerous to become familiar with that which is base and sordid. It is more subtly dangerous to become flippantly and unrespondingly familiar with the good and the true. We can be so familiar with the gospel that we become *gospel hardened,* the victims of that fed-up feeling that says, "So what?" —W. B. K.

Someone asked William Gladstone, "What is the sure remedy for the deeper sorrow of the human heart?" Gladstone replied, "I must point to something which is called in a well-known hymn 'the old, old story,' told in an old, old Book — the gospel! This is the greatest and best gift ever given to mankind!" —W. B. K.

Illustrations

God's Life Plant for the World

There is a plant in Jamaica called the "life plant." It is almost impossible to kill or destroy any part of it. If you detach a leaf from the plant and suspend it by a string to a wire, it does not wilt and die. It sends out threadlike rootlets which imbibe sustenance from the moisture of the air. New leaves begin to grow.

The gospel of the grace of God is the life plant of the moral and spiritual world. Wherever the gospel goes, it takes root in the lives and affections of the people. No climate, howsoever surcharged it may be with sin, superstition and entrenched wrong, can kill the everlasting gospel. —W. B. K.

* * *

Jesus Was Talking with Us!

Years ago, a missionary employed two Chinese scholars to translate the Gospels into the Chinese language. In time the work was complete. When they gave the translation to the missionary they said, "We are converts to Christianity! The more we studied the sacred writings of the Chinese the more obscure they became. The longer we read the Gospels the more simple and intelligible they became until at last it seemed as if Jesus was talking with us!" Wasn't He? Surely! —W. B. K.

* * *

Unused Riches

A circuit rider visited the home of a poor couple who lived in the backwoods. There he saw a framed $500 bill hanging on the wall. "Where did you get that?" he asked in surprise. "A sick man stopped at our home years ago. We tenderly cared for him. We nursed him

back to health. When he left, he gave us that little picture. It is a pretty souvenir. We keep it in remembrance of that stranger whom we became greatly attached to." How surprised the aged couple were when the minister told them of its worth! They had something of great value, but they never used it.

All who reject the gospel, with its wonderful promises of salvation, protection and comfort, are like that poor couple. They fail to cash its invaluable promises at the repository of God's limitless source of supply. —W. B. K.

* * *

How Great a Debtor

How much womankind owes to the liberating, elevating gospel of the Lord Jesus Christ! I had rather be a cur in some parts of the east than be a woman there. In some parts of India, when a husband dies, his body is cremated on a funeral pyre. When the fire is hottest, the widow runs and leaps into the center of the glowing flames! She dies horribly! If she fails to submit to this cruel ritual, called *suttee,* she is put under a curse, eeks out a wretched existence as she slinks about like a frightened animal, seeking for food, even in garbage pails! —Rev. Herbert Mitchel

* * *

A Diluted Gospel

The vigorous old Gospel has become diluted with a curious blend of humanitarianism, socialism, and every other nicey-nicey-ism to the end that it has lost its appeal to the people.

Leadership got the notion that the function of ministers is to make a perfect world, with everything sweetness and light, everything happy, everybody getting fine wages — everything just beautiful.

The idea was to be all things to all men, nobody against anybody's ideas, everybody harmonious, with the result that Protestantism has become weak. It isn't narrow enough. It has become so broad that it is shallow.

The only true Protestants left in the United States are those who believe in the Bible and Jesus Christ the Saviour and in salvation from sin. They may not have much of a social gospel, but they have a Gospel. —Dr. Vincent Peale, in a sermon at Marble Collegiate Church

* * *

Hardened

The superintendent of a city cemetery lived in a small cottage just inside the cemetery gate through which entered several funeral processions daily. "Does not this daily scene of sadness get on your nerves and interfere with your sleep?" someone asked the superintendent. "Oh, no," he said. "When I first began to work here, I often could not sleep, and when I did drop off to sleep, it was a fitful, restless sleep. I seemed to see the endless processions, and the caskets of all lengths. Now I have become so hardened to these things that I could lie down and sleep soundly in the midst of the tombstones!"

Was there a time in your experience when the preaching of the simple gospel of the grace of God set aglow God's love in your heart, and made you dissatisfied with the smallness of your sacrifice and service for Christ? Have "the spirit of the times" and "the cares of this life" blunted the keen sensitive edge you formerly had for the things of God? Hast thou a name that thou livest and art dead? —Dr. G. T. Truett

GRACE

Illustrations

Heirs and Joint Heirs

A dying judge asked a minister, "Do you know enough about law to understand what is meant by joint heirship?" "No," said the minister; "I know a little about grace, and that satisfies me." Then the judge said, "Let me explain. If you and I were joint heirs on a farm, I couldn't say to you, 'That is your field of corn, and this is mine; that is your blade of grass, and this is mine.' We would share and share alike in everything on the place. I have been thinking with deep joy that Jesus Christ has nothing apart from me, that everything He has is mine, and we will share alike throughout eternity!"

"And if children, then heirs; heirs of God, and joint heirs with Christ" (Rom. 8:17). —W. B. K.

* * *

A Good-for-Nothing Creeping Thing!

When the father of Dr. Harry Ironside lay dying, the descending sheet which Peter saw in a vision was dominant in his mind. Over and over he mumbled, "A great sheet and wild beasts, and — and — and —." Seemingly he could not recall the next words and would start over again. A friend whispered, "John, it says, 'creeping things.'" Smilingly he exclaimed, "Oh, yes, that is how I got in! Just a poor, good-for-nothing creeping thing! But I got in — saved by grace!" —W. B. K.

* * *

Mokusatsu!

During the closing weeks of World War II, the Allies issued the Potsdam ultimatum to Japan. The emperor of Japan wished to end the war in July, 1945. The proud war lords and governing body delayed. They announced a policy of "mokusatsu," which means to ignore, or to refrain from comment. The latter definition implied that there would be no comment until there was time to weigh fully the terms of the ultimatum. Unfortunately, a press dispatch translated the word "mokusatsu" to mean that the cabinet would ignore the ultimatum! The erroneous interpretation was allowed to stand! The war was prolonged. The Russians entered the war when Japan was moribund. Atomic bombs fell on Nagasaki and Hiroshima. Thousands perished. Others were horribly maimed for life — all because one word was misinterpreted!

There is an infinitely greater and more consequential word for mankind than "mokusatsu." That word is *grace!* We are in the dispensation of God's grace. This is "the acceptable year of the Lord" (Luke 4:19). "The day of vengence of our God" will surely come. It is later, dispensationally, than we think. The world is ripe for judgment. Ere long, the command will go forth, "Thrust in thy sickle, and reap . . . for the harvest of the earth is ripe." All who refuse God's grace will not escape His judgment "when the Lord Jesus shall be revealed from heaven . . . taking vengeance on them that know not God, and that obey not the gospel of our Lord Jesus Christ" (II Thess. 1: 7, 8). —W. B. K.

* * *

Why Ask for That Which Is?

A minister lost his little child. He sorrowed greatly. As he sat in his study he read through tear-filled eyes a motto on his desk: "My grace *is* sufficient for thee." The word *is* was emphasized more prominently than the other words. While he prayed, "Lord, let Thy grace be sufficient for me!" the Lord seemed to say to him, "Why ask for that which *is?* I cannot make My grace more sufficient than I have already made it. Believe it, and you will *find* it sufficient!" —W. B. K.

* * *

A Strange Gift

Strange gift indeed — a thorn to prick,
To pierce into the very quick,
To cause perpetual sense of pain;
Strange gift — and yet, 'twas given for gain.
Unwelcome, yet it came to stay,
Nor could it e'en be prayed away.
It came to fill its God-planned place.
A life-enriching means of grace.

God's grace-thorns — oh, what forms they take;
What piercing, smarting pain they make!
And yet, each one in love is sent,
And always just for blessing meant.
And so, whate'er thy thorn may be
From God, accept it willingly;
But reckon Christ, His Life, His power
To keep in thy most trying hour.

And sure, thy life will richer grow,
He grace sufficient will bestow,
And in heav'ns' morn thy joy 'twill be
That by His thorn He strengthened thee!
—J. Danson Smith

GROWTH

Short Quotes

"I ain't what I oughter be; and I ain't what I'm gonna be; but I sure ain't what I was!" —Testimony of a simple, but sincere woman.

* * *

To reach the port, we must sail, sometimes with the wind and sometimes against it, but we must sail and not drift, or lie at anchor.
—Oliver Wendell Holmes

The largest room in the world is the room for improvement.

* * *

We can't stand still in the Christian life. If we don't go on, we may go off world-mindedly like Demas: "For Demas hath forsaken me, having loved this present world" (II Tim. 4:10); destructively like Saul: "Saul took his sword, and fell upon it . . . his armour-

bearer saw that Saul was dead" (I Sam. 31:4, 5); compromisingly like Peter: "Peter sat down among them" (Luke 22:55); or morally like David: "And David . . . lay with her" (II Sam. 11:4).
—W. B. K.

* * *

Bring me higher, nothing dreading,
In the race that has no stop,
In Thy footsteps keep me treading,
Give me strength to reach the top.

* * *

The saddest day has a morrow,
The darkest night has a dawn,
So turn from yesterday's sorrow,
And press courageously on!

* * *

High in the Swiss Alps is a solitary grave. A wooden cross marks its site. On it are these stirring, revealing words: *He Died Climbing!* —W. B. K.

* * *

I'll go anywhere provided it is forward. —David Livingstone

* * *

Not enjoyment and not sorrow,
Is our destined end or way,
But to live that each tomorrow,
Find us further than today.
—Longfellow

* * *

We ought not to rest content in the mists of the valley when the summit of Tabor awaits us. How pure are the dews of the hills! How refreshing is the mountain air! How rich the fare of the dwellers aloft whose windows look into the new Jerusalem! —Spurgeon

* * *

God can grow a mushroom overnight. He can grow a radish in fourteen days. He deems it not an unnecessary expenditure of time to take thousands of years to grow the giant redwoods of California. —W. B. K.

* * *

A growing Christian is like a church steeple: the closer he gets to heaven, the smaller he becomes in his own estimation. —W. B. K.

The mule is a hardier bird than the goose or turkey and different. He wears two wings on the sides of his head. He has two feet to walk with, and two more to kick with, and is *awful backward about going forward!*
—A boy's essay on a mule

* * *

John Newton wrote the hymn *Amazing Grace.* As he thought upon the words: "By the grace of God I am what I am," he said, "I am not what I ought to be. How imperfect and deficient I am! I am not what I wish to be. Though I am not what I ought to be, I can truly say that I am not what I once was — a slave to sin and satan. I can heartily say with Paul: 'By the grace of God I am what I am'!"
—W. B. K.

* * *

Near the close of his life, Dr. Russel Conwell said these challenging words to friends: "Always remember that when you take a step toward God, God takes a step toward you!" —W. B. K.

* * *

Nothing was so feared by seamen in the days when ocean vessels were driven by wind and sail as the doldrums. The doldrums is a part of the ocean near the equator, abounding in calms, squalls, and light, baffling winds. There the weather is hot and extremely dispiriting. The old sailing vessels, when caught in the doldrums, would lie helpless for days and weeks, waiting for the wind to begin to blow.

Have *you* been caught in spiritual doldrums where you mechanically and slavishly go through the motions of outward religious ritual, but fail lamentably to "grow in grace" and Christlikeness?

* * *

Conversion is only five per cent of the Christian life. Ninety-five per cent is going on with Christ. —Dr. M. E. Dodd

* * *

People seldom improve when they have no other model but themselves to pattern after. —Goldsmith

GUIDANCE

Short Quotes

I know not where my Lord may lead,
O'er barren plain or grassy mead,
Through valley, or on mountain crest,
But where He leads, I know 'tis best.

* * *

Life is no straight and easy corridor along which we travel free and unhampered, but a maze of passages, through which we must seek our way — now lost and confused, now checked in a blind alley. But always God will open a door for us, not perhaps one that we ourselves would ever have thought of, but one that will ultimately prove good for us.
　　　　　　　　　—A. J. Cronin, M.D.,
　　　　　　　Author of *The Citadel* and
　　　　　　　　　　A Thing of Beauty.

* * *

"Every soul leaves the port under sealed orders," said the poet in speaking of our birth. "We cannot know whither we are going, or what we are to do until the time comes for the breaking of the seal."

The Christian sails on the sea of life with an invisible Captain on board. Our Captain knows our sealed orders from the moment we embark, and He will pilot us over life's tempestuous sea.

Wondrous Sov'reign of the sea,
Jesus, Saviour, pilot me.
　　　　　　　　　　　　　　—W. B. K.

* * *

Without Christ as our Pilot and without the Bible as our guide, we are like an ocean vessel without chart, compass and captain; drifting from no port to no port, "tossed to and fro, and carried about with every wind of doctrine."
　　　　　　　　　　　　　　—W. B. K.

Illustrations

Are You at Wits' End Corner?

One of God's children was passing through trial and tribulation. She said to her pastor, "I don't know what to do." "Thank God!" exclaimed the pastor. "When you don't know what to do, do nothing! Wait until the Lord gives the all-clear. You have exhausted all human expedients. You have come to the end of yourself, and you are now on the threshold of a new and deeper experience of God's grace."

Are you at wits' end corner? Wait until God gives the directive: "This is the way, walk ye in it" (Isa. 30:21).
　　　　　　　　　　　　　　—W. B. K.

* * *

Step by Step

He does not lead me year by year
Nor even day by day,
But step by step my path unfolds;
My Lord directs my way.

Tomorrow's plans I do not know,
I only know this minute;
But He will say, "This is the way,
By faith now walk ye in it."

And I am glad that it is so,
Today's enough to bear;
And when tomorrow comes, His grace
Shall far exceed its care.

What need to worry then, or fret?
The God who gave His Son
Holds all my moments in His hand
And gives them, one by one.
　　　　　　　　　—Barbara C. Ryberg

* * *

The Blind Leading the Blind

A blind man with a white cane waited at an intersection for someone to help him across the busy street. Presently another man with a white cane stopped alongside him. They began to talk. Then one took the other by the arm and both men began tapping their way across the street. Neither knew that the other was blind. Only the alertness of the drivers prevented the possible death of both blind men. The pedestrians watched with bated breath until the blind men reached the opposite side of the street.

There are many blind religious guides who have a distorted sense of spiritual values — "ungodly men . . . denying the only Lord God, and our Lord Jesus Christ" (Jude 1:4). Jesus said of them: "And if the blind lead the blind, both shall fall into the ditch" (Matt. 15:14); "Woe unto you, ye blind guides" (23:16). —W. B. K.

* * *

My Guide

There is no path in this desert waste,
For the winds have swept the shifting sands;
The trail is blind where the storms have raced,
And a stranger, I, in these fearsome lands.
But I journey on with a lightsome tread,
I do not falter nor turn aside,
For I see His figure, just ahead —
He knows the way I take — my Guide!

There is no path in this trackless sea,
No map is limned on the restless waves;
The ocean snares are strange to me
Where the unseen wind in its fury raves;
But it matters naught; my sails are set,
And my swift prow tosses the seas aside;
For the changeless stars are steadfast yet,
And I sail by His star-blazed trail — my Guide!

There is no way in this starless night;
There is naught but cloud in the inky skies;
The black night smothers me, left and right;
I stare with a blind man's straining eyes;
But my steps are firm, for I cannot stray;
The path to my feet seems light and wide;
For I hear His voice — "I am the way!"
And I sing as I follow Him on — my Guide!

—*Selected*

* * *

Step by Step

I got an early-morning emergency call to go to a distant hospital. Dur-ing the night a heavy fog had blanketed Chicago. As I went to the garage for my car, I became alarmed as I thought upon the shadowy, half-hidden dangers I would encounter on the drive to the hospital. With great apprehension I backed my car into the murky street. As I drove cautiously along I soon ob-served that the ghostly, indistinct, dis-tant objects became clearly visible when I reached them. My fears subsided. "How like the will of God," I said to myself.

As we move forward the surrounding guideposts are clearly visible. The in-distinct, unknown ones scintillate with light when we approach them. The song of our submissive hearts becomes:
Step by step to the glory land,
My Saviour guides with a loving hand;
I go to dwell with the blood-washed band,
And step by step He will lead me!
—W. B. K.

* * *

Your Way or God's Way?

Years ago an old Scottish woman went to country homes to sell thread, buttons and shoe strings. When she came to an unmarked crossroad, she would toss a stick in the air and go whichever way the stick pointed. One day she was seen tossing the stick into the air sev-eral times. "Why do you toss the stick several times?" someone asked. She answered, "It has pointed every time to the road going to the right, and I want to go on the road to the left. It looks smoother!" She kept on throwing up the stick until it finally pointed toward the road she wanted to go.

How like that old woman are many of God's children!

If we want God to order our steps and stops, we must say, "Your way, dear Lord." If you go *your* way, you could get into serious trouble and make a shipwreck of your life. —W. B. K.

* * *

A Trustworthy Guide

While crossing a dangerous swamp in Africa some years ago a native guide preceded me, and stepping from one clump of grass to another we painfully made our way across. Every clump looked alike to me, but repeatedly he warned me not to step on certain clumps of grass which seemed to me to be just as secure as those we were standing on. Through long experience he had learned which were safe and rooted to solid ground, and which were merely floating clumps that would have sunk beneath my feet and permitted me to fall into this deadly quicksand. So, as the believer goes through life it is the Holy Spirit who guides him and tells him where to place each foot on the stable foundation of truth, and how to avoid the deceitful floating clumps of falsehood and temptation.

—*Bible Expositor and Illuminator*

Churchill's Deliverance

At a meeting in London, Winston Churchill gave the story of his escape from a South African military prison in Pretoria. Churchill told how, after wandering in the region round Pretoria for two or three days, and feeling at the end of his tether, he made up his mind to present himself at the door of one of the houses whose lights were twinkling in the valley below. Although a price had been set upon his head, he thought there was a chance of some friendly soul in the heart of that enemy country, and he prayed earnestly that he might be guided to the right house. Then he went up to the door of one of the houses and knocked. A man opened the door and asked him what he wanted. "I am Winston Churchill," he replied. "Come in," said a friendly voice. "This is the only house for miles in which you would be safe." —Bernard M. Allen in *Down the Stream of Life*

My Name Is Henry Ford!

A man was riding along in a Ford. Suddenly something went haywire! He looked at the engine but saw nothing wrong. As he stood there, a car came in sight. He stopped the car and asked for help. Out from the Lincoln stepped a tall man. "Well, what is the trouble?" asked the friendly man. "I cannot get this Ford to move," was the reply. The stranger made a few adjustments beneath the hood and said, "Now start the car!" It started! The grateful man asked, "What is your name, Sir?" "My name," answered the stranger, "is *Henry Ford!*"

The one who made the Ford knew how to make it run. God made you and me. He knows, therefore, how to run you and me. We could make a shipwreck of our life without Christ! When He is at the controls, all goes well. Without Him, we can do nothing. —W. B. K.

At the Crossroads

He stood at the crossroads all alone,
  With the sunrise in his face;
He had no thought for the world unknown,
  He was set for a manly race.
But the road stretched east and the road stretched west,
And the boy did not know which road was the best.
So he took the wrong road, and his life went down,
And he lost the race and the victor's crown;
He was caught at last in a sinful snare,
Because no one stood at the crossroads there,
  To show him the better road.

Another day at the selfsame place,
  A boy with high hopes stood;
He, too, was set for a manly race,
  He was seeking the things that were good.
But one was there who the roads did know,
And that one showed him which way to go;
So he turned away from the road that went down,
And he won the race and the victor's crown.
He walks today on the Highway fair,
Because one stood at the crossroads there,
  To show him the better road.

—*Selected*

He Guides Bees and Men

Here is a little bee that organizes a city, that builds ten thousand cells for honey, twelve thousand cells for larvae, a holy of holies for the mother queen; a little bee that observes the increasing heat, and when the wax may melt and the honey be lost, organizes the swarm into squads, puts sentinels at the entrances, glues the feet down, and then, with flying wings, creates a system of ventilation to cool the honey that makes an electric fan seem tawdry — a little honey bee that will include twenty square miles in the field over whose flowers it has oversight. But if a tiny brain in a bee performs such wonders, who are you, that you should question the guidance of God? Lift up your eyes, and behold the hand that supports these stars without pillars, the God who guides the planets without collision.

—*Beams of Light*

* * *

No Need to Be Without Direction

Said Dr. George Washington Carver, "There is no need for anyone to be without direction in the midst of the perplexities of this life. Are we not plainly told, 'In all thy ways acknowledge him, and he shall direct thy path'?" It was Dr. Carver's custom to arise every day at four A.M., and seek God's guidance for his life. In speaking of the blessings of those early morning hours, he said, "At no other time have I so sharp an understanding of what God means to do with me as in those hours when other folks are still asleep. Then I hear God best and learn His plan!" —W. B. K.

* * *

He Leadeth Me

In pastures green? Not always; sometimes He
Who knoweth best in kindness leadeth me
In weary ways, where heavy shadows be,
Out of the sunshine, warm and soft and bright,
Out of the sunshine into darkest night;
I oft would faint with sorrow and affright
Only for this — I know He holds my hand,
So whether in a green or desert land
I trust, although I may not understand.

And by still waters? No, not always so;
Ofttimes the heavy tempests round me blow,
And o'er my soul the waves and billows go,

But when the storm beats loudest, and I cry
Aloud for help, the Master standeth by
And whispers to my soul: "Lo! it is I."
Above the tempest wild I hear Him say:
"Beyond this darkness lies the perfect day;
In every path of thine I lead the way."

So whether on the hilltop high and fair
I dwell, or in the sunless valley where
The shadows lie — what matters? He is there.
And more than this; where'er the pathway lead,
He gives to me no helpless, broken reed,
But his own hand sufficient for my need.
So where He leadeth I can safely go;
And in the blest hereafter I shall know
Why, in His wisdom, He hath led me so.

—*L. Fitzgerald*

* * *

Unexpected Ways

'Tis good to dwell on years now past,
  And on those problem days,
When we could only on Him cast
  The future with its maze;
To find He brought us through at last,
  By unexpected ways!

'Tis good to view, yet once again,
  And grateful songs to raise,
On all that He did for us then,
  And to His name give praise,
He wrought for us, on things and men,
  By unexpected ways!

What if today we wistful stand,
  And on the future gaze,
We see not far, nor understand,
  The road is wrapped in haze,
God still will lead, by His good hand,
  In unexpected ways!

—*J. Duncan Smith*

* * *

The Road of No Return

How careful we should be to guide and direct others to the right way. The following incident, related by a GI of World War II, illustrates this:

It was dark and the colonel and his driver were hurrying along in a jeep, anxious to return to their own lines. Coming to a fork in the road they spied a lone MP stationed there to guide traffic. Getting the necessary directions, they were on their way. After a few miles, the driver sensed something wrong and got out to investigate. He walked ahead about thirty feet in the gloom. And there, where a bridge should have been, was a yawning drop of several hundred feet. Enraged, the colonel drove back to the MP and demanded an explanation. Weary, the MP sighed: "I can't understand, Sir. I've been sending traffic that way all night and you're the first to complain." —*Digest and Review*

* * *

A Telegram from Heaven

Paul Rader had many a talk with a banker in New York, who would reply that he was too busy for religion. But the banker overworked and was sent to a sanatorium for a complete rest. One day God spoke to Paul Rader. The message was quite clear, "Go and speak to S................" Rader caught a train and went with all speed to the sanatorium.

As he drew near he saw the banker standing in the doorway. "Oh, Rader," he said, "I am so glad to see you." "I received your telegram," said Rader. "No," he said, "that is impossible. I wrote a telegram begging you to come, but I tore it up. I did not send it." "That may be so," said Mr. Rader, "but your message came by way of heaven." He found his friend was under deep conviction of sin; and he pointed him to Christ as a perfect Saviour. The banker accepted Christ as his Saviour, and his heart was filled with joy.

"Rader," he said, "did you ever see the sky so blue or the grass so green?" "Ah," said Rader, "we sometimes sing:

Heaven above is softer blue,
Earth around is sweeter green;
Something lives in every hue
Christless eyes have never seen."

Suddenly the banker leaned against Mr. Rader and fell into his arms — dead. —*Pentecostal Evangel*

HEARING

Illustrations

Hearing What We Want to Hear

A scientist and a minister walked in the midst of a throng of people on a crowded street. The scientist specialized in entomology — insect life. Suddenly he stopped. "What do you hear?" asked he of the minister. "I hear the chatter of passing people, and the clangor and clatter of traffic," said the minister. "I hear a cricket above all the sounds you have mentioned," said the scientist. Going over to a nearby towering office building, he moved a small stone which lay against the foundation walls. Under it was a cricket, making its shrill music. "How could you hear it?" asked the preacher. "Very easily," said the scientist, "but let me show you something else." He led the preacher back into the center of the rushing crowds. "Now see what happens," said he as he dropped a quarter on the cement. The quarter tingled almost inaudibly in the noise of the passing traffic. But instantly some

people stopped and listened! Said the scientist, "You hear what you want to hear and what you are trained to hear. You see what you want to see and what you are trained to see!"
—Rev. O. C. Lunholm, in *Baptist Record*

* * *

A Fly Leads to His Conversion

A hardened unbeliever went one day to *see*, but not hear, George Whitefield when he preached outdoors to a great throng. In order to have a good vantage point and yet be inconspicuous, he climbed a nearby tree. Putting his fingers in both ears, he watched with fascination the mighty preacher in action. Then a persistent fly lit on his nose. He shook his head, but the fly wouldn't move. He stood the annoyance as long as he could. Just as he removed his hand from his ear to flick the fly away, Whitefield quoted the verse, "He that hath an ear, let him hear." Then he proceeded to speak of the willful deafness of those who reject Christ. The unbeliever was so impressed by the seeming coincidence that he opened not only his ears to the gospel, but his heart, too. Before the day was over, he became by faith a new creature in Christ Jesus.

"Hear ye the word which the Lord speaketh unto you" (Jer. 10:1).

—W. B. K.

* * *

O Earth, Hear

Thousands of dollars were found by officers of the law among the belongings of a Detroit beggar. He was brought before a judge who asked him: "Where did you get that money?" "I'm deaf," replied the beggar, "I can't hear you." The judge raised his voice and asked again, "Where did you get that money?" The beggar shook his head, and said, "I still can't hear you." The judge lowered his voice and said softly, "I'll fine you $150." "I won't pay it!" yelled the beggar, suddenly forgetting all about his deafness. "And in addition to the fine, I sentence you to jail for ninety days," said the judge.

God is trying to get the ear of a world which has largely forgotten Him, pleadingly saying, "O earth, earth, earth, hear the word of the Lord" (Jer. 22:29).

—W. B. K.

H E A V E N

Short Quotes

Lord, when Thou seest that my work is
   done,
Let me not linger on,
With failing powers,
Adown the weary hours —
A workless worker in a world of work.
But, with a word,
Just bid me home.
And I will come
Right gladly —
Yea, right gladly
Will I come.

—John Oxenham

* * *

Joyously and confidently David Livingstone exclaimed on his last birthday, "I am not old! You know I am not old! No man ever had a brighter hope, or a more inviting future!" This radiant, triumphant statement was called forth by the well-wishing remarks of a friend who said to Livingstone, "You are growing old!"

How exceedingly bright are the prospects of *all* of God's children: "Eye hath not seen, nor ear heard, neither have entered into the heart of man, the things which God hath prepared for them that love him" (I Cor. 2:9). On the other hand, how dismally dark is the future of all who reject Christ. Their souls are wreathed in darkness and oftentimes paralyzed with fear as they face the coming day of reckoning. Said Thomas Hobbs, a blatant atheist, as his sinful soul passed into eternity, "About to take a leap into the dark!" —W. B. K.

* * *

An imaginary story illustrates a heart-searching truth: A millionaire stood at heaven's gate, waiting to be shown his heavenly home. He was conducted to a small cottage, located in the midst of other tiny, unpretentious homes. He complained, "Can it be that I, who have lived in a palace on earth midst scenes of luxury and comfort, must now dwell eternally in this small abode?" Replied the conductor, "We built this house out of the material you sent to us while you were on earth! We could have built a palace for you if you had sent us the material with which to build it!"

—W. B. K.

* * *

A little faith will bring your soul to heaven; a great faith will bring heaven to your soul. —Spurgeon

* * *

Will we know our loved ones in heaven? I believe so. Peter, James, and John knew Moses and Elijah on the Mount of Transfiguration without an introduction. These saints had been with the Lord for a thousand and five hundred years respectively. —W. B. K.

The only works of unregenerated man in heaven are the scars of the nails in the hands and feet of Jesus, the wound in His side, and the thorn scars on His brow. —W. B. K.

* * *

Think of stepping on shore,
And finding it heaven;
Think of taking hold of a hand,
And finding it God's hand;

Think of breathing new air,
And finding it celestial air;
Think of feeling invigorated,
And finding it immortality;
Think of passing from storm and tempest,
To an unknown calm;
Think of waking up,
And finding it home!

—*Selected*

Illustrations

Home At Last

Safe Home at last! Oh, say not he has died.
His soul has only crossed the swelling tide,
And Heaven's gates for him have opened wide —
He's Home at last!

A true and valiant warrior of the Faith,
Proclaiming Christ e'en with his latest breath,
Has laid his armor down — call it not death.
He's Home at last!

He now beholds, with eyes undimmed by tears,
The face of Him who through the passing years
Has been his stay, dispelling doubt and fears.
He's Home at last!

And though his going leaves a void within
Our lonely hearts, we can rejoice with him —
His race is run, Heav'n's glory he hath seen.
He's Home at last!

At Home, with those on earth he loved so well,
Who now within the walls of jasper dwell —
Oh, bliss beyond all mortal pow'r to tell!
He's Home at last!

Life's sun for him has set — but oh, the glow
That long will linger o'er this world of woe,

Because he lived and labored here below!
He's Home at last!
—Alvis B. Christiansen

* * *

The Wrong Medicine

A nurse on night duty in a great hospital in Chicago mistakenly gave a lethal dose of wrong medicine to a little boy. Her error was not detected until it was too late to save his life.

Was she not *sincere* in what she did? Certainly! Was she not conscientiously performing her duties? Certainly! She was sincerely — wrong! She was conscientiously — wrong!

Many sincerely say, "All religions are good. They all lead to heaven." Many say, "Let your conscience be your guide. If your conscience tells you a thing is all right, it is O.K." But they all are wrong!

All religions are *not* good. All religions do not lead to heaven. There is only *one way* to heaven. Jesus said, "I am the way, the truth, and the life: no man cometh unto the Father, but by me" (John 14:6). —W. B. K.

* * *

Safely Home

I am home in heaven, dear ones;
Oh, so happy and so bright!
There is perfect joy and beauty
In this everlasting light.

All the pain and grief is over,
Every restless tossing passed;
I am now at peace forever,
Safely home in heaven at last.

Did you wonder why I so calmly
Trod the valley of the shade?
Oh! but Jesus' love illumined
Every dark and fearful glade.

And He came Himself to meet me
In that way so hard to tread;
And with Jesus' arm to lean on,
Could I have one doubt or dread?

Then you must not grieve so sorely,
For I love you dearly still;
Try to look beyond earth's shadows,
Pray to trust our Father's Will.

There is work still waiting for you,
So you must not idly stand;
Do it now while life remaineth —
You shall rest in Jesus' land.

When that work is all completed,
He will gently call you Home;
Oh, the rapture of that meeting,
Oh, the joy to see you come!
—*Selected*

* * *

They Are Not Far!

Said one of God's aged saints, "Husband, child and brother have been taken away from me. Yet it does not seem as if they have gone far from me. When I was a child, my older sister, whom I loved dearly, married. She went to live in a house about a mile from our home. At first I cried very hard. Then one day Mother said, 'Why, Eunice, don't you see that Sarah hasn't left us. She has only gone down the road to make another home where we can go — a house as full of love and welcome as this house. Now you have two homes instead of one. Come, put on your bonnet and run down to the other home!' When I saw it that way, no more tears were shed. In this way I think of my dear loved ones who have left this earthly house. Before long, I am going to 'put on my bonnet' just as I did when I was a little girl, and go to see my loved ones in the heavenly home!"

The dear ones left behind,
O, foolish ones and blind,
A day and you will meet,
A night and you will greet!
—W. B. K.

* * *

My Father's House Is Finer!

Some years ago, Tamabana, a New Zealand chief, visited England. He was shown many places of interest, including a beautiful mansion near London. To the surprise of his guide the chief expressed no admiration for the mansion, which was replete with the costliest of furniture from all parts of the world. Before he left the mansion Tamabana said, "Ah, my Father's house is finer than this!" In astonishment the guide exclaimed, "Your father's house is finer than this mansion?" The guide understood what the chief meant when the chief began to speak of his heavenly Father, and of the "many mansions" in glory which await the children of God at journey's end.

"For we know that if our earthly house of this tabernacle were dissolved, we have a building of God, an house not made with hands, eternal in the heavens" (II Cor. 5:1). —W. B. K.

* * *

At Journey's End, What Then?

Toward the close of World War II, a soldier, who had spent more than three years in the South Pacific, sat in a railway coach with a look of joyous anticipation on his face! The train was speeding toward Chicago. "How fast are we traveling?" asked the soldier of the porter. "This is a good section of track and we are making about 105 miles an hour!" the porter answered. "How far are we from Chicago?" asked the soldier. "A little over a hundred miles, Sir." "We can't get there too quickly," said the soldier as he took his duffel bag and bundles from the overhead rack. "I'm going to be the first one off this train!"

Why was he so eager to reach his destination? His father, mother, brothers, sisters, friends, and sweetheart were all waiting to welcome him!

There was another serviceman in that same coach. His face looked like a blown-out lamp. He was a picture of gloom and dejection. He was in handcuffs and in charge of military policemen. He was not eager to reach his destination, for only judgment and punishment for crime awaited him there. There would be no friends or loved ones to greet him.

Do you look forward with joy to your home-going? Will you be received "into everlasting habitations," and be "forever with the Lord," and with loved ones in glory? Or do you look forward with fear to meeting the One whose love you spurned, and whose mercy and forgiveness you rejected?

Our eternal destination is determined by the answer we give to this question: "What shall I do then with Jesus which is called Christ?" (Matt. 27:22).

—W. B. K.

* * *

Is This the Right Road Home?

Is *this* the right road home, O Lord?
The clouds are dark and still,
The stony path is sharp and hard,
Each step brings some fresh hill;
I thought the way would brighter grow
And that the sun with warmth would
    glow
And joyous songs from free hearts flow.
    Is *this* the right road home?

Yes, child! this very path I trod,
The clouds were dark for Me.
The stony path was hard to tread,
Not sight but faith can see
That at the end the sun shines bright,
Forever where there is no night,
And glad hearts rest from earth's fierce
    fight,
    It *is* the right road home!

—Mrs. Jonathan Gorofth
in *Climbing*

* * *

The Other Side

This isn't death, it's glory!
    It isn't dark, it's light;
It isn't stumbling, groping,
    Or even faith — it's sight.

This isn't grief, it's having
    My last tear wiped away.
It's sunrise, it's the morning
    Of my eternal day!

It isn't even praying,
    It's speaking face to face,
It's listening, and it's glimpsing
    The wonders of His grace.

This is the end of pleading
    For strength to bear my pain;
Not even pain's dark memory
    Will ever live again.

How did I bear the earth life
Before I came up higher,
Before my soul was granted
Its every deep desire?

Before I knew this rapture
Of meeting face to face
The One who sought me, saved me,
And kept me by His grace!

—Martha Snell Nicholson in
Heart to Heart Talk

* * *

Let Me Hold Lightly

Let me hold lightly
    Things of this earth;
Transient treasures,
    What are they worth?
Moths can corrupt them,
    Rust can decay;
All their bright beauty
    Fades in a day.
Let me hold lightly
    Temporal things —
I, who am deathless,
    I, who wear wings!

Let me hold fast, Lord,
    Things of the skies;
Quicken my vision,
    Open my eyes!
Show me Thy riches,
    Glory, and grace,
Boundless as time is,
    Endless as space. . . .
Let me hold lightly
    Things that were mine —
Lord, Thou dost give me
    All that is Thine!

—Martha Snell Nicholson

* * *

The Only Way There!

There was a moral, debt-paying, neighbor-loving man who sincerely believed that the performance of good works was a passport to heaven. One night he had a dream which led to his conversion. In his dream he saw himself on a ladder. Everytime he did a good deed, the ladder came nearer heaven. After the performance of many good deeds, the top of the ladder was so close to heaven that he needed to take but one step and he would be there! As he took that step, however, he and the ladder crashed to earth. Then he heard a thunderous voice which said, "He that

. . . climbeth up some other way, the same is a thief and a robber" (John 10:1).

I believe in good morals. I believe that one deserves credit for paying his honest debts. I believe that one should love his neighbor as himself. I do not believe, however, that these things are a substitute for the miracle of regeneration by faith in Christ. —W.B. K.

* * *

Time Enough in Heaven

A well-known English minister preached one Sunday for Dr. Phillips Brooks in Boston. After the service he started to walk to his hotel. He needed direction so he asked a man behind him the way. "Why you're the minister I just heard. I know your voice. I am blind, but I can show you the way. I can take you to the door." The minister protested, but the blind man insisted, saying, "You will not refuse me the pleasure of helping you? I so seldom have the opportunity to render service. Everyone is so kind to me." The two men walked arm in arm for ten minutes. "Here's your hotel," said the blind man.

Before parting, the blind man said, "I live alone. I can go about the streets without a guide. I am thankful for my blindness, because I have so much time for quiet and meditation. There will be time enough in heaven for me to see everything!"

The minister said afterwards, "His face shone with contentment and serenity. What he said and did preached to me one of the profoundest sermons I've ever heard!" —W. B. K.

* * *

Lamb Carried on Before

An Eastern shepherd led his sheep
Toward a river's bank,
But when they saw the stream was broad
Their hearts with fear did shrink;
And though the shepherd went across
In view of all the sheep,
They did not dare to follow him
And ford the waters deep.

And so he took a little lamb
Right from its mother's side,
He clasped it in his shelt'ring arm
And with it crossed the tide.
The mother, missing what she loved,
Was eager now to gain
The distant shore, that she might find
Her precious lamb again.

She quickly made her way across
And soon the stream she passed,
And other sheep soon followed her
Till all had crossed at last.
She found the lamb which she had lost,
Within the shepherd's care,
And he had used her little one
In leading many there.

Oh, mother, has your little lamb
Been carried on before?
The Shepherd wants to have you, too,
Upon the farther shore.
And so He clasped your treasured one
Unto His sheltering breast,
That you might come and seek it there
And find in Him your rest.

—*Selected*

HELL

Short Quotes

Every man *has* his own place, here and
　　hereafter,
Every man *makes* his own place, here
　　and hereafter,
Every man *finds* his own place, here and
　　hereafter,
Every man *feels* that it is his own place
　　when he gets there.
　　　　—Dr. Alexander Dickson

I cannot preach on hell unless I preach with tears. —Moody

* * *

To be alone with my conscience is hell enough for me —Shakespeare

* * *

God has put innumerable blockades, including the cross of Christ, athwart the pathway to hell. —W. B. K.

In beginning a lecture one night, Robert G. Ingersoll said: "I'm going to prove conclusively that hell is a wild dream of some theologians who invented it to terrify credulous people." A man, heavily under the influence of drink, stood and said: "Make it strong, Bob. There's a lot of us poor fellows depending on you. If you are wrong, we are all lost. Prove it clearly and plainly!" —W. B. K.

* * *

One of the horrors of hell is the undying memory of a misspent life — "Son, remember" (Luke 16:25). —W. B. K.

* * *

Two young ministers preached sample sermons in a church which was seeking a pastor. The text of the first one was, "The wicked shall be turned into hell, and all the nations that forget God" (Ps. 9:17). By strange coincidence, the text of the second candidate was the same. Later, the two young ministers were being considered as possible pastors in a business session. The chairman of the deacons' board was the first one to speak. He said, "Both sermons were splendid. There was this difference, however — the first one spoke as if his heart would break because the wicked would be turned into hell. The second one spoke as if he were glad that it were so!" The candidate who displayed solicitous concern for the perishing ones received the call. —W. B. K.

* * *

Asa Keys, a former district attorney of Los Angeles County, was convicted of conspiracy to obstruct justice. He was sentenced to serve a term in San Quentin prison. When the inmates of the prison heard of his conviction and sentence, they laughed long and sardonically — he had prosecuted some two thousand of those men! Hell will be something like this as relates to the attitude of its occupants toward one another. —*King's Business*

* * *

Asked an unbeliever of a Christian, "Suppose you discover after death that there is no such place as heaven, and through the years you have been laboring under a delusion. What then?" "Well, I would still be the gainer, for I have had a most wonderful and joyous time getting there! Suppose you, on the other hand, make the discovery after death that there is a hell. *What then?*" asked the Christian. —W. B. K.

HOLY SPIRIT

Short Quotes

A lady said to an evangelist to whom she had listened with disdain and contempt, "You are not abreast with the spirit of the age." The evangelist replied, "You are quite right. I am not abreast with the spirit of the age, but I do have within me the Holy Spirit of this age!" —*Gospel Banner*

* * *

Oh, that in me the sacred fire
Might now begin to glow,
Burn up the dross of base desire,
And make the mountains flow!

* * *

Whenever in any period of the history of the church a little company has sprung up so surrendered to the Holy Spirit, and so filled with His presence as to furnish the pliant instrument of His will, a new Pentecost has dawned on Christendom. —A. J. Gordon

* * *

Lord, we can't hold much, but we can overflow lots! —From a Negro minister's prayer

* * *

If God called His Holy Spirit out of the world, about ninety-five per cent of what we are doing would go on and we would brag about it. —Rev. Carl Bates, D.D.

* * *

God is not looking primarily for better methods, but for better men — ex-

emplary, courageous men who are empowered by the Holy Spirit, and who know no fear other than the fear of incurring God's frown: "There was a *man* [not a *method*] sent from God, whose name was John" (John 1:6).
—W. B. K.

* * *

Impression without expression brings depression. —Barnhouse

* * *

One day in New York — what a day! I can't describe it! I seldom refer to it! It is almost too sacred to name! I can only say God revealed Himself to me! I had such an experience of love that I had to ask Him to stay His hand! I went to preaching again. The sermons were no different. I did not present any new truth. Yet hundreds were converted. I would not be back where I was before that blessed experience if you would give me Glasgow!
—Dwight L. Moody

* * *

When we rely on organization, we get what organization can do. When we rely upon education, we get what education can do. When we rely upon eloquence, we get what eloquence can do. When we rely on the Holy Spirit, we get what God can do.
—Rev. A. C. Dixon, D.D.

* * *

At the close of a message, a man approached Dr. Len G. Broughton and said, "As you preached, the Holy Spirit whispered in my ear and told me to ask you for fifty dollars which I badly need." Dr. Broughton answered, "That's strange that the Holy Spirit would tell you to ask me for fifty dollars, because I don't have fifty dollars."

"Beloved, believe not every spirit, but try the spirits whether they be of God" (I John 4:1). —W. B. K.

* * *

The grandest operations, in both the natural and the spiritual realms, are the most silent and imperceptible. The shallow brook babbles because it is shallow. The storm rages and alarms, but its fury is soon spent and its effects soon remedied. But the change of the seasons is silent. The dew, though gentle and unheard, is immense in quan-

tity and is the very life of large portions of the earth. The Spirit's voice is the "still small voice" and is heard only by those who are sufficiently quiescent before God to hear Him. "Be still and know that I am God" (Ps. 46:10).
—W. B. K.

* * *

"Moody speaks as if he had a monopoly on the Holy Spirit," said a critic of him. "Moody has no monopoly on the Holy Spirit, but the Holy Spirit has a monopoly on Moody," answered an admirer of Moody.

When we are filled with the Spirit, we do not have more of the Spirit, but the Spirit has all of us. —W. B. K.

* * *

We can best appraise Peter in the glow of three fires: Peter by the fire, consorting with the enemies of Christ; Peter under fire, being accused by a maiden to be a follower of Christ and disowning and denying his Lord; and Peter on fire, preaching with such power that three thousand souls were drawn into God's Kingdom! —W. B. K.

* * *

Organizations without the Holy Spirit are like mills without power. Even a church that is thoroughly orthodox and accepts biblical standards is as useless as are clouds without rain until endued with power from on high.
—Charles H. Spurgeon

* * *

Lord Cecil, an earnest Christian, spoke in a meeting in London. Wilberforce, who was also an earnest Christian, sat with William Pitt, a non-Christian, in the meeting. Afterwards, Wilberforce asked Pitt, "What is your opinion of the message?" He replied, "To tell the truth, I gave that man my most careful attention, but I was wholly unable to understand what he was talking about!"

"The natural man receiveth not the things of the Spirit of God . . . neither can he know them, because they are spiritually discerned." —W. B. K.

* * *

The early Christians were so devoid of any political or worldly "pull" that they could not stay out of jail. Yet they were so endued with the power of the Holy Spirit that no prison was strong enough to hold them! —W. B. K.

* * *

The apostles met with opposition in most places they visited. Yet one of two things usually occurred wherever they went — a revival or a revolution: "And many that believed came, and confessed, and shewed their deeds. Many of them also which used curious arts brought their books together, and burned them before all men. . . . So mightily grew the word of God and prevailed" (Acts 19:18-20) ; "These men that have turned the world upside down are come hither also" (17:6). —W. B. K.

Illustrations

A Safe Guide

Of all sailors the ancient Norsemen must have been the most daring. In their little boats they made distant voyages throughout the northern Atlantic. Centuries before the time of Columbus they are thought to have explored the route to America. When Columbus crossed the sea, he had the help of a compass. However, the Norsemen had no scientific instruments. They did have a guide that you will think strange. They carried with them on their voyages a cage containing several ravens. When they were uncertain where they were or which direction to follow, they would release one of the ravens. As the bird flew high into the air, the daring sailors would follow the same direction the bird took. They knew that the raven with its keener eyesight and higher vision would lead them to land. When we are uncertain where we are or which way to follow, the Holy Spirit, if given a chance, will show the way to go.

—*The Sunday School Times*

* * *

You See What He Does

"Daddy, how can I believe in the Holy Spirit when I have never seen Him?" asked Jim, a twelve-year-old boy. "I'll show you how," said his father who was an electrician. Later Jim went with his father to the power plant. There he was shown the generators. "This is where the power comes from to heat our stove and give us light. We cannot see the power, but it is in that machine and in the power lines," said the father. "I believe in electricity," said Jim. "Of course you do, but you don't believe in it because you see it. You believe in it *because you see what it can do!* Likewise you can believe in the Holy Spirit because you see what He does in people's lives when they are surrendered to Jesus Christ and possess His power!" —W. B. K.

* * *

The Heaven-Sent Gyroscope

Recently I went down to the lowest deck of a mighty ocean-going liner. Coming to an odd-looking mechanism, I asked the guide, "What is this?" "That's the ship's gyroscope," he answered. "When the sea is rough, the gyroscope helps to keep the vessel on an even keel. Though the waves may reach mountainous proportions, the gyroscope helps to stabilize the vessel and maintain a high degree of equilibrium."

I thought, "How like this gyroscope is the Holy Spirit! Let the storms of life break over our heads; let the enemy, Satan, come in like a flood; let the waves of sorrow, suffering, temptation and testing be unleashed upon us, our soul will be kept on an even keel and in perfect peace when the Holy Spirit dwells in our hearts." —W. B. K.

* * *

Handle Reverently!

The writer was honored by being one of the pallbearers at the funeral of "The Black Samaritan," Chaplain Raymond Lilly, who for years lived and preached Christ in the world's largest charity hospital, the Cook County Hospital, Chicago. As he with others carried the body along, he was reverently aware of the wondrous truth that he was handling the mortal remains of what had been a "temple of the Holy Ghost." Impressed anew upon his heart

161

was the thought of the sacredness of the Spirit's dwelling place, and the seriousness of allowing anything of a defiling nature to abide in the dwelling place of the Holy Spirit! —W. B. K.

* * *

Ye Do Always Resist

Dr. George W. Truett preached to a large audience on the text, "Ye do always resist the Holy Ghost" (Acts 7: 51). As he emphasized the danger of the unsaved turning an unhearing ear to the wooings of the Holy Spirit, and finally coming to the place where His voice is no longer heard, an aged man interrupted him, saying, "Dr. Truett, you are describing my case!" "Not knowingly, my brother," said Dr. Truett. "But you are," said the old man. "In my youthful years, the Holy Spirit frequently convicted me of sin and of my need of the Saviour. Each time I refused to obey the Spirit's call and continued in my sinful ways. The time came when I no longer heard His pleadings. From that time I have never had the slightest desire to turn from sin to God. I would give anything I possess if I could feel tonight as I felt years ago when the Spirit strived with me!" —W. B. K.

* * *

Our Capacity, Not God's Ability, Is the Measure

Standing on the deck of a ship in mid-ocean, you can see the sun reflected from its depths. From a little boat on a mountain lake you can see the sun reflected from its shallow waters. Looking into the mountain spring not more than six inches in diameter, you see the same great sun. Look into the dewdrop of the morning, and there it is again. The sun has a way of adapting itself to its reflections. The ocean is not too large to hold it, nor the dewdrop too small. So God can fill any man, whether his capacity be like the ocean, like the mountain lake, like the spring, or like the dewdrop. Whatever, therefore, be the capacity, there is opened up the possibility of being filled with the fullness of God. —Major D. W. Whittle

Dr. J. Wilbur Chapman's Experience

I had been struggling for five years. I had had visions of His power and glimpses of what I might be if I were "filled with the Holy Spirit"; but all this time, like the disciples at Ephesus, there was a great lacking. At last I reached the place where I felt that I was willing to make a surrender. I reached it by the path marked out by one who said, "If you are not ready to surrender everything to God, are you ready to say, 'I am willing to be made willing about everything'?" That seemed easy, and alone before God I simply said, "I am now willing." Then He made the way easy. He brought before me my ambition, then my personal ease, then my home, then other things came to me, and I simply said, "I will give them up." At last all my will was surrendered about everything. Then without any emotion I said, "My Father, I now claim from Thee the infilling of the Holy Spirit." From that moment to this He has been a living reality. I never knew what it was to love my family before. I question whether they ever knew what it was to love me, although we had called ourselves happy in the love of each other. I never knew what it was to study the Bible before; and why should I? For had I not just then found the key? I never knew what it was to preach before. "Old things are passed away" in my Christian experience; "behold, all things are become new." —*The Preacher's Magazine*

* * *

Visit That Man

A minister was inwardly urged to visit a dangerous, notorious sinner. He delayed. The Holy Spirit, however, seemed to say: "Visit that man." Finally he went with fear and trembling. The man greeted him cordially. "I am glad you have come. I have been trying for weeks to get up courage enough to send for you. In recent weeks I have been most wretched. I cannot go on like this any longer. Pray for me!"

"Grieve not the Holy Spirit of God" by failure to obey His behests.

—W. B. K.

HOME

Short Quotes

A layman has charged that overcrowded church programs are a definite hindrance to Christian home life. He held up a bulletin from an unnamed church and told how it listed thirty-five different meetings and "opportunities for service" in a one-week period. "And this," he explained, "was during Christian Home Week when emphasis was on family living in the home!"

We repeat: is your local church program overweight? Does it need a diet?
—*The Evangelical Witness*

* * *

Our nation is sadly in need of a rebirth of the simple life — a return to the days when God was a part of each household, when families arose in the morning with a prayer on their lips, and ended the day by gathering together to place themselves in His care.

If there is hope for the future of America; if there is to be peace and happiness in our homes, then we, as a nation, must turn to God and the practice of daily family prayer.
—J. Edgar Hoover

* * *

On the average three and a half marriages out of six in the United States end in divorce courts. Seven hundred and fifty thousand children become half-orphans yearly because of broken homes, some total orphans. Said a nationally known psychiatrist: "There is little or no happiness in ninety per cent of American homes!"
—Billy Graham

* * *

We have lived and loved together,
  Through many changing years;
We have shared each other's gladness,
  And wept each other's tears;
I have ne'er known a sorrow,
  That was long unsoothed by thee,
For thy smiles can make a summer,
  Where darkness else would be.
—Charles Jeffreys

* * *

A house at night looks gloomy and foreboding. Put a key in the lock and turn on the lights and gloom vanishes and the place comes alive! That's what daily Bible reading and prayer, eagerly and expectantly done within one's home, does for the home. If one's mind and heart are filled with the effulgence of God's light at home, his feet will never lead him astray, even in far places.
—Dr. George W. Crane,
  newspaper columnist

* * *

To call me a judge is something of a misnomer. I am really a sort of public mortician. In the past eleven years I have presided over the final obsequies of twenty-two thousand dead marriages. The trouble is this: I have buried a lot of live corpses. There was no sure way to discover and resuscitate the spark of life that surely remained in many of them. —A Judge of the Court of Common Pleas, Division of Domestic Relations, Toledo, Ohio

* * *

It is my conviction that the greatest single need of young life in America today is the need for restoration of the home as a dependable, godly influence. Our lads and lassies are in desperate need of sources of strength from the home. —Chester E. Swor

* * *

The beauty of a house is harmony,
The security of a house is loyalty,
The joy of a house is love,
The plenty of a house is in children,
The rule of a house is service,
The comfort of a house is God Himself.
—Dr. Frank Crane

* * *

The cornerstone of every home,
  The most important part,
Is never laid upon the earth,
  But in the mother's heart.

* * *

One-half of the church members in the nation marry outside their own faith. One-half of these mixed marriages involve Catholics. The divorce rate among inter-faith couples is more than twice as high as among those who mar-

ry within their faith — 15.2 per cent for the former, 6.6 per cent for the latter.
—*The Gospel Banner*

* * *

One per cent of the child's time is spent under the influence of the Sunday school; 7 per cent under the influence of the public school; 92 per cent under the influence of the home.
—Rev. Albert S. Taylor, President Audio Bible Society of America

* * *

Eighty per cent of our criminals come from unsympathetic homes.
—J. Edgar Hoover

* * *

A cornerstone in truth laid,
The guardian walls of honor made,
The roof of faith is built above,
The fire upon the hearth is love,
The storms descend and loud winds call,
This happy home shall never fall.
—A Scottish Writer

A *house* is built of logs and stone,
Of tiles and posts and piers,
A *home* is built of loving deeds,
That stand a thousand years.
—Victor Hugo

* * *

Home — a roof to keep out rain, four walls to keep out wind, floors to keep out cold! Yes, but home is more than that: It is the laugh of a baby, the song of a mother, the strength of a father, warmth of loving hearts, the light from happy eyes, kindness, loyalty, comradeship!
—Madame Schumann-Heink

* * *

The family altar has altered many a family!

* * *

Television has offered the brewers a unique advantage. It has opened a vast new market almost untapped — *the American home!*
—*The Reader's Digest*

Illustrations

Home Folks First

Would you like to know how always to say
The pleasantest things in the pleasantest way,
That will bring you friends you will surely need —
Friends that are true in word and deed?
Just try them on the home folks first.

Do you want to know how always to do
The things that politeness requires of you?
For courtesy is the oil, you know,
That makes the wheels of the day's work go —
Just try them on the home folks first.

For home folks are nearest and dearest and best,
And home love is surest to stand every test;
So, if you would know how to do and to say
The pleasantest things in the pleasantest way —
Just try them on the home folks first.
—*Selected*

Home, Sweet Home

Years ago the world-famed opera singer, Jenny Lind, sang in many of the cities of our nation. In Washington, D. C., she sang to many celebrities, including the president, the vice-president, members of the cabinet, and congressmen. She so thrilled her great audience that at the close of the concert the applause was thunderous and she was brought back to the stage for seventeen encore numbers. As she was about to sing her last encore, she chanced to see a man in the gallery whom she recognized as John Howard Payne, the man who wrote "Home, Sweet Home," a song which strikes a responsive chord in hearts around the world. Simply and beautifully Jenny Lind sang that song. The audience was spellbound. Deep emotion brought tears to the eyes of many. At its conclusion, the audience leaped to its feet and applauded uproariously, and hats were thrown into the air. The demonstration lasted for five minutes. Then the audience sensed the fact that the writer of the song was present! Silence suddenly pervaded the scene. All turned and looked with deferential awe at the man in the gallery who had given to the world a song that will last as long as time lasts.

—Told by Billy Graham

* * *

Toy-Strewn Home

Give me the house where the toys are
    strewn,
  Where the dolls are asleep in the
    chairs,
Where the building blocks and the toy
    balloon,
  And the soldiers guard the stairs;
Let me step in the house where the tiny
    cart
  With its horses rules the floor.
And rest comes into my weary heart,
  For I am at home once more.

Give me the house where the toys are
    about,
  With the battered old train of cars,
The box of paints and the books left out,
  And the ship with the broken spars;
Let me step in a house at the close of
    day
  That is littered with children's toys,
And dream once more in the haunts of
    play
  With the echoes of bygone noise.

Whoever has lived in a toy-strewn house,
  Though feeble he be and gray,
Will yearn, no matter how far he roam,
  For the glorious disarray
Of the little home with its toy-strewn
    floor
  That was his in the bygone days,
And his heart will throb as it throbbed
    before
  When he rests where a baby plays.

—Edgar Guest

* * *

Smiles at Church — Frowns at Home

Home is the place where we should shine most brightly for the Lord. The Bible says, "Learn first to shew piety at home" (I Tim. 5:4). Some people are all smiles at church, and gloomy and grouchy at home. "I like to go there," said Robert when he returned from a visit to a cousin's home. "Why?" he was asked. "Aunt Emma's home is just a plain cottage. The furniture is old and the carpet is badly worn." Robert

thought for a moment, and then said, "I guess it is because everybody there is kind, loving, and helpful to everybody else, and nobody scolds or says mean things to anybody!" —W. B. K.

* * *

Those We Love

They say the world is round — and yet
  I often think it's square,
So many little hurts we get
  From corners, here and there.
But there's one truth in life I've found
  While journeying East and West:
The only folks we really wound
  Are those we love the best.
We flatter those we scarcely know;
  We please the fleeting guest,
And deal full many a thoughtless blow
  To those we love the best.

—*Selected*

* * *

Non-Churchgoing Parents

Two condemned murderers were recently executed in the State of Utah. On the night of their execution they made public statements: "The principal cause for our failure in life was the lack of religious training in the home. We do not protest against the forfeiture of our lives. We are guilty of a most serious crime. For the sake of the record, however, we must say that we both came from broken homes. We grew up in neglect. We were left to shift for ourselves. We had no parental care, affection and guidance. Religious training would have pointed us in the right direction. But godless, non-churchgoing parents led us away from Sunday school and the church. While in prison, we have tried to build up in our souls what was lacking — vital faith in God and forgiveness of our great sin by the Saviour. This enables us to accept our punishment with trustful resignation!" —W. B. K.

* * *

A Crime Educational Center

A labor union in Chicago has issued a pamphlet — *Crusade for Children* — in which the union calls upon churches of all denominations to "drive completely from American homes the education in crime being given children through the medium of radio and television."

The pamphlet states further: "On nation-wide networks, millions of dollars are spent to bring into American homes, 365 days of the year, every known trick of the criminal — methods of robbing, hijacking, burglarizing and killing. These abominable crime stories, viewed by our nation's youngsters, serve as a crime educational center for the youthful mind." —*Herald of His Coming*

* * *

Do I Look Like a Henpecked Fellow?

A bachelor, well advanced in years, was greeted at the close of a service by the aged minister. He was a stranger to the pastor. In the course of the conversation the minister asked, "Are you married?" Jokingly the bachelor replied, "Do I look like a henpecked fellow? No, I'm not married. I'm my own boss!" Seriously, the minister said, "I am sorry to hear that, Sir, for you are showing contempt for a divine institution!" Later, the bachelor said to a friend, "I didn't know whether the minister was engaging in a mild form of good humor, or whether he was rebuking me!" —W. B. K.

* * *

Are There Scriptural Grounds for a Divorce?

A young couple married just before the husband went overseas. During his absence his wife was unfaithful to him. She requested her husband to get a divorce. He did. Now he has met a fine Christian girl. They are considering marriage. But can he remarry and be true to Scripture? In commenting, Dr. V. Raymond Edman said, "Bible-believing Christians disagree on Scriptural grounds regarding this problem. . . . If one uses only Mark 10:11 there seems little ground for divorce, and no right for the innocent party to remarry. However, if one takes all the Scriptures on the subject, the result is different, I am sure (cf. Matt. 19:9). It does seem that the returned soldier had Scriptural grounds for divorce, and therefore is free to marry in the Lord." —W. B. K.

* * *

What? No Family Spats?

"Is there a husband here who has never had a quarrel with his wife? If

there is, I want that man to stand," said Sam Jones in one of his meetings. Silence pervaded the audience. The male portion of the audience sat motionless. Finally one man stood. With a humorous gesture, Jones said: "Look at the biggest prevaricator in the community!"

There are times *in every home* when tempers become short and hasty words fly. This shouldn't happen, however, and it should be our *fixed* purpose to obey the injunction: "Learn first to shew piety at home" (I Tim. 5:4).
—Rev. T. W. Callaway, D.D.

* * *

To Be Noted on a Blueprint

It takes a heap of thinking
  To plan a house for two.
It takes a heap of money
  To see the project through.
It takes a heap of flooring
  To cover rooms and halls,
It takes a heap of plaster
  To smooth its many walls.
It takes a heap of labor
  And many pounds of nails;
And yet it's worth the watching
  And waiting it entails,
For when a house is finished,
  From cornerstone to dome,
It takes but happy heartbeats
  To change it to a home.
—William W. Pratt

* * *

Cumbered with Serving

Curtains fresh and snowy-crisp,
Hearthstone swept of every wisp,
Floors immaculate and shining,
Voice irascible and whining,
Puckered brow and fretful lips,
Eyes that witness joy's eclipse,
Color-blind to all but gray.
Pity that she can't one day
Leave untidy some top shelf,
While she renovates herself!
—*Selected*

* * *

A Godly Minister Gave Advice

A godly old minister, after he performed a marriage ceremony, always gave advice to the bride and groom. Some of his church officials thought he ought to discontinue the custom. One said, "It is too old-fashioned." But the chairman of the board said, "Our pastor performed our wedding ceremony twenty years ago. I didn't know the Lord then, but because of a searching question he asked me: 'Have you invited the Lord Jesus to be a guest at your wedding and bless your home?' I asked the Saviour to come into my heart and abide there! If Christian counsel was needed twenty years ago, it is more greatly needed today!" —*The Sunday School Times*

* * *

Neither Bid Him God Speed

Two callers stood at the door of a faithful Christian who recognized them as representatives of a false religion. "May we come in?" they asked. "No!" said the Christian, "I have tried to help others of your sect, but they just heckled and ridiculed me." They said, "If you will let us come in, we will not interrupt you as you talk." When seated, the Christian asked, "Do you believe that the Lord Jesus Christ was the Son of God?" "Yes, we believe that Jesus was *a* Son of God." Instantly, the Christian turned to the following verses in his Bible and read them slowly and prayerfully: "For many deceivers are entered into the world, who confess not that Jesus Christ is come in the flesh. This is a deceiver and. . . . If there come any unto you, and bring not this doctrine, receive him not into your house, neither bid him God speed" (II John 1:7, 10). In an awed voice, the zealous callers asked, "Do you wish us to leave?" "Yes!" was the short reply.

The Christian then knelt and prayed, "Father, forgive me. I received in my home those who do not believe that Thy Son was God manifested in the flesh!" —W. B. K.

* * *

A Second Honeymoon

A young couple came to a minister to get married. The minister, in keeping with his unvarying custom, asked, "Have either of you, or both of you, ever been married before, and, if so, how was the marriage tie broken?" "Yes," they both replied, "we have been married before, and were divorced." The minister said, "I am sorry, but I am unable to marry you." Then they said, "We have both been married before and were legally separated, but *we were married*

to *each other!* When we were married, we were both unsaved. Now we are Christians! We love each other devotedly! We want to retie the broken chord, establish a Christian home, and rear our dear little child for God!"

How happy the minister was to reunite a family which had been sundered by the evil of divorce!

—Told by Rev. Norman B. Jerome

* * *

God Bless My Kitchen

God bless my little kitchen,
I love its every nook;
And bless me as I do my work —
Wash pots and pans, and cook.

And may the meals that I prepare
Be seasoned from above
With Thy blessing and Thy grace,
But most of all, Thy love.

As we partake of earthly food
When the table for us is spread,
We'll not forget to thank Thee, Lord,
Who gives us daily bread.

So bless my little kitchen, God,
And those who enter in;
May they find naught but joy and peace
And happiness therein.

—*Selected*

* * *

Glamorized Vice Enters Homes!

One evening a family sat talking together. They heard a gentle rapping. Thinking that someone was knocking at the door, they opened it. No one was there, however. They listened more closely and learned that the sound was coming from somewhere in the house. With difficulty they located the noise. A picture of Christ hung in one of the rooms. An electric fan was blowing a stream of air against it. Intermittently the picture struck the wall and produced the gentle rapping.

Think of it! A picture of Christ upset a household!

Does not Christ often upset and disturb households where He is supposed to be a welcomed Guest? How many households need to be upset by Christ! Does Christ see things in our homes which dishonor Him? Does He see things which undermine the morals of our youths and blunt the sensibility which we formerly had toward evil? Too often, glamorized vice comes into our homes via radio and television.

—W. B. K.

* * *

Home Sweet Home

Happy the home when God is there,
  And love fills every breast:
When one their wish, one their prayer,
  And one their heavenly rest.

Happy the home where Jesus' name
  Is sweet to every ear;
Where children early lisp His fame
  And parents hold Him dear.

Happy the home where prayer is heard,
  And praise is wont to rise;
Where parents love the sacred Word,
  And live but for the skies.

Lord, let us in our homes agree,
  This blessed home to gain;
Unite our hearts in love to thee,
  And love to all will reign.

—*Selected*

* * *

God Absent From Family Circle

Today, too many homes have lost touch with religion. The failure to provide sympathetic guidance for the nation's youth has been most marked. The rampage of juvenile delinquency, the high incidence of crime across the nation, is a disgraceful reflection on the abdication of parent responsibility. God must be brought back into the family circle. He must become an integral part of everyday life, the unseen hand which guides the footsteps of a Christian society. —J. Edgar Hoover in *Action*

* * *

The Child in the Godless Home

Think of your child in his Christian
  home,
See him in prayer at your knees;
Then think of the child in the godless
  home,
What manner of chance has he?

What chance to learn why the Saviour
  died,
And why His blood was shed;
Will he only learn salvation's plan
Too late, when he is dead?

"As the twig is bent the tree inclines,"
A child is a tender plant,
And a child needs God as a flower needs
  light,
And a soul can die from want.

"Suffer the children to come unto Me!"
"Dear Saviour, can there be
A greater service, a sweeter task,
Than to bring a child to Thee?"

—Martha Snell Nicholson

HONESTY—DISHONESTY

Short Quotes

It is not what you say that counts,
  Nor merely what you do;
Your words may all seem genuine,
  Your works be not a few;
Yet, after all, God looks within,
  And sees the inner "you."
Your doctrine may be error free,
  Your creed be all so true;
Yet God looks past all these to see
  If you, yourself, are true.

—R. E. Neighbour

* * *

Much may be known of a man's character by what excites his laughter.

—Goethe

This above all: to thine own self be true, and it must follow as the night the day, thou canst not then be false to any man. —Shakespeare

* * *

In thy face I see the map of honor, truth and loyalty. —Shakespeare

* * *

A young man was telling his friend about a dishonest thing he had done. He said to the friend, "Of course I know that it was not exactly straight, but ...." Said the friend, "In other words, it was *crooked!*" Then the self-excusing, dishonest young man said, "Well, I wouldn't want to call it crooked, but it wasn't exactly *straight!*" "Remember this," replied his friend, "a line is either straight, or it is crooked. If it is not *exactly* straight, it is crooked. Remember also that 'ill-gotten gain never prospers'!" —W. B. K.

* * *

It is better to lose with a conscience clean
Than to win with a trick unfair;
It is better to fail, and to know you've been,
Whatever the prize was, square
Than to claim the joy of a far-off goal
And the cheer of the standers-by,
And to know down deep in your inmost soul
A cheat you must live and die.

* * *

A young attorney was just beginning his practice of law. He saw what he thought was a prospective client coming toward his office. Hastily he lifted the telephone receiver from its cradle and said, "No, no, I couldn't undertake the case for less than $5000!" He put the receiver down just as the man entered the office. "What can I do for you?" asked the young lawyer. "Oh, nothing, Sir. I just came to connect up your telephone!" —W. B. K.

* * *

Cheating is so prevalent in U. S. schools and colleges that the cheater seems almost to be the normal college student. So widespread is the practice of cribbing that many students do not look upon it as being morally wrong. They call it "The Good Neighbor Policy" or "The Wandering Eye." —*Newsweek*

* * *

One thing which we can and ought to keep after giving it is our word.
—W. B. K.

Illustrations

Efficiency of a Cape Canaveral Count-Down

I asked Billy Graham, "What do you consider the most important thing in life?"

"Integrity," he flashed.

"Suppose," I said, "you could choose between a billion-dollar gift to spend for Christian causes; Khrushchev's conversion to Jesus Christ; or an open door to evangelize the Communist world — which would you take?"

"Still integrity!" he insisted.

I believe the Gospel allows no other answer. It salutes integrity with the efficiency of a Cape Canaveral countdown. That is why men who really know the power of the Gospel are devotees of moral soundness.
—Dr. Carl F. H. Henry

* * *

It Worked

Clem Pizzutelli was a grocer. He trusted many of the townspeople, including some churchgoers. The failure of some to pay up their accounts of long standing threatened the grocer's continuance in business. "How can I pay my creditors if the people I have trusted do not pay me?" he thought. A novel idea came to him. He wrote the following ominous message on the bulletin board in front of his store: "On this bulletin board, thirty days from now, will appear the names of all persons who have been indebted to me for one year or more and who, after repeated requests, have refused to pay! Some have told me that they are unable to pay, but they are able to build homes, drive cars, and have other things that I could have if I had the money due me. I hope I don't have to put any names on the board, but I won't be put off any longer!" Results followed immediately. Many paid their old accounts while others promised to do so on the next payday! —W. B. K.

* * *

A Practical Sermon Preached

Before leaving Japan for a much needed furlough, some missionaries stopped at a gift shop to buy some presents for friends and relatives at home. The shopkeeper, a Japanese, spoke good English. He asked, "Shall I make a true bill for you to pay me, and another one for half the value for you to show the customs officer when you reach San Francisco?" The missionaries said, "We are Christian missionaries!" "I humbly beg your pardon," said the shopkeeper. "I know that Christians are truthful, but American tourists often ask me to do this. I thought you were tourists!" What a mighty and practical sermon those missionaries preached! —W. B. K.

* * *

I Was Slapped in the Face!

A certain farmer lived a defeated, joyless life. "Whenever I knelt to pray, a dishonest thing I had done would slap me in the face," he said. He had bought some hay from a neighboring farmer. Before he paid for it, the neighbor died. He went to the administrator of the decedent's estate and asked, "Have you an account against me?" "There is nothing in the records against you," he was told. For a while he dismissed the debt from his mind. As time passed, however, a shadow came over his life. He made no progress in his spiritual life. God convicted him of his dishonesty. After a sleepless night he said, "I am going to the widow, confess my sin, and pay the account in full with interest!" In getting right with another, he got right with himself and with God. And new joy and power came to him. —W. B. K.

* * *

Non-Debt-Paying Churchmen

'Twas the young minister's first pastorate. He was filled with zeal for the unsaved ones. Among those about whom he was deeply burdened was the druggist of the little town. Going to the drugstore one day, the minister, after the usual exchange of greetings, began to talk to the druggist about his soul and his need of the Saviour. The man listened respectfully, in silence. Then he took the pastor to his office in the rear of the store. There he began to shift the leaves of his ledger. Coming to a certain account, the druggist asked the minister, "Do you know that man?" "Why, yes," replied the minister. "Do you see how long this account has been unpaid?" "I do," said the pastor. Then he continued, "Is that man able to pay

this account?" "Why, yes, that man is a prosperous member of my church. I can't understand," said the pastor hesitantly. Coming to another account, the same conversation ensued between pastor and druggist. Two professing Christians, both non-debt-paying, were blocking the road to heaven for the unsaved druggist. The young minister stood speechless for a moment; then he walked dejectedly from the store. —W. B. K.

* * *

Diminishing Returns

A baker living in a village not far from Quebec bought his butter from a neighboring farmer. One day he became suspicious that the butter was not the same weight, and therefore decided to satisfy himself about it. For several days he weighed the butter, and then found that the rolls of butter that the farmer brought were diminishing in weight. This so angered him that he had the farmer arrested. "I assume you have weights," said the judge. "No, Sir," replied the farmer. "How then do you manage to weigh the butter that you sell?" "That's easily explained, Your Honor," said the farmer. "When the baker began buying his butter from me, I thought I'd get my bread from him, and it's the one-pound loaf I've been using as a weight for the butter I sell. If the weight of the butter is wrong, he has himself to blame."
—*Sunday School Chronicle*

* * *

Why He Was So Particular

An aged Christian man who mended umbrellas knocked at my back door. "Have you any umbrellas which need fixing?" he asked. "Yes," I replied, as I went for my umbrella whose cover was torn and whose ribs were broken. The old man sat on the steps and carefully removed the torn cloth. With equal care he measured the new cloth and repaired the broken ribs. I was fascinated in observing how he put his best effort into the task, and commented, "You seem most careful in your work." "Yes," he said as a smile came on his wrinkled face. "I try to do the best possible work." "But your customers would not know the difference until you

were gone. Perhaps you expect to come back this way again someday," I suggested. "No," said the old man, "I will probably never come this way again." Sensing greatness of character in the old man, and wanting him to disclose it, I asked, "Then why are you so particular to do the best work?" Said he, "So it will be easier for the man who follows me! If I do shoddy, bad work, my customers will soon find it out, and the next mender of umbrellas who comes along will get the cold shoulder!"
—Told by Dr. Harry A. Ironside

* * *

Character Cannot Be Bought

King Edward III of England wanted a governess for his children. A Scottish lady of integrity and character was recommended to him. The king offered her the position. She modestly declined his offer. "Royal children need a much more learned person than I am," she said. The king, however, refused her declination, saying, "Madam, I wish you to accept the position because you are an honest, good woman. I can employ others who are possibly better prepared scholastically than you, but I cannot buy integrity and honesty."
—*Southport Methodist*

* * *

Measuring One's Integrity

One's character is as good as the number of persons whose lives are enriched by one's action; the length of time the good influence of one's actions continues; the importance for human welfare of the issues or problems in which one is actively interested; the proportion of one's life — time, energy, thought, work — which one gives to the struggle to find a solution to these problems; the eagerness with which one seeks to gain sound judgment from the experiences of others throughout history; and the extent to which one seeks to gain strength by allying himself with the great forces of God.
—Bishop C. C. Selecman

* * *

Half-Truths May Work Havoc

An overstatement or an understatement may create a false inference. A

half-truth, with essential facts left out, may work more havoc than a whole lie.

A mate on a sailing vessel got drunk. The captain entered in the log: "Mate drunk today." The mate pleaded with the captain, "This is my first offense. Unless you put the whole truth, telling of my usual sobriety, it will cost me my post." The captain was obdurate and would not change the entry. Some days later, the mate was keeping the log. Among other entries, he made this one: "Captain sober today." The captain fumed when he read the entry. "That entry," he protested, "will create a false impression in the minds of the owners of the vessel. They'll conclude that it is an unusual thing for me to be sober!" This time the mate was obdurate and said, "It is a true fact, and it stays in the log!" Though a statement may be accurate, if it misrepresents the circumstances it is, in essence, lying. —W. B. K.

* * *

Only Six Feet of Terra Firma Needed

A conscientious Christian was transacting some business with a clever lawyer. The Christian's scrupulous honesty in his dealings with others was reflected in his instruction to the lawyer to use no weasel words in certain legal documents he had him draw up for him that might be advantageous to himself but to the disadvantage of others. "Man," said the lawyer, "if you are so particular about that, you will never possess much of this world." Said the Christian, "Six feet of it will be all I will need when I come to the end of life's journey!"

The shrewd lawyer made no reply for a moment. Then he said, "I guess you are right." —W. B. K.

* * *

A Father's Honesty

I read somewhere of a family who lived on the prairie. They were very poor. The boy in the home was ashamed to take his lunch out at school. He never had cakes, jam tarts, or extras. On one occasion a man called at the farm and offered a high price for the horse standing in the barnyard. The boy chuckled with delight at the thought

of what a difference it would make to
his daily lunch, as well as in other ways,
if such a large amount of money came
into the home. However, that boy's
father was honest. He knew there was
something wrong with the horse and
that it was not worth the large amount
offered. To the boy's amazement and
bitter disappointment he heard his
father refuse the offer. Later that boy
marveled at the honesty of his father,
who accepted his poverty rather than
trying to get rich quick — with a guilty
conscience. It was that one act of his
own father that lived over and over
again in the boy's mind and heart, and
held him to the path of rectitude. God
honored that father's testimony in the
lifelong honesty and uprightness of his
own son.   —Dr. J. B. Rowell in
The Sunday School Times

* * *

Noble Men

Men are noble when they're godly,
  When they're patient, kind and true;
Noble when they bless their fellows
  From the pulpit and the pew;
Noble when they walk uprightly
  As they journey on life's way;
Noble in their homes and nation
  When they worship God and pray.

Men are noble when they're honest,
  Never stooping to the wrong;
Noble when they're clean in spirit,
  And in manhood great and strong;
Noble when they're full of mercy
  Toward the downcast and the weak;
When they're filled with Christian
    graces,
  Tenderhearted, gentle, meek.

Men are noble when they're spotless
  In their character and name;
Noble when they love their fellows
  More than riches, honor, fame;
Noble when their deep affections
  Are upon the things above;
When they're looking up to heaven,
  Filled with God's eternal love.
    —W. E. Isenhour

I'na Trust Ye!

There was a time in Scotland when
in some communities one's word of hon-
or was all that was required to borrow
money or consummate business agreements. A farmer moved away from
such a community to another where
business transactions were consummated
by written contracts. Years later, the
farmer moved back to his old community. Needing money, he asked an old
acquaintance to lend it. When the
latter gave him the money the farmer
handed the lender a promissory note.
"What's this?" he asked. "It's a promissory note, binding me to return the
loan with interest when it matures,"
said the borrower. "My man, if ye
canna trust yoursel', I'na trust ye. Ye
canne hae my money. Give it to me!"
"But, Sir, I might die, and my sons
might refuse it to ye, but a bit of paper
might compel them." "Compel them
to sustain their dead father's honor,
and do the right and honest thing? If
this is the road ye're leading them, ye
can gang elsewhere for money," said the
incensed, honest Celt. —W. B. K.

* * *

No Double-Dealing

When a young man, R. G. (Bob) Le
Tourneau worked in a garage. The
owner of a fine car regularly brought
his car there to be serviced. Suddenly
he stopped coming. "I believe he's taking his car to my competitor," said the
boss to young LeTourneau. "Go there
under some pretext and see if it's so."
It was there. Then the owner of the
car said to him, "Don't tell your boss
my car is here." Bob said, "Okay."
"Did you see the car, Bob?" asked his
employer. Bob stalled and answered
evasively. But instantly God convicted
him of double-dealing. He knew that
a Christian cannot serve two masters.
He at once put the situation in the clear
both with the former customer and his
employer. —W. B. K.

HUMILITY
Short Quotes

Here is the path to the higher life: Down, lower down! This was what Jesus taught His disciples when they were thinking of being great in the kingdom. Do not seek or ask for exaltation — that is God's work. Let us take no place before God or man but that of a servant. —Andrew Murray

* * *

The Messiah was superbly rendered by an orchestra, chorus, and soloists while its composer, Handel, was present. At the conclusion of the performance there was thunderous applause and all eyes turned toward Handel! He, however, stood up and pointed heavenward. This was his way of saying, "To God be the glory!" —W. B. K.

* * *

There is a church in Palestine the doorway of which is so low that one must stoop to enter it. This was to prevent medieval raiders from riding their horses into the church and disrupting the worship. The door is called "Humility Gate." —W. B. K.

* * *

Just as water seeks to fill the lowest places, so God fills you with His glory and power when He finds you empty and abased. —Andrew Murray

* * *

Humility is not thinking meanly of oneself. It is not thinking of self at all. —W. B. K.

Few of us are big enough to become little enough to be used of God: "Not many wise . . . mighty . . . noble are called" (I Cor. 1:26).
—Rev. Vance Havner

* * *

He that is down need fear no fall,
He that is low, no pride,
He that is humble, ever shall
Have God to be his guide.
—Bunyan

* * *

In a class in homiletics in a theological school different students would preach their sermons before the class. After the sermon, the student would go into the office of the professor who would criticize it and offer suggestions. One day the saintly professor said to a student, "The sermon you gave yesterday was mighty fine. The truth you dealt with was well arranged and well presented. But your sermon had one omission — a grave one, too. There was no word in it for a poor sinner like me!"
—W. B. K.

* * *

The lovely things are quiet things:
Soft-falling snow
And feathers dropped from flying wings
Make no sound as they go;
And petals loosened from a rose
Quietly seek the ground,
And love, if lovely, when it goes,
Goes without a sound!

Illustrations

Sit Down, General Washington!

After America had won its freedom from England under the brave leadership of George Washington, the Speaker of the House of Burgesses extolled Washington for his courage and sacrifice. Washington at the conclusion of the speaker's eulogy stood up to make some response. He was overcome with confusion and modesty. His face flushed a deep red and he could not say a word. Instead of being proud, he was humbled by the gracious words of the Speaker. Said the Speaker, "Sit down, General Washington! Your modesty and humility are equal to your valor, and that surpasses the power of language I possess." —W. B. K.

* * *

Not from Me — from Heaven!

In 1808 Haydn's *Creation* was rendered in Vienna when its composer was present. He was so feeble, however, that he had to be wheeled into the theater in an invalid's chair. His presence thrilled the great audience so that it could not suppress its enthusiasm when the chorus and orchestra came gloriously and in full power to the passage: "And there was light!" All eyes were upon Haydn. With great effort, he stood up and with all the strength he could muster he exclaimed: "No! No! Not from me, but from heaven above comes all!" When he had ascribed all glory to God, he sank, exhausted, in his chair, and had to be carried out of the theater.

"If ye will not . . . give glory unto my name . . . I will even send a curse upon you, and I will curse your blessings" (Mal. 2:2). —W. B. K.

* * *

No Gentleman Would Do Such Lowly Work!

Hsu Chu came from a wealthy Chinese family. He entered the China Inland Mission Hospital to be trained as a nurse. He dressed immaculately. One day he was asked to perform a menial service — clean and shine some shoes. He felt insulted and refused. "No gentleman or scholar would do such lowly work," he said. The superintendent of the hospital took the shoes and shined them. Hsu Chu looked on with mingled feelings. "Come with me to my office," said the superintendent. Then he asked Hsu Chu to read the thirteenth chapter of John. His eyes filled with tears as he read the verse: "If I then, your Lord and Master, have washed your feet; ye also ought to wash one another's feet" (John 13:14). "May Jesus for-

give me," he prayed. Thereafter no one scrubbed floors, washed dishes, shined shoes, or did other lowly tasks more joyfully than Hsu Chu. —W. B. K.

* * *

You Blacked My Shoes!

"Do you remember me?" asked a prisoner of a minister who passed his cell. Before the minister could reply, the prisoner continued: "I remember you! You got me out of one of the 'dives' in New York City. You gave me a letter to a mission where I could find shelter. Before we parted, you got some clothes for me. I was shivering with delirium tremens, and couldn't dress myself. So you dressed me. And there was one thing more. After you dressed me, you said, 'You want to look nice from head to toe, so I'll shine your shoes!' This you did! I do not recall what you said about Christ. I did not want to be better. I did not go to the mission for lodging. I didn't want your religion, but to think that you cared enough for my soul to black my shoes — that has followed me ever since. I believe God has caused our paths to cross again. I have come to the end of myself, and I am now ready to give my life to the One whose love caused you, an honored minister, to perform that humble service on the night I first saw you!"

Soon a "new name was written down in glory," and there was rejoicing in the presence of the angels of God because a sinner had repented, being led ultimately to godly sorrow because a minister was humble enough for God to use him! —W. B. K.

HYPOCRISY

Short Quotes

We can be right without being self-righteous.
—General Dwight D. Eisenhower

* * *

Cromwell said to Fairfax as they rode through a cheering throng, "They would turn out with the same enthusiasm to see me hanged!" —W. B. K.

The people to fear are not those who disagree with you, but those who disagree with you and are too cowardly to let you know it. —Napoleon

* * *

"In every excavation in Palestine where we have opened up the remains of an Israelitish civilization, we have found figures of the goddess of love, and in almost every house we have found figures of Astarte, the most firmly believed in and abjectly loved goddess among all ancient deities," said Dr. Nelson Glueck.

In their hearts, the nation spurned the love and mercy of God. Outwardly they slavishly adhered to empty religious ritual.

* * *

Unless piety stems from inward righteousness it will degenerate into an outward form of religion, worn only on the sleeve for effect, with long-facedness being an ever-attendant characteristic. —W. B. K.

* * *

Righteousness without genuine love for God and others will soon degenerate into self-righteousness. —W. B. K.

* * *

Some people are so heavenly that they're no earthly use.
—Rev. J. Vance Havner

* * *

How guilty many are of singing in church words which they do not mean, words which are greatly at variance with their lives. Many sing, "I love

to tell the story," but in their contacts with non-Christians they are as silent as a sphinx about Jesus. Many sing, "Take my silver and my gold, not a mite would I withhold," while they covetously and tenaciously cling to their dollars. Many sing, "O for a thousand tongues to sing, my great Redeemer's praise," but they are not using the *one tongue* they do have to sing and speak forth His praise. How displeasing to God is mere lip service!
—W. B. K.

* * *

The meanest and most contemptible kind of praise is that which first speaks well of a man, and then qualifies it with a "but!" —Henry Ward Beecher

* * *

Hypocrites do the devil's drudgery in Christ's livery. —Matthew Henry

* * *

I do not know of anything more dreadful than to be fattened *without* and to be starved *within;* to have everything that heart could wish for, and yet not have the best thing that the heart ought to wish for. May God save us from that *appearance* of prosperity which is only a veiled desolation! —Spurgeon

Illustrations

Straight Mouths and Crooked Hearts

There are many words which cause Bible translators difficulty when translating them into the languages of tribes and nations. There is one word, however, which presents no difficulty to the translators, and that word is hypocrisy. Hypocrisy is a universal sin. The hypocrite is found everywhere. The Indian tribes in Latin America have various ways to denote the hypocrite. They designate him as "a man with two faces," "a man with two hearts," "a man with two kinds of talk," "a two-headed man," "a forked-tongue person," "a two-sided man," and "a man with a straight mouth and a crooked heart!" —W. B. K.

* * *

Don't Do It, Lord, She Leaks!

In every community there are those who are notorious for the on-and-off

manner in which they serve the Lord. In a small town, there was such a character, a woman whose life was at great variance with her high-sounding, empty professions of religion. She was always present during the annual "protracted meeting" — so they are called in some sections of the South — but absent the rest of the time. One spring, at the revival meeting, the spiritual tempo was rising. At the altar of prayer were some genuine seekers for God. The woman, too, knelt there and said, "Fill me with Thy Spirit, O Lord!" One who knew her well cried out, "O, Lord, don't do it! She leaks!"

We do not advocate rudeness of speech, but there are times when God seems to use plain words. There were times when the Lord Jesus "took the gloves off," so to speak, and denounced the sin of hypocrisy. —W. B. K.

Singing a Lie!

Two young ladies sang beautifully in a well-attended meeting. The theme of their song was the preciousness of Jesus to them and their utter dedication to Him. A minister from England listened with admiration to their beautiful singing. But as he listened, somehow he felt that the young ladies were singing only with their lips and not from their hearts. So convinced was he that his impressions were from God that at the close of the service he engaged the young ladies in loving and earnest conversation. He spoke searchingly to the hearts of those young ladies until finally they broke down and confessed that they were singing for self-glory and the praise of man. Then and there they were delivered from the deadly sin of taking emptily, or vainly, things sacred upon their lips! May we be prevented from singing, "Take my life and let it be, consecrated, Lord, to Thee," when we don't mean it! —W. B. K.

* * *

Only the Valuable Is Counterfeited

Only that which is genuine is counterfeited. As a boy in the South, I saw boxes filled with worthless Confederate currency. No one counterfeited it. As a chaplain in the U. S. penitentiary at Lewisburg, Pa., I knew some who had counterfeited U. S. currency. Christianity is genuine and invaluable. For gain, it has been counterfeited, cluttered up with "curious arts" and meaningless ritual. Blessed are God's children who can discern between the true and the false. —W. B. K.

* * *

You Can't Fool God

You can fool the hapless public,
  You can be a subtle fraud,
You can hide your little meanness,
  But you can't fool God!
You can advertise your virtues,
  You can self-achievement laud,
You can load yourself with riches,
  But you can't fool God!

You can criticize the Bible,
  You can be a selfish clod,
You can lie, swear, drink, and gamble,
  But you can't fool God!

You can magnify your talent,
  You can hear the world applaud,
You can boast yourself somebody,
  But you can't fool God!
      —Grenville Kleiser

INFLUENCE

Short Quotes
(See also: Christian Example)

A press correspondent entered a small restaurant in a European village. Later a group of workmen entered for their noonday meal. Immediately a delicate odor of perfume permeated the room. After the men left, the correspondent asked the proprietor, "Who were those men?" "They are workmen from a perfume factory nearby. They bring the perfume with them!" was the reply. Shouldn't God's children, too, "manifest the savour of (Christ's) knowledge . . . in every place" (II Cor. 2:14)?
      —W. B. K.

* * *

Dr. Shepard was a medical missionary who died in World War I in Asiatic Turkey where he labored long and faithfully. He died of typhus fever while caring for Armenians who were stricken with the disease. Many of them often said: "We have not seen Jesus Himself but we have seen Him in Dr. Shepard!"
      —W. B. K.

* * *

On a bronze tablet in Bethany Church, Philadelphia, are these words: "In loving memory of John Wanamaker — founder — By reason of him many went away and believed on Jesus."

* * *

If you are a Christian in small things, you are not a small Christian.
      —W. B. K.

So live that people who remember you will also remember Jesus Christ.

* * *

A character stripped of its helpful influence becomes not merely negative as to good, but positive as to evil.
—*Choice Gleanings Calendar*

* * *

In 1828 Franz Schubert was in the midst of his greatest work when suddenly he died. But today the world still stands in reverence and adoration when the violins and the organ and the harps and the flutes move into *The Unfinished Symphony!* "He being dead yet speaketh" (Heb. 11:4).
—Dr. L. D. Newton, in
The Mercerian

* * *

"Bury my influence with me," remorsefully pleaded a dying young man who had made a sordid mess of his life. But that is not possible. One's influence, for weal or woe, is as undying as one's soul: "Abel offered unto God a more excellent sacrifice . . . by it he being dead yet speaketh" (Heb. 11:4).
—W. B. K.

* * *

"It wasn't Livingstone's preaching that converted me," said Stanley, "it was Livingstone's living!"

* * *

A young man was summoned before the official church board for selling liquor. "It is true that I did sell liquor," he confessed, "but I did not know that it was any more wrong to *sell* it than it is to *buy* it, and I know I have sold some to several of the men in this room!" —W. B. K.

* * *

A father was one day teaching his little boy what a Christian is. When the lesson was finished, the father got a stab he never forgot. The boy asked, "Daddy, have I ever seen a Christian?"
—W. B. K.

Illustrations

Cork Moves Steel Bar

In a gun factory, an elongated bar of steel, which weighed five hundred pounds, was suspended vertically by a chain. Near it, an average-size cork was suspended by a silk thread. "You will see something shortly which is seemingly impossible," said an attendant to a group of sight-seers. "This cork is going to set this steel bar in motion!" The cork was swung gently against the steel bar which remained motionless. For ten minutes the cork, with pendulum-like regularity, struck the iron bar. Then the bar vibrated slightly. At the end of an hour, the great bar was swinging like the pendulum of a clock!

Many of God's children feel that they are not exerting a feather's weight of influence upon others, or making a dent in the bastions of evil. Not so. How powerful is the cumulative influence for good which emanates from the obscurest of God's children! —W. B. K.

* * *

She Pulled Me Through!

A young man, who had inherited a strong desire for liquor, said, "One night I attended a banquet where liquor was served. The smell of wine was so tempting, I could hardly resist it. But just about the time I began to yield, I heard a young woman say, 'No thank you!' This gave me courage! I watched her all the evening. I said, 'If she drinks, I will!' I was hoping, yet fearing, that she would. But she didn't. As often as she was asked, she refused. She didn't know it, but she pulled me through!"
—*Record of Christian Work*

* * *

An Odour of Sweet Smell!

It was only an earthen vessel of no particular beauty. But all who came near it were charmed by the exquisite, delicate odor emanating from it. Someone asked the potter, "What did you put into the clay you used to mould this vessel to make it so appealing to all who enter your shop?" "Nothing! Nothing at all! I, too, noticed the flowerlike fragrance of the clay from which I wrought the vessel. So I went to the place from where the clay came and there I found a wild rosebush growing. Its petals covered the ground and filled the atmosphere with fragrance. The petals it shed year after year must have given the clay its odor."

We should stay so close to Christ that our daily lives will radiate His grace, goodness and sweetness.

—W. B. K.

* * *

How Christ Is Expressed

Not merely in the words you say,
  Not only in your deeds confessed,
But in the most unconscious way
  Is Christ expressed.

For me 'twas not the truth you taught,
  To you so clear, to me so dim;
But when you came to me you brought
  A sense of Him.

And from your eyes He beckons me,
  And from your heart His love is shed,
Till I lose sight of you and see
  The Christ instead.

—Selected

* * *

Ah, may we join that choir invisible,
Of those immortal dead who live again,
In minds made better by their presence!
Live in deeds of daring rectitude,
In scorn of miserable aims ending in
    self,
In thoughts sublime, which pierce the
    night like stars,
And with their mild persistence,
Urge man's search to vaster issues!
So to live is sublime!"

—George Eliot

* * *

An Alcoholic Woman Transformed

An alcoholic woman was gloriously saved. Later, the pastor called on her husband, wanting to win him, too, to Christ and the church. But the man was very bitter. Contemptuously he said of his wife's conversion, "She'll get over it. She'll go back to drinking again." Six months passed. Then the husband went to see the pastor. He said, "I have read all the leading books on the evidences of Christianity, and I can answer their arguments. But for the past six months I have had an open book before me — my wife, whose life has been utterly changed. I have been wrong. There must be something divine about a religion that can take a

slave to drink, like my wife was, and change her into the loving, patient, prayerful, singing saint that she now is! I, too, want the thing that has worked the miracle in her life!"

—W. B. K.

* * *

He Being Dead Yet Speaketh

Because of his zeal for missions and outspoken advocacy of missions, David Brainerd was expelled from Yale College. He became a missionary to the American Indians. After his death, his diary fell into the hands of William Carey who was so impressed with the life and work of Brainerd that he went as a missionary to India. Of David Brainerd we can say: "He being dead yet speaketh!"

An aged, obscure minister in Scotland prayed earnestly one day that God would cause someone to accept Christ during the service. Someone did accept the Saviour that day — a little boy, Robert Moffat, who became a pioneer missionary to South Africa. When Moffat came home, years later, on a furlough, a young student, David Livingstone, heard him lecture and dedicated himself to God to go as a missionary to Africa. Another student, Mackay, read Moffat's life story and went to Uganda as a missionary! Of these mighty servants of God, we can say: "They being dead yet speak!"

—W. B. K.

* * *

He Lived What He Taught

While giving a challenging message in a Sunday-school conference where many Sunday-school teachers were present, a well-known minister told the following story:

"I was a boy from a broken home. I had a Roman Catholic background. I became a member of a Sunday-school class in which there were thirteen boys. Five of the boys were from broken homes. They knew little of love and kindness. Our teacher was a big man. He wore a size fourteen shoe. There were no discipline problems in that class — we had respect for that large shoe! Our teacher had never gone beyond the sixth grade in school, but he knew the Lord and he loved the boys in his class. He gave me love that I had never known before. He played with me and with the other boys. All of the thirteen boys became Christians. Eleven of them entered into full-time Christian service. How great is the influence of the Christian teacher who knows the Lord and who loves the pupils in his or her class!" —Alice M. Knight

* * *

Irresistible Power of a Holy Life

"I want you to teach me your language," said Gordon Maxwell, a mis-

sionary in India, to a Hindu. "No, sahib, I will not teach you my language. You would make me a Christian," said the Hindu. Maxwell replied, "You don't understand me. I am only asking you to teach me your language." Replied the Hindu, "No, sahib, I will not teach you. No man can live with you and not become a Christian!"

Lord Peterborough, a skeptic, spent a night with Fenelon. In the morning he hurried away, saying, "If I spend another night with that man, I shall be a Christian in spite of myself!"
—W. B. K.

INTERCESSION

Illustrations

Here and There

We could not triumph over sin down here if Christ were not living for us up there, and talking to the Father for us: "Wherefore he is able also to save them to the uttermost that come unto God by him, seeing he ever liveth to make intercession for them" (Heb. 7:25). —Rev. Paul Reese, D.D.

* * *

Great and Greater

Talking to men for God is a great thing, but talking to God for men is greater still. One will never talk well and with real success to men for God who has not learned well how to talk for men. —Rev. R. A. Torrey, D.D.

* * *

An Unknown But Mighty Intercessor

An American minister became the pastor of a London church. On the first Sunday there were several converts. He preached with such power he had never before experienced. About a year later, he was called to the bedside of an obscure member of his church who told him the following story:

"I should not tell you, pastor," he said, "but I know that my time is come, and I do not want my work to cease when I go. I passed through a period of rebellion and spiritual darkness because of my poverty and lameness. It

seemed that there was little that I could do for my Master. But God revealed to me that He had given me the privilege of intercession. Saturday night, before you preached your first sermon, I spent all night in prayer for you; and I have done that every Saturday night since. Someone will take up the work that I am about to lay down, surely."

When the weak voice ceased, the pastor knew what had been the secret of his power. —*The Christian Business Men's League Bulletin*

* * *

I'm Sure He Will Be Saved!

At a prayer meeting one night a burdened wife requested those present to intercede for her unsaved husband. "Let's pray right now," said the pastor. It was the husband's custom to call for his wife at the close of prayer service. As he stood near the door, he heard different ones interceding for an unsaved husband. "For whom were they praying?" he asked his wife later. "Oh, it was the husband of one of our workers," she said. "I'm sure he will be saved. God must answer prayers like that," he said. That night the husband was convicted of sin. He awakened his wife, and pleaded, "Pray for me!" He was joyously saved!

One of the greatest of ministries is the ministry of intercessory prayer.

Lord, help me to live from day to day
In such a self-forgetful way,
That even when I kneel to pray,
My prayer may be for others!
                              —W. B. K.

* * *

An Invalid Intercessor

During my pastorate in Orlando,
Florida, one of my most faithful members was a helpless invalid. Lifting
her from the car, the loving husband
would bring her in his arms and place
her in a front pew.

After some years, I left Orlando for
a pastorate elsewhere. Later, I visited
Orlando. Among the first ones I went
to see was my invalid friend. She told
me her cherished secret: "Mr. Knight,
never has there been a day since I first
met you that I have failed to pray for
you. For years I have interceded for
you, calling upon God to protect you and
use you in His service!"

Surely, when God's children appear
before the judgment seat of Christ, His
"well done good and faithful servant"
will also go to an invalid who faithfully
prayed for others. —W. B. K.

* * *

Do It Yourself!

John Hyde, a missionary to India, was
called "Praying Hyde." He was a
mighty intercessor. "How can we enlist a body of intercessors in America?"
asked an American friend. Said Hyde,
"I have tried to enlist intercessors without success. I have found that the *only
way* to get other people to pray is to
do it myself." It is believed that over
100,000 people were saved in the Pun-
jab district alone because of Hyde's
intercession for them!

Make me an intercessor, Lord,
    Hidden, unknown, and apart,
Thought little of by those around,
    But satisfying Thine heart!
                              —W. B. K.

* * *

What Changed Dr. Wilson

After his conversion, Dr. Walter Wilson became a member of the church.
Each night and morning he read in a
desultory way a few verses from the
Bible and prayed for power to live the
Christian life. In time he began to feel
that he was making very little progress.
When he entered college he didn't tell
others that he was a Christian. Then
something happened which proved to
be a great blessing to him. His room-
mate had an almost fatal fall in the
gymnasium. He was taken to his room
in a critical condition. He was bleeding profusely from his nose and mouth.
He whispered, "Wilson, pray for me!"
They were alone. Wilson kneeled down.
He prayed for God to help his friend.
Said Wilson later, "I was surprised to
see the change in him, and still more
surprised at the wonderful change which
took place in me. That faltering prayer
opened to me the whole wide vista of
intercession! I saw that my Christian
faith had languished because I had never
prayed enough for *others*!" —W. B. K.

* * *

Bring Him Hither to Me

A girl became deeply burdened for
her wild, wayward brother. She went
one Sunday morning to church with the
feeling that her deep distress would
make her unfit for the service. A visiting minister occupied the pulpit. He
preached with great feeling on the luna-
tic whom the disciples could not help.
Then he emphasized the request of Jesus,
"Bring him hither to me" (Matt. 17:17).
"Ah," thought the burdened sister, "this
command of Jesus is God's message for
me. In prayer, I'll bring my unsaved
brother to the Saviour. He is now as
accessible as He was in the long ago."
With calmness and confidence she began to talk to Jesus about her brother.
Ere long he was joyously saved and
wonderfully delivered from his sinful,
enslaving habits! —W. B. K.

* * *

Please, Father, for My Sake

During the Civil War, a soldier was
found asleep while on picket duty. He
was sentenced to die. A delegation
appealed to President Lincoln to spare
the soldier's life. Lincoln felt, however,
that the sentence should be carried out
to maintain army morale. As the group
turned sorrowfully away, little Tad
Lincoln, who had been in the room, un-
observed, crept to his father and said,

"Please, father, *for my sake*, don't let them shoot that poor man!" The President could not resist his little son's plea. He reversed his decision and spared the soldier's life!
—Rev. T. W. Callaway, D.D.

JESUS

Short Quotes

We do not know what the future holds, but we know the One who holds the future, the One in whose pierced hands reposes all power in heaven and on earth. —W. B. K.

* * *

"Thou art a teacher come from God," said Nicodemus of Jesus. Jesus was more — He was God come to teach!
—Barnhouse

* * *

The mother of Bernard M. Baruch, adviser to presidents, often attended the services of the Reverends Thomas Dixon and Henry Ward Beecher. Someone asked her, "How is it that you, a Jewess, go into a church where the worship of Christ is a part of the creed?" She replied, "If He was not divine, all His actions, His life, and His death were!"
—W. B. K.

* * *

Joan of Arc was burned at the stake as a witch. As the flames enveloped her she said, "Jesus! Jesus! Jesus!" The passport to heaven is the name "Jesus!" —Dr. George W. Truett

* * *

A young Chinese Christian was traveling from China to America to study at one of the universities. A fellow passenger noticed him reading his Bible on the deck of the ship. He engaged the Chinese in conversation. He spoke disparagingly of the Bible, endeavoring to create doubt in it, adding, "I would not like to disturb your faith in Christ, however." The Chinese replied, "Sir, if you could disturb my faith in Christ He would not be a big enough Saviour for me!" —J. Stuart Holden in *The Alliance Witness*

* * *

God will never be known unless He reveals Himself in human form.
—Zoroaster

I cannot do it alone,
The waves run fast and high,
The fogs close chill around,
And the light goes out in the sky;
But I know that we two shall win in the end —
Jesus and I.

Coward and wayward and weak,
I change with the changing sky,
Today so eager and brave,
Tomorrow not caring to try;
But He never gives in, so we two shall win —
Jesus and I.
—Dan Crawford

* * *

Oh, that someone would arise, man or god, to show us God. —Socrates

* * *

In Stuttgart, Germany, is a famous statue of Christ by Dannecker, inspired by the sculptor's desire to express in a statue the words — "God manifest in the flesh." What an impossible task the sculptor set before him! How can one put love in cold stone? How can one express infinite being in marble? How can one capture the glory of God and congeal it in rock?
—*Christian Victory*

* * *

I know not how that Bethlehem's Babe
Could in the Godhead be,
I only know the manger Child,
Has brought God's love to me!

* * *

He came to bless, He came to give
Eternal life that we might live,
He came His grace on us to pour,
He came that we might sin no more,
Oh, let us bless His wondrous name,
This day our Saviour came!

* * *

Shortly before his death, Charles Darwin, with whom began the theory of organic evolution, said, "I was a young man with unformed ideas. I threw out queries and suggestions. To my astonishment, they took like wildfire!" Later, he suggested to a Christian friend that she speak to the servants, tenants and neighbors. "What shall I speak about?" "Christ Jesus," replied Darwin.

—*The Watchman-Examiner*

* * *

Said Franklin Roosevelt before the 1936 election: "There's one issue in this campaign — it's myself. People must be either for me or against me!"

Concerning our relationship to the Saviour, we are either for Him or we are against Him — "He that is not with me is against me" (Luke 11:23).

* * *

We need an experience of Christ in which we think everything about Christ and not about the experience. We need preachers who shall not keep demanding either a faith or love that we cannot rise to, but shall preach a Christ that produces and compels both.

—Peter T. Forsyth in *Positive Preaching and the Modern Mind*

* * *

Why is He silent when a word,
Would slay His accusers all?
Why does He meekly bear their taunts,
When angels wait His call?
"He was made sin," my sin He bore
Upon the accursed tree,
And sin hath no defense to make,
His silence was for me!

* * *

I cannot conceive that a time will come when the figure of Jesus will no longer be a star of the first magnitude in the spiritual heavens, when He will no longer be regarded as one of the greatest religious heroes and teachers whom the world has seen!

—Claude G. Montefiere, spokesman for English Liberal Judaism

* * *

I am ready to admit after contemplating the world and human nature for sixty years that I see no way out of the world's misery but by the way which would be found by Christ's will.

—George Bernard Shaw

Why talk piously about getting back to Jesus when so few of us have caught up with Him? —W. B. K.

* * *

A careful study of the Scriptures reveals the astounding fact that more than fifty per cent of the record of all that Christ said and did was directed at everyday problems — attitudes, afflictions and the eternal well-being of individuals. His was a *personalized* ministry.

—R. H. Kells

* * *

Exclaimed little four-year-old Terrie, "He is not!" Startled, the mother asked, "He is not what, Terrie?" Terrie replied: "That man on the radio said he was going to sing 'Jesus Is Mine,' and He is not, 'cause Jesus is everybody's!"

—*Contact*

* * *

When Marie Antoinette was on her way to Paris to become queen, orders were given that all sick and infirm ones be kept away from the roads along which she was to pass. How glad we are that no such commands were given when the Lord Jesus passed along any road! The waysides were always thronged with sufferers who came or were brought in the hope that they might be healed. Many of His miracles were performed "as He passed by."

—Harold F. Sayles

* * *

In his book, *When Iron Gates Yield*, Geoffrey Bull speaks of the joy which came to him when he was released from solitary confinement in a Chinese Communist prison where he was kept for months and deprived of all possessions, including his Bible. One day he heard a prisoner in a cell below sing, "Onward Christian Soldiers!" How thrilled he was to hear the name of Jesus. Exultantly, he exclaimed, "Praise the Lord! That's the sweetest sound I've heard during my months of imprisonment. His name shall ever thrill and entrance us!"

—W. B. K.

* * *

At Christ's birth, "the high and mighty were unaware that a miracle was happening beneath their upturned noses!"

—Peter Marshall

I marvel that whereas the ambitious dreams of myself, Caesar, and Alexander should have vanished into thin air, a Judean peasant — Jesus — should be able to stretch His hands across the centuries and control the destinies of men and nations. —Napoleon

* * *

A vessel was wrecked one stormy night off the coast of England. All were drowned except an Irish boy. The waves swept him onto a great rock. In the morning he was rescued. "Lad, didn't you tremble out there on the rock during the night?" "Sure I trembled, but the rock didn't tremble once all night long!"

How safe are God's children on the Rock, Christ Jesus! —W. B. K.

* * *

A burglar broke into a seaside mansion. He put the valuable things he gathered from different rooms on the living-room floor. As he began to put the loot into a bag, he chanced to look up. On the wall above the mantle hung Guido's "Ecce Homo," the painting of the thorn-crowned Christ. The tender, penetrating gaze of Christ caused him to stop bagging the loot. He could not continue his thieving venture until he had turned the face of Christ to the wall. —W. B. K.

* * *

When Henry Drummond rode with a coachman one day, he asked, "Friend, if your team were running away with you, after you had done your best to stop them, what would you do if you suddenly learned that a person was sitting beside you who knew exactly how to control your team and save you from disaster?" The coachman answered, "I'd instantly hand over the reins to him!" Then Mr. Drummond told him about Jesus Christ, and urged him to enthrone Him in his heart, and turn over the reins of his life into His mighty hands. —W. B. K.

Illustrations

Dead Man on a Stick

A South American was asked, "Who is Jesus?" He thought for a moment and then replied, "Jesus is a dead man hanging on a stick!" Had he not all of his life seen statues and paintings of the Saviour writhing in anguish on the cruel cross? His soul was darkened and superstitious. He knew nothing about the triumphant, glorified Lord. He told all he knew when he said, "Jesus is a dead man hanging on a stick!" How desperately do this man and millions of his fellow countrymen need the gospel of God's grace!

High on the front of a massive cathedral in the heart of the Loop in Chicago is a life-size statue of the Saviour, writhing in anguish, with a look of indescribable horror on His soot-begrimmed face! Whenever I look at that sight, a verse from God's Word comes irresistibly to mind: "They crucify to themselves the Son of God afresh, and put him to an open shame" (Heb. 6:6). Do not such representations cause many to think of Jesus as "a dead man hanging on a stick"? —W. B. K.

What Christ Is to Me

What the hand is to the lute,
What the breath is to the flute,
What the fragrance is to the smell,
What the spring is to the well,
What the flower is to the bee —
    That is Jesus Christ for me.

What's the mother to the child,
What's the guide to pathless wild,
What is oil to troubled wave,
What is ransom to the slave,
What is water to the sea —
    That is Jesus Christ to me.

—Spurgeon

* * *

One Solitary Life

Here is a Young Man who was born in an obscure village, the Child of a peasant woman. He grew up in another village. He worked in a carpenter shop until he was thirty, and then for three years He was an itinerant preacher. He never wrote a book. He never held an office. He never owned a home. He never had a family. He never went to college. He never put His foot inside a big city. He never traveled two hundred miles from the place where He was born. He never did one of the things that usually accompany greatness. He had no credentials but Himself.

While He was still a Young Man, the tide of public opinion turned against Him. His friends ran away. He was turned over to His enemies. He went through the mockery of a trial. He was nailed to a cross between two thieves. While He was dying, His executioners gambled for the only piece of property He had on earth, and that was His coat. When He was dead, He was laid in a borrowed grave through the pity of a friend.

Nineteen wide centuries have come and gone, and today He is the central figure of the human race and the leader of the column of progress.
—Phillips Brooks

* * *

I've Tried in Vain!

A man was all his life an atheist. In word and action he said, "There is no God!" One morning he was found dead in his bed. In one hand he held a piece of white paper. On it were written in a scrawling handwriting the following words:

I've tried in vain a thousand ways,
My fears to quell, my hopes to raise,
But what I need, the Bible says,
Is ever only Jesus!
My soul is night, my heart is steel,
I cannot see, I cannot feel,
For light, for life, I must appeal,
In simple faith to Jesus!

His atheism may have brought a measure of satisfaction to the man in life, but it failed him in death. Then he apparently turned to the only One who can help us when we come down to the valley of the shadow of death.
—Told by Robert Harkness

* * *

Blessed with All Spiritual Blessings

When a certain wealthy man died, no will could be found. The man's wife and only son had preceded him in death. In due time the effects of the deceased were sold at auction. Everything was disposed of except a picture of the son. Nobody seemed to want it, until an

elderly woman approached. Seeing the unsold picture, she pleaded with the auctioneer to let her have it for the few pennies she had. When he gave her the picture, she drew it to her heart. She had been the son's nurse in his infancy and boyhood days. Attached to the back of the painting was an envelope addressed to an attorney. The woman took it to the lawyer. He read it and exclaimed, "Woman, you have a fortune! This is the rich man's will. In it he bequeathed a vast sum of money to anyone who loved his son enough to buy the picture!"

To all who love and honor His dear Son, the heavenly Father gives "all spiritual blessings" and every needed material blessing. How rich are God's children — "heirs of God and joint-heirs with Christ Jesus!" —W. B. K.

* * *

Does Jesus Really Care?

One gray morning, Dr. Philpot had the sad duty to go and tell a Christian woman that her husband had fallen in battle. After greeting her he said, "I am the bearer of sad tidings. Your dear husband has been slain in battle!" She fell to the floor and wept uncontrollably. The faithful pastor did all he could to bring comfort and consolation to her sorrowing heart. The grief-stricken woman, seemingly oblivious to his words, would cry out intermittently, "Is it true after all?" Thinking that she doubted the sad news he had brought her, Dr. Philpott said, "Yes, my good woman, it is true. Your husband has given his life in the service of his country." "Oh, Pastor," sobbed the woman, "I know my lover is no more, but is it really true that there is a God who cares?"

"Casting all your care upon him; for he careth for you" (I Peter 5:7).
—W. B. K.

* * *

What About Jesus Christ?

Arthur James Balfour, a former prime minister of England, addressed the students of the University of Edinburgh on "The Moral Value Which Unites Nations." He said that common knowledge, commerce, diplomatic relations, friendship and understanding are things which bind nations in one-ness. At the conclusion of his address, a Japanese student asked the pertinent question: "But, Mr. Balfour, what about Jesus Christ?" The audience waited in silence for the prime minister to reply. Obviously embarrassed, he did not answer.

How strange it was that a prime minister of a leading self-acclaimed Christian nation would fail to include the essential bond which unites men and nations in Christian brotherhood — Jesus Christ. How significant, too, that the deserved rebuke should come from a student of a country in which there are relatively few Christians. —W. B. K.

* * *

The Unchanging Foundation

One Sunday I went to worship in the little church that stands by the shore at Aberdaron. It has stood there for fourteen hundred years. The sand has drifted all round it, the wintry storms have beaten upon it, but it is set firm on the rock underneath. The church has been altered and enlarged during the centuries, but the walls of the old church are built into it. As I worshiped there, I tried to imagine the sort of people who came there fourteen centuries ago and prayed to the same God and loved Jesus as I do. Almost everything has altered since then, but God hasn't changed, and Jesus Christ is "the same yesterday, and today, and for ever"! On the shore by the old church the children play, making castles and houses in the sand. They look fine, but the next high tide will sweep them away. But love and truth and goodness and God will last forever. His "words shall not pass away." The firm "foundation of God standeth sure." —G. Osborn in *The Methodist Recorder*

* * *

Only the Messiah Could Be Born in a Grave

During the Nürnberg War-Crime Trials, a witness appeared who had lived for some time in a Jewish cemetery in Wilna, Poland. He had miraculously escaped from the gas chamber. The cemetery was the only place in which he could hide in safety. There

were also others hiding there for safety. One day, in a grave nearby, a Jewish woman gave birth to an infant boy. The old Jewish gravedigger, aged eighty years, assisted at the birth. When the newborn baby uttered his first cry, the devout old gravedigger said, "Good God, hast Thou finally sent the Messiah to us? For who else than the Messiah can be born in a grave?" After three days, however, the witness said he saw the baby sucking the mother's tears because she had no milk for the child!
—S. Barton Babbage, in *Christianity Today*

* * *

Christ, a Kind of Aladdin's Lamp!

Within the past few years, Christ has been popularized by some as one who, if proper amount of prayer were made, would help the pious prize-fighter knock unconscious in the ring his opponent, or help the big-league pitcher get the proper hook on his curve, or assist the runner to come in first in a track meet, or help men to beat a competitor in a deal, or underbid a rival and secure a coveted contract to the discomfort and loss of someone else trying to get it, or lend succor to a movie actress in her salacious role. Thus our Lord becomes the Christ of utility, a kind of Aladdin's lamp to do minor miracles in behalf of anyone who summons Him to do his bidding! —Rev. Chester A. Tulga

* * *

God Manifested in the Flesh

Dr. Len G. Broughton was a medical doctor before God's call came to him to be a minister. As a medical student, he rejected the supernatural birth of Christ. Later he began to practice medicine among country folk. One Sunday morning he heard an obscure, backwoods preacher in a country church. "That uneducated preacher knocked out of me more skepticism in half an hour than I had gotten during the years of my medical course. This is how he did it. In his sermon he said, 'If there is anybody here troubled about the mystery of God becoming man, I want to take you back to the first chapter of Genesis and the first verse. The opening words are, "In the beginning

God!" ' I felt that he was looking directly at me when he said, 'Let me ask you this: Do you believe God was in the beginning? Do you believe that before the beginning began, God was?' I said to myself, 'Yes, I believe that.' 'If you believe that God was ahead of the beginning, you believe the only mysterious thing of this universe!' "

Dr. Broughton said, "If I can believe that, God knows I can believe anything else the Bible says. I had gone to college and traveled through the mysteries of the theory of reproduction and cell formation. I believed the one supreme mystery of this mysterious universe — 'in the beginning, God.' The greater mystery included all lesser mysteries!"

—W. B. K.

* * *

No Fault With Christ

A former schoolmate of Robert Ingersoll entered promisingly upon the legal profession. He married a lovely woman and was the father of two children. Then he began to drink. He sank to the lowest depths and lost everything. One night a Christian worker found him lying drunk in an alley. He brought him to a mission. There Christ saved him. He was utterly transformed. He rebuilt his home. One day he learned that Ingersoll was to give a lecture against God and the Bible. The converted alcoholic wrote to him, saying, "Old friend, would you tell the people that you are against the religion that came down to the lowest depths of hell and found me? Would you speak against the Saviour who stooped and lifted me, rebuilt my home and brought joy to my wife and children?" Mr. Ingersoll read the letter that night before a large audience and then said, "I have nothing to say against a religion that will do this for a man. I am here to talk about a religion that is being preached, *but not practiced by so many*. You can find fault with the church, but there stands One supreme! No man can point his finger at Christ and find any fault with Him!" —W. B. K.

JEW

Short Quotes

About 75 per cent of the world's Jewish population — 11,820,000 — are in three countries: 5,200,000 are in the United States; 2,000,000 are in the Soviet Union; 1,760,000 are in Palestine.

—*The Gospel Banner*

* * *

Someone asked Daniel Webster, "Can you give me one reason why you believe the Bible is the inspired Word of God?" Instantly he replied, "The Jew!" He couldn't have given a more convincing answer. Through the centuries, the Jew has maintained his racial identity. Like Jonah in the belly of the great fish — undigested, unassimilated — the Jew has remained unassimilated, unamalgamated, undigested, though he has wandered among all nations. —W. B. K.

* * *

Queen Victoria asked her Jewish prime minister, Benjamin Disraeli, "Can you give me one verse in the Bible that will prove its truth?" He replied: "Your Majesty, I will give you *one word* — Jew! If there was nothing else to prove the truth of the Bible, the history of the Jews is sufficient!" "Then you take the Bible literally?" asked the queen. "Oh, yes, Your Majesty. God said what He meant!"

* * *

The Bible tells us that the Jews are God's measuring stick *geographically*: "When he gave the nations their inheritance he set their boundaries according to the number of the children of Israel" (Deut. 32:8). They were brought into a place of intimacy such as no other nation has ever known: "You only have I known among the nations of the earth." Indeed, "they are beloved for the fathers' sake" (Rom. 11:28).

—F. Kendal

The mineral content of the Dead Sea is estimated at two billion tons of potassium chloride; twenty-two billion tons of magnesium chloride, and six billion tons of calcium chloride. During the first seven months of 1957, a potash works located there produced sixty thousand tons of potash.
—*Jewish Agency Digest*, quoted by Dr. J. Wilbur Smith

* * *

You can't keep the Jew down! Wherever he has wandered, no matter how much the odds may have been against him, he has always emerged on top — financially, educationally, and commercially. One of my highly esteemed friends, the late M. Gubin, came to a city in Pennsylvania, where I was once pastor. He sold shoestrings and buttons from a pushcart. At his death, he owned and operated a fine mercantile business. The Jews were the recipients of the oracles of God. They gave us the written Word and the incarnate Word, the Saviour. Besides that, many have been their other contributions to the world. —W. B. K.

* * *

Although the Jordan River pours several million gallons of fresh water into the Dead Sea every day — it has no outlet — the water never rises nor grows less salty. It is a valuable storehouse of mineral wealth, estimated at more than twelve hundred billion dollars! —"Strange As It May Seem" section, *The Chicago Daily News*

Illustrations

Statue of Christ Becomes Animate!

There is an allegory whose setting is in one of the most horrible and blood-drenched periods of earth's history — the rise and rule of Hitler — during which some six million Jews perished. Hitler was to visit a cathedral on a specified day. In preparation for his entrance into the cathedral, the officiating clergyman announced to the audience: "All whose fathers are Jewish will now withdraw from the cathedral!" Many arose and moved toward the exits. Then the clergyman announced: "All whose mothers are Jewish will leave the sanctuary!" With this announcement, according to the allegory, the marble statue of Christ at the front of the cathedral became animate. He crawled down from His cross and sorrowfully and silently left the cathedral! —W. B. K.

* * *

The Navel of the World

In a monkish map, contemporary with the Crusaders, which still hangs in Hereford Cathedral, Jerusalem is marked as the geographical center, the navel of the world. On the floor of the Holy Sepulcher at Jerusalem, they will show you to this day the precise spot which is the center. Our study of the geographical realities, as we now know them in their completeness, is leading us to right conclusions. The medieval ecclesiastics were not far wrong. The hill-citadel of Jerusalem has a strategic position with reference to world realities not different essentially from its ideal position in the perspective of the Middle Ages.
—Sir Halford J. MacKinder, British founder of the study of geopolitics, in *U. S. News and World Report*

* * *

A Different Interpretation

A minister preached on the fifty-third chapter of Isaiah. At the conclusion of the service a Jew said to him, "We Jews have an interpretation of the chapter that is different from what you preached today." The minister asked, "What is it?" The Jew replied, "We hold that the third-person pronouns of the chapter apply to the nation Israel." The minister replied, "That's interesting, but why and when did God lay my iniquities upon the nation of Israel? In what manner was Israel chastised for my sins?" The Jew was stymied and speechless for a moment. Then he confessed, "I cannot answer such questions, but I do not believe that the chapter is a prophecy concerning Jesus Christ!" Then the minister asked, "What do you think of Christ?" "He was our greatest

Rabbi," the Jew answered. The minister further asked, "Are you not obligated then to believe His teaching?" The Jew replied, "Yes." Thereupon the minister commented upon the statement of the Samaritan woman — "I know that Messiah cometh, which is called Christ," and on what Jesus said — "I that speak unto thee am he." The Jew said, "But I don't believe that, either!" —W. B. K.

* * *

There Is No Difference

God had implanted in the heart of a friend of mine a deep love and concern for Jewish people. One day she became concerned for a Jewish student at a university near her home. She went to the school. On the university campus she made inquiry of three different students as to where she might locate the Jewish student. Though she sought diligently for him, she did not find him. Relating her disappointment to me, I asked her, "Though you did not locate the student whom you wanted primarily to see, I am sure that, as you inquired of the three other students, you spoke to them of Christ and gave them Gospel tracts?" "Oh, no," she exclaimed, "I only asked them to help me locate the Jewish student!"

It is right for us to have a *deep* concern for the souls of Jewish people. It is wrong, however, to have any *less* concern for those of other nationalities. —W. B. K.

* * *

All Things Are Mortal but the Jew!

Jews constitute but one per cent of the human race. It suggests a nebulous dim puff of star dust in the blaze of the Milky Way. Properly the Jew ought hardly to be heard of. But he is heard of. He is as prominent on this planet as any other people. His commercial importance is extravagantly out of proportion to the smallness of his bulk. His contributions to the world's list of great names in literature, science, art, music, finance, medicine and abstruse learning are also altogether out of proportion to the weakness of his numbers. He has made a marvellous fight in the world in all the ages, and

has done it with his hands tied behind him. He could be vain of himself and be excused for it. The Egyptian, the Babylonian, and the Persian rose, filled the planet with sound and splendour, then faded to dream stuff and passed away. The Greek and the Roman followed and made a vast noise and they are gone. Other people have sprung up and held their torch high for a time, but it burned out and they sit in twilight now or have vanished. The Jew saw them all, but beat them all and is now what he always was — exhibiting no decadence, no infirmities of age, no weakening of his parts, no slowing of his energies, no dulling of his alert and aggressive mind. All things are mortal but the Jew. All other forces pass, but the Jew remains. What is the secret of his immortality?

"Thus saith the Lord, which giveth the sun for a light by day, and the ordinances of the moon and of the stars for a light by night. . . . If those ordinances depart from before me, saith the Lord, then the seed of Israel also shall cease from being a nation before me for ever" (Jer. 31:35, 36). —Mark Twain

* * *

Anti-Jewish Feeling in the United States

The following statements of Dr. Paul Tillich, professor at Harvard Divinity School and erstwhile professor of theology in German universities, were given in an interview with a news correspondent in Chicago:

"Jews were much more received in the social life of the well-to-do in Germany before Hitler than they are in the United States today." He further declared that anti-Jewish feelings are stronger in the United States than they were in Germany before Hitler, and added, "One thing for Christians to remember is that the very existence of Judaism is a corrective against pagan dangers. This is important, because when Christianity becomes too much interwoven in the nation which accepts it, Christianity will easily become pagan."

"Pray for the peace of Jerusalem: they shall prosper that love thee." —W. B. K.

J O Y

Short Quotes

You cannot glorify God better than by a calm, joyous life. Let the world know that you serve a good Master! If you are in trouble, do not let anyone see that the trouble touches your spirit. Nay, more, do not let it trouble your spirit! Rest in God, and keep on praising Him! —Spurgeon

* * *

During an earthquake, an elderly lady was serene and unafraid. Someone asked her afterwards, "Were you not afraid?" "No," she replied, "I rejoiced to know that I have a God that can shake the world!" —*Prophecy Monthly*

* * *

During a test a submarine remained submerged for many hours. When it surfaced the commander was asked, "How did the storm affect you last night?" "Storm? We knew nothing of any storm," said the surprised captain. God's children are "hid with Christ in God!" In this secure hiding place, life's storms cannot mute the joy bells in our soul! —*Moody Monthly*

* * *

The world is like a mirror,
Reflecting what you do,
And if your face is smiling,
It smiles right back at you!

* * *

Resolve to keep happy, and your joy shall form an invincible host against difficulty. —Helen Keller

* * *

God has given us memories that we might have roses in December.
—James M. Barrie

* * *

There is no personal charm so great as the charm of a cheerful and happy temperament. —Henry Van Dyke

* * *

Joy is something that is multiplied when it is divided!

* * *

A smile and a scowl are known and read in every language and dialect.
—Walter L. Eberly

Where is the blessedness I knew,
When first I saw the Lord?
Where is the soul-refreshing view
Of Jesus and His Word?

What peaceful hours I once enjoyed,
How sweet their memory still!
But they have left an aching void
The world can never fill!

* * *

Though vine nor fig tree neither
Their wanted fruit shall bear,
Though all the fields should wither,
Nor flocks nor herds be there,
Yet God the same abiding,
His praise shall tune my voice,
For while in Him confiding,
I cannot but rejoice!
—G. Campbell Morgan

* * *

As a man thinketh in his heart, so is he outwardly. The products of his brain are tinctured by the thoughts of his heart. Stephen Foster had melancholic thoughts, and his songs reflect his feelings of sadness and loneliness. Haydn had bright, cheerful thoughts, and his compositions are surcharged with gladness and good cheer! —W. B. K.

* * *

It takes sixty-four facial muscles to make a frown, but only thirteen to make a smile. Why work overtime?

* * *

The devil is a chronic grumbler. The Christian ought to be a living doxology.
—Martin Luther

* * *

When a little girl was asked, "Why do you like Miss Siewerth so well?" she replied, "Because her eyes twinkle just as if she is laughing inside her all the time!" —W. B. K.

* * *

The religion that makes a man look sick certainly won't cure the world!
—Phillips Brooks

* * *

Some people bring happiness *wherever* they go. Others bring happiness *when* they go. —Dr. Wendell P. Loveless

Cheerfulness and contentment are great beautifiers, and are famous preservers of youthful looks.

—Charles Dickens

* * *

A Hindu once asked a native Christian of India, "What medicine do you put on your face to make it shine so?" "I don't put anything on it," said the Christian. "Yes you do. All you Christians do. I've seen shining faces wherever I have met Christians!" Then the Christian said, "I will tell you what 'medicine' makes our faces shine — it is the joy in our hearts because Jesus dwells there."

"A merry heart doeth good like a medicine!" —W. B. K.

Illustrations

Sour-faced Christians

One who had just begun the Christian life attended a religious convention. After a few sessions a friend who accompanied him asked, "How are you enjoying the convention?" The man replied, "Let me speak frankly. If I had still been unsaved when you brought me here, I would have thought, 'How defeated and dejected this group looks. There's something wrong, isn't there?' Please don't think I want to find fault, but 'droopy' Christians always puzzle me. They do so much harm! I am only a new Christian, but by God's grace I want to show forth the praises of Him who called me out of darkness into His marvellous light!" —W. B. K.

* * *

The Happiest Church Folk

One Sunday morning a Christian layman from Louisville, Ky., walked down the streets in St. Louis, Mo., trying to find a place of worship. The streets were rather deserted, but he saw a police officer; so he went up to him and said, "Officer, I'm a stranger in St. Louis. I'm a Protestant, and I want to go to church to worship. Could you suggest a place?" The officer said, "I will," and he named a church and gave him directions how to get there. The man thanked him and started to go; then suddenly he stopped, turned around, and said, "By the way, officer, there must be several churches on your beat. Why have you named this particular one for me to go to?" And the officer said, "I'll tell you why! I'm not a very religious man; I'm not a church man. There are several churches on my beat. I'm sending you to this one because I've observed for years that the people who come out of that church are the happiest-looking church people in St. Louis!" How little those people realized that an ungodly police officer had taken notice of the fact that there was the evidence of the joy of the Lord upon their countenances, as they came out of His sanctuary. —Rev. Paul Rees, D.D.

* * *

Happy on the Way!

An expression often used by the late Dr. R. E. Neighbour was, "Happy on the way!" Friends in greeting him would ask, "How are you?" His usual reply was, "Happy on the way!" One day Dr. Neighbour was riding in his car in a funeral procession. A bystander, recognizing him, asked, "How are you, Brother Neighbour?" He replied, "Happy on the way!"

Since "eye hath not seen, nor ear heard, neither have entered into the heart of man, the things which God hath prepared for them that love him," why shouldn't all of God's children be *"happy on the way"*? —W. B. K.

* * *

A Happy Man

The Happy Man was born in the city of Regeneration, in the parish of Repentance unto Life. He was educated in the School of Obedience, he works at the trade of Diligence and does many jobs of self-denial.

He owns a large estate in the country of Christian Contentment and wears the plain garments of humility. He breakfasts every morning on spiritual prayer and sups every evening on the same. He also has "meat to eat that the world knows not of."

He has Gospel submission in his conduct, due order in his affection, sound peace in his conscience, sanctifying love in his soul, real divinity in his breast, true humility in his heart, the Redeemer's yoke on his neck, the world under his feet, and a crown of glory over his head. In order to obtain this, he prays fervently, believes firmly, waits patiently, works abundantly, redeems his time, guards his sense, loves Christ, and longs for glory. —John Bunyan

Christ Makes the Difference!
Heaven above is softer blue,
  Earth beneath is sweeter green,
Something lives in every hue,
  Christless eyes have never seen!

Birds with sweeter songs o'erflow,
  Flowers with newer beauty shine,
Since I know as now I know
  I am His and He is mine!
—*Selected*

A Happy Man
A gentleman going along a country road met a man to whom he courteously wished, "Good morning."

"I have never had a bad morning," replied the man.

"That is very singular; I wish you may always be so fortunate."

"I was never unfortunate," said he.

"Dear me! I wish you may always be happy."

"And I am never unhappy," said the other.

"I wish," said the gentleman, "that you would explain yourself a little."

"That I will certainly do. I never had a bad morning, for every morning I praise God. If it rains or snows; whether the weather be bright or stormy, I am still thankful to God. You wish that I might be always fortunate, but I cannot be unfortunate, for nothing befalls but according to the will of God.

And His will is always good, in whatever He does or permits to be done. You wished me always happy, but I cannot be unhappy while resigned to the will of God, and as long as His peace rules in my heart." —*Faithful Words*

I Have Only Joy!
All loved and believed Mother Stetler who daily lived a beautiful Christian life. As the passing years exacted their toll upon her, her health began to fail. One day she said to her pastor, "I am God's own through grace, but, Pastor, I must confess to you that I have a great fear of death!" "You'll have no fear, Mother, as you enter the valley. The One for whom you have lived over a long span of years will not forsake you when you come to the portals of death."

Some days thereafter the pastor stood by her bed. A smile of ineffable glory wreathed her face. Her lips started to move and she said, "Pastor, soon I shall behold the King in His beauty. I have only joy, not fear!" So saying, a redeemed and radiant soul passed to be forever with her Lord. —W. B. K.

The Heart That Sings!
Of all life's good and lovely things
Most precious is a heart that sings;
That, like a bird in winter's tree,
Chirps anthems of expectancy,
Or in the darkness of the night
Steadfastly proclaims the light.

God's rare and holy gifts abound,
His loving-kindness wraps us round;
But of all gifts that I would praise,
The peaceful nights, the fruitful days,
All true and good and lovely things,
Most precious is a heart that sings.
—R. G. Grenville

JUDGMENT
Short Quotes

God demands an account of the past, which we must render hereafter. He demands an improvement of the present, and this we must render now.
—Jay

It may be that "The Book of Remembrance" is the divine messenger on whose pages the soul meets and relives much of its immortal experience.
—Coleridge

A burgler entered a U.S.O. center in St. Paul, Minnesota. His theft netted him $23.50. The thief left a note addressed to Mrs. Margaret Wood, the director, which read : "I am sorry I did this. There is coming a day when I will pay!"

How true! Is there not a day coming when all impenitent evil-doers will have to pay? —W. B. K.

* * *

I believe there are two forces which move us. One is a belief in a last judgment when every one of us has to account for what he did with God's great gift of life on earth. The other is belief in an immortal soul, a soul which will cherish the award or suffer the penalty decreed in a final judgment.

—Dr. Wernher von Braun

For years we have been told that humanity is at the crossroads. Humanity stands today before an abyss. Unless God intervenes, how soon we will be hurled into the abyss no one knows. What makes things infinitely worse is that the religious leaders insist on continuing to act as if nothing had happened! —Evangelist Leonard Ravenhill

* * *

There is a point where God and man must meet, either in grace or judgment, and at that point both are revealed as they are. —Dr. George W. Truett

* * *

When we stand before the judgment seat of Christ, He is not going to look for medals, but for scars. Who of us can say with Paul: "I bear in my body the marks of the Lord Jesus" (Gal. 6:17). —W. B. K.

Illustrations

Found at Post of Duty

Nearly two centuries ago, a nightlike pall one day settled over parts of New England. Cows wended their way to barns. Chickens went to roost. The people were terrified! Many fell on their knees, believing that the day of judgment had come. In Hartford, Connecticut, the State Council was in session. One member proposed a motion to adjourn. All were frightened except one — Abraham Davenport. He said, "I object to the motion. If this is the day of judgment, I want to be found at my post of duty! I move that candles be brought in, and that we proceed with the business at hand!" —W. B. K.

* * *

Judged for Rejecting Christ

A Christian, as he entered a barber shop, heard a man say, "I was born a sinner. It was no responsibility of mine. It would, therefore, be unjust for God to judge or condemn me for that in which I had no responsibility whatever, no matter what the Bible or preachers say!" The Christian pointed out that the Bible does not say God will condemn us because we are born sinners, but that He will do so if we remain sinners, rejecting the Saviour, by whom He has opened the way of escape for us.

He used this illustration: "Suppose someone has occasion to pass your door at midnight, and notices that fire has broken out in your house. You are asleep, unaware of the danger you are in; the alarm is given and you are awakened. In this circumstance, what would your responsibility be?" "Well," the man answered, "surely I would be responsible to heed the warning and escape as quickly as possible." "But supposing you were to answer the one who warned you, 'I didn't set this building on fire, and have no responsibility for it,' and so remain in the house. What then?" "In that case," he said, "I would be a fool, and responsible if I lost my life." —Tom M. Olson, in *Now*

* * *

Too Heavy at the Judgment

An old Arabian story tells how a royal prince once seized the land of a poor widow and made it part of his palace garden. The destitute woman complained to the chief judge of the country and asked for justice. The judge was sympathetic and fair, but he faced a very difficult situation. How could he condemn the rich and powerful prince who ruled the land? However, the judge had courage, and he was a staunch champion of the right. He decided on a daring step. He came to the palace of the prince with a large sack in his hand. To the amazement of the prince, the judge asked permission to fill his sack with earth from the palace garden. Deeply mystified, the prince agreed and the judge laboriously filled the huge sack to the brim. Then the judge asked the prince to lift the sack to his shoulder. The prince protested that the sack was much too heavy for one man to lift. "This sack," firmly replied the honest judge, "which you think too heavy to bear, contains only a small portion of the land which you took from the rightful owner. How then, at the day of judgment, will you be able to support the weight of the whole?"

—Earnest Worker

* * *

God Does Not Afflict Willingly!

At an early morning hour, the phone in the home of a devout Christian woman rang. "I knew intuitively," she told me later, "that something awful had happened! As I lifted the receiver a voice informed me that my son, recently honorably discharged from the service of his country, had been tragically killed in an automobile wreck. My heart was overwhelmed with sorrow. My son, when he entered the service, was an exemplary Christian, the joy of my heart. While in service, he began to drink. The destroying evil tightened its grasp upon my son. When he was traveling at a high speed under the influence of alcohol, his car went out of control, and was utterly demolished, hurtling him into eternity!"

Since the mother told me of that heart-rending tragedy, I have often thought about the warning words God gave primarily to His children: "To deliver such an one unto Satan for the destruction of the flesh, that the spirit may be saved in the day of the Lord Jesus" (I Cor. 5:5); "If any man defile the temple of God, him shall God destroy; for the temple of God is holy, which temple ye are" (I Cor. 3:17).

—W. B. K.

* * *

Suddenly Destroyed!

As a mocker emerged from a coal mine in Shamokin, Pennsylvania, a vio-

lent wind and rain storm swept the mountain side. Forked, zigzag flashes of lightning streaked across the dark storm clouds, and the thunder rolled ominously. Mockingly the man said, "God must be having a beer party in heaven. That noise is from beer kegs colliding with one another!" Then, with clinched fist, he cursed God! As he did so, a bolt of lightning struck him dead.

—W. B. K.

* * *

Is Your Name Written There?

In the Chapel of St. George, in Westminster Abbey, is a memorial of World War II. It consists of four bound volumes that contain the names of the 60,-000 civilians who were killed in the city of London by enemy action. One volume lies open on the shrine and a light shines down upon the typescript names that appear on that opened page. Each day a page is turned. Thus will the names of those who were rich or poor, titled or of the common people, old or young, healthy or ill, sound of body or crippled, famous or infamous, stand together to be revealed in the light for all to see as a page of the book is turned each day. It is a book of death. There is another book — the Book of Life. It is in heaven. In that book, too, will be found the names of men and women from all classes and conditions on earth. All will be in the light, and all will be honored of God. For the Book of Life will reveal, in that coming day, the names of all those who through faith in God and His Christ will have been regenerated from death to life.

—*Our Hope*

* * *

Our Judge or Advocate, Which?

When he was a young man, Judge Warren Candler practiced law. One of his clients was charged with murder. The young lawyer went all out in his effort to clear his client of the charge. There were some extenuating circumstances, and the lawyer made the most of them in his plea before the jury. Too, there were present in the court the aged father and mother of the man charged with murder. The young lawyer wrought greatly on the sympathies and emotions of the jury by frequent

193

references to the God-fearing parents. In due course the jury retired for deliberation. After reaching a verdict, they returned to the jury box. Their verdict read, "We find the defendant not guilty!" The young lawyer, himself a Christian, had a serious talk with his cleared client. He warned him to steer clear of evil ways, and trust God's power to keep him straight. Years passed. The man was again arraigned. Again the charge was murder. The lawyer who had defended him at his first trial was now the judge on the bench. At the conclusion of the trial the jury rendered its verdict: "Guilty!" Ordering the condemned man to stand for sentencing, Judge Candler said, "At your first trial I was your lawyer, your advocate. Today I am your *judge*. The verdict of the jury makes it mandatory for me to sentence you to be hanged by the neck until you are dead. May God be merciful to your soul!"

Oh, ye unsaved rejecters of Christ, accept Him *now*. He who may now be your Advocate will later be your Judge!

—Told by Dr. T. W. Callaway

* * *

Sodom — Judgment of Sin

The site of Sodom, at the lower end of the Dead Sea area, has been for many centuries a disputed point in Biblical geography. Today not only is the exact location known, but the scene is one of modern development and activity. The government of Israel has set up road markers at three hundred historic sites within its national boundaries. The marker for Sodom reads as follows: "Sodom is the lowest point of habitation in the world, 1,286 feet below sea level. Sodom, primitive scene of the most terrible judgment on human sin, was the dwelling place of Lot, 'Abraham's brother's son,' before its classic destruction with its sister city, Gomorrah. Today, Sodom is the center of Israel's potash production." —Edgar Ainslie in *The Sunday School Times*

* * *

The Brain Contains Permanent Record!

Dr. Wilber Penfield, director of the Montreal Neurological Institute, said in a report to the Smithsonian Institute,

"Your brain contains a permanent record of your past that is like a single continuous strip of movie film, complete with sound tract. This 'film library' records your whole waking life from childhood on. You can live again those scenes from your past, one at a time, when a surgeon applies a gentle electrical current to a certain point on the temporal cortex of your brain." The report goes on to say that as you relive the scene from your past, you feel exactly the same emotions that you did during the original experience.

Could it be that the human race will be confronted by this irrefutable record at the judgment bar of God when "God shall judge the secrets of men by Jesus Christ" (Rom. 2:16)?

This we know in reference to the guilty past of God's children that God hath "blotted out, as a thick cloud [their] transgressions, and, as a cloud [their] sins" (Isa. 44:22); their past is buried in the ocean of His forgetfulness; and "their sins and their iniquities will [he] remember no more." —W. B. K.

* * *

No Escape by Silencing the Messenger

An African chief had done something for which the English government wished to punish him and sent a gunboat for this purpose. A runner brought him word that the boat had entered the river. He had the courier killed. The next day a second runner arrived to tell him how far the boat had come up the river. This poor fellow also lost his head. And the same fate was met by the other couriers who arrived the following days. This did not, however, keep the English boat away nor delay the day of judgment. Suddenly the jungle echoed with thunder of cannon and the huts of his kraal collapsed as if made of cardboard. How do we treat the messengers of God who come to tell us of approaching judgment? We may have silenced them, but the judgment day is coming. You may have silenced your conscience, grieved the Holy Spirit, left unopened the Holy Bible, and turned your back on your Christian friends — but the judgment day is coming.

—*The Sunday School Times*

JUSTICE

Illustrations

Innocent Man in Prison Sixteen Years

Rom E. Eaton spent sixteen years in prison for a crime he did not commit. What a strange miscarriage of justice! Afterwards he said, "I didn't have a dime in my pockets or a friend in the world when they put me on trial for armed robbery. That's why I spent sixteen years in prison for a crime committed by two other men while I was 1,700 miles away. I am free now, completely vindicated. Life played a dirty trick on me in Circuit Court at Rock Island, Illinois, in 1940!"

Though there are occasional miscarriages of justice in earthly courts, there will be no miscarriages of justice in the assize of heaven. When men appear before God to give account for deeds done in the body, "every transgression and disobedience [will receive] a just recompence of reward" for God, the Judge of all the earth, will do right! When you appear before Him, will it be, "Come ye blessed of my Father, inherit the kingdom prepared for you from the foundation of the world," or will it be, "Depart from me, ye cursed, into everlasting fire, prepared for the devil and his angels"? —W. B. K.

* * *

Judge Paid Penalty

Two men who had been friends in their youth met years later in the police court of a great city, one on the judge's bench, the other in the prisoner's dock. Evidence was heard and the prisoner was found guilty. The ties of friendship were still strong between the two men. The sentiment of friendship would enter into the judge's verdict, it was believed. Said the judge, "I cannot fail to pass sentence upon you, my friend. That would not be justice. Justice must

be done, and I must uphold the law." So he sentenced his friend, imposing a fifty-dollar fine, or fourteen days at hard work. The condemned man had nothing with which to pay, so prison was before him. Then the judge, having fulfilled his duty, stepped down beside the prisoner, paid his fine, put his arm about him, and said, "Now, John, you are coming home with me to dinner!"

God cannot overlook sin. He is not only faithful, but He is also just. So in order to set us free, He laid our iniquities upon His Son, who bore the penalty for us. —W. B. K.

* * *

A Modern Dr. Jekyll and Mr. Hyde

Old John was an eccentric character. He had a small farm on which he raised turkeys. One time a motorist accidentally killed one of his turkeys. The man stopped and said that he was sorry about the accident. But old John was angry and threw a stone through the windshield, so the motorist had him arrested. Old John appeared before the judge. He said, "Your Honor, it was not the new John who threw that stone. It was the old John!" The judge did not understand. So John carefully explained how that when he became a Christian, he became a dual personality; that he still had his old nature, but that he also had a new one. It was the bad, old John who threw the stone, not the new, good one. The judge said, "I see! I see! You are a kind of double personality, modern-day Dr. Jekyll and Mr. Hyde. It was the old John, not the new John, who threw the stone!" "Yes, that's it, Your Honor," agreed old John. "I'm sorry," said the judge, but I am afraid that both Johns will have to go to jail!" —W. B. K.

KINDNESS

Short Quotes

No tranquilizer can be found
Through any magic art
As fine as that which must abound
Within a peaceful heart.

No drug or dope can take the place
Of peace within the mind,
Of those who have the friendly grace
To be gentle, just, and kind.
—Edith H. Shank

* * *

Kind hearts are the gardens,
    Kind thoughts are the roots,
Kind words are the flowers,
    Kind deeds are the fruits.

Take care of your garden,
    And keep out the weeds;
Fill it up with sunshine,
    Kind words and kind deeds.
—Longfellow

* * *

"Where's your dad?" asked a patient of a doctor's boy. "I don't know, Sir, but he must be out helping somebody," replied the lad. —W. B. K.

* * *

The life that counts must helpful be,
The cares and needs of others see,
Must seek the slaves of sin to free,
This is the life that counts.

* * *

You cannot do a kindness too soon, because you never know how soon it will be *too late!*
—*Highways and Happiness*

* * *

Do all the good you can
By all the means you can
In all the ways you can
In all the places you can
At all the times you can
To all the people you can
As long as ever you can!
—John Wesley

* * *

The only people with whom you should try to get even are those who have helped you and those to whom you are indebted.

Kindness is a language that the dumb can speak and the deaf can hear and understand.

* * *

Life is a boomerang. What we are and do comes back to us: "Cast thy bread upon the waters: for thou shalt find it after many days" (Eccl. 11:1). Each one is the inheritor of himself.
For life is the mirror of king and slave,
    'Tis just what we are and do;
Then give to the world the best you have,
    And the best will come back to you!
—W. B. K.

* * *

I shall pass through this world but once. Any good, therefore, that I can do, or any kindness that I can show to any human being, let me do it now! Let me not defer it, or neglect it, for I shall not pass this way again.

* * *

Doing nothing for others is the undoing of one's self. We must be purposely kind and generous or we miss the best part of existence. The heart that goes out of itself gets large and full of joy. This is the great secret of the inner life. We do ourselves the most good doing something for others.
—Horace Mann

* * *

If we knew the cares and trials,
    Knew the efforts all in vain,
And the bitter disappointment,
    Understood the loss and gain;
Would the grim, eternal roughness
    Seem, I wonder, just the same?
Should we help where now we hinder?
    Should we pity where now we blame?
—Rudyard Kipling

* * *

Some say that God helps those who help themselves. God also helps those who help others. —W. B. K.

* * *

Join the great company of those who make the barren places of life fruitful with kindness. Carry a vision of heaven in your hearts, and you shall make your name, your college, the world, correspond to that vision. Your success and happiness lie in you. External conditions are the accidents of life, its outer wrappings. The great, enduring realities are love and service. Joy is the holy fire that keeps our purpose warm and our intelligence aglow. Resolve to keep happy, and your joy and you shall form an invincible host against difficulty. —Helen Keller

* * *

Speak kind words and you will hear kind echoes. —Bahn

* * *

When I am wrong, dear Lord, make me easy to change, and when I am right, make me easy to live with.
—Peter Marshall

* * *

A man was hurrying along the street one night when another man, also in haste, rushed out of a doorway, and the two collided with great force. The second man was infuriated, and spoke abusively, while the first man, taking off his hat, said very quietly, "My dear sir, I don't know which of us is to blame for this encounter, but I am in too great a hurry to investigate. If I ran into you, I beg your pardon; if you ran into me, don't mention it." And he tore away with redoubled speed.
—*Forward*

* * *

Kindness always pays, but it pays most when you do not do it for pay.

A youthful giant slouched into an Illinois schoolroom one day after school. The teacher, Mentor Graham, looked up and recognized the young husky standing there awkwardly as the new young buck who had recently moved to town and who had whipped the daylights out of all local toughs. Graham looked up and down the six-foot-four-inches of muscle and ignorance before him and offered to help him read and to lend him a few books. No one remembers Mentor Graham nowadays. He was one of the quiet men, but his pupil will be remembered for a long time. His name was Abraham Lincoln. —William P. Barker

* * *

Centuries ago, a young man, who had renounced great earthly riches to follow Christ, met a leper on the road.

His first impulse was hastily to turn away. Suddenly his heart was filled with love and Christlike pity for the suffering outcast. He opened his pocketbook and emptied its contents into the bony hands of the leper as he spoke comforting words to the sufferer.

That young man was St. Francis of Assisi.

"Inasmuch as ye have done it unto one of the least of these my brethren, ye have done it unto me" (Matt. 25:40).
—W. B. K.

* * *

In a prayer meeting a deacon prayed with great fervor. The burden of his prayer had to do with a family which had suddenly been bereft of the father and husband. "O God," pleaded the intercessor, "do send someone to that grief-stricken family to touch them for You!" Suddenly the man lapsed into silence. Quietly he withdrew from the group. Before the prayer meeting concluded, he returned. Asked why he concluded his prayer so abruptly, and why he withdrew without explanation, he said, "As I prayed that God would touch that sorrowing family, He seemed to say to me, '*You* are My finger! You go and touch them for Me.'" —W. B. K.

* * *

There were two barber shops in a small town. One was operated by an Italian, one by a Russian. One week there was a large increase in Tony Sachetti's business. He learned that his competitor was ill. Tony worked late Saturday night. On Sunday morning he put on his best suit. He took all the money he had made above his regular intake during the week, and gave it to his competitor. "Little cash for you, Ivan," he said, as he poured out the bills and coins on the bed. "Get well quick!" With a laugh and warm handclasp, Tony was gone! —W. B. K.

* * *

"I once knew two pastors," says W. P. White, "one a Fundamentalist, and one a Modernist who severely criticized his brother minister. By an accident the Modernist's wife was horribly burned, and the Fundamentalist immediately raised two hundred dollars among his business friends for special

197

medical treatment. Within half an hour
the Modernist minister knocked at his
study door. With tears rolling down
his cheeks, he said, 'May I join your
Monday-night Bible class, my brother?
I want to study your theology.' Today
that man is preaching the Gospel of
Jesus Christ, a thoroughgoing Fundamentalist. Love won him."
—*The Sunday School Times*

* * *

One day I was visiting the gnarled,
lame, and blind people who lived in the
Chicago Home for the Incurables. How
friendless and forgotten some of them
were! I came to the bed of an aged German Jew whose face was scarred and
mottled as a result of having been
beaten within an inch of his life by
Hitler's Gestapo. An attendant told
me that he couldn't understand a word
of English. I beamed compassion and
kindness upon him. His face wreathed
in smiles and reflected good will back to
me. Linguistic barriers seemed to vanish. The unarticulated language of love
and kindness fused together the hearts
of two men who were so different ra-
cially. —W. B. K.

* * *

A new pastor and the superintendent
of his Sunday school were walking together down a street. They came to a
drunken man lying on the edge of the
sidewalk. The superintendent said,
"Sit up, my man. I want to talk to
you." Sitting down beside the alcoholic,
the superintendent lovingly told him of
Christ and of His mightiness to save.
As the pastor and superintendent re-
sumed their walk, the pastor asked, "Do
you think it does any good to speak to
a man when he is under the influence
of drink?" The superintendent replied,

"Yes, it does! I know from experience!
I was once just like that man. Many
times I was so drunk that I had to be
carried home, but even in times like that
God spoke to me. Thanks to Him for
His redeeming love, I have become a
new man!"

* * *

Kindness is a mark of the well-bred.
It reveals itself at all times and under
all circumstances.

One Sunday a scholarly-looking man,
plainly dressed, went into a church in
Holland and took a seat near the pulpit.
In a few minutes a lady approached the
pew, and seeing the stranger in it curtly
asked him to leave. He took one of the
seats reserved for the poor, and joined
devoutly in the service.

When the service was over, one of the
woman's friends asked her if she knew
who it was whom she had ordered out
of her seat. "No," she replied, "but it
was only some stranger, I suppose." "It
was King Oscar, of Sweden," replied her
informant; "he is here visiting the
queen." —*The Motor*

* * *

Samuel Bradburn was a co-worker of
John Wesley. One time Bradburn was
in difficult circumstances. Wesley
learned of his situation and sent him a
five-pound note accompanied by the following letter: "Dear Sammy: 'Trust in
the Lord, and do good; so shalt thou
dwell in the land, and verily thou shalt
be fed.' Yours Affectionately, John
Wesley." Bradburn replied promptly to
the letter. He wrote, "Reverend and
Dear Sir: I have often been struck with
the beauty of the Scripture quoted in
your letter, but I must confess that I
never saw such useful expository notes
on it before!" —W. B. K.

Illustrations

My Name Is Paganini!

It was a bitter, cold day in London.
An old blind man sat on a little stool
near the corner of a street. His fingers
were blue with cold. He tried to play
a cheap violin. Few paid any attention to him, or put any money in his
tin cup. Then two well-dressed men

stopped. One said in broken English:
"No luck, eh? Nobody give money?
Make them. Play till they open!" Then
he said: "Give me your violin!" The
old man gave it to him and he began
to play. The cheap violin seemed to
come to life. Beautiful, heavenly music
flowed from it. Men, women, boys and

girls listened, spell-bound! When the music stopped, a hat was passed. It was filled with money for the blind man. When the stranger returned the violin and bow, the blind man said: "Oh, Sir, you have my undying thanks! What's your name?" As the stranger walked away, he said, "My name is Paganini!"
—W. B. K.

* * *

Here Is Half of That Blanket!

General Marquis de Lafayette was a Frenchman. He helped General Washington when the thirteen American colonies were fighting for their freedom. After the war Lafayette returned to France. In 1824 he visited America. An old soldier went up to him and said, "Do you remember me?" "No," Lafayette said. "Do you remember the frosts and snows of Valley Forge?" asked the soldier. "I shall never forget them," answered Lafayette. "One bitterly cold night," continued the soldier, "when you were going the rounds, you came upon a sentry who was thinly clothed. He was slowly freezing to death. You took his gun and said, 'Go to my hut. There you will find clothes, a blanket and a fire. After warming yourself, bring the blanket to me. Meanwhile I will keep guard for you. When the soldier returned to you, you cut the blanket in two pieces. One piece you kept. You gave the other part to the sentry!" Tears ran down the cheeks of the old soldier as he said, "General, here is that half of the blanket. I am the sentry whose life you saved!" —W. B. K.

* * *

When I Helped a Nun

A heavy snow had just fallen when I started out for my accustomed daily hike. As I trudged through the heavy snow, I saw a nun shoveling snow from a long sidewalk alongside the convent. Approaching her, I said, "Let me shovel the snow for you, sister." Sweat was beading on her grateful, smiling face. Taking the shovel, I made a quick job of removing the snow. Then I said to the grateful nun, "It was a pleasure to have given you a helping hand, sister. God's children should have not only helping hands, but also disseminating hands. May I have the pleasure of giving you some of the little booklet-meditations I wrote?" I gave her the booklets, including the one which has been greatly blessed of God — "Knowing Christ as Saviour, Lord and Friend."

With a hearty, "Thank you," she received the booklets, adding, "May the Saviour richly reward you for your kindness!" —W. B. K.

* * *

An Unsullied Name

A man once caught another in the very act of picking his pocket. The thief excused himself by saying that he was workless and starving, and how, after he had served a term of imprisonment, nobody would employ him. Whenever he gave his name his reputation became known, and no one would trust him. "Well," said the other, "take my name, which I have never yet sullied. I give it to you. Take it and keep it clean." He then took steps to find the man employment. Fifteen years later he was told that a gentleman was waiting to see him. A glance at his visiting card revealed that he bore the same name as himself, and when he opened his lounge door to see his visitor, he was confronted by a man of fine and noble appearance, who said, "I have called to tell you that today I have been made a partner in the firm to which you recommended me fifteen years ago, and all you see me to be, I owe to your noble generosity, and above all to the gift of your name which is still unsullied. God bless you, Sir, and reward you."
—*Methodist Recorder*

* * *

In the Shoes of Priest and Levite

Moody and Sankey were traveling in a railway coach, going west. A drunk recognized Moody. He had heard him preach, and began to mimic him. Moody became angry and demanded that the conductor eject the drunk. The conductor spoke kindly to the man, helped him to a seat, sat beside him and talked calmly to him. Presently the drunk was sound asleep. Moody sat thinking about what had occurred. God convicted him of his hastily spoken words and unChristlike attitude. He said to Sankey, "Last night I preached on the Good Samaritan, and here I find that my feet are in the shoes of the priest and the Levite! I have missed a chance to *practice* what I preached last night. May God forgive me!" —W. B. K.

* * *

He Acted Out the Meaning!

A little girl in Boston became critically ill. She was visited by Dr. Phillips Brooks whose Sunday school she had attended. As he stood at her bedside he noticed how uncomfortable she looked as she lay propped up in her bed. The pillow was sagging and the sheets were wrinkled. "Little girl, let me lift you clear off your bed while mother smooths it and makes it comfortable for you," he said tenderly. After the bed was tidied up, he gently laid her down. Soon she fell asleep.

When the little girl awakened she said to her mother, "Oh, Mother, how good it felt to have someone lift me who is strong enough to feel no strain!"

That night the nurse read this verse from the Bible to her little patient: "The eternal God is thy refuge, and underneath are the everlasting arms." Said the little girl, "I now know what that verse means. Dr. Brooks acted out its meaning when he visited me!"

—W. B. K.

* * *

Kindness Rewarded

Some eighty years ago, in a rural community a farmer was caught putting water in his milk. In those days that offense was considered as great a crime as horse-stealing. The farmer was a member of the church. He was not prosecuted, but he and his family were shunned by the other church folks.

On Christmas day, an elder of the church said to his wife, "I'm going over to our shunned neighbor, and try to move a load from his heart!" "May the children and I go with you?" his wife asked. "Indeed you may," said the modern Good Samaritan, "and let us share with him and his family some of the good things we have received at this glad season!"

When they met the farmer and his wife, the women embraced each other with tears. And the elder said to the erring brother, "We need each other, and we ought to love one another." The farmer broke down and began to weep. He started to pray, but he couldn't finish his prayer. His wife had to finish it for him.

The two families parted with joy, knowing that the Christmas message of good will had been proclaimed in a neighborly and joyous manner.

—W. B. K.

* * *

Ye Have Done It Unto Me

A Christian lady, well advanced in years, was forced by circumstances to seek outside employment. After meeting with several discouragements, she was given a job. She had no special qualifications, and it was with difficulty that she did the work expected of her. Later she related: "As a Christian, I wanted to do my best. I would have been a failure had it not been for the kindness and help given me by a Christian lady in charge of the department where I worked. One day, after I had sincerely thanked her for all she had done for me, she said, "God expects His children to bear one another's burdens. I have found great joy in helping you. In helping you in my Saviour's name, it was just the same as helping Him!'"

—W. B. K.

* * *

I Could Be a Dangerous Man

A man had been out of work for some time. He and his family were in dire need. He began to walk to a distant town. In seeking directions to his destination, he knocked at a door. It was the home of the minister of a small church nearby. The minister lived alone. He had just prepared his noonday meal, so he said to the stranger, "Come in! Have something to eat with me!" The minister gave thanks for the meal and concluded his prayer by saying, "And Lord, bless the guest whom You have graciously sent to me!" The stranger was deeply touched. He said, "Why, Sir, you don't know me. I could be a dangerous person for all you know!" "Even so," said the minister, "but for years I have put my day in God's hands, asking Him to fill it as He wishes, and to send to me those in need of help and those to whom I can show the kindness of the Lord." —W. B. K.

Pass It On

If you hear a kind word spoken
Of some worthy soul you know,
It may fill his heart with sunshine
If you only tell him so.

If a deed, however humble,
Helps you on your way to go,
Seek the one whose hand has helped you,
Seek him out and tell him so.

If your heart is touched and tender
Toward a sinner, lost and low,
It might help him to do better
If you'd only tell him so.

Oh, my sisters, oh, my brothers,
As o'er life's rough path you go,
If God's love has saved and kept you,
Do not fail to tell men so.

—*Selected*

LAW

Illustrations

Stop! You're Wrong!

A young man was riding along a highway with an aged minister. Sneeringly he said, "I do not believe in the Ten Commandments. I hate to have a 'thou shalt' and a 'thou shalt not' flung in my face continuously." The minister said nothing. When he came to an intersection, he deliberately took the wrong road. "Stop!" demanded the young man, "you've taken the wrong road. The other sign said, 'This way to Toronto.'" The minister replied, "But I want no arbitrary sign telling me which way to go!"

The young man got the point.

—W. B. K.

* * *

God's Wise Reminders

A king gave his little son a silver arrow to carry about with him wherever he went. Whenever the prince was going to do something wrong, the arrow would prick him, and he didn't like that at all. So, one day, the prince left the arrow at home, and, oh, the trouble he got into! He was glad to get his arrow back again! God, in His infinite wisdom, gives us His Law to keep us from sorrow and sin, and guide us in the way of right and happiness. When God says, "Thou shalt," or "Thou shalt not," He is only saying, "Do thyself no harm!" —*Methodist Recorder*

* * *

That "Dangerous" Doctrine

A young Christian had been taught that while a person gets saved through faith in Christ, he must obey the law of Moses in order to keep saved. When she saw that God's Word teaches that Christians are not under law but under grace, she said, "It's almost too good to be true!" Then she added, "The Bible does seem to say that, but don't you think it is a dangerous doctrine to teach? If Christians knew that, they might go out and do just anything." I said, "*You* see that that is what the Bible teaches; are you going out now to do all the bad things you can think of?" I wish you could have seen her look of horror as she said, "No, of course not." "Why not?" I asked. She answered quickly, "Because I love the Lord Jesus." That is the secret of the Christian life. —Vivian D. Gunderson, in *The Sunday School Times*

* * *

The Wicked Flee!

A state patrolman cruising down the highway looking for speedsters came up behind a seemingly law-abiding car and would have passed on without trouble had not the guilty conscience of the driver betrayed him. On seeing a state patrolman so near, the guilty driver immediately thought of his load of whiskey, and decided to outrun the officer. The patrolman knew from the man's actions that there was something amiss, and so gave chase. The liquor-laden car sideswiped three cars, crashed red lights, endangering the lives of all who met him, and finally was completely demolished in a one-car wreck. The driver barely escaped death because the patrolman was a terror to his sinful works. In contrast, a few friends and I approached a dangerous intersection near Asheville, N. C. Someone in the car remarked, "There sits a state pa-trolman." The driver's answer was, "Fine, I'm glad he's watching this dangerous place." The law held no fear for her because she loved her fellow man and appreciated the state's effort to make our highways safer for all.

—*The Sunday School Times*

LIGHT

Short Quotes

I'd rather light a candle than curse the darkness. —James Kelley

* * *

Give me a Bible and a candle and shut me up in a dungeon, and I will tell you what the world is doing.

* * *

Said a woman in India to a friend, "One night as I walked home, a panther followed me. Because I carried a lantern and walked in the circle of light, I was safe. A panther won't attack you while you are in the light!" We, too, are safe when we walk with Jesus, "the light of the world." —W. B. K.

* * *

I said to a man who stood at the gate of the year: "Give me a light that I may tread safely into the unknown." He replied: "Go out into the darkness and put your hand into the hand of God. That shall be to you better than a light and safer than a known way."

—Minnie L. Haskins in *The Dexter*

* * *

The General Electric Company has perfected a light bulb with an alleged life expectancy of a million hours. It is said that the bulb will burn eight hours a day every day for 342 years, or until the year 2295! The Bible tells us of an infinitely superior light: "The Lord shall be unto thee an *everlasting light*" (Isa. 60:19). —W. B. K.

* * *

A Christian girl found it difficult to be true to her Christian principles where she worked. One day she told her pastor about it. "Where do you put lights? In a bright place?" "Why, no," she said, "in a dark place, to make it light."

Then she saw that the Lord had put her in those difficult surroundings, and she resolved to be faithful and let her light shine. —*Baptist Standard*

* * *

Light is the source of all life. All vegetation would wilt and die without light. Light and joy are inseparably related. Birds greet light at dawn with joyous song. Light imparts loveliness — redness to the cherry and tints to the rose. Spiritual life, joy, and beauty come from Jesus: "I am come that they might have life" (John 10:10); "I have spoken . . . that my joy might remain in you, and that your joy might be full" (15:11); "He will beautify the meek with salvation" (Ps. 149:4).

—W. B. K.

* * *

Centuries ago in England lanterns were hung in some of the church steeples at night. They were also hung in front of homes. When the lantern was missing or had gone out, the night watchman would cry, "Hang out your light," or, "Light your lantern." The lighted lanterns helped to guide those walking at night through London's fog and darkness.

Jesus said, "Ye are the light of the world." Lights are made for dark places. Shine for Jesus wherever you may be. —W. B. K.

* * *

One of the Easter ceremonies in Jerusalem is "The Sacred Fire." From within the tomb enclosure of the Church of the Holy Sepulcher a high church dignitary thrusts through an aperture a torch. The nearest light their candles at the tomb. From these, others light their candles until the entire church and its vicinity are ablaze with thousands of candles. As a religious ceremony Protestants take no stock in the spectacular performance. As a parable, however, it holds a message for everyone: Transmitted light, passed from one to another, is a great Christian principle.

Have you found the heavenly light?
Pass it on!
Souls are groping in the night,
Daylight gone!
Lift your lighted lamp on high,
Be a star in someone's sky,
He might live who else would die,
Pass it on!
—Christian Herald

* * *

"Who are these people?" asked a little girl as she sat with her mother in church. She was looking admiringly at the figures on the stained glass windows, vivified and glorified by the rays of the sun shining through them. "They are saints," replied the mother. As they left the church, the little girl said, "Mother, I now know what a saint is: A saint is one through whom the light shines!" She was right! Even the carnal Corinthian Christians were designated "saints," but how unsaintly were some of them! How unlike saints do all of us act at times! —W. B. K.

* * *

A missionary took a sundial with him to his mission station. The superstitious natives thought it was a miraculous gadget to be venerated or worshiped. They built a roof over it to protect it from the sun!

Some build a roof of tradition over Jesus, "the Sun of Righteousness," and obstruct the light, and leave sin-darkened souls to flounder in the fog banks of doubt and unbelief. —W. B. K.

* * *

A. W. Milne labored as a missionary in a section of New Guinea where there were cannibals. There he died preaching the gospel of Christ. His converts, some of whom were former cannibals, asked permission to place a marker on his grave on which they inscribed: "Here lie the remains of A. W. Milne. When he came to us there was no light. When he died there was no darkness."
—W. B. K.

Illustrations

A Christ that Shines in Darkness

A father took his son into an art shop to buy a picture of Christ for him. The boy was shown different pictures of Christ but he didn't like any of them. "No, Daddy, these are not what I want." The father, thinking that his son didn't want a picture of Christ after all, asked, "What kind of a picture of Christ do you want?" Promptly the boy replied, "I want a Christ who shines in darkness!" The boy had seen a luminous picture of Christ which shone in the darkness.

We greatly need Christ to shine in the night of sorrow, suffering, testing and temptation. Only He can illumine life's dark pathway. As we follow Him, our way grows increasingly bright: "But the path of the just is as the shining light, that shineth more and more unto the perfect day" (Prov. 4:18).
—W. B. K.

Deliverance from Darkness

Darkness has a paralyzing power. Try to envision the condition of the millions in the regions where the "Sun of Righteousness," Jesus, is unknown! When I was a boy, I came home late from work one night. Like all growing boys, I was continuously hungry. Going into the dining room, I took my place at the table near a window. Without, the darkness was unrelieved by any ray of light. As I sat eating, I heard a hissing noise just outside the window. The lateness of the hour, the dense darkness without, and the unearthly hissing sound — all conspired to freeze my heart in terror. I sat motionless for a moment, which seemed like an eternity. Then I heard the honking of some geese which had strayed from our Jewish neighbor's yard. Knowing now the source of my fright, my fears subsided. Spiritual darkness, with its attendant fear, held sway in my heart through the years of my boyhood. Then, one never-to-be-forgotten night, God, "who commanded the light to shine out of darkness," shined into my sin-darkened heart! —W. B. K.

* * *

No Shadows Permanent

Dr. Jowett, the noted preacher, once saw a total eclipse of the sun, while he was traveling through a foreign mission field. The superstition-ridden natives thought that a great monster was swallowing up the sun, so they beat their drums and cried out in fear. When the eclipse was over, and the sun was shining again, Dr. Jowett went home and wrote his famous sermon, "No Shadows Permanent." In it he pointed out that while the love of God seems sometimes to be in a state of eclipse, there is a law of the spirit by which the bright hopes of the Gospel always return. There are no permanent shadows. Even the temporary shadows are behind us, if we face the light and walk towards it.
—*God's Revivalist*

* * *

A Lighted Candle Inside

While preaching in Soul's Harbor, Columbus, Ohio, I noticed a nurse under deep conviction of sin. She sat night after night the picture of dejection and distress. One night she yielded herself to Christ. The burden of sin fell from her heart. She became radiant. On the way home that night, she stopped at a store to do some shopping. A clerk who had known her for some time said, "Why, you look as if someone had just lighted a candle inside you!" "That's right," said the converted nurse. "What I mean," said the clerk, "is that you look as if you had just fallen in love!" "I have!" exclaimed the nurse. "I have fallen in love with the One who loved me when I didn't love Him — Jesus!"
—John Linton, in
Christian Readers Digest

* * *

They See Not

A businessman, 45 years of age, was driving along a Canadian highway. The sun was shining brightly. He saw what appeared to be drops of rain begin to fall on the upper part of his windshield. Within seconds, all became dark! Quickly he turned his car to the side of the road. Blindness settled permanently upon him!

His experience was not unusual. Yearly, in Canada and the United States, some 30,000 people, 92 per cent of them adults, go blind.

Only God knows how many go blind to spiritual and eternal things. They have physical eyesight, "but they see not." "The god of this world," said Paul, "hath blinded the minds of them which believe not, lest the light of the glorious gospel of Christ, who is the image of God, should shine unto them" (II Cor. 4:4).

What a privilege is ours, who have seeing eyes, to help the unseeing ones to see the "Light of the world," the Lord Jesus! —W. B. K.

* * *

Lamps

I met a stranger in the night
Whose lamp had ceased to shine.
I paused and let him light
His lamp from mine.

A tempest sprang up later on
And shook the world about.
And when the wind was gone,
My lamp was out.

But back to me the stranger came —
His lamp was glowing fine!
He held the precious flame,
And lighted mine!
—*Selected*

* * *

Making Holes in the Darkness

One evening at dusk, Robert Louis Stevenson stood as a boy at the window of his home and watched the darkness envelop the city. "Robert," his nurse said to him, "come and sit down. You can't see anything out there."

But young Stevenson insisted, "I can see something wonderful. There is a man coming up the street making holes in the darkness." It was the lamplighter.

In the truest sense, Jesus Christ is the Divine Lamplighter. He came into the world to make holes in the darkness of sin, ignorance, and despair. "I am the

light of the world," He said. "He that followeth me shall not walk in darkness, but shall have the light of life."
—Gwynne W. Davidson, D.D.

* * *

Their Minds Were Blinded!

Years ago, young mules were lowered into coal mines. There they remained until old age rendered them useless for further service. When they were brought up into God's sunlight, it was detected that they were totally blind. They had

been in darkness so long that they had gone blind.

Men may stay away from Jesus so long, going headstrong in the ways of sin and darkness, that they ultimately forfeit the possibility to become spiritually enlightened. Paul said, "But if our gospel be hid, it is hid to them which believe not, lest the light of the glorious gospel of Christ . . . should shine unto them" (II Cor. 4:3, 4). There is a point at which the light on the road to hell goes out! —W. B. K.

LORD'S DAY

Illustrations

Quaint, or Is It?

A notice was recently found which appeared in 1854 on the bulletin board of the great Wananaker store in New York City. It read:

"The store must not be open on the Sabbath day unless absolutely necessary, and then only for a few minutes. Any employee who is in the habit of smoking Spanish cigars, getting shaved at the barber shop, going to dances and other places of amusement will most surely give his employer reason to be suspicious of his integrity and all-around honesty.

"Each employee must not pay less than $5 per year to the church and must attend Sunday school every Sunday.

"Men employees are given an evening a week for courting purposes, and two if they go to prayer meeting regularly.

"After 14 years of work in the store, the leisure time must be spent in reading good literature."
—*The Sunday School Times*

* * *

Missing Its Blessing

A Jewish rabbi's parable tells of seven brothers who lived together. Six worked and the seventh cared for the house, having the meals ready and the house bright for his brothers in the evening. But the six said that the seventh must work, too. So in the evening they returned home and found the house dark

and no meal prepared. They then saw how foolish they had been, and quickly restored the old way. The Sabbath is a day among the seven which provides light, comfort, and good for all the others. Drive it out to work, and all the rest will miss its blessing.
—*Christian Herald*

* * *

Stealing the Seventh Day Also

It came to pass that a man went to market with a string of seven coins. Seeing a beggar who asked him for alms, he gave the poor man six of the coins and kept one for himself. The beggar, instead of being thankful, followed the good man and stole the seventh coin also. What an abominable wretch! Yes, and would you, to whom God has given six days, steal the seventh also?
—A Chinese pastor

* * *

Perfectly Balanced

During the French Revolution the Christian Sabbath was abolished in France. One day in ten as a day of rest was substituted for one day in seven. "We cannot destroy Christianity until we first destroy the Christian Sabbath," said Voltaire. The experiment worked disastrously for man and beast. Horses, going for ten days without rest, broke down in the streets under the strain. In writing about God's beneficent law, providing rest on one day in seven, a writer of that time said:

"So transcendent is the harmony between six days for work and one day for rest, we would be guilty of intellectual dishonesty to say that Moses gave the regulation by chance, apart from divine guidance. Diminish the week by a single day, the work is too small to require the rest. Increase it by a single day, the work is too great to go without rest." —W. B. K.

* * *

A Sure Way to Lessen Sunday Work

Bill usually attended church regularly. So when he had been absent for several Sunday mornings, his pastor was deeply concerned. He went to see Bill and said, "I haven't seen you in church lately. Is there any reason for your continued absence?" "Yes, there is a reason. As you know, I handle perishable commodities. Someone must handle them, even on Sundays. My employees want to attend their church, so I take over on Sundays, though I greatly miss the fellowship of God's people. But, Pastor, since I am doing this necessary work on the Lord's Day, I am going to give to the Lord all the money I make on His time — thirty-five dollars!"

How little work there would be on the Lord's day if all Sunday workers had to follow Bill's example! —W. B. K.

* * *

What Would You Have Done?

When studying the Hebrew New Testament with a class of Jewish boys, the question was raised about Jesus healing a man on the Sabbath of an infirmity of thirty-eight years' duration. I asked them what they thought about Christ's action. One boy said that as the man's infirmity was of long standing, he could easily have waited one day more. Another said it would have saved trouble if Jesus had deferred the cure until the next day. A third said that there had been no infringement of the Sabbath law because the act of healing involved no manual operation. The discussion abruptly ended when a blind boy in the class asked, "What would you have preferred if you had had an infirmity for thirty-eight years?"
—George M. Mackie

* * *

What Kept Her Going

Granny Stewart was a cheerful, hardworking person. She dearly loved her Lord. She was poor and so she had to work, although she was advanced in years and suffered from arthritis. She was a cleaning woman in a large hotel in Edinburgh.

As she scrubbed the hotel lobby one day, a guest said to her, "So you wash this floor six mornings a week?" "I do that," cheerfully replied Granny. "Well, I hope you at least sleep late on Sunday, and get plenty of rest on that day," said the guest.

"No," said Granny, "that is the morning when I get up early, too, to take my grandchildren to Sunday school and kirk!"

A look of distress came to the face of the guest. He said, "But surely you've earned your right to a good rest on one morning of the week. Wouldn't that help you to keep going?"

Granny beamed with joy as she said, "Och! It's going to the kirk on the Lord's day that keeps me going the other six days of the week!" —W. B. K.

LORD'S SUPPER

Illustrations

Has Anyone Been Overlooked?

"Has anyone been overlooked?" asked a pastor as he looked over the audience at the conclusion of the Lord's Supper. One of God's children who was present had a vision of a lost world in his soul. He arose and said feelingly, "Yes, pastor, there are millions in the regions beyond who are starving for Jesus, the 'Bread of life!' They are going into a lost eternity at the rate of eighty-three per minute. Some two thousand years ago, Jesus said, 'Go ye into all the world and preach the gospel to every creature.' Some of them plead, 'Come, help us!' Pastor, they have been over-looked!" —W. B. K.

* * *

A Cup of Hallowed Memory

Recently I came across a badly nicked enamel cup which, for years, had been among the odds and ends in a seldomly opened drawer. How junky were some of the things in that drawer! As I sorted the things and discarded unwanted things the badly nicked cup was tossed out too. But as I looked at that little, old cup, a train of happy and hallowed memories raced through my mind: My three daughters, when babies, had learned to drink milk and orange juice from that cup. Instantly and reverently I recovered it from the heap. Tenderly caressing it with my hands, I said, "This cup will find its place among my treasured possessions, for when I look at it, memories of the joyous babyhood days of my daughters fill my being with grateful and precious thoughts!

I am thinking now of another cup, a cup which is most sacred to God's children, a cup which the Saviour blessed.

How prone we are to forget! To keep in memory His vicarious death and sure promise to return again, the Lord has left with His children the communion cup and the command, "This do in remembrance of me" (Luke 22:19); "Drink it, in remembrance of me" (I Cor. 11:25); "For as often as ye eat this bread, and drink this cup, ye do shew the Lord's death till he come" (I Cor. 11:26). —W. B. K.

* * *

I Must Confess First

The Lord's Supper was going to be observed in a church in India. The minister first gave a searching preparatory message. A tall Indian stood and said tearfully to one of the missionaries: "I am so sorry, Memsahib, but when I was working for you, I took a gunny sack. I didn't mean to steal it. I only meant to borrow it. But it's burned up. Please forgive me. I will pay for it. I want to take Communion, but I couldn't until I had confessed this!" "I freely forgive you," said the

missionary, as both went to the altar and partook of the sacred elements.
—W. B. K.

* * *

Guilt Cleansed Away

A member of the Rev. Thomas Guthrie's church said, "Pastor, I said to myself this morning that I would not partake of Communion. I was distressed by my guilt and unworthiness. However, when I got ready for church, and while I was washing my hands, the Lord seemed to say to me, 'Cannot I, in my blood, wash your soul as easily as you wash your hands?' I came to Communion this morning, and sat under Christ's shadow with great joy!"
—*United Presbyterian*

* * *

A Peek at the Early Christians

When Pliny was governor of Bithynia, he wrote a most interesting letter to the Roman Emperor Trajan, asking why Christians were being exterminated, and added: "I have been trying to get all the information I could regarding them. I have even hired spies to profess to be Christians and become baptized in order that they might get into the Christian services without suspicion. Contrary to what I had supposed, I find that the Christians meet at dead of night or at early morn, that they sing a hymn to Christ as God, that they read from their own sacred writings and partake of a very simple meal consisting of bread and wine and water (the water added to the wine to dilute it in order that there might be enough for all). This is all that I can find out, except that they exhort each other to be subject to the government and to pray for all men."
—Dr. Harry A. Ironside

* * *

Don't Stay Away

A man called his pastor on the telephone and said, "I'm not coming to the Communion service this time. I don't feel prepared; and since I've been sick, I'm so shaky and low in spirits; and somehow I just feel I've failed the Lord so much." The wise minister answered, "My friend, I'm afraid it's your feelings you are going by. You know there's a good place to prepare, and that's in the secret place of prayer where none but the Lord sees and hears. And no matter what your feelings are, remember 'He ever liveth to make intercession' for you. Don't stay away from the Lord's Table, friend, because of your feelings; that's just what the devil wants you to do. Meet the Lord at His Table and let it be a time of heart-searching and revival for you. It will be, if you will it."

* * *

Preparation Before Participation

The writer has been reading recently the "Memoirs of Thomas Boston." He was one of the Marrow Men in Scotland and the pastor of Ettrick two hundred years ago. When he became pastor of Ettrick he found such carelessness of life among the members, and such gross indifference to the ordinances of God, that he refused to allow the Lord's Supper to be administered for the first three years of his pastorate. Then, at the first Communion, he gave tokens only to fifty-six persons whom he deemed ready to come to the Lord's table. Twenty-four years later he held his last Communion. After three days of preaching and preparation, on the Saturday afternoon he, and his elders, gave tokens to 777 persons to commune the next day. They came seeking Jesus. The Communion to them meant putting away sin, and renewing their covenant with their Lord, and experiencing His grace in their hearts. Those Communion seasons were to them times of refreshing from the presence of the Lord.

—*United Presbyterian*

LOST

Short Quotes

He who provides for this life, but takes no care for eternity, is wise for a moment, but a fool forever.

—Tillotson

* * *

Your fairest pretensions must be waived,
Your best resolutions be crossed,
You can never expect to be perfectly saved,
Till you know yourself utterly lost!

* * *

Two men rode by the estate of a wealthy man who had recently died. "What is the value of this estate, including the mansion on the hill?" asked one of the men. The other replied, "I don't know what its value is, but I know that it cost its owner his soul!"

—W. B. K.

* * *

A man found an Indian wandering aimlessly in the woods and asked, "Are you lost?" The Indian replied. "No! No! Indian not lost. Wigwam lost!" How like that Indian are many who are too proud to acknowledge their lostness and to pray: "God be merciful to me a sinner!" —W. B. K.

Robert Service, poet of Yukon, died at eighty-four. He was the author of *The Shooting of Dan McGrew* which netted him about $500,000. At the age of eighty, Service gave an *Associated Press* reporter a verse that expressed his state of hopelessness. The verse reads:

"E'er death shall slam the door
will you, like me,
Face fate and count the score —
futility?"

—W. B. K.

* * *

A man said to a high-school student, "Well, your high-school course is finished." "Yes," said the young man, "I graduate today." "And then what are you going to do?" "Oh, I shall go through college and take up a profession." "And then?" "Then I'll marry a fine woman, make a fortune, and succeed in the world." "And then?" "Then I shall retire, travel, see the world, take life easy." "And then?" "Well, old age will come; but I hope to enjoy that,

too." "And then?" "Well, then I shall have to die, I suppose." "And then?" But the young man had no answer ready for that question. Have you?
—*Power*

* * *

Some time ago a boy fell into an old well. In a short while $40,000 was raised in the small community to bring in the necessary earth-moving equipment for his rescue. In 1937, Amelia Earhart, attempting a round-the-world flight, was reported lost. For the following ten days, our government and others spent over $250,000 daily searching for her. We place highest value on this life. We spend comparatively little on seeking lost souls!
—*The Brethren Evangelist*

* * *

A faithful pastor was called to the bedside of an officer in his church. "Oh, Pastor," pleaded the dying man, "I have sent for you to tell me how to be saved!" "What!" exclaimed the pastor, "is it possible that you have sat under my ministry for these many years and do not know the way of salvation?" "Yes, Pastor, it is true. While you preached my thoughts were on business. Rarely did I give attention to your messages!"   —Dr. George W. Truett

Illustrations

Just a Minute

If you should wake some dreadful day
Before His throne, and hear Him say:
"I am the Way you did not take,
Although I died once for your sake;
I am the Truth you did not heed,
You were not sure you had a need;
I am the Light you did not see —
Now, darkness for eternity!"
You cannot say, "I did not know";
He plainly wrote and told you so.
And if you would not read His Word?
That Word still stands, "Thus saith the
    Lord!"
—*Martha Snell Nicholson*

* * *

Religious, But Lost!

Dr. Harry A. Ironside and his family were going to the Pacific coast by train one summer. His oldest son walked down the aisle giving tracts to the passengers. Later a passenger came and sat down by Dr. Ironside. "That was your little son who gave me that tract, I believe." "That's right," answered Dr. Ironside. The woman said, "I am so glad to know that there are other religious people on the train beside myself. I have been religious all my life. My uncle and my two brothers are clergymen." "That's interesting, but have you been converted yourself?" "Why, you don't seem to understand. My father was a Bible-class leader and my uncle and two brothers are earnest clergymen," she said. "But you don't expect to go to heaven hanging on their coattails, even if they were born-again Christians, do you?" "No," she said, "but I thought if I put it that way, you would understand that religion runs in our family!" —W. B. K.

* * *

Emptiness Without the Saviour!

Had I wealth and love in fullest measure,
    And a name revered both far and near,
Yet no hope beyond, no harbor waiting,
    Where my storm-tossed vessel I could
        steer;
If I gained the world, but lost the
        Saviour,
    Who endured the cross and died for
        me,
Could then all the world afford a refuge,
    Whither, in my anguish, I might flee?

Oh, what emptiness — without the Saviour
'Mid the sins and sorrows here below!
And eternity, how dark without Him! —
Only night and tears and endless woe!
What, though I might live without the
        Saviour,
When I come to die, how would it be?
Oh, to face the valley's gloom without
        Him!
And without Him all eternity!
—V. Raymond Edman

* * *

Only Two Classes

In 1912 the great ocean liner the *Titanic* struck an iceberg in the north

Atlantic and sank. Some were saved but the majority was lost. Some hours afterwards, the names of those known to have been saved and the names of the lost were placed on two bulletin boards outside the office of the White Star Line in Liverpool, England. Friends and relatives knew that there were but two classes among those who had been on the *Titanic* — the saved and the lost!

When God looks upon the people of the world, He sees but two kinds of folk — the saved and the unsaved.

"He that believeth on the Son hath everlasting life: and he that believeth not the Son shall not see life; but the wrath of God abideth on him" (John 3:36). —W. B. K.

* * *

Microphone in Your Heart

According to *Newsweek* the stethoscope, commonly used by doctors to listen to one's heart, is due to become obsolete. A new invention unveiled recently by the Heart Association is a microphone that can record the sound waves from within the heart on a mike's ceramic plate. This tiny microphone can be slipped through the veins right up into the heart itself and the vibrations are amplified as sound or as a diagram on a picture tube.

This is a marvelous advance in the science of medicine. However, science has not been able to compare its findings with the knowledge and the accurate appraisal and diagnosis of the human heart as God has revealed it in the Bible: "The heart is deceitful above all things, and desperately wicked: who can know it?" For confirmation, read your daily newspaper!

—J. B. Tweter in *Christian Life*

* * *

Why Will Ye Die?

The dreadful scourge of sleeping sickness struck a certain section of Africa. This sickness is caused by the bites of the tsetse fly, which lives in the dark, dense forests. Many natives succumbed. The Belgian government sent in a remedy for the sickness. Missionaries were supplied with it, and went in all directions into the villages to inoculate the natives. At their approach, however, many of the natives in the faraway villages would scamper away. They were afraid of the white man and his needle. The sure remedy for their sickness had been provided, but they refused it!

God, in mercy, has provided an unfailing remedy for sleeping, sin-sick souls. Yet many refuse the remedy. Jesus provided the remedy for the scourge of sin. All who reject Him will die in their sins. Jesus said to those who rejected Him: "And ye will not come to me, that ye might have life" (John 5:40).

—Told by a missionary

* * *

I Tried to Save Her!

During the blitz in London a woman stood in an open window in the top story of a blazing building. An escape ladder was quickly run up. A brave fireman made his way to the top. He leaned into the window with outstretched arms to take the woman to safety. The more he pleaded with her, the more she retreated in terror. The flames enveloped her. The noble fireman had to return without her! Weeping, he said, "I tried to save her, but she wouldn't let me!"

If you are eternally lost, it won't be because God failed to make every provision for your eternal safety and salvation. Pleading, He asks you to flee from the wrath to come to the Saviour, who, by the grace of God, tasted death for every man. You'll die in your sins if you refuse to come to Him —W. B. K.

* * *

Bony Finger Points to Text

Emperor Charlemagne was interred in the tomb of the emperor at Aix-la-Chapelle, France. His body was placed in a sitting posture in the marble coronation chair in the death chamber beneath the floor of the tomb. He wore his imperial robes. In his left hand was a scepter, and on his head was a jeweled crown. His right hand rested on a Bible that lay open on his lap. The burial chamber was sealed for centuries.

When the tomb was opened, what changes the passing of the centuries had wrought! The scepter had slipped from the hand. The crown had toppled to the floor. The robes had become dust. The finger of the skeleton still pointed to the verse of Scripture: "For what is a man profited, if he shall gain the whole world, and lose his own soul?"
—W. B. K.

• • •

Self-Made Trap

Recently the word was spread in Livingston, Montana, that mountain lions had been spotted on a nearby ranch. The chase was on and before the hunt was over, two large cats had been treed and shot. One measured seven feet and weighed 125 pounds and the other was seven feet six inches and weighed 145 pounds.

The interesting part about these native lions is that they always head for the false security of a tree when the hounds are after them, thus assuring their ultimate destruction. They cannot reason that immediate security is not always the best — that the only

escape from the tree is down, into a trap of their own setting.

Many persons reason as poorly in the important matter of their eternal welfare. When pursued by an awakened conscience and the fear of death, they seek the false security of the home-made tree of their own good works.
—*The Log*

• • •

African and American Pagans

An Ethiopian was asked: "Do you believe in God? He replied, "Yes, I believe in God, but I don't offer sacrifices to Him. God is far away and will not harm me. I offer sacrifices to the lions because they are near. They will kill and eat my cattle and maybe my children if I do not offer sacrifices to them!"

An American merchant was asked: "Do you believe in God?" He replied, "Surely, I believe in God, but 'business is business.' I go to church only occasionally, for I must consider my business." In reality, he meant, "I sacrifice to my business."

One was an African pagan. The other was an American pagan. —W. B. K.

LOVE FOR CHRIST

Illustrations

That's Why I Love Him!

An old Indian chief constantly spoke of the Lord Jesus and what He meant to him. "Why do you talk so much about Jesus?" asked a friend. The old chief did not reply, but slowly, deliberately gathered some sticks and bits of grass. He made a circle of them. In the circle he placed a caterpillar. Still silent, he struck a match and lit the sticks and bits of grass. They watched the caterpillar. As the fire caught around the circle, the trapped caterpillar began to crawl around rapidly, seeking a way of escape.

As the fire advanced, the helpless caterpillar raised its head as high as it could. If the creature could have spoken, it would have said, "My help can come only from above."

Then the old chief stooped down. He extended his finger to the caterpillar which crawled up his finger to safety. "That," said the old chief glowingly, "was what the Lord Jesus did for me! I was lost in sin. My condition was hopeless. I was trapped. Then the Lord Jesus stooped down, and in love and mercy He drew me out of the 'horrible pit' of sin and shame. How can I help but love Him and talk of His wondrous love and care?"
—Told by Dr. John R. Rice

• • •

The Motive

I will not work my soul to save,
For that my Lord has done,
But I will work like any slave,
For love of God's dear Son!

Moody's Love for Jesus

"The first time I saw Mr. Moody," said Mr. Reynolds, "was in a little shanty that had been abandoned by a saloon keeper. Mr. Moody had gotten the place to hold a meeting in at night. I was there a little late, and the first thing I saw was a man standing up, holding a Negro boy, and trying to read to him the story of the prodigal son. A great many of the words he could not make out and had to skip them. I thought: 'If the Lord can use such an instrument as that for His honor and glory, it will astonish me!' After the meeting was over, Moody said to me: "Reynolds, I have only one talent. I have no education, but *I love the Lord Jesus Christ!* I want to do something for Him. Pray for me!'" —*Dawn*

* * *

Loving Him Who First Loved Me

Saviour! teach me day by day,
Love's sweet lessons to obey;
Sweeter lessons cannot be,
Loving Him who first loved me.

With a childlike heart of love,
At Thy bidding may I move;
Prompt to serve and follow Thee,
Loving Him who first loved me.

Teach me all Thy steps to trace,
Strong to follow in Thy grace:
Learning how to love from Thee,
Loving Him who first loved me.

Love in loving finds employ —
In obedience all her joy;
Ever new that joy will be,
Loving Him who first loved me.

Thus may I rejoice to show
That I feel the love I owe;
Singing, till Thy face I see,
Of His love who first loved me.
—*Selected*

* * *

Convinced Intellectually

I had been convinced intellectually of a Supreme Being. All nature pointed to it, all science affirmed it. But God to me had been an impersonal power and heretofore I flinched from anything *mysterious.* Universal laws readily enough point to a Supreme Intelligence. But one does not *love* a Supreme Intelligence, a Universal Truth, or a Divine Law. Not until God becomes a loving Father intimately concerned with your personal problems are you able to love your God with your heart, your mind, and your soul.
—Mayling Soong Chiang

* * *

Love and Service

As Gustave Doré was putting the finishing touches on the face of Christ in one of his paintings, an admiring friend stepped quietly into the studio. She looked with bated breath upon the painting. Doré sensed her presence and said graciously, "Pardon, madam, I did not know you were here." She answered, "Monsieur Doré, you must love Him very much to be able to paint Him thus!" "Love Him, madam?" exclaimed Doré, "I *do* love Him, but if I loved Him better I could paint Him better!"

If we loved Him better, we could serve Him better. —W. B. K.

* * *

I Want to Love Thee

As an old man was walking to work one morning, Jesus' question to Peter came to his mind: "Simon . . . lovest thou me?" He wished with all his heart that he could answer as Peter did. He felt sad that he couldn't. Then this thought came to him: "If I cannot say so much as Peter, perhaps I could say, 'Lord, Thou knowest that I do *not* love Thee.'" He found some comfort in his honest confession. But as he walked along he said, "Lord, Thou knowest that *I want* to love Thee." He began to think of Christ's great love for him. He thought of Christ's life and of His death as his substitute. From his heart burst forth the affirmation, "Lord, Thou knowest that I do love Thee!" He asked Christ to come into his heart and make him a child of God. He went on his way rejoicing — a new creature in Christ Jesus! —W. B. K.

LOVE FOR OTHERS

Short Quotes

"Give my love to the world," said John Greenleaf Whittier as he died.

* * *

Let us raise our standard of loving the higher, the better.

* * *

If I could choose but one great gift,
Dear God, what would it be?
I diligently searched my heart
And then prayed fervently:
"God, give me charity!'"
—Elaine Watson

* * *

There are two ways of being united —frozen together, and melted together. What Christians most need is to be united in brotherly love. —Moody

* * *

It is no chore for me to love the whole world. My only real problem is my neighbor next door.
—*The Defender*

* * *

One Christmas William Booth, founder of the Salvation Army, wanted to send a message of encouragement to Salvationists throughout the world. A lengthy message was prohibitive, so he chose a message of but one word: *Others!*
—W. B. K.

* * *

I am sick of opinions. Give me a humble, gentle lover of God and man — a man full of mercy and good fruits, without partiality or hypocrisy. Bigotry is too strong an attachment to our own creed or opinion. How unwilling men are to allow anything good in those who do not agree with them in all things. We must not narrow the cause of God to our own beliefs, but rejoice in goodness wherever it appears.
—John Wesley

* * *

He drew a circle that shut me out,
Heretic, rebel, a thing to flout,
But love and I had a mind to win,
We drew a circle and took him in!

* * *

Said a New York socialite to Mrs. Fritz Kreisler; "You don't seem to get much 'kick' out of social life!" "No," said Mrs. Kreisler, "I get more 'kick' out of feeding poor children. I get my 'kicks' in a different way, that's all!" —W. B. K.

* * *

Ah, how skillful grows the hand
That obeyeth love's command,
It is the heart, and not the brain,
That to the highest doth attain,
And he who follows love's behest
Far excelleth all the rest.

* * *

Love this world through me, Lord,
This world of broken men,
Thou didst love through death, Lord,
Oh, love in me again!
Souls are in despair, Lord,
Oh, make me know and care;
When my life they see,
May they behold Thee,
Oh, love the world through me.
—Dr. Will Houghton

Illustrations

One Thing More I Ask

Dear God, another day is done
And I have seen the golden sun
Swing in the arch from east to west
And sink behind the pines to rest.
I thank Thee that Thou gavest me
The power of sight that I may see
The tinted glories of Thy skies,
An earthly glimpse of Paradise;
The power to hear the evening breeze
Swelling in organ harmonies;
The power to feel the tender grasp
Of loving hands in friendship's clasp;
I thank Thee for these gifts to me,
But one thing more I ask of Thee:
From out Thy bounteous, gracious hand
Give me the power to understand,
To understand — to sympathize —
To note the pain in others' eyes;
To have the power rightly to read
The kindly motive of each deed.
And this I humbly ask of Thee
Because I know Thou lovest me. Amen.
—*Selected*

213

Love Never Faileth

A little five-year-old boy in an orphanage habitually stole things from the other children and hid them in his locker. The superintendent reasoned with him, but to no avail. Then he tried different kinds of discipline. Still the child continued his thievery. "Possibly the child takes things which do not belong to him to compensate for the lack of parental love," suggested one. "Let's lavish love on him!" In different ways, the officials of the orphanage demonstrated to the child that they had genuine love for him. Within a short while a wonderful change was observed! He no longer took things from the other children. "Love never faileth." Try it! —W. B. K.

* * *

How Many Commandments Are There?

Years ago a bishop, wanting to test the hospitality of the members of one of the churches over which he had the oversight, dressed as a tramp and started on his unusual mission. Some rudely rebuffed him, saying, "Be gone!" Others showed kindness. One housewife began to lecture him, asking, "How many commandments are there?" Hesitantly, the "stranger" mumbled. "Eleven!" "I thought I hadn't misjudged you! Here, take this catechism, and the next time anyone asks you how many commandments are there say, 'Ten.'" The bishop went heavy-heartedly away!

The following Sunday in the pulpit of the community church he read his text: "A new commandment I give unto you, That ye love one another; as I have loved you, that ye also love one another" (John 13:34). Then the bishop said, "Friends, it would appear that with this *new commandment*, there are *eleven* commandments!"

The face of a certain woman in the audience crimsoned! Can you guess why?
—W. B. K.

* * *

I Put Myself in Their Shoes

It was the custom of an Indian tribe to appoint a judge to go into the Indian villages and try evildoers. One time a young brave was chosen for the task. He wanted to judge righteously. He went into a dense, dark forest and prayed, "O Great Maker of Men, forbid that I judge any man until I have walked for two months in his moccasins!"

I know a minister whose life is dedicated wholly to God and to helping people who are in trouble. He cheerfully responds at any hour of the day or night to the calls of distressed people. "How can you respond so readily to calls for help from people whom you do not know, and who are so unworthy of your help?" someone asked. The minister replied, "Here's the reason: In imagination I put myself in the shoes of needy, troubled ones and say to myself, 'I may be down tomorrow and in need of an encouraging word and a helping hand.' This consideration deepens my pity for the needy ones, and the constraining love of Christ impels me to do as I do!" —W. B. K.

* * *

Love Doesn't Count the Cost

William Gladstone, in announcing the death of Princess Alice to the House of Commons, told a touching story. The little daughter of the Princess was seriously ill with diphtheria. The doctors told the Princess not to kiss her little daughter and endanger her life by breathing the child's breath. Once when the child was struggling to breathe, the mother, forgetting herself entirely, took the little one into her arms to keep her from choking to death. Gasping and struggling for her life, the child said, "Mamma, kiss me!" Without thinking of herself, the mother tenderly kissed her daughter. She got diphtheria and some days thereafter she went to be forever with the Lord.

Real love forgets self. Real love knows no danger. Real love doesn't count the cost. The Bible says: "Many waters cannot quench love, neither can the floods drown it" (Song of Sol. 8:7).
—W. B. K.

* * *

Though I Have

If I have the language perfectly and speak like a native, and have not His love for them, I am nothing. If I have diplomas and degrees and know all the up-to-date methods, and have not His touch of understanding love, I am nothing. If I am able to argue successfully against the religions of the people and make fools of them, and have not His wooing note, I am nothing. If I have all faith and great ideals and magnificent plans, and not His love that sweats and bleeds and weeps and prays and pleads, I am nothing. If I give my clothes and money to them, and have not His love for them, I am nothing.

If I surrender all prospects, leave home and friends, make the sacrifices of a missionary career, and turn sour and selfish amid the daily annoyances and slights of a missionary life, and have not the love that yields its rights, its leisures, its pet plans, I am nothing. Virtue has ceased to go out of me. If I can heal all manner of sickness and disease, but wound hearts and hurt feelings for want of His love that is kind, I am nothing. If I can write articles or publish books that win applause, but fail to transcribe the Word of the Cross into the language of His love, I am nothing.
—*The South African Pioneer*

* * *

How He Found Joy and Contentment

There was a wealthy nobleman in Italy who had grown tired of life. He had everything one could wish for except happiness and contentment. He said, "I am weary of life. I will go to the river and there end my life." As he walked along, he felt a little hand tugging at his trousers. Looking down, he saw a frail, hungry-looking little boy who pleaded, "There are six of us. We are dying for want of food!" The nobleman thought, "Why should I not relieve this wretched family? I have the means." Following the little boy, he entered a scene of misery, sickness and want. He opened his purse and he emptied all of its contents, saying, "I'll return tomorrow, and I will share with you more of the good things which God has given to me in abundance!"

He left that scene of want and wretchedness, rejoicing, with no thought of ending his life. —W. B. K.

* * *

We Then That Are Strong Ought to Bear

God, in His inscrutable and unerring wisdom, sent to a Christian home an afflicted baby boy. "Should he be placed in an institution?" was the question that presented itself. After prolonged prayer it was unanimously decided that little Tommy would stay at home and be the special object of tender care and love!

Wherever the family went, little Tommy was carried along. Intermittent drooling and manifestations of idiocy evoked no feeling of shame in that noble family. They held their heads high as their love and care for the weaker one deepened.

For years they exemplified the Scriptural admonition: "We then that are strong ought to bear the infirmities of the weak, and not to please ourselves" (Romans 15:1).

In his thirteenth year, God took little Tommy home to be forever with the Lord.

It was the unanimous feeling of each member of that family that in lavishing love, kindness, understanding, affection and Christlike sympathy upon little Tommy, they became more loving, more understanding, more Christlike and kinder to each other.

In the church of Christ there are weaker ones, too. Not until we awaken in glory will we fully understand how indispensable to God's over-all, eternal purposes are these weaker ones.

"Nay, much more those members of the body, which seem to be more feeble, are necessary" (I Cor. 12:22).
—Told by a pastor

* * *

What a Challenging Field, Chalmers!

When he was still a young man, Dr. Chalmers left his great church and a host of admiring friends in Forfarshire, to labor in the slums of Edinburgh. It was a dreary day when he reached his new work. Clouds hung oppressively low and the rain descended in a dismal drizzle. Rags and pillows were stuffed in broken windows. Dr. Chalmers became sad and heavy-hearted. As he trudged along, he heard a cheerful voice saying, "Greeting, Chalmers!" It was Dr. Thomas Guthrie, who added, "what a fine and challenging field you have in which to work!" "Why I never thought of it in that light," said Dr. Chalmers. "I saw the needy people through my eyes, and not as the Lord sees them — a flock that somebody must shepherd!" Seeing those people in the

Edinburgh slums as God saw them, his heart was filled with love and compassion for sinful men and women, boys and girls. And his work was crowned with success. —W. B. K.

* * *

Love

To kiss the hands that smite,
     To pray for them that persecute,
To hear the voice of blame,
Reap undeserved shame,
     And still be mute —
       Is this not love?

To give for evil good,
     To learn what sacrifice can teach,
To be the scoffer's sport,
Nor strive to make retort
     To angry speech —
       Is this not love?

To face the harsh world's harms,
     To brave its bitterness for years,
To be an unthanked slave,
And gain at last a grave
     Unwet by tears —
       Is this not love?
            —Susie M. Betts

* * *

Where Lincoln Put the Emphasis

A budding high-school orator delivered Lincoln's Gettysburg Address. Calmly he began, "Fourscore and seven years ago." He glowed with fervency when he came to the climactic words ". . . that government *of* the people, *by* the people, and *for* the people shall not perish from the earth!" The audience applauded uproariously! An old man hobbled slowly through the crowd and said to the young orator, "You did a grand job, son! You will be interested to know that I was present at Gettysburg when Lincoln delivered that memorable speech. What an occasion it was. But, son, you didn't say it just like Lincoln did. You said, 'Government *of* the people, *by* the people, and *for* the people.' When Lincoln spoke these words — it seems I can hear him still — he said, 'Government of the *people*, by the *people*, and for the *people* shall not perish from the earth!' His emphasis and concern were on *people*. Your emphasis is on prepositions!"

It was the need of *people* — not the slavish, legalistic observance of the Sabbath — which was of paramount con-

cern to the Saviour. The sight of hungry, shepherdless *people* moved the heart and hand of the Saviour in their behalf.

The spiritual and temporal needs of *people* are of greater concern to God than any institution, no matter how hoary and venerable the institution may be. This fact was enunciated with authority and finality in Christ's words: "The sabbath was made for man, and not man for the sabbath" (Mark 2:27). In countries where this principle is reversed, *people* become pawns of the state and are degraded to the level of pack animals!

When religious institutions lose their primary concern for the spiritual and temporal needs of *people*, heaven weeps and the zest to carry on fades and dies. Such institutions become soulless and are a distorted image or caricature of what they ought to be! Our major emphasis must ever be on *people*. We must love, respect, and have an unfeigned concern for people, wanting their highest and best welfare everywhere.
            —W. B. K.

* * *

Love for Mexicans!

Years ago a young woman went from Dr. Bob Shuler's church as a missionary to Mexico. Her heart was aglow with God's love for the Mexicans. Wherever the word "love" occurred in I Corinthians 13, she interpolated: "love for the Mexicans." She read, for instance, "Though I speak with the tongues of men and of angels, and have not love for the Mexicans, I am become as sounding brass, or a tinkling cymbal." Her unfeigned love for the Mexicans enabled her to win many of them to the Saviour. After years of unselfish service she succumbed to illness. Hours before her death she was unconscious. As her Mexican converts gathered about her bed, the sight of their tearful faces brought her back to consciousness. Before she passed to be forever with the Lord she requested her converts not to bring flowers, but Spanish Bibles and New Testaments to the funeral. They were stacked high around her casket. Later, her converts gave them to those who did not have the Word of God.
            —W. B. K.

LOVE OF GOD

Short Quotes

There is an eye that never sleeps,
  Beneath the wing of night;
There is an ear that never shuts,
  When sink the beams of light;
There is an arm that never tires,
  When human strength gives way;
There is a love that never fails,
  When earthly loves decay.

—*Selected*

* * *

If any church would be content to have Jesus' teaching of love as its creed, I would join that church.

—Dr. Albert Einstein

* * *

Among the first glimpses we get of God is that of a *Seeker*: "Adam . . . Where art thou?" (Gen. 3:9). Someone said to a young minister, "You can never be a preacher if you read the question 'Where art thou?' in the tone of a policeman, as if God were seeking a fugitive from justice. You must read it as though God were a broken-hearted Father looking for a lost child!"

—W. B. K.

Though I have a scientific mind and a university degree in sociology and philosophy, and although I am an expert in social service and an authority on Browning, and though I use the language of the scientific laboratory so as to deceive the very elect into thinking I am a scholar, and have not a message of salvation and the love of Christ, I am a misfit in the pulpit and no preacher of the gospel!

—An anonymous minister

* * *

In St. Paul's Cathedral, London, is a life-size, marble statue of Christ writhing in anguish on the cross. The statue is subscribed: "This is how God loved the world!" —W. B. K.

* * *

A mother, in reprimanding her naughty little girl, said: "Bonnie Jean, if you are bad, God won't love you!" The mother was wrong. God loves bad people, but He doesn't love their bad ways.

—W. B. K.

Illustrations

God So Loved

A young woman went to the ticket office in an English railway station. She had lived only for the sinful pleasures of life. She was weary of her empty, sinful life. Above the ticket window were printed these words: "God So Loved!" Said she to the ticket agent, "I never heard that before. Where did those words come from?" "They are in the Bible, Miss," said the agent. "Where can I get a Bible?" she asked. "Across the street at the bookstore."

The young woman bought a Bible and returned to the station in time to take her train. She asked a passenger to find the place in her Bible where it said, "God so loved." She was shown John 3:16. She read it over and over again!

Reaching her home, the young woman rushed in. She showed the verse to the man with whom she lived. "Isn't this

wonderful!" she exclaimed as she showed him the verse. "I've known that verse was in the Bible for a long time. What's wonderful about it?" asked the one who, like herself, had lived a sinful life.

"Well, if God loves me like that, I am going to forsake my sinful life, and love and serve Him with all my heart!" she said.

She became a joyous Christian. She won the man to the Saviour. They were united in Christian marriage, and their home in London became a center of a rich influence for Jesus Christ!

—W. B. K.

* * *

Where God's Love Is Seen

I see God's love in simple things,
Enjoyed by common folk and kings;
I see it in the trees and flowers,
In sunlight and the summer showers,
In those who give me loving care,
And those who will my troubles share.

I know my friends who are so kind,
Are prompted by a Divine mind,
And I give thanks for them each night,
When velvet darkness hides the light;
I see it in the mountain peaks,
And hear it when the small child speaks.

I see it in the rainbow's hue,
Green moss and misty morning dew;
In dragonflies' transparent wings,
I hear it when a choir sings;
In bird songs at the break of dawn,
In sunrise in the early morn.

And when I long for quiet spells,
I read the Book that clearly tells
Of the great Love who gave His all,
To save poor sinners great and small;
And love, with faith and truth combined,
Who dares to say that love is blind.

O, Holy Blessed Trinity,
Enter my heart and set me free
From sin and all base things impure,
That I too might this life endure;
And give me grace that folk may see
In me Thy perfect charity.
—Sadie Tanner, who for many years
was hospitalized, and unable to move
more than a finger. Its composition
took weeks of dictation and effort of
memory.

* * *

God Hates Our Bad Ways

Little Gloria had a tantrum. She
screamed and jerked off her bedding
and threw it on the floor. When her
anger subsided, she felt very badly
about the way she had acted. She went
into her mother's room and sat beside
her. Both sat silently for a moment.
Then Gloria leaned her head on her
mother's shoulder and asked, "Mommy,
does God love me after I acted so bad?"
"Yes, Gloria, God loves you very much,
even now. But always remember that
God does not like the bad things we
do!" —W. B. K.

* * *

Too Far Down!

The captain of a ship crossing the
Atlantic said to a minister aboard, "We
have just crossed over the place where
the *Titanic*, the alleged unsinkable ship,
went down!" Later the minister said,
"I thought of all the wreckage beyond
the power of man to recover and re-

deem. I thought of the great bed of
the deep sea, with its treasures that
are too far down for man to reach and
restore. Too far down! And then I
thought of all the human wreckage engulfed and sunk in the depths of nameless sin. Too far down! For what?
Not too far down for *the love of God!*"
—W. B. K.

* * *

The Unfailing Motive

A young lady was deeply stirred by
a missionary address. She felt that the
Lord was calling her to work among
children in the foreign field. She could
hardly wait until she got to the mission
field, learn the language, and begin her
work. On her first trip into the interior,
she traveled by ox cart. About an hour
before reaching her destination it began
to rain. "I can go no further. The mud
is too deep," said the driver. She was
horrified! How could she spend the
night out in the rain on the road? All
of her baggage would be ruined. She
pleaded, but the driver paid no attention. All her love for these dear people
evaporated! She began to think that
they were horrid, stubborn creatures.
Finally, the man said that if she would
give him five dollars more, he thought
the ox could pull the cart to town. She
had to pay it, but from then on her
rosy vision of the mission field and
its glamor grew very dim. Later she
went to a village to try to reach the
children whom she loved, and they all
ran from her, calling her a "foreign
devil"! She realized at last that she had
come to the mission field because of her
own natural pity and love for people.
Then she knew that mere human love
and pity will not stand the tests of the
realities of life. If she had gone to the
mission field because Christ loved the
lost, not because she loved them, the
situation would have been different. Even
though the driver had left her in the
mud, Christ's love for his soul would
not be altered. He was unlovely because he did not yet know Christ!
—Raymond Frame, in *His*

* * *

Can't Get In Unless It Can Get Out

A minister was discussing electricity
with an electrician. "Is it true," asked
the minister, "that electricity cannot

get into you unless it can get out of you?" "That's absolutely right," answered the electrician. "Let me illustrate. When I worked in the coal mines in Pennsylvania, my brother operated one of the coal cars. I was standing on the rear of the car, singing in a carefree manner. Coming to a point where the tracks divided, my head got caught in the overhead 'frog.' There I dangled for a moment, my feet just clearing the ground! That explains my being here today. The high voltage current couldn't get into me because it couldn't get out of me!"

God's love, like electricity, can't get into us unless it can get out of us and share itself with others. —W. B. K.

* * *

Profit and Loss

I counted dollars while God counted crosses,
I counted gains while He counted losses,
I counted my worth by the things gained in store
But He sized me up by the scars that I bore.
I coveted honors and sought for degrees,
He wept as He counted the hours on my knees;
I never knew until one day by the grave
How vain are the things that we spend life to save;

I did not yet know until my loved one went above
That richest is he who is rich in God's love.
—*The Brethren Evangelist*

* * *

Thou Lovest Me

Grant me, O Lord, a heart content
To face each trial as it is sent.
That I may see in all Thy ways
A love that governs all my days.

Save me from doubt and dark despair.
Teach me to trust Thy tender care.
The distant scene I would not see,
Suffice to know Thou lovest me.

Thy love so vast, so full, so free,
That reaches down to even me,
In this assurance I am blest
No matter what may be the test.

I cannot drift beyond Thy care,
My every burden Thou wilt share.
Grant me this rest of faith, dear Lord,
According to Thy precious Word.

Open mine eyes that I might see
Each promise written there for me;
When Thou dost speak, attune my ear
That I might hear Thy accents clear.
—Rev. Walter E. Vater, D. D.

MISSIONS

Short Quotes

Yearly, the world's population increases by forty-two million. It is estimated that by the year 2000, with the increase of the birth rate over the death rate, incident to the discovery of life-prolonging antibiotics, there will be more Chinese than the population of the world is today.
—Bob Pierce

* * *

William Carey had high hopes that his son Felix would become a missionary. Official honors in Burma caused the young man's soul to shrivel toward divine things. The disappointed father requested prayer for his son, saying,

"Pray for Felix. He has degenerated into an ambassador of the British government!"

* * *

A mother of twelve children came to a minister and said, "I feel that God wants me to be a missionary!" The minister replied, "I believe you are right! God does want you to be a missionary, and He has already given you a mission field right in your own home!"
—W. B. K.

* * *

Five million New Yorkers are immigrants, or the children of immigrants. There are more Italians in New York

City than in Rome, more Irish than in Dublin, more Germans than in Berlin, more Puerto Ricans than in San Juan, and a tenth of the Jewish population of the world.

—Billy Graham

* * *

A young missionary, after spending some years in China, came home an invalid. His health had failed him, but he still had the yearning, burning heart of a true missionary. His heart was with the perishing millions of China. In speaking of them he said: "I can't sleep for thinking about them!"
There are ninety and nine that safely lie,
In the shelter of the fold,
But millions are left outside to die,
For the ninety and nine are cold!
Away in sin's delusive snare,
Hastening to death and dark despair,
Hastening to death and none to care,
For the ninety and nine are cold!

—W. B. K.

* * *

The rich man wasn't in hell long before he became an ardent believer in missions: "I pray . . . that thou wouldest send him to my father's house: For I have five brethren; that he may testify unto them, lest they also come into this place of torment" (Luke 16:27, 28).

—W. B. K.

* * *

A visitor from America saw a young Korean Christian kneeling and praying most fervently, while his breast heaved with emotion. The visitor whispered to a missionary, "What can that young fellow be praying about that agitates him so greatly?" Said the missionary, "He is praying that the salvation which has come to the Korean people may be carried to the other nations of Asia."

—W. B. K.

* * *

We've not only a story to tell to the nations, but also a *pardon* to deliver for the Saviour to the nations!
We've a pardon to give to the nations,
Which was purchased at infinite cost,
A pardon as yet undelivered,
Which leaves them eternally lost!

—*The Prairie Overcomer*

* * *

Dr. Wilfred Grenfell, medical missionary to Labrador, was guest at a dinner in London, together with a number of socially prominent British men and women.
During the course of the dinner, the lady seated next to him turned and said, "Is it true, Dr. Grenfell, that you are a missionary?"
Dr. Grenfell looked at her for a moment before replying, "Is it true, madam, that you are not?"

—*Sunday School Promoter*

* * *

There are a hundred thousand churches in America, and not far from its shores there are thousands of tribes without a missionary. There are more preachers in Los Angeles than there are missionaries in all of Japan. There are millions of dusty Bibles in homes and attics. Yet there are seventeen hundred languages and dialects without one word of Scripture.

—*Stewardship Bulletin*

* * *

God had only one Son, and He was a missionary.

—Livingstone

* * *

That land is henceforth my country which most needs the gospel.

—Count Zinzendorf

* * *

In North America there are 1,448 ministers per million people. In Latin America there are 19 missionaries per million people, and there are 87 million unevangelized. In Africa there are 56 missionaries per million people, and there are nearly 68 million unevangelized. In India and Pakistan there are 10 missionaries per million people, and there are 261 million unevangelized. Much of Europe, with its 480 million people, is largely unevangelized. All Russian-held territory is closed to missionaries. —W. B. K.

* * *

One-third to one-half of the first-term missionaries do not return to the foreign field for a second term.

—Harold Lindsell in
*Missionary Principles
and Practices*

* * *

Every heart without Christ is a mission field. Every heart with Christ is a missionary.

On with the message, on with the light,
On to the regions still shrouded in
night,
On to the nations which never have
heard,
On with the life-giving, soul-saving
Word!

* * *

"Wouldn't you rather be in Africa
preaching to a people with their face
toward the light, coming out of paganism, than in America preaching to
people with their backs to the light,
going into paganism?" asked an African
Christian. —W. B. K.

* * *

"I have long ago ceased to pray,
'Lord Jesus, have compassion on a lost
world,'" said Dr. A. J. Gordon, "for
the Lord seemed to say to me, 'I have
compassion on a lost world. Now it is
time for you to have compassion on
it. I have given My heart. Now give
your heart."

* * *

Take back my interest in Thy blood
unless it flows for the whole race.
—John Wesley

* * *

What are churches for, but to make
missionaries? What is education for,
but to train them? What is commerce
for, but to carry them? What is money
for, but to send them? What is life itself for, but to fulfill the purpose of
missions — the enthroning of Jesus
Christ in the hearts of men?
—Dr. Augustus H. Strong

* * *

I will go down, but remember that
you must hold the ropes.
—William Carey

* * *

A missionary does not necessarily go
outside of his country, his state or even
his own community. A true missionary
needs only to go outside himself.

* * *

In the mind of God there is no distinction between home missions and
foreign missions. Wherever there is a
lost soul there is mission ground.

* * *

Dr. Walter Wilson and a missionary
friend were praying for a car which
was greatly needed for the missionary's

work in Africa. The missionary prayed,
"O God, You know how badly I need
a car for my work. Do, Lord, send me
a car. Any kind of an old, ramshackle
car will do!" Dr. Wilson interrupted.
"Stop praying that way, brother! God
is not in the junk business!" —W. B. K.

* * *

Down beneath the mighty ocean
Divers plunge for treasures rare,
But men hold the ropes above them,
So they breathe the upper air.
Seeking pearls of richest value,
Braver hearts have dared to go,
But our hands must every moment,
Hold the ropes that go below!

* * *

I would that I had a thousand lives
and a thousand bodies that I might devote them all to no other employment
than preaching the gospel to those who
have never heard the joyful sound!
—A Missionary

* * *

Almost half of the world's population
can neither read nor write.
—Clarence W. Hall in
*Two Thousand Tongues
to Go*

* * *

A boy told the pastor of his church
that his ambition was to be a missionary.
"Are you saved?" asked the pastor.
"Yes," said the boy. "Then you are a
missionary *now*," said the pastor. "The
field is the world, and wherever you
live after you are saved, you are a
missionary. Don't expect God to make
you a missionary somewhere else, unless you are a missionary for Him
where you are," added the wise pastor.
—W. B. K.

* * *

Eighty-three percent of the money
given to missions is given by Canada
and the United States.
—Dr. Bob Pierce

* * *

We spend 96c on ourselves out of
every dollar and give only 4c to missions.
—Dr. Bob Pierce

* * *

"Mr. Taylor, why do you travel fourth
class?" someone asked Hudson Taylor.
"I travel fourth class because there is
no fifth class," was Mr. Taylor's answer.
—W. B. K.

221

India is a racial mosaic of 360 million persons who speak 180 distinct languages and 540 dialects.

—Rabbi Abba Hiller Silver

* * *

India has a population of approximately 360 million. Of these, 10 million are nominal Christians. This means that 350 million know nothing of Christ.

—Frederick G. Schwarz, in
Christianity Today

* * *

A one-legged schoolteacher from Scotland came to J. Hudson Taylor to offer himself for service in China. "Why do you with only one leg, think of going as a missionary?" asked Mr. Taylor. "I do not see those with two legs going, so *I must go!*" replied George Scott. He was accepted.

* * *

I cannot, I dare not, go up to the judgment until I have done the utmost God enables me to do to diffuse His glory through the world.

—Dr. Asahel Grant

* * *

If I had ten lives, I would gladly lay them down for Christ in the white man's grave to gain by the grace of God the black man's resurrection.

—Canon Taylor Smith

* * *

A United Nations estimate reports a net gain in the world population of 129,600 during every twenty-four-hour period.

* * *

There are some three billion people in world. Two-thirds of them are colored. Seven-eighths of the world's surface is uncultivated. Two-thirds of the colored people live in the uncultivated areas.

—Governor Collins (Fla.)

* * *

A United Nations report indicates that by the year 2000 the world population will be between six and seven billion.

* * *

The sob of a thousand million of poor heathen sounds in my ear, and moves my heart. And I try to measure, as God helps me, something of their darkness, something of their blank misery, something of their despair. Oh, think of these needs! I say again, they are ocean depths. And, beloved, in my Master's name, I want you to measure them, I want you to think earnestly about them, I want you to look at them, until they appal you, until you cannot sleep, until you cannot criticize.

—Charles Inwood

* * *

The only one among the twelve apostles who did not become a missionary became a traitor.

—Wm. Adams Brown

* * *

There are 1,700,000,000 people that today are living without sufficient food, shelter, clothing and health facilities. They are not going to remain quiescent. They are just going to have an explosion.

—*Time*, Nov. 30, '59

* * *

Five-ninths of the world is closed to Christian missions.

—Dorothy Farrier, Field
Representative of
International Students, Inc.

* * *

In the United States, there is one minister for every 1100 people.

—Dr. William Culbertson,
President Moody Bible Institute

* * *

O matchless honor, all unsought,
High privilege, surpassing thought,
That Thou shouldst call us, Lord, to be
Linked in work-fellowship with Thee!

To carry out Thy wondrous plan,
To bear Thy messages to man,
"In trust" with Christ's own word of
    grace,
To every soul of the human race!

* * *

A baby is born every eight and two-thirds seconds. The world has more than doubled its population in the last century. The world's population may reach four or five billion within the life span of those now living.

—Bob Pierce

* * *

Many will never reach the mission field on their feet, but all of God's children can reach it on their knees!

—W. B. K.

More than two billion of the earth's inhabitants are either pagan, atheistic or non-Christian. There are 800,000,000 Communists, all militant atheists. There are 700,000,000 Moslems, all anti-Christians, and there are almost a billion Indians and Chinese and other kindred Asiatics.
—Commander H. H. Lippincott, United States Navy (retired)

* * *

Six-sevenths of the world is without Christ.
—Rev. Charles E. Scott, D.D.

* * *

One-third of the world's people earn only one dollar a week. Two-thirds of the world's people go to bed hungry every night. Our problem is dieting. Their problem is living.
—Bishop Fulton J. Sheen

* * *

A missionary was homesick and discouraged. "My work is in vain, and I am spending my strength for nothing," he lamented. Then suddenly the cloud of discouragement lifted. Joy filled his heart! "What does this mean?" he asked. As he thought, he said, "Oh, I know! Somebody is praying for me. Prayer is being offered by friends at home."
—*The Brethren Missionary Herald*

* * *

Forget not that your first and principal business, as a disciple of Christ, is to give the gospel to those who have it not. He who is not a missionary Christian will be a missing Christian when the great day for the bestowing of rewards for faithful service comes.
—Dr. A. J. Gordon

* * *

Many of you have asked to know our real prayer needs. We missionaries go from daylight to midnight in a terrific heat witnessing for Christ but seeing little response. Sickness strikes many of our homes. Depression sweeps new missionaries. We see need after need that must be filled, and yet we have no immediate answer. Our need is not financial, for we are well provided for. Our greatest need is for the power of the Holy Spirit to saturate our lives.
—Paul Box, missionary to Malaya.

Illustrations

Unprayed-for Missionaries

James Gilmore was a foreign missionary. He felt that mission work could not succeed without prayer by God's children in the homeland. He said, "Unprayed for, I feel like a diver on the bottom of the river with no connecting line to the surface and no air to breathe; or like a fireman with an empty hose on a burning building. With prayer, I feel like David facing Goliath!" —W. B. K.

* * *

Except They Be Sent

A young medical doctor came to his pastor one day and joyously said, "Pastor, I have volunteered for mission service. How thrilled I am to obey the Saviour's command, 'Go *ye* into all the world, and preach the gospel to every creature.'" The pastor was delighted. He warmly congratulated the young doctor. Continuing, the doctor said, "I have dedicated my profession, my life, my *all* to God. I have entered into sacred covenant with God to earn money for Him and expend it in sending out missionaries into the regions beyond with the Gospel of the grace of God!"

Before the judgment seat of Christ, the young doctor will be *equally* rewarded with the missionaries whom his dollars sent to faraway places: "For who will hearken unto you in this matter? but as his part is that goeth down to the battle, so shall his part be that tarrieth by the stuff: they shall part alike" (I Sam. 30:24).
—W. B. K.

* * *

Do Not Say!

Years ago there was a young engineering student whose name was Fraser. He was just about to graduate with honors when a fellow student gave him a little booklet entitled, *Do Not Say*. It was written by a missionary in

China. It dealt with the excuses some give for not obeying the Lord's command to preach the gospel to every creature. Fraser surrendered to God's call and went to China. He was the first missionary in Lisu where he led thousands to Jesus! —W. B. K.

* * *

Jesus Is Here

Out where the loneliness presses around me,
 Looking on sights that are sordid and drear,
Strangely abiding — yet surely God called me,
 Why do I wonder if Jesus is here?

Strangeness of living and strangeness of people,
 Have I not come with the Gospel of cheer?
Why is my heart then depressed with its burden?
 Isn't my Comrade — my Jesus — out here?

God! Teach me quickly to do without friendships,
 How to let go of those things that were dear,
How to be rid of this self that is binding me,
 Surely my Master, my Jesus, is here.

Wilt Thou forgive me for failure in serving;
 Heartache, depression, regrets, disappear.
Born of the Cross, a new courage infills me;
 Jesus, my Victory, my Life, is now here!

—*Selected*

* * *

How God's Word Is Translated

It is interesting to observe how missionaries translate God's Word into the language of Indian tribes in Central and South America. "God's love" is translated "God hurts in His heart for us." "Doubt" becomes "Thinking two things." "Our hope is in God" becomes "We hang on God." "Heap coals of fire on his head" is translated "Make him ashamed by your friendliness."

Extreme caution must be exercised in translating the Bible into multi-tonal words, because often only the inflection of the voice indicates which word is meant. The word "sinner" is almost synonymous with "a fat person." One day a teacher said, "God loves the sinner." A look of bewilderment clouded the Indian faces. They understood it to mean, "God loves a fat person." None of them were fat, so they concluded that they were not the objects of God's love.
—W. B. K.

* * *

For Country, for Christ

For seven days, Airman Don Farrel underwent severe and dangerous tests, making make-believe trips to the moon. After the exhausting tests he repeated his offer. He said, "I would really and truly like to make that first trip to the moon! I am available if you want me!"

If others bravely do so much for their country, shouldn't God's children bravely go forth to the dark places on earth where Christ has never been named?
—W. B. K.

* * *

You're Now a Missionary

The false attitude which sidetracks hundreds of young people from the foreign field is expressed in the words, "I am going to be a foreign missionary." At the core of such a statement there is a basic misconception. The fact is, you are now a missionary or you are not a missionary. To put missionary service out in the future is to defeat the very purpose of missions. A missionary is fundamentally a soul-winner despite time or place. To conceive of the missionary as one who, after years of Bible school, college or seminary training, boards a plane and leaves for a foreign field is to misunderstand the entire proposition. To determine to be today the missionary that you hope to be in the future is the only true attitude.

—*Moody Monthly*

* * *

A Dying Mother's Request

The mother of Christian Schwartz died as he was born. Before her death she exacted this promise from her husband: "When my baby becomes a man and God calls him to be a missionary, promise me that you will not stand in his way!"

In those days, foreign missionary enterprise was almost unknown. Years passed. One day a brilliant young man came from the university and said, "Father, God has called me to be a missionary!" Tears filled the father's eyes as he recalled the promise he gave to his dying wife. "Answer the call, my son, and may God's blessings be continually upon you," said the father.

Christian Schwartz went to India, a pioneer missionary in the generation before William Carey. —W. B. K.

* * *

The Foreigner in the Midst

God has brought the mission field of the world right to our door. My church in Chicago was near the University of Chicago. Oftentimes I walked on the campus of the university where I encountered students from many nations. They were of the "upper crust" of society in their respective countries — leaders and potential leaders.

One afternoon, as I walked on the campus, I first encountered a Negro. Going on a little further, I engaged a Chinese in conversation. Still further, I met a man from Bagdad. Finally, I encountered four Arabs! I spoke to all of them about the Saviour, and gave them Gospel tracts.

Are these foreigners at our door less precious to God than their compatriots across the seas?

The mission field for all of us is where we are; besides, we can pray and give, and thus help to send the Gospel to the ends of the earth.

"Go not and glean in another field" (Ruth 2:8). —W. B. K.

* * *

No Pity Where Christ Is Unknown

How devoid of pity and compassion are a people who have no knowledge of God and of death's Conqueror, the ever living Saviour!

In the section of Africa where I was a missionary for more than a decade, it was not uncommon for the natives to kill, by a most torturous and slow death, aged ones who could no longer work. Their legs were broken and the protruding, splintered bones exposed to burning embers.

One day word came to the dispensary that an aged woman was at the nearby riverside, writhing in indescribable agony. The trail along which she had dragged herself was bespattered with blood. I took her on my back and brought her to the dispensary. The natives, totally devoid of any concern or sympathy, looked in amusement upon what I did.

How accurately does the Word of God depict those calloused souls — "past feeling!"

What a change is wrought in them when they become new creatures in Christ!

"We've a story to tell to the nations." Let's hasten forth with its liberating message.

—Told by Rev. C. Leslie Miller

* * *

A World Without

Our wealth in Christ is for ever incalculable. A missionary in China writes: "A great 'without' is written on heathenism. Men and women are *without* a Bible, *without* a Sunday and *without* righteousness. They have homes *without* peace, marriage *without* sanctity. Their young men and women are *without* ideals, the little children *without* purity, the mothers *without* wisdom or self-control. There is poverty *without* relief, sickness *without* skill or care, sorrow *without* sympathy, sin *without* remedy, death *without* hope. All this is wrapped up in the words, '*without* Christ.' This is why Christ has told us to go "into all the world, and preach the gospel.' This is why we urge you to give and pray *without* stint, for the only answer to the world *without* is to have Christ *within*."

—D. M. Panton

* * *

Mission-Minded

Every church is the product of someone's missionary activity. Every church is a monument to the missionary impulse. Every church should be reminded that it has been set down in the midst of a mission field — whether in the heart of Africa or in the heart of Washington, D.C.

Every church should be reminded that it has fallen heir to the Great Commission which Christ gave to His disciples in the long ago.

—Rev. Edward Hughes Pruden

We Forget So Soon!

There are about three billion people in the world. Many of them are without God and without hope, having never heard the name of Jesus. Many are saying, "Come and help us!" A heathen woman said to a missionary, "Tell your people how fast we are dying. Ask them if they cannot send the gospel a little faster!" An Indian woman pleaded, "Oh, tell us again who Jesus Christ is. Tell us slowly, for we forget so soon!" An Eskimo made this appeal: "Tell it to me once more for I want to be saved!" A Burmese boy pleaded: "Tell me where I can find Jesus! Tell me, oh, tell me!" —W. B. K.

* * *

Like a Flash from Heaven

A friend asked Judson, "Was it faith or love that influenced you most in going to Burma?" Judson answered, "There was in me at that time little of either. In thinking of what did influence me, I remember a time when I was greatly discouraged. Everything looked dark. No one had gone out from our country as a foreign missionary. The way was not open. I didn't know what to do. Then, with a flash, Christ's command, 'Go ye into all the world, and preach the gospel to every creature' seemed to come to my heart directly from heaven. I determined on the spot to obey Jesus at all costs." —W. B. K.

* * *

Why Didn't You Hurry?

When a father, who lived on the Western prairies, came home one night, his little boy ran through the long grass to meet him. Suddenly the boy disappeared. Running through the grass to the point where his boy vanished, the man heard a gurgling cry. His son had fallen into an old well. The father barely reached the well in time to save his boy. When the lad revived from his fright, he asked, "O Daddy, why didn't you hurry?" Said the father later, "That boy's question made a missionary out of me. I seemed to hear the piteous, pleading cry of myriads in the regions beyond, 'Why don't you hurry? We are dying without God and without hope. Why don't you hurry with the gospel?' " —W. B. K.

* * *

Even As Ye Were

British Christians ought to recollect that their ancestors were blind idolators, serving them that by nature are no gods. In Scotland stood the temple of Mars; in Cornwall, the temple of Mercury; in Bangor, the temple of Minerva; at Maldan, the temple of Victoria; in Bath, the temple of Apollo; at Leicester, the temple of Janus; at York, where St. Peter's now stands, the temple of Bellona; in London, on the site of St. Paul's Cathedral, the temple of Diana; and at Westminster, where the Abbey rears its venerable spire, the temple of Apollo. Through the mercy of God our country is now blessed with thousands of Christian churches and multitudes of Gospel ministers. The land is full of Bibles; and British Christians sensible of their privileges are engaged in diffusing the light of divine truth among the benighted nations.

—*Biblical Museum*

MOTHERS

Short Quotes

An aged, white-haired mother sat with a smile on her face in the White House, waiting for her famous son, Dwight, to arrive. Someone said to her, "You must be very proud of your great and illustrious son." Upon which she asked, "Which son?" Each one was equally great to that noble mother.

My sainted mother taught me a devotion to God and a love of country which have ever sustained me in my many lonely and bitter moments of decision in distant and hostile lands. To her, I yield anew a son's reverent thanks.

—General Douglas MacArthur

Who ran to help me when I fell,
And would some pretty story tell,
Or kiss the place to make it well?
My Mother!

* * *

Dr. G. Campbell Morgan had four sons. They all became ministers. At a family reunion, a friend asked one of the sons, "Which Morgan is the greatest preacher?" While the son looked at the father, he replied, *"Mother!"* —W. B. K.

* * *

A great Christian mother testified, "I was not content with my private prayer for my children, nor with our family prayers for them. Therefore, as my children grew old enough to make a personal decision for Christ, I took each one to my private place of prayer. There I poured out my soul for that one individually!"

Is it any wonder that all her children were converted early in life, and that two of them became ministers of the gospel? —W. B. K.

* * *

A widow, left with five little boys, was honored at a banquet. She had reared the boys to be noble, upright men. "Explain to us how you did it," asked the toastmaster. She said, "The secret lies in an occasional pat on the back. It gets positive results if given young enough, often enough, and low enough!" —W. B. K.

* * *

Susannah Wesley was a great Christian mother. Despite the fact that she had nineteen children, she found time to give each child an hour's religious instruction each week. Her most renowned sons were Charles and John. They turned the spiritual tides of England toward God in a dark hour.

             —Home Life

* * *

A mother was asked: "Which of your thirteen children do you love the most?" She replied, "The one who is sick until he gets well, and the one who is away until he gets home."

* * *

After the world-renowned opera singer Amelita Galli-Curci had won fame, she lamented one day to a young aspirant understudy, "How gladly I would have given it all up to hear a baby call me "Mother!" —W. B. K.

* * *

After a hard-fought battle in the late war, a chaplain moved among the seriously wounded soldiers. "Can I do anything for you, soldier?" he asked one whose life was rapidly ebbing away. "I want you to return thanks for me." "What shall I thank God for?" asked the chaplain. "Thank Him for giving to me a devout Christian mother, whose life and teaching brought me to the Saviour!" —W. B. K.

* * *

When all is said, it is the mother, and the mother only, who is a better citizen than the soldier who fights for his country. The successful mother, the mother who does her part in rearing and training aright the boys and girls, who are to be the men and women of the next generation, is of greater use to the community, and occupies, if she only would realize it, a more honorable as well as a more important position than any man in it. The mother is the one supreme asset of the national life. She is more important, by far, than the successful statesman, or businessman, or artist, or scientist.

             —Theodore Roosevelt

Illustrations

A Ninth, Ma'am

The more children a woman has, the more unselfish she is sure to be. A teacher said to a little boy, "James, suppose your mother made a peach pie, and there were ten of you at the table — your mother and father and eight children — how much of the pie would you get?"

"A ninth, ma'am," James answered.

"No, no, James. Pay attention," said the teacher. "There are ten of you — ten, remember. Don't you know your fractions?"

"Yes, ma'am," said James, "I know my fractions, but I know my mother, too. She'd say she didn't want no pie."

             —Mrs. Theodore Roosevelt

A Huge Bouquet

If I could take the heartaches
　You have had along the way,
And change them into roses,
　I would make a huge bouquet.
I would place it on a mirror
　Close beside your easy chair,
And kneel in silence by it
　With my heart reflected there.
Then you'd know the truths you taught
　me,
　In your kindly, patient way,
Have been my guide and anchor
　Through every troubled day.
And you could read life's record
　With neither shame nor fear,
For I made it by the pattern
　That you gave me, Mother dear.
Then this shall be my tribute,
　The best I have to give:
I'm grateful to you, Mother,
　That you taught me how to live!
　　　　　—Clara Ross Baxter in
　　　　　　The Wesleyan Methodist

* * *

A Mother's Song

A Scottish sailor became ill in an American port. A chaplain to seamen visited him. "Christ died for our sins. If you will trust Him as your Saviour He will give you eternal life," said the chaplain to the critically ill seaman. Then he sang a Scottish version of a psalm. Tears came to the sailor's eyes. "My godly mother taught me that song years ago. She prayed for me and taught me the right way to go. I've gone into bad, sinful ways, but now God, because of what she did for me, is bringing me to Himself!" God spared the sailor's life. He proved by faithful Christian living that his conversion was real. —W. B. K.

* * *

A Mother of Nineteen Children

An aged Welshman guided some tourists to a hallowed spot in Bunhill Cemetery, London — the grave of one of the noblest mothers of religious history, Susannah Wesley, the mother of nineteen children. The most famous of them were John and Charles Wesley, who, under God, gave to the world Methodism. All stood in silent reverence. Near her grave stands a marble monument, fourteen feet high. The gnawing tooth of time will ultimately reduce this marble memorial to dust but the influence of this devout mother will live as long as time lasts.

God give us better mothers that we might have better men! —W. B. K.

* * *

To Mother

You painted no Madonnas
　On chapel walls in Rome,
But with a touch diviner
　You lived one in your home.

You wrote no lofty poems
　That critics counted art,
But with a nobler vision
　You lived them in your heart.

You carved no shapeless marble
　To some high-souled design,
But with a finer sculpture
　You shaped this soul of mine.

You built no great cathedrals
　That centuries applaud,
But with a grace exquisite
　Your life cathedraled God.

Had I the gift of Raphael,
　Or Michelangelo,
Oh, what a rare Madonna
　My mother's life would show!
　　　　　—Thomas W. Fessenden

* * *

One Year to Live

Mrs. Lucille McFarland Fray, of Ottumwa, Iowa, thirty-three years of age, succumbed to a fatal illness. God had sent to her humble home, a three-room rented cottage on the edge of the town, ten children. She was told that she could not live longer than a year. What could she do with her small children? Her husband was almost a total invalid. He could not care for them. The noble mother could not countenance the thought of placing them in an orphanage. She took her "secret" to God in prayer. Her condition and the burden of her heart became known. Let's listen as she tells her story: "One night, I began to turn the problem over in my mind. Suddenly I got a feeling that there was some kind of wonderful Presence right beside me. And I knew then what I must do. There are enough good people in the world to provide loving homes for all my children. I will find them before it is too late." She told her minister of her plans. Only homes and foster parents meeting the mother's high standard could qualify. One by one, the brave mother found homes for her children. As she parted with them, she would say, "Be a good child, just as you always have been!" During the year, the heroic mother suffered great pain, but she did not complain. A few hours before her death she said to her pastor, "My house is in order!" Who could say that it wasn't? Of all who die in the Lord, we can say that they "rest from their labours." Of all true mothers, we can say, "Her children rise up, and call her blessed."

—W. B. K.

• • •

God made a wonderful mother,
  A mother who never grows old,
He made her smile of the sunshine,
  And molded her heart of pure gold!
In her eyes He placed shining stars,
  In her cheeks, fair roses you see,
God made a wonderful mother,
  And gave that dear mother to me.
—Pat O'Reilly

• • •

The Sweetest Flower

The sweetest flower that ever grew
Is mother love, so kind, so true;
Conceived in God's infinite mind,
Placed in the breast of womankind.
Its buds in morning rich and rare,
At noonday blooms divinely fair;
When evening skies are red and gold
Its true magnificence doth unfold.

When wintry skies are chill and gray,
It blooms as sweetly as in May.
'Tis found in every race and clime,
Its beauty is a thing sublime.
It blooms in sickness and in health,
And thrives in poverty and wealth.
It is the light of every home,
The light that scatters all the gloom.

No sky so threatening above
That it would daunt true mother love;
No wintry blast has ever blown
That made such love forsake its own.
No night too long, or shadows deep,
For her to silent vigil keep
At the maternal shrine, despite
The silent watches of the night.

Its fragrance fills the earth and skies,
It may be crushed, but never dies;
The sweetest flower that ever grew
Is mother love, so kind, so true.
—Selected

• • •

My Mother's Bible

This book is all that's left me now!
Tears will unbidden start, —
With faltering lip and throbbing brow
I press it to my heart.
For many generations past,
Here is our family tree;
My mother's hands this Bible clasped,
She, dying, gave it me.

As well do I remember those
Whose names these records bear;
Who round the hearth-stone used to close
After the evening prayer,
And speak of what these pages said,
In tones my heart would thrill!
Though they are with the silent dead,
Here are they living still.

My father read this holy book
To brothers, sisters dear;
How calm was my poor mother's look
Who leaned God's word to hear!
Her angel face — I see it yet!
What vivid memories come!
Again that little group is met
Within the halls of home.

Thou truest friend man ever knew,
Thy constancy I've tried;
Where all were false I found thee true,
My counsellor and guide.
The mines of earth no treasures give
That could this volume buy:
In teaching me the way to live,
It taught me how to die.
—George Pope Morris
From *The Mother's Anthology*
Compiled by William Lyon Phelps

• • •

Woman's Greatest Function

Unless God wills differently, woman's greatest function is to bear children and rear them for God.

Dr. Frederick H. Falls, president of the American Committee on Maternal Welfare, and famous obstetrician and gynecologist says, "A woman hasn't fulfilled her highest function until she has had a child — unless she can substitute a creative activity that to her is just as important. It is the distinct difference between a woman who fulfills her destiny and one who doesn't. It is the difference between a rosebush that blooms and one that doesn't. The stay-at-home mother who makes her family the core of her life is the backbone of America. A woman who has had a baby and rushes back to her job without the spur of economic necessity should be certain she is not cheating herself of one of life's greatest satisfactions."

"I will . . . that the younger women marry, bear children, guide the house, give none occasion to the adversary to speak reproachfully" (I Tim. 5:14).
—W. B. K.

* * *

Bouquets!

Whose gentle voice when childish heart
    Was pierced by disappointment's dart,
Did consolation, sweet, impart?
    It was the voice of — Mother.

Whose sacrifice, whose smile and tears
    Have brought their blessings through
        the years
In sharing all our joys and cares?
    The sacrifice of — Mother.

The memory of whose constant care,
    Whose self-forgetfulness, whose pray-
        ers
A halo spreads across the years?
    'Tis those of precious — Mother.

Whose counsel and whose tenderness
    Come back today our lives to bless —
To teach us true unselfishness?
    The tenderness of — Mother.

Whose blessed face in vision bright,
    Like beacon gleaming through the
        night,
Is here today to lend us light?
    The gentle face of — Mother.
—H. W. Ellis, in *Western Recorder*

* * *

Bouquets for the Living

Dr. Arnot Walker, when a student in the Jefferson Medical College, heard Dr. Clarence E. Macartney preach a sermon on the text, "Do thy diligence to come before winter" (II Tim. 4:21). The text continued to linger in his thoughts as he sat in his room. He decided, "I had better write a letter now to my

mother. Perhaps the winter of death is near for her." He wrote to her and expressed gratitude for her exemplary Christian life. Two days later while he sat in class a telegram was given to him. It read, "Come at once. Your mother is critically ill!" Hurriedly he went to the country home. His mother was still living. A smile of recognition and satisfaction was on her face. Under her pillow lay a treasured possession — the loving letter her son had written her after the Sunday service. It had cheered and comforted her as she entered "the valley of the shadow of death"!
—W. B. K.

* * *

A Kiss That Made a Missionary

Dr. Joseph Parker once said that when Robert Moffat was added to the Kingdom of God, a whole continent was added with him. A mother's kiss did it. He was leaving home, and his mother was going with him part of the way. At last she could walk no farther, and she stopped. "Robert," she said, "promise me something." "What?" asked the boy. "Promise me something," she said again, and he replied, "You will have to tell me before I will promise." "It is something you can easily do," she said. "Promise your mother." He looked into her face, and said, "Very well, Mother, I will do anything you wish." She clasped her hands behind his head and pulled his face down to hers, and said, "Robert, you are going out into a wicked world. Begin every day with God. Close every day with God." Then she kissed him, and Robert Moffat said it was that kiss that made him a missionary.
—*Methodist Recorder*

* * *

I Gave Them Myself

A mother said one day, "When my children were young, I thought the very best thing I could do for them was to give them myself. So I spared no pains to talk with them, to read to them, to teach them, to pray with them, to be a loving companion and friend to them.

"I had no time to indulge myself in many things which I would have liked to. I was so busy adorning their minds and cultivating their hearts with affections, that I could not adorn their bodies in fine clothes, though I kept them neat at all times.

"I have my reward now. My sons are ministers of the Gospel. My grown-up daughter is a Christian woman. I have plenty of time now to sit down and rest, and keep my house in order; plenty of time to go about my Master's business, wherever He has need of me.

"I have a thousand beautiful memories of their childhood to comfort me now that they have gone out into the world. I have the sweet consciousness of having done all I could to make them ready for whatever work God called them to do."

—The Burning Bush

* * *

An Undying Memory

Wesley L. Gustafson once related that as a boy his mother would never go to bed until he came home. Even if it were dawn — he would creep up the stairs, but she would still have her light on and he knew she was praying for him. After he was in bed, she would come into his room. He would pretend to be asleep and would not answer her. "Wes!" she would call his name softly again and again, but he would not let her know he heard. Then she would stand there — he could see her against the windowpane — and pray audibly, "O God, save my boy." "That memory will *never* leave me," Gustafson said. "I myself am quite sure that the prayers of a good mother never die."

—Christian Digest

* * *

Tell Mother I'll Be There!

When President McKinley heard that his mother was dying, he wired home saying, "Tell Mother I'll be there." The message was headlined by the American newspapers, and Charles M. Fillmore was moved to compose a hymn that has moved the hearts of millions. Charles M. Alexander, the great gospel singer, sang it around the world on his evangelistic tour with Dr. R. A. Torrey. No other gospel song ever written, said Alexander, brought so many men to conviction and decision for Jesus Christ. It has been sung with convicting power in more than a score of languages. Following are the words of this famous, soul-stirring song:

When I was but a little child how well
    I recollect
How I would grieve my mother with
    my folly and neglect;
But now that she has gone to heav'n I
    miss her tender care:
O Saviour, tell my mother, I'll be
    there!
CHORUS:
Tell mother I'll be there in answer to
    her pray'r,
This message, blessed Saviour, to her
    bear!
Tell mother I'll be there, heav'n's joys
    with her to share,
Yes, tell my darling mother I'll be there.

—The Watchman-Examiner

* * *

Never Through

The one whose work is never through,
Whose love is ever strong and true,
    Is mother.
The one who sleeps with waking eye,
And listens for the faintest sigh,
    Is mother.
The one who washes off the dirt,
And heals, with kisses, every hurt,
    Is mother.
Though age puts wrinkles in her face,
There's beauty time cannot erase,
    In mother.
Of all the name of earth we hear,
The one that seems to be most dear,
    Is "Mother."

—Selected

* * *

My Heart Aches to Hear It

A proud mother showed a friend a picture of her fine-looking boy. The friend said, "If I had a lad like that my pride could know no bounds. He is the most beautiful boy I have ever seen. I speak sincerely!" Tears came to the eyes of the mother. She bit her lip. The friend said to himself, "Have I misjudged that boy, or is there something hidden in his life that is breaking her heart?" The mother seemed to sense the thoughts of her friend. She quickly said, "Don't feel hurt. He is just as sweet and beautiful and wholesome as you believe him to be. Here's why I weep. Until about four years ago there was never a day in his life but he climbed upon my knees, put his arms around my neck, kissed me, and said,

'O Mother, how dear you are! How I love you!' But it is now two or three years since he has done that. I believe he loves me, but I tell you my heart is aching to hear it from his lips!"

—Told by Dr. W. B. Riley

* * *

Mother Keeps Promise

Going to Grandmother's for Christmas was a delight that had suddenly loomed among prospective possibilities. But the children, eagerly discussing it, were not sure. One little girl slipped away to Mother, and throwing soft arms around her neck, asked coaxingly: "Mother, are we really going to Grandmother's house for Christmas? Are we, Mother?" "Christmas is only two days away. Wait and see," answered the mother. But the child went dancing back to her companions, calling through the hall: "We're going! We're going! She said, 'Wait and see,' and you know she would never let us keep expecting just to disappoint us at last!"

—*Forward*

* * *

Too Late!

A mother had been very ill for some time. One day she had to reprimand her daughter for some misconduct. Instead of accepting the rebuke, the girl began to fume inwardly. She did not speak to her mother that day. As she started to go to her room that evening, she heard her mother calling, "Will you please bring me a drink of water, dear?" The girl silently and sullenly closed the door of her room without complying with her mother's simple request. Soon she fell asleep. With the coming of the dawn, her anger had subsided. "I must go now and tell mother how very sorry I am for my unlovely attitude!" Softly she tapped on her mother's door. But the usual "Come in, dear" was not heard! The girl pushed open the door and rushed to her mother's side. But instead of seeing the usual warm, friendly smile, she saw her mother's features set in the cold stare of death. Brokenheartedly, the girl sobbed, "Oh, Mother, I didn't intend to hurt you! I love you! I love you! Please forgive me for being so mean!" But the loving lips could no longer speak words of par-don. Even in her middle age, the memory of that incident troubled that daughter and brought hurting pangs of conscience. —The Rev. Elmer J. Knoernschild, in *The Lutheran Hour*

* * *

God's Helpers

God could not be in every place
With loving hands to help erase
The teardrops from each baby's face,
And so He thought of mother.

He could not send us here alone
And leave us to a fate unknown
Without providing for His own
The outstretched arms of mother.

God could not watch us night and day
And kneel beside our crib to pray,
Or kiss our little aches away;
And so He sent us mother.

And when our childhood days began
He simply could not take command,
That's why He placed our tiny hand
Securely into mother's.

The days of youth slipped quickly by,
Life's sun rose higher in the sky,
Full grown were we, yet ever nigh
To love us still, was mother.

And when life's span of years shall end,
I know that God will gladly send,
To welcome home her child again,
That ever faithful mother.

—George W. Wiseman

* * *

My Mother's Hands

In Mother's dear old wrinkled hands
  So plainly do I see,
A story clearly written there,
  And read by only me.
Of days wherein they rested not
  From early morn to night,
Nor did they ever pause to choose
  The labor that was light.

With patience and with willingness
  They toiled 'mid hope and tears,
That mine would be a better life
  Throughout the coming years.
For me, they paved a thorny path
  With bricks of purest gold
That came from honesty and strife,
  Of which I've ne'er been told.

They're wrinkled, old, and knotty now,
No one could call them fair,
Yet in my eyes they're beautiful,
And every scar they bear
Means absolute unselfishness
Upon the road she trod —
They mark her God's best gift to man,
And man's best gift to God.

—Alice Whitson Norton

* * *

Mother Knows

How many days have you cried for me?
How many tears have you dried for
me?
How many days have you worried long?
How many years have you filled with
song?
Nobody knows but you, Mother.

How many times have I hurt your heart?
How many times have we had to part?
How many prayers have you said for
me?
How many miles have you walked for
me?
Nobody knows but you, Mother.

How many times will your heart be
glad?
How many times will you say of your
lad,
"I knew he'd repay me for all of my
pain;
I knew my work would not be in vain"?
Nobody knows but you, Mother.

And so we're giving this day to you,
Tho' the hours are short and the minutes
few,
That you may know on this sacred day
We are thinking of you, and pray
As nobody can but you, Mother.

—*Selected*

* * *

Mothers Who Keep Young

We read about the mothers
Of the days of long ago,
With their gentle, wrinkled faces
And their hair as white as snow;
They were "middle-aged" at forty,
And at fifty donned lace caps,
And at sixty clung to shoulder shawls
And loved their little naps.

But I love the modern mother
Who can share in all the joys,
And who understands the problems
Of her growing girls and boys;
She may boast that she is sixty,
But her heart is twenty-three, —
My glorious bright-eyed mother
Who is keeping young with me.

—Florence Howard

* * *

A Little Parable for Mothers

The young Mother set her foot on
the path of life.

"Is the way long?" she asked.

And her Guide said: "Yes. And the
way is hard. And you will be old before you reach the end of it. But the
end will be better than the beginning."

But the young Mother was happy, and
she would not believe that anything
could be better than these years. So
she played with her children, and gathered flowers for them along the way,
and bathed with them in the clear
streams; and the sun shone on them and
life was good, and the young Mother
cried, "Nothing will ever be lovelier
than this."

The night came, and storm, and the
path was dark, and the children shook
with fear and cold, and the Mother drew
them close and covered them with her
mantle, and the children said, "Oh,
Mother, we are not afraid, for you are
near, and no harm can come," and the
Mother said, "This is better than the
brightness of day, for I have taught my
children courage."

And the morning came, and there was
a hill ahead, and the children climbed
and grew weary, and the Mother was
weary, but at all times she said to the
children, "A little patience and we are
there." So the children climbed, and
when they reached the top, they said,
"We could not have done it without you,
Mother." And the Mother, when she
lay down that night, looked at the stars
and said: "This is a better day than
the last, for my children have learned
fortitude in the face of hardness. Yesterday I gave them courage. Today I
have given them strength."

And the next day came strange clouds
which darkened the earth — clouds of

233

war and hate and evil, and the children groped and stumbled, and the Mother said: "Look up. Lift your eyes to the Light." And the children looked and saw above the clouds an everlasting Glory, and it guided them and brought them beyond the darkness. And that night the Mother said, "This is the best day of all, for I have shown my children God."

And the days went on, and the weeks and the months and the years; and the Mother grew old, and she was little and bent. But her children were tall and strong, and walked with courage. And when the way was hard, they helped their Mother, and when the way was rough, they lifted her, for she was as light as a feather; and at last they came to a hill, and beyond the hill they could see a shining road and a golden gate flung wide.

And the Mother said: "I have reached the end of my journey. And now I know that the end is better than the beginning, for my children can walk alone, and their children after them."

And the children said: "You will always walk with us, Mother, even when you have gone through the gates."

And they stood and watched her as she went on alone, and the gates closed after her. And they said: "We cannot see her, but she is with us still. A Mother like ours is more than a memory. She is a living presence."

—Temple Bailey in
Log of the Good Ship Grace

* * *

A Wise and an Unwise Mother

A mother sat by a hearthside place,
Reading the Bible with a pleasant face,
Till a child came up with a childish frown,
And pushed the Bible, saying, "Put it down!"
Then the mother, slapping his curly head,
Said, "Troublesome child, go off to bed,

The words of the Bible I must know,
To train you up as a child should go."
And the child went off to bed to cry,
And hated religion by and by!

Another mother, perusing the Book,
With a smile of joy and an intent look,
Till a child came up and jogged her knee,
And said of the Book, "Put it down, take me!"
Then the mother sighed as she stroked his head,
Saying softly, "I never shall get it read,
But I'll try by loving to do God's will,
And His love into my child instill!"
That child went to bed without a sigh,
And loved the Lord by and by!

—*Selected*

* * *

If Only There Might Be

Just yesterday it seems my tots
  Were playing on the floor,
And I wiped countless fingerprints
  From windowpane and door.

I kissed away a thousand tears
  And darned sock after sock,
And tried to keep pace with the hands
  That raced around the clock.

And often when at end of day,
  Too tired to sleep in bed I lay,
I'd think how nice when, children grown,
  My time again should be my own.

So now I sit and rock alone,
  My hands at rest, the work all done;
No little tots upon the floor,
  No fingerprints upon the door.

No socks to mend, no hurts to kiss —
  Ah, me! How could I know I'd miss
The very things I grudged to do
  When I was young, and sturdy too.

Dear God, if only there might be
  Someone again who needed me!

—*Selected*

NATURE

Illustrations

All Things Beautiful

All things bright and beautiful,
All creatures great and small,
All things wise and wonderful,
The Lord God made them all.

Each little flower that opens,
Each little bird that sings,
He made their glowing colors,
He made their tiny wings.

The purple-headed mountain,
The river running by,
The morning and the sunset
That lighteth up the sky.

The tall trees in the greenwood,
The pleasant summer sun,
The ripe fruits in the garden,
He made them, every one.

He gave us eyes to see them,
And lips that we might tell
How great is God Almighty,
Who doeth all things well.
— Keble, in *The Burning Bush*

* * *

The Lesson

A man sat in the heat of the day under a walnut tree looking at a pumpkin vine. He began to muse, "How foolish God is! Here He puts a great heavy pumpkin on a tiny vine without strength to do anything but lie on the ground. He puts tiny walnuts on a tree whose branches could hold the weight of a man. If I were God, I could do better than that!" Suddenly a breeze knocked a walnut from the tree. It fell on the man's head. He rubbed the bump, a sadder and wiser man. He remarked: "Suppose there had been a pumpkin up there instead of a walnut! Never again will I try to plan the world for God. I shall thank Him that He has done it so well!" —Dr. Frank S. Mead

* * *

Ocean Sunset

The sinking sun drops slowly down
To meet the sea's wide way;
And all of earth is hushed to watch
The ending of the day!

A lone bird calls a single note,
His throat a golden lyre;
Then silence as the sea becomes
A bank of molten fire!

The colors fade, the breakers turn
To heavy midnight black;
As ceaselessly they race along
The white sand's silver track!

Once more the flaming sunset sky
Is blotted out by night;
But thankful hearts still hold and thrill
To the magic of its light!
— Lillian E. Miles

* * *

Secret of the Snow

Softly now the snow is falling
In a world so still and white;
Even time has been arrested:
There is neither noon nor night.

There is neither spot nor wrinkle,
Not a branch stands stark and nude:
Leveled are each field and fence post
To a common altitude.

How the heart takes joy in seeing
Beauty by His hand prepared,
How the heart finds peace in knowing
Secrets of the snow are shared!

Even as the earth around us
Clothes itself in borrowed dress,
So the soul that trusts the Saviour
May put on His righteousness —

Not to glory in His presence,
Nor to cower with the clod,
But to wait in white before Him —
Leveled by the grace of God.
— Helen Frazee-Bower

* * *

Things Worth Remembering

A lovely sky at daytime's close,
Of lavender and pink and rose
And lots of gold and amethyst,
Commingling with a silver mist.

A cedar on a rocky crest,
An eagle, sheltering a nest,
A mountain capped with ermine snow —
A candle with a Christmas glow.

The ocean, with its ebb and flow,
A winding river moving slow,
The sun, the moon, the stars, the sod —
And first and last and always —God.
        —Alice Whitson Norton

* * *

Eventide

At cool of day, with God I walk
  My garden's grateful shade;
I hear His voice among the trees,
  And I am not afraid.

He speaks to me in every wind,
  He smiles from every star;
He is not deaf to me, nor blind,
  Nor absent, nor afar.

His hand that shuts the flowers to sleep,
  Each in its dewy fold,
Is strong my feeble life to keep,
  And competent to hold.

The powers below and powers above,
  Are subject to His care —
I cannot wander from His love
  Who loves me everywhere.

Thus dowered, and guarded thus, with
    Him
  I walk this peaceful shade;
I hear His voice among the trees,
  And I am not afraid.
        —Mrs. Caroline Atherton Mason

* * *

What It Takes to Make a Life!

He takes the sound of the dropping nuts,
  And the scent of the wine-sweet air,
In the twilight time of the year's long
    day,
  When the spent Earth kneels in
    prayer,
He takes a thousand varied hues
  Aglow in an opal haze,
The joy of the harvests gathered in —
  And makes the autumn days.

He takes the years — the old, the new,
  With their changing scenes and brief,
The close-shut bud and the fruiting
    bough,
  Flower and fading leaf;
Grace and glory and lack and loss,
  The song, the sigh, the strife,
The joy of hope and the hope fulfilled —
  And makes of the years a life.
        —Annie Johnson Flint

Indian Summer

A silken curtain veils the skies,
And half conceals from pensive eyes
The bronzing tokens of the fall;
A calmness broods upon the hills,
And summer's parting dream distils
A charm of silence over all.

The stacks of corn, in brown array,
Stand waiting through the tranquil day,
Like tattered wigwams on the plain;
The tribes that find a shelter there
Are phantom peoples, forms of air,
And ghosts of vanished joy and pain.

At evening when the crimson crest
Of sunset passes down the West,
I hear the whispering host returning;
On far-off fields, by elm and oak,
I see the lights, I smell the smoke, —
The Campfires of the Past are burning.
        —Tertius and Henry van Dyke

* * *

They All Belong to You

Ye cannot shut the trees in,
  Ye cannot hide the hills,
Ye cannot wall the seas in,
  Ye cannot choke the rills.
The corn will only nestle
  In the broad arms of the sky,
The clover crop must wrestle
  With the common wind, or die.
And while these stores of treasure
  Are spread where I can see,
By God's high, bounteous pleasure,
  They all belong to me.
        —Eliza Cook in
      The Watchman-Examiner

* * *

The Overture to Spring

A handful of jonquils, waving in the
    breeze,
Their golden heads uplifted beneath the
    leafing trees,
Like a breath of sunshine across the
    patterned lace
The leaf-shadows are making in this
    grassy place.
It makes the heart soar upward, like a
    bird on wing —
It is all so lovely! The overture to
    spring!
        —Ruth J. Dimmitt

God's Autograph

I stood upon a hill one night
And saw the great Creator write
His autograph across the sky
In lightning strokes, and woods too far
    apart
To witness this magnificent
Tumultuous, Divine event!

I stood one morning by a stream
When night was fading to a dream.
The fields were bright as fields may be
At spring, in golden mystery
Of buttercups — then God came on
And wrote His autograph in dawn.

One afternoon long years ago,
Where glacial tides had ebbed and flowed,
I found a cliff which God had smitten;
I scanned its breast where He had writ-
    ten
With some great glacier for a pen
His signature for time and men.

One night I stood and watched the stars;
The Milky Way and ranging Mars,
Where God in letters tipped with fire
The story of His tall desire
Had writ in rhyme and signed His name
A stellar signature of flame.

Creation's dawn was deep in night,
When suddenly: "Let there be light,"
Awakened grass, and flower, and tree,
Chaotic skies, the earth, the sea;
Then, to complete creation's span
In His own image, God made man,
And signed His name, with stroke most
    sure —
Man is God's greatest signature!
      —William L. Stidger

   • • •

Autumn Rain

The autumn rain fell through the night,
And slipped away at dawn;
It flushed the valley's stagnant pools
Before the night was gone.

It washed the buildings till they stand
Like children fresh and clean,
And clothed the rolling pasture lands
With cloth of jeweled green.

It bathed the flowers with gentle hand;
It combed the forest's locks;
It set the trees like maiden gowned
With multicolored frocks.

It touched the earth with magic brush
Such as no artist wields,
And left a feel of glad content
Upon the furrowed fields.
    —W. Everett Henry, in *Friends*

   • • •

Free to All Mankind

As I beheld the crimson sun
Stretched o'er the western sky,
A picture only God could paint,
A painting none could buy,
I tho't, tho' man be rich or poor,
Or bare his walls of art,
God's hung a canvas in the sky
To satisfy each heart.

He made within the woodland fair
A symphony of song;
We need not go to concert halls
When birds sing all day long;
No music with their song compares
For they sing not for fame,
They only sing to glorify
Their great Creator's name.

Like gleaming jewels beneath the sun
The shimm'ring waters flow,
No diamonds ever brighter shone
And not for worldly show;
Upon these beauties we may feast,
They shine for all to see
That some things money cannot buy,
Some things in life are free.

And as we down life's pathway tread,
We learn that, after all,
The things that satisfy the most
Upon our lives will fall;
If we just look to God alone
Within our reach, we'll find,
That music, art, and rarest jew'ls
Are free to all mankind.
    —Hope Evangeline

NEGLECT

Illustrations

A Burning Shame!

There are 750,000 people in mental hospitals in America. I'm convinced ... that 80 per cent of those people could be out if enough of us cared.

—Dr. William C. Menninger

* * *

Is It Nothing to You?

Sigismund Goetze's great painting "Despised and Rejected of Men" was first displayed in the British Royal Academy in 1904. The painting vividly portrays Christ crowned with thorns and dying in anguish upon His cross. The surging, restless crowd is seen passing by, seemingly heedless of the Sufferer's presence. All segments of human society pass by — unchallenged, unconcerned. Only one person of the milling crowd has her face turned toward the abandoned Figure on the cross — a nurse on her way to minister to suffering ones. For a moment she pauses and looks reverently at the awesome scene!

What a representation this is of Christ today — neglected, unrecognized, despised, dishonored! "Is it nothing to you, all ye that pass by?" —W. B. K.

* * *

Did He Pray in Time?

In the city of Macon, Georgia, one of the leading hotels had become notorious for its harboring of vice and crime. One tragic night an explosion occurred in the hotel. Many leaped to certain death into the streets below. Many perished in the flames. A young man in an upper story was seen by the horrified throngs in the streets below, running from room to room, then into the hallway, trying to find some exit, only to be thrust back by the merciless flames. Seeing that there was no way of escape, he knelt and prayed just before the flames enveloped him. Did he pray in time? So far as his physical salvation was concerned, he prayed too late. Was his prayer too late for his soul's salvation? Only God knows. This we do know, however: "He that being often reproved hardeneth his neck, shall suddenly be destroyed, and that without remedy" (Prov. 29:1). —W. B. K.

* * *

Will Jesus Understand?

One of God's children came to the end of life. It was evident that he was in great distress. A minister spoke comfortingly and assuringly to him. The dying man listened as if in a trance. Then he said, "I believe I am saved, and that soon I will stand in the presence of my Lord, but what can I say to Him about the wasted years? Will He understand?" It is possible to have a saved soul and a wasted life! —W. B. K.

* * *

Do-nothing-ism

We are not told that the unprofitable servant who hid his talent was a murderer, or a thief, or even a waster of his Lord's money. But he did nothing. This was his ruin. Let us beware of a do-nothing Christianity. Such Christianity does not come from the Spirit of God. "To do no harm," said Baxter, "is the praise of a stone, not of a man!" And Burke said, "The only thing necessary for the triumph of evil is for good men to do nothing!" —W. B. K.

NEW YEAR

Illustrations

The Past Is Future

Somewhere in South America there is an Indian tribe whose concept of the past and future seems to be exactly opposite that of ours. We refer to the past as being behind us, and the future ahead of us.

To this particular tribe, however, the

past is thought of as being ahead of them, and the future as being behind them. At first this may seem very strange to us, and many will undoubtedly wonder how anyone could possibly be so foolish as to think in this manner.

The reasoning of these Indians, however, is quite logical. All that they have experienced — their mistakes, failures, lessons learned, etc. — is considered as being in front of them, and it is there for their contemplation and betterment. The future, on the other hand, is behind them because it has not yet been experienced. —John W. Brawand, Wycliff Bible Translator

* * *

His Unfailing Presence
Another year I enter
Its history unknown;
Oh, how my feet would tremble
To tread its paths alone!
But I have heard a whisper,
I know I shall be blest;
"My presence shall go with thee,
And I will give thee rest."

What will the New Year bring me?
I may not, must not know;
Will it be love and rapture,
Or loneliness and woe?
Hush! Hush! I hear His whisper;
I surely shall be blest;
"My presence shall go with thee,
And I will give thee rest."
—*Selected*

* * *

Forget and Remember
Forget the word of slander heard;
Forget the harsh, the cruel word;
Forget the strife, the bitter test;
Forget it all, in Him find rest.
Forget the storms of yesteryear;
Forget the rocks, the days so drear;
Forget the clouds you must pass
    through;
Forget it all, He loveth you.
Forget the foe, the woundings had;
Forget the rain, the weather bad;
Forget the snow, the days so cold;
Forget it all as time grows old.
Remember this, His sovereign grace
Sufficient is for every place;
O'er every foe with Christ within,
We shall o'ercome, the vict'ry win.
—Ernest O. Sellers

My Book of Life
I closed another chapter
In my book of life today,
And paused for meditation
As I laid the book away.

I thought of smudgy pages
Where the record was not clear,
And dreary lines of trouble
Clouded o'er by doubt and fear.

It's now too late to alter
Any script that's dried and set:
The story's far from perfect,
But it's vain to stew and fret.

I asked the Lord to pardon
The mistakes that mar the book,
And give me grace and courage
By a hopeful, Christ-ward look.

So now, there lies before me
A new chapter clean and white.
And I hope to write its pages
So the plot will turn out right.

I trust the final chapters
Will the Master's plan reveal,
And weave the many fragments
To depict a life that's real.
—*Selected*

* * *

The Best Memory System
Forget the kindness that you do,
As soon as you have done it;
Forget the praise that falls on you,
The moment you have won it.
Forget the slander that you hear,
Before you can repeat it;
Forget each slight, each spite, each sneer,
Wherever you may meet it.

Remember every kindness done,
To you, whate'er its measure;
Remember praise by others won,
And pass it on with pleasure.
Remember every promise made,
And keep it to the letter;
Remember those who lend you aid,
And be a grateful debtor.

Remember all the happiness
That comes your way in living;
Forget each worry and distress,
Be hopeful and forgiving.

Remember good, remember truth,
Remember heaven's above you,

And you will find through age and youth,
True joy and hearts to love you!

—*Selected*

OBEDIENCE—DISOBEDIENCE

Short Quotes

In the North Pacific lies the little island of Iwo Jima. Its dry surface of volcanic ash has been likened to a landscape on the moon. For this tiny but vital piece of land we paid the price of some 21,000 casualties in our war with Japan. For the men who took it, it was never a question of a feeling of adequacy or inadequacy, courage or lack of it. They took it in obedience to a command.

How strange it is that we Christians can so easily cast aside the fact that we are commanded to speak for Jesus Christ.

—Rev. W. Carter Johnson in
Christianity Today

* * *

It is better not to know than to know and not to do: "For it had been better for them not to have known the way of righteousness, than, after they have known it, to turn from the holy commandment delivered unto them" (II Peter 2:21). Most of us *know* better than we *do*. —W. B. K.

* * *

The battle raged, the cannons roared,
  I stood to see the fight—
And, lo, behold, I saw the Lord,
'Twas He who fought and won the day—
  'Twas He who gave the word:
"Stand still, my child, stand still, I say,"
  And yet another word I heard,
'Twas only this: "Obey."

"Aboard a man-of-war," said an old sailor, "there's only two things — duty or mutiny." The same is true of the Christian life — duty or mutiny.

* * *

Said Lord Nelson to a young officer, "You must always implicitly obey orders without attempting to form any opinions of your own respecting their propriety."

* * *

How ready is the man to go,
  Whom God hath never sent,
How timorous, diffident and slow,
  His chosen instrument.

—Wesley

* * *

A father wanted his boy to do certain things for him. He told his boy simply how to do them. "Now do you understand?" asked the father. The father was surprised when the boy said, "No!" "Why not?" asked the father. "Because I don't want to," said the boy.

* * *

The foolish and the dead alone never change their opinions.

—James Russell Lowell

* * *

Some people are like the man who went through a political campaign with a saucerlike "button" on his coat lapel which read: "My mind is made up! Don't confuse me with facts!"

—Billy Graham

Illustrations

They Follow Me

Near twilight I was strolling with a GI friend in the environs of Casablanca, North Africa. Lifting our eyes toward the horizon, we saw a great billowing cloud of dust. As it neared us, we could vaguely discern the shadowy forms of sheep. A moment later we saw thousands of sheep making their way to the watering troughs. What a sight it was to see all those sheep plunge their heads into the sparkling, refreshing waters! Having slaked their thirst, the sheep stood lazily and contentedly. Then some half-dozen bronzed shepherds walked off in different directions. One, in a trilling, singsong way uttered a call which was totally unintelligible to me, but not to a sizeable number of those mixed-up sheep. Instantly they perked up their ears and ran toward their shepherd! The other shepherds did as the first one had done, until all the sheep had disentangled themselves from the other sheep, and had rallied to the call of their respective shepherds.

How thrilled I was to see that never-to-be-forgotten sight! Before my eyes had been portrayed the meaning of the words spoken by the Good Shepherd: "My sheep hear my voice, and I know them, and they follow me. They know not the voice of strangers."

—Told by Rev. C. Leslie Miller

* * *

The Last Words Danny Ever Heard

Is there a greater care than parental care? Is there a greater sorrow than parental sorrow?

A watchful, dutiful mother looked out of the window on the snow-covered driveway. She saw her seven-year-old son, Danny, sled into the street. She called him into the house and reprimanded him, saying, "I've told you never to sled into the street! You will have to stay in the house the rest of the day!"

Throughout the day, Danny heard the laughter of happy neighborhood children as they romped and sledded in the snow.

When the day was almost gone, Danny pleaded, "Can't I go out now, Mom?" Mother relented. She bundled him up warmly. As Danny dashed toward the door, Mother warned, "Remember what I told you about going into the street. Stay in the yard!"

They were the last words Danny ever heard his mother speak. Five minutes later Danny was dead — he was crushed by a car when he sledded into the street!

Obedience could have saved Danny's life!

"Children, obey your parents in the Lord: for this is right" (Eph. 6:1).

—W. B. K.

Plowing Crooked Furrows

During my college days at Mercer University, an aged Baptist minister greatly influenced my life. It was this minister who challenged me to memorize much of God's Word. This he himself had done. I learned another lesson from his life. When he was a young man, he felt that God had called him to go to a foreign field. He prepared himself and, in time, entered the field of service. I do not know why he became disobedient "unto the heavenly vision" but before long he returned to the homeland. Thereafter his life was cast in the shallows. He was seemingly a misfit everywhere. He was unsought, unwanted, and unrecognized. He had put his hands to the plow and looked back, and thereafter he plowed a crooked furrow!

His life, in which God's first and best plan was thwarted, is an apt illustration of the warning words of the Apostle Paul, "Lest . . . when I have preached to others, I myself should be a castaway," or "disapproved" (I Cor. 9:27).

—W. B. K.

* * *

I Have Missed God's Best!

"I have enjoyed the meetings this week, but I am sorry I attended them," said a well-to-do businessman to a minister. "Why?" asked the astonished minister. "Here's why. These meetings have reminded me afresh that I have missed God's best for my life. I was called to Africa. I intended to answer God's call. I began to earn money for my passage and outfit. I earned more and more money. I stayed and entered business. Today I am the owner of a large business concern. I have everything money can buy. I have a beautiful home and a lovely wife and children. Down in my heart, however, there is a great void. My life has been a failure, not from the standpoint of the world, but from God's point of view!"

—*Prairie Overcomer*

* * *

Did I Please You?

Some years ago in a Southern city I saw a large group of people standing at a street corner. Going closer, I saw a hound performing stunts so amazing as to be unbelievable! At first I didn't see anyone giving commands to the dog. Then, as I looked around, I saw a Negro boy whose lips barely moved standing nearby. He was speaking to the dog in soft undertones. When the performance was over, the dog went to his master, with tail awag and eyes fixed on him. Could the dog have articulated his thoughts, I am sure he would have said, "Did I please you? Did I fully obey you?"

The boy caressingly stroked the dog's head, as he said, "Good doggie! Good doggie!"

Going to the boy, I said, "I love dogs. How I would like to own your wonderful dog! I'll give you fifteen dollars for him." (That was when fifteen dollars were worth much more than they are today.) The boy said, "If you would give me a hundred times that much, you couldn't have my dog. I wouldn't sell him to anybody!"

Tears suffused my eyes as I walked away. I prayed silently, "Heavenly Master, make me as subservient to Your will as that dog is to his master's will! May I so fully obey Thee that when I stand in Thy presence I may hear Thy 'Well done, good and faithful servant!'" Since that day, I have never ceased to pray that prayer. —Dr. Lee Roberson

* * *

Master, Speak!

Master, speak! Thy servant heareth,
Waiting for Thy gracious Word;
Longing for Thy voice that cheereth,
Master, let it now be heard.
I am listening, Lord, for Thee:
What hast Thou to say to me?

Speak to me by name, O Master,
Let me know it is to me;
Speak, that I may follow faster,
With a step more firm and free,
Where the Shepherd leads the flock,
In the shadow of the Rock.

Master, speak! Tho' least and lowest,
Let me not unheard depart;
Master, speak! for, oh, thou knowest
All the yearnings of my heart,
Knowest all its truest need;
Speak! and make me blest indeed.

Master, speak! and make me ready,
When Thy voice is truly heard,
With obedience glad and steady,
Still to follow every word.
I am listening, Lord, for Thee;
Master, speak, oh, speak to me!
    —F. R. Havergal

* * *

A Keen Regret

Before my conversion, I had a jazz orchestra. A member of the orchestra later became the leader of a jazz band. One day the Holy Spirit deeply impressed me to go to a clubhouse where he and his band were playing and speak to him about his soul. Though I intended to speak to him, I delayed to do so. Great was my sorrow when I read the headlines on the front page of a newspaper: "Popular Orchestra Leader Killed Instantly!" Under the influence of liquor, when driving home from the clubhouse, he crashed into a culvert. One of my keenest regrets is that I didn't immediately obey the Spirit's voice.
    —Told by H. E. Fox

* * *

Warning Unheeded

Many years ago, the steamer *Portland* left Boston harbor when all the danger signals were flying. The weather was stormy. The government agent in the signal office had advised all vessels to remain in port. The captain of the *Portland* was heedless of all warnings. Before sailing he said to the keeper of the lighthouse, "Keep your light burning brightly tonight. We may come back!" But neither he, his crew, nor his vessel came back! When they were just outside the harbor, a mighty storm broke in fury. The vessel was torn to pieces. Not one on board ever saw friends or loved ones again.

The shores of time are strewn with moral and spiritual wrecks, men and women who defiantly went in their own willful ways with no thought of God, and no sense of need of His directing, molding hand.

Lest we make a shipwreck of our lives, may this be our daily prayer:
Jesus, Saviour, pilot me,
Over life's tempestuous sea!
    —W. B. K.

Who Walks With God

Who walks with God must take His way
Across far distances and gray
To goals that others do not see,
Where others do not care to be.
Who walks with God must have no fear
When danger and defeat appear,
Nor stop when every hope seems gone,
For God, our God, moves ever on.

Who walks with God must press ahead
When sun or cloud is overhead,
When all the waiting thousands cheer,
Or when they only stop to sneer;
When all the challenge leaves the hours
And naught is left but faded powers.
But he will some day reach the dawn,
For God, our God, moves ever on.
—*Heart and Life*

OLD AGE

Short Quotes

Retirement can be the severest shock that the human organism can sustain. —Dr. Edwin Zabriskie, one of the world's leading neurologists

* * *

You are young at any age if you are planning for tomorrow.

* * *

The reason so many retired men die mentally is because they stop doing everything they do not want to do. When they do that, they also stop growing. Growth is the result of assuming obligations and responsibilities. Retirement is too often a state of slow decay and death. The minds of too many retired men become stagnant pools. —Thomas Dreier, in *Clinical Medicine*

* * *

What great things some men have done in the later years of their life. Michelangelo painted the ceiling of the Sistine Chapel lying on his back on a scaffold when almost 90; Paderewski at 79 played the piano superbly; at 88 John Wesley preached every day; Tennyson, when 83, wrote "Crossing the Bar." Booth Tarkington wrote sixteen novels after 60, some of them when he was almost totally blind. Benjamin Franklin went to France in the service of his country when 78, and wrote his autobiography when over 80!
—W. B. K.

* * *

Sixty-five is too early for any man to retire. If I had retired at sixty-five I wouldn't be here today. Keep busy. I was lucky in my choice of parents, because I had to go to work before I could play. —Frederick H. Eckner, 90 years old and Honorary Chairman of the Metropolitan Life Insurance Co.

* * *

I am drawing near to the close of my career. I am fast shuffling off the stage. I have been perhaps the most voluminous author of the day. It is a comfort to me to think I have tried to unsettle no man's faith, to corrupt no man's principle, and that I have written nothing which on my deathbed I should wish blotted. —Sir Walter Scott

* * *

As soon as you give in to inertia and indolence, you are on the toboggan and can slide into a semi-invalid's chair very quickly! Stay on your feet and fight. Agitate — don't vegetate! Don't listen to the "Be careful" or "Take it easy" comments of your solicitous children. They mean well, but if you follow their loving advice, you'll be bedfast before you know it. —Dr. Frank Crane

* * *

He who dwells in the past grows old before his time. He who lives in the future remains forever young.

* * *

We justify our existence not by adding years to our lives, but by adding life to our years!

* * *

The hoary head is a crown of glory if found in the way of righteousness. It is a fool's cap if found in any other way.
—W. B. K.

Two men were sharing a seat in a railway coach. One of them was eighty-one years of age. His eyes were keen and he displayed vigor in every movement. "I envy you your vigor," said the other man. "What is the secret of your astounding vitality?" Laughing, the octogenarian said, "I'm living on the interest of a well-invested youth!"

—W. B. K.

* * *

Grow old along with me!
The best is yet to be,
The last of life, for which the first was made:
Our times are in His hand
Who saith "A whole I planned,
Youth shows but half; trust God; see all nor be afraid!"

—Browning

Because of the remarkable advances by modern science, the average lifespan is lengthening. Millions of folks past 65 are now living in enforced idleness by the political doctrine that a man is on the shelf when he happens to celebrate his 65th birthday. The doctrine is definitely not scientific. You are never on the shelf until you put yourself there. —Dr. Frank Crane, in
The Chicago Daily News

* * *

People grow old by deserting their ideals. Years may wrinkle your skin, but to give up interest wrinkles the soul. When the wires are all down and your heart is covered with the snows of pessimism and the ice of cynicism, then, and then only are you grown old.

—General Douglas MacArthur

Illustrations

The Secret of a Happy Life

We occasionally meet a woman whose old age is as beautiful as the bloom of youth. We wonder how it has come about — what her secret is. Here are a few of the reasons. She knew how to forget disagreeable things. She kept her nerves well in hand, and inflicted them on no one. She mastered the art of saying pleasant things. She did not expect too much from her friends. She made whatever work came to her congenial. She retained her illusions and did not believe all the world wicked and unkind. She relieved the miserable and sympathized with the sorrowful. She never forgot that kind words and a smile cost nothing, but are priceless treasures to the discouraged. She did unto others as she would be done by, and now that old age has come to her and there is a halo of white hair about her head, she is loved and considered. This is the secret of a long life and a happy one. —*United Presbyterian*

* * *

Retire and Die!

Often we hear the comment, "If he retires, he'll curl up and die." This is literally true. Studies show that older people who hold jobs from which they do not have to retire get along best. Those who have a chance to do something creatively after they retire get along second best. Those with less chance to do something creatively go down most quickly. The body is a closed unit with lots of energy in it. Unless the individual has a way to discharge the energy, he gets into difficulty, and the difficulty is sickness and death.

—Dr. Ewald W. Busse

* * *

Man's Inhumanity to Man!

Our public mental hospitals are being used increasingly to dispose of feeble and dying old folks. One out of every two persons, age 65 and over, committed to a state institution does not belong there. These unfortunates are suffering from nothing more than deterioration of age, poverty and rejection by their families. They are in mental hospitals because there is no other place for them to go. These are the facts apparent in a pilot study conducted by Dr. Otto L. Bettag, state welfare director, as reported in *The Chicago Daily News*.

—W. B. K.

Too Young for the Position

A professor at an Eastern law school recently wrote to Dean David E. Snodgrass of the University of California's Hastings College of Law to ask about an opening on the faculty. The professor explained that he was 63, and, although he was approaching retirement age, he wanted to go on teaching.

"He was flabbergasted," Snodgrass said with a smile, "when I told him that he was still *too young* for the job!"

For the past 17 years, Dean Snodgrass has, with two exceptions, hired professors only after they have been forced out of their jobs at other schools by iron-clad retirement rules. Because every one of the ten full-time professors at Hastings is over 65, its faculty has become famous as the "65 Club." The oldest member was hired in the winter of 1957 at the age of 80. The average age is 73.

"This notion that a man is through just because he has celebrated an arbitrary number of birthdays is idiotic," Snodgrass says.

The change was summed up recently by the most famous living American professor of law, the venerable Roscoe Pound, who was once Snodgrass' law dean at Harvard. Dean Pound stated, "On the whole, I am inclined to think you have the strongest law faculty in the country." —*Coronet*

* * *

You're Not So Old

Are you getting along in years and haven't yet made a name for yourself? Here are some words of comfort from some research people who looked into the histories of about 400 famous men, each one the most outstanding statesman, painter, warrior, poet or writer of his time. Of the group's greatest achievements, 35 per cent came when the men were between 60 and 70; 23 per cent when they were between 70 and 80; and 8 per cent when they were more than 80. In other words, 66 per cent of the world's greatest work has been done by men past 60. Feel better? —*Gospel Banner*

* * *

Grandmother's Prayer

A tiny room, a rocking chair,
Warmth for old bones, clean clothes to
     wear,
A reading lamp, a soft white bed,
A pillow for my weary head.
Sufficient good plain food to eat,
A little love, a friend to greet,
A shining faith, a useful task . . .
Dear Lord, is that too much to ask?
                    —Alice MacKenzie

* * *

Beating One's Record

One day the great photographer, Edward Steichen, was in the sculpture garden of the Museum of Modern Art in New York, shooting from different angles the statue of Balzac by Rodin. Said he to a friend, "I first photographed that statue by moonlight in Paris more than fifty years ago. This background is terrible! Those big buildings, you know."

As he talked, he kept maneuvering for the best angle to shoot the statue.

Think about it — Steichen, who is the greatest living photographer and who was now seventy-eight was seeking to improve on a job he did more than half a century before.

Not until God's children awaken in the likeness of Christ should they be satisfied with their accomplishments. To live on past glories and laurels already won arrests progress and is spiritually disastrous! "Forward" is the command of the Captain of our salvation.

Not enjoyment and not sorrow,
     Is our destined end or way;
But to live that each tomorrow,
     Finds us further than today!
                    —W. B. K.

OPPORTUNITY

Short Quotes

It is a good and safe rule to sojourn in every place as if you meant to spend your life there, never omitting an opportunity of doing a kindness, or speaking a true word, or making a friend.
—John Ruskin

For each of us who have traveled the road
Of sorrow, misfortune and sin,
There's a wonderful place of courage and hope
Called the Land of Beginning Again!

When God writes opportunity on one side of an open door, He writes responsibility on the other side.

Listen to the water-mill
Through the live-long day,
How the clicking of its wheel
Wears the hours away. . . .
And a proverb haunts my mind
As a spell is cast —
"The mill cannot grind
With the water that is past."
—Sarah Doudney

Opportunity often goes around disguised as hard work. That's why so many people fail to find it.

There is nothing so powerful in this world as an idea whose time has come.
—Victor Hugo

There is a tide in the affairs of men
Which, taken at the flood, leads on to fortune;
Omitted, all the voyage of their life
Is bound in shallows and in miseries.
—Shakespeare

Master of human destinies am I!
Fame, love, and fortune on my footsteps wait.
Cities and fields I walk; I penetrate
Deserts and fields remote, and, passing by
Hovel and mart and palace, soon or late,
I knock unbidden once at every gate!

If sleeping, wake; if feasting, rise before
I turn away. It is the hour of fate,
And they who follow me reach every state
Mortals desire, and conquer every foe
Save death; but those who doubt or hesitate,
Condemned to failure, penury or woe,
Seek me in vain and uselessly implore—
I answer not, and I return no more.
—Senator John J. Ubgakks

PARENTAL RESPONSIBILITY

Short Quotes

America is running on the momentum of a godly ancestry. When that momentum goes, God help America!
—Dr. J. Gresham Machen

"Have you anything to say before I sentence you?" asked a Canadian judge of a youth, seventeen years old, who had committed murder and who himself

was soon to hear the death sentence pronounced. "Yes, Your Honor, I have something to say. Am I alone responsible for the crime I committed? My father put the first bottle of liquor in my hand. My parents taught me that there is nothing to religion. I never saw a Bible in my home. I never heard my parents pray. May God have mercy on their souls and mine!" —*The Dry Legion*

Illustrations

Teach Them Diligently

My earliest conceptions of religion were developed in a Christian home. I came from a family of hard-working pioneers. We earned a livelihood from land purchased from the Government in the rugged hill country of southwestern Wisconsin. There was not much variety in the menus but we had plenty to eat and did not know that we were "economically underprivileged." A lumber wagon without canopy was our only transportation, so church attendance was a rare experience indeed. Steep hills and many miles separated us from the nearest church. Yet the stories of the early Hebrews, the achievements of Abraham, Moses, and Gideon, the glory which came to David and Solomon, the courage and faithfulness of the prophets, and, above all, the redemptive love of Jesus, were quite familiar to us as children in the home. When my parents read the command, "And ye shall teach them to your children," they did not think God was talking to the government or the school, or even the Sunday school or church. They knew He was talking directly to parents. Christian fathers and mothers are the most effective teachers of religion on earth.

—As told by a member of the family

* * *

An Orphan in His Own Home

Dr. John Sutherland Bonnell relates a telling story in his book, *Pastoral Psychology*, concerning a ten-year-old boy whose father was a very popular and enterprising young doctor. The father had no time for his family. The two younger sisters received the attention and affection of the mother, but the boy, for all practical purposes, became an orphan in his own home. He lost interest in his studies as well as in his family. He quarreled continually with his sisters. The distracted mother brought him to Dr. Bonnell for counseling help. After several sessions, the boy was drawn out of his shell, revealing his utter loneliness and craving for love. The parents, quickly apprised of the situation, took the boy into their heart and lavished their attention and affection upon him. As a result, the lad was rescued from awful consequences, and the home was saved from an inevitable tragedy. How often children are taken for granted. How often it is assumed they are already adults. How quickly they gather the impression they are not wanted or needed. How many homes have suffered disintegration due to a lack of family loyalty or interest! —*The Brethren Evangelist*

* * *

Drawing the Line

Where should we draw the line, and
  how?
This is the question we parents face
  now,
In a day when nothing seems very
  wrong —
When "Christians" are much the same
  as the throng.

These, our children, have truly not
  known
Of things true Christians would never
  condone
Back in the days before their time —
Could we have failed to draw the line?

"Father above," today we cry,
"Is it too late yet to rectify
The mistake we have made in drifting
  along
With no move against what we once
  thought wrong?

We parents must bow our heads in
  shame,
While Thy mercy and help we humbly
  claim
To still be able to draw the line
In a way that will help in plenty of
  time!"
        —Genevieve Perrine Cheney

* * *

Blocking the Way

A teen-age girl was genuinely converted. Coming home from the church, she broke the glad news to her mother who was only a nominal church member. The mother became enraged. She went to the telephone and called the minister in whose church the daughter had found the Saviour. She spoke contemptuously of what she called the girl's emotional upset. The daughter, however, held fast to her profession of faith in Christ. Shortly thereafter the mother went to the daughter's room. There she saw her on her knees with an open Bible before her on her bed. The mother was very angry. She snatched the Bible and demanded that her daughter change her "peculiar ways."

The girl was deeply distressed. She bared her heart to the minister, calling his attention to the following command: "Children, obey your parents in the Lord; for this is right" (Eph. 6:1). The minister yearned to be a true friend to the girl. "Let's look closely at that verse. It says, 'Children, obey your parents *in the Lord.*' If a parent demands of a child anything which goes contrary to the Word of God, the child is to obey God. Remember that the Bible says, 'We ought to obey God rather than men'" (Acts 5:29).

—W. B. K.

• • •

Is There Forgiveness for Me?

A greatly distressed mother came to a minister and asked, "Is there forgiveness for a sin such as mine? Years ago on a Sunday night I was out walking with my ten-year-old daughter. We passed a large tent where a gospel meeting was in progress. 'Let's go in, Mommie,' said my little girl. We did. As the minister closed the service, he said, 'Anyone who will accept Christ as Saviour stay for a while.' My little girl said, 'Mommie, I'll stay, if you will,' but I said No, though I knew I needed Christ and His forgiveness. My daughter has grown up to be a profane person. She is a heavy smoker and drinker, with no thought of God whatever."

—W. B. K.

• • •

What Is It to You?

A leading churchman recently said: "To our forefathers Christian faith was an experience. To our fathers it was an inheritance. To most of us it is an inconvenience. To our children it has become a nuisance!"

No doubt he was generalizing. But there is much truth in what he said. Many a person today is living on the afterglow of his parents' faith — and his own children are doomed to live on the afterglow of the afterglow. One shudders to think of the diluted faith which will be passed along to the grandchildren of today's adult generation.

—*Messenger of Peace*

• • •

Crops and a Child

I have seed to raise and I plow the field
   And I plant my crops with care,
And I thank the Lord for the rain He sends,
   As I watch them growing there.
But I don't sit down with a book by day
   And let my crops run wild,
For crops won't grow by themselves, I know;
   Is it different with a child?

I've a boy to raise and I want a man
   When his growing days are done;
And a man must work for the crop he seeks —
   Is it different with a son?
Will strangers care for my wheat out there
   When the weeds grow rank and wild?
If my crop would shrink if I idled here,
   Dare I idle with my child?

Yes, I'll work for him and I'll pray for him,
   And I'll do the best I can,
For the Lord has given me a son to raise,
   And I want to raise a man.
Yes, my eyes are set on the harvest years
   When the long, hard task is done,
So I'll pull the weeds from the life, myself,
   For I dare not shirk my son.

—*The Missouri Counsellor*

• • •

Religious Training of Prime Importance

Judge Allen Ardell of the Municipal Court of Council Bluffs, Iowa, states: "The Juvenile Court considers religious training of such prime importance in the determination of the cause of delinquency and the possibility of rehabilitation, that one of the first matters inquired into is the child's attendance at Sunday school, and church attendance by the parents.

"Rarely does the parent of delinquent children attend church, and even smaller is the number of parents who could be considered active church members. Less than ten per cent of our delinquent children attend Sunday school, and only a few of these could be listed as regular in their attendance." —*National Voice*

* * *

My Boy's First Bible

A little boy's first Bible
  Is the greatest thrill he's known,
There's a sweet, unique excitement
  In a Bible all his own!

And yet my heart is smitten
  As this touching sight I see,
Has his reverence for that Bible
  Depended much on me?

As I see him with his Bible,
  I bow my head and pray,
May he always love that Bible
  The way he does today.

Then I hear a voice within me
  Speak in solemn words and true,
How he cherishes that Bible
  Will depend a lot on you.

I love my Bible better
  Since I've seen the beaming joy
This wonderful possession
  Has afforded to my boy.

May I seek to give mine daily
  A devotion he can see,
For the love he bears his Bible
  Will depend a lot on me.
          —*United Presbyterian*

* * *

A Child Left to Himself

"You are too strict with your son," said a well-intentioned mother to a friend. "You are too old-fashioned. You do not allow your boy to go with rougher boys, and you require him to be at home by nine o'clock at night. Times have changed, you know." The boy's mother answered, "We are responsible to God for the training of our boy; and what a responsibility it is! I take this verse with great seriousness 'A child left to himself bringeth his mother to shame.' "

The son of the strict mother grew into manhood, entered college, and became a highly respected Christian citizen. The son of the other began to drink, committed a crime, and was sent to prison.
          —W. B. K.

* * *

What If Lads and Lassies Be Not There?

"I had a most realistic dream last night," said a mother to me when I was visiting her home. I asked what her dream was and she said, "I dreamed that I went to heaven and made the heartbreaking discovery that not one of my five boys were there! Then I awoke, weeping bitterly!" Seldom had I known a mother who displayed so little concern for the spiritual welfare of her sons, though she was a professing Christian. Having for years been deeply concerned for the souls' welfare of these boys, I felt that I should speak searching words to her. "Mother," I said, "God, in goodness, may have given you this dream to stir you with concern for the salvation of your unsaved sons. The dream could become an *actuality* if you fail to agonize in prayer for their salvation!"

Mothers and fathers, how do you expect to go up to your heavenly Father without urging your lads and lassies to go with you? —W. B. K.

PATIENCE

Short Quotes

The promises of God are *certain*, but they do not all mature in ninety days: "For he is faithful that promised" (Heb. 10:23). —Dr. A. J. Gordon

Keep me from bitterness, dear Lord. It is so easy to nurse sharp, bitter thoughts each dull, dark hour! O "Man of Sorrows," defend me from self-pity.

Impart Thy deep sweetness and gentle power. Out of my hurt, pain and heartbreak, help me to harvest a new sympathy for suffering humankind and a wiser pity. Give me great love for those who lift a heavier cross with Thee.
—*War Cry*

* * *

The outstanding characteristics of the great New England preacher Phillips Brooks were poise and imperturbability. His intimate friends, however, knew that, at times, he suffered moments of frustration and irritability. One day a friend saw him pacing the floor like a caged lion. "What is the trouble, Dr. Brooks?" asked the friend. *"The trouble is that I'm in a hurry, but God isn't!"*
—W. B. K.

* * *

How most of us are forever in a hurry. Like the Psalmist, we impatiently plead, "Make haste, O God!" Remember that the cogs of our lives are geared to the cogs of God's workings. The gear teeth of God's plans are stronger than our own. When we speed up while God keeps His own pace we strip our gears. We wear out. We crack up nervously, mentally and physically. Is this maybe the explanation of the fact that increasing numbers of ministers are "falling apart?" —W. B. K.

* * *

Be assured that if God waits longer than you could wish, it is only to make the blessing doubly precious. God waited four thousand years, till the fullness of time, ere He sent His Son. Our times are in His hands; He will avenge His elect speedily; He will make haste for our help, and not delay one hour too long. —Andrew Murray

* * *

Inspire me with the knowledge that a man may at times be called to do his duty by doing nothing, to work by keeping still, to serve by waiting.
—George Matheson

* * *

"I marvel at your patience," said a friend to Susanna Wesley. "You have told that child the same thing twenty times!" "Yes," said the noble mother, "and had I spoken only nineteen times, I should have lost all my labor!"
—*The Brethren Evangelist*

* * *

They also serve who only stand and wait. —Milton

* * *

If, but one message, I would leave behind
One single word of courage for my kind,
It would be this: "Oh! brother, sister, friend;
Whatever life may bring, what God may send —
No matter whether clouds lift soon or late,
Take heart and wait!"

* * *

The Talmud tells the story of an aged man whom Abraham invited to share his tent but who refused to join Abraham in prayer to the one God. Learning that the man was a fire worshipper, Abraham drove him from his door. That night God appeared to Abraham in a vision and said, "I have borne with that ignorant man for seventy years; could you not have patiently suffered him one night?"

Illustrations

Stop Hurrying

The Bible seldom speaks, and certainly never its deepest, sweetest words, to those who always read in a hurry. Nature can tell her secrets only to such as will sit still in her sacred temple till their ears are attuned to her voice. And shall revelation do what nature cannot? Never. The man who shall win the blessedness of hearing the voice of divine wisdom must watch daily at her gates, and wait at the posts of her doors. —F. B. Meyer

* * *

Failure to Hold the Line

"Have you, perchance found a diamond pendant? I feel sure I lost it last night in your theater," asked a woman who did not identify herself to the manager of the theater. "Not yet, madam," said the manager, "but we will search diligently for it. Please hold the line for a minute while I make inquiry." Returning a few moments later to the telephone, the manager said, "I have good news for you! The diamond pendant has been found!" There was no reply, however. "Hello! Hello! Hello!" said the manager but the woman who made the inquiry about the lost diamond pendant had failed to wait. The manager endeavored to trace the call, but without success.

Many of God's children are like that woman. They fail to wait on the Lord. His answer to our prayers will come in His good time. The promise is sure: "Call unto me, and I will answer thee" (Jer. 33:3). —W. B. K.

* * *

What Waiting Does

The Rev. William Gray, when he was in the Alps, visited a glacier grotto that was reached by a tunnel bored through the solid ice.

"As we penetrated into the chilly depths," he said, "away from the outside sunshine, the light became dimmer and dimmer, and when we stood in the narrow chamber at the end of the passage, the darkness was as black as pitch. 'Wait,' said the guide, 'and in five minutes you shall see light clearly.' We waited, and it was just as he had told us. What happened was this: as the eye got accustomed to its new surroundings, the atmosphere gradually brightened, the walls and roof of the grotto glimmered into pure translucent green, and in the clear soft light that encircled us we could recognize the faces of our companions and read our guidebooks." That is what waiting can do. It can open our eyes to see the beautiful things of God all around us, but which only patient waiting eyes can see. I have known people laid aside by sickness, people baffled and troubled; everything was dark about them; but when at last they stopped striving, and simply waited, waited on God, then the light came, and they saw God's kindness and loved Him more and better for the quiet waiting time He pressed upon them.

—*"The Children's Preacher,"* by the Rev. J. Reid Howath

He Keeps the Key

Is there some problem in your life to solve,
Some passage seeming full of mystery,
God knows, who brings the hidden things to light.
    He keeps the key.

Is there some door closed by the Father's hand
Which widely opened you had hoped to see?
Trust God and wait — for when He shuts the door,
    He keeps the key.

Is there some earnest prayer unanswered yet,
Or answered not as you had thought 'twould be?
God will make clear His purpose by-and-by.
    He keeps the key.

Have patience with your God, your patient God,
All-wise, all-knowing, no long tarrier He,
And of the door of all thy future life
    He keeps the key.

Unfailing comfort, sweet and blessed rest,
To know of *every* door He keeps the key
That He at last, when just He sees 'tis best,
    Will give it thee.
              —*Selected*

* * *

Wait My Soul

Wait, my soul, upon the Lord
    To His gracious promise flee,
Laying hold upon His Word,
    "As thy days thy strength shall be."

If the sorrows of thy case
    Seem peculiar still to thee,
God has promised needful grace,
    "As thy days thy strength shall be."

Days of trial, days of grief,
    In succession thou mayst see;
This is still thy sweet relief,
    "As thy days thy strength shall be."

Rock of Ages, I'm secure,
    With Thy promise full and free;
Faithful, positive, and sure —
    "As thy days thy strength shall be."
           —*The Baptist Examiner*

One Day at a Time

One day at a time, with its failures and
    fears,
With its hurts and mistakes, with its
    weakness and tears,
With its portion of pain and its burden
    of care;
One day at a time we must meet and
    must bear.

One day at a time — but the day is so
    long —
And the heart is not brave and the soul
    is not strong.
O Thou merciful Christ, be Thou near
    all the way;
Give courage and patience and strength
    for the day.

Swift cometh His answer, so clear and
    so sweet:
"Yea, I will be with thee, thy troubles
    to meet;
I will not forget thee, nor fail thee, nor
    grieve;
I will not forsake thee; I never will
    leave."

One day at a time, and the day is His
    day;
He hath numbered its hours, though
    they haste or delay.
His grace is sufficient, we walk not
    alone;
As the day, so the strength that He
    giveth His own.
    —Annie Johnson Flint

PATRIOTISM

Short Quotes

Nine-tenths of the calamities that have befallen humanity have no other origin than the union of high intelligence with low desires. —Lord Macaulay

* * *

Make us to see that our liberty is not the right to do as we please, but the opportunity to do right.
    —Peter Marshall, in a prayer in
    U. S. Senate

* * *

The history of the once flourishing and now decadent nations can be briefly told: drunkenness, licentiousness, and forgetfulness of God. Alarmingly and increasingly existent in our nation today is this trinity of monstrous evils!
    —W. B. K.

* * *

To live under the American Constitution is the greatest political privilege God ever gave to mankind.
    —Calvin Coolidge

* * *

A dread disease is gnawing at the basic structure of American existence — the home. The moral breakdown has already reached an acute state. There is but one ray of hope — God! He, long ago, laid down the principles of family life. —J. Edgar Hoover

Without a moral regeneration throughout the world, there is no hope for us! We will suddenly disappear in the dust of a terrific atomic explosion!
    —General Dwight Eisenhower

* * *

Sir Robert Peel was found by a friend while he was praying over a bundle of letters. The friend apologized for disturbing him in his private devotions. "No," said Peel, "these are my public devotions. I was just giving the affairs of state into the hands of God, for I cannot manage them myself!"
    —W. B. K.

* * *

Our government has continued to grow until big government threatens to become, not the government for the people, but in place of the people.
    —Dr. Clyde W. Taylor,
    Secretary Public Affairs, N.A.E.

* * *

Knowledge is not enough. Unless we can anchor our knowledge to moral foundations, the ultimate result will be dust and ashes. The towering enemy of man is not his science, but his moral inadequacy.
    —Dr. Raymond B. Fosdick

Our knowledge of science has already outstripped our capacity to control it. We have too many men of science and too few men of God. We have grasped the mystery of the atom and rejected the Sermon on the Mount. Man is stumbling blindly through a spiritual darkness while toying with the precarious secrets of life and death. The world has achieved brilliance without wisdom, power without conscience. Ours is a world of nuclear giants and ethical infants. —General Omar N. Bradley

* * *

There is a rank due to the United States among nations which will be withheld, if not absolutely lost, by the reputation of weakness. If we desire to secure peace, one of the most powerful instruments of our rising prosperity, it must be known that we are at all times ready for war.
—George Washington

* * *

America does not consist of groups. A man who thinks of himself as belonging to a particular national group in America has not yet become an American. —Woodrow Wilson

* * *

The American Constitution is the most wonderful work struck off at a given time by the brain and purpose of man. —William Eward Gladstone

* * *

Democracy is based upon the conviction that there are extraordinary possibilities in ordinary people.

* * *

The banners of Christ can lead the way to the moral and spiritual rebirth of our great nation. In the forefront of His standard-bearers are the Sunday schools. —J. Edgar Hoover

* * *

We and all the nations stand at this hour in human history before the portals of supreme catastrophe. What ought we to do? Which way can we turn to save our lives and the future of the world? It does not matter so much to old people. They are going to die soon anyway. But I find it poignant to look at youth in all its activity and ardour, and, most of all, to watch little children playing their merry games, and wonder what would be before them if God wearied of mankind. Mankind is placed in a position both measureless and laden with doom!
—Sir Winston Churchill

* * *

Unless spiritual security goes hand in hand with military security, the United States will find itself passing into obscurity! What will destroy our country is the delusion that military defense will save it. Every civilization that has fallen has destroyed itself.
—Luther W. Youngdahl

* * *

America was born a Christian nation for the purpose of exemplifying unto the nations of the world the principles of righteousness found in the Revelation of God. —Woodrow Wilson

* * *

America is in the midst of a frightening moral slump. During the past fourteen years, our statistics show that major crimes have increased about three times as fast as the population.
—Herbert Hoover

* * *

It is paralyzing to think of the average American family going on from the rising sun to the retiring hour as if God had no existence.

Sunday is a day for extra sleep, motoring, Sunday papers in many volumes, comic supplements, etc.

If American children are not taught God in the schools and He is unnamed in the homes, what can we expect but at this moment the United States is developing into a non-Christian nation.
—*The Literary Digest*

* * *

My country owes me nothing. It gave me, as it gives every boy and girl, a chance. It gives me schooling, independence of action, opportunity for service, and honor. In no other land could a boy from a country village, without inheritance or influential friends, look forward with unbounded hope.
—Herbert Hoover

* * *

If we abide by the principles taught in the Bible, our country will go on prospering and to prosper. But if we and our posterity neglect its instruction and authority, no man can tell how suddenly a catastrophe may overwhelm us and bury our glory in profound obscurity.

—Daniel Webster

• • •

No one has ever devised a method by which the public can get something out of government for nothing.

—*Chicago Daily Tribune*

• • •

Religious liberty in America is being slowly and surely taken away. There seems to be a code of platitudes that have been prepared by certain people who, in many cases, make no profession of true Christianity. You either use these platitudes or you are silenced, or, if permitted to be heard, smeared as a bigot or fanatic.

—Dr. Albert J. Lindsey

• • •

A shocking intelligence concerning our armed forces was presented in the *Saturday Evening Post* by Hanson W. Baldwin, U. S. Naval Academy graduate and military editor of the *New York Times*. Our fighting men, Baldwin charged, have gone soft. He attributes this to the inequities of the draft, civilian meddling and physical pampering. Draft statistics from September 1948 to November 1958 show the rejection rate for draftees for physical, mental or moral reasons was 38.3 per cent. In the same period there was a further rejection by the armed forces of 6.6 per cent of those passed by the draft boards. —*The Plain Dealer*

• • •

There was a day when the individual was responsible for his own welfare and for that of his family, for his own advance in responsibility and in remuneration. Today the state assumes vast areas of our worries and responsibilities. It will care for us if we are unemployed, and when we grow old. Unions will protect one's job. Millions of young people in this country have no conception of what it is to be in want. Their every need has been provided *for* them rather than *by* them.

—Dr. V. R. Edman

• • •

The true Christian is the true citizen, lofty of purpose, resolute in endeavor, ready for a hero's deeds, but never looking down on his task because it is cast in the day of small things, scornful of wrongdoing, awake to his own duties as well as his rights, following the higher law of reverence, and doing all that lies in his power, so that mankind is in some degree better because he lived. —Theodore Roosevelt

Illustrations

Science and God

To me in youth, science was more important than either man or God. I worshiped science. I was awed by its knowledge. Its advances had surpassed man's wildest dreams. In its learning seemed to lie the key to all mysteries of life.

It took many years for me to discover that science, with all its brilliance, lights only a middle chapter of creation. I saw the science I worshiped, and the aircraft I loved, destroying the civilization I expected them to serve, and which I thought as permanent as earth itself.

Now I understand that spiritual truth is more essential to a nation than the mortar in its cities' walls. For when the actions of a people are unguided by these truths, it is only a matter of time before the walls themselves collapse.

The most urgent mission of our time is to understand these truths and to apply them to our way of modern life. We must draw strength from the almost forgotten virtues of simplicity, humility, contemplation, prayer. It requires a dedication beyond science, beyond self, but the rewards are great and it is our only hope.

—Charles A. Lindbergh in
Of Flight and Life

• • •

Internal Decay

America will not be slain by the Soviets, but America can commit suicide. Great nations rarely fall to the batterings of their enemies. They wither from within from loss of soul. Sixteen out of the nineteen civilizations that have passed away from the beginning of time *decayed from within.* Very often an attack from without strengthened them. If there was an enemy invasion at the end, as there was in the Roman Empire, it was merely the visit of the vultures to the carcass!

—Bishop Fulton J. Sheen

* * *

Why Lincoln Was Serene

The fate of the nation was hanging precariously in the balances. General Lee and his army had surged forward to the environs of Gettysburg, where the fateful, decisive battle of the Civil War was in the making. The sorrows and burdens of the war-torn nation had exacted its terrible toll on the occupant of the White House, Abraham Lincoln. Yet, on the eve of the crucial Battle of Gettysburg, he was calm and assured. His serenity was reassuring to his generals. When they inquired, "How can you be so self-possessed in this hour of the nation's mortal peril and darkness?" Lincoln said, "I spent last night in prayer before the Lord. He has given to me the assurance that our cause will triumph and that the nation will be preserved!" —W. B. K.

* * *

This Is Our Flag

I think the sun will never shine
Upon a flag like yours and mine.
A flag that's never known defeat,
Whose guardians never sound retreat.
And so, tyrants, near and far,
Who would bedim one single star
Of this our flag, take solemn heed,
That we will fight, and die if need,
To make this land a steady shrine
For this our flag, both yours and mine.

—*Selected*

* * *

Our Source of Life

America and its institutions came largely out of the Bible, and its future depends to a great extent upon keeping this once forbidden book open as a guide to its life. . . . One of the best things American parents can do to promote the American way of life is to teach their children to love this Book

by reading it to them, keeping an attractive appearing copy of it where it can be seen and read, and familiarizing themselves with its contents so they may guide their children into satisfying and useful lives that will promote their happiness and well-being.

—Sydney W. Powell, D.D.

* * *

American Colleges Began Christian

It was God from the beginning. Take our educational institutions, Harvard, for example. In the bequest of Mr. Harvard, he gave several rules and precepts that were to be observed by Harvard College, and the second rule reads as follows:

"Let every student be plainly instructed and earnestly pressed to consider well the main ends of his life and studies; to know God and Jesus Christ which is eternal life and therefore to lay Christ in the bottom as the only foundation of all knowledge and learning and see the Lord only giveth wisdom. Let everyone seriously set himself by prayer in secret to seek Christ as Lord and Master."

Yale College was founded by Christian ministers in the interest of religious education. Columbia University, in an advertisement dated July 3, 1752, in the *New York Gazette*, stated: "The chief things that are aimed at in this college are to teach and engage the children to know God and Jesus Christ and to love and to serve Him in all sobriety, godliness, righteousness, in life with a perfect heart and a willing mind."

A president of Dartmouth said: "Dartmouth College was conceived in the fervor of a religious revival and born in the throes of a great missionary zeal dedicated to Christ, our Redeemer."

—Billy Graham

* * *

A Challenging Inscription

The inscription on the Plymouth Rock monument is a challenge to every generation of Americans: "This spot marks the final resting place of the Pilgrims of the *Mayflower.* In weariness and hunger and cold, fighting the wilderness and burying their dead in common graves that the Indians should not know how many had perished, they here laid the foundations of a state in which all men for countless ages should have liberty to worship God in their own way. All you who pass by and see this stone remember, and dedicate yourselves anew to the resolution that you will not rest until this lofty ideal shall have been realized throughout the earth."

—*The Watchman-Examiner*

* * *

America

One bleak day in February, 1832, a young theological student sat in his room at Andover Seminary. Samuel Francis Smith was going over a sheaf of German songs for children, given him by a friend, the composer Lowell Mason. Sunset shadows crept into the room and Smith was tired from a strenuous day of study. He was relieved to spend a few relaxed moments going over his friend's music.

As he hummed over one after another, one struck his fancy. He glanced at the words at the bottom of the page and his knowledge of German told him that the words were patriotic, but they did not appeal to him. He decided to write his own words. He searched around on his desk until he found a scrap of paper, about five or six inches long and two and one half inches wide. On this, as he tapped out the rhythm of the music, he began to write,

My country, 'tis of thee,
Sweet land of liberty,
Of thee I sing:
Land of the pilgrims' pride,
Land where my fathers died,
From every mountain side
Let freedom ring.

Thus was born the hymn — *America!*

* * *

Patriotism

Patriotism is not a hand waving a flag. It is not flowery speeches, or chest-thumping. It is not a swaggering, aloof people looking down on the less fortunate.

Patriotism is a humble, inner feeling of kinship for all that is our land and our people, a pride in the good and a hopeful tolerance for the bad. It is a willingness to sacrifice that we may preserve what the earlier patriots gave us;

it is courage to lead others when the world is dark.

Only real patriots see the flag. Others merely see a brightly-colored piece of cloth. Only patriots can speak with understanding of freedom; others recite empty words. Only patriots can walk with respect among the world's unfortunate; others are scorned and ignored.

—*Christian Herald*

* * *

What Makes a Nation Great?

Not serried ranks with flags unfurled,
Nor armoured ships that gird the world,
Not hoarded wealth, nor busy mills,
Not cattle on a thousand hills,
Not sages wise, nor schools, nor laws.
Not boasted deeds in freedom's cause —
All these may be and yet the state
In the eye of God be far from great.

That land is great which knows the Lord,
Whose songs are guided by His word.
Where justice rules 'twixt man and man,
Where love controls in act and plan,
Where breathing in his native air
Each soul finds joy in praise and
        prayer —
Thus may our country, good and great,
Be God's delight — man's best estate.

—Alexander Blackburn

* * *

American Paganism

Often as one rides along the highways he sees the words, "Jesus Saves." Someone commented, "The words must be advertising a savings bank!" A fourteen-year-old boy was given a Gospel of John. "What's that?" he asked. "It's a part of the Bible," he was told. "What is the Bible?" he then asked. A child attending a vacation Bible school for the first time reported to her mother, "The teacher was swearing." The teacher had used the name of Jesus several times while telling Bible stories. A woman was invited to attend a neighborhood Bible class. She declined, saying, "I don't think I would be interested. I'm a Democrat." A youngster, after hearing the creation story, "corrected" the teacher by saying, "But Adam is God, and Adam and Eve created this world!" She was quoting her Mormon father. Someone may say, "These are but isolated cases!" No, indeed! They

are representative of a cross-section of a vast area of America, two generations removed from practicing Christianity!
—*The Sunday School Times*

* * *

A Time to Preach — A Time to Fight!

Good Christians make good citizens.

Peter Muhlenberg was pastor of the Woodstock Lutheran Church during the days of the Revolution. Preaching as was his custom in clerical gown, he threw back his clerical robe at the end of the sermon and appearing before his congregation in the regimentals of a Revolutionary officer, said, "There is a time to preach and a time to pray and there is also a time to fight, and that time has come now." He then went out on the lawn of the church and recruited and inducted almost every able-bodied man present into the ranks of Washington's army.

General Muhlenberg recognized the fact that as a Christian he owed allegiance both to God and to country. He did not try to evade the responsibilities of Christian citizenship as do many people today.
—*The United Evangelical*

* * *

Will History Repeat Itself?

The Roman Empire was once powerful and proud. People thought it would last forever. No one dreamed it would ever fall. But it did. It fell and it fell hard. We in America should read the reasons listed below why the Roman Empire fell, and then do some serious thinking about our own country.

In 1787 Gibbon completed his masterful book, *The Decline and Fall of the Roman Empire*. He gave the following reasons for its fall: the rapid increase of divorce with resultant undermining of the home; higher and higher taxes and the spending of public money for free bread and circuses for the people; the mad craze for pleasure and sports which became more and more brutal; the building of gigantic armaments, and the decay of religious faith which faded into formalism and became impotent.

Shall we ignore today the causes which brought about the decay and disintegration of once mighty nations? Shall we go on to disaster, refusing to repent

and return to the God of our fathers? Repent or perish! Which will it be?

"If my people . . . shall humble themselves, and pray, and seek my face, and turn from their wicked ways; then will I hear from heaven, and will forgive their sin, and will heal their land" (II Chron. 7:14). —*Exchange*

* * *

Lord of the Nations

Lord, while for all mankind we pray
 Of every clime and coast,
O hear us for our native land,
 The land we love the most.

O guard our shores from every foe;
 With peace our borders bless;
With prosperous times our cities crown,
 Our fields with plenteousness.

Unite us in the sacred love
 Of knowledge, truth and Thee;
And let our hills and valley shout
 The songs of liberty.

Lord of the nations, thus to Thee
 Our country we commend;
Be Thou her refuge and her trust,
 Her everlasting Friend. Amen.
—J. R. Wreford

* * *

Lest We Forget

When God made the oyster, He guaranteed it economic and social security. He built the oyster a house — a shell — to protect it from its enemies. When hungry, the oyster simply opens its shell and food rushes in upon him.

But when God made the eagle, He said, "The blue sky is the limit. Go build your house," and the eagle built on the highest mountain crag, where storms threaten him every day. For food he flies through miles of rain and snow and wind.

The eagle, and not the oyster, is significantly the emblem of the United States! —*Christian Cynosure*

* * *

Dead Men Can't Help.

During World War I a member of the State Council of Defense in an Illinois city received a stack of posters from the Government with the request that he stick them up wherever he could find a vacant space. He called in an over-enthusiastic boy and told him to go and put them up wherever he could find a dead wall. At noon an elderly, indignant gentleman called and said, "Did you send out a boy to stick up posters?" "Yes, sir," replied the patriot. "Well, come with me," said the man. He took him to the cemetery, and there on the walls of a mausoleum which contained the last mortal remains of one of the city fathers, he saw, in flaming red letters a foot high, this thrilling command — "Wake up, Citizen! Your country needs you!" No more can *spiritually* dead men save a country.

—From an old clipping

* * *

Keeping in Touch with God

It is *good* for our President to keep in touch with the rulers of nations. It is *better* for him to keep in touch with God.

One night one of the guests in the White House had difficulty in sleeping. Is was during the darkest days of the Civil War. It was on the eve of the battle of Bull Run. His room was near President Lincoln's. The guest heard an agonized voice. It was the voice of the President. He was on his knees, praying. "O Thou God, who heard Solomon in the night when he prayed and cried for wisdom, hear me! I cannot guide the affairs of this nation without Thy help. I am poor and weak and sinful. O God, save this nation!" Later, Lincoln said, "I am not depending upon my constituents, my generals, my army and navy, but upon the God of our fathers who raised up this nation, and will not suffer it to perish!"

—W. B. K.

* * *

Needed: Old-Fashioned Patriotism

The apathetic attitude of the general public between wars has made it possible for Communist domination to extend to one out of every three persons on earth. The only reason this is possible is that people in the United States don't realize that Communism is at war with everything we stand for. How timely are the following words of General Douglas MacArthur: "The best memorial we can give our soldiers, alive and dead, is a fervent revival of old-fashioned, year-around patriotism." —Clarence Manion, former Dean of Notre Dame University Law School

* * *

Where Wealth Accumulates and Men Decay

No other nation has received greater physical blessings from the hand of God than has America. The United States has 6 per cent of the world's population. We have 72.8 per cent of the automobiles in the world. We have 56.5 per cent of the telephones in the world. We have 50.9 per cent of the radios in the world. We produce 44.3 per cent of the world's oil. There is one radio for every person in the United States. There is one telephone for every sixty people in the rest of the world. There is one automobile for every three people in the United States. There is one automobile for every 128 people in the rest of the world. —W. B. K.

* * *

The People's Favorite

On each schoolday in the later years of Samuel Francis Smith's life, he hoisted the Stars and Stripes up the pole in front of his house, and stood at attention, listening, as across the Common of Newton Centre, Massachusetts, came the voice of schoolchildren singing:

My country, 'tis of thee,
Sweet land of liberty,
　Of thee I sing:
Land where my fathers died,
Land of the pilgrim's pride,
From ev'ry mountain side
　Let freedom ring!

His heart responded with joy and pride, for many years ago, in his youth, he had written the words to this song. He had written it merely to express his own patriotic feeling, but those who heard it felt it also expressed their feelings and joined him. Now 150 years later, 173,000,000 Americans are still expressing their patriotism by singing it. —Dorothy C. Haskin

PEACE—PEACEMAKERS

Illustrations

Hid with Christ in God

In the north Atlantic, icebergs are often seen in the wintertime. Ships sailing the Atlantic are often caught in violent storms. Mighty vessels are tossed about like chips by the mountainous waves. How different it is with the icebergs! Like majestic, white castles, they glide placidly through the heaving sea. They are defiant of the mighty waves which are hurled against their towering walls and glistening heads. They do not bob about like a cork because the lower part is deep in the ocean where there is calm. Only one-ninth of an iceberg is above the ocean.

When our lives are hidden with Christ in God, the storms of life are powerless to take from us the peace and repose we have in Christ. —W. B. K.

* * *

He Giveth Peace!

He giveth peace!
Though storms may rage, the billows roll
And beat upon thy weary soul;
The storm will not forever last.
He giveth peace!

Dear restless heart, be still and know
That He who walked life's path below
Will surely understand and care,
And all thy heavy burden share.

Thy loving Father knows thy heart;
He sees the tears that often start;
With arms outstretched He yearns for thee
To come to Him that you might see —
He giveth peace!

Whatever He may send, 'tis best;
It may be that it's meant to test
Thy willingness to follow Him.
Press onward then, though faith be dim!
He giveth peace!
                                   —Georgia B. Adams

* * *

Peace 'Midst Life's Storms

Two artists put upon canvas their concepts of peace. One artist painted a placid rural scene in the center of which was a country home. Adjacent to the home were fertile fields and an abundant harvest. The undulating roads stretched in different directions from the home toward the horizon. A lazy haze hovered over glen and dale. One could almost hear the rustle of the ripened wheat, swayed with the kiss of the gentle breeze. A friendly sun shone upon the blissful picture of calm and contentment. Cows lay lazily under a shade tree, chewing their cuds.

The other artist gave a totally different concept of peace. A destroying tempest raged in his painting. Trees swayed to and fro on the storm-lashed mountainside and in the valley. The sky was ominous and gloomy, relieved only by the zigzag flashes of lightning. A roaring waterfall lunged furiously over the precipice, working disaster in the valley below! Why could the artist call this violent, turbulent scene a representation of peace? On a rock projecting from the cliff, sheltered by an overhanging boulder, sat a little bird calmly on its nest, seemingly unmindful of the howling storm or of the raging waters which plunged downward nearby. There the little bird sat in peace, with no fear, unperturbed and undisturbed!

In this world, God's children live and move and have their being amidst scenes of turmoil, tribulation, strain, stress, and storm. Inwardly, their hearts and minds are kept by God in ever deepening peace and calm. Daily they prove the genuineness of the promise, "Thou wilt keep him in perfect peace, whose mind is stayed on thee: because he trusteth in thee" (Isa. 26:3). —W. B. K.

* * *

I'm Going to Be a Peacemaker

Two members of a church disagreed over a trivial matter. The disagreement hardened into ill will and hatred. A mutual friend became distressed about the situation. "I'm going to be a peacemaker and do what I can to heal the breach between my friends," he said to himself. He called on his friend Brown first and asked him, "What do you think of my friend Thompson?" "Think of him?" flashed Brown. "He is contemptible in my sight!" "But," said the peacemaker, "you must admit he is very kind to his family." "Yes, that's true. He is kind to his family." Next day, the peacemaker called to see his friend Thompson. "Do you know what Brown said about you?" "No, but I can imagine the dirty, unkind things he would say about me!" "Well," said the peacemaker, "he said that you are very kind to your family!" "What! Did he say that?" exclaimed Thompson. "He surely did. Now, what do you think of Thompson?" "I think he is a scamp and a rascal," said Brown. "But," said the peacemaker, "you will have to admit that he is an honest man." "Yes, he is honest, but what has that to do with it?" The next day the peacemaker called on Thompson and said, "Do you know that Brown said that you are a very honest man?" "You don't mean it," said Thompson. "I do mean it. I heard him say it with my own ears!"

The next Sunday, Brown and Thompson sat together in church, rejoicing in each other's fellowship! —W. B. K.

* * *

He Giveth Peace!

Fierce raged the tempest o'er the deep,
Watch did Thine anxious servants keep,
But Thou wast wrapped in guileless sleep,
    Calm and still.

"Save, Lord, we perish," was their cry,
"O save us in our agony!"
Thy word above the storm rose high,
    "Peace, be still."

So, when our life is clouded o'er,
And storm-winds drift us from the shore,
Say, lest we sink to rise no more,
    "Peace, be still." —Godfrey Thring

* * *

The Quiet Heart

When seeking for a word or phrase for "peace" in the language of the Chol Indians of South Mexico, translators discovered that the words, "a quiet heart," gave just the meaning of "peace," so that "the way of peace" becomes "the road of the quiet heart." So far as he knew, Peter was on the road of a violent death at the hands of Herod, but it was still for him "the road of the quiet heart," for here he was on the eve of execution at peace and asleep. —*The Sunday School Times*

* * *

I Have the God of Peace!

The following conversation ensued between two men: "I'm glad to tell you," said one, "that I've got peace with God at last. I've taken Jesus Christ as my Saviour."

"I'm glad to hear that," said the other, "but I've got something better than that."

"Better than peace with God?" asked the first in surprise.

"Yes," was the reply, "for I have not only peace with God, but I have the peace of God."

"I see," said the first, "that is better."

"But wait a minute; I have something better still," went on his friend.

"What do you mean?"

"Why," was the answer, "I have the God of peace." —*Baptist Standard*

* * *

Peace, It Is I!

Fierce was the wild billow, dark was the night,
Oars labored heavily, foam glimmered white,
Trembled the mariners, peril was nigh,
Then said the Son of God, "Peace, it is I."

Ridge of the mountain wave, lower thy crest,
Wail of Euroclydon, be thou at rest!
Sorrow can never be, darkness must fly
When saith the Light of Light, "Peace, it is I."

Jesus, Deliverer, come Thou to me,
Soothe Thou my voyaging over life's sea.
Then when the storm of death roars sweeping by,
Whisper, O Truth of Truth, "Peace, it is I." —Anatolius

Perverse People

It is no great matter to associate with the good and gentle, for this is naturally pleasing to all, and everyone willingly enjoyeth peace and loveth those best that agree with him. But to be able to live peaceably with hard and perverse people, or with such as go contrary to us, is a great grace, and a most commendable thing. —Thomas A. Kempis

PERSECUTION

Illustrations

I Wiped Away the Blood and Went Right On

One day John Wesley preached to a great throng in an outdoor meeting. He pleaded with the unsaved to flee from the wrath to come. Later Wesley said, "Many of the people acted like beasts and did their best to disturb the meeting. They tried to drive a herd of cows into the crowd, but without success. Then they began to throw stones —showers of them. One of them struck me between the eyes. I wiped away the blood, and went right on, declaring that God has given to them that believe, 'not the spirit of fear, but of power, and of love, and of a sound mind.' By the spirit which now appeared . . . I saw what a blessing it is when it is given us, even in the lowest degree, to suffer for His name's sake!" —W. B. K.

* * *

Words that Change People

One day, which happened to be a Jewish holiday, I was returning from Temple. At the time I was eleven. As I approached a corner, four boys challenged my progress and after making harsh comments about my holiday suit and my holiday appearance, beat me up.

When I got to my feet I wrapped my torn garments around me and made a headlong flight home, feeling extraordinarily sorry for myself. Why had I been chosen for this unprovoked attack?

My mother comforted me and began to clean me up. The words she spoke to me then have stayed with me all my life and prevented me from bcoming cynical, bitter or disillusioned when events went against me. Her words went something like this:

"Son, it's the beatings you do not deserve that are always the hardest to bear. When you do something wrong and you are punished, it does little good because you know you did something wrong and you know you deserve the punishment. But when you take a beating for no reason at all, then you must be stronger and more patient because it is these beatings that will give you the understanding and strength to cope with life." —Dore Schary, in *Guideposts*

* * *

Not Counted Worthy to Suffer,

Some years ago Japan took over Korea. Many of the leading Christians were bitterly persecuted. Some were imprisoned in Japanese jails. Those who were not persecuted felt that they were somehow lacking in their Christianity. A native Methodist pastor went to a missionary and said, "Maksa, there must be something wrong with us Methodists. I fear that we are not living as godly as we ought to live. There are thirty-seven Presbyterians in jail and only one Methodist! Does not the Lord count us 'worthy to suffer shame for His name'?" —W. B. K.

* * *

Sheepskins and Goatskins

What indignities and satan-devised tortures have God's faithful ones suffered throughout the ages gone by! Could any mind, other than a depraved, satan-possessed mind concoct a more cruel method of torture than the one depicted in the verse: "They wandered about in sheepskins and goatskins" (Heb. 11:37)? It is said that the "green" or unshrunken skins of these

animals were sown around the bodies
of God's ancient heroes and that then
they were banished to desert wastes. As
the hot rays of the merciless sun shone
upon them, the skins became dehydrated
and shrunk more and more until the
life of the encased victims was slowly
crushed to death. Truly the world was
not worthy of these illustrious worthies!
Their daring deeds of valour shame us
who sacrifice too little for Him who
gave His all for us! —W. B. K.

* * *

Orthodox But Dead

In one of my churches was a former
missionary to India. She was in the
evening of life and was joyously and
actively awaiting the summons to depart
from this life and be forever with the
Lord. She was living a beautiful and
exemplary Christian life but, according
to the reckoning of two elderly women
in the church, she was in error in one

phase of her belief. How those women
persecuted her. With cold disdain, they
looked down their Pharisaic noses on her.
These women were thoroughly orthodox
and established in the faith. There
was little, however, of tenderness and
Christlike compassion about them. They
were devoid of the "milk of human
kindness."

It is right for us to be orthodox, believing all of God's Word. But there
is something radically wrong when our
assenting to God's Word fails to produce in us the fruit of the Spirit: "Love,
joy, peace, longsuffering, gentleness,
goodness, faith, meekness, temperance."
What havoc is wrought by loveless con-
tenders of the faith! There is little or
nothing they can acceptably do for
Christ when they have ceased loving
Christ first. What is deader than dead
orthodoxy? "Thou hast a name that thou
livest, and art dead!" —W. B. K.

POWER

Short Quotes

Great men are they who see that the
spiritual is stronger than any material
force; that thoughts rule the world.
—Ralph Waldo Emerson

* * *

Many Christians estimate difficulties
in the light of their own resources, and
thus attempt little and often fail in the
little they attempt. All God's giants
have been weak men who did great
things for God because they reckoned
on His power and presence with them.
—J. Hudson Taylor

* * *

"There is enough atomic energy in the
body of one man to destroy the City of
New York," said a prominent physicist.
Man's real strength, however, is never
in himself. It comes from God: "He
giveth power to the faint; and to them
that have no might he increaseth
strength" (Isa. 40:29); "But ye shall

receive power, after that the Holy Ghost
is come upon you" (Acts 1:8).
—Rev. Bruce Slack

* * *

After all, it is not so much what we
do for God that counts as it is what we
let Him do for us. —Dr. F. B. Meyer

* * *

Responsibility is man's response to
God's ability.
—Dr. W. H. Griffith Thomas

* * *

Just so sure as you keep drawing
out your soul's currency without making
new deposits, the next thing will be:
"No funds." Soul deposits and checks
must more than balance if we are to be
spiritually dynamic.
—Oliver Wendell Holmes

* * *

Christianity is not the truth on ice,
but the truth on fire.
—*News Letter Release*

Illustrations

Go Back and Tarry

"Tarry ye in the city of Jerusalem until ye be endued with power from on high" (Luke 24:49).

The last word from Jesus was, Go back! Go back to Jerusalem and tarry, tarry until ye be endued with power from on high. But, Master, the world is dying! Let it die! But men are hungry! Let them be hungry! But hearts are breaking! Let them break! But multitudes are being lost! Let them be lost rather than you attempt the Divine work without the Divine power!

Go back, go back to that upper room, back to your knees, back to searching your own heart, back to waiting and back to praying, back until you have come to the condition of heart and of life where your personal Pentecost shall come, and *then* go. Oh, then you will find that the works that Christ did you can do. . . . Filled with the Spirit, miracles shall become the commonplace of your daily experience.

—Samuel Chadwick

*   *   *

Noiseless But Powerful

Two men visited a factory. They were shown the rooms where huge machines were running and making much noise. Then the guide conducted the men to a smaller room. It was very quiet in there. One of the men asked, "There is not much going on here, is there?" The guide smiled and replied, "This is the most important room of all. This is where the power comes from to run the great machines. We call this room, 'the Quiet Room.'" The visitors looked in wonderment upon the great, almost noiseless dynamos!

The power room in our lives is the place where we daily meet with God. Here we receive power to meet the testings and temptations of life.

—W. B. K.

*   *   *

Greater Pressure — Greater Power

Some automobiles are equipped with motors of 325 horsepower. How is this increased power produced?

The cylinder head is milled, or ground, as much as a twenty-thousandth of an inch to give a smaller cubic inch displacement in the cylinder head of the engine. This results in an increase in the compression ratio and a substantial increase in horsepower. To say it more simply, the greater the pressure, the greater the power.

This is also true in the spiritual realm. The greater the pressure upon us, the greater is our realization of our helplessness, with the result that our dependence upon God is greater and we receive spiritual power. Said Paul, "We were pressed out of measure, above strength," that is, human strength. When thus pressed, we press closer to the One whose "strength is made perfect in weakness," and who gives us "more grace."

Pressed out of measure and pressed to all length,
Pressed so intensely it seems beyond strength;
Pressed in the body and pressed in the soul,
Pressed in the mind till the dark surges roll;
Pressure by foes, and pressure by friends,
Pressure on pressure, till life nearly ends;
Pressed into loving the staff and the rod,
Pressed into knowing no helper but God;
Pressed into liberty where nothing clings,
Pressed into faith for impossible things;
Pressed into living a life in the Lord,
Pressed into living a Christ-life out-poured!

—W. B. K.

*   *   *

Wilberforce and God

Nearly two hundred years ago there lived in England a man whose name was William Wilberforce. God seemed to say to him, "I want you to free all the slaves in the British Empire!" Humanly speaking, Wilberforce could not do it. He was a cripple, and a hunchback. His body was so twisted that a writer of that day said he looked like a human corkscrew. The majority of the leaders did not want the British Empire to stop the slave trade. Wilberforce believed that nothing was impossible with God. He believed he could do all things in Christ's strength. On the day of his funeral, when his worn-out body was put beneath the flagstones of Westminster Abbey, the British Parliament passed a law that every slave who lived beneath the British flag be freed.

—W. B. K.

* * *

God's Works Declare His Greatness
The spacious firmament on high,
With all the blue ethereal sky
And spangled heavens, a shining frame,
Their great Original proclaim.
The unwearied sun, from day to day,
Does his Creator's power display,
And publishes to every land
The work of an Almighty hand.

Soon as the evening shades prevail.
The moon takes up the wondrous tale,
And, nightly, to the listening earth
Repeats the story of her birth;
Whilst all the stars that round her burn,
And all the planets in their turn,
Confirm the tidings as they roll,
And spread the truth from pole to pole.

What though in solemn silence all
Move round the dark terrestrial ball:
What though no real voice nor sound
Amid their radiant orbs be found?
In Reason's ear they all rejoice,
And utter forth a glorious voice,
Forever singing, as they shine,
"The Hand that made us is divine."

—Joseph Addison in
"Treasures of Poetry"

* * *

Christians Are Like Locomotives
A minister was being shown through a large plant where locomotives were built. Pointing at one completed locomotive, the guide said, "This locomotive is the last word in engine building!" The minister exclaimed with admiration, "What a mighty thing!" "Yes," said the guide, "if there are three things attending it. It must have power generated by internal combustion of crude

oil. It must be on the rails, for its power would bring destruction if it is derailed. It must have a good engineer, for it will run efficiently only when rightly handled." The minister replied, "That's just like a Christian. We are powerful and useful only when we are filled with the fullness of God, walking in His way, and utterly under the Holy Spirit's control!" —W. B. K.

* * *

A Puzzled Agnostic
An agnostic set out to save a drunkard from his besetting sin, just to prove that it was possible to do so without the aid of religion. He found the task much harder than he had imagined, for no appeals to his manhood, or arguments about the power of mind and will had any effect. The drunkard had lost all strength to resist temptation, and his would-be savior found he had to be with him constantly, and even take him by the arm to get him past a public house. Still the optimistic unbeliever persevered, declaring that eventually he would save him without any Christian help. One day a friend met him alone, and asked him how the experiment was going on. He replied: "I was doing fairly well when a group of fellows singing at a street corner got hold of him. I don't really know what happened, but somehow they persuaded him to kneel and pray with them. Anyway, he can pass a public house by himself now." —Told by Dr. T. R. Glover

* * *

He Giveth Power to the Faint
Dr. F. B. Meyer, a prince of exegetes and a powerful preacher, was on his last visit to America. A large audience had assembled in a New York City church to hear him speak. Weak and wobbly, Dr. Meyer was helped to the platform by two men, one on either side. Sitting in an elevated chair and with great physical exertion, he began his message. The audience thought, "Will he be able to go through the service?" As he spoke, a miracle of God's enabling power was enacted before their wondering eyes. Dr. Meyer stood to his feet. The heyday and vigor of his earlier

years returned, and for one and a quarter hours words of graciousness and wisdom flowed from his lips.

All left that memorable meeting knowing in their hearts that they had the answer to the ancient question, "Where is the Lord God of Elijah?" and rejoicing in the sure promise of God to His physically enfeebled children, "He giveth power to the faint!"

—W. B. K.

* * *

Power Belongeth to God

When Dr. J. H. Jowett preached from his pulpit in Newcastle-on-Tyne, an elderly man usually sat near the pulpit. As Dr. Jowett repeated the Lord's Prayer, the elderly gentleman would quietly repeat it along with him. When they came to the place where all power is ascribed to God, the old man would say, "Hallelujah! Hallelujah! Hallelujah!" Said Dr. Jowett, "He never said it anywhere else — only there. I knew what he meant — that to God belongeth power, always and everywhere!"

—W. B. K.

* * *

The Power Within

We were looking out over the sea on a rough and stormy day. "I have been watching a steamer," said someone to me, "fighting her way onward in the face of that terrible wind and those high-crested waves. How she keeps on her course at all is a mystery to me; how does she do it?" There was only one answer to that question, and I said, "Because the power within her enables her to overcome the opposing forces without." It is so with God's children. They are hindered by obstacles, thwarted by the keen cutting winds of misfortune; buffeted and bruised by the surging waves of sorrow, bereavement, disappointed hopes; and we wonder how they can keep on their course so bravely and brightly. They hold the secret in their hearts; they are conscious of a power within, one which is not theirs by nature. They have learned to say with St. Paul, "I can do all things through Christ which strengtheneth me."

—*The Christian Herald*

* * *

Smelly Lamps

There was a Welsh woman who lived in a valley far away from any town or city. She was a simple-minded, hardworking person who knew little about the ways of the world. At a great sacrifice to herself, she had electricity installed in her little cottage. "You use the electric lights so little, I wonder if it was worth what it cost you to have them put in," said a neighbor. "Oh, yes," answered the woman, "I switch them on every night to see to light my lamps. Then I switch them off!" Think of it! With great power at her command with the flip of a switch, she continued the weary task of trimming wicks, pouring oil and lighting smelly lamps!

Christ's strength is ours for the asking. Yet, there are many who continue to serve the Lord in weariness and weakness, "sometimes up, but most times down!" —W. B. K.

* * *

Connected to the Power

A delicate little lady, who had obviously seen better days, continued to go to work as a seamstress, although past the traditional threescore and ten years. The daughter of one of the families in which she was employed, marveling at her quiet endurance, asked her one day how she managed to work so hard and so steadily. "Well, my dear," replied the patient voice, "sometimes it seems hard. Often I get up in the morning feeling so weak and faint that it seems impossible to go through the day's work. But, you see, I'm like a tram car before it is connected with the power wire. The first thing I do is to *connect with the Power*. When I have said my prayers, I feel my hand in God's, and the power of His Spirit passing into me, and then I can go on and do what I have to do." —*The Sunday Circle*

PRAYER

Short Quotes

When the disciples locked the doors, Christ knew He was sure of a welcome. He could not get their ear because of the din and confusion that came through the open doors. Closing the door to the world is opening the door to the Master. Don't be afraid of shutting the door. It is the best invitation for the Master to enter. —*Christian Herald*

* * *

There is a law that I am learning
That is helping me each day,
That our Lord sends something better
For each thing He takes away.

* * *

It was the custom of Judge Glenn of Missouri to stand and pray with his eyes open. A friend tactfully asked him, "Why do you pray with your eyes open?" He replied, "Does not the Bible tell us to watch as well as pray? Did not the Saviour lift up His eyes to heaven in giving thanks? After all, it is not the posture of the body or the closing of our eyes which causes God to answer our prayers. Rather, it is the posture of our heart. If there is no iniquity therein, God will surely answer our prayers." —W. B. K.

* * *

An eight-year-old boy sat on top of a load of wood in a wagon. The wagon was drawn by two horses which ran swiftly down a steep hill. After the frightening ordeal, the child's mother asked him, "Well, my boy, what did you do?" The boy said, "I prayed to God and hung on like a beaver!"

* * *

Our God has boundless resources. The only limit is in us. Our asking, our thinking, our praying are too small. Our expectations are too limited.
—A. B. Simpson

* * *

Prayer gives you courage to make the decisions you must make in a crisis and then the confidence to leave the result to a Higher Power.
—General Dwight Eisenhower

Undertake great things *for* God and expect great things *from* God.
—William Carey

* * *

Prayer is a safety valve for the mind and the soul. If Christianity were practically applied to our everyday life it would so purify and vitalize the race that at least one-half of our sickness and sorrow would disappear.
—Dr. William Sadler

* * *

Yes, hands and feet and eyes may share
The work which helps to answer prayer!
We pray the hungry may be fed,
To Christ the weary may be led,
The poor be clothed — 'tis good to pray,
And help somebody every day!

* * *

In prayer, delays are not denials: "When . . . he heard . . . that he was sick, he abode two days still in the same place where he was" (John 11:6). Denials are sometimes the best answers to our prayers: "Ye know not what ye ask" (Matt. 20:22). —W. B. K.

* * *

Praying mothers are America's greatest assets. —Theodore Roosevelt

* * *

George Muller said that the most important part of prayer was the fifteen minutes after he had said "Amen."

* * *

Prayer isn't a monologue. It is dialogue — our talking to God and God talking to us: "I will hear what God the Lord will speak" (Ps. 85:8).
—W. B. K.

* * *

Too few of us are sufficiently quiescent before God to hear the still, small voice of the indwelling Holy Spirit. Often the best disclosures God has for His children are spoken in a whisper.
—W. B. K.

* * *

"I suppose the greatest thing in the world is loving people, and wanting to destroy the sin but not the sinner, and not to forget that when life knocks you to your knees, that's the best position in which to pray. That's where I learned." —Ethel Barrymore

* * *

There is seemingly little power in prayer. There is a marked absence of travail. There is much phrasing but little pleading. Prayer has become a soliloquy instead of a passion.
—*Sunday School Times*

* * *

Prayer is the greatest force we can wield. It is the greatest talent God has given. He has given it to every Christian. What right have we to leave unappropriated or unapplied the greatest force which God has ordained for the salvation and transformation of men? —John R. Mott

* * *

As one whose whole life has been concerned with the sufferings of the mind, I would state that of all the hygienic measures to counteract disturbed sleep, depression of spirits, and all the miserable sequels of a distressed mind, I would undoubtedly give the *first place* to the simple habit of prayer."
—Dr. Hysloop

* * *

What various hindrances we meet
In coming to a mercy seat!
Yet who that knows the worth of prayer
But wishes to be often there!
—William Cowper

* * *

Much kneeling keeps us in good standing with God. We cannot stumble when we are on our knees. A Christian on his knees sees more than the philosopher on tiptoes.

* * *

When the glory of the Father
Is the goal of every prayer,
When before the throne in heaven
Our High Priest presents it there,
When the Spirit prompts the asking,
When the waiting heart believes,
Then we know of each petition —
Everyone who asks receives.

* * *

God respects not the arithmetic of our prayers — how many they are; not the rhetoric of our prayers — how ele-

gant they are; not the music of our prayers — how melodious they are; not the logic of our prayers — how methodical they are; but the *sincerity* of our prayers — how heartfelt they are.

* * *

My prayers seem to be more of an attitude than anything else. I indulge in no lip service, but ask the great God silently, daily, and often many times a day, to permit me to speak to Him. I ask Him to give me wisdom, understanding and bodily strength to do His will. Hence, I am asking and receiving all the time.
—Dr. George Washington Carver

* * *

In God's name I beseech you to let prayer nourish your soul as meals nourish your body. —Fenelon

* * *

We can pray, believe, and receive, or we can pray, doubt, and do without.

* * *

"If I were to live my life over again, I would spend less time in service and more time in prayer," said Adolph Saphir, famed Hebrew teacher, as he neared death.

* * *

Sometimes, when our souls are overwhelmed by sorrow, our prayers lie so deep in our innermost being that we are powerless to articulate them in words. How comforting it is to know that we do not need words to pray prevailingly: "Thou hast heard my voice: hide not thine ear at my breathing" (Lam. 3:56).
—W. B. K.

* * *

The privilege of prayer is to me one of the most cherished and loved of privileges. God answers prayer, and I never venture to criticize His answers. When I finally pass through the valley of the shadow of death, I expect to pass through it in conversation with Him.
—Dr. Grenfell

* * *

Prayer does not always change things, but it always changes us. Things outward may continue the same, but if we are changed, outward things do not matter greatly. —W. B. K.

I never prayed earnestly for anything but it came sooner or later, and oftentimes in the way I least imagined. But it came. —Adoniram Judson

* * *

Thou art coming to a King,
   Large petitions with thee bring;
For His grace and pow'r are such,
   None can ever ask too much!

* * *

If I could hear Christ praying for me in the next room, I would not fear a million enemies. Yet distance makes no difference. He *is* praying for me: "He ever liveth to make intercession."
   —Robert Murray McCheyne

* * *

Prayer is not an all-out effort to overcome God's unwillingness to "do exceeding abundantly above all that we ask or think" (Eph. 3:20). God has been waiting to fill us with all the fulness of God, and to grant to us the blessings for which we pray. There is no unwillingness on God's part to bless us, but often there is unreadiness on our part!
   —W. B. K.

* * *

When thou prayest, rather let thy heart be without words than thy words without heart. Prayer will make a man cease from sin, or sin will entice a man to cease from prayer. —Bunyan

* * *

Then let us earnest be,
   And never faint in prayer;
He loves our importunity,
   And makes our cause His care.
   —John Newton

On a very dark night in my life these words came to me: "Praise waiteth for thee, O God, in Zion" (Ps. 65:1). I had been waiting in prayer for months. God was waiting for me to take this final step of faith. When I began to praise Him for the answer, He began to answer "exceeding abundantly above all" that I could ask or think! Praise changes things! Praise changes *you!* Try it!
   —Mrs. Charles E. Cowman

* * *

A violent storm struck Tupelo, Mississippi. The following day a Negro asked his friend if he had prayed while the storm raged. The man replied in his unique and fascinating way, "Co'se I did! Who wouldn't pray in a storm lak dat?" A third Negro, hearing what was said added, "I 'spec de Lawd heard plenty strange voices roun' here las' night!" —W. B. K.

* * *

Two little girls from Christian homes had been taught to pray and ask God to help them in time of need. One morning, as they walked leisurely to school, they looked at a big clock in a window and saw that they were late. They were very distressed. The one girl said, "Let's kneel down and ask God to help us to get there on time!" "No," said the other girl, "let's run as fast as we can, and pray as we run!"
   —W. B. K.

* * *

The sun has never risen upon China without finding me at prayer. In 40 years I saw 700 missionaries and 1000 native workers in China.
   —J. Hudson Taylor

Illustrations

Ask for Big Things

A rich man went Christmas shopping to toyland with a little girl from a very poor home. How thrilled the girl was! She was filled with wonder as she looked at the large display of toys. "Little girl," said the man, "choose anything you wish and I will buy it for you." But the little girl thought, "That's too good to be true!"

For an hour, clerks trailed the man and the girl, hoping that she would select some high-priced item. They looked at a three-hundred-dollar doll house. They looked at an expensive talking doll. Finally the girl asked the rich man, "Can I really have anything I want?" Her benefactor smiled and said, "Yes, my little girl, you can have anything you want." The clerks smiled expectantly. Then the little girl said, "This is what I want," and pointed to a little plush squirrel, marked twenty-five cents!

God is a great God. We honor Him greatly by asking big things of Him.
—W. B. K.

* * *

A Hallowed Spot to Billy Sunday

"I had better check on that bird. He's acting queerly," said a burly Irish cop as he walked toward a well-dressed man who stood near the curb with head bowed, eyes closed and mumbling. "Had a little too much, comrade?" he asked the stranger. "No, officer. I'm Billy Sunday. This is the spot where, years ago, I was converted fom sin to the Saviour. Whenever I come to Chicago, I come to this spot so sacred to me and thank God for His marvelous grace in saving me!"

"Put it here, Billy," said the genial cop as he extended his hand. "Stay here and pray all you want to. I'll stand by and see that nobody molests you. And say a little prayer for me, too!"

There is no spot to me more dear
Than native vale and fountain;
A spot for which affection's tear
Springs grateful from its fountain!

'Tis not where kindred souls abound,
'Though that were almost heaven;
But where I first my Saviour found
And felt my sins forgiven!
—W. B. K.

* * *

Mueller's Testimony

I spend hours in prayer every day. But I live in the spirit of prayer. I pray as I walk and when I lie down. I pray when I awake. The answers are always coming. Thousands of times have my prayers been answered. When I am persuaded that a thing is right, I go on praying until the answer comes. I never give up. I have been praying every day for fifty-two years for two men, sons of a friend of my youth. They are not converted yet, but they will be. How can it be otherwise when we have the unchanging promises of God!
—*God's Revivalist*

* * *

Working on Your Knees

A minister was watching some men repairing a section of a highway. His attention was especially drawn to an elderly man who knelt as he broke stones for the hole in the highway. The minister observed that this man did more work than the ones who were standing while breaking stones. Then he said to the kneeling man, whom he knew well, "John, I wish I could break the stony hearts of my hearers as easily as you are breaking those stones!" With a twinkle in his eyes John said, "Pastor, you could if you worked on your knees!" —W. B. K.

* * *

Earth's Last Prayer Meeting

The prayer meeting is, in many churches, defunct or dead. It is only a lingering memory in the minds of some of the older saints. Yet I would remind you that earth's best attended prayer meeting is yet future. How different it will be from any other prayer meeting! See who they are who are praying — "And the kings of the earth, and the great men, and the rich men, and the chief captains, and the mighty men, and every bondman and every free man" (Rev. 6:15f.c.). Observe to whom this unique assemblage will address its prayer — "the mountains and rocks." Hear what they unitedly and fervently pray for — "Hide us from the face of him that sitteth on the throne." We need but three words with which to describe their prayer — dead in earnest! Their prayer, even if they would address it to God, would be *too late*. The day of grace will have been superseded by the day of God's wrath! —W. B. K.

* * *

Whisper a Prayer

Whisper a prayer in the morning,
Whisper a prayer at noon,
Whisper a prayer in the evening,
To keep your heart in tune.

God answers prayer in the morning,
God answers prayer at noon,
God answers prayer in the evening,
To keep your heart in tune.

Jesus may come in the morning,
Jesus may come at noon,
Jesus may come in the evening,
So keep your heart in tune.
—Bishop Charles V. Fairbairn

Down on Your Knees — Pray Now!

"Who is there?" cried a sentinel one night to a British soldier who was creeping stealthily back to his quarters from a nearby clump of trees. The sentinel was not satisfied with the soldier's explanation, so he took him to the commanding officer. There the soldier explained, "I went into the woods to pray alone. That is my only defense." The officer asked, "Have you been in the habit of spending hours in private prayer?" "Yes, Sir," answered the soldier. "Then down on your knees and pray now," demanded the officer. The soldier knelt. He prayed earnestly and without hesitancy. When he had finished his prayer, the officer said, "You may go. I believe your story. If you hadn't often prayed alone, you couldn't have done so well here!" —W. B. K.

* * *

God Answered the Other Way

Frank Sheriff, a former superintendent of the Christian Business Men's Association in Chicago, and his little girl prayed earnestly for the recovery of the wife and mother. But, after much suffering, she died. The little girl sought to comfort her father. She said, "Daddy, God answered our prayers *the other way*, didn't He?" She meant that God had answered their prayers, but not the way they had prayed. Sometimes God, in infinite wisdom, answers our prayers with a *no!* But this is certain — He always answers our prayers in keeping with His wondrous plans and eternal purposes. —W. B. K.

* * *

All Night Prayer

How greatly impressed I was, in the beginning years of my Christian life, with the custom of the pastor of the church where I was saved occasionally to pray all night with his deacons and other consecrated Christians. One night, as they were praying in the pastor's study in the church, a drinking dentist passed by on his way home. The hour was late. Seeing a light beaming from the pastor's study, he went to investigate. He was told that he had been one of those for whom they had unitedly prayed during the hours of the night.

It wasn't long before the dentist was on his knees crying to God for mercy and forgiveness.

Oh, the power of *united* prayer! "If *two* of you shall agree . . . as touching *any thing* that they shall ask, it *shall* be done for them of my Father which is in heaven" (Matt. 18:19). What wouldn't God do for us if there were more of us emulating the example of our Lord who often continued all night in prayer.
—W. B. K.

* * *

Prayers Answered the Other Way!

I asked God for strength, that I might achieve,
I was made weak, that I might learn humbly to obey. . .
I asked for health, that I might do greater things,
I was given infirmity, that I might do better things. . .
I asked for riches, that I might be happy,
I was given poverty that I might be wise. . .
I asked for power, that I might have the praise of men,
I was given weakness, that I might feel the need of God . . .
I asked for all things, that I might enjoy life,
I was given life, that I might enjoy all things . . .
I got nothing that I asked for — but everything I had hoped for,
Almost despite myself, my unspoken prayers were answered.
I am among all men most richly blessed.
—An Unknown Confederate Soldier

* * *

God Hears Every Language

A missionary, after using a telephone in the presence of a group of natives, was asked by one of them, "Where was that wonderful thing made?" Upon being told that it was manufactured in America, the man said, "Then it is no use for me to have one in my shop, for it cannot speak our language." Calling at the home of a mutual friend, the missionary placed the instrument against the man's ear. He listened, and then exclaimed, "Oh, it speaks our language, too!" This discovery opened the way for the missionary to tell of the God who

hears and understands the languages of
all His people of every race and tongue.
—*Free Churchman*

* * *

Keep the Fire Burning

Keep the altar of private prayer burning. This is the very life of all piety.
The sanctuary and family altars borrow
their fires here, therefore let this burn
well. Secret devotion is the very essence,
evidence, and barometer of vital and
experimental religion.

Burn here the fat of your sacrifices.
Let your closet-seasons be, if possible,
regular, frequent, and undisturbed. Effectual prayer availeth much.

Let us examine ourselves on this important matter. Do we engage with
lukewarmness in private devotion? Is
the fire of devotion burning dimly in our
hearts? Do the chariot wheels drag
heavily? If so, let us be alarmed at
this sign of decay. Let us go with weeping, and ask for the Spirit of grace and
of supplication. —Spurgeon

* * *

Obituary

Died — in Laodicea, the *prayer meeting*, aged one year.

The health of this little meeting was
poor; most of the year its life was
despaired of. But a few anxious friends
kept it alive, and sometimes it would so
revive as to encourage them. Discouragement at last prevailed; now the
prayer meeting is dead.

It died from neglect; not a Christian
was present when it died; over forty
were living within a mile of it, and not
one of them was there.

Had two or three been there, its life
might have been saved, for "where two
or three are gathered together . . ."
(Matt. 18:20).

Two-thirds of the forty *might* have
been there had they been so disposed.
But they were not, and so the prayer
meeting died. —*Scattered Seed*

* * *

He Cannot Be Disturbed!

The superintendent of a large factory
wanted to talk with the company's manager about an urgent business matter.
He went to the manager's office. The
secretary said, "The manager is in con-

ference now, and cannot be disturbed."
"But how can he be in conference when
there is no one in the office with him?"
asked the superintendent. "I must see
him now on a matter of great importance." "You may come back in fifteen
minutes if you wish," said the secretary,
"or you may leave your message with
me. At present, he is not to be disturbed." The irate superintendent
pushed by the secretary and quickly
opened the door to the manager's private
office. After a quick glance within, he
quickly and quietly closed the door. Said
he apologetically to the secretary, "Why,
he is on his knees! He is praying!"
"Yes, he is *in conference*, as I told you,"
answered the secretary. —W. B. K.

* * *

Did Jesus Speak Spanish?

An evangelist sat beside an elderly
woman in a railway coach. The woman
spoke only Spanish. So also did the
evangelist. She asked, "Don't you think
that Adam and Eve spoke Spanish in
the Garden of Eden?" He answered,
"No, I don't think they did." Then she
thought for a moment and asked, "Don't
you think that Jesus spoke Spanish when
He was here on earth? You know in
all His pictures He is dark, like we are,
and He has dark hair and dark eyes."
"No, Jesus did not speak Spanish when
He was here upon earth." Then quick
as a flash she said, "Well, if He didn't
talk it then He talks it now, because He
talks to me. He answers my prayers
and He understands me." Thank God
for a wonderful Saviour who makes
Himself known to any, in his own
tongue, who will listen.

—*Sword of the Lord*

* * *

How He Knew

General Stonewall Jackson had in his
service a Negro who had become so accustomed to his ways that he was able
to discern whenever the General was
about to start on an expedition. "How
do you know the General's plans without his telling you?" someone asked him.
"Here is how," replied the Negro, "he
always prays every night and every
morning. But when he is on the eve
of an expedition, he prays two or three
or four times during the night. When

I see him praying often during the night, I pack his baggage, for I know he is going on an expedition."
—*The Christian Index*

• • •

Lord, Speak to Me

Lord, speak to me, that I may speak
In living echoes of Thy tone;
As Thou hast sought, so let me seek
Thy erring children lost and lone.

O teach me, Lord, that I may teach
The precious things Thou dost impart;
And wing my words, that they may reach
The hidden depths of many a heart.

O fill me with Thy fullness, Lord,
Until my very heart o'erflow
In kindling thought and glowing word,
Thy love to tell, Thy praise to show.
—Frances Ridley Havergal

• • •

What Prayer Does

Prayer makes the darkened clouds withdraw;
Prayer climbs the ladder Jacob saw;
Gives exercise to faith and love;
Brings every blessing from above.

Restraining prayer, we cease to fight;
Prayer makes the Christian's armor bright;
And Satan trembles when he sees
The weakest saint upon his knees.
—Cowper

• • •

Prayer Can Be —

Prayer can be as quiet
As a falling petal,
Fragrant as a flower,
But strong as metal.

Prayer can be a crying,
As in Gethsemane.
And he who heard his Son, the Christ,
Will he not hear me?

Prayer can be the music
Of his song divine,
The miracle of harmony,
His counterpoint with mine.

And always to the Spirit-fed
Prayer can bring the Living Bread.
—Gwynnyth Gibson

Large Petitions with Thee Bring!

Carol Ann Miller, a twelve-year-old girl in Oxon Hill, Maryland, had a heart ailment which required specialized, dangerous surgery. A rare type of blood — B-negative — was needed for transfusion before the surgeons would attempt the operation.

"I'll write to President Eisenhower, and ask him to help me get the needed blood," thought Carol Ann. So she wrote: "My Dear President: The surgeons want to close up a hole in my heart. If you know anyone who has B-negative blood, please call my mother. It is very important!"

The girl's plea deeply touched the president. Immediately he had the Red Cross contacted, and also the doctors in Walter Reed Hospital. Soon twenty pints of the required blood were made available to Carol Ann's surgeons.

How glad we are that the smallest and obscurest of God's children can come to "the throne of grace" and there "find . . . help in time of need!"

Whatever our need may be, God will supply it. The Saviour's promise is sure: "What things soever ye desire, when ye pray, believe that ye receive them, and ye shall have them" (Mark 11:24). —W. B. K.

• • •

Prayer Meeting Lasts Fifty-three Hours!

Five men were entrapped in a spar and zinc mine in Salem, Kentucky, by falling rocks. They had nothing to eat. They were in utter darkness. One of the men could have saved himself had he not run back to warn the others. When the entombed men discovered that they could not escape, they began to pray and sing. Their prayer and praise service lasted for fifty-three hours! Then they were rescued. Later one of the men testified, "We lay there from Friday morning till Sunday morning. We prayed 'without ceasing.' When the rescuers reached us, we were still praying!"

When the men were brought up out of the mine, on the caps of each one were scrawled these words: "If we are dead when you find us, we are all saved!" —W. B. K.

Does God Know Chinese?

Before the days when China was under Communist rule, a little Chinese boy lived at a school where missionaries were teaching. They were all praying one night when the little boy said to the missionary, "Do you think God understands Chinese?"

"Oh, yes," replied the missionary. "Why do you ask?"

"Because," said the little boy, "sometimes when I feel bad I like to pray to God in Chinese, and I wondered if He understands, just the same as English."

"Of course," said the missionary. "God knows every language. He can hear what we *think*. He doesn't really hear the words we say. He listens to the feeling down deep in our hearts that makes us want to speak to Him. He says in the Bible: 'Before they pray, I will answer, and while they are yet speaking, I will hear.' So speak in any language, and God will hear."

—Junior Trails

• • •

A Prayer for the Day

Grant me, O Lord, the strength today
For every task which comes my way.
Cover my eyes and make me blind
To petty faults I should not find.
Open my eyes and let me see
The friend my neighbor tries to be.
Teach me when duty seems severe
To see Thy purpose shining clear.
Let me at noontime rest content,
The half day bravely lived and spent.
And when the night slips down, let me
Unstained and undishonored be;
Grant me to live this one day through
Up to the best that I can do.

—Edgar A. Guest

• • •

A Motorist's Prayer

Our Heavenly Father, we ask this day a particular blessing as we take the wheel of our car. Grant us safe passage through all the perils of travel; shelter those who accompany us and protect us from harm by Thy mercy; steady our hands and quicken our eye that we may never take another's life; guide us to our destination safely, confident in the knowledge that Thy blessings go with us through darkness and light . . . sunshine and shower . . . forever and ever. Amen.

(State Highway Patrol
North Carolina Department of
Motor Vehicles)

• • •

Pray On

To talk with God, no breath is lost;
　Talk on! talk on!
To walk with God, no strength is lost;
　Walk on! walk on!
To wait on God, no time is lost;
　Wait on! wait on!
To grind the ax, no work is lost,
　Grind on! grind on!
The work is quicker, better done;
Not needing half the strength laid on;
　Grind on! grind on!

—Selected

• • •

Call and I Will Answer

A devout Christian in Chicago developed a humanly incurable ailment — a tumor of the brain. Two of Chicago's greatest brain specialists were called in on the case. On the following Sunday, the pastor stood before his people, calling their attention to the critical illness of the fellow member. "We'll not have formal worship service this morning. Instead we will unitedly pray that the great Physician, Jesus, will work a miracle and completely restore His servant and our friend. We will trustingly claim the promise: 'And this is the confidence we have in him, that, if we ask any thing according to his will, he heareth us' (I John 5:14). Never have I felt the presence and power of the Holy Spirit as I now feel His presence! I know that God will hear our cry!" The service was turned into an old-fashioned prayer meeting. Before the meeting adjourned, the Christian doctor on the case entered and exclaimed, "Thank God! a miracle has happened! Our friend has a chance to live. God has answered prayer!" —W. B. K.

• • •

We've Done All We Can!

"We've done all we can for your boy," said two physicians to a sad father and mother. "There is no human skill that can save him!" It was Sunday. In every church throughout Lou-

isville, Kentucky, earnest prayer was
offered for little Jack. Dr. John R.
Sampey asked prayer for Jack over a
nation-wide broadcast. Merely as a
gesture of concern, the doctors returned
to see Jack on Sunday afternoon. A few
minutes later they left his bedside, saying, "It's a miracle! The fever is gone!
Jack is sleeping peacefully!"

"Today Jack is a happy Christian, a
deacon in his church and a successful
businessman," said Dr. Sampey.

—W. B. K.

* * *

How Church Was Heated in July

Five ministerial students were visiting
in London on a hot Sunday in July.
While they were waiting for the doors
to open, a man approached and asked,
"Gentlemen, would you like to see the
heating apparatus of the church?" They
thought, "How queer he is to want to
show us the heating system on a hot
day in July!" Following him, they came
to a door. He quietly opened it and whispered: "There, sirs, is our heating apparatus!" Some seven hundred intercessors were kneeling in prayer, seeking an outpouring of God's Spirit upon
the service which was soon to begin in
the Tabernacle. *That unknown guide
was Spurgeon himself!* —W. B. K.

* * *

Pray Before Storm Breaks

An elderly Negro who for many years
had faithfully served his Lord, was riding along in a buggy in the countryside
with an atheistic white man. Ominous,
black clouds began to gather and dark-
en the skies. A cyclone was in the
making. Presently trees began to sway
to and fro, houses began to topple, and
flying debris swished past. The atheist,
in terror, called to the Negro, "Pray!
Call upon God to save us!" But the
Negro replied, "I did my praying before
the storm broke."

The time to pray is now. The time
to get right with God is now. The
Bible says: "Seek ye the Lord while he
may be found" (Isa. 55:6); "Surely in
the floods of great waters they shall not
come nigh unto thee" (Ps. 32:6).

—W. B. K.

The Camel Kneels

The camel at the close of day
Kneels down upon the sandy plain
To have his burden lifted off,
And rest to gain.

My soul, thou too shouldst to thy knees
When daylight draweth to a close
And let thy Master lift thy load,
And grant repose.

Else how canst thou tomorrow meet,
With all tomorrow's work to do,
If thou thy burden all the night
Dost carry through?

The camel kneels at break of day
To have his guide replace his load;
Then rises up anew to take
The desert road.

So thou shouldst kneel at morning dawn,
That God may give thee daily care;
Assured that He no load too great
Will make thee bear.

—*Selected*

* * *

On Wings of Prayer

I breathed a heartfelt evening prayer
To God on high, and lingered there,
To see if God did truly care
    In heaven above.
Down from the heights, my answer came
A quiet peace passed through my frame,
I felt His presence, praise His Name,
    For God is love.

I sang a joyful, evening song,
It swept the stars, its way along,
And up amid that heavenly throng,
    Reached God on high:
Then, back into my spirit came,
God's presence, as a bush aflame,
I bowed again and praised His Name,
    For God was nigh.

How wonderful to have the right,
Up past the stars to take our flight,
Into God's holy, sacred light,
    Beyond the blue;
There to have access by His grace,
Into the presence of His face,
And then, to earth, our way retrace,
    With hope anew.

—Rev. R. E. Neighbour, D.D.

Earnestness in Prayer

Two African chiefs came to Chalmers and said, "We want Christian teachers. Will you send them?"

Chalmers had no one to send and he said, "I have no one. I cannot send anyone."

Two years passed and these two chiefs came to him again. Chalmers himself happened to be at liberty, and he went to their village, arriving on Sunday morning. To his surprise, he saw the whole tribe on their knees, in perfect silence.

Chalmers said to one of the chiefs, "What are you doing?"

"We are praying," he said.

"But you are not saying anything," Chalmers said.

"White man," the chief answered, "we do not know what to say. For two years every Sunday morning we have met here. And for four hours we have been on our knees, and we have been praying like that, but we do not know what to say."

How many in America are as earnest as these native Africans were?

—*The Burning Bush*

* * *

Somebody Prayed!

A thrilling incident happened in a little hut in Africa. A missionary awoke suddenly. She had a feeling of imminent danger. Fear held her in a vice-like grip. The moon's rays shone through the window, but she could see nothing wrong. She continued to have a feeling of great danger so she awoke her husband. They talked in a whisper. Looking beside the bed, they saw a fearsome creature — a giant cobra whose head was raised, ready to strike and inject venom into the flesh of the missionaries. Quickly the husband reached for his rifle and shot the cobra through its head.

Our story is not complete. One day while a friend of the missionaries was sweeping the floor in her Canadian town, she had an irresistible urge to pray for these missionaries. "They are right now in great danger," she said to herself. So she began to pray. Presently God's peace came into her heart. She knew that God had worked in behalf of her faraway friends. Later, when the missionaries told her of their frightful experience, she compared the date and time of the two experiences. The peril of the missionaries and the burden to pray for them corresponded to the minute!

"More things are wrought by prayer than this world dreams of!" —W. B. K.

* * *

A Prayer for My Pastor

"Our Father, let me be a pillar of strength to help hold him up and not a thorn in his flesh to sap his strength, nor a burden on his back to pull him down. Let me support him without striving to possess him. Let me lift his hands without placing shackles around them. Let me give him my help that he may devote more time in working for the salvation of others and less time in gratifying my vanity. Let me work for him as the pastor of all the members and not compel him to spend precious time in pleasing me. Let me be unselfish in what I do for him and not selfish in demanding that he do more for me. Let me strive to serve him and the church much and be happy as he serves me less and the church and others more."

—*The Fairmount Baptist Messenger*

* * *

Unarticulated Prayers

Words are not absolutely necessary to prevailing prayer. There are times when our souls are so overwhelmed by sorrow that we are unable to articulate our prayers: "Thou hast heard my voice: hide not thine ear at my breathing, at my cry" (Lam. 3:56).

A historian, in narrating the surrender of General Lee to General Grant at Appomattox Court House, said: "Few words were spoken by General Lee and his officers. Their lips quivered with a sorrow too deep for words."

—W. B. K.

. . .

The Button of Prayer

Recently a large hospital in a great city was completed. It is equipped with the latest and most improved gadgets. Their purpose was explained by an attendant to visitors on the opening day. Regarding a button at the bed of each patient, the attendant said: "By the old method, a patient pressed a button beside his bed, and a bell rang. Sometimes the bell was not heard, or at least unheeded. The sound of various bells was also confusing. But now the weakest patient may touch a button and instantly four lights flash — one in the office, one in the hall, and two others in different parts of the building. It is impossible for anyone to turn the lights off until the call has been answered and the patient who pressed the button has been visited!"

If human ingenuity has devised such a clever thing to bring help to needy ones, surely God will hear the cry of His children in times of weakness and great need. When the weakest hand touches the button of prayer, there is no power in hell or earth which can hinder the signal, nor bar the answer!

—W. B. K.

. . .

Where Two or Three

A dear friend of mine, Mrs. Donald B. McHenry, made elaborate preparations for a prayer meeting in her home. She invited many neighbors and friends, but only five came. How disappointed and discouraged she was! Defeated, she said to me, "Only five attended the prayer meeting. I expected at least twenty-five!" Then I said, "Praise the Lord! In reality you had two more than you needed to claim the sure promise: 'For where two or three are gathered together in my name, there am I in the midst of them.'" —W. B. K.

276

God Works Mysteriously!

When Adoniram Judson was dying, news came to him that some Jews in Turkey had been converted through reading the account of his sufferings in Burma. "This awes me," said Judson to his wife. "This is good news. When I was a young man, I prayed for the Lord to send me to the Jews in Jerusalem as a missionary. But He sent me to Burma to preach and to suffer the tortures of imprisonment. Now, because of my sufferings, God has brought some Jews in Turkey to repentance!"

Deep in unfathomable mines
Of never-failing skill,
He treasures up His bright designs,
And works His sovereign will!

—W. B. K.

. . .

When Burdened to Pray

Dr. Harry A. Ironside was asked: "If you had prayed all your life for the salvation of a loved one, and then you got word that that person had died without giving any evidence of being saved, would your belief in prayer or faith in God be shattered?"

Dr. Ironside answered by telling the story of an unsaved man who had gone to sea. One night his mother awakened with a deep sense of need. A burden for her unsaved boy rested heavily upon her heart. She earnestly prayed for his salvation.

Weeks passed. Then, one day, there was a knock at her door and there stood her son! "Mother, I'm saved!" he exclaimed joyfully. Then he told her: "A few weeks ago, our ship was caught in a fearful storm. The waves seemed mountain high. Hope of our outriding the storm vanished. Suddenly the ship gave a lurch and I was swept overboard. As I began to sink, the awful thought came to me: 'I'm lost forever! Where will I spend eternity?' In agony of heart I cried out, 'O God, I look, I look to Jesus!' Then I lost consciousness. After the storm had abated, the sailors came out to clear the deck. They found me lying, unconscious, against a bulwark!"

If God has burdened your soul for the salvation of anyone, keep on praying! God has put the burden upon your heart, and in His own good time and manner, He will answer your prayers.
—W. B. K.

PREACHERS
Short Quotes

A young dairyman from Kansas was chairman at a session of the Kansas Methodist Conference. When time came to introduce the principal speaker, he gave the speaker's name, and read the following letters which followed his name: A.B., A.M., Th.D., LL.D., Ph.D., D.D. After a slight pause he drawled, "I don't know what all this means, but with dairymen we'd say he was a registered critter!" —W. B. K.

* * *

There was a preacher who was a manuscript slave. He not only wrote his sermons, but he read them, word for word, from the pulpit. One Sunday night the lights went out in the church. The minister thought someone was playing a practical joke on him. "Turn the lights on," he demanded in a stern voice. He was told that the lights were definitely off. What could he do? He could not speak extemporaneously, even in an emergency. He wisely said, "If the power is off, it is time to pray!" The service was turned into a prayer meeting, and all went well. —Tom M. Olson

* * *

A pastor preached on a political issue. I was sorry, not merely because I could not accept his conclusions, but also because he missed an opportunity to preach the gospel to a large congregation many of whom, no doubt, were weary of the week's disturbing headlines. They needed to hear a word of peace and comfort from God's Word. Ministers who discuss *timely topics* overlook the basic desire of worshipers for the eternal truth about God and the Saviour. Unless they get a new vision of God, they go away from the sanctuary unfed with that meat which endures unto eternal life. —Dr. William T. Ellis in *Christian Herald*

* * *

Nineteen out of every twenty who receive the Lord Jesus as Saviour do so before they reach the age of 25.
Dr. Wilbur Chapman tested a meeting where 4,500 were present; the result was:

400 saved before 10 years of age
600 saved between 12 and 14
600 saved between 14 and 16
1,000 saved between 16 and 20
25 saved after 30 years of age
1,875 were unsaved
After 25, only 1 in   1,000
After 35, only 1 in   50,000
After 45, only 1 in   200,000
After 55, only 1 in   300,000
After 75, only 1 in   700,000
—*The Evangel*

* * *

A certain elder had faithfully attended his church for thirty years. One day he attended a conference at a university. There he heard a learned city pastor urge rural pastors to take a short course in agriculture. The brave elder said: "One of the things I do not want from the pulpit is a lecture on agriculture. I do not want my pastor to force his ideas of agriculture or animal husbandry upon the worshipper of our church. We farmers go to church to hear the man of God preach and teach the Word of God!" —W. B. K.

* * *

The spiritual giants of the past had no slave whip, like the threat of a pending Communist invasion, to crack over the fear-craven heads of their hearers. They had no help from the horrors of the hydrogen bomb to subdue rebellious hearts. Those God-governed men rode no theological hobby horses, but they preached with the power of the Holy Spirit.

—Evangelist Leonard Ravenhill

* * *

If preachers insist on competing with psychiatrists as counselors, with physicians as healers, with politicians as statesmen and with philosophers as speculators, then these specialists have every right to tell them how to preach. If a minister's message is not based on "Thus saith the Lord," then as a sermon it is good for nothing but to be cast out and trodden under foot of the specialists in the department with which it deals.   —John H. Gerstner, in
Christianity Today

* * *

"Very often," says our pastor, "I don't see the people I might have helped to keep out of trouble, until they come crying to me for help to get them out."

* * *

I am of the opinion that the chief dangers which confront the coming century will be religion without the Holy Spirit, Christianity without Christ, forgiveness without repentance, salvation without regeneration, politics without God, and heaven without hell.

—William Booth

* * *

An overwrought pastor went daily to a railway track to watch an express train streak by. An observer asked, "Pastor, why do you come here every day to see the Dixie Flyer go by?" "Well," he replied, "I like to see something I don't have to push!" —W.B.K.

* * *

I like to hear a man preach like he were fighting bumblebees. —Lincoln

* * *

It is not foolish preaching that brings the lost ones to Christ, but the "foolishness of preaching." —W. B. K.

* * *

Brother ministers, let not sin-sick souls, with burdened minds and battered spirits, turn away from our messages empty because, when they sought a spiritual remedy, we offered them only one

more dreary diagnosis of the crisis of the hour!

—Evangelist Leonard Ravenhill

* * *

In addressing a graduating class of ministerial students at Union Theological Seminary, John Foster Dulles said: "In Tennessee there is a plant which turns out bombs. Here is a plant which turns out ministers of the gospel. The two seem remote and unrelated. Actually the issue of all human life is this: which of the two outputs will prevail?"

—W. B. K.

* * *

In Siberia, milk is often delivered in blocks rather than in bottles, the weather being so cold that the milk freezes before it reaches the customers. Sometimes "the sincere milk of the word" is delivered in the same state and caloused, frigid hearts are unmoved and unchanged. Oh, for more burning, burdened hearts among us! —W. B. K.

* * *

Modern preaching tends to cause people to *vegetate* instead of *consecrate*. It seldom arouses to militant action.

—Roy L. Laurin in
The Alliance Weekly

* * *

The minister's wife is more sensitive to your needs than you are. She knows more about you than you do, and she knows it sooner. Pastors, enlist the help of your wives to prevent you from working yourselves into a breakdown. They will help you to get balance and harmony into your life.

—Dr. Bradford Murphy, psychiatrist, in an address to a ministerium

* * *

There is nothing the modern world needs quite so much as it needs gospel preaching. If the modern world had in it two or three Pauls, Wesleys, Whitefields, Finneys and Moodys, the downward trend of the world might be reversed and turned to God.

—*Fellowship News*

* * *

Today I went to Newcastle and I offered them Christ. Today I visited the prisoners at Bristol and I offered them Christ. This day I visited the sick, and

I gave them Christ. Today I preached on my favorite text: "Christ is made unto us wisdom, and righteousness, and sanctification, and redemption!"
—John Wesley

* * *

The preacher who is convicted of sin and failure by his own sermon is preaching the gospel. —*Ram's Horn*

* * *

God takes His workmen, but He carries on their work. —On crypt where John Wesley is buried

* * *

Spurgeon said that the greatest compliment ever paid him was spoken by one of his outspoken enemies who said: "Here is a man who has not moved an inch forward in all his ministry. At the close of the nineteenth century he is teaching the theology of the first century, and is proclaiming doctrine current in Nazareth and Jerusalem in the first century!" —*Gospel Herald*

* * *

An English bishop reprimanded John Berridge for preaching at all hours and seven days in the week. Said Berridge: "My good bishop, I preach only at two times!" "Which are they?" asked the bishop. "In season and out of season, my lord," replied Berridge.
—*The Elim Evangel*

* * *

An atheist regularly attended the services of a certain church. Someone asked him, "Why do you go to that church? You don't believe anything the minister says." "Of course I don't but I believe in that minister! He lives the way he preaches," was the reply.
—W. B. K.

* * *

Some years ago, Roger Babson, famed statistician, made a study of the heads of 100 leading industries. He found that 5 per cent of these outstanding men were the sons of bankers; 10 per cent were the sons of merchants and manufacturers; 25 per cent were sons of doctors and lawyers and over 35 per cent were the sons of preachers whose salaries at the time of his investigation did not average more than $1500 a year.
—*The Voice*

One-third of the sons of the parsonage rule the world. —Bruce Barton

* * *

Two ministers, given to arguing about their respective faiths, were in a very heated discussion. "That's all right," said one calmly. "We'll just agree to disagree. After all, we're both doing the Lord's work — you in your way and I in His. —*The Christlife Magazine*

* * *

Rash preaching disgusts; timid preaching leaves poor souls fast asleep; bold preaching is the only preaching that is owned of God. —Rowland Hill

* * *

A Negro pastor, just before he presented a visiting white minister to the members of his congregation, prayed: "O Lord, blot him out so we can see only Jesus!" Wouldn't this be an appropriate prayer for all ministers? —W. B. K.

* * *

Stand up straight, speak out boldly, and sit down quickly. —Martin Luther's advice to ministers

* * *

I believe a patient should send for his minister when he gets sick just as he sends for his doctor.
—Dr. James Means, Chief of Staff, Massachusetts General Hospital, and professor of clinical medicine, at Harvard Medical School

* * *

A six-year-old girl, returning with her father from a morning church service, asked, "Daddy, are all those men at church preachers or are some just watchers?" Every Christian should be a preacher for Christ. The life one lives often preaches the greatest sermon. Too many are just watchers. "They were all scattered . . . except the apostles . . . they that were scattered . . . went every where preaching the word" (Acts 8:1, 4). —W. B. K.

* * *

Many times I have found that when the sermon, and even the text, has been forgotten, some story has fastened itself in a hearer's mind, and has borne fruit. Illustrations are like windows to let light in upon a subject.
—D. L. Moody

279

Robert Hume, the Scottish philosopher and skeptic, would walk many miles on the Lord's Day to hear John Brown of Haddington preach. Asked why he did it, Hume said: "I go to hear him because he always preaches as though Jesus Christ is at his elbow."
—*The Watchman-Examiner*

* * *

A nearsighted minister glanced at a note that Mrs. Jones had sent to him by an usher. The note read: "Bill Jones having gone to sea, his wife desires the prayers of the congregation for his safety." Failing to observe the punctuation, he startled his audience by announcing: "Bill Jones, having gone to see his wife, desires the prayers of the congregation for his safety!"
—*Missionary Worker*

* * *

We must preach what has passed through the crucible of our own experience. We shall never produce conviction in others until the truth is a burning conviction in our own souls. Bunyan said: "I preached what I did feel, what I smartingly did feel!"
—*United Methodist*

* * *

The wrath of God and the judgment of God are muted themes in much of today's teaching and preaching. An editor of a great newspaper sarcastically said, "What is preaching doing for us today? God is love, and there is no hell. Nobody is lost and it is downhill to heaven, hallelujah! Let us eat, drink and be merry!"
—Rev. Ralph W. Neighbour

* * *

The best sermon is not the one which makes the hearers go away talking to one another, and praising the speaker, but is that one which makes them go away thoughtful and serious, and hastening to be alone. —Burnet

A sailor had just returned from a whaling voyage. He heard an eloquent preacher. Asked how he liked the sermon, the sailor replied: "It was ship-shape. The masts just high enough, the sails and the rigging all right, but I did not see any harpoons. When a vessel goes on a whaling voyage, the main thing is to get whales. They do not come because you have a fine ship. You must go after them and harpoon them. The preacher must be a whaler!"
—Dr. W. H. Griffith Thomas

* * *

Theodore Roosevelt was in Chicago one Sunday during a political campaign. He attended church, as was his custom. The pastor asked him to speak. He stood and quoted this verse: "Be ye doers of the word, and not hearers only" (James 1:22). Then he sat down. Other worshipers remembered that one-verse sermon long after they had forgotten the well-spoken sermon of their pastor.
—*The Sunday School Times*

* * *

Shortly after the conversion of Billy Sunday an aged minister said to him, "My boy, if you'll do three things daily, you'll be a victorious Christian: spend fifteen minutes daily reading God's Word, letting God talk to you; fifteen minutes in prayer talking to God; and fifteen minutes talking to someone else about God." —W. B. K.

* * *

An evangelist recently said to me: "I get so worked up over what is happening that I forget to preach the gospel!" —Vance Havner

* * *

Asked Dr. Len G. Broughton of a nationally known actor, "How is it that you and others of your profession seem to be most successful in 'putting across' your acting, while we preachers fail so often to 'put across' our preaching?" After a moment's reflection, the actor replied, "Well, we actors act fiction as if it were fact, and oftentimes the minister preaches *fact* as if it were *fiction!*"
"For if the trumpet give an uncertain sound, who shall prepare himself to the battle?" (I Cor. 14:8). —W. B. K.

* * *

A famous minister in the early years of his ministry, spoke quite loudly. As he grew older, he spoke more quietly. A friend asked why the change. The minister replied, "When I was young, I thought it was the thunder that killed people. When I grew older and wiser,

I learned that it was the lightning. So I determined to thunder less and lighten more!" —W. B. K.

* * *

I believe in comforting the afflicted and in afflicting the comfortable.
—A pastor

* * *

The shepherd's duty is to find the sheep, fold the sheep, feed the sheep, and fleece the sheep.
—Rev. Herschel H. Hobbs, D.D.

* * *

"You love to preach, don't you?" asked Henry Ward Beecher of a young minister. "I surely do," was the glowing reply. "But do you love the people to whom you preach?" Beecher then asked.

* * *

Peter, endued with power from on high, preached one sermon and three thousand were saved! Today we preach three thousand sermons and nothing much happens. "O Lord, revive thy work in the midst of the years" (Hab. 3:2). —W. B. K.

* * *

I preached as never sure to preach again,
The message of a dying man to dying men!
—Baxter

* * *

"We are not nearly so grieved that he died as we are grateful that he lived.
—Said of a faithful minister

* * *

Pray for illumination; use your imagination; go in for illustration, but beware of exaggeration.

"I have no recollection how he began his sermon," said A. C. Benson, author and son of an archbishop, referring to Moody's message, "but he had not spoken half a dozen sentences before I felt as though he and I were alone in the world!"

* * *

A prepared messenger is more important than a prepared message.
—Dr. Robert Munger,
Pastor First Presbyterian
Church, Berkeley, California

* * *

I am not tired of my work, neither am I tired of the world. Yet, when Christ calls me home, I shall go with the gladness of a schoolboy bounding away from school! —Adoniram Judson

* * *

Martin Luther's preaching aroused the church from a thousand years' slumber during the Dark Ages — the devil's millennium. Here's how. Luther said, "I preach as though Christ was crucified yesterday, rose from the dead today, and is coming back to earth again tomorrow!"
—*The United Evangelical*

* * *

Two men went to hear Dr. Joseph Parker in London. As they came away from the church, they said, "My, what eloquence! He knows how to choose the right words and say them! His oratory is simply irresistible!" The same two men went to hear Spurgeon on the following Sunday. They left the service silently and reverently. One said, "My, what a Christ!" —W. B. K.

Illustrations

Overcoming Evil with Good

One of God's servants was undergoing a time of severe testing in his church. Faction clashed with faction, and the pastor became the object of merciless criticism. The pastor said to me, "I'm going to my pulpit Sunday morning, and I'm going to take the hide off the troublemakers, especially the one who is at the bottom of it all." I pleaded, "Oh, please don't! Go to your pulpit Sunday with your heart saturated

with the Word of God, and your soul filled with tenderness for all your people, especially those who have caused the greatest trouble. If you'll do this, the peace of God which passeth all understanding (and misunderstanding, too) will flood your soul and your Christlike spirit will do much more than angry words could."

Bickering and backbiting cannot live in an atmosphere charged with genuine love for Christ and for one another.
—W. B. K.

Divers Diseases

The words "divers diseases" impressed an old Negro preacher forcibly, so he elucidated somewhat as follows: "Brethren, our doctors can scrutinize you, analyze you, and diagnose you, and can give you medicine that can cure you of rheumatism, diabetes, palsy, arthritis, and all kinds of stomach troubles, heart troubles, and liver troubles; but brethren, when you get the *divers*, you are in such bad shape that no doctor can cure you. Only the Lord is able to cure *the divers*."

I thought, when I read the old preacher's statement, that he spoke more to the point than he knew, for I noticed that "the divers" are becoming very common in our churches all over the country.

We see perhaps four hundred in Sunday school on Sunday morning. But when Sunday school is dismissed, about three-fourths or more make a *dive* for the door, and the pastor has one hundred, or not that many people, in the preaching service. This I believe is a fatal disease that will kill the spirituality of any church.

When this diving disease gets hold of folks, they hurry home from Sunday school, and many dive their noses into the Sunday newspaper. Others make a dive to the television to turn on their favorite program. As soon as lunch is over, many make a dive for the car and drive to some pleasure resort and spend the afternoon in Sunday desecration.

Yes, I believe with the old Negro preacher that "the divers" is a deadly disease, and only the Lord can cure it.
—Wendell P. Loveless, in *God's Revivalist*

* * *

What a Minister Ought to Be and Do

F. B. Meyer, in estimating the work of the minister, remarked: "The first and best thing a pastor can do is to be a pastor. Let him do the spade work of visitation. Let him give himself to his ministry and prayer. If he wants to touch public life, let him do it through the men he educates.

I am more and more assured that it is not wise for us to enter into things that distract us from our study and our church. The time may come, when a man has done spade work in earlier life, that God will give him a wider service in the great annals of public life and thought. I do not think any man in beginning his ministry ought to be ambitious for public influence. Let him feel that the public influence of his later life comes through the careful pastoral work of his early life."
—*Canadian Baptist*

* * *

Preachers Preach!

It is surprising how stoutly and stubbornly the churches insist upon preachers knowing how to preach. They will forgive almost anything else, but they will not forgive inability to preach.

They have a wholesome reverence for learning, but they would rather have a man with no diploma who can preach than a man with two diplomas who cannot preach.

They believe in experience, and acknowledge its value; but they would rather have a man with no experience who can preach than a man with years of experience who has lost the gift of presenting truth in ways which lift and strengthen.

In all this, the churches may be stiff-necked and unreasonable, but it is a frame of mind which is not likely to be changed.

Men and women judge Christianity largely from sermons. If you make your sermons dull, then religion seems dull also. Let the preacher clothe in fitting form the heavenly message entrusted to his lips! —Charles E. Jefferson

* * *

Retreat from the Ministry

"I've resigned my pastorate," said a minister recently, "and have signed a contract to teach school this year so I can get something done for God." This may seem an astonishing statement coming from a pastor, but I for one understand what he meant by it. As he later explained, he had become something of an office manager, a master of detail, an architect and a committee maneuverer; whereas, originally, he had been trained and commissioned to give himself to the Word, to prayer, to soul-winning, to Bible teaching and to visiting the sick and the lost.

"Sure," he admitted, "they let me preach on Sunday, but the real emphasis was usually on how I could organize, engineer, create publicity, and so forth." By returning to high school to teach in the chemistry labs, he believed now that he would have more time actually to witness and win souls to Christ. Surely, this is a sad commentary on twentieth-century evangelical church life, but it is representative of the feeling of many earnest ministers today.

It is high time spirit-filled pastors took the position affirmed by the twelve disciples who, torn by increasing demands, said, "It is not fit that we should forsake the word of God and minister to tables. . . . But we will give ourselves continually to prayer and to the ministry of the Word" (Acts 6). Others were appointed to attend to material matters. Did God vindicate and approve the stand taken by those disciples? The answer is found in the following words: "And the word of God increased, and the number of the disciples multiplied in Jerusalem greatly."

—Rev. Kenneth L. Miles, in *Christianity Today*

* * *

Only a Half Dozen!

Duncan Matheson . . . was asked to address a meeting. Over a thousand Christians had gathered there to hear the Word. He read a portion of Scripture that had a wonderful message for Christians and began forthwith to open it up for their edification. But as he thought of poor, needy sinners, he turned to them instead and went on to fill the whole hour with a Gospel message. At the close of the meeting one of the conveners came up to him and said: "Brother Matheson, it was really too bad. Here were a thousand Christians who came for some spiritual food, and you spent the entire hour preaching the Gospel." "Oh," said he, "were there no unsaved ones there?" "There might have been half a dozen or so." With a twinkle in his eye, the old man replied in his Scottish way, "Oh, well, ye ken Christians, if they are Christians, will manage to wiggle awa' to heaven

some way, if they never learn any more truth, but poor sinners have got to be saved or be in hell!" —From *Lectures on Acts*, by H. A. Ironside

* * *

Blessed Are the Hungry

What a joy it is to a teacher or a pastor to feed spiritually hungry folk who can say with the Psalmist: "As the hart panteth after the water brooks, so panteth my soul after thee, O God. My soul thirsteth for God" (Psalm 42:1, 2). How difficult it is to feed people who say: "I am rich, and increased with goods, and have need of nothing" (Revelation 3:17).

When our oldest daughter, Alice, was a baby, I often fed her with a spoon as she sat in a high chair. How easy it was to feed her when she was hungry, but how hard when she was not hungry! Often, when I raised the filled spoon toward her little mouth, she would turn her head so quickly that the spoon, with the baby food, landed in her ear instead of her mouth! —W. B. K.

* * *

I'm Not Mad!

A gentleman and his wife, one Sabbath, going to church in Glasgow, met a friend who spoke to them and inquired where they were going. They said, "To hear Dr. Chalmers." He said, "What! to hear that mad man?" They said that if he would agree to go with them, after that, if he persisted in talking in such a manner of him, they would never dispute the matter with him again. He accompanied them; and, singular to relate, it happened that when Dr. Chalmers entered the pulpit that day, he gave out as his text, "I am not mad, most noble Festus; but speak forth the words of truth and soberness," and the friend from that day became a changed man — a convert to evangelical Christianity. —*British Weekly*

* * *

Lincoln — Pastor and Lawyer

"Come with me," said Lincoln to Captain Gilbert J. Green. "I've got to ride into the country to draw a will for a woman who is believed to be on her deathbed."

The invitation was accepted. When

they arrived at the house, they found the woman near death. Lincoln hastily drew up the will which was signed and witnessed.

"Now," said the woman with a smile on her face, "my affairs in this world are arranged satisfactorily. Years ago, I made preparation for the other life I am soon to enter. I sought and found Christ as my Saviour, so I do not fear death, Mr. Lincoln!"

"Your faith in Christ is strong. Your hope of eternal life is bright. I congratulate you for passing through life so usefully and into the beyond so hopefully," said Lincoln.

Then, the dying woman asked, "Mr. Lincoln, won't you read a few verses from the Bible?" Instead of reading from the Bible, Lincoln began to quote the twenty-third Psalm, emphasizing the verse, "Yea, though I walk through the valley of the shadow of death, I will fear no evil: for thou art with me; thy rod and thy staff they comfort me." Then he quoted the verse, "Let not your heart be troubled: ye believe in God, believe also in me," and other comforting verses from John 14. After that he recited some stanzas from familiar, comforting hymns. He concluded with the line: "Rock of Ages, cleft for me!"

As he concluded the quotations, the woman passed serenely into the presence of her Lord.

"Mr. Lincoln, you served perfectly as a pastor and an attorney," said Captain Greene when they returned to Springfield.

Lincoln answered, "God, eternity and heaven were very near to me in that home!" —W. B. K.

* * *

Church Babies

When I was a boy, two lines of a popular song ran thus:

Everybody loves a baby,
That's why I'm in love with you!"

Everybody does love a baby. What is sweeter than a little baby?

How cute are baby monkeys, baby alligators, baby bullfrogs, baby elephants!

There is one variety of babies, however, whom we deplore — *church babies!* Some of them have been church members for decades. What a problem they

are! Paul said something about them 2000 years ago: "I . . . speak . . . unto you . . . as unto babes in Christ" (I Cor. 3:1).

Church babies cry for attention. They keep the pastor awake at night. Quarreling church babies can give a pastor ulcers and insomnia. Like babies, they are fussy — largely to attract attention to themselves. They like to be petted and pampered. They would like to be wheeled into glory in a perambulator!

The pastor is not a nursemaid. As a good minister of Jesus Christ, he is to give himself impartially to all the people. The wise pastor will lose no time pampering church babies who refuse to doff their swaddling clothes and "grow in grace and in the knowledge of our Lord and Saviour Jesus Christ" (II Peter 3:18). —W. B. K.

* * *

Getting a Favorable Verdict

A brilliant and successful lawyer said: "When I was at the bar, I used to take it for granted, when I had before me a jury of respectable men, that I should have to repeat my main position about as many times as there were persons in the jury box. I learned that unless I illustrated and repeated and turned the main points over — the main points of law and evidence — I should lose my case. Our object in addressing a jury is to get their minds settled before they leave the jury box; not to make a speech in language but partially understood by them; not to display our oratory, and then let them go. We are set on getting a verdict. Hence we are set upon being understood."

Tell me the story slowly,
That I may take it in —
That wonderful redemption,
God's remedy for sin.
—*Choice Gleanings Calendar*

* * *

Ready O'er Souls to Yearn!

One day David Garrick, the great Shakespearean actor, was going down a street. He came upon a group of people who were listening intently to a man who was pleading earnestly for souls. "I stood on the fringes of the crowd, but soon I found myself elbowing my way in," said Garrick. The man that preached was George Whitefield. As he preached Christ, tears welled in his eyes which were severely crossed. He had already preached five times in the streets that day. "Sir," said a woman in the group, "I have followed you since you preached this morning at seven o'clock, and have heard you five times in the streets of this city. Why do you weep so as you preach?" "Before Whitefield could reply, Garrick said, "I listened to George Whitefield, and I have seen his passion and earnestness. I know that he believes that men without Christ will die in their sins and be lost." When Whitefield came to the place where he could say nothing more, he lifted up his mighty arms and would yearningly say, "Oh!" Garrick said, "I would give much if I could say 'Oh' like George Whitefield!"

Can we say with Jeremiah: "Oh that my head were waters, and mine eyes a fountain of tears, that I might weep day and night for the slain . . . of my people" (Jer. 9:1)? Do we weep with Christ over a perishing world?

—W. B. K.

* * *

Christ, the Sinner's Friend

In one of his meetings in Spitalfields, John Wesley denounced the sins of the people. Two men, heavily under the influence of liquor, stood on the edge of the crowd. "He's saying mean things about us," they said; "let's do him in." With large rocks in their hands they crept to a vantage point from which they could hurl them at Wesley's head. As they were about to carry out their murderous plan, Wesley's emphasis suddenly changed from sin to the Saviour, the sinner's Friend. While he lovingly and earnestly spoke of the Saviour, his face shone, and his fervent words burned their way into the hearts of his would-be murderers. The stones dropped from their hands. They went and knelt at Wesley's feet. He put his hands on their heads and said, "God bless you, my boys! God bless you!" As they walked away one said, "Was it God Himself?" "No, Bill, but it was a man like God!" answered the other. —W. B. K.

How to Get Rid of an Undesirable Preacher!

Look the preacher straight in the eye while he is preaching and say, "Amen," once in a while. He will preach himself to death in a few weeks. Pat him on the back and speak encouragingly of his good points. He will soon work himself to death. Start paying him a living wage. Perhaps he is one of those many preachers who have gone on starvation wages for so long, he would eat enough to kill himself if he ever got the chance. Rededicate your own life to Christ, and ask the preacher for a job to do, preferably winning some lost person to Christ. He'll die of heart failure! Get the church to unite in prayer for the preacher, and he will soon become so effective, some larger church will take him off your hands!

—*Baptist Standard*

* * *

No Room for Broad-Mindedness

The preacher is sometimes accused of being narrow-minded because he insists upon the Christian forsaking all to follow Christ. But all of life is narrow and success is to be found only by passing through the narrow gate and down the straight way. There is no room for broad-mindedness in the chemical laboratory. Water is composed of two parts hydrogen and one part oxygen. The slightest deviation from that formula is forbidden. There is no room for broad-mindedness in music. There can be only eight notes in an octave. The skilled director will not permit the first violin to play even so much as one-half of a note off the written note, chord, and key. There is no room for broad-mindedness in the mathematics classroom. Neither geometry, calculus, nor trigonometry allows any variation from exact accuracy. The solution of the problem is either right or it is wrong. There is no room for broad-mindedness in the garage. The mechanic there says that the piston rings must fit the cylinder walls within one-thousandth part of an inch. How, then, shall we expect that broad-mindedness shall rule in the realm of religion and morals? —*The Sunday School Times*

You Left Nothing for God to Do!

One morning many years ago I preached in the Broadway Street Methodist Church in Orlando, Florida. A special friend of mine, an aged Baptist minister, sat in the audience. In the sermon I expended much physical energy. At the close of the service, the aged minister spoke kindly of the sermon, and then added, "But you didn't leave anything for God to do. You tried to do it all." In my youthful heart, I felt like saying, "You old fool! You'll learn a thing or two yet!" With the passing of the years, however, I came to another conclusion — the aged minister was a wise man and I was the fool. —W. B. K.

* * *

Assume That They Don't Understand

What mischief we often work when we assume that those to whom we preach have at least a little knowledge of God's Word. We assume that those listening to us are familiar with our references to sacred things. The opposite is often true. Even many professing Christians may be inexcusably ignorant of God's Word.

A minister spoke on the family altar. In his audience was a recently converted Roman Catholic. She listened with seeming understanding. Days passed. A Christian friend called at her home. To her consternation, she observed in the house a shrine on which had been placed the little images which meant something to her in her former faith. "What is this?" asked the astonished friend. "This is my family altar! Did not the pastor in his sermon urge us to establish a family altar?" "Oh, dear," said the Christian friend, "having a family altar in the home means that the family gathers daily to read God's Word and pray!" —W. B. K.

* * *

Poor Old Mrs. Hemingway!

Brother Jones was a large, florid, pompous man, so wrapped in self-conceit and arrogance as to be almost intolerable to other members of the church. One elder after another had remonstrated with him upon his monstrous vanity and reminded him that such pride was unbecoming to a Christian, but he was deaf to hints or rebukes. At last, after a solemn consultation, it was resolved that the minister should preach a sermon aimed at Brother Jones, and at him only. The rebuke was to be so severe that he would be cured of conceit for the rest of his life. The day came. The church was even more than ordinarily full of people. The sermon began. Brother Jones, with a complacent expression of face, disposed himself to listen. The man's infirmity was sketched with bold, severe strokes. He smiled with lofty superiority. As the denunciation grew more scathing, his smile deepened with a touch of complacent pity. At the conclusion of the services he swaggered down the aisle. One of the elders joined him. "What did you think of the sermon, Brother Jones?" he ventured to ask. "A great effort, sir! But personal. The pastor aimed his shots too directly. Poor old Mrs. Hemingway!" —*Earnest Worker*

* * *

A Pastor's Prayer

I do not ask
That crowds may throng the temple,
That standing room be at a price,
I only ask that as I voice the message,
They may see Christ.

I do not ask
For churchly pomp and pageant,
Or music such as wealth alone can buy,
I only ask that as I voice the message,
He may be nigh.

I do not ask
That men may sound my praises
Or headlines spread my name abroad,
I only pray that as I voice the message,
Hearts may find God.

I do not ask
For earthly place or laurel,
Or of this world's distinction any part,
I only ask when I have voiced the message,
My Saviour's heart.

       —*Selected*

* * *

Satanic Sweetness

In a Canadian city, a great daily newspaper conducts an annual poll to ascertain "the man of the year." Readers are asked to submit their nominations together with the reasons why their candidate qualifies for the honor. One reader wrote to the paper and presented the name of a popular clergyman. "He, in my opinion, deserves the title, for after listening to him for twenty-eight years, I have never heard him say one word which would offend anyone!"

We devoutly hope that the enthusiastic admirer's opinion of the minister is not true. How uncomplimentary it is to say of any minister who has preached for twenty-eight years that his utterances never offended anyone! We are disturbed when we hear of unoffensive ministers. The day any minister descends to the low level where the avoidance of offense is his sole aim, he has ceased to be a true prophet of God, a descendant of those fearless prophets of old who sealed with their life's blood the testimony of their lips. —W. B. K.

* * *

Self-Appointed Informants

It has been my custom in my initial sermon in a new pastorate to request, among other things, that no one relate to me any gossip or slander about anyone else. Is it not the pastor's prerogative to learn what he wants to know about people? Does not the Bible tell him all he needs to know about poor, sinful, weak human nature?

One elderly lady, in my Pennsylvania pastorate, didn't take the request seriously. On Monday morning she called at the parsonage in the role of a self-appointed informant. Before I could check her, she had laid low a member of the church. True, he was a snoopy sort of a fellow, as I later learned.

Before the self-appointed informant could say more, I said, "Wouldn't it be Christian charity to have the individual, of whom you have spoken so ill, present to answer for himself any further accusations you may make against him?" Then I started toward the phone as if I was going to call the man. "Oh," she pleaded, "please don't! I confess that I have been sinful and un-Christian in my attitude toward that person. Do pray that God will cleanse my heart of this sin. It has rendered me powerless,

joyless and has made me largely unusable in God's service." —W. B. K.

* * *

In Quietness and Confidence

"You can do more for that veteran than we can," said a guard to me as I entered the gate of a great veteran's hospital to visit patients in the psychopathic section of the hospital. The guard meant, of course, that the One I represent could help where human help was of no avail. The patient I visited was a brilliant Wheaton College student upon whose mind and nerves the shock and horrors of war, and also over-study, had left their scars. For at least an hour, both the student and myself called upon the Great Physician to work mightily in his behalf. God answered our prayer almost immediately! Relaxation came to the student's taut nerves, and his turbulence of mind gave place to serenity and poise. The cure was complete.

God's promise is sure: "Call unto me, and I will answer thee, and shew thee great and mighty things which thou knowest not" (Jer. 33:3). —W. B. K.

* * *

Sagacious Advice

A young minister in a college town was embarrassed by the thought of criticism in his cultivated congregation. He sought counsel from his father, an old and wise minister, saying: "Father, I am hampered in my ministry in the pulpit I am now serving. If I cite anything from geology, there is Prof. A...., teacher of this science, right before me. If I use an illustration of Roman mythology, there is Prof. B...., ready to trip me up for my little inaccuracy. If I instance something in English literature that pleases me, I am cowed by the presence of the learned man that teaches that branch. What shall I do?" The sagacious old man replied: "Do not be discouraged, preach the Gospel. They probably know very little of that."
—*Moody Monthly*

* * *

I Have a Retainer From Christ!

Charles G. Finney's conversion and call to the ministry were simultaneous. He seemed to see Christ face to face.

Finney was a young lawyer. The morning after his conversion and call, a client came into his office and asked him if he were ready to try his case which was set for 10 o'clock that day. Finney replied, "I have a retainer from the Lord Jesus Christ to plead His cause, and I cannot plead your cause." "When the client left," said Finney, "I immediately went forth to talk to those I would meet about their souls. I knew that God wanted me to preach the gospel, and that I must begin immediately. I knew it with a certainty past all possibility of doubt!" —W. B. K.

* * *

The Hearer's Responsibility

A Christian lady told at a women's meeting: "When I was a child we had a minister who preached very plain from God's Word to both saved and unsaved, but because he did this, a group of people strongly opposed him in the church, and vowed they would get rid of him. Forces of evil outside the church wanted to be rid of him, too, and life was very difficult for him. Finally, his health broke down, and he had to resign. When he was leaving, the opposition decided to give him a dinner, and the man who opposed the godly minister most was chairman of the meeting. As a child, I surely was puzzled that night when the chairman said how sorry they were because the minister was leaving. I wondered at such insincerity, but I have never forgotten the minister's reply, and I don't believe the chairman did either. "The Lord is my Judge. I gave His Word in this place. How you received it is your responsibility."
—*The Sunday School Times*

* * *

A Veteran Minister's Advice

A young minister in England had just begun his first pastorate, so he said to an aged minister, "You know by experience many things which would be helpful to me as I enter upon my work. Do tell me some of them."
The old man replied, "I will tell you about the most important one first. As you know, there is in every village and town in England a road which leads to London. Every Bible text which you may choose to preach from should lead

to Jesus Christ. Be sure to find the road in the text which leads to Christ and follow it!"
How greatly does our sinful, morally and spiritually confused world need the Saviour! Christ and Christ crucified is still the power of God unto salvation!
—W. B. K.

* * *

Preach Christ to Them!

Mr. Birch, a well-known evangelist, tells of a dying unbeliever whom he visited by request. The man had long been ill, and was in great temporal as well as spiritual need. Mr. Birch, with Christian liberality, had supplied his temporal needs, and now the dying man told him he had sent for him, not to speak about religion, for he didn't believe in it, but to thank him for his great kindness to him. "Will you answer me one question?" asked Mr. Birch. "Yes, providing it is not about religion." Lifting his heart in prayer to God, Mr. Birch said, "You know I have to preach tonight. Many will be gathered to hear me — mostly poor people, who, like you, will soon have to face death. I ask you, what shall I preach about?" There was silence for a moment. Then, with tear-dimmed eyes and trembling voice, the unexpected answer was given, "Mr. Birch, preach Christ to them! Preach Christ to them!" —*Chimes*

* * *

Why He Succeeded

A minister in Canada was called from a small church to a large city church. Someone asked: "How did he secure that prominent pulpit? What is the secret of his success? There are greater preachers than he is, more scholarly and more eloquent."
The answer was, "He has always done what many other men knew ought to be done, but neglected. He never failed to write notes of condolence to the afflicted, whether they belonged to his congregation or not. He would cross the street to speak to a burdened man. He would take an hour to make friends with a group of romping children. He would pen a sincere word of praise to the sheriff who did his duty, to the mayor who enforced the law, to the teacher in the public school who was

faithful. Nothing that might properly receive a minister's notice escaped him. This is the real secret of his success."
—*Christian Observer*

* * *

I Believe in the Munro Doctrine!

"What is your doctrine — your belief?" asked an examining committee of Melvin Trotter, a converted drunkard, as the committee sought to ascertain Trotter's qualifications for the gospel ministry. "My doctrine is the Munro Doctrine!" said Trotter. He meant that he believed in the heart-transforming power of the gospel as exemplified in the miraculous conversion of Harry Munro who had sunk to the lowest depths of sin and was a humanly hopeless alcoholic. After Harry Munro's conversion, he became superintendent of the world-famed Pacific Garden Mission of Chicago. There he brought many outcasts to a saving knowledge of Jesus Christ. Oh, that more of us believed in the Harry Munro Doctrine, and would dedicate our lives to salvaging human wrecks! —Harry Saulnier

* * *

We Preach

Some years ago there was built in an Eastern city a beautiful church and on its cornerstone were inscribed the words, "We preach Christ crucified." Later, a vine was planted at the same corner, which in the course of the years covered a part of the cornerstone so that the passers-by could only read the words, "We preach." There was never a day when there was so much preaching as in our day, but I am fearful that we have strayed far from that message that our Lord intended to be sent to a lost world. The vines of oratory, of human wisdom, of worldly ambition, of higher criticism, and the destructive vines of modernism, all have helped to cover over the one great theme of the first-century preachers.
—Rev. C. C. Grisso

* * *

Who Is My Pastor's Pastor?

It dawned on me recently that my pastor has no pastor, no human under-shepherd to whom he can turn when the days are dark.

Like most church members, I have called my pastor when there was need, and he has never failed me. But who is *his* pastor? Who rushes to *his* side when the load is heavier than he can bear alone?

Is there not something within all of us which cries out for human sympathy and understanding? Is my pastor an exception merely because he is my pastor?

The Saviour, on earth, turned aside to talk with the Father and spent long hours with Him who meets His servants in the secret places, and who never forsakes them. But our Lord also needed John and Peter and James and the others.

I have made a resolution which, by God's help, I will not break. I am determined that my pastor shall know that I love him, that he shall not lack the sympathetic understanding which I can give. As a member of my church I shall, in some way, be a shepherd's friend. I cannot but believe that there are many others like me who will, day by day, stand at the side of the man who has no pastor. —*Western Recorder;* and *The Doorstep Evangel*

* * *

I Will Close

We often hear preachers and speakers use this expression as they approach the end of their discourse. We often wonder why they do. In the first place, such a statement distracts the attention of their hearers from the subject under consideration. They will likely be watching to see how soon he will close.

It also suggests to the hearer that the speaker feels that he is talking too long. That will weaken the impression that he makes by what he says.

We have often noticed that the man who says this is likely to forget his promise and continue talking for some time, and this tends to set the hearer to wondering why he does not stop, instead of his listening to what he says.

"I shall speak very briefly," says another. Then the people watch to see how brief he will be. We have more than once heard a man make that statement as he begins and then talks for a half or three-quarters of an hour, and because of that his sermon or address loses its power.

"I shall speak very simply," says another. If he speaks simply the people will soon find it out. If he does not, after making the statement, the hearers will think he is ignorant or dishonest.

When one has something to say, the best thing to do is to say it plainly, briefly, earnestly, and when he has said it to stop without apologies or explanations. —*Presbyterian of the South*

* * *

He's Done Gone Meddling!

With fervent Amens, Mandy apparently approved of everything the Negro pastor was saying in his sermon. To be sure, she did approve as long as he spoke of the joys of one's salvation, and of the blessedness of being one of God's children. When the pastor began to speak against the filthy habit of snuff-dipping, however, Mandy's Amens ceased, and she said, "There now, he's done gone meddling; he has done gone and spoiled a good sermon!" Had he? Did John the Baptist spoil a good sermon when he said to adulterous Herod, "It is not lawful for thee to have thy brother's wife" (Mark 6:18); and did Elijah spoil a good sermon when he fearlessly said to cowardly, compromising Ahab, "I have not troubled Israel; but thou, and thy father's house, in that ye have forsaken the commandments of the Lord, and thou hast followed Baalim" (I Kings 18:18)?

God's command is, "Cry aloud, spare not, lift up thy voice like a trumpet, and shew My people their transgression, and the house of Jacob their sins" (Isa. 58:1). —W. B. K.

* * *

Dr. Meyer's Secret

From an early age I had desired to become a minister of Christ's Gospel, but was perpetually haunted by a fear that I should not be able to speak. At sixteen, the secret locked in my breast, I had been pleading with tears that God would show me His will, and especially that He would give me some assurance as to my powers of speech. Again that room at Streatham, near London, to which we had moved, is before me, with

its window toward the sun, and the leather-covered chair at which I kneeled. Turning to my Bible, it fell open at this passage, which I had never seen before: "But the Lord said unto me, Say not, I am a child: for thou shalt go to all that I shall send thee, and whatsoever I command thee thou shalt speak" (Jer. 1:7). With indescribable feelings I read it again and again, and even now never come on it without a thrill of emotion. It was the answer to all my perplexed questionings. Yes, I was the child; I was to go to those to whom He would send me; and He would be with me, and touch my lips. —Dr. F. B. Meyer in the *Illustrator*

* * *

Foreteller, or Forthteller?

There is always the danger of becoming so taken up with what the world is coming to that we forget Him who has come to the world. Studying current events and lecturing about the future is fascinating business these days when things happen with such bewildering rapidity. There is a great temptation to turn prophet exclusively. The newspaper may easily become more absorbing than the Bible, and, keeping our ears to the ground, we fail to keep our eyes on the Lord. Many of the brethren have turned foretellers instead of forthtellers, and that to their own embarrassment when their predictions go askew. Some are wringing their hands over the state of the world instead of pointing to the Saviour of the world. —*The Alliance Weekly*

* * *

Twigs and Roots

When interviewing Dr. A. J. Gordon as a prospective pastor of a Boston church, the pulpit committee asked: "If you are called to the pastorate of our church will you preach against the cards, the theater, and dancing?" "I will," solemnly affirmed Dr. Gordon. He was called. Months passed and he didn't say a word against the cards, the theater, and dancing. The official board of the church said, "Almost a year has gone by and you have said nothing against cards, the theater, and dancing. We wonder why." Dr. Gordon replied essentially as follows: "Gentlemen, it is true that I have said nothing against these things, but I have preached Christ who is the only Saviour from all evils. When He comes into one's heart all evil things vanish from the life like the mist before the hot breath of the noonday sun!"

Dr. Gordon was eminently right. His stand agreed perfectly with the teaching of his Lord: "Even so every good tree bringeth forth good fruit" (Matt. 7:17); "Either make the tree good, and his fruit good" (12:33). Lopping off a twig here and a branch there is reformation. God's method of changing wrongs is to get to the source of evil and extirpate the roots. —Told by Rev. T. W. Callaway, D.D.

* * *

Where His Sermons Had Gone

Coming to the close of many years of faithful ministry, an aged pastor tied his sermon notes in a bundle and wrote on it: "Where has the influence of all the sermons I have preached gone?" One who had been under his ministry for years and who had grown in Christlikeness and in the knowledge of God's Word, gave the following heartfelt appraisal of his sermons. "Where are last year's sunrays? They have gone into fruits and grains and vegetables to feed mankind. Where are last year's raindrops? Forgotten, of course, but they did their gracious and refreshing work. Your sermons, preached over the years, have gone into my life and into the lives of others, to make me and them better, nobler, and more Christlike. They have deepened our love for God's Word, given us a vision of and love for unsaved ones, and have challenged us to go on in the Christian life!"

—W. B. K.

* * *

What I Owe My Pastor

I owe him respect as the ambassador of God, sent to teach me a better way of living than the selfish, sordid existence I might be guilty of but for his guidance.

I owe him trust, that he may be free to serve the church, unhampered by fault-finding and criticism. I owe my pastor prayer, that God may make his services a blessing to everyone with whom he comes in contact.

I owe my pastor the protection of kindly silence by refraining from repeating in his presence the slander or unkind gossip that would worry him and prevent him from doing his best.

I owe him enough of my time to help him in his work whenever he may need me.

I owe him encouragement when vexations and annoyances make his work difficult.

I owe my pastor my attention when I go to church, that he may not be annoyed by seeing, by my careless inattentive actions, that I am not interested in what he is saying. —A layman

* * *

The Preacher's Wife
You may think it quite an easy task,
   And just a pleasant life;
But really it takes a lot of grace
   To be a preacher's wife.
She's supposed to be a paragon
   Without a fault in view,
A saint when in the parsonage
   As well as in the pew.

Her home must be a small hotel
   For folks that chance to roam,
And yet have peace and harmony —
   The perfect preacher's home!
Whenever groups are called to meet,
   Her presence must be there,
And yet the members all agree
   She should live a life of prayer.

Though hearing people's burdens,
   Their grief both night and day,
She's supposed to spread but sunshine
   To those along the way.
She must lend a sympathetic ear
   To every tale of woe,
And then forget about it,
   Lest it to others go.

Her children must be models rare
   Of quietness and poise,
But still stay on the level
   With other girls and boys.
You may think it quite an easy task,
   And just a pleasant life,
But really it takes a lot of grace
   To be a preacher's wife!

—*Selected*

Your Preaching Disturbs Me!

A man attended church regularly for months. Then he suddenly stopped. "I haven't seen you at church lately," said the pastor when he met him on the street one day. "Nor will you see me there! Your preaching on hell disturbs me. I am now attending another church where the minister is not so narrow-minded as you." The faithful minister replied, "I am sorry you aren't coming any more. But let me tell you of a personal incident. One time I found a poor fellow half-frozen in the snow. He was near death. He felt so drowsy and comfortable that I had to shake him violently to awaken him." "So what?" replied the man rudely. "Just this," said the minister. "I preach to please God, and not to make people feel comfortable, or to lull them more soundly asleep in their sins. Lovingly and earnestly I warn impenitent sinners to flee from the coming wrath!"

—W. B. K.

* * *

Are We Ministers Soft?

We know more about vitamins than John Wesley did. But who of us could stand the pace he stood. The following description is from Albert Edward Bailey's biography of Wesley.

"An undersized man of delicate appearance, he yet had nerves of iron, could ride horseback twenty to sixty miles a day — once he rode a hundred miles in twenty-four hours. He rose at four in the morning, retired at ten p.m. and never wasted a minute. He read hundreds of volumes while traveling — would drop the reins on the horse's neck and with both hands would hold the big books to his nearsighted eyes. In later years, when friends had given him a chaise, he boarded up one side of it, put in book shelves and a writing board and so kept up his incessant work. He wrote voluminously, published 233 original works beside editing and translating others. For sixty years he kept a diary which accounted for every hour of every day, and kept beside a full-length journal. He could read Hebrew, Greek and Latin and could not only read but preach in German, French and Italian. At the age of eighty-three he was piqued to discover that he could not write more than fifteen hours a day without hurting his eyes; and at the age of eighty-six he was ashamed to admit that he could not preach more than twice a day. In his eighty-sixth year, he preached in almost every shire in England and Wales and often rode thirty to fifty miles a day."

—*The Canadian Free Methodist Herald*

* * *

Minister Indispensable Says Psychiatrist

An overwrought friend of mine yielded to the fearful impulse to end his life and almost succeeded. I visited him in the psychopathic hospital. He was greatly humiliated and could hardly believe that he had tried to find the solution of life's enigma in suicide. I prayed with him, commending him to the only One who can speak peace to tempest-tossed souls. As I left his room, a psychiatrist called me into his office and said, "I presume you realize that you can do more for that man than I can do?" The doctor meant, of course, that the One whom I represented helps and heals when human help is of no avail. —W. B. K.

PRESENCE, GOD'S

Short Quotes

When God says, "Come," He goes out to meet us. When He says, "Go," He goes with us!

* * *

"I'll give you an orange if you'll tell me where God is," someone said to a little girl. "I'll give you two oranges if you'll tell me where God isn't!" answered the girl.

* * *

Regard not much who is for thee or who against thee; but give all thy

thought and care to this, that God be
with thee in everything thou doest. For
whom God will help, no malice of man
shall be able to hurt.

—Thomas à Kempis

* * *

We cannot hide from God, but we
can hide in God: "Your life is hid with
Christ in God" (Col. 3:3). —W. B. K.

* * *

A man of prominence attended the
services of an old minister in a small
church. The old minister preached with
his accustomed earnestness. At the
close of the service, some members of
the congregation said, "Pastor, we had
a distinguished visitor today, but you
did not seem embarrassed." The minister replied, "I have been preaching
in the presence of Almighty God for
forty years, and do you think with Him
as one of my constant Hearers any man,
howsoever distinguished, can embarrass
me by his presence?" —*Power*

* * *

God is a circle whose center is everywhere, and its circumference nowhere. —Empedocles

* * *

On sunlit hills where joy is,
In the heart of the wood where calm is,
In little homes where love is,
In all the world where weary souls seek,
Eager and wistful, their tryst to keep,
There is God, and sanctuary.

—Grace A. Auringer

* * *

All of God's giants have been weak
men who did great things for God because they reckoned on His being with
them. They counted on God's faithfulness. —J. Hudson Taylor

* * *

A call to God brings His answer:
"Then shalt thou call, and the Lord
shall answer" (Isa. 58:9). A cry to God
brings the Lord Himself: "Thou shalt
cry, and he shall say, Here I am"
(*ibid.*). —W. B. K.

* * *

"I feel so close to God when I am
operating that I don't know where my
skill leaves off and His begins," said
a great surgeon.

"As we come into Thy presence" are
often the opening words of the prayers
of some of God's children. Where had
they been? God's children are always
in His presence: "My presence shall go
with thee" (Exod. 33:14). —W. B. K.

* * *

God is before me, He will be my Guide,
God is behind me, no ill can betide,
God is beside me, to comfort and cheer,
God is around me, so why should I fear?

* * *

A Quakeress said to Lincoln during
the dark days of the Civil War: "Friend
Abraham, thee need not think thee
stands alone. We are praying for thee.
The hearts of the people are with thee.
The Lord is with thee!" to which Lincoln
replied, "You have given a cup of cold
water to a very thirsty man. You have
done me a great kindness!"

—Rev. J. Wallace Hamilton

* * *

"If I could see Christ through a key-
hole once in a thousand years, that
would be heaven enough for me," said
Samuel Rutherford. But it would not
be enough for the Saviour. He has
something to say in the matter. It is
this: "Father, I will that they also,
whom thou hast given me, be with me
where I am; that they may behold my
glory" (John 17:24).

—Dr. John R. Rice

* * *

A terrific noise awakened a three-
year-old boy during an air raid in
World War II. He began to cry. His
father rushed into the room. All was
dark. The child could not see his
father, but he could feel his presence
and hear his voice. "It's all right, Dad!
You're here. I'm not afraid." His confident words were almost a paraphrase
of the Psalmist's words: "I will fear
no evil, for thou art with me!"

—*Methodist Recorder*

* * *

A young man was deeply convicted
of sin and his need of the Saviour.
"Can you tell me the way to Christ?"
he asked a minister; "I want to find
Him!" The minister replied, "No!"
Astonished, the young man said: "Pardon me, Sir, but I thought you were a

293

minister." The minister replied, "There is no way to Christ. *Christ* is the way! He is not far off. He is here with us. You are a sincere seeker and He is saying to you: 'Thy sins be forgiven thee!' " —W. B. K.

* * *

Sometime ago, it became necessary to break my little girl from sleeping with me. I laid her in her crib, kissed her good night and turned out the light. She cried long and bitterly, thinking that I did not hear her cry and that I did not love her, not knowing that I was not far away — only hidden by the darkness. My mother-heart was aching for her. I heard her cries. I longed to do what she wanted, but for her own good I must hide myself. And so, in times of affliction, God hears our cry and feels for us, though for our own good He may temporarily hide His face and may seem not to be near.

—Grace C. W. Groben

Illustrations

Father's Presence

Alexander Maclaren learned this truth when he accepted his first job in Glasgow. Just sixteen was he and his home was six miles from the big city. Between home and the city there was a deep ravine, supposedly haunted — terrible things happened there. He was afraid to go through there even in the daytime. On Monday morning his father walked with him to work and in parting said, "Alec, come home as fast as you can when you get off Saturday night." Thinking of the deep ravine, Maclaren replied, "Father, I will be awfully tired Saturday night. I will come home early Sunday morning." The father was adamant. "No, Alec, you have never been away from home before and these six days are going to seem like a year to me. Come home Saturday night." All the week, Alec worried about the ravine. On Saturday night, frightened, he packed his belonging and came to the edge of the ravine. Looking into the inky blackness, he could not move. Tears came. Then suddenly he heard footsteps. He started to run, but paused, for the footsteps were familiar. Out of the darkness came the grandest man on earth. The voice said, "Alec, I came to meet you." Alec reported, "Together we went into the valley and I was not afraid of anything that walked."

"Yea, though I walk through the valley of the shadow of death, I will fear no evil: for thou art with me!"

—Dr. C. Roy Angell in *Iron Shoes*

The Lord Himself Was With Me

Years ago a young missionary had to flee from western China. An infuriated mob hotly pursued him. He hastily boarded a river boat. The mob, too, came on the boat. Then he jumped into the river. The mob began to throw spears at him. Miraculously he escaped, unharmed. When he was telling of the ordeal later, a friend asked him, "What verse from the Bible came to you as you were darting beneath the boat to escape the spears of the mob?" "Verse?" he asked in astonishment, "why, the Lord Himself was with me!" —W. B. K.

* * *

In Quietness and in Confidence

A businessman once said: "Sometimes, after waking in the morning, I am appalled by the thought of all the duties and appointments that await me in the next eight or ten hours. Then I repeat to myself the words: 'In quietness and confidence shall be thy strength'; and, 'Thou wilt keep him in perfect peace, whose mind is stayed on thee, because he trusteth in thee.' It is astonishing how quickly the load is lifted when once I become aware of God's presence and help. The strain and tension go out of me and instead there wells up within me a feeling of serenity and peace."

—W. B. K.

* * *

The Secret

A learned professor lived a Christlike, peaceful life. He exerted a profound influence upon his pupils. Wanting to learn the secret of his beautiful life, a student hid himself in the study of the professor. Entering his study at a late hour, and very weary from the day's toil, the professor opened his Bible, read therefrom for an hour and then knelt to pray. In his prayer he said, "Well, Lord Jesus, we're still on the same terms!"

To know Christ intimately and practice His presence is the secret of a triumphant, radiant life. All who thus know him shall "be strong, and do exploits" (Dan. 11:32). —W. B. K.

* * *

Very Near

In the solace after pain,
In the sunshine after rain,
When you fail — but try again:
God is very near.

In the fruit upon the trees,
In a cool midsummer breeze;
In a baby at its birth,
Any place upon the earth;
In the smile that follows tears,
In the harvest of the years,
In the conquering of fears:
God is very near.

When you help someone in need
With a single kindly deed;
When of selfishness you're freed:
God is very near.

—Carl C. Helm

* * *

Imagine Jesus in a Chair

An old Scotsman lay very ill, and his minister came to visit him. As the minister sat down on a chair near the bedside, he noticed on the other side of the bed another chair placed at such an angle as to suggest that a visitor had just left it. "Well, Donald," said the minister, glancing at the chair, "I see I am not your first visitor." The Scotsman looked up in surprise, so the minister pointed to the chair. "Ah!" said the sufferer, "I'll tell you about that chair. Years ago I found it impossible to pray. I often fell asleep on my knees, I was so tired. And if I kept awake, I could not control my thoughts from wandering. One day I was so worried I spoke to my minister about it. He told me not to worry about kneeling

down. 'Just sit down,' he said, 'and put a chair opposite you, imagine that Jesus is in it, and talk to Him as you would to a friend.' And," the Scotsman added, "I have been doing that ever since. So now you know why the chair is standing like that." A week later the daughter of the old Scot drove up to the minister's house and knocked at his door. She was shown into the study, and when the minister came in she could hardly restrain herself. "Father died in the night," she sobbed. "I had no idea death could be so near. I had just gone to lie down for an hour or two. He seemed to be sleeping so comfortably. And when I went back he was dead. He hadn't moved since I saw him before, *except that his hand was out on the empty chair at the side of his bed.* Do you understand?" "Yes," said the minister, "I understand."

—*The Sunday School Times*

* * *

It Is Better

It is better to walk in the dark with
   God
Than to run in the light alone;
Yes, better the thorniest path ever trod,
Where the briers are thick, and our feet
   unshod,
If only we follow his voice and rod,
Than without him to march to a throne.

It is better with him when the billows
   dash high,
On the breast of the mad Galilee;
Though the Master may sleep, he will
   wake at our cry,
Or he'll come on the waves saying:
   "Peace, it is I."
Better this than a calm when he is not
   nigh,
Or without him to sail a smooth sea.

—Alexander Blackburn, in
   The Watchman-Examiner

* * *

God, You Are There, Aren't You?

A grief-stricken father and his little girl stood at the graveside of the wife and mother. After the funeral solemnities, kind friends said to the sorrowing husband, "You and the little girl come home with us for the night. It will be easier for you." "No," said he, "we will go back to the scene of her suffering and trust God's grace to sustain us." That night the little girl was late in getting to sleep. Her little bed was moved alongside her father's bed. In the darkness she would say, "Daddy, it's so dark, but you are there, aren't you, Daddy?" The father placed his hand on her head and said, "Yes, Daddy is right here. Now go to sleep!" Before long the little girl fell soundly asleep. Then, in the darkness and gloom, the father weepingly said, "O, heavenly Father, it is so dark, and my heart is so overwhelmed with sorrow, but You are there, aren't You, Father?" The sure promise came instantly to his mind: "Fear thou not; for I am with thee: be not dismayed; for I am thy God: I will strengthen thee; yea, I will help thee; yea, I will uphold thee with the right hand of my righteousness" (Isa. 41:10).

—Told by Dr. George W. Truett

. . .

God Is Everywhere

Glory shining in a star,
Billows beating on the bar,
Planets whirling on their way,
Dawn unfolding into day,
Verdant meadows wet with rain,
Golden fields of waving grain,
Woodland music's sweet refrain:
God is everywhere.

Falling shade and evening glow,
Winter moonlight on the snow,
Traveler footsore on the road,
Toiler bending 'neath his load —
He who notes the sparrows fall,
Sleepless, watches over all,
Hears the helpless when they call:
God is everywhere.

Still small voice to teach us good,
Mother watching o'er her brood,
Children bowing down to pray,
Love pursuing if they stray,
Saviour in Gethsemane,
Winning holy victory,
Life laid down to make men free:
God is everywhere.

—*The Watchman-Examiner*

Not Always

In pastures green? Not always; sometimes He
Who knoweth best in kindness leadeth me
In weary ways, where heavy shadows be —

Out of the sunshine warm and soft and bright,
Out of the sunshine into darkest night;
I oft would faint with sorrow and affright —

Only for this — I know He holds my hand.
So whether in the green or desert land.
I trust, although I may not understand.

And by still waters? No, not always so;
Ofttimes the heavy tempests round me blow,
And o'er my soul the waves and billows go.

But when the storms beat loudest, and I cry
Aloud for help, the Master standeth by,
And whispers to my soul, "Lo, it is I."

Above the tempest wild I hear Him say,
"Beyond this darkness lies the perfect day,
In every path of thine I lead the way."

So, whether on the hilltops high and fair
I dwell, or in the sunless valleys where
The shadows lie — what matter? He is there.

—*Selected*

. . .

Whom Shall We Believe?

In a bulletin of a Roman Catholic church in Wisconsin this amazing statement by a priest was printed: "There have been a number of people leaving the church a few minutes after they have received holy communion. . . . This is a great dishonor to our blessed Lord. The Church tells us Jesus remains in our bodies fifteen minutes after we have received holy communion. That means that our thanksgiving should be at least fifteen minutes long. . . . We

should not leave the church until our
Lord is no longer with us!"

How grateful we are for the Saviour's
changeless promise: "Lo, I am with
you alway!"

If we live, He will be with us. If we
die, we shall be with Him: "Whether
we live . . . or die, we are the Lord's"
(Rom. 14:8). —Told by Dr. J. Wilbur
Smith in *The Sunday School Times*

* * *

His Presence

My presence shall go with thee!
So calm thy troubled fears;
My promise is unchanging
Throughout the changeful years.
'Mid scenes of gloom and gladness,
When weary or distressed,
My presence shall go with thee,
And I will give thee rest.

My presence shall go with thee!
Most blest assurance here,
While in this lower valley,
Beset by doubt and fear.
No evil shall befall thee,
Close sheltered to my breast;
My presence shall go with thee,
And I will give thee rest.

My presence shall go with thee!
Though in a foreign land,
Afar from home and kindred,
This covenant shall stand.
Nor time nor space can sever,
Love knows not East or West:
My presence shall go with thee,
And I will give thee rest.
                              —*Selected*

* * *

Once Every Hour

Dr. Frank Laubach learned to practice the presence of God by disciplining
his thoughts to think on God once every
minute. He called it "the game of minutes."

A sixteenth-century saint tells us: "If
thou dost once every hour throw thyself . . . into the abysmal mercy of
God, then thou shalt receive power to
rule over death and sin" (Jacob
Boehme).

The airplane pilot radios a message to
headquarters every hour and receives
an answer. Thus he keeps "on the

beam." Thus he keeps in touch with the
control station, receives his orders, and
reports his position. He knows that if
the station does not hear from him at
the appointed time, they will be alerted
to his danger.

As we journey the unseen way of
life, fraught with many dangers, are
we careful to keep in touch with the
unseen control? "Once every hour" to
throw ourselves into the abysmal grace
of God; once every hour to turn to
Him, relax in Him, let go of tension,
give ourselves completely to His strong
arms — What change that would make
in our lives! —Mildred Long, in
                        The Watchman-Examiner

* * *

Keeping Watch Above His Own!

In the pioneer days of our country,
there was a boy whose home was situated in the backwoods. A school had
been opened some miles away from
where the boy lived. Part of the way to
the school led through a dense forest.
The boy's father was a strong, brave
backwoodsman. He wanted his son to
grow up to be strong and brave. So he
told his son that he would have to go
to school alone! When the boy walked
through the dark forest, he always expected to meet a bear or some wild Indians.

With the passing of the days and
weeks, his fear subsided. Then, one
afternoon, he saw a great bear standing right in his pathway! The bear
growled and glowered at the boy. The
boy stood motionless, filled with fear.
Even if he had run, it would have done
no good, for the bear would have outrun him. As he stood there, a shot
rang out. The bear fell dead. Then,
from the bushes, the father emerged.
"It's all right, Son. I've been with you
all the time. Every morning I have
followed you to school, and every afternoon I have been in the shadows watching you. I kept myself hidden from you
because I wanted you to learn to be
brave!"

God has promised to His children:
"Fear thou not; for I am with thee."
                        —O. Osborn Gregory, in
                        The Methodist Recorder

A New Year Promise
Another year I enter,
  Its history unknown;
Oh, how my feet would tremble
  To tread its paths alone!
But I have heard a whisper,
  I know I shall be blest:
"My presence shall go with thee,
  And I will give thee rest."

What will the New Year bring to me?
  I may not, must not know.
Will it be love and rapture,
  Or loneliness and woe?
Hush! Hush! I hear His whisper,
  I surely shall be blest:
"My presence shall go with thee,
  And I will give thee rest."

—*Selected*

PRIDE

Short Quotes

A proud young man received a medal at school. The person who bestowed it used extravagant language to praise the student's greatness and accomplishment. Proudly the young man repeated the words to his mother. Then he asked her, "How many great men are there in the world today anyhow?" The wise mother said, "One less than you think!"
—W. B. K.

* * *

Pride is a good thing to have. Be sure, however, it is the kind that keeps your chin up and not your nose.

* * *

William Carey said on his deathbed to a fellow missionary who had spoken highly of Carey's accomplishments, "When I am gone, speak *less* of Dr. Carey and *more* of Dr. Carey's Saviour.

* * *

The greatest fault, I should say, is to be conscious of none. —Thomas Carlyle

* * *

I saw beside a copy of *Who's Who* a new volume — *Who Was Who!* How quickly we pass from hero to zero! "For all flesh is as grass, and all the glory of man as the flower of grass" (I Peter 1:24). —Dr. Vance Havner

* * *

There are many people who would not kill a mouse without publicizing it. Samson killed a lion and said nothing about it. Say much of what the Lord has done for you. Say little of what

you have done for the Lord. Do not speak a self-glorifying sentence.
—Spurgeon

* * *

A proud lawyer asked a farmer: "Why don't you hold up your head in the world? I bow my head before neither God nor man!" Answered the wise farmer: "Do you see that field of grain? Only the heads of grain which are empty stand upright. The well-filled ones bow low!"

* * *

Don't look down on anybody. Only God sits up that high.

* * *

Napoleon lived only for the fading glory of this world. In his memoirs he wrote, "I die before my time, and my body shall be given back to the earth to be devoured of worms. What an abysmal gulf between my deep miseries and the eternal kingdom of Christ. I marvel that whereas the ambitious dreams of myself and of Alexander and of Caesar should have vanished into thin air, a Judean peasant — Jesus — should be able to stretch His hands across the centuries, and control the destinies of men and nations."
—W. B. K.

* * *

There was a workman who had unusual skill and was therefore promoted rapidly. Finally he became manager of the plant. Then he became proud and oppressive. The employees of the concern hated him. One day an aged employee said to him, "You are a clever man. God has given you outstanding talents. But there is something you have forgotten." "What's that?" snapped the manager. "It's this," said the old man, "ability will help you reach the top, but you'll need character to stay there. And there is something else — you need to be big enough to acknowledge that God gave you the ability."

It is most serious to arrogate to ourselves the glory which belongs to God.
—W. B. K.

* * *

A high-ranking British official in the Orient entertained a sophisticated lady as his guest. The general's assistant seated the lady at the left of her host rather than at his right, the place of honor. She fumed inwardly until she could no longer bear it. Haughtily she said, "I suppose you have great difficulty getting your aide-de-camp to seat your guests properly!" "Not at all," said the general. "Those who matter don't mind, and those who mind don't matter!" —*Church Herald*

A highly temperamental soprano soloist was rehearsing to sing. Toscanini, the conductor, gave her instructions. This proved too much for the vanity of the soloist. She said, "I am the star of this performance!" Said Toscanini quietly, "Madame, in this performance there are no stars!"
—*Choice Gleanings Calendar*

* * *

Billie Burke was enjoying a trans-Atlantic ocean trip when she noticed that a gentleman at the next table was suffering from a bad cold. "Uncomfortable?" she asked sympathetically.

The man nodded.

"I'll tell you what to do for it," she offered. "Go back to your stateroom, and drink a lot of orange juice. Take five aspirin tablets. Cover yourself with all the blankets you can find. Sweat the cold out. I know what I'm talking about. I'm Billie Burke of Hollywood." The man smiled warmly, and said, "Thanks. I'm Dr. Mayo, of the Mayo Clinic." —*Sunshine Magazine*

Illustrations

See What I Did!

There is a little fable that expresses a big truth.

A woodpecker was pecking away at the trunk of a dead tree. Suddenly lightning struck the tree and splintered it. The woodpecker flew away, unharmed. Looking back to where the dead tree had stood, the proud bird exclaimed, "Look what I did!"

That fable reminds us of the proud man who arrogated to himself all the glory for his accomplishments — "Is not this great Babylon, that I have built . . . by the might of my power, and for the honour of my majesty?" (Dan. 4:30).
—W. B. K.

Fussy Little Christians

Dr. Vance Havner has aptly described the present generation of Christians thus: "We are a generation of proud, fussy little Christians — experts but not examples. We know too much, or we think we do. We have heard all the preachers and read all the books. It is hard these days to be converted and become like little children. We want to be thought philosophers and scholars — brilliant but not childlike. So we miss the secrets God has hidden from the wise and prudent and revealed them unto babes. How often, even among the saints, does some simple soul learn the deeper things of God and press through to heaven's best while 'the wise and the prudent' utterly miss them!"
—W. B. K.

PROCRASTINATION

Illustrations

What the Crew of the Squalas Didn't Say

The submarine *Squalas* and its crew lay helpless at the bottom of the Atlantic Ocean, two hundred and forty feet below the surface. The crew sent up smoke flares, hoping that their location would become known. The submarine *Sculpin* did locate them. A ten-ton diving bell was lowered several times, bringing to safety the thirty-three surviving members of the crew of the ill-fated *Squalas*. Not one of the thirty-three men said to their rescuers, "I will think it over," or "I will wait for a more convenient season," or "I am in good condition as I am," or "There is too much to give up," or "I don't understand the workings of that diving bell," or "I'll think about it until tomorrow!" All instantly and gratefully accepted the means of escape from death.

—Told by Dr. Robert G. Lee

* * *

How and When

We are often greatly bothered
  By two fussy little men,
Who sometimes block our pathway —
  Their names are How and When.

If we have a task or duty
  Which we can put off a while,
And we do not go and do it —
  You should see those two rogues smile!

But there is a way to beat them,
  And I will tell you how:
If you have a task or duty,
  Do it *well*, and do it *now*.

—*Selected*

* * *

Spurning God's Mercy!

In a revival meeting in Shamokin, Pa., an unsaved man, for whose conversion many had long prayed, was approached during an invitation. Pleaded the personal worker, "Won't you go forward, confess Christ as your Saviour, and seek God's mercy and forgiveness?" The man stood. A sardonic, satanic smile came to his face. Then he began to laugh so loudly that he could be heard through the church. Said he, "It's too late! I've sinned away my last chance!" Then he dashed out the door!

Apparently that man had committed the sin which knows no forgiveness. We marvel at the longsuffering forbearance of God! How long will He allow sinful man to go on spurning His offer of mercy?

—Told by Rev. C. Leslie Miller

* * *

Covered Over by Angry Sea!

Two young men were walking along a road on the far north coast of Scotland. On one side was the sea. On the other side were towering, perpendicular cliffs. The road was safe only at low tide. How enchanting were the incoming waves! How awesome were the cathedral-like cliffs! As they loitered on their way, the young men were unmindful of the incoming tide that was gradually encroaching upon the road. An observer upon the lofty cliffs cried out, "The tide is rising! Behind you and ahead of you the waters have already covered the road. If you go beyond yonder outjutting rock, you'll be swept out to sea. By this ascent alone can you escape!"

The travelers did not heed the warning words. They thought that they could reach a point where the road turned up a gorge away from the seashore. As they proceeded, they saw that the sea was rapidly covering the road. They hastened their steps but presently they saw that the sea had already cut off their escape. The billowing waves rolled on and wrapped about the feet of the young men. They cried for help, but their cries were in vain. The angry sea soon smothered their shrieks of despair and carried their dead bodies off.

What a picture this is of all who "neglect so great salvation," heedless of the gathering storm and the coming of the day of wrath!

"Seek ye the Lord while he may be found, call ye upon him while he is near" (Isa. 55:6); "Surely in the floods of great waters they shall not come nigh unto him" (Ps. 32:6). —W. B. K.

* * *

Do Not Dream It

If you have a kind word, say it,
　Throbbing hearts soon sink to rest;
If you owe a kindness, pay it,
　Life's sun hurries to the west.

If some grand thing for tomorrow
　You are dreaming, do it now;
From the future do not borrow,
　Frost soon gathers on the brow.

Days for deeds are few, my sister,
　　brother,
Then today, fulfill your vow:
If you mean to help another,
Do not dream it — do it now!

　　　　　　　　　　　—*Selected*

* * *

No Need to Hurry

A man who suffered of melancholia dreamed that he went to the abode of the lost — hell! The devil and his cohorts there were devising means whereby they could best get the lost ones on earth to continue to reject God's offers of mercy through Christ. One demon proposed, "Let's go to them and say, 'There is no God!'" Silence prevailed for a moment. Then one of the denizens of hell said, "We can never destroy them that way. 'The fool hath said in his heart, There is no God.' Most men know that there is a supreme Being." Then another suggested, "Let's tell them that there is no hell; that a man dies like a dog dies, and that there is no future punishment awaiting the wicked." "We can't get them that way," countered one. "Men know that vice and virtue cannot have the same destiny. Men do reap as they sow!" When it seemed that the conclave was to end in failure, there was a ringing cry, "I have found it! Go back to earth and tell them that there is a God; that there is a hell, and that the Bible is the Word of God. Then tell them that there is plenty of time in which to decide the question, 'Where will I spend eternity?'" Then all hell became vi-

brant with devilish glee, for the devil and his emissaries knew that if the lost ones procrastinate in the matter of being saved, they usually never decide for Christ.

　　　　　—Told by Dr. George W. Truett

* * *

Too Late!

In the old Abbey Kirk at Haddington one can read over the grave of Jane Welsh the first of many pathetic and regretful tributes paid by Thomas Carlyle to his neglected wife: "For forty years she was a true and loving helpmate of her husband, and by act and word worthily forwarded him as none else could in all worthy things he did or attempted. She died at London the 21st of April, 1866, suddenly snatched from him, and the light of his life is as if gone out." It has been said that the saddest sentence in English literature is that sentence written by Carlyle in his diary, "Oh, that I had you yet for five minutes by my side, that I might tell you all."

　　　　　　　　—*The Sermon Builder*

* * *

Which Thief?

"I'm all right," said a self-righteous, procrastinating young man to a man who sought to bring him to Christ. "Don't worry about me. It's one world at the time for me. I'll go on enjoying life while it lasts. There's time enough. Near life's end, I, like the dying thief, will turn to God!" The personal worker replied, "When the end comes, I wonder which dying thief you will be like. There were two of them, as you recall!" —W. B. K.

* * *

Wouldn't It Be Cowardly?

A brilliant college student became fatally ill. A faithful Christian implored him to turn to Christ for His mercy and forgiveness. "Don't you think it would be cowardly to turn to Him now as my life is ebbing away, when all my life I have been against Him?" "Yes, young man, it would be seemingly cowardly for you to turn to Him now, but it would be *more* cowardly for you not to turn to Him. The Bible gives us the record of one person who turned to the Saviour shortly before he died and with his latest breath asked to be remembered."

Oh the tragedy of having a *saved* soul but a *lost* life!

"Remember *now* thy Creator in the days of thy youth."

—Told by Dr. George W. Truett

GOD'S PROTECTION

Illustrations

Thorny Protection

God has devised wondrous ways to protect His creatures and children in danger. An enemy of the English sparrow is the Cooper hawk. This fearful enemy is so bold in the pursuit of sparrows, that it oftentimes follows them close to houses. The sparrows have learned that they can find safety within the thorny barberry bushes. When attacked, they whirl away to this sure refuge. The pursuing hawk swoops down, hops around the thorny bushes and then flies away, frustrated.

Through the Prophet Hosea, God gave this assuring word to His ancient people Israel, "Behold, I will hedge up thy way with thorns!"

The enemy of souls, Satan, asked God concerning His servant Job: "Hast not thou made a hedge about him, and about his house, and about all that he hath on every side?" (Job 1:10).

How protected are God's children when they are in the center of His directive will! How safe are those whose lives are hid with Christ in God!

—W. B. K.

* * *

The Third Man on the Rope

The leader, an experienced rock climber, is inching his way up a sheer wall; the second man waits on a ledge a few feet below him; a little lower the third and fourth men stand on a broader ledge. Suddenly and wordlessly the leader falls; passing the second and third men, he twists in midair and, still clutching his ice ax, lands on the shoulders of the fourth man, who collapses with him on the ledge but does not roll over. For a moment all is quiet. Then the other two move forward to help their companions. The leader is unhurt, his friend on whom he has fallen only dazed. Little is said, but each is thinking what might have been had the two gone over the ledge. The rope might have held; the other two might have checked the fall. Yet the strain of two falling bodies is very great. One thinks soberly at such a time; I know, for I was the third man on the rope. Thankfully we pulled ourselves together and went on to complete the climb. . . . I look back upon it as a wonderful example of God's gracious protection. Without question we were saved that day from what might have been a terrible accident.

—Frank E. Gaebelein, in *The Sunday School Times*

* * *

Keeping Watch

There is an Eye that never sleeps
  Beneath the wing of night;
There is an Ear that never shuts,
  When sink the beams of light.

But there's a power which man can wield,
  When mortal aid is vain;
That Eye, that Arm, that Love to reach,
  That listening Ear to gain.

That power is prayer, which soars on high
  Through Jesus to the throne,
And moves the Hand, which moves the world,
  To bring deliverance down.

—*Selected*

* * *

God's Safety Zone

Before the United States entered into World War I, the German government made known to neutral governments a

---

safety zone where ocean-going vessels could go without molestation or be attacked and sent to the bottom. God's safety zone for His children is to be in the center of His directive will.
—W. B. K.

* * *

Our Times Are in God's Hands

I take my pilgrim staff anew,
Life's path, untrodden, to pursue,
Thy guiding eye, my Lord, I view;
My times are in Thy hand.

Throughout the year, my heavenly Friend,
On Thy blest guidance I depend;
From its commencement to its end
My times are in Thy hand.

Should comfort, health, and peace be mine,
Should hours of gladness on me shine,
Then let me trace Thy love divine;
My times are in Thy hand.

But shouldst Thou visit me again
With languor, sorrow, sickness, pain,
Still let this thought my hope sustain,
My times are in Thy hand.

Thy smile alone makes moments bright,
That smile turns darkness into light;
This thought will soothe grief's saddest night,
My times are in Thy hand.

Should those this year be called away
Who lent to life its brightest ray,
Teach me in that dark hour to say,
My times are in Thy hand.
—Selected

* * *

God Cushioned the Fall

I visited one of my friends in a hospital who had fallen some thirty feet from a scaffold. It was a miracle that no bones were broken, and that he was injured only slightly. With a grateful heart he exclaimed, "There is but one explanation of my being alive — God cushioned the fall!" I left him with a deeper appreciation for the wondrous promise: "The eternal God is thy refuge, and underneath are the everlasting arms" (Deut. 33:27). —W. B. K.

There Were No Soldiers With Us

Two missionaries in Malaya walked to a distant village for some money which had been sent to a bank for them. When they were returning to their station, night overtook them. They prayed and committed themselves to God. Then they lay down to sleep on a lonely hillside. Some weeks later a man came to the mission hospital for treatment. He looked intently at the missionary doctor. "I have seen you before," he said. "No, I don't think we have met before," said the doctor. "But we have met before! You were sleeping one night on a hillside. Several of us saw you withdraw some money from the bank. We followed you, intending to rob you when it was dark. But we could not get near you because you were surrounded by soldiers." "Soldiers!" exclaimed the missionary. "There were no soldiers with us!" The bandit said, "But there were soldiers with you — sixteen of them. Their swords were drawn. We were filled with fear and ran away!"

"The angel of the Lord encampeth round about them that fear him, and delivereth them" (Ps. 34:7).
—W. B. K.

* * *

God Still Holds the Key!

To a world of bomb and bursting shell,
Sorrow, want and woe no tongue can tell,
Darkness, hunger, death, a living hell,
God still holds the key!

To an age of greed and bitter hate,
To the hearts that bleed, but hope and wait,
While the hour of time is growing late,
God still holds the key!

To the restless heart that knows no peace,
To the darkened life that nothing sees,
To the slaves of sin that need release,
God still holds the key!

To the heathen lands of deepest night,
To the hardened soul devoid of light,
To a holy life, the path of right,
God still holds the key!

To the unknown years that lie before,
To the unsolved problems yet in store,
To an untrod path, a bolted door,
    God still holds the key!

To the boundless wealth within His
        Word,
Where the trusting soul shall find re-
    ward,
To the stores of grace yet unexplored,
    God still holds the key!
                        —Haldor Lillenas

* * *

Rescued by a Robber

For days the snow fell unabated until the roofs of the homes were heavy
with snow. One night, a robber entered
a home occupied by a Christian man
and wife and their baby. As the robber moved about the room where all
three were sleeping, the baby began to
move and showed signs of awakening.
The robber, fearing that the baby might
awaken and cry, and thus betray his
presence, gently lifted the sleeping infant from his crib, and placed him just
outside the front door. The baby
awakened and began to cry. His crying awakened the father and mother.
They ran in the direction where it came
from. Just as they ran out of the
front door, the roof of their home fell
in. Later, the robber was found dead
beneath the ruins near the things he
had stolen! —W. B. K.

* * *

Keep Straight on, I'm Standing By!

During the dark days of World War
II, a British liner left an English port,
bound for America. The crossing was
very dangerous. Secret directions were
given to the liner's captain. They read:
"Keep straight on this course. Turn
aside for nothing, and if you need help
send a wireless message in this code!"
After a few days at sea, an enemy
cruiser was sighted. The captain of
the liner sent out a message in the special code. The captain's message, de-
coded, read, "Enemy cruiser sighted.
What shall I do?" Back came the reply
from an unseen ship: "Keep straight
on: I am standing by." Although no
friendly vessel could be seen, the liner
kept straight on, and at last reached

port in safety. Soon afterward, there
steamed into the same harbor a British
man-of-war. The battleship, though
unseen, had been standing by all the
time, ready to help in time of need.

God is the Protector of His children.
In danger, His mighty arms are about
us. Though we cannot see Him, we
know that He is in the shadows, keeping
watch over His own. —Adapted from
    The Sunday School Times

* * *

Sherman Was Right!

Sherman was right — "War is hell!"
As a boy, I delighted to roam and
romp through the woods, wade in the
streams, and swim in the mill pond. It
was there that I saw something of the
destructiveness of war — millstones
once whirring and grinding were now
strewn amidst the debris and wreckage
of war. The pervasive silence spoke
thunderously to my boyish imagination
— "War is hell!" Yet, even in war,
there are sometimes enduring deeds of
chivalry and healing acts of mercy.

My grandmother's humble Georgia
home stood near a road over which an
endless procession of men and muni-
tions of war went their way in "Sherman's March to the Sea." Standing at
the gate of the home, my brave grandmother gave a beseeching and tearful
distress signal which caught the eye of
a general in Sherman's army. Riding
swiftly to her assistance, the general
saluted and said, "Madam, what can I
do for you?" She replied, "Sir, I want
protection for my home and my five little
children. My husband is with Lee's
army in Richmond!" Saluting, the officer galloped away. Presently, two
sentinels took their place on either side
of the gate. For days and nights, the
rhythmic thud of myriads of marching
soldiers' feet was heard. The home,
however, was not disturbed. Grandmother had sought and secured protection for her home and children!

How protected are God's children who
live in the center of His directive will!
Above are His watchful eyes. Round
about is the delivering angel of the
Lord. Underneath are the everlasting
arms! —W. B. K.

God's Fool

Before the Communists took over China, John Ting, "God's Fool," did a mighty work for God. He was a member of the "Little Flock Evangelists." By his life and by his witnessing, he won many Chinese to Christ. He had utter faith in God's care, as the following thrilling incident attests.

One day Ting and his companions arrived at a river which had to be crossed. The river was overflowing its banks and the water was deep. Ting and his companions were being pursued by bandits. The situation seemed humanly hopeless! But Ting said, "Our God is a mighty God. He can open a way for us through the river!" He prayed simply and earnestly: "O, Lord, hold back the waters, and make a way for us to escape from our enemies!" Then he stepped into the raging water which swirled about his knees. He motioned to the others to cross as he bowed his head and prayed silently. For a moment, Ting's companions hesitated. Then, to their amazement, they saw that the water was steadily dropping. In a short while, all had crossed the river to safety!

The God who wrought this miracle in answer to believing prayer, the God who divided the Red Sea and rolled back the water of the River Jordan that His people might pass through safely, *still lives!* He still urges His children: "Call unto me, and I will answer thee, and shew thee great and mighty things which thou knowest not" (Jer. 33:3).

—W. B. K.

GOD'S PROVISION

Illustrations

How He Knew

An English woman whose Christian work incurs a large outlay every year, and who trusts to her divine Master to provide everything in response to faith and prayer, says: "I was once confronted by an infidel who demanded what proof we have that there is a God, or, rather, that we could know there was a God. I replied, 'If you had made an appeal to a person whom you had never seen, and whose existence you only knew by report, for a thousand pounds, and if he had responded to your appeal by sending you the money by the hand of some friend, would you not know that such a person must be a living reality?'

" 'Yes,' he said, with an incredulous smile, 'I think I should. Hard cash is pretty strong evidence.'

" 'Well,' said I, 'I made an appeal to God for that very sum toward building a house by the side of the sea for the benefit of His servants and He gave me the exact amount I asked for, by the hand of a friend, without my having to appeal to anyone else but Himself. I therefore claim to know that He exists.' The man changed his countenance, and turned away without answering." —*Young People's Digest*

* * *

How Faithless I've Been

A Christian man had worked for a business concern for more than twenty-five years. One day his employer said to him, "A young man will report for work today. He will be doing the same kind of work you have been doing. I want you to train him for the work." The man thought, "I have been ill and away from work much during the year. I will probably be replaced by this younger man whom I have been asked to train." At the close of the day, he went home, dejected and discouraged. He said to his wife, "Jean, my employer has asked me to train a young man for my line of work. I'm afraid that the young man will get my position. Being the president's nephew, he has strong backing!" "I see," said Jean, "and my husband has only the Lord God of hosts to back him and supply his needs!" "Oh, Jean," exclaimed the husband, "how

faithless I have been! I have the unfailing God, and His promises are
sure!" —W. B. K.

* * *

No Good Thing Will He Withhold

Steinmetz, the great scientist, never
received a fixed salary from his spon-
sors. At intervals, his backers would
give him a book of blank checks. Whatever his needs might be, whether great
or small, he needed only to fill in the
amount on a check, sign his name thereon, and present it to the bank.

The resources of heaven are at the
disposal of God's dedicated children.
God's promises are sure: "No good thing
will he withhold from them, that walk
uprightly" (Ps. 84:11); "Let your requests be made known unto God . . . my
God shall supply all your need according to his riches in glory by Christ
Jesus" (Phil. 4:6, 19).

Thou art coming to a King,
Large petitions with thee bring,
For His grace and pow'r are such,
None can ever ask too much.
—W. B. K.

* * *

God Heard the Scraping

Years ago there lived in Scotland a
Christian widow. Left with several de-
pendent "bairns," she was at length reduced to great straits, and in order to
feed and clothe her little household was
obliged to practice the strictest economy.
Yet withal, her heart was fixed upon
the Lord, and both by precept and practice she taught the lesson of trust and
confidence to her children.

But there came a day when the purse
was flat and the cupboard bare. In the
meal-barrel there was only left a handful of flour; and, like the widow of
Zarephath, she went to get it to make
a morsel of food to satisfy the craving
of the hungry little ones, knowing not
where the next would come from. As
she bent over the barrel, scraping up
the last of the flour, her heart for a
moment gave way, and in a paroxysm of
doubt the hot tears began to fall, and
she felt as one utterly forsaken. Hearing her sobs, her little boy Robbie drew
near to comfort. Plucking at her dress
till he attracted her attention, he looked

up into her face with wonder, and asked,
in his quaint Scottish dialect, "Mither,
what are ye greetin' [weeping] aboot?
Dinna God hear ye scrapin' o' the bottom o' the barrel, Mither?"

In a moment her failing faith reas-
serted itself. Ah, yes, God did hear.
All else might be gone, but He remained,
and His Word declared her every need
should be supplied. And so it was; for
help was provided from a most unexpected source when the last of what she
had was gone.
—Dr. Harry A. Ironside

* * *

I Asked and Received

A friend of ours, a deeply religious
woman, had experienced more than her
share of trouble. She was valiantly trying to support her disabled husband and
three small children, but the money
she made from washing and ironing and
caring for neighbors' children was never
enough. My wife and I decided we'd
like to help, and purchased a large-sized
order of groceries. Wishing to keep
our gift anonymous, we placed it on
Martha's doorstep at an early hour.
Later that day, accompanied by our five-
year-old son, Danny, we paid our friend
a casual visit. Martha's eyes were still
moist. "Isn't the good Lord wonderful!" she beamed. "You know, I just
didn't see how we'd make it through the
week. The cupboard was nearly bare.
Then I remembered the Scripture, 'Ask,
and it shall be given you.' So — I
asked —" She led us to the kitchen
table piled high with jars and boxes and
canned goods. Her eyes were like two
shining stars. "And I received! It was
a present from the Lord!"
—*Christian Herald*

* * *

God Knew

Said Dr. Graham Scroggie at a Keswick Convention: "Only once during
those two years did a mealtime arrive
when there was nothing in the house
to eat, but within half an hour a basket
was handed in. I took off the cover and
on a dish was a chicken covered with
sauce, and sausages all around, and
some sweets of one kind and another.
After my four-year-old had danced

around the basket he slipped away, and I heard him talking to someone. I went in the direction of the voice, and I saw him kneeling at the big arm chair where we knelt together every morning for prayer, and this is what he was saying, 'O God, thank You for the chicken, but I wish it hadn't sauce, I don't like sauce, and thank You specially for the sausages.' The friend who sent that basket did not know anything about our circumstances; but God knew, and that was what mattered." —*Keswick Week*

* * *

Really Believing

Some years ago a prominent minister came to Dr. Charles G. Trumbull at a conference and confessed that he was defeated; he did not have peace or joy in his life, nor victory over sin, nor the fruit that he longed to bear. After some moments of conversation that revealed that the man was surrendered in the sense of wanting only God's will in his life, Dr. Trumbull asked, "Do you believe the first verse of the Twenty-third Psalm?" "That is one of my favorite texts. I have preached on it many a time. Of course, I believe it." "What kind of shepherd is He? Does He take care of some of the needs of the sheep, or of all the needs of the sheep?" The minister hesitated; he was keen, and knew where the question was leading, as he answered, "Of course, He takes care of all of them." "Now look out! You are getting yourself in a corner, and it is the most blessed corner you were ever in." That minister kneeled down, and for the first time in his life he really believed "the Lord is my shepherd," meeting all his needs. From that crisis he rose in radiant victory. Previously he was doing what many Christians are doing — merely saying he believed it. —*King's Business*

* * *

Fulfillment

Fulfillment!
Ah, 'tis a lovely word!
After all the weary years,
After all the pain and tears,
After all the doubts and fears,
Fulfillment!

Fulfillment!
Yes, every promise kept!
After waiting, longing, dread,
After brightest hopes have fled,
Lo, it is done, as He hath said,
Fulfillment!

Fulfillment!
Such as ye cannot contain!
Good measure pressed down, running o'er,
All He hath shown and so much more,
A rending sky — an open door!
Fulfillment!

—Frances Metcalfe

REPENTANCE

Short Quotes

Deathbed repentance is burning the candle of life in the service of the devil, and then blowing the smoke into the face of God. —Billy Sunday

* * *

Those who wait to repent until the eleventh hour often die at ten thirty.

* * *

Mere sorrow which weeps and sits still is not repentance. Repentance is sorrow converted into action, and a movement toward a new and better life.
—Marvin Vincent

I often wondered if my message gets across until, one day, I received a telephone call from the thief who took the tape recorder from the church. He was conscience-stricken and had decided to return the recorder after listening to a recorded sermon on repentance!
—The Reverend E. W. Albrecht, a Lutheran pastor, Miami

* * *

No man ever repented on his deathbed of being a Christian.
—Hannah Moore

The Kekchi Indians of Guatemala describe repentance as "it pains my heart." The Baouli people of West Africa are more precise. They describe repentance as "it hurts so much I want to quit it," that is, the sins for which they sorrow. Remorse brings pangs of guilt which does not lead to a change in one's life.
—*American Bible Society*

* * *

"Why do you want to join the church?" asked the pastor of a little boy. "Because I want to show publicly that Jesus has saved me," said the boy. "Do you feel that you are saved? Who saved you?" The boy replied, "It is the work of Jesus Christ and myself!" "Of yourself? What was your part in your being saved?" asked the pastor. Said the boy, "I repented, and Jesus did the rest!"
—*Our Misunderstood Bible*, by H. Clay Trumbull

* * *

The Western world is standing at the crossroads. Never was the picture darker. Never was the need of divine intervention so desperate. We are facing a political crisis. Many of us are going along just as we have in the past. Christian, this is a different age! I believe God is giving the nations an opportunity to repent. If they fail, they will be destroyed. The answer for the nations is an old-fashioned, Holy Spirit endued revival in which God can speak once again as by fire!
—*Billy Graham*

* * *

A minister kept a record of the sick people he visited during a period of twenty years. Among some two thousand who recovered from their illness, and who seemingly repented and turned to God when they thought death was near, only two proved afterward that their repentance was sincere and their conversion genuine! The rest turned again to their former sinful ways.

True repentance is never too late, but seldom is late repentance true, godly sorrow for sin. —W. B. K.

Illustrations

My Common Sense Tells Me

"Do you believe John 3:16 and I John 1:9?" asked a Christian worker of an apparently sincere seeker for God. "I believe those verses," said the man. "Then you are saved," answered the Christian worker. "No, I am not," the man replied. Turning to the following verse, "Let the wicked forsake his way, and the unrighteous man his thoughts: and let him return unto the Lord, and he will have mercy upon him; and to our God, for he will abundantly pardon," the Christian worker asked the seeker to read it. Having read the verse, the man said, "I am the wicked man. I am the unrighteous man. I have to forsake sin and my wicked thoughts. I must come back from my own way to God's way. In my heart is a sin. I am hugging it and am not willing to give it up. My own common sense tells me I cannot be saved until I am so penitent that I will utterly forsake it!" "That's right," exclaimed the Christian worker, "and you have preached to me the greatest sermon I have ever heard on repentance!" —W. B. K.

* * *

The Priest Was Awed

Years ago in Ireland a priest was reading Mass at a funeral. The people were kneeling. Suddenly Gideon Ouseley rode up. Dismounting, he reverently knelt. The people couldn't understand what the priest read — he read in Latin. Ouseley, a Latin scholar, understood. He quietly translated into Irish the portions of the Mass which conveyed Scriptural truth and warning. The priest was awed. The people wept because of sorrow for sin. After the service, Mr. Ouseley pleaded earnestly with the people to get right with God by real repentance and true faith in the Lord Jesus Christ. —W. B. K.

* * *

Repent or Perish!

A young minister entered with great zest upon his first pastorate. After some "get acquainted" messages, he got down to real business. He announced a series of foundational, doctrinal messages, the first of the series being, "Except Ye Repent." With much fervor he exhorted his hearers to repent. "Repent or perish," he warned. During the days of the ensuing week, he looked for some tangible results from his sermon. Seeing no change in the attitudes and living of his members, he preached the next Sunday on "Except Ye Repent." This he did for four Sundays in a row. When asked if he had no other sermons to preach, the young pastor said gravely, "Since my first message on repentance, I have been looking for some changes in the attitudes and lives of my people. I have seen none. I know that except they repent, they will perish. Impenitent, cold, calloused hearts are powerless to receive the truths of God's Word except they *first* repent and bring forth fruit meet for repentance." The young pastor was right!

A sense of sin and a heart-rending sorrow for sin are things we seldom encounter nowadays. Who of us has the grace to acknowledge this *fact* and head a procession back to the antiquated and seldom-spoken-of altar of sorrow where pew and pulpit will repent of its pride, pretense and departures from God and "the old-time religion"? —W. B. K.

* * *

I'll Make You Repent

A hot-tempered officer in the army one day struck a common soldier. The soldier whom he struck was a young man who was noted for his courage. He felt the insult deeply, but military discipline forbade that he should return the blows. He could use only words, and he said, "I will make you repent." One day, in the heat of a furious battle engagement, the young soldier saw an officer wounded and separated from his company gallantly striving to force his way through the enemies who surrounded him. The courageous young soldier recognized his former insulter and rushed to his assistance, supporting the wounded man with his arm. Together they fought their way through to their own line. Trembling with emotion the officer

grasped the hand of the soldier and stammered out his gratitude. "What a return for an insult so carelessly given!" The young man pressed his hand in turn and, with a smile, said gently, "I told you that I would make you repent." From that time on they were buddies. —*Way of Life Journal*

* * *

Evangelism, Not Revival

Evangelism, fine as it is, is not revival. After a signally successful meeting, Billy Graham was asked, "Is this revival?" Graham replied, "No. When revival comes, I expect to see two things which we have not seen yet. First, a new sense of the holiness of God on the part of Christians; and second, a new sense of the sinfulness of sin on the part of Christians."

We might add a third and closely related indication of revival — a new working of the Holy Spirit in the local church. Why? For two big reasons, among others; first, because the Word of God calls for it; and second, because the world challenge calls for it.

—*The Moody Monthly*

* * *

I'm Going to Hell — I'm Going to Heaven

Years ago, a Methodist bishop preached on repentance. What he said was true to the Bible. However, an old circuit rider in the audience — the Reverend John W. Knight, my grandfather — felt that the bishop's learned discourse was not sufficiently clear for the audience to get the meaning of true repentance. Respectfully, the old man stood and asked, "Bishop, may I show the people what I believe repentance is?" The bishop said good-naturedly, "Very well, 'Uncle' Knight. Show us what repentance is!" The old man began to walk down the long aisle of the church, saying, "I'm going to hell! I'm going to hell! I'm going to hell!" Then he wheeled around. As he went in the opposite direction, he exclaimed, "I'm going to heaven! I'm going to heaven! I'm going to heaven!"

How literally did the old circuit rider

act out the meaning of genuine repentance. Is it not an about-face? Is it not our forsaking the downward way, and turning our feet onto the upward way. Is it not a change of heart and attitude? —W. B. K.

REST

Illustrations

Will the Lord Just Let Me Rest?

An aged mother, who had known little else than toil and care in this life, was about to slip into eternity. Her pastor spoke comforting and assuring words to her. He spoke glowingly of heaven with its many mansions, its harps, crowns, and choirs. A twinge of disappointment clouded her face as she asked, "Pastor, do you think the Lord will let me just rest for a while?"
—W. B. K.

* * *

Finding All in Thee

My Saviour, Thou hast offered rest:
   Oh, give it then, to me;
The rest of ceasing from myself,
   To find my all in Thee.

O Lord, I seek a holy rest,
   A vict'ry over sin:
I seek that Thou alone shouldst reign,
   O'er all without, within.
—Selected

* * *

I Longed for Rest

I've traveled north, I've traveled south,
   I've traveled east and west;
I've had my flings in worldly things,
   But, oh, I longed for rest!

I've earthly gems, I've jewels rare,
   Of these I claimed the best;
I have my gold, I've wealth untold,
   But, oh, I longed for rest!

One day I turned me from my sins,
   And then my soul was blest;
I gave my all, at Jesus' call,
   And, oh, He gave me rest!
—*Selected*

* * *

Rest Found in Toil

One summer evening, when Thomas Edison returned home from his work, his wife said, "You've worked too long without a rest. You must take a vacation." "But where will I go?" he asked. "Decide where you'd rather be than anywhere else on earth and go there," she said. "Very well," promised Mr. Edison, "I will go there tomorrow." The next morning he returned to his laboratory. —*Christian Science Monitor*

* * *

Until I Rest in Thee

O God of love, within my heart
Ignite love's sacred flame,
That I, by loving actions, may
Bring honor to Thy name.

O God of light, upon my path
Let truth unhindered shine,
That I may walk in confidence,
My will submerged in Thine.

O God of peace, control my life,
No longer will I flee,
For I shall never know soul-rest
Until I rest in Thee.
—Tom Roberts in *Moody Monthly*

* * *

How to Find Rest

Rest is not quitting
   The busy career;
Rest is the fitting
   Of self to its sphere.
'Tis loving and serving
   The highest and best!
'Tis onward, unswerving,
   And that is true rest.
—J. S. Dwight

* * *

Americanitis

Because of her late arrival at a railway station, a lady had but five minutes to make connection with an outgoing train. As she ran toward the train, a Pullman car porter waved her to slow down and said, "Lady, you better take it easy or you are going to come down with *Americanitis!*" "What's that?" gasped the lady. "I can't tell you what it is, but I can tell you how it acts: Americanitis is running up an escalator!"

So many of us are getting nowhere fast! Like ants disturbed on an anthill, we scurry hither, thither and yon. Taut nerves are snapping, and over-wrought minds are cracking, with the result that there are more mental patients in hospitals than any other kind of patients!

"Be still and know that I am God!" "In returning and rest shall ye be saved; in quietness and in confidence shall be your strength" (Isa. 30:15). —W. B. K.

* * *

When You Are Tired

A mother was teaching her children the meaning of the Twenty-third Psalm. She told them how the good shepherd cares for the little lambs. Impetuous Mamie, eager to speak her one thought, said, "Yes, and he drives away the lions and the bears." "Yes," said thoughtful Tiny, "and he carries them uphill when they are tired." The words went to the mother's heart with a strength and sweetness of which the little speaker did not dream, and often after thrilled her tired heart like the echo of an angel's song. It was in fulfillment of this promise that Jesus stretched out His hands to the weary laborers, returning from their toil at evening time, and called, "Come unto me, all ye that labour and are heavy laden, and I will give you rest."
—*United Presbyterian*

* * *

Rest on Promiser Himself

"For years I have been memorizing precious promises from God's Word, cherishing the comforting thought that I would repeat them as I entered the valley of the shadow of death," said an aged, dying saint to his pastor, "but now my memory has failed me completely." "My friend, do you think God has forgotten them?" "Of course not," pastor." "Then why not rest in the Promiser Himself?" said the pastor.
—W. B. K.

The Quiet Mind

I have a treasure which I prize,
  Its like I cannot find;
There's nothing like it on the earth,
  'Tis this — *a quiet mind.*

But 'tis not that I'm stupified,
  Or senseless, dull or blind;
'Tis God's own peace within my heart
  That forms my *quiet mind.*

I found this treasure at the Cross;
  And there, to every kind
Of weary, heavy-ladened soul,
  Christ gives *a quiet mind.*

My Saviour's death and risen life
  To give it were designed;
His love's the never-failing spring
  Of this, my *quiet mind.*

The love of God within my breast,
  My heart to Him doth bind;
This is the peace of Heaven on earth —
  This is my *quiet mind.*

—*Selected*

* * *

Heart Rest

My heart is resting, O my God,
  I will give thanks and sing;
My heart is at the secret source
  Of every precious thing!

Now the frail vessel Thou hast made
  No hand but Thine can fill;
The waters of this earth have failed,
  And I am thirsty still!

I thirst for springs of heavenly life,
  And here all day they rise;
I seek the treasure of Thy love,
  And close at hand it lies!

—Anna L. Waring in *Moody Monthly*

* * *

A Multimillionaire's Question

A minister said in his message, "How powerless are fountains of earthly origin to slake the soul's thirst, and bring rest and contentment. Solomon tried works, wisdom, wine, women and wealth. Of all of them he said: "Vanity of vanities; all is vanity" (Eccl. 1:2). Augustine said that God has made our hearts for Himself, and that they are restless until they rest in Him."

In the audience sat Titus Salt, a multimillionaire, who had invented the way to weave the wool of the alpaca into cloth. He was sad and dejected. At the close of the service he said to the minister, "I agree with what you said about the futility of seeking soul rest and satisfaction by pursuing passing pleasures and by accumulating wealth. My life has been saddened by these things. I yearn for spiritual rest and satisfaction!" —W. B. K.

The Power of Thirst

Two thirsty elephants broke through barriers to reach a water hole in Colombo, Ceylon. They demolished the reinforced concrete and steel fences to slake their thirst. The spiritual thirst of man for God should drive him as irresistibly to the One who said: "If any man thirst let him come unto me and drink." God made man to hunger and thirst after Himself and his soul will remain restless until he finds rest in God through Christ.

—*Christian Herald*

RESTITUTION

Illustrations

A Deacon Got Right with God

Every Sunday a certain deacon ushered in the church. When the Lord's Supper was observed, he assisted too. There was something in his life, however, which caused him at times to have a troubled conscience. Others also were troubled over his inconsistency. The deacon owned a hotel building on the main street of Salisbury, North Carolina. He rented part of it for a saloon. God deeply convicted him of the wrong of what he was doing. He knew that he could not get right with God until he had evicted the saloon. This he did. Then he computed the rent which he had received from the saloon and gave it to Dr. R. E. Neighbour, instructing him to use it to help the impoverished families of the former patrons of the saloon!

"God requireth that which is past" (Eccl. 3:15). —W. B. K.

The Love that Rights the Wrong!

One of God's servants had preached a searching sermon on forgiveness. He urged God's children to get right with God and with one another. He emphasized the fact that God's children cannot be right with God and at the same time wrong with one another, if it is within their power to right the wrong. He quoted the verse which says, "If it be possible, as much as lieth in you, live peaceably with all men" (Rom. 12:18). "Oh, that more of us had the 'love which rights the wrong!' Then more hearts would be 'filled with cheer and song!'" At the close of the service, a lady, who had harbored hatred for the pastor in her heart, openly confessed to him the wickedness and wretchedness of her heart, saying, "Your reference to the 'love that rights the wrong,' went like an arrow to my heart. Do forgive me for the wrong I have done you as I feel that God has forgiven me."

—W. B. K.

Then Jesus Came!

J. P. Bosovich, manager of the Robert Hall clothing store in Grand Rapids, Michigan, was surprised when he opened a letter and found a check for $5 for two sweaters which a woman had stolen. He was even more surprised when the woman gave her name and address in an Ohio town, and offered to send more money if she had not sent enough. "This is the first time I've ever had anything like this happen to me since I've been in the clothing business," said Bosovich. The woman concluded her letter thus: "The Lord has saved me and has made me a new person!" —W. B. K.

Not Enough to Confess

During the revival at Wamba in the Belgian Congo, the story of restitutions would make a volume in itself. The head woman confessed to pilfering rice from church supplies, not deliberate stealing, but taking small amounts over the years with the covering thought, "I am the head woman, and as such should have certain privileges." She could not rest until she had collected a large basketful of rice and returned it to the church supplies. The wife of one of our houseboys confessed to taking eggs from our fowls and presenting them to us as her gift to our wee son. "It is not enough to confess this," she said, "I will give an egg for each one I stole." One man came with a few francs, saying he had bought a New Testament nearly twenty years ago. He had not sufficient money then, but had promised to pay later. He had gone away, saying to himself, "These white people have plenty of money; why should they trouble about a few francs?" But now he saw this was a great sin, and hastened to pay his debt.

—*The Sunday School Times*

* * *

Undoing a Wrong

A professing Christian sold her house. One day she asked the sister of the purchaser, "Wouldn't you like to become a Christian?" She replied, "You sold a house with many defects to my sister. You lied about them. I am not a Christian, but I certainly wouldn't do what you did!" The professing Christian was deeply convicted. She immediately made amends for the wrongs she had done. Now she and the woman who reproved her are on the best of terms.

Let's cease pleading for "showers of blessings" until we make amends, as far as we can, for the wrongs we have done others. —W. B. K.

RESURRECTION
(See also: Death)

Short Quotes

A minister selected as the first hymn for the Sunday morning service: "Christ the Lord Is Risen Today!" "This is an Easter hymn," said the helper who published the church calendar, "didn't you make a mistake?" The minister answered: "There has been no mistake. That is the hymn I want. *Every Sunday is Easter Day!*"

—W. B. K.

* * *

He lives triumphant from the grave,
He lives eternally to save,
He lives all glorious in the sky,
He lives exalted there on high,
He lives my hungry soul to feed,
He lives to help in time of need!

—Samuel Medley

* * *

Some years ago, Dr. Will Houghton, the president of the Moody Bible Institute, was in the Holy Land during an Easter season. With great interest he watched a large crowd of people march along a street. In front of the procession was a life-size wax figure of Christ — dead! How lifelike was the wax figure! Mothers held up their little children and said, "Kiss the Christ!" Dr. Houghton became sick at heart at the hollow mockery. He thought, "It is a lie — a base, terrible lie! *He is not dead! The cross and the tomb are past! He is alive forevermore!*" —W. B. K.

* * *

A scholar frequently talked to a minister about the resurrection. He didn't believe in the resurrection. Years passed. The scholar believed in the Lord Jesus Christ and His triumph over death. One day he chanced to meet the minister, who asked him, "What do you now think about the resurrection?" "I believe in the resurrection. Two words, spoken by Paul, 'Thou fool' (I Cor. 15:36). conquered me. It wasn't argument, or any attempt to satisfy my objections, but God convicting me of the fact that I was a fool!" —W. B. K.

313

Hope we not in this life only,
  Christ Himself has made it plain,
None who sleep in Him shall perish,
  And our faith is not in vain!
Not in vain our glad hosannas,
  Since we follow where He led,
Not in vain our Easter anthem:
  "Christ has risen from the dead!"

* * *

The embalmed remains of Lenin lie in a crystal casket in a tomb in Red Square in Moscow. On the casket it says: He was the greatest leader of all peoples, of all countries, of all times. He was the lord of the new humanity. He was the saviour of the world!"

All is in the past tense for Lenin. How forward-looking, by contrast, are the triumphant words of Christ: "I am he that liveth. . . . I am alive for evermore" —W. B. K.

* * *

"I do not believe that a dead body can be resurrected," said an Orthodox Jew to a Chicago minister. "Do you believe that God in the beginning created the heaven and the earth, and that He formed Adam's body from the dust of the ground?" asked the minister. "Yes, I do," said the Jew. "Why don't you believe that God can bring back into existence a body that has returned to dust?" Thoughtfully, the Jew replied, "If you put it that way, I do believe!" —W. B. K.

* * *

Some years ago in Michigan, a little child of great promise died. In the child's lifeless hand was placed a beautiful bouquet, in the center of which was an unopened bud of the rose of Sharon. At the close of the funeral solemnities, loved ones gathered about the little casket to take their farewell look. A wonderful and revealing thing had happened. The bud had become a rose in full bloom while grasped in the dead child's hand. The beautiful rose seemed to say, "Weep not for the spirit that has gone! It has already become a full-bloomed rose in glory!" —W. B. K.

* * *

A minister stood before the window of an art store, and looked at a painting of Jesus on the cross. A little ragged, dirty boy came and stood by him. "Do you know who He is?" asked the minister. "That's Jesus. Them's the soldiers standing around. That woman crying is His mother," said the little boy. The minister walked away. The boy overtook him and said, "Say, Mister, I wanted to tell you that Jesus rose again!" Then he smiled and ran away, happy to tell the good news! —W. B. K.

* * *

Many famous people are buried in an underground vault or chamber beneath St. Paul's Cathedral in London. On tomb after tomb are seen the words, "Here lieth the body of ...." The name of some general, artist, or minister follows. How different it was at the tomb of Jesus. There it is not "Here lieth the body of Jesus," but the spoken epitaph of the angel: "He is not here: for he is risen." Earthly greatness usually ends with the grave. The greatest demonstration of Jesus' power began at the grave where He conquered death!

* * *

As I stood by the grave of one I loved devotedly, and saw the earth heaped upon the casket, I thought: "What dishonor!" But I thought again, "This is the last that sin and Satan can do!" Then I thought of the next scene. How gloriously different it will be when that which was "sown in dishonor" shall be raised in glory, and "fashioned like unto his glorious body!"
     —J. R. Caldwell, in
     The Sunday School Times

* * *

A mother and her two children, ages four and six, went into a religious bookstore. The children were greatly interested in the religious articles. "I don't like this one," said the boy to his little sister, when he called her attention to a crucifix. "I don't like it either," said the little girl, "for Jesus is living now. He isn't dead!"

How grateful we are for Christ's words of triumph: "I am he that liveth, and was dead, and, behold, I am alive for evermore!"
     —Rev. Ralph W. Neighbour

* * *

Centuries ago the coastal region of the southern tip of Africa was known

as *The Cape of Storms.* The region was a graveyard for ships. No ship had been known to round that cape and return. There was an intrepid navigator, however, who believed he could round the cape and return. He succeeded. The name of the cape was changed to *The Cape of Good Hope.* Until Jesus died and rose again, death was a cape of storms. He rounded the cape of death, and has "begotten us again unto a lively hope" by His triumph over death. Because He lives, we, too, will live everlastingly!
—W. B. K.

* * *

A song of sunshine through the rain,
Of spring across the snow,
A balm to heal the hurts of pain,
A peace surpassing woe!
Lift up your heads, ye sorrowing ones,
And be ye glad of heart,
For Calvary and Easter Day,
Earth's saddest day and gladdest day,
Were just three days apart!

* * *

When the weary ones we love
Enter on their rest above,
Seems the earth so poor and vast?
All our earth-joy overcast?
Hush! be every murmur dumb,
It is only "till He come!"

* * *

When Canadian and British soldiers had taken Fricourt on the Somme in July, 1916, the village cemetery was found to have been heaved by German shells as if by an earthquake. When the peasants of the village returned to their village, they asked, "Where are our dead?" Someone said comfortingly, "Our departed dead were never there!"
Of our loved ones who die in the Lord, we can confidently say: "Absent from the body — at home with the Lord" (see II Cor. 5:8). —W. B. K.

How thrilling was the news of the capture of Jerusalem by General Allenby during World War I! Before the Turks evacuated the Holy City, they hastened to the famous tomb of Jesus. They, according to a press dispatch, "robbed it of all its treasures." Not so! That tomb was divested of its real Treasure some two thousand years previously when the glorified Christ emerged triumphantly from it. —W. B. K.

* * *

If the heavenly Father deigns to touch with divine power the cold and pulseless heart of a buried acorn and make it burst forth from its prison walls, will He leave buried in the earth the body of man made in the image of his Creator? —William Jennings Bryan

* * *

Two little birds built their nest in a garden. Little Bonny Jean found the nest. There were four speckled eggs in it. "How pretty they are," she said. Weeks later her brother went with her to see the beautiful eggs. Looking into the nest, she saw only broken, empty shells. "Oh," she said as she picked up the broken shells, "the pretty eggs are all spoiled now!" "No, no," said her brother, "they are not spoiled. The best part of them has taken wings and has flown away!" —W. B. K.

* * *

I feel in myself the future life. I am like a forest that has been more than once cut down. The new shoots are stronger and livelier than ever. I am rising, I know, toward the sky. When I go down to the grave I can say, like so many others, that I have finished my day's work, but I cannot say I have finished my life. My day's work will begin the next morning. The tomb is not a blind alley — it is a thoroughfare. It closes with the twilight to open with the dawn! —Victor Hugo

Illustrations

What Made the Difference?

I saw a man who did not believe in Christ bid his little six-year-old girl farewell. He kissed her little face and fingered the curls about her ears for

a moment, then turned away from the little white casket in utter despair, saying, "Farewell forever!" Then the mother, who was a Christian, came. She stroked the forehead and kissed the face of the little girl. "Though you have been with us for only six years, life is richer and sweeter, my darling little girl," said the mother. "Good night! I'll be with you and with our Lord in the morning!"

—Told by Dr. George W. Truett

* * *

The Best Story in the World!

A missionary couple and their children went on a sight-seeing tour in Costa Rica. The youngest of the children was six-year-old Mark. They visited a Catholic cathedral in Cargago. The children noticed the many images, including a statue of Christ hanging on the cross. Later they visited an old Spanish mission. Some of the children were frightened when they saw a wax figure of Christ in a glass-enclosed casket.

That night, during family devotions, little Mark said, "Daddy, I have seen Jesus *dead* so many times today. Please tell me again the story of the resurrection!" After listening to the story he said, "Daddy, that's the *best story* in the whole world!" —W. B. K.

* * *

The Strife Is Over!

The strife is o'er, the battle done;
Now is the Victor's triumph won;
Now be the song of praise begun, —
Hallelujah!

The powers of death have done their worst,
But Christ their legions hath dispersed;
Let shouts of holy joy outburst, —
Hallelujah!

The three sad days have quickly sped;
He rises glorious from the dead;
All glory to our risen Head!
Hallelujah!
—*Selected*

* * *

What Easter Means to Me

The Lord who took on our life had to die to give us His divine life. But death could not keep Him, so He rose again on the third day. My deepest rejoicing is in the living Word of God assuring us of the victory of Jesus over death, for I know that the little Child who was

born in Bethlehem had to suffer before I could be saved. I cannot therefore be grateful enough to Him. I pray that I daily may know Him more and more, that I do not harden my heart when He speaks to me, that when He clearly speaks to me, I may obey Him, and that above all I may adore Him as my God and Saviour.

If we love Him above everything else in life, He will give us power to master our problems, overcome our fears and rise above every temptation and every sin. And then we shall be granted a foretaste of life eternal even in this mortal life. —Dr. Charles H. Malik, former President of the United Nations General Assembly, and former Ambassador to the United States from Lebanon, now a professor of government at Dartmouth College

* * *

They'll Live Again!

Springtime, in her royal garment,
Spreads new beauty on the hills,
I can hear her softly singing
In the valleys and the rills!

I can feel her fingers moving
Through the freshly leafing trees,
Sending forth her warm caresses,
On the flower-scented breeze!

I can see her shuttles flying
Through the fields of growing grain,
Giving credence to the story:
Though men die, they'll live again!
—Alice Whitson Norton

* * *

Bone to His Bone

In the Ryukyu Islands, a chain of islands which were formerly a Japanese possession, Dr. E. R. Bull, a missionary, found on the Island of Amajusa a mammoth grave. A boulder marked its site. An inscription on the boulder read: "Here lie the heads of 11,111 Christians," and the year 1637. That was the year the Japanese exterminated all Christians. Only the heads were placed in the grave. Their bodies were buried elsewhere. "That's queer," thought Dr. Bull. When he made inquiry in Nagasaki, he was told that when the missionaries preached the resurrection, they said the Christians would rise again, and the murderous shoguns, fearful that the resurrection was an actuality, conjured up a novel strategy. They buried the heads and the bodies of the martyred Christians separately, believing that this would make it impossible for them to rise again.

How apropos are the words of Jesus "Ye do err, not knowing the scriptures, nor the power of God" (Matt. 22:29), and also Ezekiel's realistic description of the resurrection: "The bones came together, bone to his bone" (Ezek. 37:7). —W. B. K.

* * *

Easter Day

Tomb, thou shalt not hold Him longer,
Death is strong, but life is stronger;
Stronger than the dark, the light;
Stronger than the wrong, the right;
Faith and hope triumphant say:
"Christ will rise on Easter day!"

While the patient earth lies waiting
Till the morning shall be breaking,
Shuddering 'neath the burden dread
Of her Master, cold and dead,
Hark! she hears the angels say:
"Christ will rise on Easter day!"

And when sunrise smites the mountains,
Pouring light from heavenly fountains,
Then the earth blooms out to greet
Once again the blessed feet;
And her countless voices say:
"Christ has risen on Easter day!"
        —Phillips Brooks

* * *

Mommy, If I Hold Your Hand

What interesting and thought-provoking questions little children can ask! Has not God said about them: "Whom shall I teach knowledge? and whom shall he make to understand doctrine? them that are weaned from the milk and drawn from the breast" (Isa. 28:9)?

"Mommy, if I hold your hand when you go to heaven, will I go with you?" asked a little three-year-old boy.

The valley of the shadow of death is a through way for God's children, not a blind alley, but it is so narrow that not even a little child can go through

it with his mother. "One at the time" is the order to those entering it.

There is One, however, who meets God's children at death's portals and goes with them through the valley — Jesus. Not even death can separate them from His love and tender care: "For I am persuaded, that neither death nor life . . . shall be able to separate us from the love of God which is in Christ Jesus our Lord" (Rom. 8:38, 39).
        —W. B. K.

* * *

Light After Darkness

"It was night."
Darkest that was ever seen;
Treachery, desperate and mean;
"Friends" on whom He could not lean.
    It was night!
Night for Him — and for them night
For they could not bear the sight,
So they left Him in their fright
    That dark night.

"Morning light!"
"Very early" in the dawn
Of that resurrection morn
Hope was dead. But joy was born.
    O the light!
"Mary" was the name He said;
"Master!" — Gone was all her dread;
He was living, and not dead,
    Glory light.

It will be bright!
When the Morning Star shall shine,
When the joyful "shout" is Thine,
When in Glory — "Thine are Mine."
    Gone: the dark night.
All the sin, shame, sorrow, past;
All the shadows suffering cast;
Tears all wiped away at last!
    Eternal light!
        —Selected

* * *

Glory in the Highest!

Easter flowers are blooming bright,
Easter skies pour radiant light;
Christ our Lord is risen in might,
    Glory in the highest.

Angels caroled this sweet lay,
When in manger rude He lay;
Now once more cast grief away,
    Glory in the highest.

He, then born to grief and pain,
Now to glory born again,
Calleth forth our gladdest strain,
   Glory in the highest.

As He riseth, rise we, too,
Tune we heart and voice anew,
Offering homage glad and true,
   Glory in the highest.
                          —*Selected*

The Question of a Jewess

An aged Jewess was hospitalized during the Easter season. Over the radio in her room she listened to several messages which emphasized the triumph of the Messiah over death. Sobering thoughts raced through her mind. "Could it be possible, after all, that Christ arose from the dead, and that He is the true Messiah?" So concerned was she that when her husband entered the room, she spoke to him about the thoughts which persisted in her mind. She asked him, "Could it be that we have missed something?"

Later she died. We have the fond hope that the living One revealed Himself to her as her *only hope* of eternal life. —W. B. K.

He Is Risen!

He is risen! Earth awakes
And her prison-house forsakes.
Hear the glad bird-voices sing —
"Where, O Death, is now thy sting?"
Winds their silver trumpets blow —
"He hath conquered every foe."
Soft the murmuring waters say —
"Lo, the stone is rolled away."
   He is risen, He is risen,
Christ the Lord is risen today.

He is risen! Heart rejoice,
Hear you not the angel's voice?
Though you wait beside the tomb,
There is light within its gloom;
Grave, where is thy victory?
He hath set thy captives free,
He hath robbed thee of thy prey,
They with Him shall live alway.
   He is risen, He is risen,
Christ the Lord is risen today.
               —Annie Johnson Flint

Heavenly Home Just Beyond

An aged minister was lost on an unpaved, unmarked road in west Texas. He went to a farmhouse to inquire as to how he could reach his destination. A little freckle-faced boy gave the following directions: "Go right on down the big road for several miles. It is plenty sandy and rough. Sometimes you will bog down and get stuck, but keep going until you come to a graveyard. Go right through the graveyard and just on the other side you will come to a paved highway. Turn to the right and the place you are looking for is just around the corner. When you get to the paved road beyond the graveyard, your troubles will be over!"

The old minister thought as he rode along: "I am traveling down the rough road of life. Sometimes it seems that I almost bog down. After I travel life's road for a few more miles, I will come to the graveyard, and then my troubles will all be over, for God's highway and the heavenly home are just the other side of the cemetery!" —W. B. K.

Ballistic Missile Expert Testifies

Today, more than ever before, our survival — yours and mine and our children's — depends on our adherence to ethical principles. Ethics alone will decide whether atomic energy will be an earthly blessing or the source of mankind's utter destruction.

Where does the desire for ethical action come from? What makes us want to be ethical? I believe there are two forces which move us. One is belief in a Last Judgment, when every one of us has to account for what we did with God's great gift of life on the earth. The other is belief in an immortal soul, a soul which will cherish the award or suffer the penalty decreed in a final Judgment.

Belief in God and in immortality thus gives us the moral strength and the ethical guidance we need for virtually every action in our daily lives.

In our modern world many people seem to feel that science has somehow made such "religious ideas" untimely or old-fashioned.

But I think science has a real surprise for the skeptics. Science, for instance, tells us that nothing in nature, not even the tiniest particle, can disappear without a trace.

Think about that for a moment. Once you do, your thoughts about life will never be the same. Science has found that nothing can disappear without a trace. Nature does not know extinction. All it knows is transformation!

Now, if God applies this fundamental principle to the most minute and insignificant parts of His universe, doesn't it make sense to assume that He applies it also to the masterpiece of His creation — the human soul? I think it does. And everything science has taught me — and continues to teach me — strengthens my belief in the continuity of our spiritual existence after death. *Nothing disappears without a trace.*

—Dr. Von Braun,
Development Operations
Director, Army Ballistic
Missile Agency

My Redeemer Lives

"I know that my Redeemer lives,"
  Oh, precious thought to me;
Though death abounds on every hand,
  He lives eternally.
Death cannot lay its blighting hand
Upon that Blessed One,
As Prince of Life, He conquered it,
Its sting and power are gone.

"I know that my Redeemer lives,"
  I know too that He died;
I also know He rose in power,
  And has been glorified.
And now He sits on yonder throne,
God's object of delight,
Angels and saints adore Him there
While ages take their flight.

I know that my Redeemer bore
  My sins on Calvary's tree,
He paid the debt I could not pay,
  And thus He set me free.
I know He intercedes above,
  In courts of light for me;
His life up there maintains me here,
  Whose death has made me free.
—C. C. Crowston

REVERENCE—IRREVERENCE

Illustrations

You've Undone Their Labor

Josiah Wedgwood, maker of the famous Wedgwood pottery, one day showed a nobleman through the factory. A boy who was an employee of the factory accompanied them. The nobleman was profane and vulgar. At first the boy was shocked by the nobleman's irreverence. Then he became fascinated by his coarse jokes and laughed heartily. Mr. Wedgwood was distressed. At the conclusion of the tour, he showed the nobleman a vase of unique design. The man was charmed with its exquisite shape and rare beauty. As he reached for it, Mr. Wedgwood designedly let it fall to the floor. The nobleman uttered an angry oath! "I wanted that vase for my collection," he said, "and you have ruined it by your care-

lessness!" Mr. Wedgwood answered, "Sir, there are other ruined things more precious than a vase, howsoever valuable, which can never be restored. You can never give back to that boy, who has just left us, the reverence for sacred things which his parents have tried to teach him for years! You have undone their labor in less than half an hour!"
—*Good News Digest*

• • •

They Took a Bath!

Profoundest reverence characterized the ancient copyists of the Scriptures. It is said that when they came to a name for Deity, they put new pens into their writing instruments, took a bath, and changed raiment. What a far cry from that is our present-day irreverence for things sacred. With flippant, barefaced irreverence we intrude into those places where sinless angels tread with veiled faces and hesitant steps.

—Rev. Paul Kreiss

* * *

Why Hatred Vanished

Some Scottish soldiers were cut off from their company while in fierce engagement with the enemy during World War II. They hid in the loft of an empty house. Death seemed to be inevitable. The Germans were setting fire to surrounding homes and buildings. Nearer and nearer they came to the hiding place of the Scottish lads. Said one of them, "It's time for church, partners. Let's hae a wee bit of service here. It may be oor last!" He took a New Testament from his pocket and after reading some verses, he said, "I'm no' a gude hand at this job, but let us finish it off with prayer." After a pause, he began to read reverently and feelingly — "Our Father, which art in heaven, Hallowed be thy name." About midway the prayer, they heard a click of heels. They knew the Germans were below, standing reverently at attention! After the prayer, the Scottish lads heard the door close silently, and the sounds of footsteps dying away. Marked reverence for things sacred created an atmosphere in which hatred vanished. —W. B. K.

* * *

How Big Is Your God?

"You must have a small God," said a Mohammedan to an American tourist. "Oh, no," quickly replied the American, "we have a great and mighty God, at whose word of command, the universe and all that is therein came into existence!" "Still I believe you Americans have a small God, for when you pray to Him, you do it so indifferently and irreverently. When we Mohammedans pray, we fall prone on our faces in acknowledgment of the mightiness of God." Who would say that the worshiper of the false prophet, Mohammed, did not have a talking point? Sinless angels, in approaching God, veil their faces as they adoringly and reverently say, "Holy, holy, holy, is the Lord of hosts: the

whole earth is full of his glory" (Isa. 6:3). Sinful man doesn't.

—Dr. J. C. Macaulay

* * *

Chatterboxes

A young lady, under deep conviction of sin, entered a church. She sat near the front. In the pew ahead of her was a row of young ladies who were professed Christians, the daughters of church leaders. During the service they whispered, exchanged notes and snapshots of themselves and their boy friends. Their irreverence so disturbed and distressed the convicted girl that all thoughts of seeking the Saviour vanished and she arose and went out of the church, disgusted and unsaved. Before the judgment bar of God, those flippant, frivolous girls will have to give an account for a soul convicted of sin, but not converted to God.

"But the Lord is in his holy temple: let all the earth keep silence before him" (Hab. 2:20).

—Told by Rev. C. Leslie Miller

* * *

Blazing Eyes, and Roped Heifers

In my earlier years, I was a news correspondent. Often I reported Bible conferences in which world-famed Bible teachers spoke. Once, as Dr. R. A. Torrey was speaking, two young ladies, in the rear of the auditorium, began to whisper and snicker. Dr. Torrey suddenly stopped speaking. His eyes seemed to blaze as he sternly and severely rebuked the girls for their irreverence! They were deeply wounded. Should he have dealt more kindly with them?

Billy Sunday had a similar situation in one of his meetings. Observing the misbehavior of two girls, who sat near the front of the tabernacle, he called out, "Ushers, come and rope these two heifers and carry them out of the tabernacle!"

Possibly none of us could thus speak to anyone without greatly grieving the Spirit of God, though irreverence in the house of God must not be condoned.

—W. B. K.

Ask God's Forgiveness

An army chaplain said: "Occasionally soldiers would unintentionally curse and swear in my hearing. On second thought, they would immediately say, 'Pardon me, Chaplain.' I would reply: 'I can readily forgive you for taking the name of my Lord profanely in my presence. But your sin is primarily against God. It is His name, not mine, that you profaned. You should go to God and say, 'Pardon me, merciful God.'" —W. B. K.

* * *

Worse Than the Heathen

Dr. Scudder, the missionary, after long absence, was returning from India to England with his son, a fine lad. In their presence a man on the deck of the steamship was interlarding his conversation with a great deal of foul, impious talk. "Look here, friend," the missionary said, addressing the blasphemer, "this son of mine was born and bred in a heathen country, in a land where heathen idol-worship has its home. But in all his life he has never heard a human being curse his Creator until now!" The man reddened and mumbled what had to pass for an apology.

—*The Bible Friend*

* * *

Ask God's Apology

President Woodrow Wilson took great pleasure in referring to his father, the Rev. Joseph R. Wilson, who was a distinguished Presbyterian minister. "Father was once in the company of some men who were having a heated discussion. In the midst of their animated talk a man emitted a volley of curse words, coupled with the name of God. Then he remembered that father was present! He instantly apologized, saying, 'Dr. Wilson, I had forgotten that you were present. Please pardon me.' Father's reply was, 'It is not to me that you own your apology, but to God!'" —W. B. K.

REVIVAL

Short Quotes

How impotent are movements to heal the nation's hurts which exclude God, and fail to reckon with man's sinfulness and need of the Saviour! A revival of the old-time religion, with resultant confessing and forsaking of sin, would do much to solve juvenile and parental problems. —W .B. K.

* * *

A mighty spiritual revival in the Church of Christ is the fundamental need of the hour; it is the only thing that will avail. In view of the tremendous issues involved, both to an embarrassed Church and to a dying world, unceasing prayer should ascend to God day and night from every loyal and discerning heart, for such a revival. When it comes, the problems of missionary recruits and missionary support will be solved. When it comes, a new volume of missionary intercession will release the omnipotence of God, before which every obstacle will give way, every opposing force will be rendered impotent, the whole enterprise of world evangelization will move firmly onward to its consummation and "the ends of the earth shall see the salvation of our God." —Robert H. Glover, M.D.

* * *

Revive Thy work, O Lord,
  And manifest Thy power;
O come upon Thy church and give
  A penitential shower!

Revive Thy work, O Lord,
  And make Thy servant bold;
Convict of sin and work once more,
  As in the days of old!

* * *

Mass evangelism, good as it may be, is necessary only because the church is unhealthy. The church is fundamental and orthodox, but it has little spiritual life. —Redpath

We fail oftentimes to reckon with the *expulsive* power of the gospel: "And of the rest durst no man join himself to them" (Acts 5:13). Not *quantity*, but *quality* is the crying need of the church. The true pastor's heart is often saddened by the many names of unsaved ones cluttering up the church roll. Said David Livingstone, "Nothing will induce me to form an impure church. Fifty added to the church sounds well at home, but if only five are genuine what will it profit in the day of judgment?"
—Rev. Vance Havner

* * *

Since a revival can never lay hold upon the world until it has first laid hold on the church, the need is for the fountains of sin to be broken up in the church. Backslidden Christians must be brought to repentance. They must have their faith renewed. Before the world can be moved, we must renew the image of Jesus Christ in ourselves. It is vain even to call upon the church to love others when the church has ceased loving Christ first. —Charles G. Finney

People generally are realizing that without a spiritual awakening no peace or other plans will be much good. Nations cannot be depended upon to co-operate and stick to their agreements unless *they recognize God as their real Ruler and Guide.* —Roger Babson

* * *

I am afraid of any religious movement that does not arouse the bitter opposition of entrenched evil. You will remember that our Lord once cast the demons out of a man and the demons entered the hogs. The hogs committed suicide and the hog-owners asked Jesus to leave the country. When the power of God casts out the devil, all hog-owners whose business is affected will raise a protest. A real revival today would cause a commotion in the traffic of evil.
—Rev. Vance Havner

* * *

Our scientific achievements have brought mankind to that place in history where revival of spiritual values is the basic condition for human survival. —Joseph H. Jackson, D.D.

Illustrations

Offerings for Baal

Smouldering revival fires were beginning to glow with white-hot intensity in a Southern church. God's power was upon the visiting evangelist and souls were being saved. Backslidden, worldly Christians were turning from their evil ways to God.

A unique feature of the services was that at the front of the church, in view of everyone, a large basket was placed. Above it was a placard on which was printed in large letters: OFFERINGS FOR BAAL. As God's Spirit convicted His children of their sins, they would write them on pieces of paper, read aloud what was written thereon, and then place the paper in the basket. Some wrote pride, covetousness, envy, malice, hatred, unforgiveness, prayerlessness, unfaithfulness to God and His church, backbiting, slander, lying, and other foul sins of the spirit or disposition. Others brought unused portions

of plugs of tobacco and packages of cigarettes.

Oh, that such a moving of God's Spirit were evidenced in all churches, with resultant cleaning up of lives and victorious living! Then we would have a heaven-sent, Holy Ghost empowered revival of the old-time religion, and we would experience a spiritual awakening such as the present generation has never witnessed.

God has but one recipe for revival: "If my people, which are called by my name, shall humble themselves, and pray, and seek my face, and turn from their wicked ways; then will I hear from heaven, and will forgive their sin, and will heal their land" (II Chron. 7:14). —Told by Phil Marquart, M.D.

* * *

Why There Was No Revival

Henry Morehouse, a young minister, was greatly used of God to bring souls to Christ. He preached with great power in revivals in England and America. In one of his meetings, however, everything was at a standstill. He gave himself to earnest prayer. "O God," he implored, "why am I not preaching with unction and power? Why are the people so unresponsive? Why are souls not being saved?"

God gave him the answer to his questions as he walked down a street. On a billboard he read some flattering words about himself: "Hear the most famous of all British preachers — Henry Morehouse!" God seemed to say to him, "That's why there is no revival." He went immediately to those in charge of the meeting and said, "No wonder we can't have a revival. No wonder the Holy Spirit cannot work. You have advertised me as the greatest this and the greatest that. The Spirit is grieved because we have not magnified the Lord Jesus Christ, and ascribed all glory to His mighty name. He is the wonderful One. I am only a voice saying, 'Behold the Lamb of God!'"

—W. B. K.

. . .

Where's the Revival?

Years ago God gave a great revival to the Welsh people who got right with God and with one another. Many were converted. Those coming from afar to the meetings would inquire of the policemen, "Where's the revival?" Snapping to attention, and with a glow on their faces, they would reply, as they pointed to their hearts, "Ah, the revival is here!" That is where the revival we need, *must* start — in your heart and in *my* heart. Not until God's children sincerely pray, "Create in *me* a clean heart, O God; and renew a right spirit within *me*," will we have that sleepless, solicitous concern for the lost and perishing ones about us. Draw a circle, place yourself in that circle, and as you stand there, with sorrow of heart,

pray this prayer, "O, God, send a revival, and let it start in this circle!" Then the revival will be on! —W. B. K.

. . .

Clogged Channels!

It is my firm conviction, as deepseated as my faith in God, that there is one reason why we are not having great victories and that is because the channels of our lives are clogged. My Bible still says that the fervent, effectual prayer of a righteous man availeth much. I do not care what the circumstances are. If the evangelist, if the pastor, if half a dozen people in the church are right with God, you will have some kind of victory. . . . I used to think that in order to have a revival we had to have every person in the church right. I used to scold, and nag, and drive, and criticize Christians, just beat them over the head. But I have found out that not even God can revive everybody in a church. Some of them have never been "vived" and they cannot be revived. They have nothing to revive. —Appleman

. . .

Needed — A Great Crisis

Our time suffers from moral uncertainty. We have plenty of levity but little happiness. There is searching for fun but no real joy. There is plenty of laughter but it is cruel and in bad taste. We are zealous for democracy and weak in worship. There is boasting over muscular strength but it is brutal in application. We have everything but possess nothing. We seek knowledge but lack understanding. There is plenty of struggle upward but we continue to sink lower. Our civilization needs the panic of a great crisis to shock it out of its Pharisaism. We must have a rebirth of moral conviction in order to fulfill the purpose of our being. —*Watchman-Examiner*

REWARDS

Illustrations

Barely Saved!

One time, Dr. R. E. Neighbour preached a sermon on the possibility of God's children being saved "so as by fire" and receiving no rewards when they stand before Christ. After the service, the minister walked home with a wealthy businessman who said, "I didn't like that sermon about the possibility of some Christians barely entering heaven and not receiving any rewards for faithful service. Why, I will be satisfied if I just get inside of heaven and can lean against its walls!" At that moment the two reached the palatial home of the wealthy businessman. It was filled with all the luxuries that money could buy. How different was the wealthy man's thinking about his earthly home and his thinking about his heavenly home.

Let us aspire to enter glory abundantly and triumphantly. Peter said, "For so an entrance shall be ministered unto you abundantly into the everlasting kingdom of our Lord and Saviour Jesus Christ" (II Peter 1:11).

—W. B. K.

* * *

Rewarded for Trying

Opening a window of his fifth-story room, a minister in London heard some beautiful singing below. A blind man stood on the street corner, singing and holding out a badly worn hat to passers-by. Leaving his room, the minister went to the singer, spoke cheerfully to him, and put a shilling in his hat. The blind man profusely thanked the donor and said, "I'll sing a hymn — just for you!" At close range there was no melodious beauty in the blind man's voice. The minister thought, "His voice is cracked. How different were the tones which came up to me in my room higher up!"

As the minister walked away, he mused: "If his singing was sweet to me higher up, his singing must be infinitely sweeter to God, the 'high and lofty one that inhabiteth eternity!'

Surely our songs and sincere efforts are glorified as they ascend to the heavenly Father. He rewards us for what we aspire to do for Him, even though we may fail in the effort or do it imperfectly." —W. B. K.

* * *

Czar Nicholas Rewards Hospitality

When Czar Nicholas ruled the Russians, he wanted to test the hospitality of his subjects. Dressed as a beggar, he knocked at several doors, asking for food and shelter. He was rudely rebuffed by many. Finally, at nightfall, he knocked at the humble cottage of a peasant. The peasant was poor and his wife was ill. He said to the stranger, "We have little, but what we have, we'll share with you!" Taking the "beggar" in, the peasant gave him warm, wholesome food. For sleeping accommodations, the best he could provide for the stranger was a pallet on the floor. All settled down for the night's rest. Rising early in the morning, the peasant discovered that the stranger had disappeared. Some days thereafter, as the peasant and his convalescing wife sat near the door of their cottage, they saw a group of soldiers marching on the road, coming toward their cottage. Behind the soldiers was a beautiful carriage, drawn by four magnificent horses. "Oh, wife," exclaimed the peasant, "what have I done? The soldiers are coming to arrest me!" But presently his fears turned into rejoicing! Coming to a halt before the cottage, Czar Nicholas alighted from the royal coach and greeted the peasant and his wife graciously. Then he showered rich rewards upon them as he told them that it was he who, a few nights previously, had been welcomed into their cottage as a beggar.

It is ours, in this age, to serve the "despised and rejected" One, the Lord Jesus, and "go forth ... unto him without the camp, bearing his reproach" (Heb. 13:13). When He returns as "King of kings and Lord of lords," He will richly reward us for all we have done for Him, for He has promised: "For the Son of man shall come in the glory of his Father . . . and then he shall reward every man according to his works" (Matt. 16:27). —W. B. K.

* * *

Does It Count if I Try?

It was bedtime. The room of little five-year-old Julie Ann was a shambles. Books, toys, dolls and stuffed animals were strewn all over the floor. Her mother said, "Julie Ann, you know you shouldn't scatter your playthings all over your room." Julie Ann's face looked sad. Sadly she said, "Mommie, I try to keep things straight. Doesn't it even count if I try?"

God will reward us for all we sincerely try to do for Him even though we fail. —W. B. K.

* * *

Cross-bearers and Crown-wearers

A faithful missionary was asked: "What pay do you receive for the hardships you undergo and the sacrifices you make, living and working among these people?" The missionary took from his pocket a letter, worn with much handling, and read two sentences from it, written by a Chinese student: "But for you, I would not have known Jesus Christ, our Saviour. Every morning I kneel before God, and think of you, thank God for you and pray for you!" "That," said the missionary, "is my pay!"

Spurgeon said: "There are no crown-wearers in heaven who were not cross-bearers on earth. Hast thou a cross, Shoulder it manfully. It is Christ's cross and it is an honor to carry it."

—W. B. K.

* * *

A Good Action Brings a Good Reward

Baron Rothschild was one of the richest men in the world in his day. One day he visited the studio of his artist friend, Ary Scheffer, who said, "I need a beggar to sit for a painting." "Wait until tomorrow," said Rothschild. "I'll dress as a beggar and make an excellent model." The next day, the financier appeared, dressed in rags. Just then, another friend of the artist entered the studio. He looked in pity upon the "beggar." He gave him a louis d'or — a French gold coin — which was received with thanks. Ten years later, the man who gave the coin received an order on the bank of the Rothschilds for ten thousand francs, accompanied by the following note: Sir, you one day gave a louis d'or to Baron Rothschild in the studio of Ary Scheffer. He has invested it, and made good use of it, and today he sends you the capital you entrusted to him, together with the interest it has gained. A good action is always followed by a good reward.

—James Rothschild

* * *

Penny and the Fifth of Scotch

J. C. Penny, the merchant prince, ran a butcher shop before his chain store empire came into being. He was told that if he gave a fifth of Scotch to the head chef in a leading hotel, the business of that hotel would be assured. This Penny did for some time. Then God convicted him of the wrong of the practice. He discontinued it and lost the hotel's business. He went broke. God, however, had "better things" for him, and, in time, he began a merchandise business which has grown into a nationwide enterprise!

—Howard H. Hamlin, M.D.

* * *

God's Pay

Who does God's work will get God's pay,
However long may seem the day,
However weary be the way;
Though powers and princes thunder "Nay,"
Who does God's work will get God's pay.

He does not pay as others pay,
In gold or land or raiment gay;
In goods that vanish and decay;
But God in wisdom knows a way,
And that is sure, let come what may,
Who does God's work will get God's pay.

—*Selected*

* * *

Cross Becomes Crown

God laid upon my back a grievous load,
A heavy cross to bear along the road.
I staggered on, and lo! one weary day,
An angry lion sprang across my way.

I prayed to God, and swift at His com-
mand,
The cross became a weapon in my hand.
It slew my raging enemy, and then
Became a cross upon my back again.
I reached a desert. O'er the burning
track
I persevered — the cross upon my back.
No shade was there, and in the cruel
sun
I sank at last, and thought my day was
done.
But lo! The Lord works many a blest
surprise,

The cross became a tree before my very
eyes!
I slept — I woke — to feel the strength
of ten,
I found the cross upon my back again.
And so through all my days from then
to this,
The cross — my burden — has become
my bliss.
Nor ever shall I lay my burden down.
For God some day will make my cross a
crown.

—Amos R. Wells

RICHES

Short Quotes

Make money honestly — lots of it;
use it wisely — all of it; and dedicate
it religiously — every last cent of it.
—Rev. Herschel H. Hobbs, D.D.

* * *

Earn all you can; save all you can;
give all you can.
—John Wesley

* * *

The poorest man I know is the man
who has nothing but money.
—John D. Rockefeller, Jr.

* * *

A man is rich in proportion to the
number of things he can afford to let
alone. —Thoreau

* * *

There are two ways to be rich —
one is to have all you want, and the
other is to be satisfied with what you
have: "And having food and raiment
let us be therewith content" (I Tim.
6:8). —W. B. K.

* * *

Andrew Carnegie, the multimillionaire, sat in a dining room in a swanky
hotel. Before him was untouched food.
His health was failing and his appetite
was gone. He chanced to look out of a
window and saw a working man sitting
on a curbstone, heartily enjoying his
noonday lunch. Exclaimed Carnegie:
"I'd give a million dollars to have an
appetite like that man!" —W. B. K.

Oftentimes the most discontented and
fearful people are those who have great
riches. When Calouste Gulbenkian died
in 1955, he left a fortune of $420 mil-
lion! Did riches bring him happiness
and peace? Never! He lived in constant fear. An electric barrier surrounded his home in Paris and many
private guards and spies guarded him
and his mansion.
—*The Watchman-Examiner*

* * *

To purchase heaven, has gold the power?
Can gold remove the mortal hour?
In life can love be bought with gold?
Are friendship's pleasures to be sold?
No, all that's worth a wish, a thought,
Fair virtue gives unbrib'd, unbought,
Cease then on trash thy hopes to bind,
Let nobler views engage thy mind!
—Samuel Johnson

* * *

It is not the fact that a man has riches which keeps him from the kingdom
of heaven, but the fact that the riches
have him. —David Gaird

* * *

Those who live for money spend the
first half of their lives getting all they
can from everybody else and the last
half trying to keep everybody else from
getting what they have away from them,
and they find no pleasure in either half.
—William Jennings Bryan

Special requests for prayer were being made by different people who had assembled in the place of prayer. The pastor stood up. A serious look was on his face. It was evident that something of a deep concern was on his heart. Requested he, "Oh, pray, and pray earnestly, for Brother .... He has inherited $150,000!"

"And when thy . . . gold is multiplied . . . and thou forget the Lord thy God" (Deut. 8:13, 14).

—Rev. Paul T. Stengele

* * *

Treasures in heaven are laid up only as treasures on earth are laid down.

* * *

I warn you that it will go hard with you when the Lord comes to reckon with you if He finds your wealth hoarded up in needless accumulation instead of being carefully devoted to giving the gospel to the lost. —A. J. Gordon

* * *

Someone asked John D. Rockefeller, Sr., "How much money does it take to satisfy a man?" "Just a little bit more than he has, which means that money is powerless to satisfy those who waste their life acquiring and hoarding it."

* * *

Lord Congelton heard a servant say, "Oh, if I only had five pounds! I would be contented." Lord Congelton, who heard her, gave her a five-pound note. She thanked him profusely. As she left him, she said in an undertone, thinking that her benefactor wouldn't hear her, "Why didn't I say ten!"

* * *

Money is the article which may be used as a universal passport to everywhere except heaven, and the universal provider of everything except happiness. —A London newspaper

Money and time are the heaviest burdens of life, and the unhappiest of all mortals are those who have more of either than they know how to use.

—Samuel Johnson

* * *

Though America has only 6 per cent of the population of the world, we have 50 per cent of the income of the world.

—Dr. Bob Pierce

* * *

Spoken by a saintly woman,
Dying on an attic floor,
Having not one earthly comfort:
    "I have Christ! What want I
    more?"

You may have gold and grandeur,
    And yet be counted poor,
He alone has riches truly,
    Who has Christ, though nothing
    more!

—*Selected*

* * *

I will place no value on anything I have or may possess except in its relation to the kingdom of Christ. If anything I have will advance the interests of that kingdom, it shall be given up, or kept, as by keeping or giving it I shall most promote the glory of Him to whom I owe all my hopes, both in time and eternity. —David Livingstone

* * *

Do good with what thou hast, or it will do no good. —William Penn

* * *

Money may be the husk of many things, but not the kernel. It brings you food, but not appetite; medicine, but not health; acquaintances, but not friends; servants, but not loyalty; days of joy, but not lasting peace or joy.

—Henrik Ibsen

Illustrations

Only an Empty Hole

Arthur J. Morris, banker and founder of The Morris Plan, was fond of relating a fable of a miser who buried his gold in a hole in a field. Every night he went to count it and gloat over it. A servant discovered the gold and ran

off with it. The rich man screamed in despair. A friend suggested, "You really haven't lost a thing. The money wasn't doing you or anybody else any good. You still have the hole left. Why don't you pretend the gold is there, and come and look at the hole every night?"

"Dealing with men and money for over forty years, there is one clear lesson I've learned — anyone who seeks only gold will look at an empty hole every night," said Mr. Morris —W. B. K.

* * *

Spiritual Riches

A little girl, on her way to church, was stopped by some soldiers. When the soldiers asked her where she was going she replied, "Please Sirs, I am on my way to my Father's House to hear the reading of my Elder Brother's will, for I am one of his heirs." So saying she was allowed to proceed to the church, undisturbed; for it was there that the minister read and explained the Bible, the last will and testament of our Elder Brother Jesus Christ. And He is our Elder Brother too; for we are all heirs of God and joint heirs with Jesus Christ. But, like this little Scotch girl, we must claim this inheritance if we are to enjoy it. And best of all, we live in a country where Bible reading and churchgoing are not forbidden, and where all are free to worship God according to the way He has revealed in His Word.   —M. L. Fearnow, in
The American Holiness Journal

* * *

Possessing our Possessions

Years ago a foreigner left the old country by boat for America. His valise was well stocked with dried herring, cheese and crackers. For breakfast he ate herring, cheese and crackers. For dinner, to vary the fare, he ate cheese, crackers and herring. At supper, he ate crackers, cheese and herring!

The tantalizing smell of good food coming from the ship's dining room caused the foreigner to long for the meals which the other voyagers were enjoying. Just as the ship was nearing New York harbor, the half-starved man went to the ship's purser and asked, "What would one good, square meal cost me?" "Let me see your ticket," said the purser. "Why, man," he exclaimed, "your ticket includes all meals during the voyage!"

How like this man are many of God's children! They sing:

I've reached the land of corn and wine, And all its riches freely mine! Yet, they fail to possess their possessions. God daily spreads a feast of good things, saying, "Come, for all things are now ready!" —W. B. K.

* * *

Riches Enlarge or Enslave Us

One of God's noble laymen, a doctor, was asked what he had done during the past week. He replied, "On Monday, I preached the gospel in Brazil. Tuesday, I ministered among the Mexicans in southwest Texas. Wednesday, I operated on patients in a hospital in Africa. Thursday, I taught in a mission school in Japan. Friday, I helped to establish a new church in California. Saturday, I taught classes in our seminaries. Sunday, I distributed Bibles in Korea." The astonished questioner asked, "How could you be in so many places, doing so many different things?" "I wasn't," said the doctor with a twinkle in his eye, "for I have been busy with my patients every day. But, you see, I hold the dollars God has enabled me to earn in trust for God, and some of them have been channeled into the places of need I have mentioned."
—Told by Rev. Herschel H. Hobbs, D.D.

* * *

I Have Two Footmen

When I was in England I visited Buckingham Palace. I did not go over to see the king; I don't think he knew I was there at all; but I went there with some others and we were shown around. In going through the stables, we were shown a great coach which was used for state occasions. There was a great deal of gold on the coach, and the harness cost $150,000 in our money, I was told, and was overlaid with gold. Up behind the coach were two little seats. I asked what those little seats were for, and was told that they were for two footmen. My mind immediately went back to the Psalm, "Goodness and mercy shall follow me all the days of my life." I said to myself, "They do not know it, but I am a king and I have two footmen."   —From an American correspondent's letter to the
Prophetic News

A Million Dollars and the Electric Chair

Harry S..............., twenty-nine, inherited one million dollars. He did not care about his fortune, however. The electric chair was in his way. He said, "I don't care whether it's one dollar or a million of them. I have something else on my mind!" The vision of the electric chair wouldn't go away. Harry was sentenced to die for the murder of a six-year-old boy. In Statesville Prison he learned of his inheriting the fortune. Commenting on his crime, he said, "They tell me I did it. But in my mind, I don't know. I'd do anything for the family of the boy, but I suppose money wouldn't help them. No, not now!"

"Riches profit not in the day of wrath" (Prov. 11:4). —W. B. K.

* * *

He Went to His Riches

Shortly after the death of her aged Christian father, a young lady visited his associate in business. He was not a Christian. He had lived only to amass riches. He said to the girl, "Your father was a good man. He lived for God and others. His chief joy was to bring happiness to others. I have never known a man more generous with his money. Right up to the end of his beautiful life, his thoughts were of others. In death, he went to his riches. In death, I will leave the riches which I could have used for God and others!" —W. B. K.

* * *

Misplaced Confidence

Years ago a social event of statewide interest took place in Colorado — the wedding of Charles Tabor, a pioneer millionaire miner, to "Baby Doe." Tabor had divorced his wife that he might marry the young, beautiful and popular socialite. It was a gala occasion. One source of Tabor's wealth was the Matchless Mine. For a while, things were rosy and pleasant for the newlyweds. Then reverses came. Tabor lost his vast fortune and succumbed to mortal illness. Before his death he said to his bride, "Cling to the Matchless Mine." He felt that the mine would stage a comeback. She took his advice, but the mine didn't stage the anticipated comeback. She spent the last thirty-six years of her life in poverty, waiting for the mine to bring her wealth and restore her to her former social position. She waited in vain. She died in poverty and without friends. *Her confidence was misplaced.* The question is pertinent: "Wilt thou set thine eyes upon that which is not? for riches certainly make themselves wings; they fly away as an eagle toward heaven" (Prov. 23:5). —W. B. K.

* * *

Rodeheaver Leaves $650,000

Both saints and sinners, in death, leave behind all temporal things: "For we brought nothing into this world, and it is certain that we can carry nothing out" (I Tim. 6:7).

There was much of eternal value Homer Rodeheaver went to when his Lord summoned him to his eternal home: "Eye hath not seen, nor ear heard, neither have entered into the heart of man, the things which God hath prepared for them that love him" (I Cor. 2:9).

The words of the Saviour, who had little or nothing of this world's goods, should speak to our hearts their sobering message: "Lay not up for yourselves treasures upon earth. . . . But lay up for yourselves treasures in heaven" (Matt. 6:19, 20). —W. B. K.

* * *

Idol in Their Hearts

Said a Chinese Christian: "In the city of Foochow they bring out great images and parade them along the streets. In Western lands people have gotten rid of all this nonsense, but they have not gotten rid of the idol in their hearts." "What a man loves, that is his god," wrote Luther. On his return after a journey through Europe, Li Hung Chang declared: "The European god is not so large as the Chinese; it is small, so small that one can take it in the hand, it is round, made of silver and gold, bears weapons and inscriptions, and is called money."

—*Tarbell's Teacher's Guide*

It Isn't Mine

I never look upon the money I can earn as my own. It is public money. It is only a fund entrusted to my care for proper distribution. I am constantly endeavoring to reduce my needs to the minimum. I feel morally guilty in ordering a costly meal, for it deprives someone else of a slice of bread — some child, perhaps, of a bottle of milk. My beloved wife feels exactly as I do. In all these years of my so-called success in music we have not built a house for ourselves. Between it and us stand all the homeless in the world!
—Fritz Kreisler

* * *

What a Fool I've Been!

A rich man lay dying. His little daughter couldn't understand why her big daddy was so helpless now. She asked, "Daddy, are you going away?" "Yes, dear, I am going away, and I am afraid you won't see me again," her father answered. The little girl asked, "Daddy, have you got a nice house to go to?" The rich man was silent for a moment, and then began to cry. He lamented, "What a fool I have been! I have built a great business here and have amassed riches here, but I shall be a pauper there!"
—W. B. K.

* * *

Concern for the Perishing Rich

A night watchman was making his routine rounds in a Southern resort town. It was past the midnight hour. Looking toward the end of the pier which extended into the sea, he saw a man standing. Investigating, he discovered that he who was standing there and peering into the dark waters was one of the millionaire tourists of the town. "Why, what are you doing here at this unearthly hour of the night?" asked the officer. Weeping, the millionaire confided, "I do not believe there is a person alive who cares for me with a disinterested, unselfish love!"

Oftentimes the most neglected ones about us are those who possess great riches. Fawning sycophants toady to the rich, "having men's persons in admiration because of advantage" (Jude 1:16). They often give to them prominent places on boards and committees, not especially to honor any greatness of character in the rich, but to obtain financial gain. How wrong and sinful this is! How abhorrent this is to God who is "no respecter of persons" (Acts 10:34)!

It is all right to go all out in our effort to reach the down-and-out people. It is all wrong to neglect the rich and fail to bring them to Christ. They, too, are precious to God, and we should sincerely love them. —W. B. K.

* * *

My Real Wealth

Toward the close of the last century a young businessman was accumulating riches rapidly. He said to Stephen Paxton, who had known only poverty through the years, "Come with me and we will make a fortune together!" Paxton declined the appealing offer, for God had placed upon his heart the great need of Sunday schools in the thinly populated rural sections of our country. "You are a fool to turn down such an attractive offer," said the businessman. Other people derided him, too, calling him a "crackpot" and a religious fanatic. Years passed. One day he met the man who had made him the business offer. The man said, "You wouldn't come with me. Now I am worth fifty thousand dollars and you and your family still live in a covered wagon!" "But," said Paxton, "you do not know the extent of my real wealth. More than fifty thousand boys, girls, men and women are enrolled in Sunday schools that I organized!" —W. B. K.

* * *

Riches Profit Not in Death

The thirty-year-old heir and only son of a fabulously wealthy manufacturer died a suicide according to a judge. He jumped from a twentieth-floor window to a horrible death below!

Though he was the sole heir of an enormous fortune, his riches were worthless to him when he died: "For we brought nothing into this world, and it is certain we can carry nothing out" (I Tim. 6:7).

Riches profit not in death, nor do they

profit in life if they are hoarded and not used for God and others. They shrivel and corrode the soul. How wretched are the unsaved rich! "I suppose I am the wretchedest wretch who ever lived," said J. Gould late in life after he had become a multimillionaire!
—W. B. K.

• • •

Disadvantages of Riches

Artichokes are really a delicious vegetable when properly cooked, but they are usually so "knobby" they are hard to peel and prepare. . . . "Would you mind picking me some smooth ones?" I asked the man who was selling them. "It is a difficult matter to get smooth artichokes unless you have poor soil to grow them in," he replied. "Is that a fact?" I inquired. "Yes," he replied, "if the soil is rich they grow rough and knobby, and if one wants them smooth they must grow in poor ground." "They must be like some people," I said. "I have always heard that young people who grow up in a rich environment rarely turn out as well as those who have to grow up in poverty." . . . Looking back through the ages, we know that the world has been enriched infinitely more through the poverty of its saints than by the wealth of its millionaires. —*Christian Digest*

• • •

What We Have In Christ

A love that can never be fathomed;
A life that can never die;
A righteousness that can never be tarnished;
A peace that can never be understood;
A rest that can never be disturbed;
A joy that can never be diminished;
A hope that can never be disappointed;
A glory that can never be clouded;
A light that can never be darkened;
A happiness that can never be interrupted;
A strength that can never be enfeebled;
A purity that can never be defiled;
A beauty that can never be marred;
A wisdom that can never be baffled;
Resources that can never be exhausted.
—*Selected*

ROMANS 8:28

Short Quotes

"And we know that all things work together for good to them that love God, to them who are called according to his purpose" (Romans 8:28).

• • •

If the Weaver of our life's pattern chooses another plan than the one we thought to use, is He not wiser than we? Surely it will be a pattern more beautiful than our fondest dreams!
—Rosalie Mills Appleby in
The Life Beautiful

• • •

God never takes away a gift, however small or great, that in its place He does not let another compensate.
—Katherine L. Ramsdale in
Moody Monthly

• • •

A young Christian businessman suffered great sorrow and loss. He first lost his wife and was left with the care of two little children. Then he lost a yearly income of $20,000. He lost his home. His car had to be sold. Later he said to a friend, "In looking back upon my suffering, I find that God makes no mistakes!" —W. B. K.

• • •

When gray threads mar life's pattern,
    and seem so out of line,
Trust the Master Weaver who planned
    the whole design;
For in life's choicest patterns some dark
    threads must appear
To make the rose threads fairer, the
    gold more bright and clear.
The pattern may seem intricate and
    hard to understand,
But trust the Master Weaver and His
    steady, guiding hand.
—*Selected*

331

Illustrations

He Maketh No Mistakes

My Father's way may twist and turn,
My heart may throb and ache,
But in my soul I'm glad I know,
He maketh no mistake.

My cherished plans may go astray,
My hopes may fade away,
But still I'll trust my Lord to lead
For He doth know the way.

Tho' night be dark and it may seem
That day will never break,
I'll pin my faith, my all in Him,
He maketh no mistake.

There's so much now I cannot see,
My eyesight's far too dim;
But come what may, I'll simply trust
And leave it all to Him.

For by and by the mist will lift
And plain it all He'll make.
Through all the way, tho' dark to me,
He made not one mistake.

—A. M. Overton, in
The Brethren Evangelist

* * *

Thank God One Cottage Burned!

Years ago a fishing fleet went out from a small harbor on the east coast of Newfoundland. In the afternoon there came up a great storm. When night settled down not a single vessel of all the fleet had found its way into port. All night long wives, mothers, children, and sweethearts paced up and down the beach, wringing their hands and calling on God to save their loved ones. To add to the horror of the situation, one of the cottages caught fire. Since the men were all away, it was impossible to save the home. When the morning broke, to the joy of all, the entire fleet found safe harbor in the bay. But there was one face which was a picture of despair — the wife of the man whose home had been destroyed. Meeting her husband as he landed, she cried, "Oh, husband, we are ruined! Our home and all it contained was destroyed by fire!" But the man exclaimed, "Thank God for the fire! It was the light of our burning

332

cottage that guided the whole fleet into port!"

—Told by Rev. W. W. Weeks, D.D.

* * *

God's Ways Always Right

The ways of the Lord are right. Right to all. Right to each. Right to one as much as to any other. Right on to the end. The ways of the Lord are often dark and mysterious, but they are right. They are concealed, or revealed but in part; but right. They are very various — not outwardly the same to any two individuals of the human race; but right. They are changeful to the *same* individual; but always right. They are sometimes full of trial and temptation, seeming to press men on and down to evil; but that is only in seeming, for still they are right.

The ways of the Lord are right, and the just shall walk in them.

—Dr. Alexander Raleigh

* * *

From His Hand

I will not take that bitter thrust
Which rent my heart today
As coming from an earthly soul —
Though it was meant that way.
But I will look beyond the tool,
Because my life is planned;
I take the cup My Father gives —
I take it from His hand.

He knows, and even thus allows
These little things that irk.
I trust His wisdom and His love,
Let patience have her work.
Though human means have brought the
sting,
I firmly take this stand:
My loving Father holds the cup,
I take it from His hand.

Now those who watch may wonder why
These things do not disturb.
I look right past the instrument
And see my Lord superb.
The trials which would lay me low
Must pass through His command;
He holds the outstretched cup to me,
I take it from His hand.

—Mrs. Ray Merrill

God Rules and Over-Rules!

When the missionary Barnabas Shaw was forbidden to preach in Cape Town he decided not to leave Africa, but to push into the interior. He bought a yoke of oxen, put his wife and his goods into a wagon and started out, resolved to settle wherever he would be allowed to preach.

So they journeyed for three hundred miles. Then while camping one night they discovered that a band of Hottentots were also camping nearby. In conversation with the leader Shaw learned that the heathen were on their way to Cape Town to find a missionary. The similar meeting of Philip and the eunuch (Acts 8:26-40) flashed through his mind, when he realized that God had been leading him where *He* wanted him to go. —*Gospel Herald*

* * *

It's in the Holy Writ

This verse in Holy Writ I see
Has very often puzzled me;
And many have been led to doubt
Just how this could be brought about.
How trouble as a blessing could
Work out for our eternal good,
Was more than sight of man could know,
And yet I felt it must be so.

"All things" include both dark and bright;
It means the sunshine and the night;
It means my sickness and my health;
My poverty as well as wealth.
This world is full of toil and care,
Both joys and sorrows have a share;
But One there is, a present Friend,
Who knows my life from start to end.
—*Selected*

* * *

A Disappointment Became God's Appointment

A missionary was going to an appointment to preach in a church in the mountains of Kentucky. He was hindered in filling the appointment by a raging blizzard. Wearily he trudged his way through the snow and ice to the home of a young man who was active in one of the mountain Sunday schools. He was welcomed by both him and his wife. They were very poor, but they gave the missionary the best they had.

That night, the missionary felt that God was calling the young man to enter the ministry. He persuaded him to answer God's call and go away to school and prepare himself for a life of service for God and others. The young man had no money. He walked thirty-five miles to school. "That man," said the missionary, "is now pastor of one of our large city churches. He has won hundreds of people to Christ. What a blessing that blizzard was! A disappointment became God's appointment! God ruled and overruled to work out His wondrous plan." —W. B. K.

* * *

Grateful for Traffic Ticket

Have you ever gone to your parked car and found a traffic ticket on it? The experience doesn't make one feel happy. For years, I had been parking my car in an alley near my Chicago home. Neither I nor others doing likewise had ever been ticketed, as there was no regulation against parking there. Going out one morning, I found a ticket on the car. I paid the three-dollar fine. For a while, I was hesitant to include the unpleasant experience among the "all things" which work together for good to God's children. Not until some days thereafter did I see the hand of God in the experience. During a wind storm a mammoth oak went down and fell right across the place where I had been parking my car for years. Had my car been in its accustomed place, it would have been smashed right in the middle! I humbly thanked God for the fact that nothing of a chance nature can ever befall His children who are "the called according to his purpose." —W. B. K.

* * *

An Animated Question Mark

A mother's only child, a little girl, was suddenly taken from her. The mother's soul was overwhelmed by sorrow and grief. In her deep despair, she became an animated question mark. "Why, oh, why did God take from me my darling little girl?" she asked her pastor. "Why didn't He take one of the six children of Mrs. ...., a mother who has failed so miserably to be a true mother to her children, neglecting them as she makes the rounds of the saloons, and leaving the care of them to the neighbors? She has shown that she does not care for her children and that she does not want them!"

The pastor sat speechless, not knowing the answer to the grief-stricken mother's question.

Let us not judge harshly that sorrowing mother, remembering that there was another One who asked, "My God, why?"

Let us always find comfort in the assuring words of the Saviour, "What I do thou knowest not now; but thou shalt know hereafter" (John 13:7).

Judge not the Lord by feeble sense,
But trust Him for His grace,
Behind a frowning providence,
He hides a smiling face!

Blind unbelief is sure to err,
And scan His work in vain,
God is His own Interpreter,
He will make all things plain!"
—W. B. K.

* * *

God's Handwriting

He writes in characters too grand
For our short sight to understand;
We catch but broken strokes, and try
To fathom all the mystery
Of withered hopes, of death, of life,
The endless war, the useless strife, —
But there, with larger, clearer sight,
We shall see this — His way was right.
—John Oxenham in *Bees in Amber*

God's Stories Come Out Right!

With dramatic skill, a Sunday-school teacher was telling the story of Abraham and his obedient preparation to sacrifice Isaac. As the story neared its climax, a little girl pleaded, "Oh, please don't go on! This story is too terrible!" Another girl interrupted, "Don't be silly, Mary! This is one of God's stories, and God's stories always come out right!"

God rules and overrules and causes everything to come out right for His children. —W. B. K.

* * *

God Makes No Mistakes

A Christian businessman suffered heavy financial losses. He began to doubt the goodness of God. "Why did He allow these reverses to come to me?" he questioned. One night he sat dejected and discouraged in the library before the fireplace. His little six-year-old boy came into the room and crawled in his lap.

Over the mantle hung a motto which read: "God's works are perfect." "Daddy, what does perfect mean?" Before the father could reply, the boy asked another question, "Does it mean that God never makes a mistake?"

The thought was just what the father needed. Enfolding the boy in his arms, he said, "Yes, my precious boy, that's just what it means!"

Confidence in God began to revive. Silently he prayed, "O God, do forgive me for my misgivings. I give myself anew to You. Use me for Your glory!"
—W. B. K.

SACRIFICE

Short Quotes

Robert Arthington of Leeds, a Cambridge graduate, lived in a single room, cooking his own meals; and he gave foreign missions 500,000 pounds on the condition that it was all to be spent on pioneer work within twenty-five years. He wrote these words: "Gladly would I make the floor my bed, a box my chair, and another box my table, rather than that men should perish for want of the knowledge of Christ.
—*The Wesleyan Methodist*

* * *

A Mohammedan sneeringly asked a missionary, "Where are your converts?" Pointing to a nearby cemetery, the missionary answered, "There!" In faithfully standing for their Lord, the missionary's converts gave their lives! "They loved not their lives unto death."

—Rev. William McCarrell, D.D.

* * *

"Is there some way to lessen your duties?" a friend asked a pioneer medical missionary and his wife. The wife was also a medical doctor and labored faithfully with her husband in China. Night and day they ministered to the physical and spiritual needs of the natives who came to the mission hospital. Their reply was, "We cannot lose our lives and save them, too!" Nor can we. Have we said:

> Jesus, I my cross have taken,
> All to leave and follow Thee?

—W. B. K.

* * *

"Have you found a good road to where you are? If so, we want to know how to send other men to join you," wrote a misisonary society to David Livingstone. He replied, "If you have men who will come only if they know there is a good road, I don't want them. I want men strong and courageous enough who will come even if there is no road at all!"

—*Christian Business Men's Bulletin*

Illustrations

When Jesus Had Nowhere to Go

As some missionaries were fleeing for their lives from some Chinese bandits, nightfall overtook them. They huddled together in an old abandoned building. It was filthy and vermin-infested. Among the fleeing missionaries were Archibald Glover and his family. After a wretched night, little Hendley Glover said, "Daddy, I think Jesus must have slept in a place like this when He had nowhere to go." "Yes, my boy, I think it very likely," answered Archibald. Then little five-year-old Hendley said, "Then we ought to be glad to be like Jesus, and suffer for Him!"

—W. B. K.

* * *

I Lay in Dust Life's Glory Deal

While in the heyday of his wondrous work among the Indians, David Brainerd died. Some would say, "What hopes for Christ's cause went down to the grave with the wasted form of that totally dedicated missionary. All there was to show for his sacrificial labors were a few score Indian converts!" Such deduction might be measurably true if we failed to reckon with the fact that one's influence never dies. After Brainerd's death, Jonathan Edwards wrote the memorials of Brainerd in a little book. It found its way across the sea, and was placed on the table of a brilliant Cambridge student, Henry Martyn. The little book brought great inspiration and challenge to him. For the Lord's sake, he utterly dedicated himself as a missionary. Concerning Him the world would ask, "Why should he throw away his scholarship and worldly honors and riches for the sufferings and privations of a missionary?" He labored for many years. Then, when broken in health, he trekked northward. Reaching the Black Sea, his triumphant soul left his broken body.

Out of the early graves of Brainerd and Martyn sprung the noble army of modern missionaries. We can say of them, "For the Lord's sake, 'they loved not their lives unto the death.'"

—W. B. K.

* * *

They Voluntarily Became Slaves

When Moravian missionaries went with the Gospel message to the West Indies, it was almost impossible to reach the natives because at the break of day the natives were driven to their hard work where they remained until darkness settled over the land. At night, they would eat their coarse meal and fall, exhausted, onto their beds. After much waiting before God in prayer, the Moravian missionaries decided that they would voluntarily become slaves and work alongside the natives so that they could tell them the story of Jesus!

The world today is almost totally pagan because so many are only half Christian when it comes to self-crucifying service for God and man.

—W. B. K.

* * *

He Took With Him Burial Clothes!

An African, who is a Mohammedan, has twice made the pilgrimage to Mecca, and has earned the title "Al Haji," which means "The Pilgrim." So devoted is he to his religion that he has planned to make the long and arduous journey a third time. On this last trip he will take along his burial clothes, for he expects to die on the road to Mecca!

Does not such devotion shame us who know little or nothing of sacrificial service for the Lord Jesus? Who of us can say with Paul, "Christ Jesus my Lord: for whom I have suffered the loss of all things" (Phil. 3:8)?

—Rev. William McCarrell, D.D.

* * *

The Supreme Sacrifice

Christians everywhere were shocked and saddened by the tragic deaths of five young missionaries: Youdarian, Saint, Elliot, Fleming and McCully. They were killed by the Auca Indians said to be the worst people on earth, according to a scientist. Believing the Indians to be friendly to them, the missionaries landed hopefully on a stretch of sandy beach by the River Curaray. One of the missionaries radioed, "Oh, here come some Aucas we haven't seen before! I'll call you back at four o'clock!" Four o'clock brought only silence. Five noble martyrs for Christ's gospel had been sent into the presence of their Lord. The father of one of the martyred men said, "God makes no mistakes," and another said, "I feel more sorry for those poor Indians than for my son!" —W. B. K.

* * *

Tyndale's Sacrifice

Four hundred and twenty-five years ago, it was a crime to own a Bible in English. The ban was broken by a few courageous men of God whose eyes were open to the need of the people for a Bible they could read. One of the greatest of this little company of heroes was William Tyndale. Because he vowed, "Every plowboy should know the Scriptures," he was forced to leave his native England, never to return. Working in Europe, he labored long years to translate the Bible into English. He printed the first English New Testament in 1525 and with the help of friends smuggled thousands of copies into England. Finally he was arrested and held in solitary confinement in a cold, dark jail in Vilvorde, Belgium. Then he was choked and burned at the stake. William Tyndale gave his life to give us our Bible. His last words were, "O Lord, open Thou the King of England's eyes." —From a tract, "Tyndale Gave His Life," by the American Bible Society

* * *

Hast Thou No Scar?

Hast thou no scar
No hidden scar on foot, or side, or hand?
I hear thee sung as mighty in the land,
I hear them hail thy bright ascendant star?

Hast thou no wound?
Yet I was wounded by the archers, spent,
Leaned me against a tree to die; and rent
By ravening beasts that compassed me, I swooned:
Hast thou no wound?

No wound? No scar?
Yet, as the Master shall the servant be,
And pierced are the feet that follow Me;
But thine are whole: can he have followed far
Who has no wound nor scar?

—*Selected*

* * *

He Counted the Cost

I remember an earnest and effective layman in Ecuador who felt called to God's service in the ministry, but his wife would not hear of it. She threatened all kinds of reprisals if he should leave his lucrative employment to become a servant of the Lord Jesus. One evening he came to me, with a bundle under one arm and tears in his eyes. I read the following verses to him: "Verily I say unto you, there is no man that hath left house, or brethren, or sisters, or father, or mother, or wife, or children, or lands, for my sake, and the gospel's but shall receive an hundredfold, now in this time, houses, and brethren, and sisters, and mothers, and children, and lands, with persecutions; and in the world to come eternal life" (Mark 10:29-30). After prayers and tears, I inquired, "And what have you in the bundle?" "It contains my. working clothes. I left my employment today!"

He had counted the cost, and had set himself to leave all. . . . And do we wonder that he won his wife to full allegiance to the Master, and that together they have become pillars in the house of God? —Dr. V. Raymond Edman

* * *

Where Are the Men?

One of God's. heroines, a missionary nurse to Africa, didn't *die* for Christ — she *lived* for Him. She deemed herself expendable, daily wearing down as she responded to the incessant calls from suffering ones. Let us follow her on a typical day's work: She arose at daybreak and began her daily routine. Already scores of outpatients were then gathered at the nearby mission compound. For hours she dressed their sores, speaking a word to each one of them of the great Physician, Jesus. Having treated 308 patients, she went over the hills and through the valleys where others awaited her healing ministry. She had not gone far, however, until she toppled over through sheer fatigue. The native helper accompanying her asked a question which should shame and challenge us, "Why don't men come out here to help you?"
—Told by Rev. R. F. Haggerty

* * *

All or Nothing

"When a Buddhist becomes a Christian, he recognizes that he has chosen a path of no compromise. Acceptance has to be all or nothing. To accept Christ is to break caste, to deny one's cultural heritage. It means to be dead

to one's family with disinheritance and funeral rites marking the finality of this death. Thus for the Asian, Christianity necessarily calls men to crucifixion with Christ, no less in the family than in the nation."

The author of these words, Ritasarani Rajanayagam, knows whereof she speaks. She came to the United States from Asia as a Buddhist. During the course of her studies here, she began to read the Bible and, as a result, she accepted Jesus Christ as her Saviour. When she sent word of her decision back to her family, they conducted a funeral pyre and burned her body *in absentia*. She is now legally dead in her home country and cannot go back as the same person again. She has been disinherited, disowned, and declared dead.
—*Conquest for Christ*

* * *

God's Appointment

During a time of persecution in Korea, a young church member was accused by the police and put in jail as a suspect. He was placed in a cell by himself and he grieved because he was restrained from speaking of Christ to the other prisoners. Soon he was banished to one of the neighboring islands. When he was released after the breakdown of the accusation, he said with shining face, "Just think, I have been longing for a chance to speak of Christ, and was mourning because I could not speak in jail. Then God sent me off to an unevangelized island, where there was plenty of work to do, and the government paid my fare."
—*King's Highway*

* * *

How Little I Have Sacrificed!

Someone dreamed that he died and went to heaven. He found himself in the midst of a great multitude. "Who are you?" he asked someone standing near him. "I am a Roman Christian. I was put to death during Nero's reign," that person answered. "How awful!" said the dreamer. "No, I was glad to give my life for Jesus who gave His life for me," was the reply. "And who are you?" the dreamer asked someone else. "I am from a South Sea island.

John Williams came there and told me about Jesus. I became a Christian. I was killed for my faith in Jesus!" Just then, the dreamer awoke. "How little I have sacrificed for Jesus," he sobbed. "O God, forgive me! I'll take my cross and live for Him who died for me!" —W. B. K.

• • •

No Strength to Sacrifice

At the close of a Lord's day which had been filled with loving service for God and others, a weary mother sat quietly in church for the evening service. The pastor's message was an earnest plea to sacrifice one's money and life. Who would say ought against any servant of God pleading for sacrificial giving and living when most of us live like kings, and when few, if any, of us can say with Paul: "Christ Jesus my Lord: for whom I have suffered the loss of all things" (Phil. 3:8)? The overworked mother, whose life had been fully dedicated to God from her earliest childhood days, remarked as she wearily went homeward, "Honestly, I am so tired in body and mind that I have no strength to sacrifice anything." The one to whom she spoke understood fully, and so did her heavenly Father.

—W. B. K.

Jesus, I'm Doing This for Thee

Mrs. Comstock was a great missionary to India. When it came time for her children to go to her native land to be educated, she had to make a heartwrenching decision: "Shall I send them there and stay here with my chain of mission stations? Or shall I go with them and be separated for years from the mission field?" It wasn't an easy decision for her to make. Children are gifts from God. All of them need a mother's care and love. She fought the battle out and said, "I will stay here by the task. I will put my children in the care of loved ones and in the care of the Saviour!" The day came for their departure. She prayed for them. She placed them on a ship. She saw her children going farther and farther from her and waving their handkerchiefs. When she could no longer see them, she knelt on the sand and said over and over again: "Lord Jesus, I am doing this for Thee. I am putting Thee before my girls!" She went back to her work. She had the joy of seeing many people "delivered . . . from the power of darkness, and . . . translated into the kingdom of [God's] dear Son!" —W. B. K.

SALVATION

Short Quotes

An old man testified that it took him forty years to learn three simple things: that he couldn't do anything to save himself, that God didn't expect him to, and that Christ had done it all.

—*King's Business*

• • •

There are only two kinds of religion in the world. The one says, "Nothing in my hands I bring"; the other says, "Something in my hands I bring."

—W. B.K.

• • •

Said Spurgeon of his conversion, "I looked at Him, and He looked at me, and we became one forever!"

Augustine prayed, "Lord, save me from all my sins, but not yet." There was no answer. Later he prayed, "Lord, save me from my sins, except one." Still there was no answer. Finally he prayed, "Lord, save me from *all my sins*, and save me *now!*" God answered instantly! —W. B. K.

• • •

Salvation has three tenses: past, present, and future. We *have been* saved from sin's penalty by Christ's vicarious death on the cross: "But he was wounded for our transgressions" (Isa. 53:5); we *are* being saved from sin's power by Christ's intercession on high: "He ever liveth to make intercession for them" (Heb. 7:25); and we *shall be saved* from sin's presence: "And there shall in no wise enter into it anything that defileth" (Rev. 21:27). —W. B. K.

* * *

Many, like the prodigal son, are starving in the far country when Jesus, the Bread of Life, may be had for the asking! —W. B. K.

* * *

To educate a man in mind and not in morals is to educate a menace to society. —Theodore Roosevelt

* * *

The unsaved have eternal existence, but they do not have eternal life: "And this is life eternal, that they might know thee the only true God, and Jesus Christ whom thou hast sent" (John 17:3). —W. B. K.

* * *

"There wasn't anything I had not tried," testified Melvin Trotter, who was once a humanly hopeless alcoholic. "I had taken cure after cure. I could no more stay sober than I could jump over the moon. But one glimpse of Jesus Christ, and I have never wanted a drink from that instant to this!" —W. B. K.

* * *

God forms man, sin deforms him, the school informs him, but only Christ transforms him.

* * *

"Christ Jesus came into the world to save *cinders*," misquoted a small boy. Yet, is it not true? —W. B. K.

* * *

A young man in Chicago entered an insurance office with his pockets bulging with burglar tools. The policeman caught him red-handed as he endeavored to open the safe. When the young man was investigated, it was learned that he was highly educated, having three college degrees. His latest degree was a degree in psychology, earned from the University of Kansas. He had studied law for a year, and, when apprehended by the authorities, he was working on a doctorate in psychology. An education is valuable, but it is not

man's basic need. Jesus said to a cultured, educated man, "Ye must be born again." —W. B. K.

* * *

Two rude stones in the Sahara Desert mark a tragedy of thirst. The wealthy Egyptian merchant, Ab Ishay, paid his camel driver Arik 10,000 ducats ($22,500) for a mouthful of water. Within an hour both died of thirst. Yet only a thousand steps distant was a well which would have saved them! "If any man thirst, let him come unto me, and drink" (John 7:37). —*The Burning Bush*

* * *

God never alters the robe of righteousness to fit the man, but He alters the man to fit the robe.

* * *

A Communist was haranguing a group of people in Columbus Circle, New York, who had gathered around him. In extolling the so-called virtues of Communism, he cried out, "Communism can put a new suit on a man!" One of God's children, ever on the alert to turn any situation in such a way as to bring glory to his Lord, said in a clear, earnest voice, "And Christ can put a *new man* in the new suit!"
"Therefore if any man be in Christ, he is a new creature" (II Cor. 5:17). —W. B. K.

* * *

When man is reduced to his constituent chemical elements he is worth something less than eight dollars. Spiritually speaking, however, man is of infinite worth: "For what is a man profited, if he shall gain the whole world, and lose his own soul?" (Matt. 16:26). —W. B. K.

* * *

In our present-day evangelism, men are urged to be saved before they know they are lost; to believe without being convicted of their need. The fruit is picked before it is ripe, and the work is sure to come undone. The Holy Spirit must convict of sin before men can truly believe. This "accepting Christ" theory without conviction is not the new birth. It is not a "born again" experience. What a mockery it is! —Dr. Oswald Smith

"Sign the pledge and keep it," admonished a friend to an alcoholic. "But," replied the humanly hopeless man, "I can't keep it. I need something to keep *me*!"

* * *

"What have you found in Christianity that you did not have in Hinduism?" asked an agnostic professor in a Hindu college of a *sadhu*, or holy man, who had recently become a Christian. "I have found Christ!" was the answer. The professor, hoping to involve him in some philosophical argument, replied, "Yes, I know, but what particular principle have you found that you did not have before?" The *sadhu* replied, "The particular thing I have found is Christ!" —W. B. K.

* * *

Countess de Crudener said to Czar Alexander: "Sire, if you come to God as the Czar of all the Russians, you will get nothing. If you come to Him as an undeserving sinner, trusting the Saviour who died for you, you will get all the blessings of the gospel." —W. B. K.

* * *

A converted soldier was asked, "How were you saved?" He replied, "The Lord said to me, Halt! Attention! Rightabout-face! March! That was all there was to it!" —W. B. K.

* * *

George Whitefield, when asked why he preached so often on the text, "Ye must be born again," replied that it was because *ye must be born again.*
—W. B. K.

* * *

The major emphasis of all false religions is on man's search for God. The major emphasis of Christianity is on God's search for man: "For the Son of man is come to seek and to save that which was lost" (Luke 19:10).
—W. B. K.

* * *

A dog was barking furiously at a little girl. It ceased its barking only when the owner said to stop. The dog, however, glowered menacingly at the little girl. In his efforts to rid the girl of further fear, the man said, "You needn't have any fear. See, the dog has quit barking!" "Yes," replied the little girl, still uncomforted, "but look at the dog's eyes! The bark is on the *inside*!"

Isn't that the case with the man whose outward appearance belies the inward wickedness of a "deceitful and desperately wicked" heart? —W. B. K.

* * *

The Bukidnons who live in the Philippine Islands are an extremely backward people. It is said that their bodies are indescribably filthy and repulsive. "We never tell them to clean up. We exhort them to be cleaned *inwardly* by the blood of Christ," said Mr. and Mrs. Henry DeVries, missionaries who labor among them. "When inward cleansing takes place, the outward cleansing follows. Another missionary gave them tooth paste and soap, but it simply didn't work that way. The gospel must do the cleansing work inside first."
—W. B. K.

* * *

A missionary in India spoke near a fountain on the subject, "Jesus, the Water of Life." A Moslem interrupted, "Your religion is like this little stream of water, but Mohammedanism is like a great ocean!" "Yes," said the missionary, "but there is this difference: when men drink ocean water they die of thirst. When they drink the water of life which Christ gives they live forever!" —W. B. K.

* * *

"To win real peace and a world without war in the atomic age, the hearts of men must be changed," said Dr. Arthur H. Compton, noted atomic scientist to the 100th anniversary graduating class of Lake Forest College. "True peace is yet afar off. Hates continue. Ambition for power and for dominance still burns in our breasts. . . . To win real peace the hearts of men must be changed," he said.

It is only through the miracle of the new birth that sinful hearts are changed. Christ plumbed to the depth the basic need of sinful man when He said, "Ye must be born again."
—W. B. K.

Illustrations

Christ Made the Difference

A young man came to an evangelist with a long list of questions. "I will answer your questions if you will promise me to do one thing," the evangelist said. "What's that?" asked the young man. "It is this," said the minister, "Give your heart to Christ, and then come to me with your questions."

The young man went silently away. Two days later, he returned with a radiant face which told its own story. "Where are your questions?" asked the evangelist. "I have none! The moment I accepted Christ as my Saviour, I had the answer to most of them, and the others appeared so insignificant that no answer to them was necessary!"

—W. B. K.

* * *

I Was That Bit of Mud

A so-called higher critic spoke scornfully of the Bible story of man's creation. With a grin on his face he said, "Think of God taking a piece of mud in hand, breathing on it, and changing it into a man!"

In the audience was a man who had sunken low into the muck of sin, but who was now transformed by the wondrous grace of God. He stood fearlessly to his feet and said to the critic of God's Word: "I will not discuss the creation of man with you, but I will tell you this: God stooped down and picked up the dirtiest bit of mud in our town. He breathed upon it by His Spirit. It was newly created. It was changed from a wicked wretch into a man who now hates his former sins and loves the God who saved him. *I was that bit of mud!*" —W. B. K.

* * *

Dog Sense

A man saw a dog running on three legs down the street of a city. The fourth leg was bound in a splint. The dog did its best to keep the injured leg from touching the ground. Presently it entered a large building through the open door. The building was a *general hospital!* The onlooker smiled when he saw what the dog did. As he walked along, he chanced to see a discarded newspaper on a bench. Bold headlines told about our morally and spiritually sick world, mentioning crime, wars and rumors of wars!

Oh, that our sick world had as much "dog sense" as that mongrel displayed, and would go to the Great Physician, Jesus, for healing of body, soul, and mind! God's diagnosis of sick souls is this: "The whole head is sick, and the whole heart faint" (Isa. 1:5). God's remedy for sin-sick souls is this: "The blood of Jesus Christ his Son cleanseth us from all sin" (I John 1:7).

There is a balm in Gilead,
    To make the wounded whole;
There is a balm in Gilead,
    To heal the sin-sick soul!

—Told by Ken Anderson

* * *

The Living Stone

On Christ salvation rests secure:
The Rock of Ages must endure;
Nor can that faith be overthrown
Which rests upon the Living Stone.

No other hope shall intervene;
To Him we look, on Him we lean;
Other foundation we disown
And build on Christ, the Living Stone.

In Him it is ordained to raise
A temple to Jehovah's praise;
Composed of all the saints who own
No Saviour but the Living Stone.

View the vast building, see it rise;
The work how great! the plan how wise!
Oh, wondrous fabric! power unknown!
That rears it on the Living Stone.

—Samuel Medley

* * *

Let Go — Let God!

A traveler upon a lonely road was set upon by bandits who robbed him of his all. They then led him into the depths of the forest. There, in the darkness, they tied a rope to the limb of a great tree, and bade him catch hold of the end of it. Swinging him out into the blackness of surrounding space, they told him he was hanging over the brink

341

of a giddy precipice. The moment he let go he would be dashed to pieces on the rocks below. And then they left him. His soul was filled with horror at the awful doom impending. He clutched despairingly the end of the swaying rope. But each dreadful moment only made his fate more sure. His strength steadily failed. At last he could hold on no longer. The end had come. His clenched fingers relaxed their convulsive grip. He fell — *six inches*, to the solid earth at his feet! It was only a ruse of the robbers to gain time in escaping. And when he let go it was not to death, but to the safety which had been waiting him through all his time of terror.

Friend, clutching will not save you. It is only Satan's trick to keep you from *being* saved. And all the while is your heart not full of fear? *Let go!* *That* is God's plan to save you. "And will I not fall to death?" you say. Nay. Underneath is — *Jesus!*
—James McConkey

* * *

They Gave Him All the Works

"Let's go down to skid row, find a vagrant derelict in great need of a shave and haircut, bring him before us and demonstrate to our group the change we can make in him," suggested someone at a convention of The Midwestern Barber's Association meeting in Chicago. They found a man and gave him "all the works." The barbers took a collection and bought him a new suit, tie, shoes and underwear. How good he looked outwardly! A hotel manager, impressed by what had been done, offered the man a job. "I'll report for work at eight A.M. tomorrow," the man said. He didn't report for work, however. Later he was found in skid row, dead drunk.

Man's greatest need is inward cleansing. "Ye must be born again."
—W. B. K.

* * *

Out With the Life-Line

A farmer near Milton, Pennsylvania, was getting chunks of ice from the Susquehanna River to put in his ice house. A floating mass of ice struck his small boat and broke the rope which was fastened to a tree on the bank. The boat was set adrift on the swollen river, amidst the churning ice. Someone, seeing his danger, mounted a horse and rode swiftly downstream, calling for helpers. Many hastily got ropes, went out on the bridge downstream, and suspended a line of dangling ropes from the bridge across the river. Presently the farmer was seen standing in his boat which was half filled with water. He was wet and cold and frantic. Then he saw the dangling ropes. When the rapid current brought him to the bridge, he seized the nearest rope and was drawn up to safety!

Imperiled souls are floundering on life's tempest-tossed sea. The black waters of defeat and despair will overflow them unless we "throw out the lifeline with hand quick and strong."
—W. B. K.

* * *

Only One Hope for Man

Clarence Darrow, the famed criminal lawyer, said, "You can make nothing of man but man — selfish, mean, tyrannical, aggressive. That's what man is and a lot more. It is useless to try to change him!"

And a phrenologist said to a group of people, "I can tell you what a man's character is by the bumps on his head. Who'll volunteer?" A man went forward. After a thorough examination, the lecturer said, "This man is hard and cold. He has many disagreeable traits." The audience laughed derisively. "You've miserably failed to judge that man's character. He is kind and genial, and he lives an exemplary life," they said. The one who was examined, wanting to give the Saviour the honor for any good there was in him, said, "Friends, you have heard what my nature *was* before Jesus Christ changed my life. Before He came into my heart, I was guilty of graver sins than the lecturer mentioned!" —W. B. K.

* * *

Dirty Rags Preach a Sermon

Queen Victoria once visited a large paper mill. She was shown, among other places, the "rag room" where tons of offensively filthy rags were stored. "How can these dirty rags ever be made white and pure?" she asked. "I have a chemical process by which I can remove all the grime and uncleanness from those rags, and make them immaculately white," answered the superintendent. Sometime later, the Queen found on her writing desk some of the most beautiful writing paper she had ever seen. Accompanying the paper was a note which read: "Will Her Majesty be pleased to accept a specimen of my paper with the assurance that every sheet was manufactured out of the dirty rags which she saw? Will Her Majesty also allow me to say that I have had many excellent sermons 'preached' to me as I have seen filthy rags changed into the most elegant bond paper? I can understand now how Christ can make the vilest sinner clean — white as snow — though his sins be as scarlet!"

—W. B. K.

* * *

No Substitute

There was a mail carrier who used a canoe in the course of his rounds among homes along a river. One day a Salvation Army man said to him, "Can you swim?" "Oh," replied the man, "there's no need for me to learn to swim. I've paddled this canoe up and down the river for years. I'll be all right." Some time after the conversation the newspapers reported that this man's canoe had capsized; and, because he could not swim, he was drowned. All his knowledge and experience at paddling a canoe did not suffice for him at the critical moment; he had neglected the means of his salvation. How often we hear people say when spoken to about their souls, "I'm all right; I live a good life." Yet they neglect salvation through Christ; and there is no salvation for the soul from eternal death when it refuses the "one thing needful." —*War Cry*

* * *

Cleansing the Inside

While walking down a street one day, I passed a store where a man on the pavement was washing the large plate-

glass window. There was one soiled spot which defied all efforts to remove it. After rubbing hard and using much soap and water and failing to remove it, he found out the trouble. "It's on the inside," he called out to someone in the store.

Many are striving to cleanse the soul from its stains. They wash it with tears of sorrow; they scrub it with the soap of good resolves; they rub it with the chamois of morality; but still the consciousness of it is not removed. The trouble is, "*It's on the inside.*" Nothing but *the blood of Jesus*, applied by the mighty power of the Holy Spirit, can cleanse the inside. —*Rod and Staff*

* * *

It Was the Cat's Nature

Timmy was just an ordinary cat. We liked Timmy because Alice, our girl, liked him. There was one thing, however, which we all greatly disliked in Timmy — he preyed upon the birds which nested in the trees in our back yard. One day, Timmy was eating a robin. I snatched the unconsumed portion of the bird from the cat. I sprinkled it with red pepper. Then I dangled the morsel temptingly before the cat. Instantly the cat's sharp teeth closed upon it, only to drop it the next instant! The cat sputtered and ran away, meowing.

Did that rather drastic procedure break the cat's habit of catching and killing more birds? No. It was the cat's nature to catch birds. I could not break his bad habit by working on him *externally*.

Man's heart is deceitful and desperately wicked. It is his nature to sin. For confirmation, read your daily newspaper. Lopping off a twig or a branch here and there does not change man's sinful nature. Man must be changed *inwardly* before he will act right *outwardly*. Not external reformation, but inward regeneration is the answer to man's sin question. —W. B. K.

* * *

Absolutely Free

In Mexico those who sell bread often carry it in a large basket on their heads. As a Christian man left his bakery one day, he tucked his Bible under the white cloth which covered the basket. As he walked along the street, he shouted, "Bread, bread." "What kind of bread do you have?" asked a woman standing in a door. The baker replied, "I have bread that costs money and bread that is free!" "What! You have bread that you give away?" Without replying, the baker opened his basket, took the Bible from it and read this verse, "I am the bread of life: he that cometh to me shall never hunger."

—W. B. K.

* * *

Glory for Christ, Too

Some years ago, a mammoth fireman's parade was held in New York City. Fire-fighting apparatus of all kinds were entered in the parade. In several of the vehicles rode men, women, boys and girls. Large streamers were fastened on both sides of the vehicles, bearing the words: "These were rescued from burning buildings by New York City firemen!" Their rescue brought glory to the brave firemen.

In heaven, great glory will redound to the One who rescued us from the eternal burning by His infinite grace and precious blood! Paul spoke of "the riches of the glory of his inheritance in the saints" (Eph. 1:18). Our arriving in heaven by His infinite grace will be glory for us — and for Him, too!

—Told by Dr. George W. Truett

* * *

Daddy, Get Me Out!

Years ago, near Electra, Texas, a child fell into a defunct oil well. It was 180 feet deep and twelve inches wide. From below, the child pleaded, "Daddy, get me out!" Ropes were tied about the father's body, and an effort was made to lower him into the narrow well, but to no avail. Fainter and fainter, the child pleaded, "Daddy, get me out!" The plea finally ceased! Grab-hooks finally brought to the surface the lifeless body of the child.

Man, in his lost condition, is in a horrible pit of sin from which he may be extricated by praying from his heart: "Lord save me, I perish!" —W. B. K.

Can Brain Surgery Eradicate Sin?

Sometime ago a most unusual operation was performed upon a six-year-old "problem child" in the Wesley Memorial Hospital in Chicago. The operation is called hemispherectomy. It took nearly five hours to perform it. It is claimed that "a mean brat" was transformed by the operation into "a lovable, sweet angel!" The child could not be tolerated by either her parents or teachers. Her seizures could not be controlled by any kind of medicine. She was described as being "disobedient, disruptive, destructive, and so antagonistically unruly that teachers sent her home." She was such a behavior problem that her parents were contemplating putting her in an institution. Now, it is claimed, "all is changed. She is co-operative and gracious!"

Perhaps surgery can bring about temperamental changes in children, but it takes the soul-transforming grace of God to change sinful hearts. —W. B. K.

* * *

Christ a Myth?

"I tell you Jesus Christ is a myth," shouted an atheistic lecturer as he concluded his talk in which he ridiculed the Bible and denied the existence of God. A miner, who had come to the meeting in his grimy clothes, stood up and said, "I'm only a workingman. I don't know what you mean by the word 'myth.' But can you explain *me?* Three years ago I had a miserable home. I neglected my wife and children. I cursed and swore. I drank up all my wages. Then someone came along and told me of the love of God, and of deliverance from the shackles of sin by turning to Christ. Now all is different! We have a happy home. I feel better every way. A new power has taken possession of me since Christ came into my life! *Sir, can you explain me?"*

—Told by Rev. R. E. Neighbour, D.D.

* * *

Publicans and Harlots

For eleven years, it was my privilege to preach in the world-famed Pacific Garden Mission in Chicago. The audiences were composed largely of drunkards and harlots. They were a conglomerate mass of down-and-out men and women who had sunken low in sin and shame. As I preached Christ to them, my heart was filled with tenderness and love for them. Often I said to them, "You won't go to hell because you drink. You will go to hell because you reject Christ. When Christ comes in, drink goes out!" I always gave an invitation for the unsaved to come to Christ. Often scores responded to the loving appeal and went into the inquiry rooms where they were personally dealt with. Some were genuinely saved and later gave evidence of being new creatures in Christ Jesus.

Oftentimes it is easier to reach the down-and-out people for Christ than religious people who have only a "form of godliness." —W. B. K.

* * *

Stoop Down, Drink and Live

The skeleton of a woman was found on the hot sands of the Mojave Desert. Before death, she had written a note which read: "I am exhausted and must have water! I do not believe I can last much longer!" She died of thirst and exposure just two miles from Surprise Springs where water flowed in abundance.

None needs to die of spiritual thirst. All may accept the all-inclusive invitation of the Saviour: "And whosoever will, let him take the water of life freely" (Rev. 22:17). —W. B. K.

* * *

From Sin's Depth to Heaven's Glory

A bit of human flotsam was brought by policemen into the emergency room of a city hospital. After examination, the doctor said, "Stand aside. She'll die!" But a kind, Christian nurse didn't "stand aside." *She stood by!* She sat at the bedside of the dying girl, waiting for an opportunity to speak to the girl of the love and care of God. "Does God care for anybody like me?" asked the dying girl. Assured by the nurse that He did care for her, the sinful girl said, "I've been such a bad girl. Tell me straight, does God care for a bad girl like me?" Tenderly the nurse replied, "Yes, dear, God loves you and cares for you. A God who so loved you that He

gave His dear Son for your sins and my sins on His cruel cross does care for you!" As the nurse spoke further words of assurance into ears rapidly dulling in death, a smile of confidence wreathed a face which, though marred by sin, now became beautiful. Then a forgiven, triumphant soul passed into the presence of the One who said to a sinful woman in the long ago, "Neither do I condemn thee: go, and sin no more!"

—Told by Rev. Paul Rees, D.D.

* * *

He Brought Me Up

Richard Almo of Pittsburgh was walking home after working on a night shift of the Jones and Laughlin Steel Works. Looking in a ravine alongside the Penn-Lincoln Highway, he saw protruding what seemed to be a man's head. Descending into the ravine, he saw that it was a living man's head. The man had been entrapped in the bog for eighteen hours. He had slowly sunk in the morass until it was almost up to his chin. He could not speak. His mouth was full of mud. He could move only his eyes. Richard dashed away for help. Nearby police and fire departments were notified. Descending into the ravine, brave men, supported by branches cut from nearby trees, crawled to where the imperiled man was and tied a rope beneath his shoulders. Then he was extricated from what would have been his grave in a short while if his plight had not been discovered. He was hospitalized for shock and pneumonia.

How aptly this incident illustrates our plight before the Saviour extricated us from the quagmire of sin and degradation! With glowing, grateful hearts we say with David: "I waited patiently for the Lord; and he inclined unto me, and heard my cry. He brought me up also out of an horrible pit, out of the miry clay, and set my feet upon a rock, and established my going" (Ps. 40:1, 2). —W. B. K.

* * *

Too Much Pyruvic Acid in Thalamic Calls

Recently a biochemist announced that within a hundred years neurologists would cope with the inherent evils of mankind on a scientific, physiological basis. He said, "Then we will not say a man is vicious, criminal, or immoral because he commits crime or immoral acts. Instead we will know that he has too much pyruvic acid in his thalamic cells, or that there is no carboxylase in his tyalamus. We will be able to tell whether or not he grew enough association neurones to descend from his cortex so that he has enough acetylcholine in his midbrain or mesencephalon!"

Do not ask me to explain these terms. I am as ignorant of them as you are. I know, however, that biochemistry cannot change the depraved heart of man which is "deceitful above all things, and desperately wicked" (Jer. 17:9). Nor can the religious hocus-pocus of any priest or parson stay the ravages of sin or do away with man's basic need of becoming a new creature in Christ Jesus by the miracle of regeneration: "Can the Ethiopian change his skin, or the leopard his spots? then may ye also do good, that are accustomed to do evil" (Jer. 13:23). —W. B. K.

Then Jesus Came

Masagr, a benighted African pagan, was guilty of the basest sins — lying, stealing, polygamy, slavery, gluttony, drunkenness and murder. Then Jesus came! Hearing the heart-transforming gospel of the grace of God, Masagr believed it, and trusted Christ to save him from sin. The change was so miraculous that all marveled. He immediately began to tell others of Christ's saving power. For months he saved every penny, and even sold his cow to buy a second-hand bicycle. He said to a missionary, "I am old. I cannot go far to tell my people about Jesus. There is a young man in your school. He is full of zeal. Put him on this bicycle, and send him to my fellow tribesmen that they may hear of the wonderful Saviour!" —W. B. K.

Bread Enough and to Spare

Many die of spiritual hunger when Jesus, "the bread of life," may be had for the asking. During the Revolu-

tionary War, a half-starved Indian found his way into a Western settlement. "Bread! Bread!" he piteously said. "Give me bread! I am starving!" As an officer questioned him, the Indian drew from his pocket a dirty, worn wallet in which the officer found a regular discharge from the Federal army, signed by General Washington. That discharge, which the Indian thought was worthless, entitled him to ample provision which he immediately received. How like that Indian are millions of starving souls! —W. B. K.

Getting the Slums out of the Slummer

In the wake of horrible crime — the murder of two teen-age girls — the *Chicago Tribune* came out with a front-page cartoon whose ostensible purpose was the disclosure of the cause of the widespread and ever mounting crime wave in that great city. In the background of the cartoon were skyscraping, palatial apartment buildings and modern, stately, office structures. In the forefront of the cartoon were ratty, ramshackle, tottering tenement structures, whose approaches and surroundings were littered with rubbish and debris. Hovering over the slum scene was the shadowy form of a monstrous, red-eyed devouring wolf with claws aspread and mouth agape, ready to pounce upon its prey.

Slum clearance is good. We must remember, however, that it is one thing to get the slummer out of the slums, and another thing to get the slum out of the slummer. Turn degenerate man, whose heart is "deceitful and desperately wicked," loose and he will, in time, turn a Garden of Eden into a shambles and a swine sty! —W. B. K.

Hold on! Let go! Watch for Light!

A young man went forward and knelt at an altar of prayer. A well-wisher came and knelt beside him and said, "Just hold on!" Presently another well-meaning man came and said, "I, too, am happy that you are seeking the Lord. Just let go!" Still a third came and said, "I, too, was at this altar. I stayed here until I saw in the distance a great light, and then I knew I had it!" Going home that night, unrelieved and unsaved, the young man, who was later converted, said, "With one hand I was trying to *hold on.* With the other hand I was trying to *let go.* All the while I was peering into the darkness, looking for some mysterious light. As I walked along, I cried to God for mercy and forgiveness. Then this verse flashed into my mind, 'But as many as received him, to them gave he power to become the sons of God.' By faith I received Him, and He received me!"

—Told by Rev. Roy Gustafsen

* * *

Anchored in Safe Harbor!

The old captain of the historic *Merrimac* was an inmate of the Pennsylvania Soldiers' Home. He was a skeptic and an unbeliever. The chaplain in the home tried to get him to read the Bible, but he refused to do so. At last the chaplain said to the old captain, "Read the Bible and mark in red anything that you do not believe. Begin with the Gospel of John." The captain accepted the challenge. He was sick at the time and confined to his bed. Every few hours the chaplain, passing his door, would come in and ask, "Have you marked anything yet, captain?" The old captain would grin and say nothing. Several days later, when the chaplain stepped into the old captain's room, he found him dead, with his Bible open beside him. The chaplain leafed through the Gospel of John. Nothing was marked in red in the first chapter, or the second, or the third, until John 3:16. This verse was circled in red, and beside it was written, "I have cast my anchor in a safe harbor, thank God!"

—W. B. K.

* * *

I Believe in the Golden Rule

A self-righteous farmer boasted, "I am a good moral man. I pay my debts. I believe in the Golden Rule. It is true that I sometimes get angry and swear, but I am doing pretty well on the whole." The farmer hired a Christian carpenter to build a fence around the pasture where his cattle grazed. "Build the fence securely so none of my cattle can get out," instructed the farmer. Upon completion of the fence, the farmer asked, "Is the fence good and strong?" The carpenter said, "Sir, I cannot say it's all good and strong, but it's a good average fence. I may have left a little gap here and there. I dare say the cattle will find it a good fence *on the whole,* though I cannot say the fence is perfect in every part!" "What!" demanded the farmer angrily, "do you mean to tell me you built a fence around my pasture with weak places and gaps in it? My cattle will surely find them and escape. Don't you know that a fence must be perfect or it is worthless?" The carpenter answered, "I used to think so, but I've heard you talk so much about averaging matters with the Lord, and about being pretty good on the whole that I built the fence pretty good on the whole!"

It began to dawn upon the farmer that his righteousness was as filthy rags in God's sight, and that salvation is "not by works of righteousness which we have done," but by becoming new creatures in Christ Jesus. —W. B. K.

* * *

Is There Any Chance for Me?

When I was holding meetings in Canton, Ohio, a man asked me, "Is there any chance for me? I am the biggest scoundrel and sinner who ever lived. I make good money. When I get it, I go to a tavern and there spend my money for drink, though my wife and children sorely need it. My wife is a good Christian, but she has told me that she cannot take it any longer and for me not to come back home." While he spoke, he wept. "Can you do anything for me?" he pleaded. I told him that I knew One who could transform him, and give him a happy home — Jesus. He called upon the Lord to save him and his cry was heard. Immediately his thoughts were of his home and wife. He asked, "Do you think my wife will take me back?" I said, "I believe she will." Then he asked, "Will you go with me and tell her what has happened to me and ask her to take me back?" We went to his home. The wife met us. There was a scared look in her eyes. I told her that she had a *new husband*. I told her that Christ had saved him. I then called him in. They fell into each other's embrace, and both wept for joy!

—Told by Evangelist Fred Brown

• • •

Psychiatrist and Alcoholic Saved

A humanly hopeless alcoholic was placed under the care of a psychiatrist. He received little help. During the Billy Graham meetings in London, the alcoholic was induced to attend. He listened in wonderment to the gospel messages. "Possibly there is some hope for me," he thought. One night, when the invitation was given, he, with several others, went forward. Christ saved him. A new power came into his life. That night, before going to sleep, he reached for the nearby bottle of liquor. Something, or rather, *Someone*, held back his hand. Getting out of bed, he took the bottle of liquor and emptied it down the drain. When he awakened in the morning, through force of habit, he reached for the usual morning "bracer." It was not there. There was no feeling of disappointment, however. He phoned the psychiatrist and said, "You have lost a patient! Christ has saved me from drink. I am now a new man!" The psychiatrist said, "That sounds fine! Maybe I can find help where you found it!" He began to attend the meetings, and he, too, accepted Christ as his Saviour. Some days thereafter, in a lobby of a fashionable London hotel, the psychiatrist and the former alcoholic testified along with some fifty others, of the saving power of Christ.

—Told by Rev. Herbert Mitchell, Director *Family Altar League*

• • •

Milk-fed Lion Cubs Unchanged

Walter Beckworth was a famous lion trainer. One time he tried to change the nature of some lion cubs by feeding them only milk. When the young lions were ten months old, something happened which caused him to know that he could not change their nature by raising them on milk. "Come quickly, Walter," called his wife. Answering her call of distress, he saw a burro feeding on the grass nearby. One of the milk-fed young lions was slinking towards it. Suddenly the lion pounced on the burro's shoulder, hung on with one paw and reached for the animal's nose with the other paw. Jerking the head of the burro back, the lion threw it to the ground and with bared teeth plunged for the helpless burro's jugular vein. It was the lion's nature to do as he did.

We are born with sinful natures: "Behold I was shapen in iniquity; and in sin did my mother conceive me" (Ps. 51:5); "The wicked are estranged from the womb: they go astray as soon as they are born, speaking lies" (Ps. 58:3). Only the Saviour can change our sinful natures and give us a new nature: "If any man be in Christ, he is a new creature" (II Cor. 5:17). —W. B. K.

• • •

Opened From the Inside

Holman Hunt painted the picture "Christ the Light of the World." It portrays Christ in a garden at midnight, holding a lantern in his left hand. With His right hand He is knocking at a massive door with heavy panels.

When the painting was unveiled, several critics were present. They looked with admiration at the great production. One critic detected what he thought was lacking, namely, a knob on the door. He said, "You haven't finished your work." "It is finished," said the artist. "But there is no knob on the door," protested the critic. "Ah!" said the artist, "that is the door to the human heart. It can be opened only from the inside!" —W. B. K.

• • •

The Problem of Genesis

"I wish to discuss with you some of the problems I am having with the book of Genesis. I do not believe the first three chapters of the book," said a young man to a minister who had spoken to a group of students in an Eastern college. The minister asked him to attend a meeting which he was holding in the city, agreeing to spend some time with him after any service. One evening the minister gave an invitation to the unsaved to receive Christ as their personal Saviour. The doubting young man went into the inquiry room. After a searching talk with him, the minister asked, "Now tell me what your problems about the book of Genesis are. I want to help you if I can." The young man replied, "I have no problems with Genesis now. They are all gone!"

In obeying Christ's command to repent and believe the gospel, he had received salvation. Salvation safeguards the mind and makes the heart receptive to *all* of God's Word. —W. B. K.

* * *

The Heavens Must Do This, Or Else

How powerless are self-effort, self-mortification, and self-imposed tortures to justify sinful man before God! Martin Luther fasted, scourged himself and underwent all manner of privations. He became emaciated in body and broken in health. Then the light broke upon his darkened soul. He exclaimed, "He that made the heavens must do this, or it will remain forever undone." Coming to the end of all self-effort, and so-called "works of righteousness," God revealed to him the glorious truths: "The just shall live by his faith" (Hab. 2:4); "But to him that worketh not, but believeth on him that justifieth the

ungodly, his faith is counted for righteousness" (Rom. 4:5). —W. B. K.

* * *

Would He Rob Me of My Endeavors?

A humble Moravian workman asked John Wesley before his conversion the searching question, "Do you hope to be saved?" "Yes, I do," replied Wesley. "On what ground do you hope for salvation?" asked the Moravian. "Because of my endeavors to serve God," said Wesley. The Moravian made no reply. He only shook his head and walked silently away. Wesley, in speaking of the incident later said, "I thought him very uncharitable, saying in my heart, 'Would he rob me of my endeavors?'" Later, Wesley saw the light — that salvation is solely of grace, "not by works of righteousness which we have done," or can do. He saw what his brother, Charles, saw and expressed in these words:

Could my tears forever flow,
Could my zeal no languor know,
These for sin could not atone;
Thou must save, and Thou alone:
In my hand no price I bring,
Simply to Thy cross I cling.
—W. B. K.

SECOND COMING OF CHRIST

Short Quotes

Frankly I see no way out of this spiritual and moral torpidity and actual turpitude apart fom either the Spirit of God or the coming of the Son of God.
—Dr. William Culbertson,
President Moody Bible
Institute

* * *

Many are looking for signs of Christ's coming when they should be looking for souls. The disciples were *gazing* when they should have been *going.*
—Rev. A. W. Bailey

* * *

I have felt like working three times as hard since I came to understand that my Lord is coming again.
—D. L. Moody

The only hope for a peaceful world is the coming of the Lord Jesus Christ.
—Lt. Gen. William K. Harrison

* * *

We are now in the twilight of the great apostasy, and perilous times are gathering like the hurrying regiments of a mobilizing army.
"This know also, that in the last days perilous times shall come" (II Tim. 3:1).
—Dr. C. H. Morrison

* * *

In 1860 the French scientist, Pierre Berchelt, said, "Within a hundred years of physical and chemical science, man will know what the atom is. It is my belief that when science reaches this stage, God will come down to earth with

His big ring of keys and will say to humanity: *'Gentlemen, it is closing time.'* —*Flame*

* * *

There was a father whose business took him away from home for weeks and months. One day, as he was leaving, his little boy asked him, "When are you coming back, Daddy?" He replied, "When you see the green leaves on the trees turning yellow and red and brown, you may know that I am coming soon!" The little boy couldn't understand dates, but he could see the change in color of the leaves. When he saw the leaves put on their dresses of yellow, red and brown he was very happy, for he knew his daddy's coming was near!

Jesus said, "And when these things begin to come to pass, then look up . . . for your redemption draweth nigh" (Luke 21:28). —W. B. K.

"Till He come!" Oh, let the words
Linger on the trembling chords;
Let the little while between
In their golden light be seen;
Let us think how heaven and home
Lie beyond that "Till He come!"

Clouds and conflicts round us press;
Would we have one sorrow less?
All the sharpness of the Cross,
All that tells the world is loss —
Death, and darkness, and the tomb —
Only whisper, "Till He come!"

See, the feast of love is spread,
Drink the wine and break the bread —
Sweet memorials — till the Lord
Call us round His heavenly board;
Some from earth, from glory some,
Severed only "Till He come!"

—*Selected*

Illustrations

The Night Is Far Spent

When the slaves were emancipated in the British West Indies there was great jubilation and thanksgiving. On the night before the day of their freedom, thousands gathered in their places of worship for prayer and praise to God. Some went to nearby hilltops to catch the first glimmering of the dawn. They shouted to those below when the day of their deliverance from thraldom was dawning!

From the eminence of the prophetic Scriptures, we can "see the day approaching," and the glorious coming of the day of the Lord! We herald the glad and glorious news: "The night is far spent, the day is at hand. The coming of the Lord draweth nigh."

—W. B. K.

* * *

The Boss May Be Here Today!

When Shackleton was driven back in his attempt to reach the South Pole, he was forced to leave some men on Elephant Island, promising to come back for them. Time and again he tried, but was unable to reach them. At last, although it was the wrong time of the year, he made another great attempt.

An open channel formed between the sea and where he left his men. He rushed in his boat at risk of being "nipped" by the ice, got his men, and rushed out again before the ice crashed together. It only took half an hour! Afterwards he turned to one of the rescued men and said, "How was it you were able to come so quickly?" The man answered, "Sir, Mr. Wild (Shackleton's second-in-command) never let a chance slip; you had promised to come and we were waiting for you. Whenever there was a chance of your coming, Mr. Wild said, 'Boys, roll up your sleeping bags, the boss may be here today,' and, Sir, our sleeping bags were all rolled up; we were ready!"

Jesus has said, "I will come again!" We do not know *when* He will come. We know that He *will* come. Let us be ready for His coming!

—*Wonderful Word*

* * *

On the Brink!

Dr. Paul A. Schilpp, professor of philosophy at the University of Wisconsin said, "For a number of years, we have almost incessantly been told that 'humanity is at the crossroads.' Aside

from the fact that we have all grown
tired of this old cliché, the slogan is no
longer true. Humanity stands today before the abyss! How soon we may be
hurled into this abyss, as a result of
the inventive power of our own creative
minds, no one actually knows. But
among people who know the facts, the
fear is growing that the time is very
short indeed, so short, in fact, that we
can no longer speak in terms of generations, or even in terms of decades,
but probably only in years below two
digit figures. What seems to me, however, to make it infinitely worse is the
fact that leaders of the church, of science, and of the universities insist, in
general, upon continuing to act as if
nothing has happened!"
—Rev. Ralph W. Neighbour

* * *

Perhaps Today

Perhaps today our Lord will come
To bear us to our much loved Home:
Before the evening shadows fall
May sound the longed-for clarion call;
Then out of sorrow, tears and strife,
We'll rise to realms of joy and life.

Perhaps today will be the last,
And time shall be forever past.
Our light affliction will be o'er,
Then Glory! Glory! evermore!
These days of toil and pain will cease
And faithful workers rest in peace.

Perhaps today mine eyes shall see
The Lamb of God who died for me:
Oh, nothing else will matter then,
If unto Him I've faithful been.
Live for that day, O soul of mine,
And joy eternal shall be thine.
—Annie Lind Woodworth in
The Witness

* * *

**When Dr. Philpott Accepted the
Purifying Hope**

In the earlier years of his Christian
ministry, Dr. P. W. Philpott didn't believe in the premillennial return of
Christ. He believed that the Church
would save the whole world, taking the
world for Christ! His courage weak-
ened, however, as he observed "evil men
and seducers [waxing] worse and worse,
deceiving, and being deceived" (II Tim.

3:13). Then a change occurred! He
heard a stirring message on the second
coming of Christ. The message was
sane and Scriptural. He said, "The
message gripped my soul and set it on
fire for the lost ones. From the study
of God's Word, I saw that the mission
of the Church is not to take the world
for Christ, but to take Christ to the
world! Rarely in my teaching and
preaching did I fail to emphasize this
verse: 'And now, little children, abide
in him; that, when he shall appear, we
may have confidence, and not be
ashamed before him at his coming.'
The church I was serving at the time
grew from fifty believers to more than
two thousand. Of that number sixteen
young people were converted and went
forth as foreign missionaries. Souls
were saved in increasing numbers, and
Christians were cleansed from sin. How
could it have been otherwise when God's
Word says: 'And every man that hath
this hope in him purifieth himself, even
as he is pure'" (I John 3:3)?
—W. B. K.

* * *

I Am Waiting

I am waiting for the dawning
Of the bright and blessed day,
When the darksome night of sorrow
Shall have vanished far away;
When forever with the Saviour,
Far beyond this vale of tears,
I shall swell the song of worship
Through the everlasting years.

I am looking at the brightness —
See, it shineth from afar —
Of the clear and joyous beaming,
Of the "Bright and Morning Star";
Through the dark, gray mist of morning
Do I see its glorious light;
Then away with every shadow
Of this sad and weary night.

I am waiting for the coming
Of the Lord who died for me;
Oh, His words have thrilled my spirit,
"I will come again for thee."
I can almost hear His footfall
On the threshold of the door,
And my heart, my heart is longing,
To be His forevermore.
—*Selected*

Lo, He Comes

Lo, He comes, with clouds descending,
  Once for favored sinners slain;
Thousand, thousand saints attending,
  Swell the triumph of His train;
Hallelujah! Hallelujah!
  God appears on earth to reign!

Yea, Amen! Let all adore Thee,
  High on Thine eternal throne:
Saviour, take the power and glory;
  Claim the kingdom for Thine own.
O come quickly, O come quickly,
  Hallelujah! Come, Lord, come!
                    —*Moody Monthly*

* * *

If Christ Should Come Sunday

If Christ should come next Sunday,
  And it may be that He will,
Would the thing that I'll be doing
  Set the Master's heart athrill?

If the Christ should come next Sunday
  Would He find me loyal, true,
In my place with my influence
  Doing what He'd have me do?

If the Christ should come next Sunday,
  Let's suppose He came at ten,
Would He hear me answer "present"
  In the class I should attend?

If the Christ should come next Sunday,
  If He came just at eleven,
Would He find me in His service,
  Singing praises unto heaven?
                    —*Selected*

* * *

We Shall Be Like Him

Spurgeon received one day a copy of Andrew Bonar's commentary on Leviticus. Spurgeon was greatly blessed as he read it. He returned it to its author with this request: "Dr. Bonar, please autograph this book, and paste your picture on the title page. Then return it to me." Bonar did as requested. Below the picture he wrote, "Dear Spurgeon: Here is the book with my autograph and my photograph. If you had been willing to wait a short season you could have had a better picture. When I see Christ, I shall be like Him." —W. B. K.

352

Fuse Religions or Die

Thus counseled Arnold Toynbee, the British historian in the Gideon Seymour memorial lecture in Northrup Auditorium of the University of Minnesota. Toynbee said that living together as a single family is the only future mankind can have now that Western technology has simultaneously annihilated distance and invented the atomic bomb. The alternative, he added, is mass suicide. The only alternative to the destruction of the human race is "a worldwide social fusion for all the tribes, nations, civilizations, and religions of man."

How significant are these words to the student of the "sure word of prophecy," as given us in the eternal Word of God! We believe that the stage is now being set for the coming of the world dictator, the antichrist, under whose sway world religion, in all of its falsehood and antagonism to God and His Christ, will hold universal sway.

Long ago, Nebuchadnezzar "made an image of gold," and commanded all to "fall down and worship the golden image," death being the penalty for disobedience to his decree. Universal worship will be a decree of the antichrist, and the trend is unmistakably in that direction now.
                    —Rev. Ralph W. Neighbour

* * *

Dr. A. B. Simpson Tells Why

A news correspondent called on Dr. A. B. Simpson, wanting to learn the explanation of the great zeal for missions which characterizes the Christian and Missionary Alliance Church. "The members of this group," said the correspondent, "are people of average income, yet they give large sums of money to send missionaries into faraway places. What is the explanation? Also tell me how you know when Christ will come again."

Dr. Simpson answered, "I'll answer your second question first, and this will tell you why our people are so zealous to give the gospel to all the world as quickly as possible. Put this down just as I say it: 'And this gospel of the kingdom shall be preached in all the world for a witness unto all nations; and then shall the end come' (Matt. 24:14). Have you written down the reference?" "Yes, what more?" asked the reporter. "Nothing more!" replied Dr. Simpson. "Do you mean to say that you believe that when the gospel has been preached to all nations Jesus will return?" asked the correspondent. "Just that," said Dr. Simpson. "Then," replied the reporter, "I think I now see the motive and the motive power for this movement!" Said Dr. Simpson, "Then you see more than some of the doctors of divinity!" —W. B. K.

* * *

Unintentional Depiction of Coming Events

With little or no knowledge of eschatology, editors and writers sometimes depict future events and characters with uncanny accuracy. Did the editor of *Harper's Magazine*, for instance, realize how accurately the coming of antichrist was portrayed in the following item which occurred in his magazine?

"There will arise *The Man*. He will be strong in action, epigrammatic in manner, personally handsome and continuously victorious. He will sweep aside parliaments and demagogues, carry civilization to glory, reconstruct it as an empire, and hold it together by circulating his profile and organizing further successes. He will codify everything, rejuvenate the papacy, or, at any rate, galvanize Christianity. He will organize learning into meek academics of little men and prescribe a wonderful educational system. And the grateful nations will deify a lucky and aggressive egotism!"

The above excerpt appeared in *Harper's Magazine* in 1902, but it is more intelligible and up-to-date now than when it was first published.

Of the antichrist, the Bible says: "And through his policy . . . he shall cause craft to prosper in his hand: and he shall magnify himself in his heart" (Dan. 8:25); "And they worshipped . . . the beast, saying, Who is like unto the beast? who is able to make war with him?" (Rev. 13:4). —W. B. K.

* * *

Work, for the Day Is Coming

Work, for the day is coming!
Day in the Word foretold.
When, 'mid the scenes triumphant,
Longed for by saints of old,
He who on earth a stranger
Traversed its paths of pain,
Jesus, the Prince, the Saviour,
Comes evermore to reign.

Work, for the day is coming!
Darkness will soon be gone;
Then ere the night of weeping
Day without end shall dawn.
What now we sow in sadness,
Then we shall reap in joy;
Hope shall be changed to gladness,
Praise be our blest employ.

Work, for the Lord is coming!
Children of light are we;
From Jesus' bright appearing
Powers of darkness flee.
Soon will the strife be ending,
Soon all our toils below,
Not to the dark we're tending,
But to the day we go.

—*Selected*

SELF-CONTROL

Short Quotes

No form of vice does more to unchristianize society than the evil temper. For embittering life, for breaking up communities, for destroying the most sacred relationships, for devastating homes, this evil stands alone!

—Henry Drummond

Nothing external to me can have any power over me. —Walt Whitman

* * *

Most powerful is he who has himself in his power. He moves forward as tranquilly as a ship on a placid stream.

—Seneca

Our temper is one of the few things that improves the longer we keep it.

—W. B. K.

* * *

Quiet minds cannot be perplexed or frightened, but go on in fortune or misfortune at their own private pace, like a clock during a thunderstorm.

—Robert Louis Stevenson

* * *

If we knew as much about mental health as we do about physical health, an epidemic of hate would be considered as dangerous as an epidemic of typhoid!

—Dr. Howard A. Kelley

* * *

The Chinese have a story based on three or four thousand years of civilization. Two Chinese coolies were arguing heatedly in the midst of a crowd. A stranger expressed surprise that no blows were being struck. His Chinese friend replied, "The man who strikes first admits that his ideas have given out." —Franklin Delano Roosevelt

Illustrations

Easy Albert!

A young father was pushing a baby buggy down the street. He seemed to be unruffled by the bawling of the baby and softly said, "Easy, Albert! Control yourself! Keep calm!" The baby bawled more loudly. "Now, now, Albert, keep your temper!" the father went on. A mother, passing by, said, "I must congratulate you on your self-control. You surely know how to speak to a baby — calmly and gently!" She patted the crying baby on the head, and asked soothingly, "What's wrong, Albert?" "No, no!" exclaimed the father, "the baby's name is Johnny. *I'm* Albert!"

—W. B. K.

* * *

Hot or Cool Temper?

When temper is out of control,
It is a menace to one's soul,
It rages where peace should abound
And reason is no longer sound.

When tempers rise to angry heat,
Love goes down in dire defeat
And will-power wanes impotent
Until temper's madness is all spent.

When temper is controlled and cool
One's not induced to play the fool,
Conscience resumes its proper role
As mentor to one's will and soul.

—Dr. Albert Leonard Murray

How Far Is It to Heaven?

Late one Sunday night, a young minister entered a crowded bus with his Bible under his arm. Some rough fellows began to make sneering remarks about him. The minister didn't lose his temper. He didn't give the fellows a piece of his mind, but sat quietly and prayed silently for the rough fellows. As the minister left the bus, one of the fellows yelled, "Say, guy, how far is it to heaven?" Still in control of himself, the minister gently and earnestly said, "It is only a step! Will you take it now?" Because he had kept his temper, that minister had the joy of later bringing that young man to Christ. —W. B. K.

* * *

Flying Off the Handle!

When in Africa, I knew a missionary with an uncontrollable temper. One day he was out working with a group of natives. He became angry with one of them and, with his booted foot, kicked him over. That missionary — and I apologize for calling him a missionary — might as well have packed up his belongings and gone home, for that one fit of temper forever spoiled any possibility he may have had to help bring the natives to God.

Keep your temper — nobody wants it!

—As told by a missionary

SELFISHNESS—UNSELFISHNESS

Short Quotes

If you want to be miserable, think much about yourself, about what you want, what you like, what respect people ought to pay you, and what people think of you. —Charles Kingsley

* * *

All ambitions are lawful except those which climb upward on the miseries or credulities of mankind. —Joseph Conrad

* * *

Forget yourself for others, and others will never forget you.

* * *

There is a foe whose hidden power
The Christian well may fear,
More subtle far than inbred sin,
And to the heart more dear:

It is the power of selfishness,
It is the willful I;
And ere my Lord can live in me,
My very self must die.
—*Selected*

* * *

It is when we forget ourselves that we do things that are remembered.
—Eugene P. Bertin

* * *

How abhorrent to God is the self-life, including self-seeking, "And seekest thou great things for thyself? seek them not" (Jer. 45:5); self-exaltation, "I will exalt my throne above the stars of God" (Isa. 14:13); self-ease, "Woe to them that are at ease in Zion" (Amos 6:1); self-glory, "How much she hath glorified herself" (Rev. 18:7); "Is not this great Babylon, that I have built . . . by the might of my power, and for the honour of my majesty?" (Dan. 4:30). —W. B. K.

* * *

Let self be crucified and slain,
And buried deep, and all in vain
May efforts be to rise again,
Unless to live for others!

* * *

Jesus was the most selfless person who ever lived. He lived for others: "He went about doing good, and healing all that were oppressed of the devil" (Acts 10:38). He made the sorrows and sufferings of others His very own: "Himself took our infirmities, and bare our sicknesses" (Matt. 8:17). He died for others: "But he was wounded for our transgressions" (Isa. 53:5). In heaven He now intercedes for others: "He ever liveth to make intercession for them" (Heb. 7:25). At God's appointed time, He will come for others: "I will come again, and receive you unto myself" (John 14:3). —W. B. K.

* * *

Others, Lord, yes, others,
May this my motto be,
Help me to live for others,
That I may live like Thee!

Illustrations

Abandon Ship!

The ominous, frightful command, "Abandon ship!" was given. The so-called "unsinkable ship" — the Titanic — was sinking. Then came the order, "Women and children go to the lifeboats!" The ship's band began to play "Nearer My God to Thee." There were many deeds of heroism and unselfishness that night, but there was one exception. What appeared to be a stooped and feeble old lady, with a shawl drawn closely over her face and shoulders, pressed with the women and children toward a lifeboat. A sharp-eyed officer on the ship observed the agility of the "old woman." He grabbed the shawl and snatched it away, uncovering the face, not of an aged, decrepit grandmother, but of a despicably selfish young man! Pointing his pistol at the cowardly fellow the officer commanded him to go away.

Gladstone said: "The greatest curse of the human race is selfishness."

We are naturally selfish. Supernaturally, we become unselfish. —W. B. K.

An Illusion

There's a heap o' joy in living,
  When we're living as we should;
And the greatest joy is giving,
  Where it does the greatest good;
And we come to this conclusion,
  As the more of life we see,
It is merely an illusion,
  When we live it selfishly!

It's the old, but truthful story,
  If we strive for great success,
And we win, it lacks the glory,
  If we win by selfishness,
For we find life's sweetest pleasure,
  After all is said and done,
When we give in fullest measure,
  Of the riches we have won!
                —Frank C. Nelson

* * *

Motives

"What can I do for you, Madam?" Abraham Lincoln asked an elderly lady who had been ushered into his private office. Placing a covered basket on the table she said, "Mr. President, I have come here today not to ask any favor for myself or for anyone. I heard that you were very fond of cookies, and I came here to bring you this basket of cookies!"

Tears trickled down the gaunt face of the great President. He stood speechless for a moment; then he said, "My good woman, your thoughtful and unselfish deed greatly moves me. Thousands have come into this office since I became President, but you are the *first one* to come asking no favor for yourself or somebody else!" —W. B. K.

* * *

Man Is Like an Onion

"Much of our spiritual life has a great deal of the leaven of self corrupting it," said Dr. A. T. Pierson. "We seek self-advantage and self-glory on a higher level, and of a more refined sort. Nothing is so hard to kill as pride and selfishness. Man is like an onion —

layer after layer, and each a layer of self in some form. Strip off self-righteousness, and you will come to self-trust. Get beneath this, and you will come to self-seeking, and self-pleasing. Even when we think these are abandoned, self-will betrays its presence. When this is stripped off, we come to self-defense, and last of all, self-glory. When this seems to be abandoned, the heart of the human onion discloses pride that boasts of being truly humble!"

* * *

The Crust That Faileth Not

Is thy cruse of oil failing?
  Rise and share it with another,
And through all the years of famine
  It shall serve thee and thy brother.

Love Divine will find thy storehouse,
  Or thy handful still renew;
Scanty fare for one will often
  Make a royal feast for two.

For the heart grows rich in giving;
  All its wealth is living grain;
Seeds, which mildew in the garner
  Scattered, fill with gold the plain.

Is thy burden hard and heavy?
  Do thy steps drag wearily?
Help to bear thy brother's burden;
  God will bear both it and thee.

Art thou stricken in life's battle?
  Many wounded 'round thee moan;
Lavish on the wounds thy balms
  And that balm shall heal thine own.

Is thy heart a well left empty?
  None but God its void can fill;
Nothing but a ceaseless fountain
  Can its ceaseless longings still.

Is thy heart a living power?
  Self-entwined, its strength sinks low;
It can only live in loving,
  And by serving love will grow.
                —*Christian Monitor*

SERVICE

Short Quotes

The greatest danger for most of us is not that our aim is too high and we miss it but that our aim is too low and we reach it.

* * *

My mind was so full of service
I had drifted from Him apart,
And He longed for the old confiding,
The union of heart with heart.
I sought and received forgiveness,
While my eyes with tears were dim,
Now, though the work is still precious,
The first place is kept for Him!

* * *

The world measures a man's greatness by the number who serve him. Heaven's yardstick measures a man by the number who are served by him.
—Rev. Herschel H. Hobbs, D.D.

* * *

"When does the service begin?" whispered a visitor to someone sitting beside him in a Quaker's meeting. "Sir, service begins just after the meeting ends," was the reply.

Is your place a small place?
Tend it with care!
He set you there!

Is your place a large place?
Guard it with care!
He set you there!

Whate'er your place, it is
Not yours alone, but His,
Who set you there!
—John Oxenham

* * *

Fret not because thy place is small,
Thy service need not be,
For thou canst make it all there is,
Of joyful ministry.

The dewdrop, as the expansive sea,
In God's great plan has part,
And this is all He asks of thee:
Be faithful where thou art.

* * *

An elderly lady of wealth gave liberally to provide services for the poor in a mission in London. She was deaf, but nevertheless she was a radiant, joyful Christian. She faithfully attended the services of the mission. "What is your part in this work?" asked a visiting minister at the close of an evening service. "Oh," she replied, "I smile them in and I smile them out!" "Ah!" exclaimed the minister, "how valuable is such service in a place like this where so many are downcast and discouraged!" —W. B. K.

* * *

A little girl dearly loved Jesus and she wanted to serve Him. "How can I serve Him? I am so little and weak," she thought. One day she read a sentence in her Sunday-school paper which caused her to enter upon a life of service for Jesus. The sentence read: "An engine of one-cat power, working all the time, can do more for Jesus than an engine of forty horse-power standing idle." She said, "I will not have many chances to serve Jesus while I am small. But I will use the one-cat power I have, and serve Him all I can!"
—W. B. K.

* * *

Do all the good you can, by all the means you can, in all the ways you can, in all the places you can, at all the times you can, to all the people you can and as long as you can.
—John Wesley's rule

* * *

If I can do some good today,
If I can serve along life's way,
If I can something helpful say,
Lord, show me how!

If I can do a kindly deed,
If I can help someone in need,
If I can sow a fruitful seed,
Lord, show me how!

* * *

A writer for a great newspaper visited India. One day he met a missionary nurse who lived among the lepers and helped them. How tender and loving she was to the poor lepers. The reporter looked upon her with amazement. He said, "I wouldn't wash the wounds of these lepers for a million dollars!" "Neither would I," answered the missionary nurse, "but I gladly do it for Christ. I have no thought of any reward other than His smile of approval upon me!" —W. B. K.

Shamgar had an ox goad,
  Rahab had a string,
Gideon had a trumpet,
  David had a sling,
Samson had a jawbone,
  Moses had a rod,
Dorcas had a needle —
  All were used of God!

Illustrations

What's Full-time Christian Service?

The Moody Monthly editoralized thus: "Everyone isn't called to be a preacher or a missionary. Yet every person in Christian work whether stenographer, accountant, engineer, scientist, copywriter, teacher, janitor or in any one of many other classifications is truly in full-time service. Each makes a valuable contribution to the cause of Christ. At Moody we have more than four hundred full-time employees, and everyone is doing business for God. They make it possible for others to prepare for the ministry, mission field, Christian education or a ministry of music."

* * *

Serving Only for God's Glory

There was a humble shoemaker who was a devout Christian. One day a young minister called to see him, to enjoy his fellowship and talk with him about the things of God. Ineptly, the young minister said, "How good it is to meet a Christlike Christian in such a lowly occupation." The shoemaker answered, "Brother, don't call this occupation lowly." Before the shoemaker could say more, the minister, thinking that he may have unintentionally offended him, said, "Excuse me, my brother, I didn't mean to reflect on what you do to earn a living." To which the shoemaker replied, "You didn't hurt me, brother. I believe that my making shoes with an eye single to God's glory is just as great and holy as your preaching a sermon. I believe that when I stand before the Lord, He will ask me, 'What kind of shoes did you make?' He will ask you, 'What kind of messages did you deliver, and for whose glory did you deliver them?'" —W. B. K.

Pots, Pans and Things

Lord of all pots and pans and things,
Since I've no time to be
A saint by doing lovely things,
Or watching late with Thee,
Or dreaming in the dawnlight, or storm-
   ing heaven's gates,
Make me a saint by getting meals,
And washing up the plates.

Although I have Martha's hands,
I have a Mary's mind;
And when I black the boots and shoes,
Thy sandals, Lord, I find.
I think of how they trod the earth,
Each time I scrub the floor.
Accept this meditation, Lord,
I haven't time for more.

Warm all the kitchen with Thy love,
And light it with Thy peace;
Forgive me all my worrying,
And make all grumbling cease.
Thou who didst love to give men food,
In a room or by the sea,
Accept this service that I do —
I do it unto Thee.
           —*Selected*

* * *

Will No One Come to Help Him?

At Eastertime, many years ago, several paintings of things which happened during the week of Jesus' crucifixion were displayed in an art gallery in London. "Christ Before Pilate" was one of the paintings. People stood silently before the painting. A little girl was among the group. She could bear the silence no longer. She cried out, "Will no one come to help Him?" That little girl was Evangeline Booth. When she grew to womanhood, she spent a long busy life helping Jesus to help others. In time, she became commander in chief of the Salvation Army, which world-wide organization carries on the healing, saving ministry which Jesus began. —W. B. K.

* * *

Start Doing Something for God!

In Chicago one Sunday morning a minister in the course of his sermon pointed to a young woman who had been converted about a year and a half, and said, "What are you doing for God? Why don't you do something for God?"

To give emphasis to his words, he stepped down from the pulpit, went to where the young woman was sitting, took her hand, conducted her out to the middle aisle, made her turn toward the door, and giving her a push, said to her, "I want you to start doing something for God."

That push sent the young woman to the other side of the globe. She turned from her occupation, which was washing clothes, and began to study in preparation for Christian service. Later she went to Africa as a missionary.

In Africa she won to Christ many British people, including General Allenby.

The pastor who gave the young woman the push was D. L. Moody; the young woman was Miss Malla Moe, a missionary under the Evangelical Alliance Mission, who died in recent years at the age of ninety.

—Lydia Jacobson in *Moody Monthly*

SIN

Short Quotes

Christians should avoid all appearance of evil instead of doing a balancing act on the line of demarcation between good and evil: "Abstain from all appearance of evil" (I Thess. 5:22).

—W. B. K.

* * *

Psychologists say that if you put a frog into a pail of hot water he will jump out, but if you put him in a pail of cool water and then gradually heat it up, the frog will permit himself to be cooked. Apparently he is unable to decide when the water is so hot as to be unbearable. When sudden heinous temptations rear their ugly heads, most people instinctively shrink back; but the thing that causes many to get away from God is the almost imperceptible day-by-day drifting. The best protection is to get out of the pot when the water even begins to get warm.

—*Christian Victory*

* * *

A young African convert was given a position of trust in the mission station. He violated the trust and stole. The missionaries were distressed. "Why did you take what didn't belong to

you?" they asked him. He replied, "It wasn't I who stole. It was grandfather in the bones!" That was the way he spoke of his old nature. In time, he became an overcoming Christian. When asked, "How is grandfather in the bones?" he would reply, "Well, grandfather in the bones isn't dead yet, but he doesn't get about like he used to."

—W. B. K.

* * *

A minister's text for his message was, "There is no difference: for all have sinned, and come short of the glory of God" (Rom. 3:22, 23). A cultured, educated gentleman asked the minister, "Did you mean that there is no difference between a moral man and an immoral man?" Said the minister, "I did not mean that there is no room for comparison between two such men. There is this difference between them — one is a moral sinner and the other is an immoral sinner. One is a superior sinner and the other is an inferior sinner. Both are equally lost before God. Don't forget that it was to a moral, religious sinner to whom the Saviour said, 'Ye must be born again.'" —W. B. K.

God forgets and forgives the sins of all who repent of them and turn to the Saviour: "For I will be merciful to their unrighteousness, and their sins and iniquities will I remember no more" (Heb. 8:12). Shouldn't we forget them, too? —W. B. K.

* * *

Dost thou behold thy lost youth all aghast?
Dost reel from righteous retribution's blast?
Then turn from blotted archives of the past,
And find the future's pages white as snow!

—Walter Malone

* * *

There are a hundred men hacking at the branches of evil to every one who is striking at the roots of evil.

—Henry Ward Beecher

* * *

I think there is no doubt that this idea of sin creates much havoc in our relationships with other cultures. We should begin to think far more clearly and more extensively than we have in the past about it. We must remember that it is only in some cultures that sin exists. For instance, the Eskimos didn't have this concept until quite recently. Now they have it. They caught it from us!

—Dr. G. B. Chisholm in
Prescription for Survival

* * *

We are capable of every sin that we have seen our neighbor commit unless God's grace restrains us. —Augustine

* * *

The devil is an artist — he paints sin in very attractive colors.

* * *

Would you judge the lawfulness of a pleasure? Take this rule: Whatever weakens your reason, impairs the tenderness of your conscience, obscures your vision of God, or takes away the relish of spiritual things or increases the authority of your body over your mind, *that is sin.*

—John Wesley's mother

All sin is primarily against God: "Against thee, thee only, have I sinned" (Ps. 51:4). Sin is a clenched fist and its object is the face of God!

—W. B. K.

* * *

Men of culture no longer bother about their sins. —Sir Oliver Lodge

* * *

"My hardest job," said the warden of a great penitentiary, "is to convince youthful delinquents that they have done something wrong."

* * *

We are inclined to look upon bad temper as a very harmless weakness. The Bible, however, condemns it as one of the most destructive elements in human nature. —Henry Drummond

* * *

Sin is so deep and horrible a corruption of nature that no reason can comprehend it, but upon the authority of the Scriptures, it must be believed. The original sin is not like all other sins which are committed. The original sin *is*. It is the root of all sin. It can be restrained by no law or punishment, even though there were a thousand hells. Only the grace of God can purify and renew the nature. It is the heritage of all who are born into the world, Christ alone excepted. —Martin Luther, in
Converted Catholic Magazine

* * *

Eight-year-old Richard Mains, an English child, suffers from a rare disease — ganglineuropathy. Otherwise normal, he has no sense of feeling or touch. He is, therefore, immune to pain. His is a rare case of physical insensibility. But there is another insensibility not at all rare. In fact it is rampant and raging! It is destroying more children and youths in our land than polio. No Dr. Salk has discovered a vaccine to prevent it — it is insensibility to sin and conscience!

—Dorothy Dix

* * *

All sinners are *potential* saints. Oftentimes the greatest sinners become the greatest saints: "She loved much: but to whom little is forgiven, the same loveth little" (Luke 7:47). —W. B. K.

It is said that on his deathbed Vanderbilt, the multimillionaire, asked someone to sing the old hymn, "Come Ye Sinners." At the conclusion of the verse
Come ye sinners, poor and needy,
    Weak and wounded, sick and sore;
Jesus ready stands to save you,
    Full of pity, love and pow'r,
Vanderbilt said, "I am a poor and needy sinner!" —W. B. K.

* * *

Sin pays — it pays a wage, namely *death*: "For the wages of sin is death" (Rom. 6:23). Sin's wage is never reduced. The pleasures of sin are "for a season," but sin's wages are for eternity. —W. B. K.

* * *

If we want God to cover our sins, we must uncover them, confess them to God and to others against whom we may have sinned: "He that covereth his sins shall not prosper: but whoso confesseth and forsaketh them shall have mercy" (Prov. 28:13). It is not enough to say, "We have sinned." We must pinpoint our sins, and never excuse ourselves or blame others for them.

—W. B. K.

* * *

I dreamed last night that I had come
To dwell in Topsy-Turveydom,
Where vice is virtue, virtue vice,
Where nice is nasty, nasty nice,
Where right is wrong, and wrong is right,
Where white is black, and black is white!
"Woe unto them that call evil good, and good evil; that put darkness for light, and light for darkness; that put bitter for sweet, and sweet for bitter." (Is. 5:20).

Illustrations

Only Sin Separates From God

An apparently sincere seeker for truth came to a minister and said, "There is so much about the Bible that I don't understand. It contains so many difficulties. For instance, where did Cain get his wife?" "Yes, there are some things in the Bible whose full meaning God's children will not know until they awaken with the likeness of Christ in heaven. However, if I show you where Cain got his wife, will you renounce your sins and ask Christ to come into your heart and save you?" The man would not commit himself. The minister made investigation. He learned that it was not Cain's wife who was keeping the man from God, but some other man's wife!

"But your iniquities have separated between you and your God, and your sins have hid his face, that he will not hear" (Isa. 59:2).

—Told by Dr. R. A. Torrey

* * *

A Harmless Tiger?

During the rainy season in India, a valley near a populous community flooded. The natives fled to the highest peak. As they waited for the waters to subside, they saw a huge Bengal tiger swimming toward them. As the tiger neared the natives they became terrified! Often children and adults in India are killed and eaten by tigers. When the tiger reached the peak where the natives were, it showed no sign of molesting them. Instead, it lay down peaceably. The raging waters had frightened the ferocity out of him, but an English army officer, knowing the nature of a tiger, sent a bullet through its head. The natives naively asked, "Why did you kill it? The tiger was not going to hurt us." "You're wrong," snapped the officer. "Its true nature was only temporarily subdued by fright. When its old nature would have asserted itself, it would have surely pounced upon some of us!" —W. B. K.

* * *

I Know How Far to Go!

The scene of this awesome tragedy was in Georgia at Stone Mountain, the largest boulder in the world. Atop the mountain, a young man walked unsuspectingly along, oblivious of the gradual and almost imperceptible downward curvature of the domelike mountain. Suddenly he became aware of the fact that he was powerless to retrace his steps to safety. He had gone to the point of no return. Frantically he cried, "Help! Help!" His piteous plea was to no avail. Horrified spectators saw him hurtle to his death below.

The shores of time are strewn with moral and physical wrecks whose vain boast was, "I know how far to go! I know where to draw the line!" They didn't, however. "Let him that thinketh that he standeth take heed lest he fall." —W. B. K.

* * *

Eleven Miles Off Course — 135 Die!

"The United Air Lines DC jetliner, involved in history's worst aviation disaster, was eleven miles from where it should have been when it collided with a Trans World Airlines constellation," the administrator of the Federal Aviation Agency said.

The tragedy resulted in the deaths of 135 persons.

Speaking aeronautically, eleven miles are infinitesimal. Yet 135 people would be alive today if the jetliner had been where it ought to have been according to instructions.

Disastrous results often follow when God's children deviate even a little from the straight and narrow way. Warningly God's Word says, "Enter not in the path of the wicked, and go not in the way of evil men. Avoid it, pass not by it, turn from it, and pass away" (Prov. 4:14, 15). —W. B. K.

* * *

Abhor That Which Is Evil!

A woman of wealth wanted to hire a coachman. Three persons applied for the job. When she spoke to the applicants, she asked each the same question: "Tell me, if you drove my coach around a steep corner with a precipice on one side, how near could you go to the precipice?" The first applicant said, "I think I could keep within twelve inches of the precipice and we would be perfectly safe!" The next man said, "I could take you a hair's breadth and we would still be safe!" The third man said, "Madam, if I'm going to get

this job and you want me as your coachman, I'm telling you that when we go around that corner, I'm keeping as far from that precipice as I can!" He was employed. —W. B. K.

* * *

Sin Depersonalizes

For years, I was chaplain of the U. S. N. E. Penitentiary, in Lewisburg, Pennsylvania. Oftentimes, while chapel service was in progress, an officer would quietly pass to me a slip of paper on which no name occurred — only a number. I would announce, "Call for number so and so." The inmates were known only by numbers. Such was the depersonalized relationship of a prisoner to the government whose laws had been broken. Sin had degraded the prisoners from persons to mere numbers.

How different is the personalized relationship which the sheep of Christ's pasture sustain to the Good Shepherd: "He calleth his own sheep by name." —W. B. K.

* * *

No Longer Sensitive to Sin

I think television is having a detrimental effect on Christians. They are no longer sensitive to sin! Television has brought the night club into the home along with violence and sex, things which Christians looked upon ten years ago with abhorrence. They are gradually becoming desensitized, and I can cite case after case where Christians now watch these things on television without feeling any twinge of conscience! —Billy Graham

* * *

How Can the Leopard Change His Spots?

Screaming from daily papers were the tragic words — Doctor Tells of Killing Four! An unsigned note, in the doctor's handwriting, read: "Despair, frustration, restlessness — all haunt and tantalize me. Have I sinned? I do not believe my plight is due to sin. I think it is the result of being born a bad apple, a cross, brooding, mean dog, instead of a happy, friendly dog. How can the leopard change his spots? This is the question!"

The young heart specialist had gone into the rooms where his wife and three children were sleeping, and taken their lives. Then, in a futile effort to hide his crime, he had set fire to the home.

How grateful we are that there is an answer to the doctor's question. "How can the leopard change his spots?" Here is the one and only way: "Come now, and let us reason together, saith the Lord: though your sins be as scarlet, they shall be as white as snow; though they be red like crimson, they shall be as wool" (Isa. 1:18). —W. B. K.

* * *

Insensitiveness to Sin

A little girl in London held up her broken wrist and said, "Look, Mommy, my hand is bent the wrong way!" There were no tears in her eyes. She felt no pain whatever. That was when she was four years old.

When she was six, her parents noticed that she was walking with a limp. A doctor discovered that the girl had a fractured thigh. Still she felt no pain.

The girl is now fourteen years old. She is careful now, but occasionally looks at blisters and burns on her hands and wonders, "How did this happen?" She is insensitive to pain! Medical specialists are baffled by the case. It is called ganglineuropathy.

There is another insensitiveness which is deadlier and more dangerous — insensitiveness to sin! Paul said of this malady: "Having their consciences seared as with a hot iron" (I Tim. 4:2). —W. B. K.

* * *

Virtue and Decency Are Not Old-Fashioned

A distracted mother wrote to Dorothy Dix, world-famed columnist: "I have a very attractive daughter who has had a good environment all her life and devoted parents. Yet she does things and has ideas that distress us greatly. She resents our efforts to control her. She calls us old-fashioned. When we try to keep her from doing things of which we disapprove, she says, "Oh, Mother, can't you become up-to-date?"

Am I out-of-date when I tell her not to go to the apartment of two young men, that it will lead to no good?"

"Tell your daughter," replied Miss Dix, "it isn't virtue and decency that are 'old-fashioned' — it is wrongdoing. There hasn't been a new sin invented since the fruit-eating experience in the Garden of Eden. . . . The young people of today think that they are the first people in all the history of the world who ever strayed off the straight and narrow path. Everybody has always been doing it. There isn't a frank sex novel, hot from the press, whose plot isn't foreshadowed in the Ten Commandments, nor a vice that wasn't old when its warnings were thundered from Sinai. Girls think they show how ultramodern they are when they boast about how many cocktails they can drink, but there is nothing new in a drunken woman. Generation after generation has seen the poor, bleary-eyed, straggle-haired, frousy creatures stumbling along the streets, muttering to themselves, or living in a gutter!"

—W. B. K.

* * *

What Is Sin?

Man calls it an *accident;* God calls it an *abomination.*

Man calls it a *blunder;* God calls it a *blindness.*

Man calls it a *defect;* God calls it a *disease.*

Man calls it a *chance;* God calls it a *choice.*

Man calls it an *error;* God calls it an *enmity.*

Man calls it a *fascination;* God calls it a *fatality.*

Man calls it an *infirmity;* God calls it an *iniquity.*

Man calls it a *luxury;* God calls it a *leprosy.*

Man calls it a *liberty;* God calls it *lawlessness.*

Man calls it a *trifle;* God calls it a *tragedy.*

Man calls it a *mistake;* God calls it a *madness.*

Man calls it a *weakness;* God calls it *willfulness.*

—*Moody Monthly*

Death at the Controls

There was gaiety in the huge turbojet plane as it streaked on its way toward Miami. At the airport in Miami, husbands, wives, sweethearts, fathers and mothers were awaiting the arrival of their loved ones. The plane never arrived! Death was at the controls of the ill-fated plane that night! In midair, a terrific explosion occurred. The countryside was strewed with bits of mangled bodies and wreckage.

Who is at the controls of your life — the Saviour or Satan? Either one or the other is your master. The Bible says: "Know ye not, that to whom ye yield yourselves servants to obey, his servants ye are to whom ye obey; whether of sin unto death, or of obedience unto righteousness?" (Rom. 6:16).

The pathway of life is strewn by human wrecks who once boasted of their self-sufficiency. They felt no need of having Christ at the controls. "I know where to draw the line," they said. But they didn't! —W. B. K.

* * *

A Deadly Guest

A traveler in Ceylon was being entertained in the hut of a missionary. As they ate dinner, a deadly cobra noiselessly slithered into the room and coiled itself about the ankle of the host. "Quickly and quietly place a bowl of milk on the deerskin beside my chair," said the missionary to the servant. He knew that a cobra likes milk above everything else. The servant tiptoed for the milk. Any hasty movement or unusual noise would have meant sure death to the missionary. All sat like statues! Presently the cobra uncoiled itself and glided toward the bowl of milk, where it was killed.

Sin is a deadlier guest than a cobra. It is the enemy of our souls.

—W. B. K.

SINGING

Short Quotes

There's something about a fine old hymn,
That can stir the heart of a man,
That can reach the goal of his inmost soul,
Such as no mere preaching can!

It's more than the tune of the song he sings,
And it's more than the poet's rhyme,
It's the spirit of God working through them,
That gives them their power sublime!

So we thank Thee, Lord, for the grand old hymns,
May we use them again and again,
As we seek to save from a hopeless grave,
The souls of our fellow men!

—J. B. H.

* * *

A missionary sat solitarily in a prison cell. Suddenly, out of the stillness, a beautiful Chinese voice was heard singing, "O Come, All Ye Faithful, O, Rest in the Lord," followed by several carols. The missionary could not sing, but he could whistle. He whistled, "God Be With You Till We Meet Again!" Back came the answer, clear as a flute, "Blest Be the Tie." The missionary didn't know who the other singing prisoner was who lifted his soul onto a plane of jubilant praise! —*The Missionary Link*

* * *

Beware of singing as if you were dead or half asleep! Lift up your voices with strength. Be no more afraid of your voice now, or more ashamed of its being heard, than when you sang the songs of Satan. —John Wesley

* * *

Benjamin Flower was an English journalist. Some considered him too radical for his times. He was imprisoned for six months. An English girl, whom he later married, frequently visited him in prison. Their daughter was Sarah Flower. She was brilliant and had varied talents. Because of poor health, she dismissed all thoughts of a career she had long dreamed about. She began to write. In the field of writing she gained her greatest achievement. The hymn, *Nearer, My God, to Thee,* will immortalize her as long as time lasts. It is said to be the greatest hymn ever written by a woman.

—*Power*

* * *

A serious menace is present among us! It goes about in the disguise of religion. It finds favor among some people. I refer to the so-called "religious songs," some of which are totally false to God and the Bible. I give but one jolting example:
"The bells of hell go ting-a-ling,
Where, O death, is thy sting-a-ling?"

This bit of doggerel is often sung at square dances to the accompaniment of clapping hands! The God and Father of our Lord Jesus Christ is not the god of the square dance. The buddy-buddy-with-God cult has taken over the popular mind. May God help us.

—A Congregational minister

* * *

I was born with music in my system. I knew musical scores instinctively before I knew my ABC's. It is a gift of Providence. I did not acquire it. So I do not even deserve thanks for the music. Music is too sacred to be sold. The outrageous prices which musical celebrities charge today are truly a crime against society! —Fritz Kreisler

Illustrations

Greatest Earthly Music

What is the most inspiring music you ever heard? An old man wrote of his being present in Boston in 1869 at the great Peace Jubilee in commemoration of the ending of the Civil War. There was a chorus of ten thousand voices and an orchestra of one thousand pieces. Two hundred anvils had been placed on the platform for use in the Anvil Chorus.

There were huge bells. Outside, in the park, was artillery to be fired electrically in harmony with the chorus. At the head of the violin section, two hundred in number, stood the world's greatest violinist — Ole Bull. Their bows moved up and down as if in the hand of one man.

Parepa Rose was the soloist of whose singing Dr. Talmage said, "It was never equalled on earth!" When, in the "Star-Spangled Banner," she sang the high C with the fortissimo accompaniment of the full chorus and orchestra, the bells and cannon, it was so loud and clear that it seemed to bury the accompaniment!

The old man's letter closed thus: "I am an old man now, but am looking forward to the music of heaven where there will be music infinitely superior to the marvelous chorus I listened to that day!"

We shall sing on that beautiful shore
The melodious songs of the blest,
And our spirits shall sorrow no more,
Not a sigh for the blessings of rest!
—W. B. K.

* * *

Dear Lord, Do Not Pass Me By!

Blind Fanny Crosby wrote many beautiful hymns. She dearly loved her Lord. She would go anywhere to tell others of Jesus. One day she spoke in a prison to the convicts about Jesus. "He will come into your heart and make your life anew if you will ask Him for His mercy and forgiveness!" she said. As she spoke, a poor man who had been in the prison for many years, cried out, "O, dear Lord, don't pass me by. Do be merciful to me a sinner. O, do not pass me by!" The earnest plea went right to the heart of Miss Crosby. She went to her room and wrote the hymn, "Pass Me Not." Let us quote a verse of this hymn:
Pass me not, O gentle Saviour,
Hear my humble cry;
While on others Thou art calling,
Do not pass me by.
—W. B. K.

* * *

Jesus, Lover of My Soul

Charles Wesley was one day sitting by an open window, enjoying the fresh spring air and the fragrant breath of his garden below. Suddenly his attention was diverted to the frantic flutterings of a sparrow attempting to elude a pursuing hawk. The little sparrow flew straight to him and hid itself in the ample folds of his coat. Wesley himself was full of grave cares and anxieties at the time. He saw in the incident a parable of his own deliverance from fear. Inspiration came instantly to him to write a hymn which will last as long as time lasts: "Jesus, Lover of My Soul"! Thousands of tempest-tossed souls have found a comfort in this beautiful song. —*Service*

* * *

My Name Is Martin Luther, Sir!

A weary choirmaster closed his organ at the end of a rehearsal. As the choristers were preparing to leave, a boy's clear voice rang out in joyous song in the street outside the Eisleben church. "Bring that singer in! I want to speak to him," said the choirmaster. Search was made for the singer. Presently a boy stood attentively before the choirmaster who asked, "What is your name?" "Martin Luther, sir," replied the boy.

"Who taught you to sing?"

"No one taught me, sir. I like to sing. I often earn a few coins by singing in the streets."

"Would you like to sing in my choir?"

"I'd be very glad for the chance, sir," Martin answered gratefully. "Then report for rehearsal Saturday afternoon," the choirmaster said.

In this manner Martin Luther was introduced to the Eisleben church choir and to the world of song. —W. B. K.

* * *

Hymns Could Not Be Spanked Out of Him

In the period following the Reformation, singing in churches was confined mostly to psalms. It was thought wrong and even sinful to make up new hymns.

One man who made many contributions to the change from psalm singing to hymn singing was Isaac Watts. By the age of seven, he was composing so many poems that his father became annoyed and ordered him to quit. But Isaac refused. So his father took him

to the woodshed to "spank poetry out of him." But poetry was too deeply ingrained in Isaac for that.

When he was eighteen, Isaac complained to his father that the hymns in the church service were uninspiring. "Well," said his father, "if you could improve on them, why don't you try?"

Isaac did try. After much prayer, he wrote a hymn which was sung the following Sunday. During the following two years he wrote a new hymn for each service. At first, his hymns met opposition, for people considered them emotional, but Isaac Watts wrote on. Today his hymns are sung in churches throughout the world. The Lord guided his pen to write such never-to-be-forgotten hymns as "When I Survey the Wondrous Cross."

—*The Watchman-Examiner*

* * *

Brighten the Corner

This gospel song truly had its origin in a testing experience of its author — Mrs. Ina Dudley Ogdon. As a girl she saw visions and dreamed dreams. But her well-made plans and cherished ambitions had to be abandoned. She had an invalid father. Her dreams of reaching great audiences and swaying them by her eloquence in large auditoriums melted away and in their place she saw just one — her father. It was a struggle undoubtedly to reconcile her great ambition and a humble task, but at last she found her peace in God's perfect will. The transition from resentment to quiet resignation was made at last. She describes it in the little song so popular in the Billy Sunday revival campaigns:

Do not wait until some deed of greatness
    you may do,
Do not wait to shed your light afar,
To the many duties near you ever now
    be true,
Brighten the corner where you are.

Just above are clouded skies you may
    help to clear,
Let not narrow self your way debar
Tho' into one heart alone may fall your
    song of cheer,
Brighten the corner where you are.
    —*The Sunday School Times*

Singing Two Thousand Feet Below

The late Charles M. Alexander and the writer were on one occasion inspecting a gold mine in Bendigo, Australia, my native town. We descended to a depth of two thousand feet. Then we groped our way along a narrow, tortuous drive, aided by the dim light of candles, until we reached an open space where the miners were working on the gold reef. One of the miners, George Bartlett by name, asked Mr. Alexander to sing a verse of the "Glory Song." Together we sang the last verse.

Friends will be there I have loved
    long ago,
Joy like a river around me will flow;
Yet just a smile from my Saviour, I
    know,
Will thro' the ages be glory for me.

As we sang, Bartlett knelt and began to pray. As the strains of the song ceased, Mr. Alexander and I knelt beside him, and spoke to him about his personally accepting Christ as his Saviour. Definite prayer was offered; the way of life was clearly explained, and that day, George Bartlett was definitely led to a definite acceptance of Christ as his personal Saviour! —Robert Harkness, in
The Sunday School Times

* * *

Song Above the Field of Battle

It was on the eve of one of the great battles of Flanders. About midnight, the quiet was suddenly broken by the roar of German artillery. A shower of shells fell upon the British trenches. The British batteries replied and for several hours there was an incessant thunder of great guns. The air was filled with death's messengers. Toward morning, the bombardment ceased almost as abruptly as it had begun. The hush of night fell upon the field of death! Then, another and altogether different sound was heard. Somewhere, far above, a lark began to sing. Wearied with the noise of confusion and strife, the little herald of the dawn had mounted up until he caught the first gleam of the coming day, and called down the good news to those who were still in the darkness!

—Rev. W. W. Weeks in
The Heart of God

SMALL THINGS

Short Quotes

"For who hath despised the day of small things?" (Zech. 4:10).

* * *

Often the most useful Christians are those who serve their Master in little things. He never despises the day of small things, or else He would not hide His oaks in the acorns, or the wealth of a wheat field in bags of little seeds.
—Theodore Cuyler

* * *

Your ability is the measure of your responsibility: "Unto whomsoever much is given of him shall be much required."
—*New York Observer*

* * *

Little deeds of kindness,
    Little words of love,
Make our earth an Eden,
    Like the heaven's above.

For the want of a nail, a shoe was lost;
For the want of a shoe, a horse was
    lost;
For the want of a horse, a rider was
    lost;
For the want of a rider, a message was
    lost;
For the want of a message, a battle
    was lost;
For the want of a battle, a kingdom
    was lost;
All for the want of a nail!

* * *

Little masteries achieved,
Little wants with care relieved,
Little words in love expressed
Little wrongs at once confessed,
Little graces meekly worn,
Little slights with patience borne,
These are treasures that shall rise
Far beyond the shining skies.

If we cannot do great things, we can do small things in a great way.

* * *

Nothing is great without God, and nothing is small with God. When God is in it, little is much.

* * *

So many of us are not big enough to become little enough to be used of God.
—Rev. Vance Havner, D.D.

* * *

He stopped to pat a small dog's head —
A little thing to do;
And yet, the dog, remembering,
Was glad the whole day through.

He gave a rose into the hand
Of one who loved it much;
'Twas just a rose — but, oh, the joy
That lay in its soft touch.

He spoke a word so tenderly —
A word's a wee, small thing;
And yet, it stirred a weary heart
To hope again, and sing.
—Lois Snelling

* * *

Thank God for all the little things,
For butterflies with gauzy wings,
For hummingbirds that dart and fly
Among my flowers low and high;
For myriad blooms in Queen Anne's lace
And for each smiling pansy face;
For little babies, very wee,
I lift my special thanks to Thee
Who lovest all things great and small,
But maybe wee things best of all!
—Ruth Wheeler Wilcox

* * *

Little self-denials, little honesties, little passing words of sympathy, little nameless acts of kindness, little silent victories over temptations — these are the silent threads of gold which, when woven together, gleam out so brightly in the pattern of life that God approves.
—Dean Farrar

When I was young, I said to God, "Lord, tell me the mystery of the universe." God seemed to say, "That knowledge is reserved for Me alone." So I said, "God, tell me the mystery of the peanut." God seemed to say, "Well, George, that's more nearly your size!" And the Lord told me!
—Dr. George Washington Carver,
in *The Gospel Banner*

* * *

Do not wait to do a great thing. The opportunity may never come. But since little things are constantly claiming your attention, do them for a great motive — for the glory of God, and to do good to others. —Dr. F. B. Meyer

* * *

A holy life is made up of a multitude of small things. It is the little things of the hour — not the great things of the age — that fill up a life like Paul, John, Rutherford or Brainerd or Martyn. The avoidance of little evils, little inconsistencies, little indiscretions, little foibles, little acts of indolence — this goes far to make up the negative beauty of a holy life.
—Horatius Bonar in
The Watchman-Examiner

* * *

"I cannot do much," said a little child,
"To make this dark world bright;
My little feet cannot reach far
To make this dark world bright."
But Mother said, "Darling, do all you can,
For you are a part of God's great plan!"

So she helped another child along,
When the world was rough to its feet.
And she sang in her heart a little song,
That we all thought wondrous sweet.
And her father, a weary, toil-worn man,
Said, "I, too, will always do all that I can."
—*Selected*

Illustrations

How Chicago Fire Started

Many years ago, in 1871 in Chicago a woman was milking her cow, and there was a little lamp of oil, a little flickering flame. The cow kicked over the lamp, and the flame kindled a wisp of hay, and another wisp, until all the hay in the stable was on fire, and the next building was on fire, and the next, and the next! The fire spread over the river to the main part of Chicago and swept on until, within a territory one mile wide and three miles long, there were only two buildings standing. The little flame from that lamp had laid Chicago in ashes! If the fire of God shall fall now, you may be only a little wisp of hay, but if it sets you on fire, the fire will communicate itself to another, and that to another; it will burn on and on, till the remotest part of the earth is touched by the holy fire of God. —Rev. R. A. Torrey, D.D.

* * *

Mighty Little Things

Do you know that one speck of dust in an automatic flight-control instrument is sufficient to cause a multimillion-dollar supersonic jet airplane to veer widely off its course?

Do you know that lint from clothing and moisture from fingerprints can make a guided missile, zooming along at twice the speed of sound, go awry, and miss its mark?

Do you know that smog and humidity can cause intricate flight instruments to fail and endanger the success of vital military missions?

G. M. Giannini, a noted American scientist, says all this is so! This is a reminder that there are many tiny things that can cause the finest specimen of humanity to go awry and miss the glorious destiny which his Maker has made possible for him to enjoy. It is not necessary to commit some glaring evil in order to become a failure spiritually. —*Now*

* * *

What Can I Do?

It is my joy to do the task
That I can find to do.
I cannot sing an anthem sweet,
But I can find an empty seat
And listen with devoted care
While someone lifts his heart in prayer.

I cannot play the organ grand,
But I can clasp a stranger's hand
And smile and say a word of cheer.
Who knows? It may dispel a fear
And help that one upon his way,
If I can just the right word say.

I cannot preach a sermon great,
But when the offering they take
I can be honest with my Lord
And freely give of my small hoard.
And I can bring a flower fair,
So God's own house will look less bare.

These little things that I can do
Seem, oh, so small, and far too few,
But if I'm watchful of them all,
When His dear voice to me shall call,
I'll say, "Here, Lord! And all I bring
Is faithfulness in little things."
—Rosilyn C. Sture

* * *

Little Things

It takes a little muscle
And it takes a little grit,
A little true ambition
With a little bit of wit.
It's not the "biggest" things that count
And make the "biggest" show,
It's the little things that people do
That makes this old world go!

A little bit of smiling
And a little sunny chat,
A little bit of courage
To a comrade sliding back.
It's not the "biggest" things that count
And make the "biggest" show,
It's the little things that people do
That makes this old world go!
—*Selected*

* * *

Little Becomes Much

Robert Hill, 13, recently read a book about the renowned Africa medical missionary, Dr. Albert Schweitzer. The Negro lad was so impressed that he sent a bottle of aspirin from his home in Waycross, Ga., to Lt. Gen. Richard C. Lindsay, commander of Allied Air Forces in southern Europe where Robert's sergeant father is stationed. The letter asked Lindsay if "any of your airplanes" could drop the aspirin over Lambarene, Gabon Republic, where Schweitzer runs his jungle hospital in French Equatorial Africa. Robert added, "Maybe some other people feel like I do."

And they did! The Italian press and radio made public Robert's letter, and soon Lt. Gen. Lindsay had $400,000 worth of donated medicine to send by Italian and French government airliners to the jungle hospital. Robert was also given a trip to Lambarene where he

shyly shook hands with Schweitzer. Smiling, the doctor looked at the young American and quoted the Bible as he said, ". . . a little child shall lead them."
—E. P. Service

SORROW, SUFFERING, CHASTENING

Short Quotes

Have courage for the great sorrows of life, and patience for the small ones.
—Victor Hugo

* * *

No physician ever weighed out medicine to his patients with half so much care and exactness as God weighs out to us every trial. Not one grain too much does He ever permit to be put in the scale. —Henry Ward Beecher

* * *

God doesn't comfort us in our sorrow to make us feel comfortable, but "that we may be able to comfort them which are in any trouble, by the same comfort wherewith we ourselves are comforted of God" (II Cor. 1:4). —W. B. K.

* * *

"When I left Springfield," said Lincoln, "I was not a Christian. When I buried my son, the severest trial of my life, I was not a Christian. But when I went to Gettysburg, and saw the graves of thousands of soldiers, I then and there consecrated myself to Christ. Yes, I do love Jesus!"

* * *

I learn, as the years roll onward
And I leave the past behind,
That much I had counted sorrow
But proves that God is kind;
That many a flower I had longed for
Had hidden a thorn of pain,
And many a rugged by-path
Led to fields of ripened grain.

* * *

A jewel is a bit of ordinary earth which has passed through some extraordinary experiences.

* * *

There are two ways of getting out of a trial. One is simply to try to get rid of the trial, and be thankful when it is

over. The other is to recognize the trial as a challenge from God to claim a larger blessing than we have ever had, and to hail it with delight as an opportunity of obtaining a larger measure of divine grace. —A. B. Simpson

* * *

Life is not a cloudless journey,
Storms and darkness oft oppress,
But the Father's changeless mercy
Comes to cheer the heart's distress;
Heavy clouds may darkly hover,
Hiding all faith's view above,
But across the thickest darkness
Shines the rainbow of His love.

* * *

The writer knew a Jewish brother who was a good Hebrew scholar. When he took a stand for Jesus, his wife spurned him. His children turned against him. Time and again he pleaded with his loved ones to listen to the appeals of their Messiah. They were obdurate. He died in a hospital of cancer. —F. Kendal in *Bible Expositor and Illuminator*

* * *

For twelve long years Bunyan's lips were silenced in Bedford jail. It was there, however, that he did his greatest and best work of his life, for there he wrote the book that has been read most next to the Bible — *Pilgrim's Progress*. Bunyan said, "I was at home in prison, and I sat me down and wrote and wrote, for the joy did make me write."

* * *

The Reverend Leslie Weatherhead dedicated his book, *Why Do Men Suffer?* to his mother and sister in the following touching words: "Dedicated in unfailing remembrance to Elizabeth Mary Weatherhead, my mother, and

Muriel Weatherhead, my sister, whose bodies were defeated in the battle of painful disease, but who wrested from that defeat a *spiritual victory* which challenged and inspired all who knew them, and made glad the heart of God."

—W. B. K.

* * *

For every hill I've had to climb,
For every stone that bruised my feet,
For all the blood and sweat and grime,
For blinding storms and burning heat
My heart sings but a grateful song —
    These were the things that made me
    strong!

For all the heartaches and the tears,
For all the anguish and the pain,
For gloomy days and fruitless years,
And for the hopes that lived in vain,
I do give thanks, for now I know
    These were the things that helped me
    grow!

'Tis not the softer things of life
    Which stimulate man's will to strive;
But bleak adversity and strife
    Do most to keep man's will alive.
O'er rose-strewn paths the weaklings
    creep,
    But brave hearts dare to climb the
    steep.
—*Occidental United Presbyterian*

* * *

Bud Robinson, a unique evangelist of the other years, spoke thus of God's refining fires:

"God put me into His crucible. The fires got hotter and hotter. Then God began to ladle off the skimmings. I began to think that there was nothing but skimmings, and that there would be nothing left of Bud Robinson!"

When God saved us, He began to conform us to the image of His Son. It is in the crucible of trial and temptation, sorrow and suffering that the heavenly Father transforms us "from glory to glory," and grows us into Christlikeness.

—Rev. James Seward

* * *

O blessed storm, thou hast brought me to the knowledge of Christ! O happy starless night, thou hast conducted me to the Light of the world! O tumultuous sea, thou hast tossed me furiously on thy bosom only to bring me to rest on the bosom of God!

—Rev. H. M. Freleigh

* * *

The ancients used an interesting little instrument, called the *tribulum*, to beat grain to divide the chaff from the wheat. The word "tribulation" comes from this word. Tribulations truly separate the chaff from the wheat in human character.

"And not only so, but we glory in tribulations also: knowing that tribulation worketh patience; and patience, experience; and experience, hope" (Rom. 5:3, 4). —W. B. K.

Illustrations

I Shall Come Forth As Gold!

Derby china is made in Derby, England. It is also called Crown Derby, because a royal warrant is issued authorizing its manufacture. It is widely sought and is highly prized by those who possess it. One day a minister visited the factory where Derby china is made. He saw artisans apply varicolored paints to the china — yellowish-brown, bluish-black and dirty-looking red. They circled the edge of the china with black paint. How unattractive was the china when it was put into the furnace. But the fire wrought an amazing transformation. When it was taken from the furnace, the minister looked in wonderment upon the exquisitely beautiful pieces of china! The black had become a bright gold. The blue and the red had become lustrous and bright.

In the unerring wisdom of God, some of His choicest saints are disciplined and conformed to the image of Christ in the furnace of sorrow and suffering: "Behold, I have refined thee, but not with silver; I have chosen thee in the furnace of affliction" (Isa. 48:10).

—W. B.K.

God's Way Is the Best Way

God never would send the darkness
  If He knew you could stand the light,
But you would not cling to the Guiding
    Hand,
  If the way were always bright;
And you would not care to walk by faith,
  Could you always walk by sight.

'Tis true He has many an anguish
  For your sorrowful heart to bear,
And many a cruel thorn-crown
  For your tired head to wear;
He knows how few would reach heaven
    at all
  If pain did not guide them there.

So He sends you the blinding darkness,
  And the furnace of sevenfold heat,
'Tis the only way, believe me,
  To keep you close to His feet;
For 'tis always so easy to wander
  When our lives are glad and sweet.

So nestle your hand in the Father's
  And sing, if you can, as you go,
Your song will cheer someone behind
    you,
  Whose courage is sinking low;
And — well, if your lips do quiver,
  God will love you the better, so.
               —*Selected*

* * *

That Was Some Trick!

The man on the hospital bed had lost his left leg. He was bitter. As I walked slowly toward him, he began, "Well, Chaplain, start cheering me up! You're a navy specialist; so do your stuff." I felt helpless to help him that day.

Next day a young marine corporal in a wheel chair rolled up to his bed. The marine was grinning generously, though both his legs were missing. No sarcasm came from the navy man this time. Here suffering had met suffering and understood; courage had encountered despair and won.

On my visit that afternoon, the navy man looked at me accusingly through a smile. "Chaplain," he said, "that was some trick — sending me that marine amputee. But it worked, I guess. The nurse just said I have become a pretty decent fellow."

In our witnessing we can be more ef-

fective if we get self out of the way and present the One who understands because He suffered and overcame.
       —Chaplain Wyatt Willard

* * *

I Know How It Feels

Dr. Stuart Nye Hutchison tells us about a boy whom he knew who had lost his right hand. He felt so badly about it that he did not want to see anyone. His father said, "I'm going to bring the minister in to see you." The boy said, "I don't want to see him." But the father brought the minister. When the boy looked up, he saw that the minister had no right arm; there was an empty sleeve. He came over to the boy and said, "I haven't any hand, either. I lost mine when I was a boy, and I know how it feels." It wasn't hard for the boy to get acquainted with the minister who knew how it felt.

So Christ has suffered for us and knows our temptations.
       —*The Sunday School Times*

* * *

The Unexpected

I know not what may come today,
Some needy soul may cross my way;
Lord, give me words of cheer, I pray,
  To meet the unexpected.

Perhaps some loss may come to me,
Some care, or some perplexity,
Then He my strength and stay shall be
  To face the unexpected.

How oft within the trivial round
So many trying things are found;
But He can make all grace abound
  For all the unexpected.

No matter what the call may be,
Or changes that may come to me;
His hand of love in all I see
  From sources unexpected.
               —Buckley

* * *

Sorrows Polish and Refine Us

On the coast of Pascadero, California, is the famed Pebble Beach. There the waves dash with a ceaseless roar and thunder among the stones on the beach. The pitiless waves toss and grind the stones together and hurl them against the rugged cliffs. Day and night, the wearing down of the stones continues unabated. Tourists from all over the world gather the beautiful, round, polished stones for ornaments on mantels. Near Pebble Beach is a towering cliff which breaks the force of the dashing waves. In the quiet cove, sheltered by the cliff, is an abundance of stones. These are unsought, unwanted. They have escaped the turmoil and beating of the waves. Hence they are rough, angular and devoid of beauty.

Billows of sorrow and trouble polish and refine us, and give to us the opportunity to prove the genuineness of the Saviour's comforting, healing words.

—W. B. K.

* * *

In His Steps

"The road is too rough," I said,
"Dear Lord, there are stones that hurt me so."
And He said, "Dear child, I understand,
I walked it long ago."

"But there's a cool green path," I said,
"Let me walk there for a time."
"No, child," He gently answered me,
"The green road does not climb."

"My burden," I said, "is far too great,
How can I bear it so?"
"My child," He said, "I remember the weight,
I carried My cross, you know."

But I said, "I wish there were friends with me,
Who would make my way their own."
"Ah, yes," He said, "Gethsemane
Was hard to bear alone."

And so I climb the stony path,
Content at last to know
That where my Master had not gone,
I would not need to go.
And strangely then I found new friends,
The burden grew less sore,
And I remembered, long ago
He went that way before.

—*Selected*

* * *

Little Vexations

Toiling through a great hot valley in Ethiopia, far from civilization, we once came with gratitude to the top of a hill, where it was much cooler. Surely the camp could not be far away. The ground was covered with short, dry grass, and after the difficult mountain, we began to rejoice. But we rejoiced too soon. After a short ride everyone began to start itching and smarting in the most intolerable fashion. Even the mules were affected and stamped angrily. A careful examination showed that each seed stem of grass had a myriad of sharp little bayonets that would penetrate the skin and would work up through the clothing, causing intense discomfort. Life's school is full of experiences like that. Not one great trouble, but a thousand little ones cause pain and vexation. Yet this is God's school. —Dr. Thomas A. Lambie

* * *

The Storm's Mad Havoc

I wonder why God's wisdom sees
The storm's mad havoc with the trees,
The broken vines and trampled grass,
And does not end the holocaust.

But when the sun shines once again
The flowers appear because of rain,
And so my life may brighter be
When God's wild rainstorms batter me.
—William Bennett

* * *

Blest Be the Sorrow

If, through unruffled seas,
Toward heaven we calmly sail,
With grateful hearts, O God, to thee,
We'll own the favoring gale.

But should the surges rise,
And rest delay to come,
Blest be the sorrow — kind the storm,
Which drives us nearer home.

Teach us, in every state,
To make thy will our own;
And when the joys of sense depart,
To live by faith alone.
—*Selected*

* * *

Songs in the Night

In his "Hunting for the Nightingale in England," John Burroughs tells of listening one dark night to the song of the sedge warbler in the hedge. It was a singular medley of notes, hurried chirps, trills, calls, warbles. When it stopped singing, a stone flung into the bush set it going again, its song now being so persistently animated as to fill the gloom and darkness with joy. Samuel Rutherford's most gladsome letters are those from his prison. The saints have sung their sweetest when the thorn has pierced their heart. Sorrow produces songs in the night.

—The Sunday School Times

* * *

Pruning

One of God's children was passing through the dark waters of sorrow and suffering. "God has forgotten to be gracious to me. I don't understand His judgments," he said. The pastor came to see him. He found him in the back yard, pruning a grapevine of its superfluous twigs and branches. The man said, "Pastor, because of the heavy rains of late, this vine has become overgrown with worthless twigs and branches. It is necessary to remove them so the vine can bring better fruit to maturity." "Does this vine resist and oppose you?" asked the pastor. "Of course not," he said. "Then why should you complain about the chastening hand of God when He does for you what you have done to this vine?" asked the pastor.

—W. B. K.

* * *

Thou Hast Enlarged Me

The cocoon of the emperor moth is flasklike in shape. To develop into a perfect insect, it must force its way through the neck of the cocoon by hours of intense struggle. Entomologists explain that this pressure to which the moth is subjected is nature's way of forcing a life-giving substance into its wings. Wanting to lessen the seemingly needless trials and struggles of the moth, an observer said, "I'll lessen the pain and struggle of this helpless creature!" With small scissors he snipped the restraining threads to make the moth's emergence painless and effortless. The creature never developed wings. For a brief time before its death it simply crawled instead of flying through the air on rainbow-colored wings!

Sorrow, suffering, trials, and tribulations are wisely designed to grow us into Christlikeness. The refining and developing processes are oftentimes

slow, but through grace, we will emerge triumphant: "Thou hast enlarged me when I was in distress" (Ps. 4:1); "When thou hast tried me, I shall come forth as gold" (Job 23:10). —W. B. K.

* * *

From Glory to Glory

Years ago, the world's most valuable diamond was found in an African mine. It was to be given to the king of England to blaze in his crown. When it was found, the diamond was shapeless. A lapidary notched it, and struck it with a hard blow from his instrument. For months he had studied that blow. The lines of cleavage of the diamond had been planned with minutest care. The blow brought the gem to its most perfect shapeliness, radiance and beauty.

Sometimes the Lord, in unerring wisdom, allows the blows of sorrow and suffering to fall on us that we might shine with brighter luster when He comes to "make up [his] jewels."

It is in the crucible of sorrow and suffering that God transforms us "from glory to glory," and grows us into Christlikeness.

—Told by Dr. Harry A. Ironside

* * *

He Shall Sit As a Refiner

In medieval times, the goldsmiths had a unique method to determine when the refining fire had purged away all extraneous matter from 'he precious metal.

They would stand patiently and peer intently into the seething, molten mass, meantime making the fire hotter and hotter. At last, a smile of satisfaction would lighten up the perspiring face of the goldsmith. He could see his face reflected in the molten mass of gold. Seeing his face mirrored there, he knew that the refining fire had wrought its purifying purpose.

Of the heavenly Father, the Bible says: "And he shall sit as a refiner and purifier of silver: and he shall purify the sons of Levi, and purge them as gold and silver" (Mal. 3:3a).

Peter admonished: "Beloved, think it not strange concerning the fiery trial which is to try you" (I Pet. 4:12a).

When God sees the image of His dear Son reflected in our lives, He knows that His purifying fires have wrought their intended purpose.

—Rev. R. E. Neighbour, D.D.

* * *

Trace the Rainbow Through the Rain

When George Matheson was entering upon a promising career, a doctor said to him, "You had better see your friends soon, for erelong darkness will settle upon you and you will see them no more forever!" That was the doctor's way of saying that soon Matheson would become totally blind. Matheson was engaged to a beautiful young lady. He told her of the calamity which would soon befall him and gave her permission to break the engagement. She did. The great sorrow deepened his devotion to God. During that soul-refining trial, Matheson gave to Christ's church a hymn which will inspire others whom God, in unerring wisdom, has chosen to go through the "furnace of affliction" (Isa. 48:10):

O love that wilt not let me go,
  I rest my weary soul in Thee,
I give Thee back the life I owe,
  That in Thine ocean depths its flow
    May richer, fuller be!

O joy that seekest me through pain,
  I cannot close my heart to Thee,
I trace the rainbow through the rain,
  And feel the promise not in vain,
    That morn shall tearless be!

—W. B. K.

* * *

Can't You Trust Him?

A mother was passing through difficult, testing times. When her pastor visited her, he found her deeply depressed. Her baby was fretful. Her husband had gone to work although he was not well. Her daughter, Mary, was in the hospital. "Everything has gone wrong with me, pastor. God has forgotten to be gracious, and has forsaken me," lamented the mother. The wise pastor replied, "So the baby is a nuisance now that he's teething?" "Yes, that's right, pastor," she answered. "Then why don't you get rid of the baby? I'll open the door, so you can throw him out!" said the minister. "Not for all the gold in the world would I do a thing like that!" replied the mother. "You wouldn't?" queried the pastor. "You know I wouldn't," said the mother as she wiped tears from her eyes. Then the pastor said, "And do you think that you love your baby more than God loves you? Can't you trust Him to see you safely through your troubles?" "Why, of course, I can," said the mother with a smile.

—W. B. K.

* * *

Called Aside

Called aside—
From the glad working of thy busy life,
From the world's ceaseless stir of care
  and strife,
Into the shade and stillness of thy heavenly Guide
For a brief space thou hast been called aside.

Called aside—
Perhaps into a desert garden dim;
And yet not alone, when thou hast been
  with Him,
And heard His voice in sweetest accent
  say:
"Child, wilt thou not with me this still
  hour stay?"

Called aside—
In hidden paths with Christ thy Lord
  to tread,
Deeper to drink at the sweet Fountainhead,
Closer in fellowship with Him to roam,
Nearer, perchance, to feel thy heavenly
  home.

Called aside—
Oh, knowledge deeper grows with Him
  alone;
In secret oft His deeper love is shown,
And learnt in many an hour of deep
  distress
Some rare, sweet lesson of His tenderness.

Called aside—
We thank Thee for the stillness and the
  shade;
We thank Thee for the hidden paths Thy
  love hath made,

And, so that we have wept and watched
with Thee,
We thank Thee for our dark Gethsemane.

Called aside—
Oh, restful thought, He doth all things
well;
Oh, blessed sense with Christ alone to
dwell;
So in the shadow of Thy cross to hide,
We thank Thee, Lord, to have been
called aside.
—*Selected*

* * *

Life-saving Tears

Tears are one of God's good gifts to
His children. Tears are escape valves
for pent-up sorrow.

According to modern medical science,
pent-up grief can be disastrous.

Dr. Erick Lindemann, psychiatrist-
in-chief of the Massachusetts General
Hospital and a pioneer in the investigation of repressed sorrow, tells of a
young nurse who tended her father
through the long months of his final illness. She was very devoted to her
father, and often fought back tears as
she nursed him.

When he died, a well-meaning friend
sternly forbade her to show any grief
for the sake of her mother who had a
weak heart. Within hours, the emo-
tionally-repressed nurse developed a case
of ulcerative colitis. She slowly cor-
roded inwardly because of the disordered
impulses of her nervous system. Eventually she died, killed by the suppressed
grief she would not allow herself to
express in copious tears. —W. B. K.

SOUL WINNING—PERSONAL WORK

Short Quotes

The following taunting statement by
an atheist made William Booth a zealous Salvationist: "If I believed what
you Christians say you believe about
a coming judgment, and that impenitent rejectors of Christ will be lost, I
would crawl on my bare knees on
crushed glass all over London, warning
men, night and day, to flee for refuge
from the coming day of wrath!"
—Rev. T. W. Callaway, D.D.

* * *

Talk to the Lord about sinners. Then
talk to sinners about the Lord.

* * *

We cannot all be evangelists, but we
can all be soul winners. Try it! There
is no work so romantic, so enduring! I
covet above all gifts to win souls.
—Samuel Chadwick

* * *

Every atom in the universe can act
on every other atom, but only through
the atom next to it. If a man would
act upon every other man, he can do it
best by acting, one at a time, upon those
beside him. —Henry Drummond

Count that day lost
Whose low, descending sun
Views from thy hand
No soul for Jesus won!

* * *

Before a condemned criminal was
electrocuted in Cook County, Illinois, he
was given the opportunity to say anything he wanted to say. This is what
he said: "No man cared for my soul!"
Can we say with Paul, "My heart's desire and prayer to God . . . is, that they
might be saved"?

* * *

Lead me to some soul today,
Oh, teach me, Lord, just what to say;
Friends of mine are lost in sin,
And cannot find their way.
Few there are who seem to care,
And few there are who pray;
Melt my heart and fill my life,
Give me one soul today.
—Will H. Houghton

* * *

I would think it a greater happiness
to gain one soul to Christ, than mountains of silver and gold to myself. If

376

God suffers me to labour in vain, though I should get hundreds a year by my labour, it would be the constant grief and trouble of my soul; and if I do not gain souls, I shall enjoy all my other gains with very little satisfaction.

—Matthew Henry

* * *

Years ago on a street in Chicago a man stepped up to a young fellow and asked, "Are you a Christian?" "Mind your own business," was the reply. "This is my business — my main business," said the man, Dwight L. Moody. He never let a day pass without speaking to someone about Jesus.

It is the main business of *each* Christian to tell others about Jesus and do his best to bring others to the Saviour.

—W. B. K.

* * *

If we work upon marble, it will perish. If we work upon brass, time will efface it. If we rear temples, they will crumble into dust. But if we work upon immortal souls, if we imbue them with principles, with the just fear of God and love of fellow men, we engrave on those tablets something which will brighten all eternity. —Daniel Webster

* * *

Where are the tears for the lost? Where is our concern for men who are confused, frustrated, lost, sinful and destined for hell? —Billy Graham

* * *

I wish that I could televise
A Sunday school to all,
I'd have a class in every home,
I'd reach the great and small!
But though I have no telecast
To cross the hill and plain,
I'm very thankful I can reach
The folks along my lane!

* * *

The bringing of one soul to Jesus is the highest achievement possible to human life.

—Rev. George W. Truett, D.D.

* * *

"Are you winning souls to Jesus?" Dr. R. A. Torrey asked a young man. "That's the preacher's business," quickly replied the self-excusing lad. "You are right," replied Dr. Torrey, "but not

exclusively. The main business of every Christian is daily to witness for Christ, and bring perishing souls to Him."

* * *

How few there are who will weep with Christ over a sick, sinful, and sorrowing world! Oh, for less organizing, and more agonizing. Oh, for more solicitous concern for others. "And when he was come near, he beheld the city and wept over it." —W. B. K.

* * *

I remember no one sin that my conscience doth so much accuse and judge me for as for doing so little for the saving of souls, and for not dealing with the lost ones more fervently and earnestly for their conversion.

—Richard Baxter

* * *

"It has been a long time since I drove you home, sir," said the cabman to Charles H. Spurgeon. "But," replied Mr. Spurgeon, "I do not recollect you." "Well," said the cabman, "I think it was about fourteen years ago —" and then he pulled a New Testament from his pocket. It was faded and worn. "Perhaps you will remember this. You gave it to me and asked me to read it. I read it and it led me to the Saviour. I have been trying to serve Him through all these years." —W. B. K.

* * *

Oh, give me, Lord, Thy love for souls,
For lost and wand'ring sheep,
That I may see the multitudes,
And weep as Thou dids't weep.

Help me to see the tragic plight
Of souls far off in sin,
Help me to love, to pray, and go,
And bring the wand'ring in.

* * *

Suppose I were to see a blind man unknowingly approaching the brink of a high precipice, and that I were to sit by without concern or any effort to warn or save him from certain death, would I not be as guilty of his death in God's sight as though I had murdered him outright? The death of a body, which might have been (but was not) prevented, is a terrible thing, but what about the preventable death of a hu-

man soul — perchance of many souls — for which *God may hold me responsible?*
—Redpath

* * *

To win men to an acceptance of Jesus Christ as Saviour and Lord is the only reason Christians are left in this world.
—Dr. R. A. Torrey

* * *

The chief business of the church is to win lost people to a saving knowledge of Jesus Christ. —Arthur Flake

* * *

Two fellows, Tact and Contact, were courting the same girl. How different were their methods of approach! While Tact was engaging the girl's father and mother in conversation at the front door, Contact was at the back door proposing to the young lady! Do I need to tell you which one won the heart and hand of the fair young lady?
—Rev. T. W. Callaway, D.D.

* * *

It is the sob of God.
It is the anguished cry of Jesus as He weeps over a doomed city.
It is the cry of Paul, "I could wish that myself were accursed from Christ for my brethren, my kinsmen according to the flesh."
Evangelism is the heart-winning plea of Moses, "Oh, this people have sinned . . . yet now, if thou wilt forgive their sin — and if not, blot me, I pray thee, out of thy book which thou hast written."
It is the cry of John Knox, "Give me Scotland or I die."
It is the declaration of John Wesley, "The world is my parish."
It is the sob of parents in the night, weeping over a prodigal child.
—*The Cumberland Presbyterian*

* * *

Princess Eugenie of Sweden sold her diamonds to build a home for incurables. On a visit to the home she met a wicked woman to whom she talked about Christ. She told the matron that she hoped special attention would be given to that poor creature, for the princess was anxious that before she died she should become a Christian. One day she found the invalid with bright face because her heart was radiant with hope. With tears in her eyes the princess said to her husband on returning to the palace, "I saw the glitter of my diamonds today." —A. C. Dixon, D.D.

* * *

When I was a missionary in Africa, a strapping, naked savage approached me. He was carrying an emaciated, sickly baby in his arms. He almost threw the child at me as she said, "I am giving you my child. It is your responsibility whether he lives or dies!"
Children of God, our heavenly Father has given to each one of us an infinitely greater responsibility — to warn and yearn over never-dying souls, souls which will spend eternity in hell if we fail to warn them to flee from the wrath to come, and bring them to the Lamb of God who taketh away the sin of the world! —Told by a missionary

* * *

When I returned from college, I went immediately to my pastor and gave him a fervid account of my recent Christian awakening. He began to write down a list of names. He gave them to me and said, "I have here a long list of young people of our town, mostly unconverted. Now take this list and see what you can do. Just go about and tell them what the Lord has done for your own soul." Such work was new to me, but I dared not flinch. The first young woman I visited, a special friend of mine, was converted that very day. She ran to a friend of hers, and that night she yielded her life to Christ. Then the two went to others, and within a week a whole class of young women in the Sunday school were brought in a way that stirred the entire church, and some other churches.
—Henry Clay Maie in
Romance of Reality

* * *

A little girl who had recently come to know the Lord as her Saviour had a deep longing that her father should know Him too. She begged him to come with her to church, but in vain. At last he said, "I will go just once, to please you." The child was delighted, and when they got near the door of the church, the father felt a tiny push. It was his daughter, who said aloud, "Here he is, Jesus, save him." The prayer of faith was answered. The father, too, was saved. —*The Messenger*

* * *

Mr. Billhorn had been wanting to know for some time the secret of Mr. Moody's power and success as a soul winner. So one morning he asked him. Modestly, Moody answered, "Billhorn, I will tell you this much: I made a promise to God that I would speak to at least one man every day about his soul's salvation." "But the opportunity does not always present itself," said Mr. Billhorn. Quickly Moody replied, "It does if you keep in touch with God and keep your eyes open for the opportunity!" —W. B. K.

* * *

Some years ago a convention was held in Indianapolis to discuss the topic "How to Reach the Masses." After listening for hours to discussions about methods of reaching sin-sick souls, a young man, filled with zeal to reach the multitudes, could take it no longer. He dashed from the auditorium, stood on a street corner where the milling multitudes passed by, and began to proclaim the glorious gospel of Christ. Soon a crowd gathered. Spiritually hungry people listened intently as the young man spoke of the mightiness and ready willingness of Christ to transform lives, and give peace to troubled hearts.
—W. B. K.

* * *

The average insurance agent makes forty-five weekly calls on prospects. Only fifteen listen to him. Of those fifteen, only *two* put their names on "the dotted line."
"If an insurance agent calls on forty-five people and sells only two policies, should soul winners be discouraged if they make a thousand calls, and bring only *one* soul to Jesus? Never!
—Stanley Tam

* * *

There is one race I wish we would get more excited about — the race for souls. When American history is read in the light of eternity, this is the one race we will wish we had won more than all the others.
"And they that be wise shall shine as the brightness of the firmament; and they that turn many to righteousness as the stars for ever and ever" (Dan. 12:3). —Dr. Edward Simpson, Dean Buffalo Bible Institute

* * *

Charles Simeon of Cambridge was summoned to the dying bed of his own brother. Conversing together, the dying man said, "You never warned me of my danger." "Nay, my good brother," said Charles, "I took every reasonable opportunity, and often alluded to it in my letters." "Yes," exclaimed the dying man, "but that was not enough. You never came to me, closed the door, took me by the collar of the coat, and told me that I was unconverted, and that if I died in that state I would be lost. Now I am dying, and but for God's grace in reaching me by other means, I would have been forever lost!"
—*Assembly Annals*

* * *

Dr. John McNeill once told a group of ministers how he had come upon a drunken man fast asleep between the railway tracks — and the midnight express was due. "What would you have done?" he demanded of the ministers. One said, "Man, I would get him off the track. I would not be mild in dealing with him. I would not invite him to get himself off. I would be rough and seize him, and by main strength I would drag him off though I dropped exhausted by his side." "Even so," said McNeill, "that is the state of every unsaved soul — asleep between the tracks, and God's judgment express is almost due." (Eph. 5:14).
—*United Evangelical*

* * *

A minister visited the editor of a great daily city newspaper. After an exchange of greetings, the minister said, "I have come to talk to you about your soul and ask you to become a Christian." The editor did not reply. He walked slowly to the window and looked through tear-dimmed eyes at the milling multitude below. The minister thought, "Oh, I have offended him!" After a moment, the editor turned and said, "Thank you! With the exception

of my mother, when I was a little boy, nobody has ever talked to me about becoming a Christian. I thought no one cared!" —W. B. K.

Illustrations

Go Out Quickly!

One Sunday morning, in 1856, a congregation of well-dressed people had been ushered to their rented pews in Chicago's Plymouth Congregational Church. Suddenly there was a commotion near the door. Many turned and looked. Something occurred which had never before been seen by that elite congregation. In walked a young man — a nineteen-year-old salesman. Following him was a motley group of tramps, slum people and alcoholics. The young man led them into four pews he had personally rented for the visitors. He continued to do this important work each Sunday until God called him into a world-wide ministry. You ask the name of that young man? *Dwight L. Moody!* —W. B. K.

* * *

Suicides Averted

God spoke to a Chicago minister in reference to going to the unreached ones in their homes, the majority of whom never cross the threshold of any church. One day, when he knocked at the door of an apartment, a man answered the call. A frightened look of despair was on the man's face. He asked what the caller wanted. The minister replied, "I want to talk to you about the Lord Jesus!" The man burst into tears and said, "Man, God must have sent you here! Just before you knocked, my wife and I had closed all the doors and windows of our small apartment, intending next to turn on the gas and end our lives. You see, we just buried our darling child who was the idol of our hearts. We felt that our sorrow was more than we could bear!" Entering the apartment, God's servant told the despairing couple of the Saviour, and how in Him they could find peace and healing for their sorrowing hearts.   —Rev. Herbert Mitchell, Director of Family Altar League

You Gave Christ to Me!

Shortly after the Reverend Charles R. Goff became pastor of the Methodist Temple in the heart of Chicago's Loop, he felt the need of a Christian painting to impress the endless stream of visitors to the Temple. He arranged for an interview with Warner Sallman. The result was that Sallman's "Head of Christ" was given a place of honor in the Temple.

During the interview Sallman told the pastor, "I have been waiting for years to tell you that it was you who gave me that picture! You gave Christ to me!"

Years before, Dr. Goff had delivered a series of Bible talks in a Y.M.C.A. One of these talks caused Sallman to get a vision of the wondrous Saviour. That night, while asleep, he saw a vision of the head of Christ. When he awoke, he made a sketch of what he had seen, and from that sketch he painted the picture. Fifty million copies of this painting have been made — more than of any other picture, modern or medieval.

What a joy will be ours when we stand before the judgment seat of Christ and we meet there even one who can say, "You gave Christ to me!"
—W. B. K.

* * *

As the Stars For Ever!

Shortly before Moody left for Kansas City, where he died of a heart attack, he preached from the text: "And they that be wise shall shine as the brightness of the firmament; and they that turn many to righteousness as the stars for ever and ever" (Dan. 12:3).

Among others who spoke at Moody's funeral service was Dr. C. I. Scofield. While he was in the midst of his message, the sun burst through a leaden sky. A ray of light shone through a window and rested on Moody's face in the casket. Scofield paused and made reference to it. He and the sorrowing friends and loved ones thought of the words: "And they that be wise shall shine as the brightness of the firmament."

Moody was interred at the close of a short, bleak, wintry day. When the words of committal were spoken at his graveside, the overcast sky was rent and revealed the bright evening star above the western horizon. Then the thoughts of friends and loved ones reverted to the words: "And they that turn many to righteousness as the stars for ever and ever." —W. B. K.

* * *

I Must Find Peace

Dr. Walter Wilson, a great soul winner, was a manufacturer of tents before God called him into full-time gospel ministry. In his office he took care of minor injuries of employees. One day a woman came into his office. The needle of a machine had deeply pierced her finger. Dr. Wilson dressed the injured finger. Before she returned to her work, Dr. Wilson asked the superintendent to examine the safeguards on the machine. "There's nothing wrong with them," reported the superintendent. "I can't understand how the accident occurred."

Some days later, the same woman came to Dr. Wilson's office again, wringing her hand in pain. Dr. Wilson scolded her mildly for her carelessness. She burst into tears. "Oh, Dr. Wilson, for weeks I have been most miserable. I knew you were a very busy man. I deliberately injured my hand that I might have an excuse to talk to you. I'm not ready to die and I am so wretched I don't want to live unless I can find peace. I heard you could help me!"

Dr. Wilson had the joy of bringing her to the Saviour!

—Told by Stanley Tam

* * *

A Dream Transforms Minister

There was a minister who neglected to deal personally with the unsaved. One night he had an awful dream. When he came to the breakfast table, his wife noticed that he looked very distressed. She asked: "Why are you distressed?" He replied: "I had an awful dream!" "Dreams don't mean anything," said the wife. "There was something to this one. I dreamed that I was standing before the judgment seat of Christ. He asked me, 'Where are the souls of the children I gave you?' I replied, 'I do not know, Lord.' 'Where are the souls of the servants who lived in your house?' Again I said, 'I do not know, Lord.' 'Where are the souls of the congregation to whom I sent you as a pastor?' With sorrow, I said, 'O Lord, I know not! I never spoke personally to them about their souls!' As I said these words, I seemed to sink into hell where I was mocked by these lost souls. Then I awoke! Now, I am a changed minister!" —W. B. K.

* * *

Only Man in America

An aged farmer visited his son, a popular senator in Washington, D.C. The farmer was a zealous Christian. When introduced to the ambassador from Belgium, he earnestly asked: "Sir, are you a Christian?" His son was greatly embarrassed by this. Before the ambassador could reply the son changed the conversation. Shortly thereafter the father became ill and after a while he died. Hearing of his death, the ambassador sent flowers. A note attached to them brought tears to the eyes of the senator. The note read: "He was the *only man* in America who asked me if I was a Christian."

—W. B. K.

* * *

I'd Go If I Had to Swim!

A girl from New Zealand went to England to study. There she became a true Christian. Immediately she became deeply concerned for her unsaved loved ones. When she graduated, friends said to her, "You have made many friends in England and are now accustomed to our ways of life. Why do you wish to go back to New Zealand? You will miss our shady lanes and clover fields. Too, you may be shipwrecked on the return voyage." The girl replied, "Here I became a Christian. Do you think I could be contented not to go and tell my father and mother how they may experience the joy of salvation and have eternal life through faith in Christ? I *must* return to New Zealand and do my best to bring them to the Saviour! I will go even if I have to swim to get there!" —W. B. K.

* * *

"Who Put Sin in Sinclair?"

Dr. Walter Wilson, ever on the alert to speak to men about their souls and need of the Saviour, asked an attendant at a service station who had filled his car with gas: "How did sin get in Sinclair?" pointing to the lighted sign atop the gas pump. "I do not know, sir, how sin got into Sinclair; but, sir, I have wished many times that I knew how to get sin out of my life!"

It was then that Dr. Wilson had the opportunity to tell the young man of the One who is the sinner's friend and of whom it is written: "And thou shalt call his name Jesus: for he shall save his people from their sins" (Matt. 1:21).

—Told by Willis Cook

* * *

The One Essential Thing

Though I speak with the tongues of scholarship and though I use approved methods of education, and fail to win my pupils to Christ, I become as a cloud of mist in an open sea, as the moan of the wind in a Syrian desert.

And though I have the best teaching skill and understand all mysteries of religious psychology, and though I have all Biblical knowledge, and lose not myself in the task of winning others to Christ, I become as a vapor on a warm summer morning.

And though I read all Sunday-school literature, and attend Sunday-school conventions, and institutes, and summer schools, and yet am satisfied with less than winning my pupils to Christ and establishing them in Christian character and service, it profiteth nothing.

The soul-winning teacher, the character-building teacher, suffereth long and is kind; he envieth not others who are free from the teaching task; he vaunteth not himself, is not puffed up with intellectual pride.

Such a teacher doth not behave unseemingly between Sundays, seeketh not his own comfort, is not easily provoked. He beareth all things, believeth all things, hopeth all things.

And now abideth knowledge, methods, evangelism, these three, but *the greatest of these is evangelism.*

—*Riverside Evangel,* Tampa, Fla.

* * *

Your Message Changed My Life!

A commercial traveler named Rigby was compelled to spend a weekend every quarter in Edinburgh. He always worshiped in Dr. Alexander Whyte's church and always tried to persuade some other visitor to accompany him. On one occasion, having taken a Roman Catholic traveler there who accepted Christ, he called on Dr. Whyte to tell him of the conversion. The doctor then asked his name, and on being told that it was Rigby, he exclaimed, "Why, you are the man I've been looking for for years!" He then went to his study and returned with a bundle of letters from which he read such extracts as this: "I was spending a week end in Edinburgh some weeks ago, and a fellow commercial named Rigby invited me to accompany him to St. George's. The message of that service changed my life."

Dr. Whyte said that twelve of the letters were from young men four of whom entered the ministry.

—*Record of Christian Work*

* * *

A Father's Joy

Bruce Crozier, a seven-year-old boy, wandered from his father's hunting camp in Arizona. He was lost for six days and six nights. At last he was found, thirty-two miles from the camp. When the mother embraced him, she exclaimed, "It is almost impossible to believe I have my boy back!" Then she fainted. The father, who had directed a thousand searchers for the boy from his hunting camp, received by phone the joyous news, and he, too, lapsed into unconsciousness. We cannot measure the greatness of the joy of that mother and father. Nor can we measure the "joy in the presence of the angels of God over one sinner that repenteth." —Adapted from *Now*

* * *

Go, See the Colonel!

The fading sound of taps seemed to echo in the lieutenant's ears. As he sat wearily on his cot, an irresistible urge came upon him that he should go and see his colonel and speak to him about his soul. "It would result only in a reprimand and possibly court-martial to wander about the camp after taps," he reasoned as he tried to throw off the feeling. Still the urge persisted. A few minutes later, the lieutenant stood trembling before the barracks where the colonel stayed. "What are you doing here?" the colonel asked. Falteringly the lieutenant told him of the irresistible urge he felt to come and talk to him about the Saviour. Without saying a word, the colonel opened a drawer and took out a revolver. Then he said to the lieutenant: "If you had knocked at my door five minutes later, I couldn't have answered your call. I was about to take my life when you interrupted me. What you have said gives me hope. Come again tomorrow and tell me more about your Christ!" Then he added, "No, I won't use the pistol!'

The following morning, both knelt in prayer. They arose with deep joy in their hearts — one because God had used him to save a soul from death, the other because he had become a "new creature" in Christ Jesus. ——W. B. K.

* * *

A Sure Indication

One of the surest indications that we have become new creatures in Christ Jesus is our deep, solicitous concern for the unsaved about us. Years ago a German servant girl presented herself for membership in the First Baptist Church of Dallas, Texas. The Pastor, Dr. George W. Truett, explained to her that it was the custom of the church to examine those applying for membership in the church before receiving them. The girl burst into tears. Dr. Truett, a kind-hearted man, was deeply distressed. Instantly he tried to explain further the rule of the church. "Oh," said the bur-

dened girl, "it was not that. I was just thinking about my unsaved father and mother, brothers and sisters. I want to see them saved, too, and I am so burdened for them!" A deacon arose and said, "Pastor, let's receive her right now into the full fellowship of this church. She has shown us, beyond a doubt, that she is truly a child of God."

Lord, lay some soul upon my heart,
   And love that soul through me;
And may I nobly do my part,
   To win that soul to Thee!
            —W. B. K.

* * *

Awake Thou That Sleepest

Years ago in a Southern city, a young man, intent on suicide, took a lethal dose of a drug. He was rushed to a hospital. In those days, the treatment of such patients was most drastic. After administering a counteracting antidote, the young man was taken into an enclosure at the rear of the hospital. There two strong men, on either side of the would-be suicide, held him erect. A third man to the rear applied a lash on the patient's bare back if he stopped walking and tried to slump down into sleep. "Leave me alone! Leave me alone!" he pleaded piteously. Had he been left alone, he would have slept the sleep that knows no awakening on earth.

How typical of many rejecters of Christ. As they sleep in deadly unconcern and indifference, they want to be left alone. In their spiritual deadness they say, "Are we not rich and increased with goods? We have need of nothing. One world at a time for us!" Let us *not* leave them alone. Let us do our *best* to arouse them and cause them to see their need of the Saviour.

          —Rev. T. W. Callaway, D.D.

* * *

Forsaken

In a little cemetery beside the English church in Fatehpur, India, lie buried some English, Indian and American folk, all victims of mutiny. A single monument has been erected near their graves. Engraved on the monument is just one word: FORSAKEN. No names are mentioned. No next of kin are mentioned, because the bodies interred there are unknown and forsaken.

There could be erected, in every country on earth, a monument to the memory of countless precious souls, and that monument could bear the one word: FORSAKEN. Myriads of lost ones are neglected by God's people and they have died and gone out into the darkness of a lost eternity, utterly forsaken by a careless and an indifferent church which is too unconcerned to make any effort to save them. —W. B. K.

* * *

Downward and Upward Reach

Two phases of Christian truth are vividly portrayed by two artists. Each artist painted a picture of a huge cross surrounded by storm-churned, angry waves. Clinging with both hands to the crossbar of one cross is an imperiled seaman. His only purpose is self-preservation. On the other cross is portrayed a seaman, clinging tenaciously with one hand to the crossbar of the cross, while reaching down with the other hand to rescue a struggling mate from the tempest-tossed waters. Which picture more accurately represents what Christ wants each one of us to do amidst the waves of "life's restless sea"? As we "cling to the old rugged Cross" with one hand, let us keep one hand stretched out to lift the fallen ones and bring them to the "wondrous Sovereign of the sea," Jesus! —W. B. K.

* * *

Consistent About the Greatest Thing

Dr. Wayland Hoyt had prepared a special sermon for a leading citizen who was not a Christian and seldom came to church. This man's wife was a devout Christian. "Tell your husband I especially want him to come to church tonight," said Dr. Hoyt to her. When the invitation was delivered, the man immediately phoned the pastor, thanked him for the invitation and said, "I will be there tonight." By nightfall, the clouds blackened and the rain poured down steadily. Only a few who lived near the church came. The specially invited person didn't come and Dr. Hoyt was discouraged. "What a failure I am in reaching that man," he said, self-ac-

cusingly. Then God seemed to say to him, "Why not emulate the example of your Saviour, and go to the man and preach your sermon to him as Jesus preached on the new birth to Nicodemus?" It was after midnight. He hesitated. Then God seemed to say to him, "If you knew that man's house was on fire, wouldn't you go and arouse him? Why not be consistent about the most important thing of all?"

Going out into the torrential downpour, Dr. Hoyt made his way to the house. The man greeted him tearfully and said, "Thank God, Dr. Hoyt! God sent you here to tell me how to be saved. The word you sent me stirred my heart. I could not sleep!" Both knelt and prayed. In five minutes the man was rejoicing in Jesus Christ, the Lord. —Dr. George W. Truett

* * *

Not Many Mighty!

An alcoholic asked his brother, who was a Christian, for two dollars, so that he could buy drink. His brother said, "There is a Sunday-school contest on at the Temple Baptist Church, and if you will take someone there next Sunday I will give you the two dollars." "It's a deal," said the alcoholic. He indeed took someone to the Sunday school but left immediately himself. As he was going out of the church, a boy, who had a harelip, spoke to him about his soul and pleaded with him to invite Jesus to come into his heart, and asked him to stay for Sunday school. The alcoholic rudely rebuffed the boy and hurried away. God's Spirit, however, used the effort of that afflicted boy to bring conviction to the drunkard. He was later visited by two earnest soul winners and won to the Saviour, who delivered him utterly from the evil which had all but wrecked his life.

—Told by Willis Cook

* * *

Where Christ Is Not Known

Some Africans were getting on a river boat, carrying in their hands sacks and baskets of vegetables. They were going to market. One of them slipped and fell into the water. She grabbed for the side of the boat and held on until her fingers became numb. Finally she could hold on no longer and sank beneath the turgid waters. Not one native made a move to rescue her. They were stonily indifferent to her cries for help.

When the boat captain learned what had happened, he swore and cursed at the heartless natives. "Why didn't you reach down and lift her from the water?" he asked. They replied in chorus, "If we had, what would have become of our fruits and vegetables?"

Before we pass judgment on these cruel, benighted heathen, let us do a bit of heart-searching. All around us are those who are going into eternity without God and without hope — forever lost. Too many Christians sing about rescuing the perishing, but do little or nothing about it.

—Told by a missionary

* * *

Nobody Cared Enough to Tell Me

A conscienceless, sinful father taught his children to steal. "If you return home empty-handed, I'll flog you!" he would threaten them. Some time ago, a student of the Moody Bible Institute gave this man a gospel tract, and earnestly pleaded with him to repent of his sins, receive Christ, and live for Him. The Holy Spirit convicted the man of sin so that he cried to God for mercy. Christ heard his cry and transformed his life. Later he said, "I'm sixty years old and it is the first time I have ever made a start in the right direction. Until that Christian worker told me about Jesus, nobody ever cared enough to tell me." —W. B. K.

* * *

She Didn't Give Up

Out on the great American desert, an Indian child was lost. There was great fear and excitement. For hours, many searched for the lost child, but to no avail. The searchers began to go silently and sorrowfully away. There was one, however, who would not give up the search — the child's mother. "Not until death reaches me will I stop searching for my lost child," she said. Trudging onward, she finally slumped on the desert sands. When her ear was

close to the ground, her keen sense of hearing revealed the faint voice of her crying child. She jumped to her feet and exclaimed, "I have heard my child's cry!" She ran in the direction where the cry came from and mother and child were soon in each other's joyous embrace.

The Bible says that there is joy in the presence of the angels of God when lost souls are found, and when they turn with sorrow to God. How glad we are that the Lord Jesus came to earth to seek and to save that which was lost. Oftentimes even God's children stray, and need to plead the prayer, "I have gone astray like a lost sheep; seek thy servant; for I do not forget thy commandments" (Ps. 119:176). —W. B. K.

* * *

A Wayside Opportunity

Years ago, as Bishop McCabe alighted from a bus, he paid his fare and said to the driver, "Good night, my friend! I hope to meet you again, if not here, then in glory!" The bishop thought nothing of the incident as it was his custom always to speak cheerily to others about things eternal. About midnight that night there was a knock at his door. Going to the door, the bishop recognized the man there as the driver of the bus to whom he had spoken of heaven. Said the man, "If I am to meet you in glory, I have got to turn around. I have come to ask you to pray for me!" Before long a new name was written down in glory — a soul had passed from death to life in Christ! —W. B. K.

* * *

Why Gladstone Was Joyous

Early one morning William Gladstone was at his desk at No. 10 Downing Street, London. A timid knock on the door called him from preparing an important speech he was to deliver that day in Parliament. Standing at the door was a little boy whose friendship Gladstone had won by little deeds of kindness. The boy said, "My brother is dying. Won't you please come and show him the way to heaven?" Leaving his important work for the most important work any Christian can do,

Gladstone went to the bedside of the dying boy. In a matter of moments the boy was rejoicing in his newly found Saviour! Returning to his office, Gladstone wrote at the bottom of the speech he had been preparing: "I am the happiest man in London today!" He had been the human instrumentality, in the hands of God, to lead a boy from darkness into the wondrous light and liberty of Christ.

—Rev. R. E. Neighbour, D.D.

* * *

Alert to Opportunity

Harry always participated in the different activities of the church. Often he sang special musical numbers with others and alone. He professed to be a Christian, and it wasn't mine to question his sincerity.

One day Harry was practicing a solo with a pianist. The emphasis of the solo was that one can never know peace until he knows Jesus. Suddenly Harry sighed, "How I wish I knew the peace Jesus gives!" The pianist was a fine Christian girl who was always alert to win others for Jesus. She said, "Harry, you may know that peace, in ever-deepening blessedness, by asking Jesus to come into your heart and make your life anew!"

Then and there, Harry passed from the low plane of a mere profession onto the jubilant plane of full assurance. He had passed from death into newness of life in Christ.

—Told by Rev. Earl Leiby

* * *

Old Truths Given New Dresses

Someone asked a young man, "Have you ever been saved?" A puzzled, questioning look came upon the face of the young man. He became thoughtful, and then he said, "Oh, yes, sometime ago I came pretty close to drowning, and a friend, hearing my frantic cry, swam to my rescue and brought me safely to shore!"

Wouldn't it have been better for the personal worker to have asked, "Have you ever asked Christ to come into your life and make you one of God's children?"

We are living in a world that is very different from the world in which prior generations of Christians lived. Religious terms and phraseology are not understandable to many worldly people, but are like an unknown tongue. Ask a run-of-the-mill individual on the street, "Have you been born again?" and he will not have the remotest idea what you are talking about.

I am not pleading for a new Gospel, nor am I remotely suggesting that we throw overboard any of God's changeless Word. I only say that we must express eternal truths in words intelligible to the persons whom we are trying to win for Jesus, or else we will not reach them. —W. B. K.

* * *

Where Hast Thou Gleaned Today?

Where the population is densest over the world, the harvest of the fields is hand-reaped. In India, China, Japan, the islands of the sea, wheat, rice, and other harvests are garnered in the hard, back-breaking way — by hand. Not since the days of Ruth has this method of gathering the yield of the fields been changed in some places.

Souls are best reaped in this way — hand reaped. They must be individually won and individually nurtured. Souls do not come to Christ *en masse*. Even in "mass evangelism," souls must come to God personally, and must have the personal touch. Henry Ward Beecher once said, "The longer I live, the more confidence I have in those sermons where *one man* is the congregation and *one man* is the minister; where there is no question as to who is meant when the preacher says: 'Thou art the man!' "

—Rev. Herbert Mitchell

* * *

Dr. Poling Alerted

Some years ago, Dr. Daniel Poling returned home after an absence of a few days. He entered a taxicab. As he rode along, the taxi driver, who did not know Dr. Poling, asked, "Have you heard about the boys who are adrift in a rowboat, and who at latest reports have not been found?" "No," replied Dr. Poling, seemingly not too much concerned. Then he added, "The boys should have been more careful." After a moment, he asked, "Do you know the names of the boys?" "No, not all of them. I know only one. His name is Poling." Instantly Dr. Poling became all attention as it dawned upon him that one of the lost youths was his own boy!

Oh, that we could feel deeply moved toward every lost soul, taking each upon our hearts, and doing everything to bring him to Christ.

—Told by Rev. C. Leslie Miller

* * *

Thirty Years a Silent Christian

A businessman said to Billy Graham, "Paul has been in my employ for some thirty years, and I have never said one thing to him about his becoming a Christian." "Oh, the shame of it!" exclaimed Graham. "Let's get down on our knees and ask God's forgiveness for the failure!" After prayer, Graham said, "When you go to your place of business in the morning, go immediately to Paul and speak to him about his soul. Ask him to invite the Saviour to come into his life and make it anew." "I will," said the man. Going to the office of Paul the next morning, he walked back and forth — speechless. Paul asked, "Jim, you are very nervous. What's the trouble?" "I am nervous, for the thing I know I ought to do isn't easy." Jim answered, "What is it?" asked Paul. Finally, with great effort, Jim said, "I want to talk to you about your soul. I want you to give yourself to Jesus Christ." There was silence for a moment. Then, as tears welled in his eyes, Paul said, "For years I have wanted you to talk to me about my soul. I will ask Jesus to come into my life and make it anew. I will go to church with you Sunday and publicly confess my faith in Him." —W. B. K.

* * *

How They Reached the Unreached

The need of reaching the unsaved and unchurched multitudes of a great city in Texas became a matter of prayerful concern to some Christian laymen. They decided to conduct Bible classes in homes in different neighborhoods. And God blessed their efforts.

A teacher from a theological seminary taught a group in one of the homes. On the first evening he saw one of the women smoking cigarettes. On her lap lay an open Bible upon which fell the cigarette ashes. As he observed this, he almost exploded. "What barefaced irreverence!" he said to himself. Then a Voice seemed to say to him: "Are you better than your Lord? Did He not eat and mingle with publicans and sinners? Did He not come to call sinners to repentance?" As he thought upon these searching questions, the feeling of self-righteous indignation gave place to Christlike pity and compassion for her. Before long she as well as others became changed creatures.

—W. B. K.

SOWING AND REAPING

Short Quotes

They enslave their children's children who compromise with sin: "Visiting the sins of the fathers upon the children unto the third and fourth generation of them that hate me" (Exod. 20:5).
—Lowell

* * *

The hereditary consequences of alcoholism are of all the most dreadful. Not only do the children of alcoholics die prematurely in great numbers, but those who survive are most often weak, degenerate, doomed to nervous and mental sicknesses, epileptics and unbalanced criminals. One cannot too often repeat it. Alcohol heredity is one of the most evident causes of antisocial tendencies — idleness, indecency, dishonesty. —Sicard de Plauzoles, M.D.

* * *

American teen-agers are being infected with venereal disease at the rate of one a minute. It is alarming to consider that more females are infected at the age of high-school graduation than at any other age period.

—Elmer Hess, M.D., a former president of the American Medical Association

* * *

I have had my will,
Tasted every pleasure,
I have drunk my fill
Of the purple measure.
Life has lost its zest,
Sorrow is my guest,
Oh, the lees are bitter, bitter!
Give me rest.
Love once filled the bowl,
Running o'er with blisses,
Made my very soul
Drunk with crimson kisses.
But I drank it dry,
Love has passed me by.
Oh, the lees are bitter, bitter!
Let me die!

—George Arnold

* * *

An educator said to a class of boys: "So live that your future self — the man you ought to be — may, in his turn, be actual and possible. In your future he is waiting his turn. His body, brain and soul are in your boyish hands. What will you pass on to him? Will it be a brain and body unspoiled by lust or dissipation? Will you let him come as a man among men in his time or will you throw away his inheritance before he has had the chance

to possess it? Every boy has his future in his own hands." —W. B. K.

* * *

A young man who was living a dissolute life was asked, "Are you still getting a kick out of your sinful, immoral living?" Dejectedly he replied, "A kick? I'm getting a kickback!" The kickback of sin always comes. God's law is immutable: "For he that soweth to his flesh shall of the flesh reap corruption" (Gal. 6:8).

* * *

Some people sow wild oats during the week and then slip into church on Sunday to pray for a crop failure.

—Rev. Rex Humbart

* * *

This is the debt I pay
Just for one riotous day,
Years of regret and grief,
Sorrow without relief!

—Paul Laurence Dunbar

* * *

We are shown, with terrifying clearness, that chronic alcohol poisoning not only destroys individuals, but stamps the coming generation in the germ cell with the mark of degeneracy.

—Emil Kraepelin, M.D.

* * *

Inherited alcoholism creates epileptics, imbeciles, idiots, dipsomaniacs, degenerates, hypersensitives to alcohol, weaklings, mental weakness and engenders tuberculosis. All this appears to me beyond discussion.

—Maurice Roch, M.D.

Illustrations

The Deacon's Troubled Conscience

An aged deacon came to me at the close of a sermon. He was deeply distressed. I had said in the message that each one of us will inescapably reap what we have sown. In his earlier years, the deacon had sown to his flesh. He had gone deeply into ways of sin. For years, however, he had lived an exemplary Christian life. "I shudder to think what I'll have to reap," he said. He was greatly relieved, however, when I told him that another — Christ — had reaped and suffered for his sins in

his stead; that God had put upon His Son the iniquity of us all; that He, the just, had suffered for the unjust, and that God had blotted out his guilty past.

How greatly should we love Him; how wholeheartedly should we serve Him! How wonderful are God's promises: "All his transgressions that he hath committed, they shall not be mentioned unto him" (Ezek. 18:22); "For I will be merciful to their unrighteousness, and their sins and their iniquities will I remember no more" (Heb. 8:12).

—W. B. K.

Harvest Day

When we come to the reaping time in
   life,
And our harvest is full-grown,
Will our hearts be glad, or spirits sad,
As we view the things we've sown?

For the things that we do and say to-
   day,
And the deeds of yesterday,
Are the deeds we sow as we onward go
Toward our final Harvest Day.

There'll be many a long-forgotten word
That cheered some heart distressed,
Many deeds of love only known above
Yet whose fruitage God has blessed.

'Tis for us to choose in the sight of God
For the good or evil way;
And the life we live will our witness
   give
In that last great Harvest Day!
      —Mary V. Harris, in
    The Watchman-Examiner

* * *

The Scars Remain

John B. Gouch was a humanly hopeless and helpless drunkard before his
conversion. One Sunday morning he
lay in the gutter of a street where
churchgoers passed. What a pathetic
sight he was! His face was covered with
flies. Some kind-hearted person placed
a clean handkerchief over his bloated
face. When Gouch sobered up, he removed the handkerchief from his face.
Looking at it, he exclaimed, "Somebody
cared enough for me to stop and place
this handkerchief over my face!" His
slumbering soul began to awaken. He
came to God for mercy and forgiveness.
Later he became a mighty power for
God and the cause of temperance. He
could, however, give only the fag end
of his life to God. This was the great
regret of his life and he used to say,

"The scars remain! I have been snatched
as a brand from the burning, but the
scars remain — scars never to be eradi-
cated, never to be removed this side of
glory!" —W. B. K.

* * *

A Roseate or Jaundiced World, Which?

A small, snarling terrier stood before a large mirror. He worked himself
into a frenzy over "another terrier" who
was exactly like him and did exactly
the things he did. Then the mirror
was removed and the terrier quieted
down and went away.

Sometimes we complain bitterly about
the world's ill-humor. Is not most of
it the reflection of our own sullen ill-
humor? If we look at the world through
yellow spectacles, we will see a jaundiced world. If we look at the world
through rose-colored spectacles, we will
see a roseate world.

Then life is the mirror of king or slave,
  It is just what you are and do,
Then give to the world the best you
   have,
And the best will come back to you.
      —W. B. K.

* * *

When Justice Speaks

Three men went out one summer night,
No care had they or aim,
And dined and drank; "Ere we go
   home,"
They said, "We'll have a game."

Three girls began, that summer night,
A life of endless shame,
And went through drink, disease and
   death,
Swift as the racing flame!

Lawless, homeless and foul they died,
Rich, loved and praised, those men,
But when they all shall meet with God,
And justice speaks, what then?
      —*Selected*

TEMPERANCE—ALCOHOL

Short Quotes

"I had always believed that every man had a right to drink if he wanted to, and it was nobody's business. Now my work as sheriff has convinced me that it *is* somebody's business. It is every citizen's solemn duty to prevent his neighbor from getting anything that will ruin him." We have legislation against sale of firearms, narcotics, and drugs that would destroy people. Yet our government licenses the sale of liquor, which destroys mind and body. —A Southern sheriff

* * *

The liquor business is the most dangerous and ruinous of all human pursuits. —William McKinley

* * *

The death rate, crime rate, accident rate in a given community varies according to the average alcohol consumption; and, when alcoholism decreases, so do the death, crime, and accident rates. Relaxation of restrictions on alcohol is followed by a rise in commitments to asylums, hospitalizations, and delinquency.   —Dr. E. M. Jellinek, formerly of Yale

* * *

Drivers are safer when the roads are dry, and the roads are safer when drivers are dry.

* * *

Twenty million people in America are offended every day by the alcoholic advertising that comes to their homes consistently and continually without even knocking at their doors, entering the very impressionable minds of boys and girls with the obvious purpose of making more customers for an industry that destroys, dooms, and damns human personality as it rolls along.
—*The Sunday School Times*

* * *

There are no depths of cruelty and criminality in the history of the human race to which people have not descended when under the influence of liquor.
—Dr. Robert G. Lee

The meat, pork and poultry producers would quickly eradicate any toxic agent which would produce as much disease, crippling and misery among their cattle, pigs and chickens as alcohol does among human beings.
—Andrew C. Ivy, Ph.D., M.D.

* * *

A cabled release dated, Paris, October 2, 1959, said that alcoholism is now costing the French nation $500,000,000 a year. The government is so disturbed about this that it is sponsoring a poster program pleading with fathers to abandon their addiction to alcoholic beverages for the sake of their children.
—Dr. Wilbur M. Smith

* * *

All the umpires put together have not put as many ball players out of the game as "old man booze."
—Connie Mack

* * *

If all the combined forces of hell should assemble in conclave and with them all the men on earth who hate and despise God, purity and virtue — if all the scum of the earth could mingle with the denizens of hell to try to think of the deadliest institution to home, church and state, I tell you, sir, the combined forces of hell could not conceive of or bring an institution that could touch the hem of the garment of the tavern to damn the home, mankind, womanhood, business and every other good thing on God's earth. —Billy Sunday

* * *

Alcoholism is reported as being 155 times more prevalent in our nation than polio. There are six times as many alcoholics as active cases of tuberculosis. Every year we raise millions of dollars to fight cancer, tuberculosis and polio, but millions are spent to help spread alcoholism. —Rev. R. W. Neighbour

* * *

I stand with the Bible. To be true in our convictions any true minister must make bold to declare what the Word of God says about this social evil — alcohol. Any sin that can keep men from inheriting the Kingdom of God, I must denounce and decry. The Bible says: "Nor thieves, nor covetous, nor drunkards . . . shall inherit the kingdom of God" (I Cor. 6:10). —Billy Graham

* * *

The chronic alcoholic and excessive drinker is a graduate of the moderate drinker. —Judge Lewis Drucker, Cleveland Municipal Court

* * *

Today the total number of taverns, bars, or what-have-you, plus retail stores that sell liquor exceed the combined total of churches and schools by nearly 30,000. The ratio of liquor outlets to American homes across the United States is one tavern or liquor store to every 80 American dwelling units. —*Christianity Today*

* * *

Friedemann Bach, the most gifted son of the great German composer, Johann Sebastian Bach, went to pieces through drink. Michael Haydn, younger brother of Joseph Haydn, and hardly less gifted, was ruined by drink. Franz Schubert became an inveterate wine drinker and died in his early thirties. Robert Schumann's dipsomania led to a nervous breakdown. After the death of his wife, Rembrandt, then thirty-six, became an alcoholic. Said Upton Sinclair, "I call drink the greatest trap that life has set for the feet of genius!"
—*The Sunday School Times*

* * *

Because of his addiction to alcohol, Charles Lamb, English essayist, spoke of himself as gliding into the abyss with open eyes and bound will, seeing his own destruction before him without having strength of will to break away, and with all good drained out of his heart.
—*The Sunday School Times*

* * *

At a social function, J. C. Penney, the merchant prince, took ginger ale, and someone mistakenly reported that he drank a cocktail. So he said, "I am sure that a reputation which I value has been endangered by my drinking ginger ale. Hereafter it will be plain water or tomato juice for me."

In all countries where the alcohol drinking habit reigns, it accounts for from half to three-quarters of the crime, a great share of suicides, of mental disorders, of deaths, of disease generally, of poverty, of vulgar depravity, of sexual excesses, of venereal diseases, and of dissolution of families.
—Auguste Forel, M.D.

* * *

At least forty per cent of automobile accidents involving death or serious personal injury are directly traceable to use of liquor.
—Judge Harry Porter, chairman National Safety Council's Committee on Intoxication Tests

* * *

A Wisconsin brewer is marketing to high-school students a "Teen-Brew!" It contains alcohol. It's bottled like beer, foams like beer, tastes like beer and looks like beer. Although it contains some alcohol, it does not have enough to be taxable as a fermented liquor. It is certainly planned to create a taste for alcoholic liquor.
—Methodist Board of Temperance, quoted in *Gospel Banner*

* * *

Ira Hayes, a Pima Indian and a former marine, died from exposure, alcoholism and tuberculosis. The man who never quailed before enemy fire failed to learn to cope with or leave alone the firewater of his race. He was arrested scores of times for drunkenness. Hayes was one of the six men in the famous photograph by Joe Rosenthal in the flag raising on Iwo Jima's Mount Suribachi. He was slain in his thirty-second year by the mother of crimes — alcohol!
—W. B. K.

* * *

In Poland, 1700 children were questioned during an investigation of the alarming increase of alcoholism in that nation. Only two out of the 1700 children questioned had never tasted vodka.
—Given in newscast by Douglas Edwards

* * *

"I cannot speak for temperance more effectually," said Booker T. Washington, "than to quote old Uncle Calhoun

Webster. He said, 'When I sees a man a-goin' home wid a gallon o' whiskey, and a half-pound of meat, dat's temperance lecture enough for me, an' I sees it ebery day. An' I knows dat ebery-t'ing in dat man's house am on de same scale — a gallon o' misery to ebery half-pound o' comfort!'"

— *Baptist Standard*

* * *

Henry L. McCarthy, Commissioner of Welfare of New York City, in an interview on a CBS television program, said that ten thousand welfare families in that one city, costing the local government forty million dollars a year for food and shelter, can be traced to alcoholic fathers who were confined either to prison or mental institutions, or died prematurely. He estimated that there are now 300,000 alcoholics in New York City, and one out of every five is a woman, whereas a few years ago the ratio was one out of every twenty-five. —Dr. Wilbur Smith, in *The Sunday School Times*

* * *

History shows that nineteen of twenty-one civilizations crumbled when the people lost their sense of responsibility. One of the motives of our nation's seven million heavy drinkers — addictive or chronic — is the drowning of responsibilities. I do know where history shows it will end — *the destruction of our democracy!*

—Dr. Andrew Ivy

* * *

Every day and every hour,
Booze gets someone in its power,
Strips him of his self-respect,
Leaves his life completely wrecked!

* * *

The consumption of alcoholic beverages in our nation continues as a cause for alarm. Manufacturers of alcoholic beverages spent $38,000,000 for spot advertisements of beer, wine, and ale on television in 1957, which places this industry third among all manufacturers using this medium of advertisement. The total amount of money spent for advertising by the liquor industry last year was $400,000,000.

—Dr. Wilbur M. Smith

The great Canadian physician, Sir William Osler, was lecturing one day on alcohol.

"Is it true," asked a student, "that alcohol makes people able to do things better?"

"No," replied Sir William, "it just makes them less ashamed of doing them badly." —*The Dry Legion*

* * *

Dr. Irving Sunshine, toxicologist (poison specialist) attached to the Cuyahoga County coroner's office in Cleveland, Ohio, said: "Half the victims of the traffic accidents have alcohol in their systems, and 60 per cent of the victims of homicide have been drinking. Alcohol is a complicating factor in 60 per cent of the home accidents that come to the attention of the coroner's office. In industrial accidents alcohol shows up in 15 per cent of the accidents. Don't believe the old adage that you can't get drunk on beer. Alcohol is alcohol whether it is in beer, whiskey, wine or gin." —W. B. K.

* * *

Is alcoholism a sickness? If so, it is a sickness which is self-imposed, and, unlike other sicknesses, it produces murder, rape, broken homes, and broken hearts. —W. B. K.

* * *

In a well-documented study, the Metropolitan Life Insurance Company, which naturally has much at stake in the number of deaths directly or indirectly attributable to the consumption of beverage alcohol, states that there are now 65,000,000 people in the United States who drink.

* * *

"If alcohol could be divorced from driving, possibly half of our 40,000 people doomed to die each year on the highway could live, and half a million more could be spared from painful and crippling injuries."

—Harold Hutchins in *The Chicago Daily Tribune*

* * *

"Do you drink?" a young man asked a stranger. "No, sir," the stranger replied. "Why don't you drink?" the young man asked again. "My boss doesn't like it, my customers won't stand for it, and my conscience won't let me," replied the stranger. "Those are three wonderful and practical reasons," said the questioner, "what's your business?" "I'm a bartender," was the surprising reply. —W. B. K.

＊ ＊ ＊

In an editorial in the *Christian Herald*, Dr. Daniel Poling protests liquor's "organized campaign to recruit teenagers as drinkers." Liquor knows no code of morals other than that thrust upon her by the indignation of the righteous. On a recent tour, members of a city chamber of commerce gave out materials representing their various businesses. One member gave out to school children beaded Indian headbands. Emblazoned on them were the words, "I am whooping it up for ———— Brewing Company." How long will God and righteous men withhold their wrath?

＊ ＊ ＊

Strong drink, the curse of all curses, is a wicked wrecker. It turns gold into dross, mentality into derangement, health into misery, beauty into caricature, honor into shame. You can say nicer things about a rattlesnake than about booze. —Dr. Robert G. Lee

＊ ＊ ＊

America is committing suicide, slowly but surely. The lethal weapon is ethyl alcohol in whiskey, beer, and wine. Over eighty million citizens of our great country are imbibing this poison that is spelling our doom and bringing down on us the curse of God. Is it possible to halt this death march when the liquor industry is spending over 250 million dollars a year in advertising over radio, TV, newspapers, and magazines, while the apathy on the part of leaders in government is at such a shocking level? —Dale Crowley, a Washington Newscaster

＊ ＊ ＊

The legalized liquor business is the tragedy of our civilization. Alcohol is the greatest and the most blighting curse of our modern civilization. The liquor seller is simply and only a privileged malefactor — a criminal.
—Abraham Lincoln

We have nearly twice as many outlets for alcohol as we have churches in the United States. Americans spend five times as much on alcohol as they give to all churches.
—*The Wesleyan Methodist*

＊ ＊ ＊

There is, by weight, precisely the same quantity of alcohol in one jigger of whiskey — or in one glass of wine — or in one bottle of beer.

One ounce of alcohol retards muscular reaction 17.4 per cent;

Increases time required to make a decision 9.7 per cent;

Increases errors due to lack of attention 35.3 per cent, and due to lack of muscular co-ordination 59.7 per cent.
—Paul Harvey, in *Listen*

＊ ＊ ＊

Drink is America's number-one enemy. So entrenched has this deadly evil become in our national life that there are few politicians brave enough to lift their voice against it! —W. B. K.

＊ ＊ ＊

For others, I abstain for an unquestionable reason, namely, I desire to avoid completely any responsibility for causing, by example, my own children or the sons and daughters of other parents to become victims of alcoholism, and all the other tragedies that result from the use of alcoholic beverages.
—Dr. Andrew Ivy

＊ ＊ ＊

The alcoholic commits suicide on the installment plan. —Rev. Vance Havner

＊ ＊ ＊

An Indian was seriously injured in an automobile accident. Later he told a friend how it happened: "Drive out big car, buy gas, buy liquor, tank up on both, step on gas, trees and fences fly by fast, big bridge coming down road, turn out to let bridge pass! Bang! And here I am!

＊ ＊ ＊

The requirement of our society that drinking is a social obligation to which one must conform is one of the major causes of alcoholism in our country.
—Dr. Marvin Block,
Chairman American Medical
Committee on Alcoholism

The War Department would do well to have real courageous teetotalers among the officers to preach and practice abstinence in order to educate the Army in sobriety. Only a sober Army is worth the pay of the taxpayers. Anything short of this is unworthy of the name American.
—Col. (Ret.) James E. McDonald, U. S. Army

* * *

Oh! that men should put an enemy into their mouths to steal away their brains! O God, that we should with joy, pleasure, revel, and applause transform ourselves into beasts!
—Shakespeare

* * *

Drinking was involved in almost every crime involving teen-agers in my district. . . . Almost every time I tell a parent that his boy had been drinking before he got into trouble, the parent replied that his son didn't drink!
—Captain Ralph Petacque, Chicago Police Force

* * *

Before today is over, 16 people will be killed, and 1500 will be hospitalized by drivers who have had a few drinks!
—*Guideposts*

* * *

Behind the attractive advertisements that lure youths, men and women to drink, is the other side which is visible to only those who are willing to look — sickness, suffering, crime, economic loss, broken homes, broken hearts and poverty. How satanically subtle and misleading is the representation of the man of distinction holding a whiskey glass in his hand! —W. B. K.

* * *

A New York City patrolman went berserk one Saturday night. He entered a tavern and with no provocation killed four men who stood there drinking. What deranged the patrolman, and caused him to commit this terrible crime? The following sentence from the *Associated Press* account of the terrible deed answers the question: "An investigation showed that McDermott had been drinking in several bars in the area Saturday evening." —W. B. K.

The secretary of the Ohio Wholesale Beer Association told a group of his distributors, "Let's not wait until 1960 or 1970. Let's try to sell the American people now on the advantages of drinking a refreshing glass of beer. In reading the trade journals, we note that many experts and authorities are looking forward to the future, to 1960-65, when a large segment of our population will become twenty-one years of age. Let's not wait until 1960. Let's try today." —*The Sunday School Times*

* * *

The price they [women alcoholics] pay is even more terrible than the male alcoholics. The woman easily becomes a social outcast. . . . The alcoholic woman frequently contributes to our soaring divorce and crime rates. Physically . . . the woman addict degenerates much faster than the male alcoholic. . . . He may drink for ten or twenty years before he becomes a physical wreck, but a woman alcoholic often ruins her health in a matter of months. Amnesia, or "blackouts," mental illness, cirrhosis of the liver and neuritis are the price one in every four pays for drinking.
—Sidney S. Greenberg, M.D., of the Consultation Clinic for Alcoholism, Bellevue Medical Center, New York

* * *

Seventy-five per cent of the world's population does not drink. The twenty-five per cent that do drink are found mostly in the Western world among people of the so-called "Christian" world.
—*The Sunday School Times*

* * *

Sixty per cent of the arrests for all causes in American towns and cities are hauled in annually on charges associated with heavy drinking, drunkenness, drunken driving, disorderly conduct and vagrancy.
—*U. S. News and World Report*

* * *

The American people spend more for alcohol than twice the sum given annually to all churches combined. Our alcohol bill for one year would support Methodist missions at home and abroad for 112 years! —*The Dry Legion*

According to the Pardon and Parole Board of Texas, eighty-seven per cent of the inmates of prisons of that state are there because of alcohol-related crimes.

* * *

"Singer Slain — GI a Suicide!" A drink-crazed GI beat and stabbed to death his consort in sin. A note, found in the room, told the tragic story: "I killed her because of passion and drink. We were both drunk. I killed her and I am sorry. Life is not worth living."
—W. B. K.

* * *

Alcoholics are being produced in the United States at the rate of more than 1200 a day — over 50 an hour around the clock. Dr. Andrew C. Ivy, chairman of the department of clinical sciences, University of Illinois, said, "Alcoholism is now the nation's number three health problem from the standpoint of incidence, lives lost, and people disabled. It ranks immediately behind heart disease and cancer in its toll in American society. —*Action*

* * *

Here is one man who made whiskey, another who sells it, another rents a house for the sale of it, another who votes a party to license it, another dies drunk. Now if you can fix that up so that some of the crowd will go to heaven and some to hell, you are a more profound philosopher than I have been.
—Sam Jones

* * *

If a natural choice between drunkenness and sobriety were possible in our civilization, I should leave the people free to choose. But when I see an enormous capitalist organization pushing drink under people's noses at every corner and pocketing the price, whilst leaving me and others to pay the colossal damages, then I am prepared to smash that organization and make it as easy for a poor man to be sober, if he wants to, as it is for his dog.
—George Bernard Shaw

* * *

We resent this invasion [by liquor advertising] of our homes, and especially the insidious campaign to exploit and seduce the youth and children in our homes. . . . Drinking is pictured as glamorous and gracious, the smart thing to do, an absolute must if one is to be the life of the party. . . . Never, never is the real truth told or pictured — no skid rows; no men of distinction who have become men of extinction; no winos; no wrecked cars with broken, bleeding victims mixed with broken, flowing bottles. Never are the end results of this product shown.
—Mrs. W. J. H. McKnight in
The United Presbyterian

* * *

On the last day of Lincoln's life, the great emancipator said: "We have cleared up a colossal job. Slavery is abolished. After reconstruction the next great question will be the overthrow and suppression of the legalized liquor traffic."

That evening, Mr. Booth stopped in a saloon, filled himself with liquor to nerve himself for his planned tragedy. That night Lincoln's bodyguard left the theater for a drink of liquor at the same saloon. While he was away Booth shot Lincoln. Those two drinks were the most costly drinks in American history. Liquor is the greatest enemy of mankind.

* * *

"I have made five thousand dollars during the last three months," said a saloonkeeper, boastfully, to a crowd of his townsmen. "You have made more than that," quietly remarked a listener.
"What is that?"
"You have made wrecked homes — women and children poor and sick and weary of life. You have made my two sons drunkards," continued the speaker with trembling earnestness. "You made the younger of my two sons so drunk that he fell and injured himself for life. You have made their mother a brokenhearted woman. Oh, yes, you have made much — more than I can reckon up, but you'll get it some day."
—*Clipsheet*

* * *

Speaking of strong drink, magazine and television ads always picture drinkers as prosperous, healthy and happy, people, apparently without a worry in the world.

When we see these ads, memories return to countless ragged, begging, drunken derelicts we have seen on Skid Row in Los Angeles, New York, Chicago, and New Orleans. However, you only see drunks in real life, never in advertisements. —*Baptist Record*

* * *

Any man who studies social conditions of the poor knows that liquor works more ruin than any other one cause.
—Theodore Roosevelt

* * *

To sell drink for a livelihood is bad enough, but for a whole community to share the responsibility and guilt of such traffic seems a worse bargain than that of Judas. —Horace Greeley

* * *

Let me tell you from the very outset, and speaking as a medical man, that I personally know of no greater curse on God's earth than alcohol, and there is no greater curse that we know of in the world. —L. P. Bosman, M.D.

* * *

If the increase of the ravages of alcohol in our country is to be halted and reversed, the pulpit and Sunday school must be reconsecrated to a militant doctrine of abstinence.
—Dr. Andrew C. Ivy, President, University of Illinois

* * *

A nationally known psychiatrist said that science does not know the answers concerning either the causes or cure of alcoholism. People of even average intelligence know that people become alcoholics by imbibing drinks of alcoholic content. It is not possible for non-drinkers of alcoholic beverages to become alcoholics. —W. B. K.

* * *

The liquor business is a business that tends to lawlessness on the part of those who conduct it and criminality on the part of those who patronize it.
—Theodore Roosevelt

* * *

Cake and ice cream at state-employees' parties are fine, but liquor is definitely

out. There must be no drinking, no liquor, no parties or celebrations of that character.
—Governor Goodwin Knight

* * *

There are many ways of murdering men. One who kills a man on the street corner at least risks the guillotine. Those who distill poison, though they are not liable to human courts, should be assured of our contempt. They await the judgment of God. —M. André Monteil, French Minister of Public Health

* * *

"How can I live if I give up this business?" asked a bartender. "The real question is, How will you die if you keep on in it?" answered a friend. "Nor thieves, nor covetous, nor drunkards . . . shall inherit the kingdom of God" (I Cor. 6:10).

* * *

Kathleen Anne, a two-months-old baby, began to cry at three a.m. Her drinking father gave her her milk bottle, but the baby refused to take it. "The baby kept crying, so I shot her!" confessed the intoxicated father.
—W. B. K.

* * *

"I'll have one more beer to finish and then I'll be on my way," phoned Allen Marvin Bourgeois from a saloon to Mrs. Ruth Ronco. A little later, Bourgeois' auto slammed into a concrete abutment while traveling 75 miles an hour! Killed in the car with Bourgeois were Everett Gillian, Jr., and Miss Joyce Ann Patenaude. —*Chicago Daily Tribune*

* * *

I do not know a solitary case in the widest range of medical practice in which alcohol is the best remedy that can be supplied.
—Howard A. Kelly, M.D.

* * *

I do not drink alcoholic liquors. I have a better use for my head. To put alcohol in the human brain is like putting sand in the bearings of an engine.
—Thomas A. Edison

* * *

I'm notorious as being a "teetotaler" and a "dry" in all the circles with which I come in contact. I've talked to medi-

cal and lay groups in every state in the Union except two. In every instance but one there has been a cocktail party. I've never taken a cocktail! When it comes to things that lead to real evil, we must have the courage of our convictions. On the battlefield we have to manifest real courage. This is a battle-field. The battle is with alcohol and the misery it produces.
—Andrew C. Ivy, M.D., President,
University of Illinois

• • •

The shortest line between life and death is the walk between the bar and the car. —Walter Winchell

Illustrations

America's Deadliest Enemy — Alcohol!

"Crash Kills 'Safe Driver' and Five Others," ran the headline of a news story which stated: "A national highway safety leader, his wife and a son died in a two-car crash which took six lives. Another son is in critical condition. On a straight stretch of highway an oncoming car swerved across the center line and slammed into the car coming in the opposite direction. State Patrol Sgt. T. H. Embry said all three of the men in the weaving car had been drinking heavily. The official report said the trio had been refused more beer at two different places shortly before the wreck."

The Chicago newspaper which carried the tragic story also carried a full-page beer advertisement and several other liquor advertisements.

Has this destroying, dehumanizing evil become so entrenched in the nation that nothing short of God's judgment and outpoured wrath will awaken our nation to the fact that alcohol is a deadlier foe than even atheistic Communism? —W. B. K.

• • •

If There Had Been No Tavern

A nineteen-year-old boy, twice torpedoed and rescued at sea, a merchant marine veteran, was sentenced to forty years in prison by a Chicago judge for having beaten a girl to death with his fists and having left her nude body in an alley. The evidence brought out in the trial showed that the youth, visiting relatives in the city, had spent a considerable part of a night at a tavern, had been served six whiskies and four bottles of beer within one hour, and was never asked for his age or identification papers. In commenting, the judge said: "If he had not been served with intoxicating liquor at the age of nineteen he would not be standing before me today. If there had been no tavern open at 4 a.m., the girl would have been alive." The tavern keeper was not brought into court, and his place is still open, with his bartenders still behind the bar selling more liquor to other men. —Charles E. Fuller in *Heart to Heart Talk*

• • •

Sin When It Is Finished!

"Kills Husband in Family Quarrel," screamed the headlines of a great city daily recently. The tragic story continued. "Four children were sleeping shortly before midnight when ...., the wife, reached that point of no return, and took the life of her drinking husband. The tragedy was the culmination of an argument about the husband's continual drinking and bringing little, or no, money home." The woman said, "The first two years of our married life were happy. After that he started to get laid off from work and to drink!"

Thus another home went on the rocks, and innocent children were bereft of the care and protection of a father. While the mother, charged with first-degree murder, sits in jail, four children will have to shift for themselves, with a good possibility of their joining the ever mounting number of juvenile delinquents.

Have the home and childhood a deadlier and more cruel enemy than alcohol? Having been a chaplain of one of the nation's largest penitentiaries, and having been a pastor for more than thirty years, I unhesitatingly say, "No!"

Before the judgment bar of God, how much will the greedy, murderous, and conscienceless brewers and saloon keepers, along with a government which protects and licenses this monstrous evil, have to account for. —W. B. K.

* * *

The Real Criminal Goes Unapprehended, Uncondemned

Going from a saloon to the scene of their horrible crime — the humble home of a hard-working Amish farmer — two drunken brutes murdered cold-bloodedly the peace-loving farmer. He had worked hard in the field from sunrise to dusk. Sitting quietly at the kitchen table, he was enjoying a late snack in the companionship of his devoted wife. Then it happened! The two youthful drunks first assaulted the wife. When she resisted she was mercilessly beaten. Then they took the husband into the yard and demanded money. They were told to take all they wanted. They found four dollars. Then they sent two bullets through the man's head.

Before the killers went to the farm, "they had had a couple of beers and played the juke box," said the owner of a tavern. Prior to that they had been drinking, it was said.

Later they were apprehended. But the real criminal, to whom can be traced this and numberless crimes of all kinds — alcohol — goes unapprehended, uncondemned, unindicted, condoned, commended, licensed and protected.

—W. B. K.

* * *

If She Could Only See Herself!

Hour after hour, day after day, from early morning to closing time, this new character — woman — is a fixture of the tavern. The bartender and male habitués regard her with an attitude of mingled contempt to predatory interest. Most of them have husbands and homes. Many of them have children of tender age. The majority of them have jobs. A few of them are in school. She is making herself unfit for the duties of homemaking and rearing children. She is dulling her mind against knowledge and poisoning her body against

normal, healthy functions. She is the laughingstock of the very men whose casual society she welcomes over a glass of liquor. Obviously she contributes to juvenile delinquency because mothers who spend their time in these places neglect their homes and their children while saturating themselves with drink. *Something must be done about this potential social cancer!*

—*New York Journal-American*

* * *

From Saloon to Morgue

One of the saddest funerals I ever conducted was that of a father and mother who had left a tavern in a drunken condition, gotten in their car and sped away into the night. Shortly thereafter their mangled bodies were removed from the wrecked car. At the funeral solemnities, I sorrowed for their souls which departed so suddenly into the hereafter. My deepest sorrow, however, was for the four little children bereft of a father's care and a mother's love! The fell blow of this deadly evil so often strikes little children.

—Told by a pastor

* * *

Realistic Advertisement

The manufacturers of a well-known brand of beer never knew whether their parade in Waco, Texas, helped their cause or hurt it. The parade was the beginning of a five-day appearance of the famed hitch of eight immense Clydesdale horses, and was planned with all possible advance publicity. The horses led the parade, pulling a giant wagon of dummy beer cases. But the parade had a surprise ending. A trailer truck, bearing a demolished automobile, with ketchup-splattered young people hanging from its windows, followed close behind. Placards proclaimed that beer and automobiles equal death. For three hours, as the parade wended its way through Waco's business district, the deadly reminder of highway death trailed the beer advertising. As thousands of pepole paused to admire the horses, they gasped in horror at the view of havoc caused by drunken driving. Four university students in the car played their roles so well that many

believed the car actually contained corpses. City police granted the same rights to the dry campaigners as to the Anheuser-Busch display. Following the float was a string of cars carrying signs telling of the devastating effects of alcohol. A number of policemen along the way voiced their approval of the float — they had seen with their own eyes many similar wrecks — and greeted the dry campaigners with handshakes. The demonstration for abstinence was planned by the Rev. Tilson F. Maynard, president of the McLennan County Drys, and a Baptist minister.
—*Good News Broadcaster*

* * *

The Little White Shoes

So depraved and dehumanized by drink was Melvin Trotter that he sneaked into the room where his baby lay in a little white casket, and removed the little white shoes from its feet. He went to a saloon, plopped the little shoes down on the counter and said, "Give me a drink! I'm dying for a drink!" However, not every spark of humanness had died in the sordid soul of the saloon keeper, because he said, "Here's a drink, but you go and put those shoes back on the feet of your dead baby!"

Sometime thereafter this slave of alcohol came to know Jesus Christ. Let Trotter tell what happened:

"There was not anything that I knew about that I had not gone through. I had taken cure after cure. I had taken everything known to science, and had made resolution after resolution. But just one glimpse of Jesus Christ, and I have never wanted a drink from that instant to this!" —W. B. K.

* * *

A Statesman Speaks Out

Liquor advertising is deceptive. The advertisements make drinking appear attractive. They cleverly conceal the end results. They print pretty labels in glorious colors, and show men of successful business and professional types drinking in attractive home or club surroundings with beautiful women. If the artists told the whole truth, they would portray also, for instance, a wreck of humanity, possibly still young, incapable of holding a job, or of supporting his heartbroken wife and homeless children. There are certain streets here in Washington where pictures could be obtained for truthful liquor advertising that would balance the glamor with the inevitable sordidness.
—The Honorable Joseph Bryson

* * *

330,000 New Chronic Alcoholics Every Year!

Whether we like it or not, you and I are in the business, legal business, of producing alcoholics. There are approximately 1,000,000 chronic alcoholics in our country, deteriorated individuals; 3,000,000 addicted drinkers, and an additional 3,000,000 heavy drinkers, persons who are under the influence of alcohol throughout their waking hours. And since the average length of time elapsing from social drinking to heavy drinking and alcoholism is somewhere between ten and twelve years, that means that we are increasing the number of addicted drinkers and chronic alcoholics at the rate of 33,000 every year! —Dr. Frederick Lemere

* * *

I Found My Father's Bottle

"I wondered what liquor tasted like," said a fifteen-year-old boy in juvenile court who had attempted to murder a woman. "I found my father's bottle and drank about a pint of liquor. Afterwards I wandered around until it was dark. I saw a woman and followed her. I hit her over the head with a bottle." The judge ordered a psychiatric test but was silent in reference to the evil which deranged the boy and unleashed murderous tendencies in him. Nor did the judge speak words of reprimand to the father of the boy. —W. B. K.

* * *

Good Lord, I Wish I Knew What Happened!

"A bar-room fight at a fashionable golf club ended with a Joliet executive dead, and a friend of thirty-five years standing charged with his murder." Thus began the story of a tragic occurrence which started according to the sheriff "with a drunken brawl." As the fog of alcohol lifted from the addled brain of the murderer, he tearfully said, "I don't know what happened! I've known him for thirty-five years, and I don't remember hitting him. Look, there isn't a mark on me. Good Lord, I wish I knew what happened!" —W. B. K.

* * *

If Brewers Paid the Bills

The liquor business is the only business I know that keeps a one-sided ledger — that deals with receipts and ignores legitimate expenditures. It takes the profits and leaves the expenses to someone else. Within one year in Vancouver I buried three young people who had been killed by alcohol on the highways. That is not my assumption; that is the verdict of the jury. At not one of those funerals was there a representative of the business that killed them. They did not pay the funeral expenses or look after the orphans. If it had been a railway accident, the fault of the road, they would have been there. Had it happened in an industrial plant, they would have been there, but this accursed business grasps its privileges but takes no stock in its obligations. Some foolish people seem to think it pays. If it met its legitimate bills, it would go bankrupt in a year.

　　　　—Dr. Willard Brewing in
　　　　　　　　Church Herald

* * *

C. I. Scofield Unshackled!

As a Christian businessman concluded his business with a lawyer in St. Louis some years ago, he said to the lawyer: "I have often wanted to ask you a question, but I have been a coward." "Why?" replied the lawyer, "I did not think you were afraid of anything. What is the question?" The man said, "Why are you not a Christian?" The lawyer hung his head. He said, "Is there not something in the Bible that says no drunkard shall have any part in the Kingdom of God? You know my weakness." "That is not my question," answered the Christian man. "I am asking you why you are not a Christian?" "Well," answered the lawyer, "I cannot recall that anyone ever asked me if I were a Christian, and

I am sure nobody ever told me how to become one." Then the Christian drew his chair close to the lawyer, read him some passages from the Bible, and said simply, "Let us get down and pray." The lawyer prayed first: "O Jesus, Thou knowest what a slave I am to drink. Here this morning Thy servant has shown me the way to God. Oh, break the power of this habit in my life." Giving his testimony later, this drinking lawyer said, "Put it down big, put it down plain, that God broke that power instantly." Who was this drunken lawyer? Dr. C. I. Scofield, famous editor of the Scofield Reference Bible!

　　　　　　—Dr. P. W. Philpott in
　　　　　　　Evangelical Christian

* * *

When Saloon Keepers Capitulated

In 1873 a group of women at Hillsboro, Ohio, met and prayed and then read the 146th Psalm. Then they went directly to the saloons of the town. There they prayed and pleaded with the saloon keepers to give up their business. Church bells tolled simultaneously with the crusade of prayer and persuasion. On the second day one saloon keeper capitulated. He gave his entire stock to the woman, saying, "Do as you please with it." At the end of eight days, every one of the eleven saloons in the town closed. The brewers of Cincinnati offered $5,000 reward to anyone who would break up the movement. One unusually courageous male tried to do so. In four days he threw up his hands and surrendered to the women. This crusade of prayer and persuasion led to the formation, in 1874, of the *Women's Christian Temperance Union*.

　　　—Prohibition and Common Sense
　　　　　　　　　　　　by Douglas

* * *

Something Radically Wrong

The dangers from radioactive fallout are guarded against and every effort to protect the public is made, whereas very little is being done to protect the public from the disastrous effects of alcoholism. The number of alcoholics is increasing at the rate of 450,000 a year. There are eight million known alcohol-

ics, and 20,000 persons die and 400,000 are injured annually in accidents caused by drunken drivers. Only a handful of people have been seriously exposed to radioactive fallout, and few, if any, deaths have resulted despite the worldwide outcry against atomic testing. There must be something drastically wrong with our sense of values when we, as a nation, allow without protest the terrible ruination of human life caused by the use of alcoholic beverages.
—Dr. Andrew C. Ivy, head of the Clinical Science Department, University of Illinois

* * *

Snozzlewobbles!

Alcohol is a tricky drug. . . . Everyone has a different tolerance. . . . Alcohol undergoes chemical changes after being absorbed. The liver has the job of detoxification. But that organ can handle only so much at a time. When cocktails go down the hatch too fast and too often, hours elapse before the body rids itself of the substance. This is the major cause of hangovers. . . . The ensuing snozzlewobbles serve one good purpose: the punishment is a form of repentance.

Americans annually spend more money on alcohol and tobacco than on medical care — 14.2 billions versus 10.2 billions!
—Columnist in *Chicago Daily Tribune*

* * *

Guilty as Charged!

Gladstone said strong drink was "more destructive than war, pestilence and famine."

Sir Wilfred Lawson said it was "the devil in solution."

Cardinal Manning said it was a "public, permanent agency of degradation."

Abraham Lincoln said it was "a cancer in human society, eating out its vitals and threatening its destruction."

Robert Hall said it was "distilled damnation."

Lord Chesterfield said it was "an artist in human slaughter."

Ruskin said it was "the most criminal and artistic method of assassination ever invented by the bravos of any age or nation."

General Pershing said "drunkenness has killed more men than all of history's wars."

General Robert E. Lee said, "My experience through life has convinced me that abstinence from spirituous liquors is the best safeguard to morals and health."

President Taft said, "He who drinks is deliberately disqualifying himself for advancement."

The United States Supreme Court said that it "tends to produce idleness, disease, pauperism and crime."
—*Baptist Standard*

* * *

Is Liquor a Disease?

If it is —

1. It is the only disease that is contracted by an act of the will;

2. It is the only disease that requires a license to propagate it;

3. It is the only disease that is bottled and sold;

4. It is the only disease that requires outlets to spread it;

5. It is the only disease that produces a revenue for the government;

6. It is the only disease that provokes crime;

7. It is the only disease that is habit-forming;

8. It is the only disease that is spread by advertising;

9. It is the only disease without a germ or virus cause, and for which there is no human corrective medicine; and

10. It is the only disease that bars the patient from heaven.
—*The Gospel Banner*

* * *

Show Me the Way to Hell

A minister stood on a street corner as a funeral procession passed by. A drunk emerged from a tavern, approached him and in a thick, raucous voice asked, "Say, pal, can you show me the way to hell?" The minister paid no attention to him. The drunk, however, persisted and repeated his question loudly, "I say, pal, can you show me the way to hell?" The minister, pointing to the tavern just a few feet away, said, "There is the way to hell; but, sir, you may forsake the dark, downward way by coming to the Saviour. He stoops to the *guttermost* to save to the *uttermost!* Won't you trust Him to break the shackles of sin which you are powerless to break?" —W. B. K.

* * *

The Most Guilty Ones Go Free

"Hammer Killer of Boy Gets 50 Years!" screamed the headline on the front page of *The Chicago Daily Tribune.* The murderer, a teen-age boy, with eleven other youngsters, had cruised around in a car, seeking a victim for their murderous designs. Spotting an innocent victim, a boy waiting for a bus, the murderer held the victim in the crook of his arm, while he mercilessly pummeled his head with a peen hammer!

The killer admitted that before his horrible crime, he had drunk a quart of beer and a quantity of wine.

His sentence was just, but I wish that the brewers and saloon keepers could be sentenced along with the youth. —W. B. K.

* * *

A Twisted Sense of Values

Just suppose there were 170 million cows in America. Let's suppose there is an industry doing a great business selling a certain kind of hay, called *Old Scarecrow.* While made entirely from loco-weed, this hay is alluringly described as a blend of old straw aged in the cornfield. As a result, cows by the million turn from their sober diet of alfalfa and begin chewing *Old Scarecrow.*

Now let's suppose that this stuff makes the cows do silly things such as running into barbed wire fences,

jumping off bridges, or running into automobiles — so much that a half million are killed or injured each year.

Suppose milk production is cut down because the users of *Old Scarecrow* lose fifty million "cow-days" a year. Suppose the life expectancy of the cows who chew it regularly is reduced by an average of twelve per cent. Suppose that it makes eight million of the cows so sick that much of the time they are useless, and suppose that for every one that is cured, the industry makes ten more *Old Scarecrow* addicts. Suppose that caring for the victims of *Old Scarecrow* requires eighty per cent of the farmer's time.

And now, just suppose that in spite of all this, the merchants of this fatal fodder are allowed to advertise the stuff in every pasture, so that on almost every fence there appears large pictures of contented "Cows of Distinction" munching away on *Old Scarecrow.* And suppose that the manufacturers of *Old Scarecrow* are making a tremendous profit out of all this trouble and tragedy they cause the farmer.

How would you expect the farmers to take to all this? Would you expect them to take it sitting down? Or would you expect them to stand up and say to the producers of *Old Scarecrow*, "That ain't hay," and then put forth an effort to protect their cows by banning the advertising and promotion of *Old Scarecrow* from the range?

And now suppose that you cared as much about your *children* and your *fellow men* as you would expect the farmer to care about his cows? *What would you do about drinking?*
—Rev. Gwynne W. Davidson, D.D.
in *The Defender*

TEMPTATION

Illustrations

Jesus and I Went By

A farmer accepted Christ as his Saviour. The next morning he had to go into town. He parked his car and got out. Then he started to go to the hard-

ware store. Suddenly he smelled liquor fumes coming out of a tavern. The fumes were strong. He began to wonder if he could resist going into the tavern and getting a drink like he had always done when he came to town. Then he remembered that he now had Christ to help him. He prayed out loud, saying, "Jesus, You must help me *go by* that tavern and not *go in!*" Christ heard and responded to his call for help. He went *by* the tavern and did not go *in.* In relating his experience to a friend, the farmer said, "The Lord came and helped me. *We* went by the saloon, and *we* have been going by ever since!"

"The Lord knoweth how to deliver the godly out of temptation" (II Peter 2:9). —W. B. K.

* * *

How We Are Made Strong

An elderly man asked a boy to go with him into the woods to cut down some hickory trees to make ax handles. They soon came to several young hickory trees. The boy said, "These trees would make good ax handles. Let's cut them down."

The old man said, "These trees in the lowlands have been protected from the storms which rage higher up. Let's go to the heights where the trees have been rocked back and forth by fierce winds. Those trees have been hardened by the tempest and they will make much stronger ax handles!"

Those who have been exposed to temptations — rocked to and fro by the tempter, Satan, but who have not yielded — are made stronger. We can be "more than conquerors through him that loved us!"

Job said, "When he hath tried me, I shall come forth as gold." —W. B. K.

* * *

More Than Conquerors

Two alcoholics were converted. One testified, "From the moment I trusted Christ to save me, and deliver me from the enslaving habit of strong drink, I have never had the slightest desire to drink anything of alcoholic content. I would have to learn all over again to love the evil which, for more than thirty years, was the greatest love of my life. Even the smell of liquor nauseates me!" The second testified, "How I wish my experience corresponded with the experience of the brother who has just testified. Every day I have a terrific struggle not to partake of the evil which for years all but wrecked my life. I am depending solely upon the mighty Saviour to keep me in temptation. Pray for me!"

Though severely tempted, we may be "more than conquerors" by looking to the One who neither sleeps nor slumbers and who knows "how to deliver the godly out of temptations" (II Pet. 2:9). —W. B. K.

* * *

The Place Is Occupied!

A saintly teacher was held in great admiration by his pupils. His poise and peace, even in times of strain and stress, registered greatly with his pupils. In class one day a student asked him, "Sir, we want to know the secret of your serenity, even under provocation which would cause us to go down in defeat. You always seem to be unperturbed and untroubled. Do not testings and temptations phase you? Do not the pleasures of sin ever cause you to go into forbidden paths?" Smiling, the teacher replied, "I know something of the things of which you speak. The appealing enticements to sin that trouble you do come to me, too, but when these temptations knock at the door of my heart, I simply say to the tempter, Satan, 'The place is occupied!' Ever remember this fact: 'Ye are of God, little children, and greater is he that is in you, than he that is in the world' (I John 4:4), and you will emerge victoriously from temptation."

—W. B. K.

THANKSGIVING

Short Quotes

A bit of praise is one of the best ways of dispelling a dark mood. I knew a man who lost his speech during the war. It was a case of shell shock. One Sunday evening he was at a religious service in which the 100th Psalm — a Psalm of praise — was quoted. Forgetting his loss of speech, the veteran began to praise God for His goodness. His speech had come back!
—James Reid

Blow, blow, thou winter wind,
Thou art not so unkind
As man's ingratitude;
Thy tooth is not so keen,
Because thou art not seen,
Although thy breath be rude.
—Shakespeare

When we bless God for mercies, we prolong them. When we bless God for miseries, we usually end them. Praise is the honey of life which a devout heart extracts from every bloom of providence and grace. —Spurgeon

Praise changes things. Praise changes *you.* Try it! A song of praise in the prison of gloom or depression can open its doors: "And at midnight Paul and Silas prayed, and sang praises unto God . . . and immediately all the doors were opened, and every one's bands were loosed" (Acts 16:25, 26). —W. B. K.

Thou hast given so much to me,
Give one thing more — a grateful heart,
Not thankful when it pleaseth me,
As if Thy blessings had spare days,
But such a heart
Whose pulse may be Thy praise.
—George Herbert

Illustrations

This Is More Than You Deserve!

A farmer's wife in Iowa worked hard to prepare good, wholesome meals for a gang of men who worked in the fields. Coming into the dining room from their work, they would sit down and wolf the food without thanking either God or the one who had prepared it. "I'll teach those ingrates a lesson," said the woman to herself. One day she put hay and oats on the large dining room table. "What does this mean?" angrily demanded the hungry men as they approached the table. "Some practical joke you have played on us!" they said. "This is no joke! This is more than you deserve! During the hot days of the summer I have done my best to give you good, wholesome food, but not one of you has uttered a word of thanks to God or to me!" said the brave woman.
Who without prayer sits down to eat,
And without thanks then leaves the table,
Tramples the gifts so good with feet,
And is like mule and ox in stable!
—W. B. K.

But Where Are the Nine?

I meant to go back, but you may guess
I was filled with amazement I cannot express
To think that after those horrible years,
That passion of loathing and passion of fears,
By sores unendurable — eaten, defiled —
My flesh was as smooth as the flesh of a child.
I was drunken with joy; I was crazy with glee;
I scarcely could walk and I scarcely could see,
For the dazzle of sunshine where all had been black; . . .
But I meant to go back, — oh, I meant to go back!
I had thought to return, when my people came out.
There were tears of rejoicing and laughter and shout;

They embraced me, — for years I had
   not known a kiss;
Ah, the pressure of lip is an exquisite
   bliss!
They crowded around me, they filled the
   whole place;
They looked at my feet and my hands
   and my face;
My children were there, my glorious
   wife,
And all the forgotten allurements of
   life.
My cup was so full I seemed nothing
   to lack! . . .
But I meant to go back, — oh, I meant
   to go back!

                        —*Selected*

* * *

A Thanksgiving Prayer

For those who bravely dared to face
   The wolf-fangs of the sea,
To find a land where they might dwell
   In faith and liberty.
For pioneers who blazed the trails
   And broke the virgin sod
With strength and spirit, firm and sure,
   Today, we thank thee, God!
For ancestors with a vision
   As wide and deep and high
And as filled with stars of promise
   As the eternal sky,
For health and homes and country
   And laughter, sweet and gay,
For all of these — and love and faith
   We thank thee, God, today!

            —Blanche Lea Walden

* * *

Mommy, No Blessing Here?

Celeste Sibley, columnist for the *Atlanta Constitution*, took her three children into a small restaurant for breakfast one morning so they would not be late for school and she for her work. The place was crowded. They had to take separate seats at the counter. Little eight-year-old Mary sat at the end of the line. When she was served, she paused and called to her mother, "Mommy, don't people ask the blessing in this place?" Silence followed. The mother was embarrassed. Before she could hush the child, the counter man replied, "Yes, we do, sister! You give thanks!" Mary bowed her head. All heads were lowered in reverence and silence while Mary prayed: "God is great and God is good, let us thank Him for our food! Amen!" —W. B. K.

* * *

Oh, How Much We Owe!

When this passing world is done,
When has sunk yon glorious sun,
When we stand with Christ in Glory,
Looking o'er life's finished story:
   Then, Lord, shall I fully know,
   Not till then, how much I owe.

When I stand before the Throne,
Dressed in beauty not my own,
When I see Thee as Thou art,
Love Thee with unsinning heart:
   Then, Lord, shall I fully know,
   Not till then, how much I owe.

E'en on earth, as through a glass,
Darkly, let Thy Glory pass;
Make forgiveness feel so sweet,
Make Thy Spirit's help so meet;
   E'en on earth, Lord, make me know,
   Something of how much I owe.

Chosen not for good in me,
Wakened up from wrath to flee;
Hidden in the Saviour's side,
By the Spirit sanctified;
   Teach me, Lord, on earth to show,
   By my love, how much I owe.

         —Robert Murray McCheyne

* * *

One Thing More — A Grateful Heart!

In honoring the memory of their son who was killed in World War II, the parents gave a sizable check to their church. When the presentation was made, a mother whispered to her husband, "Let's give the same amount for our boy!" "What are you talking about?" asked the husband, "our boy didn't lose his life!" "Ah," said the wife, "that's just the point! Let's give it as an expression of our gratitude to God for sparing his life!"

George Herbert prayed: "Our Father, Thou hast given us so much. Do please give us one more thing — a grateful heart!" —W. B. K.

* * *

Ceaseless Praise of a Leper

David was a Negro preacher, a leper, and a patient in the National Leprosarium at Carville, Louisiana. He was crippled, deformed, and blind. Yet he was cheerful and thankful. He sang hymns of praise and greatly inspired other sufferers. The note of thanksgiving was dominant in his prayers. An old-fashioned radio brought joy to him. He turned it on and off with his lips because his fingers were useless.

How blessed we are, no matter what our condition may be, if we have a grateful heart! —W. B. K.

* * *

In Everything Give Thanks

For all that God in mercy sends —
For health and children, home and
    friends;
For comforts in the time of need,
For every kindly word and deed,
For happy talks and holy thoughts;
For guidance in our daily walk —
    In everything give thanks!

For beauty in this world of ours,
For verdant grass and lovely flowers,
For song of birds, for hum of bees,
For the refreshing summer breeze,
For hill and plain, for stream and wood,
For the great ocean's mighty flood —
    In everything give thanks!

For the sweet sleep which comes with
    night,
For the returned morning light,
For the bright sun that shines on high,
For the stars glittering in the sky —
For these and everything we see,
O Lord, our hearts we lift to Thee;
    In everything give thanks!
                                    —*Selected*

* * *

Where to Find Gratitude

A businessman said, "People are ingrates. It took me 61 years to find it out. I have 175 employees, men and women. At Thanksgiving, I sent them 175 choice turkeys. Only four thanked me. Two thanked me by notes and two said, 'Thank you' when they chanced to

meet me in the hall. Because of their thanklessness, I've decided never to go out of my way to be nice again."

Someone has said, "If you want to find gratitude, look for it in the dictionary. The reward of giving comes from the good feeling it gives the giver. Don't expect any other returns."
                                    —W. B. K.

* * *

It Feels Good to Be Thanked

"Central" was tired, her head ached; she had just succeeded, after repeated efforts, in getting the number eagerly wanted by a woman — and here the woman was calling again! "Can't that woman be quiet a minute?" she soliloquized while she reiterated, "Number, please?" trying not to speak crossly. "Central," said a pleasant voice, "I want to thank you for taking so much trouble to get me that last number. You are always very kind and obliging, and I do appreciate it." The surprise was so great, so overwhelming, that Central could only murmur confusedly, "I — oh, yes, ma'am." Nothing like this had happened before. Suddenly her headache was better; suddenly the day was brighter; suddenly, too, there came a lump in her throat, and she reached for her handkerchief. It felt so good to be thanked.
                        —*The Sunday School Times*

* * *

The Magic Word — Thanks!

A postal employee opened and read the mail which came to the Dead Letter Office in Washington addressed to Santa Claus. In the three months before Christmas, there were thousands of letters asking for something. In the months after Christmas, there was only *one card* addressed to Santa Claus thanking him. How quick we are to ask and receive. How slow we are to speak the magic word — thanks!
                                    —Harold Ruoff in
                                The Chicago Daily News

TIME

Short Quotes

The life span of the average American is 57 years. We work 15 years and 5 months. We spend 8 years in recreation and cultural pursuits. Five years are required for meals and 5 more for travel. Three years we are sick. We spend 2 years in getting dressed: "So teach us to number our days that we may apply our hearts unto wisdom" (Ps. 90:12).

* * *

When as a child
I laughed and wept —
Time crept!
When as a youth
I dreamed and talked —
Time walked!
When I became
A full-grown man —
Time ran!
Then as with the years
I older grew —
Time flew!
Soon I shall find
As I travel on —
Time gone!"

—*Selected*

* * *

Enjoy the blessings of this day, as God sends them, and the evils of it bear patiently and sweetly! This day only is ours; we are dead to yesterday, and we are not born to the morrow. He, therefore, that enjoys the present, if it be good, enjoys as much as is possible, and if only that day's trouble leans upon him, it is singular and finite.

—Jeremy Taylor

* * *

Life is an eternal today. Its happiest moment is now. Yesterday was experience, but today is reality! It is everything! It is life! —Preston M. Nolan

* * *

One of the illusions of life is that the present hour is not the critical, decisive hour. Write it on your heart that every day is the best day of the year. He only is rich who owns the day, and no one owns the day who allows it to be invaded with worry, fret,

and anxiety. Finish every day, and be done with it. You have done what you could. —Ralph Waldo Emerson

* * *

Strength for today, in house and home
To practice forbearance sweetly;
To scatter kind words and loving deeds,
Still trusting in God completely.

Strength for today is all that we need,
For there never will be a tomorrow;
For tomorrow will prove but another today,
With its measures of joy and sorrow.

* * *

So often do the spirits of great events stride on before the events, and in today already walks tomorrow.

—Coleridge

* * *

Had I but this one day to live,
One day to love, one day to give,
One day to work and watch and raise
My voice to God in joyous praise,
One day to succor those in need,
Pour healing balm on hearts that bleed,
Or wipe the tears from sorrow's face,
And hearten those in sad disgrace —
I'd spend, O God, much time with Thee
That Thou might'st plan my day for me.
Most earnestly I'd seek to know
The way that Thou would'st have me go,
For Thou alone canst see the heart —
Thou knowest man's most inward part.

—Alice M. Muir

* * *

Time is God's gift to mortal man;
It is that fleeting little span
Between our birth and heaven's door
Where we begin God's evermore
When time is o'er.

How then should we our time employ,
In service, or, in passing joy?
Can we afford to throw away
And squander time in passing play,
O men of clay?

—Rev. R. E. Neighbour, D.D.

* * *

"So little done — so much to do" regretfully said Cecil Rhodes, the great empire builder of South Africa, as he lay dying.

"I must work the works of him that sent me, while it is day: the night cometh when no man can work," said the Lord Jesus. —W. B. K.

* * *

Turn backward, turn backward,
  O, time, in thy run,
For now I can see
  How it should have been done.
                    —Elinor K. Rose

Today is the golden tomorrow that you dreamed of yesterday. So it will be to the end of time. Today, then, is your day of opportunity.

* * *

We live in deeds, not years; in thoughts, not breaths; in feelings, not in figures on a dial. We should count time by heartbeats. He most lives who thinks most, feels noblest, acts the best.
                    —Phillip P. Bailey

Illustrations

For What Is Your Life? . . . A Vapour!
Time's a handbreadth; 'tis a tale,
'Tis a vessel under sail;
'Tis an eagle in its way,
Darting down upon its prey;
'Tis an arrow in its flight,
Mocking the pursuing sight;
'Tis a short-lived fading flower;
'Tis a rainbow on a shower;
'Tis a momentary ray,
Smiling in a winter's day;
'Tis a torrent's rapid stream;
'Tis a shadow; 'tis a dream;
'Tis the closing watch of night,
Dying at the rising light;
'Tis a bubble; 'tis a sigh —
Be prepared, O man, to die.
                    —Frances Quarles

* * *

What Have You Done Today?
We shall give so much in the years to come,
  But what did we give today?
We shall lift the burden and encourage some,
  But what did we do today?
We shall comfort hearts and dry the tear,
We shall plant a hope in the place of fear,
We shall speak the words of love and cheer,
  But what did we speak today?

We shall be so kind in the after-a-while,
  But what have we been today?
We shall bring to each lonely life a smile,
  But what have we brought today?
We shall give to truth a grander birth,

And to steadfast faith a deeper worth,
We shall feed the hungering souls of earth,
  But whom have we fed today?

We shall reap such joys in the by-and-by,
  But what have we sown today?
We shall build us mansions in the sky,
  But what have we built today?
'Tis sweet in idle dreams to bask,
But here and now do we do our task?
Yes, this is the thing our souls must ask,
  "What have we done today?"
                    —Selected

* * *

Just For Today
Lord, for tomorrow and its needs,
  I do not pray;
Keep me, my God, from stain of sin,
  Just for today!

Now, set a seal upon my lips,
  For this I pray;
Keep me from wrong, or idle words,
  Just for today!

Let me be slow to do my will,
  Prompt to obey;
And keep me, guide me, use me, Lord,
  Just for today!
                    —Selected

* * *

Two Awful Eternities
There are two days in every week about which we should not worry — two days which should be kept free from fear and apprehension.

One of these days is yesterday, with

its mistakes and cares, its aches and pains, its faults and blunders. Yesterday has passed forever beyond our control. All the money in the world cannot bring back yesterday. We cannot undo a single act we performed, we cannot erase a single word we said.

The other day we should not worry about is tomorrow, with its possible adversities, its burdens, its large promise and performance. Tomorrow also is beyond our immediate control.

Tomorrow's sun will rise either in splendor or behind a mask of clouds — but it will rise. Until it does, we have no stake in tomorrow, for it is yet unborn.

That leaves only one day — today. Any man can fight the battles of just one day. It is only when you and I add the burdens of those two awful eternities — yesterday and tomorrow — that we are liable to break down.

—Illinois Medical Journal

TITHING

Illustrations

O Lord, Shrink His Income!

A pastor led a man to tithe his weekly salary of ten dollars. He continued to tithe as his income mounted, but when his tithe amounted to $500.00 weekly, he asked the pastor to tell him how to get free of his promise to God. He said, "I can't afford to give away money like that." The pastor said, "I'm afraid we can't get release from the promise, but kneel here and ask God to shrink your income so you can afford to give Him a dollar." —*Evangelical Friend*

• • •

It Works!

A businessman always gave a tenth of his income to the Lord's work. One day he was informed that within a year he would have to vacate the property which he was renting for his manufacturing business. For six months he sought another building to rent but with no success. Naturally, his business could not be carried on without a suitable building. In the meanwhile he was informed that a bank would put up a building for him if he could obtain a suitable site. He found an ideal property with a railroad siding. However, there was one drawback: the price. They wanted $30,000 for the site. He had $30,000, but he felt that $10,000 of it was money he owed the Lord, and which he had allowed to accumulate for a very definite service. He tried to get the site for $20,000, but without suc-

cess. One day he was strongly tempted to pay the $30,000. He prayed earnestly, however, about the matter. After prayer, he picked up his Bible. He read, "Bring ye all the tithes . . . I will . . . open the windows of heaven, and pour you out a blessing." "That settles it! The Lord shall have His $10,000 no matter what happens!" He went to the phone and called a Christian friend, saying, "That $10,000 is waiting for you whenever you need it!" He had hardly cradled the receiver when the phone rang. The real estate man was on the line. He said, "I have good news for you. You may have the piece of ground for $20,000." The Lord got His $10,000, and he got his lot and his factory, and his business prospered!

—J. Nieboer in
How to Be a Happy Christian

• • •

Withholding His Due

Suppose a master gardener should give you a beautiful garden and say, "I will provide the seed, the soil, the sunlight, the air, and all the other things necessary to make it beautiful. All I ask in return is one blossom of each ten, that they may be mine, and that with them I may cheer others who have not. The other nine you may do with as you will." Then, suppose when the garden grew and became beautiful, you selfishly kept all the blossoms for yourself and those whom you loved, giving only a leaf or a bud to the master whenever it happened to please you to do so. What would the master of the garden think of you? Yet God is the Master Gardener! —*The Watchman-Examiner*

* * *

They Paid the Tithe, but Not to God!

A pastor asked another pastor, "How many church members have you?" "I have 1900 members," was the reply. "How many of them are tithers?" he further asked. "All of them are tithers!" said the pastor. "How did you get them all to sign pledge cards, agreeing to pay the Lord's tithe?" the first minister inquired. "I didn't," was the prompt reply. "Only 347 signed the tither's pledge, and they have faithfully kept their pledge. The other members are tithers, too, for God has many ways of collecting the tithe — through adversity, sickness, unemployment. They pay the tithe all right, but not to God!" —Rev. R. W. Neighbour

* * *

My Happiest Christian Experience

Several years after he started tithing, a Tennessee automobile dealer wrote: "I have learned that, by forming a partnership with Christ and paying more attention to spiritual things and less to material things, everything works out much better. I am much better off financially now than I was before I started tithing, but even if I had less money I would continue to tithe, for it has been the source of my happiest Christian experience. I have learned that being a partner with Christ and having the privilege of handling a small portion of His business is worth more than all the world has to offer." —*Moody Monthly*

* * *

Shortchanging God

One of God's children, who was a tither, passed through a difficult time financially. He could hardly make ends meet. It was toward the close of the year. "I'll not pay my tithe to the Lord in the new year," he shortsightedly resolved. During the new year he carried out that ill-advised decision to his own spiritual injury and financial loss. He became ill and had to be hospitalized. It turned out that his hospital and doctor's bill totaled just forty cents more than his tithe would have been.

Would he have had this medical bill if he had dealt squarely with God in the matter of tithing? Only God knows the answer. This we do know: it never pays, either spiritually or financially, to shortchange God. —Told by a pastor

TONGUE

Short Quotes

An author by the name of Theodore Reinking faced execution in 1646 because he had offended King Christian IV of Denmark with a book he had written. King Christian offered him the alternative of "eating his book" or being executed. Reinking tore the book into shreds, soaked it in soup . . . and started munching away until he had devoured the whole book.

We are not quite so fortunate, for our words, once gone forth out of our mouths, are part of the eternal record. They will meet us at the judgment. Vast issues hang on our words:

"But I say unto you, That every idle word that men shall speak, they shall give account thereof in the day of judgment. For by thy words thou shalt be justified, and by thy words thou shalt be condemned" (Matt. 12:36, 37). —*Evangelical Friend*

* * *

Psychology has proved that if you keep your voice soft, you will not become angry. Psychology has accepted as scientific the Biblical dictum: "A soft answer turneth away wrath." —Les Giblin in "How to Have Confidence and Power in Dealing With People

Unless we yield our tongues as instruments of righteousness unto God, Satan will use them to his advantage, and to our spiritual impoverishment. Some people pride themselves that they have the gift of gab. But one thing is certain — what little spirituality such people possess may soon dribble away via the mouth. —W. B. K.

* * *

To know when to keep silent is one of the finest of arts. The atmosphere of life is darkened by murmuring and whispering over the non-essentials, the trifles that are inevitably incident to the hurly-burly of the day's routine. Things cannot always go our way. Learn to accept in silence the minor aggravations. Cultivate the gift of quietude and consume your own smoke with an extra draught of hard work so that those about you may not be annoyed with the dust and soot of your complaints.
—William Osler, M.D.

* * *

There are no idle rumors. Rumors are always busy.

* * *

"My talent is to speak my mind," said a woman to John Wesley. To which Wesley answered, "I am sure, sister, that God wouldn't object if you buried *that* talent."

* * *

Meekness is giving a soft answer to a rough question. —W. B. K.

* * *

A farmer was late one day in delivering his butter and eggs. One of his customers told him just what she thought of him. With bowed head, he calmly listened. When the tirade was over he said, "I'm sorry if I caused you any inconvenience, but I had the misfortune to have to bury my mother yesterday." But these words of apology made no impression on the woman. Wrath has no understanding.
—Told by the daughter of the farmer

* * *

Someone who knew George Washington well gave the following description of him. When Washington was twenty-six years old: "He is as straight as an arrow, a little over six feet tall and weighs 175 pounds. His head is well shaped, and is graciously poised. He has a large, straight nose, blue eyes and heavy eyebrows. He has a pleasing, though commanding, countenance, and *a large mouth which is usually firmly closed.*" How interesting is the reference to his mouth. There is nothing opened more often by mistake than the mouth! —W. B. K.

* * *

A dog has many friends because the wag is in his tail, and not in his tongue.
—W. B. K.

* * *

A prominent government official, against whose policies the late Senator McCarthy had been so outspoken, was informed of the latter's death and asked to comment. He said, "*De mortuis nil nisi bonum,*" which means, "Of the dead nothing unless good."

What is good for the dead is *better* for the living: "Of the living, nothing unless good!"

What wouldn't happen among God's children if a moratorium were declared against speaking evil of one another! How few of us truly obey the command: "Speak evil of no man." —W. B. K.

* * *

If a soft answer will turn away wrath, only God knows what no answer will turn away. Oftentimes no answer is the right answer: "And when he was accused of the chief priests and elders, he answered nothing" (Matt. 27:12).
—W. B. K.

* * *

Here are the names of seven "Mischievous Misses" who are responsible for most of our troubles: Misinformation, misquotation, misrepresentation, misinterpretation, misconstruction, misconception, misunderstanding. Don't listen to them! Beware!
—William J. H. Boetcker

* * *

I have never been cursed by the things I left unsaid. —Calvin Coolidge

* * *

I will speak ill of no man, not even in the matter of truth, but rather excuse the faults I hear, and, upon proper occasions, speak all the good I know of everybody. —Benjamin Franklin

Wise is the man who knows what not
to say and remembers not to say it.
If any little word of mine
  May make a life the brighter,
If any little song of mine
  May make a heart the lighter,
God help me speak the little word,
  And take my bit of singing,
And drop it in some lonely vale
  To set the echoes ringing.
                              —*Selected*

· · ·

These words are razors to my wounded heart: "There is that speaketh like
the piercings of a sword" (Prov. 12:18).
                              —Shakespeare

· · ·

Better to remain silent and be thought
a fool than to speak out and remove all
doubt. "Even a fool, when he holdeth
his peace, is counted wise" (Prov. 17:
28). —Lincoln

· · ·

The older he grew, the less he spoke,
and the more he said.
              —Said of an aged minister

· · ·

Talkativeness is utterly ruinous to
deep spirituality. The very life of your
spirit passes out in your speech. Hence,
all superfluous talk is a waste of vital
forces of the heart. The cure for lo-
quacity must be from within by an over-

mastering revelation to the soul of the
awful majesty of God and eternity.
              —George D. Watson, in
                Pilgrim Holiness Advocate

· · ·

Guard well thy tongue —
  It stretches far;
For what you say
  Tells what you are.

· · ·

In company guard your tongue; in
solitude, your heart. Our words need
watching. So also do our thoughts and
imaginations which grow most active
when we are alone. —Spurgeon

· · ·

Be not concerned, nor be surprised,
If what you do is criticized;
There's always folks who usually can
Find some fault with every plan;
Mistakes are made, we can't deny,
But only by the folks who try.

· · ·

If someone calls you a fool, don't
"blow your top." Go off into solitude
and meditate. He may be right.
                              —W. B. K.

· · ·

It's easy to make a mountain out of
a molehill — just add a little more dirt.

· · ·

If you have a soft voice, you don't
need a big stick. —A Chinese proverb

Illustrations

The Thunderous Power of Silence

During World War II some Quakers
walked boldly into the Berlin Gestapo
office of Reinhard Heydrich, Himmler's
deputy chief. They implored Heydrich
for permission to take persecuted Jews
out of Germany. Heydrich listened stonily to the Quakers. Then he asked them
to wait in an adjoining room for his
reply. There the Quakers sat silently,
prayerfully and meditatively. The room
where they silently sat was undoubtedly wired! Their request would have
been peremptorily refused had they
spoken against the cruelties which were
being perpetrated against the helpless
Jews. Their prayerful silence was
broken by the dramatic announcement:
"Your request has been granted!" The

Quakers knew the thunderous power of
silence.   —Stephen Thiermann in
                      The Chicago Daily News

· · ·

Nagging

Nagging has sent many a man to destruction and driven some women to
despair. You can nag in any language
that human lips have spoken. You can
nag when your lips are tight shut by
lifting the eyebrows, tossing the head,
or sneering a sneer. It is not confined
to sex. It is due to disposition. The
one who nags injures himself and is
cruel in the extreme to the one attacked.
A good, old-fashioned quarrel is preferable. If the continual dropping of water
wears away a stone, it is no less true

that constant nagging will ruin the best disposition.

If you have a complaint, make it, but don't nag. If you have been injured, say so, don't nag.

—Rev. R. E. Neighbour, D.D.

• • •

Either Life or Death

It staggers the mind to try to appraise the power of words, either for good or evil. In the momentous, fateful days, when Nazism was in its nascent stage, Hitler spoke to a group of people in a beer cellar in Munich. His inflammatory words, which bristled with hate, were mirrored in the hardened faces of the evil group, and soon they engulfed the world in war.

An artist has portrayed the scene, putting on canvas the facial reactions of the group to Hitler's fiery words. He gave this title to the painting: "In the Beginning Was the Word."

What a blasphemous distortion of John's words which referred to the Prince of Peace, who came not to destroy life, but that all might have life through faith in His Name.

—W. B. K.

• • •

Wild Rumors

It is never safe to depend on snap judgments. . . . Half the scandal that goes around among members of the Church of Christ is simply the result of jumping at conclusions. Not long ago I read a little article in a church bulletin in which the pastor explained that he had been greatly troubled by a rumor going around to the effect that his wife had attended a meeting of some heretical group and that he had gone there in great indignation and dragged her out by the hair of her head and brought her home and beat her. He undertook to explain that he had not dragged his wife out of that meeting, that he had never at any time dragged her about by the hair, and that he had never beaten her, and also that his wife had never attended that meeting, and finally that he was a bachelor and had never had a wife!

—From *Lectures on Acts*, by H. A. Ironside, Litt.D.

I'll Give You a Tongue-Lashing!

When still a boy, Spurgeon offended a quarrelsome woman who did not know him. Angrily she said to him, "I'm going to give you a tongue-lashing!" She made good her threat. "You good-for-nothing rascal," she began. Young Spurgeon pretended to be deaf and, smiling, he said, "Yes, thank you, I am quite well. I hope you are the same!" Then came another burst of vituperation, to which young Spurgeon, still smiling, replied, "Yes, it does look like it might rain. I think I had better be getting on!" The infuriated woman calmed down and said, "He's as deaf as a post; what's the use of storming at him?"

—W. B. K.

• • •

Twisted Words

One day a dog stole a Quaker's roast. Said the Quaker to the dog, "I will not whip thee, or stone thee, but I will give thee a bad name!" As the dog ran away, the Quaker shouted, "Bad dog! Bad dog! Bad dog!" Soon a group of people were chasing the dog and shouting, "Mad dog! Mad dog! Mad dog!" A blast from a shotgun ended the dog's life.

How easily our words are twisted, sometimes to our embarrassment, but more often to the injury or even death of others!

If you would keep your lips from slips,
Five things observe with care:
To whom you speak, of whom you speak,
And how and when and where.

—W. B. K.

• • •

Listening with Kneecap

An infuriated woman called me on the phone one day. Hardly had I said, "Hello," when she began to slander a fine Christian couple. I quickly switched the receiver from my ear to my kneecap. The angry woman spoke so animatedly and loud that I could hear her voice, although I didn't get what she was saying. Finally she became silent. Then I lifted the receiver from my kneecap to my ear and asked softly, "Is there anything else?" "Well, I guess not," she replied. It was evident that she had cooled off considerably. The soft answer seemed to turn away what unspent wrath was left in her. As I cradled the receiver, I said, "Thank God, I didn't let my ear be used as a garbage can."

"Take heed *what* we hear!"

—W. B. K.

* * *

They Say

"They say!" Ah, well, suppose they do;
But does that make the story true?
Suspicion may arise from naught
But malice, envy, want of thought.
Why count yourself among the "they"
Who whisper what they dare not say?

"They say!" But why the tale rehearse,
And help to make the matter worse?
No good can possibly accrue
From telling what may be untrue.
And is it not the better plan
To speak of all the best you can?

"They say!" Well, if it should be so,
Why need you tell the tale of woe?
Will it the bitter wrong redress,
Or make one pang of sorrow less?
Will it the erring one restore
Henceforth to "go and sin no more"?

"They say!" Oh, pause and look within,
See how thy heart inclines to sin;
Watch, lest in dark temptation's hour
Thou, too, shouldst sink beneath its
    power.
Pity the frail, weep o'er their fall,
And speak of good, or not at all!

—*Selected*

* * *

Blessed Are the Deaf

At personal sacrifice, a loving married daughter procured a hearing aid for her aged mother. To the daughter's keen disappointment, she learned that her mother seldom used it. When she visited her mother the latter would quickly put on the hearing aid until her daughter left. Finally the daughter asked, "Mother, why do you so seldom use the hearing aid I bought you? Is it not good?" "Oh, no, my darling daughter! The hearing aid is all right. *It's the people!* I can't bear to hear them. I had forgotten how they talked. I had forgotten the awful things they say, and the cruel, cutting criticism! Oh, that people's tongues could be

curbed!" Later the daughter said, "As my dear mother thus 'sounded off,' she took off her hearing aid and pressed it into my lap, pleading, "Take it away!' Her burden was gone at last. Then she sat up and beamed with delight."

—W. B. K.

* * *

A World of Iniquity

A lady had incurred the dislike of some members of a certain family. They were discussing her at the dinner table one day. "I hope she never speaks to me again," said one. "I hope our paths will never cross again," said another. The father had remained silent. When all had had their turn at voicing their grievances, he said, "You'll not see her again, nor will your paths cross hers again. She died an hour ago. I learned of her passing as I left the office." The faces of the slanderous ones crimsoned with shame and remorse. —W. B. K.

* * *

Nothing Deadlier

A woman, highly agitated, came into a pastor's study. She instantly began to speak abusively of a mutual acquaintance who had just been in conversation by phone with the pastor. He had failed, however, to put the receiver properly back into its cradle and his phone was still connected with the phone of the abused woman. And so she heard the terrible things that were said about her to the pastor. This incident was the beginning of an intense hatred between the two women. To this day they refuse to speak to each other and hatred continues to poison their hearts. Is there anything so destructive and deadly as the unbridled tongue?

—Told by a pastor

* * *

A Word Fitly Spoken

Walter's school report was disappointing to his Mom and Dad. It indicated that he was only average and below average in his studies. However, there was one hopeful and encouraging thing about the report — the words added by the wise and discerning teacher: "*Walter works hard and shows much promise!*"

Oh, that more of us were quick to speak encouraging words! Of some people of old it was said: "They helped every one his neighbour; and every one said to his brother, Be of good cheer" (Isa. 41:6). —W. B. K.

TRACTS—PRINTED WORD

Short Quotes

Wear the old coat and buy the new book. —Austin Phelps

* * *

Books are the quietest and most constant of friends. They are the most accessible and wisest of counsellors, and the most patient of teachers.
—Charles W. Eliot

* * *

When we are collecting books, we are collecting happiness. —Vincent Starrett

* * *

Even in life the best friendships are based not so much on propinquity and contact as on the touching of minds and spirits. This is almost completely obtainable in a book.
—Mary Wright Plummer

* * *

Books are lighthouses erected in the great sea of time. —E. P. Whipple

* * *

A taste for books is the pleasure and glory of my life. I would not exchange it for the riches of the Indies! —Gibbon

* * *

Except a living man, there is nothing more wonderful than a book! A message to us from the dead from human souls whom we never saw who lived thousands of miles away. Yet these, on those little sheets of paper, speak to us, teach us, comfort us, open their hearts to us as brothers. —Charles Kingsley

* * *

Sneeringly a young man said to a Christian who had given him a tract, "Tracts everywhere!" "No," answered the Christian, "there are no tracts in hell!"

* * *

According to a United Nations report, India now stands fourth in the publication of books, exceeding such western lands as France, Italy, and the U.S. The number of titles by the top four countries are as follows: Soviet Union, 60,-000; Japan, 24,500; Great Britain, 19,-000; and India, 18,559. —*Gospel Banner*

* * *

Communism is now conquering the world. They have 800 million souls under their control. The greatest single contributing factor to this incredible advance has been the distribution of literature. The pen has preceded the sword! —Dr. Fred Schwarz

* * *

Missions have entered the era of the written word. In five years missionary literature will be talked about as much as medical missions are today. Here are some factors.
1. It can be secured and studied in secret.
2. It gets undivided attention in quiet hours.
3. It leaps language barriers and race tensions that hamper personal contacts.
4. It has permanency.
5. It goes where the missionary cannot go.
6. It lives after the spoken words are lost.
7. It's the most economical means of carrying out Christ's Great Commission: "Go ye into all the world and preach the gospel to every creature."
—A veteran missionary

* * *

There are virtually no doors closed to literature around the world.
—Dr. Clyde W. Taylor

* * *

Rufus Choate said: "A book is the only immortality on earth." Plato said: "Books are immortal sons deifying their sires." Kingsley said: "Except a living man, there is nothing more wonderful than a book." Bulwer said: "A thousand ages were blank if books had not evoked their ghosts and kept the pale unbodied shades to warn us from fleshless lips."

* * *

The greatest foreign missionary who ever led a soul to Christ was not Paul or one of the Reformers or one of the missionary pioneers such as David Livingstone. The greatest foreign missionary is the *printing press.* We must use it more. —Dr. Donald Gray Barnhouse in *Eternity*

* * *

In a rack in a Y.M.C.A. building in Bombay some literature was displayed. There were fifteen different publications in the rack. Fourteen of them were communists brochures whose format was attractive, and whose contents were slanted toward the capturing of youthful minds. The one other periodical was *The Christian Herald.* —W. B. K.

* * *

I promised the Lord I would never publish anything which would be a denial of my Christian principles. I have adhered to that promise. If there needs to be any explanation for the success of our operations, it lies in the fruit of that promise.
—William B. Eerdmans, Sr., dean of publishers of religious books in Grand Rapids, Michigan

* * *

Literature is undoubtedly God's strategic weapon for the evangelization of the world in these last days.
—Field director Davis of the Sudan Interior Mission

* * *

"Give me twenty-six lead soldiers, and I'll conquer the world," said Benjamin Franklin. "The pen is mightier than the sword."

* * *

If you would not be forgotten, either write things worth reading or do things worth the writing. —Benjamin Franklin

* * *

The world of books is the most remarkable creation of man. Nothing else that he builds ever lasts. Monuments fall. Nations perish. Civilizations grow old and die, but in the world of books are volumes that have seen this happen again and again, and yet live on, still young, still fresh as the day they were written, still speaking to men's hearts by men centuries dead.
—Clarendy Day in *Modern Woodman*

* * *

Just as good literature has the power to uplift, ennoble and transform character, so also does bad literature have the power to corrupt, drag down and destroy character. The assassin of Lord Russell said that the reading of one bad book made him a criminal and a murderer. John Angell James, one of England's noblest Christians, said when an old man that he had never fully recovered from the ill effects of fifteen minutes' reading of a bad pamphlet when he was a boy!
—Dr. George W. Truett

* * *

The printed word is in the end the great temporal power in the world. The missiles of dictators can shatter cities thousands of miles away, but the printing press can shatter an empire at the range of a thousand years.
—Professor T. C. McGrew in *The Graphic Arts Monthly*

* * *

There are only two powers in the world — the sword and the pen, and, in the end, the former is always conquered by the latter. —Napoleon

* * *

The battle for men's minds will be won by printer's ink, make no mistake about it! —G. Christian Weiss

* * *

I fear those newspapers more than a thousand bayonets. —Napoleon

* * *

If religious books are not widely circulated among the masses in this country I do not know what is to become of us as a nation. —Daniel Webster

* * *

For more than thirty years I have prayerfully considered the problem, "How can we evangelize the world in a space of one generation?" . . . There must be a way. After travel and study in fifty-three countries I have come to this conclusion — the only way we are going to be able to carry out the Great Commission will be by means of the printed page. —Dr. Oswald J. Smith in *Christian Business Men's League Bulletin*

Seventh-Day Adventists spend 15 million dollars a year for literature, producing it in over 200 languages. In their world correspondence school there are more than 3 million students!
—Carl J. Tanis, Christian Life Missions Executive Director

Illustrations

It Witnesses Daringly

Said Dr. Samuel M. Zwemer, "No other agency can penetrate so deeply, abide so persistently, witness so daringly, and influence so irresistibly as the printed page. Nearly all the inquirers in Moslem lands had first been led to Christ by means of a book or tract. Books go where evangelists are barred. Books stay when evangelists must leave. Wise indeed is the evangelist who leaves with every listener a written word with the permanence of print!"
—Cora Martinson in *Bible Society Record*

* * *

Just Anything!

A minister was in a bookstore one day, when a woman came in to buy a book. When asked as to the kind of book she wanted, she replied, "Oh, just anything." So the clerk handed her a worthless story. She rapidly glanced through the book, and then said, "That looks good. I will take it."

A half hour later, the minister was in a meat market, when that same woman came in and demanded a steak. She scornfully refused the first cut and the second that was offered, insisting rather loudly upon "the best that you have." When she finally received and paid for a most expensive cut, she announced for all to hear, "I am particular about what I eat."

Is it not too frequently true that many people feed their bodies upon the best, while their minds and souls are fed upon "just anything" — worthless and pernicious though it be?
—*The Watchman-Examiner*

* * *

The Printed Page Is a Missionary

The gospel in print is a "missionary." It never flinches nor shows cowardice.

It is never tempted to compromise. It never tires, never grows discouraged.

It travels cheaply and requires no hired hall. It works while others sleep. It never loses its temper. It continues to minister long after the present generation has passed on.

The gospel in print is effective. It gains entrance to both the lowly hut and the lofty palace.

It speaks to a man at the right time, only when he is reading it. It sticks to what it says and never answers back.

It reaches those who otherwise might never be reached. It carries the only authoritative answers. It points the way to eternal life through Jesus Christ.

The gospel in print is far-reaching. A pamphlet written by Martin Luther fell into the hands of John Bunyan, and by this means he was converted. "Pilgrim's Progress" came from his pen, and through that excellent work thousands were saved.

This missionary — the gospel in print — should have the prayerful support of every Christian. Those who make it possible become missionaries of the Printed Page.
—*The Standard Bearer* (S. Africa)

* * *

Do You Agree?

More people are led to Christ through tracts than by great preachers. When the judgment shall come and the King shall sit on His throne and the redeemed ones stand before Him, there will be more people in that throng who, in answer to the question, "What led you to Christ?" will reply in chorus, "A tract" than will point to Spurgeon, or Wesley, or Whitefield, or even the Apostle Paul, saying, "That man!"
—Rev. W. B. Riley, D.D.

How a Communist Was Converted

A missionary who labored faithfully for thirty years in China, a man of excellent reputation for accuracy, told me that the Communist regime in Red China has assigned to various students the rewriting of a number of biographies of the more famous Christian missionaries of former decades in that country, in an effort to besmirch their names, reveal them to have been tools of capitalistic enterprises, and so forth. But, my friend told me, the man who was assigned to rewrite the life of the great Hudson Taylor actually became converted to Christ as he read the material that it was necessary to survey for this task. No one knows what has happened to the man, but he is in Christ.

—Dr. Wilbur M. Smith in
The American Holiness Journal

TRUST

Short Quotes

Great is God's faithfulness and I will fear no evil about the future. There is no room for the word *disappointment* in the happy life of entire trust in Jesus and satisfaction with His perfect and glorious will.

—Frances Ridley Havergal

• • •

It's frightening when you think that one person out of every ten is going to be a mental patient! —Jack Mabley, in
The Chicago Daily News

• • •

Four things a man must learn to do
If he would make his record true:
To think without confusion clearly;
To love his fellowmen sincerely;
To act from honest motives purely;
To trust in God and heaven securely.

—Henry Van Dyke

• • •

One of Cromwell's officers was given to the sin of anxious care. One day his godly servant who knew how to live in the today and leave the tomorrow to the care of his Lord said to his worrisome master, "Master, the Lord ran this world before you came into it," to which his master quickly assented. "You expect Him to run it after you leave it, do you not?" Again the master nodded assent. "Then how would it do to let Him run it while you are in it?"

—James McConkey

• • •

Trust Him when dark doubts assail thee,
Trust Him when thy strength is small;
Trust Him when to simply trust Him
Seems the hardest thing of all.

• • •

Trust God's wisdom to guide,
Trust His goodness to provide;
Trust His saving love and power,
Trust Him every day and hour;
Trust Him as the only light,
Trust Him in the darkest night;
Trust in sickness, trust in health,
Trust in poverty and wealth;
Trust Him living, dying too,
Trust Him all the journey through.

—*Selected*

Illustrations

I Sleep When the Wind Blows!

A ranch hand applied for work. "I sleep well when the wind blows," he said to the ranchman. His cryptic words puzzled the ranchman. He employed him, however, as he needed help badly. A few nights later, high winds swept across the prairie. The ranchman arose hastily. He found the windmill properly adjusted to ride out the storm, the gate tied with an extra rope, a tarpaulin tied securely over the strawstack and pegged down tightly. Everything was shipshape. When he reached the bunkhouse, he found the ranch hand sound asleep! Then he understood the meaning of the cryptic words, "I sleep well when the wind blows!"

We, too, can sleep when the winds of adversity blow. We can confidently say: "I will trust, and not be afraid" (Isa. 12:2).

* * *

My Times

My times are in Thy hands;
My God, I wish them there;
My life, my friends, my soul I leave
Entirely to Thy care.

My times are in Thy hand,
Whatever they may be;
Pleasing or painful, dark or bright,
As best may seem to Thee.

My times are in Thy hand,
Jesus, the Crucified!
Those hands my cruel sins had pierced
Are now my guard and guide.

My times are in Thy hand,
I'll always trust in Thee;
And after death, at Thy right hand
I shall forever be.

—*Selected*

* * *

Trust God, Too

A minister was driving up a narrow mountain road behind a long line of cars. A large moving van was ahead. No one dared to pass the man as a car might be approaching from the opposite direction. At the crest of the mountain, the driver of the van waved his hand, indicating that all was clear ahead. Probably this man was a stranger to all those whom he waved past. They saw only his hand. The minister said, "More than a dozen people trusted their lives and the lives of their families to that total stranger! We trust one another with our lives many times a day — on buses and trains, in cars and in airplanes. But few are willing to trust themselves to the care of God whose eye is always upon them." —W. B. K.

* * *

Scared and Worried

A little girl said to her mother, "Mommy, you and Daddy acted awful worried and scared at the supper table last night. Was it because you thought that the bad men would blow up the world? Mommy, when I'm worried and scared, you comfort me. God will comfort you. I'm sure He will tell you He is looking after things, just like you tell me. He will take care of us!" The mother was an earnest Christian. She felt rebuked by her girl's sweet trust in the provident care of God so she said, "I guess we did act worried and scared. I am sorry, dear." —W. B. K.

* * *

The Mark of True Greatness

A bishop gave some lectures at a college. The students were greatly impressed by his deep spirituality. "What's the secret of his quiet mien and spiritual depth? Maybe if we could hear him pray at the close of the day, we'd know," said one.

Going to his room after a busy day the bishop fell wearily across his bed. Before he fell asleep, he prayed simply and with childlike trust:

"Now I lay me down to sleep,
I pray the Lord my soul to keep,
If I should die before I wake,
I pray the Lord my soul to take!"
The eavesdropping students went away silently. They felt they had the answer to their questions.

Childlike trust is always a characteristic of great Christians. Jesus taught that the symbol of greatness is the child in the midst, and that we must possess childlike trust to enter the kingdom of God.

—Told by Rev. Gordon E. Markey

* * *

If We Trust!

When the frosts are in the valley,
  And the mountain tops are grey,
And the choicest buds are blighted,
  And the blossoms die away,
A loving Father whispers,
  "This cometh from My hand,
Blessed are ye if ye trust,
  Where ye cannot understand!"

If, after years of toiling,
  Your wealth should fly away,
And leave your hands all empty,
  And your locks are turning grey,
Remember then your Father,
  Owns all the sea and land,
Blessed are ye if ye trust,
  Where ye cannot understand!

—*Selected*

Hitherto

When our soul is much discouraged
　By the roughness of the way,
And the cross we have to carry
　Seems heavier each day,
When some cloud that overshadows
　Hides our Father's face from view,
Oh, 'tis well then to remember,
　He hath blessed us hitherto.

Looking back the long years over,
　What a varied path — and yet
All the way His hand hath led us
　Past each hindrance we have met,
Given to us pleasant places,
　Cheered us all the journey through;
Passing through the deepest waters,
　He hath blessed us hitherto.

Surely then our souls should trust Him,
　Though the clouds be dark o'erhead;
We've a Friend that draweth closer
　When our other friends have fled.
When our pilgrimage is over,
　And the gates we're sweeping through,
We shall see with clearer vision
　How He's blest us hitherto.
　　　　　　　　　—*Selected*

• • •

No Confidence in Man

　The king of Italy and the king of
Bohemia promised John Huss safe trans-
port and safe custody. They broke their
promises, however, and Huss was martyred. Thomas Wentworth carried a
document signed by King Charles I
which read, "Upon the word of a king

you shall not suffer in life, honour, or
fortune." Shortly afterwards, however,
his death warrant was signed by the
same monarch. "Put not your trust in
princes," were his last words.
　"It is better to trust in the Lord"
than in anyone or anything else.
　　　　　　　　　—W. B. K.

• • •

Leave It to God

Does the path seem rough and steep?
　Leave it to God.
Do you sow, but fail to reap?
　Leave it to God.
Yield to Him your human will,
Listen humbly and be still,
Love divine your mind can fill,
　Leave it to God.

Is your life an uphill fight?
　Leave it to God.
Do you struggle for the right?
　Leave it to God.
Though the way be drear and long
Sorrow will give place to song,
Good must triumph over wrong,
　Leave it to God.

If in doubt just what to do,
　Leave it to God.
He will make it plain to you,
　Leave it to God.
Serve Him faithfully today,
He will guide you all the way,
Simply trust Him, watch and pray,
　Leave it to God.
　　　　　　　　—Grenville Kleiser

UNSHACKLED

Illustrations

A Would-Be Suicide Saved

　"When I was unsaved, my soul was
often in despair," said someone who is
now a faithful minister of the gospel.
"In anguish I would cry out, 'O wretched
man that I am! who shall deliver me
from the body of this death?' One night
I said, 'I'll seek the answer to life's
enigma by death. I'll take my own life!'
As I trudged my way to the place where
I planned to commit the awful deed, I
passed a mission. I heard singing with-

in. Some power seemed to draw me,
even against my will, into that mission.
There I saw nine people. They were
singing gospel hymns. How joyful they
seemed to be! I knew that they had
something, Someone, I desperately needed. The Holy Spirit convicted me of my
sins, and gave me a vision of the lovely
Lord, waiting and willing to save *even
me*. I cried to God for mercy and forgiveness. He gloriously answered my
plea. I was instantly and gloriously

transformed! Twenty-four hours thereafter I began to preach the gospel of Christ. Since that time it has been my joy to tell others of His mightiness to save!" —Rev. Harold Walker

Transformed by Grace Divine

In speaking of the transforming power of God, Dr. Lawes, who labored for God in New Guinea, said, "I have heard savages pray. They had tattooed marks on their chests which indicated that they were murderers. I have heard them pouring out their prayers to God as children holding converse with their Father. I knew that they were indwelt by the Spirit of God, and had been taught by the Spirit. The outward marks of their former lives of depravity and cruelty still remained, but I knew they were now new creatures in Christ Jesus, 'transformed by grace divine!'"
—W. B. K.

Help of the Helpless

When Dr. P. W. Philpott was pastor of the Moody Church, Chicago, a young man came to his office and told him what had happened on the preceding Sunday. He said, "My mother and I were sitting in Lincoln Park. As we started to leave, my attention was caught by the electric sign bearing the words, 'Moody Memorial Church.' I said to my mother, 'I would like to go to that church.' As we entered the church, a large congregation was singing. You preached a sermon on 'Hope.' As I sat there, you had no idea that I was a dope addict, bound by a chain I could not break, and getting more discouraged about myself all the time. Then, suddenly, you reached a point in your sermon where you said, 'Jesus Christ can put hope into a hopeless heart. With Him there are no hopeless cases!' Then and there I opened my heart to Christ. I took Him by faith as my Saviour. When I got outside, I stepped over to a drain on Clark Street and dropped my drugs and equipment down through the iron grating." —W. B. K.

O Lord, if It Is Not Too Late

Years ago a unique character was converted in the Water Street Mission in New York. It was "the Old Colonel." Through drink he had sunk very low. At the time of his conversion he was sixty years old. He looked as if he were one hundred. He looked more like an animal than a human being. He was clothed in rags. The overcoat he wore was fastened with a nail. He was a caricature of the man he had been — a college graduate and a brilliant law student in the office of E. M. Stanton, Lincoln's Secretary of War. On the night of his conversion, he cried, "O Lord, if it is not too late, forgive and save this poor old sinner!" God heard the cry of his heart. He was gloriously saved. God vouchsafed His promise to him: "And I will restore to you the years that the locust hath eaten" (Joel 2:25). God restored his intellect. That which had been his greatest love and had almost ruined his life — strong drink — became his greatest hate. He became an honored and beloved Christian gentleman! —W. B. K.

Sir, I'm That Man!

A young minister spoke one Sunday night in Whitefield's Tabernacle. "There may be someone in my audience who is drink-ridden, lust-sodden, demon-possessed. If such is present, Christ can instantly save you!" An incident occurred at that moment which electrified the minister and the large audience. A man rose and said, "Sir, I am that man! I am drink-ridden, lust-sodden, demon-possessed! Is there any hope for me? Can your Christ save me?" The minister answered, "Yes, He can! God's promise is sure: 'Look unto me, and be ye saved, all the ends of the earth.'" That humanly hopeless and helpless man came to Christ. "Old things . . . passed away; . . . all things . . . [became] new!"
—*The Sunday School Times*

Sermon Averts Self-Destruction

God gives to His servants, from time to time, positive proof that His Word is "quick and powerful." The following incident illustrates this. A young lady was present in a Sunday-morning service when I was pastor in Chicago. Before the service, she asked for Dr.

Phil Marquart, a Christian psychiatrist, who was a deacon in my church. He was away, speaking in another church. The young lady, obviously under great stress, expressed some disappointment, but stayed for the morning service. I prayed that God would give me a message for that distressed soul. I spoke of the healing power of the great Physician, Jesus. I emphasized the fact that utter trust in His wondrous care is the unfailing remedy for taut, overwrought nerves and sin-sick hearts. At the close of the service, I had prayer and a long talk with her. She returned for the night service. At the close of the service, she joyfully said to me, "I came to Chicago today from St. Louis with the fixed purpose of ending my wretched life in Lake Michigan. God, in mercy, put your two messages today across my dark, downward way!" —W. B. K.

VICTORY

Short Quotes

Yielding to disdain can destroy us; disdaining to yield can delight us.
—Dr. V. Raymond Edman

* * *

To feel the tempter's mighty power — without appeal;
To know the pull that money has — and never yield;
To be entranced by honor's glare — and have no urge;
To hear the voice of passing pomp — and not submerge;
To be uplifted, lauded high — and sense no pride;
To gain an orator's great fame — and never stride;
To be exalted to the skies — yet self disdain;
To be condemned and set aside — and not complain,
This is victory!
—Rev. R. E. Neighbour, D.D.

* * *

Who has accomplished his task? He who has left the world better than he found it, whether by an improved machine, a perfect poem, or a rescued soul; who has never lacked appreciation of earth's beauty or failed to express it; who looked for the best in others and has given the best he had; whose life was an inspiration; whose memory is a benediction. —*Fraternal Monitor*

* * *

Martin Luther sometimes succumbed to depression. During a time when he was passing through a "fiery trial" his wife, Cathy, dressed in black and entered his study. She said, "God is dead!" "Nonsense, woman, God lives!" answered Luther. Then she replied, "If you believe that God is living, act like it! Live like it!"

* * *

From a life of sin and shame,
Into joy and peace I came,
Through the power of Jesus' name,
Into Victory!

From a path as dark as night,
Into glorious Gospel Light —
With a heart made pure and white,
Into Victory.

* * *

John Burroughs, the naturalist, says that when a hawk is attacked by crows or kingbirds, he does not make a counterattack, but soars higher and higher in ever widening circles until his tormentors leave him alone. Do not God's children overcome their enemies by living on the higher plane of fellowship and communion with their Lord and by prayerfully waiting before Him for daily renewal of strength? —W. B. K.

* * *

Observers in the full enjoyment of their bodily senses pity me, but it is because they do not see the golden chamber in my life where I dwell delighted; for, dark as my path may seem to them, I carry a magic light in my heart. Faith, the spiritual strong searchlight, illumines the way, and although sinister doubts lurk in the shadow, I walk unafraid toward the Enchanted

Wood, where the foliage is always green, where joy abides, where nightingales nest and sing, and where life and death are one in the Presence of the Lord.

—Helen Keller

* * *

Are you an overcome or an overcoming Christian? Be an overcoming one: "But thanks be unto God, which giveth us the victory through our Lord Jesus Christ" (I Cor. 15:57). —W. B. K.

* * *

When Samuel Chadwick yielded himself utterly to God he said: "There came into my soul a deep peace, a thrilling joy and a new sense of power. My mind was quickened. Every power was alert. Either illumination took the place of logic, or reason became intuitive. My bodily powers also were quickened. There was a new sense of spring and vitality, a new power of endurance, and a strong man's exhilaration in big things. Things began to happen. What we had failed to do by strenuous endeavor came to pass without labor. It was as when the Lord Jesus stepped into the boat that with all their rowing had made no progress,

immediately the ship was at the land whither they went. It was gloriously wonderful." —*Gospel Banner*

* * *

In his prayer, a Negro minister exclaimed: "Lord, we can't hold much but we can overflow lots!" It is God's will or desire that each one of His children be "filled with all the fulness of God" and live radiantly and victoriously over known sin. —W. B. K.

* * *

A young, brilliant college student contracted poliomyelitis. However he was always friendly and cheerful. A friend asked him, "With a misfortune, how can you be so cheerful and face the world so confidently and without bitterness?" Smilingly the young man said, "You see, it never touched my heart!"

* * *

If we resist the devil without first submitting ourselves to God, he will fly *at* us, and not *from* us: "Submit yourselves . . . to God. Resist the devil, and he will flee from you" (James 4:7).

—Rev. Vance Havner

VISION

Short Quotes

We stand today at one of those decisive moments in history when we begin to see what the late H. G. Wells called "the shape of things to come." The clouds thin, the mist rises, and we see heaven or hell. We cannot yet know which. —*The New York Times*

* * *

Day by day, dear Lord,
Of Thee three things I pray:
To see Thee more clearly,
Love Thee more dearly,
Follow Thee more nearly,
Day by day.

* * *

Said a teacher to a class of boys in a school in Germany long ago: "Boys, when I meet you on the street, I am wont to remove my hat in your presence, for who knows but that from this class of boys will come, one day, a man who

will change the course of human history!" Martin Luther was a boy in that class. —W. B. K.

* * *

The rule that governs my life is this: Anything that dims my vision of Christ, or takes away my taste for Bible study, or cramps my prayer life, or makes Christian work difficult, is wrong for me, and I must, as a Christian, turn away from it. —*J. Wilbur Chapman*

* * *

The Sunday-school lesson was on Gethsemane. Both the teacher and her class of boys were treading cautiously, reverently, knowing that they were on holy ground. Asked one of the boys, "Teacher, why did Jesus finally say to His disciples, 'Sleep on now, and take your rest'?" The teacher seemed lost for an answer and silence ensued. Then the boy said, "Teacher, I think I know. Jesus had seen the Father's face, and did not need any help from the disciples any more." —W. B. K.

* * *

Just a *look back* o'er the path we have
   travelled,
Just to remember His kindness and
   grace,
See how He led us each step of the
   journey,
How we rejoice as His goodness we trace.

Now a *look forward*, no fear for the
   future
Since He will strengthen and guide us
   each day,
Cheering us, loving us, leading us onward —
Into the light of Eternity's day.

Now a *look upward* — His coming is
   nearing,
Soon in His presence forever we'll be,
Satisfied then every heart's deepest
   longing,
When in the glory His face we shall see.
       —*Christian Victory Magazine*

* * *

Look away from things that perish,
   Wood and stone will soon decay,
Fix your eyes on things eternal,
   God and heav'n will stand for aye.
He is able, He is willing,
   He will guide you all the way;
Take your eyes off things that perish,
   Look to Him and trust and pray.

* * *

Open my eyes, that I may see
This one and that one needing Thee:
Hearts that are dumb, unsatisfied;
Lives that are dark, for whom Christ
   died.
Open my eyes in sympathy
Clear into man's deep soul to see;
Wise with Thy wisdom to discern,
And with Thy heart of love to yearn.
Open my eyes in power, I pray;
Give me the strength to speak today,
Someone to bring, dear Lord, to Thee;
Use me, O Lord, use even me.
       —Betty Scott Stam

* * *

A news correspondent recently wrote — "News is either about something

changing or something unusual. Life, however, is largely about something *not* changing and *not* unusual. Follow the news diligently enough and you will become stone-blind to the greater part of reality and to most of the values of living." —Vance Havner

* * *

Look for the beautiful,
   Look for the true;
Sunshine and shadow
   Are all around you;
Looking at evil,
   We grope in the night;
Looking at Jesus,
   We walk in the light;
Look for the beautiful,
   Look for the right.
       —F. E. Belden

* * *

Someone asked Thorwaldsen, the noted Danish sculptor, "Which is your greatest statue?" He promptly replied, "The next one!"

* * *

"If you want to be distressed, look to yourself. If you want to be perplexed, look to others. If you want to be radiant, look to Jesus: "Looking unto Jesus the author and finisher of our faith" (Heb. 12:2).

* * *

One day I looked at myself,
   At the self that Christ can see;
I saw the person I am today,
   And the one I ought to be,
I saw how little I really pray,
   How little I really do;
I saw the influence of my life,
   How little of it was true!
I saw the bundle of faults and fears
   I ought to lay on the shelf;
I had given a little bit to God —
   But I hadn't given myself.
I came from seeing myself,
   With my mind made up to be
The sort of person that Christ can use,
   With a heart He may always see.

       —*Selected*

* * *

A young artist named Tucker painted the picture of a forlorn woman and child out in the storm. This picture took such a hold on him that he laid away palette and brush, saying, "I must go to the lost, instead of painting them." He prepared for the ministry and for some time worked in the city's slums. At length he said, "I must go to that part of the world where men seem to be most hopelessly lost." That young artist was none other than Bishop Tucker, of Uganda, Africa. Painting is not enough. We must obey the command, "Go," or help send others instead.

—*Christian Herald*

Some years ago, a missionary returned from the Orient. He spoke to a large audience of having seen many starve for lack of food, and of others who were starving spiritually — without God and without hope. In closing his stirring message, he asked his audience: "Do you see those people, see them as Christ saw them, shepherdless and lost?" Then he said, "I see them! I see them every time I close my eyes!" —W. B. K.

Illustrations

I Saw Also the Lord

Humboldt, in his *Travels*, describes his experiences during a mighty earthquake and accompanying tornado. He was filled with fear when he saw the churning waters receding from the bay. His vessel toppled over on the beach. Huge trees were uprooted. Ominous, black clouds darkened the sky. The scene was terrifying. He chanced to look up through a rift in the dark cloud and there he saw the sun shining in its glory! Soon the earth ceased to throb. The wind subsided. The sky cleared, and the sun brought warmth and cheer.

As we look about us today, we see much to alarm and dismay us. We, like Isaiah, see tottering, crumbling thrones. But Isaiah saw "also the Lord." Midst upheavals, God is unchanged and unchanging — the same yesterday, today and forever. "Thou remainest!"

—W. B. K.

* * *

At Heart, an Eagle

A farmer caught a young eagle and placed it with his chickens. The eaglet ate with them and soon adapted itself to their ways. One day a naturalist visited the farmer. Seeing the eagle, he said, "That's not a chicken. That's an eagle." "That's right," said the farmer, "but he's no longer an eagle in his nature. He's a chicken now, for he eats chicken feed and does everything chickens do. He'll never fly again!" "You're wrong," said the naturalist. "He's an eagle still, because he has the heart of an eagle." After making several unsuccessful efforts to get the eagle to fly, the naturalist carried the eagle to the foot of a high mountain just as the

sun was rising. The instant the eagle got a vision of the rising sun, he uttered a wild scream of joy, stretched his wings, and mounted higher and higher into the sky — never to return to the farmer.

Oh, for a vision of Jesus, "the Sun of righteousness," that we may "mount up with wings as eagles . . . run, and not be weary . . . walk, and not faint."

—W. B. K.

* * *

Looking Unto Jesus

A group of people listened to a student, who had been a navigator in a crew of giant bombers in World War II. He said, "My guiding my ship across the uncharted oceans was a simple matter indeed. Why, all I had to do was take a couple looks at the stars, and then look in a book. That book would tell me right where we were, making it the easiest thing in the world to get to our destination!"

God's children will always be guided aright when they do two things: Look to Jesus whom the Bible calls "a Star of Jacob," and "the bright and morning star," and to the Book, God's imperishable Word, which is "a lamp" that "shineth in a dark place." —W. B. K.

* * *

He Grabbed for the Branch!

An acquaintance was on the critical list in a Chicago hospital. The doctors gave no hope for his recovery. In his earlier years the patient had confessed Christ as his Saviour. His life had been characterized by neglect and failure to live a consistent Christian life. Coming close to death's door, God, in mercy, was seeking him. In vision, he saw himself on the edge of a deep, dark chasm, into which he began to slip. In his helplessness he cried to God to save him. Immediately he saw an overhanging branch which he grabbed, and to which he clung tenaciously! Could it be that the branch which he saw was the Branch of Jeremiah's prophecy, the Saviour-King? "I will raise unto David a righteous Branch" (Jer. 23:5). The patient began to pray. He recovered and gave God the glory for answering prayer and delivering him from the "horrible pit!" —W. B. K.

* * *

'Twas a Look!

What can strip the seeming glory
  From the idols of the earth?
Not a sense of right and duty,
  But a sight of peerless worth.
'Tis the look that melted Peter,
  'Tis the face that Stephen saw,
'Tis the heart that wept with Mary
  Can alone from idols draw.
Draw, and win, and fill completely,
  Till the cup o'erflows its brim,
What have we to do with idols
  Since we've companied with Him?
        —J. Stuart Holden, in
        The Watchman-Examiner

* * *

Potential Saints!

Agostino d' Antonio, a sculptor of Florence, Italy, wrought diligently but unsuccessfully on a large piece of marble. "I can do nothing with it," he finally said. Other sculptors, too, worked with the piece of marble, but they, too, gave up the task. The stone was discarded. It lay on a rubbish heap for forty years.

Out strolling one day, Michelangelo saw the stone and the latent possibilities in it. It was brought to his studio. He began to work on it. Ultimately, his vision and work were crowned with success. From that seemingly worthless stone was carved one of the world's masterpieces of sculpture — *David!*

On the rubbish heaps of the skid rows of our cities are humanly hopeless and helpless discarded degenerates who are *potential saints!* Oh, for the vision to see them and others, not as they are, but as they may become by the transforming grace of God!
    —Told by Rev. James Seward

God, Grant Us the Vision!

Nate Saint wrote a short while before he and four other young men were martyred by the savage Aucas Indians, as they sought to take the gospel to them:

"As we have a high old time this Christmas may we who know Christ hear the cry of the damned as they hurtle headlong into the Christless night without ever a chance. May we be moved with compassion as our Lord was. May we shed tears of repentance for those whom we have failed to bring out of darkness. Beyond the smiling scenes of Bethlehem may we see the crushing agony of Golgotha. May God give us a new vision of His will concerning the lost and our responsibility. Would that we could comprehend the lot of these Stone-Age people who live in mortal fear of ambush on the jungle trail. . . . Those to whom the bark of a gun means sudden, mysterious death. . . . Those who think all the men in the world are killers like themselves. If God would grant us the vision, the word 'sacrifice' would disappear from our lips and thoughts. We would hate the things that now seem dear to us, our lives would suddenly be too short, we would despise time-robbing distractions, and charge the enemy with all our energy in the name of Christ. May God help us to judge by the eternity that separates the Aucas from the comprehension of Christmas and Him who, though He was rich yet for our sakes became poor, so that we through His poverty might be made rich."
    —*The Sunday School Times*

* * *

That He Might Have the Pre-Eminence

Years ago, there lived in Switzerland a great schoolmaster whose name was Pestalozzi. He was held in highest esteem and greatly loved, especially by the children who came under his character-molding influence.

At his death, it was generally felt that a monument, commemorative of his life of selfless service, should be erected, though the schoolmaster had erected an enduring memorial in the hearts of others.

The monument was erected. The day for its unveiling came. The sculptor had succeeded so well in reproducing the likeness of the schoolmaster that all looked upon the statue with hushed reverence and admiration. The teacher was shown looking down upon the kneeling form of a little child whose uplifted gaze focused upon the face of the teacher.

Though the statue was a wonderful work of art, the schoolmaster's most intimate friends felt that the sculptor had failed to represent the dominant desire of the pedagogue — not to have those he taught to look with wonderment upon him, but to look upward to the challenging heights of goals as yet unattained, and to God.

So a change was made. At the second unveiling all were pleased to see a kneeling child, looking, not at the face of the teacher, but to the beckoning beyond.

Any Sunday-school teacher and preacher is an eminent success who so exalts Christ that all will see the One whose worthiness is extolled and whose praise ceaselessly sung in glory — "that in all things he might have the preeminence!" —W. B. K.

* * *

The Mysterious Visitor

'Twas just before Christmas. A pastor sat in his study meditating upon the words, "The knowledge of Christ Jesus my Lord." Looking out the window, he saw people scurrying hither, thither and yon, like ants disturbed on an anthill. He asked himself, "What knowledge of Christ do these hurrying people have? What knowledge of Him do the people to whom I preach have? What are their innermost attitudes toward Him?" As he pondered these searching questions, he seemed to see in vision a caller who asked, "Shall I tell you what Christ means to your people?" The caller spoke calmly and solemnly. "Can you?" asked the pastor; "and how did you know what I was thinking about?"

The caller began, "Some of your people think of Christ as they would think of a generous rich uncle. Ceaselessly they ask Him for things. Others think

of Him as a great teacher. They are stimulated intellectually to hear learned discourses about Him. Some think of Him as an errand boy whom they flippantly order to help them."

"Oh, mysterious caller, is this an accurate picture of my people?" asked the minister.

"Yes," said the caller sadly but firmly. Then he concluded, "But to some He is an ever-present, never-failing friend and confidant! To some, He is the fairest among ten thousands and the altogether lovely One!" As the caller said this, he receded and vanished, disappearing as mysteriously as he had appeared.

"Was I asleep?" asked the startled pastor, "or has an angel visited me, or has Christ Himself been here?"

—W. B. K.

* * *

The Christian's Horizon

What do I see as I look back?
Millions of mercies along life's track;
God's love shining where all was black;
    That's what I see,
      Looking back.

What do I see as I look within?
A heart by my Saviour redeemed from sin;
A hope, through His grace, heaven's joys to win;
    That's what I see,
      Looking in.

What do I see, looking forth today?
Blessings granted before I pray;
A sheltering arm, a guiding ray;
    This do I see,
      Today.

What do I see as I look on?
Burdens lifted and trials gone;
A light at even, surpassing dawn;
    That's what I see,
      Looking on.

What do I see as I look above?
God's own banner, whose name is Love:
Love unspeakable, wonderful love;
    That's what I see,
      Above!

—Mary Wardlaw in *The Presbyterian*

WAR

Short Quotes

Within the time of authentic history war has claimed the lives of fifteen thousand millions! What a pyramid of skulls their fleshless heads would make!
—Governor Hanley

* * *

War leaves a country with three armies — an army of cripples, an army of mourners, and an army of thieves.
—A German proverb

* * *

President Eisenhower received a letter from an eight-year-old boy, Kevin Aiken of Trumbull, Connecticut, which read as follows:
"After listening to news about the cold war, I am worried about the people in the world. In thinking it over, I have a plan. Get all these leaders who want war together and put them in a ring and let them fight it out."
—*The Gospel Banner*

* * *

World peace will come only when all mankind turns wholeheartedly to God in complete humility and voluntary unconditional surrender. Until human nature is changed, we'll have war.
—Dr. Robert M. Page, director of research, U. S. Naval Research Laboratory

* * *

One out of every eight Americans is a war veteran!

* * *

There are only two powers in the world — the power of the sword and the power of the spirit. In the long run, the sword will always be conquered by the spirit. —Napoleon

Napoleon once asked Metternich's opinion on a proposed military expedition. "Why, Sir, that campaign would cost you 100,000 men!" Metternich said. Napoleon snarled, "What are 100,000 men to me?" Calmly Metternich went to the window, flung the shutters open, and said, "Let all Europe hear that infamous declaration!" —W. B. K.

* * *

Columnist Sidney Harris tells of a Hindu who asked him, "How do you people interpret the words of Jesus? I mean, how do you reconcile His plain doctrine of nonresistance with your guns and your planes and your wars every few decades?"
Harris concludes his column by saying, "Maybe you can answer the Hindu; I could not in all honesty."

* * *

There are no warlike peoples — just warlike rulers. —Ralph J. Bunche

* * *

In the last 3000 years, the world has had only 227 years of peace.
—M. Odysse-Barot, French historian

* * *

"The problem with the world is not with the bomb. The problem of the world is man," said Clement Attlee in the House of Commons. Did not Christ in the long ago strike at the basic need of man when He said, "Ye must be born again"?

Illustrations

How Do Wars Begin?

"How do wars begin?" a little boy asked his father. With a show of wisdom, the father began, "Well, take the 1914 war; that began because Germany invaded Belgium." At this point, his wife interrupted him, and said in a demanding voice, "Tell the boy the truth. It began because somebody was mur-dered." The husband, with an air of superiority, retorted, "Are you answering the question or am I?" The wife bristled with anger. She stomped out of the room, and slammed the door shut. When the room stopped vibrating, a tense silence followed. At length, the boy said, "Daddy, you needn't tell me how wars begin. I know how!"
—W. B. K.

Hot Again

Do you recall that tranquil night
We walked a while in lunar light,
The long, lone country road ahead,
The talk of brave men helmeted?

Do you recall the prayer we made?
"Dear God: Let not this brightness fade,
But soon, where armies fight and die,
Bring peace like that which rules Your
    sky."

Now we have lived to see a peace
When dangers mount and fears increase,
And in the veins of jungle-men
The blood of war is hot again.

So now, dear God, we pray anew:
"Your sky today is calm and blue,
And may Your earth beneath accent
The saneness of Your firmament."

—Ivan Clyde Lake

WILL OF GOD

Short Quotes

I had rather be in the heart of Africa in the will of God than on the throne of England out of the will of God.
—David Livingstone

* * *

Samuel said, "Speak; for thy servant heareth." Some say, "Listen; for Thy servant speaketh." —W. B. K.

* * *

To know the will of God is the greatest knowledge. To do the will of God is the greatest achievement.
—Dr. George W. Truett

* * *

Nothing lies beyond the reach of prayer except that which lies outside the will of God.

* * *

There is great safety in the perils God chooses for us. A missionary was asked, "Is it safe to work among lepers as you do?" "Yes," was the reply, "it is safer to work among the lepers, if it's my job, than to work anywhere else!" —*Sunday Circle*

* * *

Lord, of the years that are left to me,
I give them to Thy hand,
Take me and break me and mould me,
To the pattern Thou hast planned!

* * *

An astronomer specialized in the study of snowflakes. Through a microscope, he photographed more than two thousand. Each snowflake was a geometrically perfect design and each one was unique. No two were identical. God,

in manifesting His glory fashioned each snowflake from a new pattern. Is it conceivable that He would have no definite personal pattern for each of His children? —W. B. K.

* * *

True devotion to God consists in doing all His will precisely at the time, in the situation, and under the circumstances in which He has placed us.
—Fénelon

* * *

A dewdrop does the will of God as much as a thunderstorm.

* * *

I am no longer anxious about anything, as I realize the Lord is able to carry out His will, and His will is mine. It makes no matter where He places me, or how. That is rather for Him to consider than for me; for in the easiest positions He must give me His grace, and in the most difficult, His grace is sufficient. —J. Hudson Taylor

* * *

I once saw a painting of a large boat laden with cattle that were being ferried across an angry, swollen river in time of storm. The artist had so cleverly pictured the dark, threatening clouds and the play of the treacherous, jagged lightning that I instantly concluded that the freight of the poor dumb cattle was marked for destruction. But the title of the painting was simply "Changing Pasture." Many times we imagine that God's plans mean disaster and affliction,

but He is only "changing pastures" for our good and the good of others.
—Dr. James M. Gray

* * *

To do Thy will is more than praise,
As words are less than deeds,
The simplest trust can find Thy ways,
We miss with chart of creeds.
—Whittier

* * *

Some build spiritual shacks on a foundation intended for a skyscraper. Every Christian is a full-time servant of the Lord. —Dr. H. Henderson

* * *

When we want to know God's will, there are three things which always concur: the inward impulse, the Word of God and the trend of circumstances!

God in the heart, impelling you forward; God in His Book, corroborating whatever He says in the heart; and God in circumstances, which are always indicative of His will. Never act until these three things agree. —F. B. Meyer

* * *

Just where you stand in the conflict,
There is your place;
Just where you think you are useless,
Hide not your face.
God placed you there for a purpose,
Whate'er it be;
Think He has chosen you for it,
Work loyally.

Gird on your armor, be faithful,
Always your best,
Whate'er it be, never doubting,
God's way is best.
Out in the fight or on picket,
Stand firm and true.
There is a work which your Master
Gives you to do.

The end of life is not to do good, although many of us think so. It is not to win souls, although I once thought so. The end of life is to do the will of God whatever it may be.
—Henry Drummond

* * *

If you cannot cross the ocean
And the heathen lands explore,
You can find the heathen nearer,
You can help them at your door.

If you cannot give your thousands,
You can give the widow's mite,
And the least you do for Jesus
Will be precious in His sight.

With your prayer and with your bounty
You can do what God demands;
You can be like faithful Aaron,
Holding up the prophet's hands.
—Selected

* * *

Thou, God, each day help me to find
The work that Thou wouldst have me do.
Keep me from sullenness of mind,
Grant unto me good thoughts and true.
And if Thy will be not my choice,
Some duty I would rather shun,
Then teach me to sincerely voice,
"Thou art my God, Thy will be done."
And grant me vision enough to see
Within the task Thy plan for me.
—Exchange

* * *

No service in itself is small;
None great, though earth it fill,
But that is small that seeks its own
And great that seeks God's will.
Then hold my hand, most gracious God;
Guide all my goings still
And let it be my life's one aim
To know and do Thy will.

Illustrations

Be What God Wants You to Be

A little boy rather thoughtlessly said, "Mommie, I am going to be a preacher when I am big!" The mother was elated. Frequently during his boyhood days the mother would proudly say, "My boy is going to be a preacher!"

How much better it would have been if the mother had said, "My boy is going to be what God wants him to be."

In time the boy entered a theological seminary. Some months later, he came into the office of the dean, a picture of defeat and dejection. "I'm a total misfit here. I have no interest in going further with my studies. God hasn't called me to be a preacher!" The heart of the dean went out in sympathy to the young man. He knew that he, like many others, had been pressurized into the ministry where God had never intended him to be. —W. B. K.

* * *

My Jesus as Thou Wilt!

How variable are the ambitions of growing boys! A minister's little boy said, "I'm going to be a streetcar conductor." Later he said, "I'm going to be an engineer." Still later he said, "I'm going to be a ball player." One day he saw the garbage collector dumping garbage into a big truck. He was fascinated and said, "I'm going to be a garbage collector!" His daddy was wise. He said to the boy, "My boy, you must be what God wants you to be. God needs ministers and missionaries. He also needs Christian school teachers, Christian nurses, Christian doctors, Christian judges and lawyers, and Christian businessmen. God has a plan for your life. Ask Him, 'Lord, what wilt thou have me to do?'" —W. B. K.

* * *

Storm

God washed the world last night
  With sweet, refreshing rain;
And thirsty earth reached up to drink
  Of that life-giving gain.

God washed my heart last night
  With tears, both bitter, sweet;
He probed in hidden corners, dark
  And washed it clear, complete.

"My child," His voice spoke sweet and
    low,
  "This storm came as a grace;
Lean hard upon my breast, dear one,
  And look into my face."

Completely spent, I looked and prayed,
  "Dear Father, be it Thine,
To mold and make me as Thou wilt,
  Thy will forever mine."
                    —Althea S. Miller

* * *

Being Where God Wants You

One day Queen Victoria visited, unaccompanied and unannounced, some cottagers in Balmoral, Scotland. Among those she visited was an aged, lonely, bedridden man. He didn't recognize Her Majesty. He said, "I am alone. All the folks went away today, hoping to get a glimpse of the Queen."

The Queen chatted pleasantly with the old man. She read a chapter from the Bible to him. Then she gave him a five-pound note. As she left she said, "When your people come back, tell them that the Queen visited you!"

We often miss great blessings by not being where God wants us to be. Elijah would have missed the service of the ravens had he not been in the place God sent him: "I have commanded the ravens to feed thee *there*" (I Kings 17:4). —W. B. K.

* * *

His Plan for Me

When I stand at the judgment seat of
    Christ,
And He shows me His plan for me,
The plan of my life as it might have
    been
Had He had His way, and I see

How I blocked Him here, and I checked
    Him there
And I would not yield my will —
Will there be grief in my Saviour's eyes,
Grief, though He loves me still?

He would have me rich, and I stand
    there poor,
Stripped of all but His grace,
While memory runs like a hunted thing
Down the paths I cannot retrace.

Then my desolate heart will well-nigh
    break
With the tears that I cannot shed;
I shall cover my face with my empty
    hands,
I shall bow my uncrowned head.

Lord of the years that are left to me,
I give them to Thy hand;
Take me and break me, mold me to
The pattern Thou hast planned.
            —Martha Snell Nicholson, in
                    "Wings and Sky"

* * *

Anywhere Except Chicago

"When I was a youth, I used to say, 'I'll go wherever the Lord calls me, but not to Chicago,'" said Dr. George L. Robinson, who for forty-one years was professor of Hebrew and Old Testament at McCormick Theological Seminary in *Chicago*! "McCormick wrote and wired me, wanting me to come," reminisced the nonagenarian. "After two and one-half years, I went. There were no strings attached to my going where God wanted me to go, and I've been thankful ever since!"

Standing now in the effulgent glow of life's setting sun, and facing a rising sun of a joyous hereafter, the aged professor testifies: "I do not fear death . . . I live by faith!"

"At evening time it shall be light" (Zech. 14:7). —W. B. K.

* * *

God Holds the Future

God holds the future in His hand.
 O heart of mine, be still!
His love will plan the best for thee,
The best, or light or dark it be —
 Then rest thee in His will.

God holds the future in His hand.
 Why should I shrink or fear?
Through every dark and cloudy day —
Yea, all along my pilgrim way
 His love will bless and cheer.

God holds the future in His hand,
 And I can trust His love.
His past declares His faithfulness;
His eye will guide, His heart will bless,
 Till I am safe above.

God holds the future in His hand.
 I leave it all with Him.
I know one day He will explain
The "wherefore" of each grief and pain,
 Though reasons now are dim.
                    —*A King's Messenger*

* * *

Beware of Short Cuts

A plane crashed in Mint Canyon. Nine occupants perished. That tragic end was not the design of the builder of the plane. It was intended to be a servant of human need, carrying messages of peace and passengers to happy home-comings. The pilot, however, decided to take a short cut across the Sierra Madras. God's children are "his workmanship, created in Christ Jesus unto good works, which God has before ordained that we should walk in them" (Eph. 2:10). As long as we stay "on the beam" and go into the pathway of

service He chooses, we are safe. Let us avoid short cuts which would take us "off the beam" which could bring disaster.   —Wade C. Smith in
             The Sunday School Times

* * *

God's Will

I asked the New Year for some motto sweet,
Some rule of life by which to guide my feet;
I asked and paused. It answered soft and low:
 "God's will to know."

"Will knowledge then suffice, New Year?" I cried;
But ere the question into silence died,
The answer came, "Nay, this remember, too,
 God's will to do."

Once more I asked, "Is there still more to tell?"
And once again the answer softly fell:
"Yes, this one thing, all other things above,
 God's will to love."

                              —*Selected*

* * *

Not a Calamity

"Oh, General, what a calamity!" exclaimed his chaplain to General "Stonewall" Jackson when the latter lost his left arm in battle; to which the General, thanking him for his sympathy, replied: "You see me wounded, but not depressed, not unhappy. I believe it has been according to God's holy will, and I resign entirely to it. You may think it strange, but you never saw me more perfectly contented than I am today, for I am sure my heavenly Father designs this affliction for my good. I am perfectly satisfied that either in this life or in that which is to come I shall discover that what is now regarded as a calamity is a blessing. I can wait until God, in His own time, shall make known to me the object He has in thus afflicting me. But why should I not rather rejoice in it as a blessing and not look on it as a calamity at all? If it were in my power to replace my arm

I would not dare to do it unless I could know it was the will of my heavenly Father." —L. E. Maxwell, in *Christian Digest*

* * *

A Judge's Prayer

A very remarkable testimony is given by Judge Harold R. Medina. It appears in the August number of the *Reader's Digest* (1951) under the title, "Someone Else on the Bench." The judge achieved fame in presiding at the trial of the eleven Communists in 1949. He says that he has followed the habit of prayer since boyhood, but since his elevation to the bench he has realized more than ever his need for God's grace and guidance. He is conscious of the unfailing presence of God in the courtroom. During the trial of the Communists there were deliberate efforts by their supporters to wear down the judge until he would lose self-control that would result in a mistrial. Judge Medina declares that the one thing that saved him and saved the trial, in a desperate crisis hour, was the strange and wonderful power that came to him when, in his

weakness, he "asked God to take charge of things and that His will be done."

—*United Presbyterian*

* * *

There, We Are Safe!

Typhoons and monsoons occur frequently in the Indian Ocean. These violent cyclonic storms swirl around in a circle. Before navigators learned how to cope with them, there was a frightful loss of ships and lives. In explaining how navigators learned to cope with typhoons and monsoons, a sea captain said, "When we run into them we locate the center, and we go around it. We narrow the circle until we get into the center where there is a dead calm! There, we are safe!"

Christ speaks with finality and authority to us. When we are in the center of His will, we are safe. There, He keeps our hearts and minds in "perfect peace!"

In the center of the circle
Of the will of God I stand,
There can come no second causes,
All must come from His dear hand.

—W. B. K.

WITNESSING

Short Quotes

A miracle has happened to me which makes me accept the miracles of the Bible. This miracle is the new birth which every Christian has experienced. It is the application of God's power which brings about this change!

—Dr. John R. Brobeck, professor of physiology, Medical School of the University of Philadelphia

* * *

Let me consider at the age of eighty-three what have been life's best gifts. Surely not health or wealth or knowledge of science important as these are. Supremely best has it been to know the God of the Bible as Father and Jesus Christ who bore my sins on the cross and by His resurrection has given me eternal life and His Holy Spirit as my daily Guide. —Howard A. Kelly, M.D.

Some years ago in a wealthy residential section of Richmond, Virginia, some residents complained of the singing of a small Christian church, saying that it disturbed them. A petition to be presented to the city council was circulated. It was brought to a Jewish resident for his signature. He read it and said, "I cannot sign it. If I believed as do these Christians that my Messiah had come, I would shout it from the housetops and on every street in Richmond, and nobody could stop me!"

—*Moody Monthly*

* * *

I came to Christ as a country boy. I did not understand all about the plan of salvation. One does not have to understand it. He has only to stand upon it. I do not understand all about electricity, but I do not intend sitting around in the dark until I do!

—Fleming H. Revell

* * *

It is wonderful to be a believer in the Lord Jesus Christ! I am exceedingly thankful that God has graciously led me to saving faith in Christ. In the Bible, God has promised eternal life to anyone who believes in His only-begotten Son. —Lt. General (Ret.) William K. Harrison, Jr.

* * *

I know I am saved, not by anything that is of character or of the works of the human heart, but by the blood of Jesus Christ alone.

—Emperor Haile Selassie

* * *

Two professed Christians worked for ten years in the same business office. Over the years, neither of them knew that the other was a Christian. Said one of these men to a minister one day, "Wasn't it funny that Bill and I were so intimately related to each other in business, and neither of us knew until today that the other was a Christian!" "Funny?" sadly questioned the faithful minister. "Why, that's not funny! It's tragic! In my opinion neither of you have ever experienced the miracle of regeneration. Let us get down on our knees and let us both ask that God will make you a new creature in Christ Jesus." —Dr. F. B. Meyer

* * *

I now regard my task as finished, namely, to give you a picture of how my whole life was guided and had significance in Christ's high plan. . . . I pray that Christ's joy may descend on His whole humanity and that mankind's joy may be fulfilled in Him. He stands at the door of its heart, and knocks. If mankind hears His voice and opens the door, He will enter. —Princess Wilhelmina of the Netherlands

* * *

For me 'twas not the truth you taught,
　To you so clear, to me so dim,
But when you came to me you brought
　A sense of Him!

And from your eyes He beckons me,
　And from your heart His love is shed,
Till I lose sight of you and see
　The Christ instead!

Illustrations

General Grant's Last Wish

General Grant was stricken with a fatal illness. As he approached the end of his life, he felt his need of the Saviour and His sustaining presence. He called for a minister. Simply the minister presented the gospel to him. "General," he said, "God in love sent the Saviour to seek and to save that which was lost. If you will sincerely call upon Him from your heart, you will receive from Him mercy and abundant pardon!" When the minister knelt and prayed, God opened the heart of the general and he was joyfully converted. God cleansed his heart from sin. The minister was elated. "God's kingdom has gained a great acquisition in your conversion, General," said the minister. Immediately General Grant protested, saying, "God does not need great men, but great men need God! There is just one thing that I now greatly desire since Christ's great peace has come to me. . . ." "What's that, General?" asked the minister. "I would like to live one year more so that I might tell others of this wonderful gift of God's love!"

—W. B. K.

Lest We Forget

A Christian girl loved a missionary. Before he left for India he wrote and asked her to become his wife. "If I do not hear from you, I'll know you have other plans," he wrote. She immediately wrote a letter and accepted his proposal. She asked her brother to mail the letter for her, but it was never mailed! The girl never heard from the missionary again. Years later, she found the letter in the lining of her brother's coat, yellow and crumpled. It had slipped there when the brother had put it into his torn pocket and he had forgotten to mail it.

Jesus has given us a message to take to others. It is John 3:16. If we fail to deliver it, others may never hear about Him. —W. B. K.

• • •

I'd Rather Have Jesus!

When King George VI and the queen visited Washington, D. C., a state dinner was given in their honor. Chief Whitefeather, an Indian, began the program by singing the British anthem. After the applause the chief sang, to the surprise of those present, the hymn whose opening words are, "I'd rather have Jesus than silver or gold!" Later in the evening, the chief sat near the king and queen. Tactfully he asked the queen, "Do you believe on Jesus?" The queen replied graciously, "He is the Possessor of my heart, and of my husband's also!" The king, smiling, added, "I'd rather have Jesus than silver or gold!" —W. B. K.

• • •

Judge Pleads with Murderers

Two condemned murderers stood before Justice A. C. Saunders to be sentenced. The judge said, "The retribution for your crime is settled by the law of the land. On me reposes the duty of carrying it into effect. May I remind you that you will appear before another Judge, the great Judge of all the world? Before you pass into His presence, may I, in all sincerity, urge you to prepare for that great day. The way is through repentance of your sins, confession of them, and embracing Christ's forgiveness assured you through His blood. I beseech you to accept Christ now so you may walk with Him through all eternity!" —W. B. K.

• • •

Let's Speak Out for God

One afternoon I was asked to go immediately to see a Communist who was dying in a distant hospital. His Communism had seemed to satisfy his sin-darkened heart in life, but in death it failed him. He asked for God's servant to come. The hospital was several miles from my home, and the rain was pouring down. When I reached the hospital, I found the man in a coma. As the fog lifted intermittently from his mind, I told him of the penitent malefactor who, with a fleeting breath, called for God's

mercy and received forgiveness. Soon he passed into eternity.

A few days thereafter, I had his funeral. The most memorable thing about the service was the outspokenness of the brother of the deceased for atheistic Communism. I had spoken to him of his lost condition and need of a Saviour. My speaking for God and His eternal truth seemed to make him only more vehement in his denunciation of Christianity.

When lost men, under the dominance of "the prince of this world," Satan, are so outspoken for error, let God's children be instantly ready to open their mouths for their God and His imperishable truth! —W. B. K.

• • •

A Soul-winning Judge

I have a friend who is a federal judge. He was a United States congressman for twenty-two years. In the summer he was working on his farm with one of his Negro employees. The man said to him, "Judge, have you ever talked to Tom about his soul?" Tom was the white manager of the farm who, with his family, had lived there for many years.

"Why, no," said the judge, "I don't believe I have."

"Well," persisted the questioner, "why haven't you, Judge? I have, and Tom is thinking about it, but it would mean so much more if it came from you. Why don't you do it now, Judge?"

"Well," said the judge, "I will sometime."

But the man was relentless. "Why don't you do it now, Judge? He is up by the barn. Why don't you go and talk to him now?"

The judge said he did some fast thinking, but he couldn't find any real reason not to do so, so he dropped his pruning shears and went up and had a talk with Tom. He told him what Christ had meant to him and to his family, and what He could mean to this man and his family. Tom made the great decision, and two weeks later the judge had the joy of seeing Tom and his family baptized and received into the church. "But," concluded the judge, "the thing that is on my conscience is this: Why hadn't I spoken to Tom before? And how many others might be in the Kingdom if only I had been a more faithful witness?"

—As told by a pastor

* * *

That's None of Your Business!

An aged Christian stood before a fount, waiting his turn to quench his thirst. As a lady turned away from the fount, he said, "Pardon me, lady, but have you ever drunk living water which Jesus gives to those who ask Him for it?" The woman was offended. Angrily she said, "That's none of your business!" Months passed. The gentleman was asked to visit a dying woman in a nearby hospital. When he came to her bed, she asked, "Do you recall asking a woman if she had ever drunk living water which Jesus gives?" "Yes, I do," he said. "I'm that woman!" replied the lady. "Forgive me for being so unkind to you. I was without peace. I asked Christ to save me. I expect to die shortly. Be as faithful in witnessing to others about Christ as you were to me!"

—W. B. K.

* * *

I Just Loves to Point Him Out

Some years ago two boats glided past each other on the Mississippi. An aged Negro was conversing with a white friend on deck of one of the boats when suddenly he said with zest, "Look! Yonder's the captain!" Asked the white friend, "Why are you so enthusiastic while you call my attention to the captain?" The grateful Negro replied, "Well, sir, years ago, as we were going along like this, I fell overboard. I couldn't swim and I began to sink, but the captain rescued me. Since that day, I just loves to point him out!"

When we were still lost in sin, the waves of sin all but overwhelmed us. But the Captain of our salvation, the Lord Jesus, rescued us. Should we not joyously "point Him out" to others?

—W. B. K.

* * *

Nzambe, Yesu Kristu, Molino Bipuru

At Adi, in the former Belgian Congo, lives a great and faithful Christian. He is deaf and dumb. He has found an effective way to witness for his Lord, however. Whenever he meets anyone on a path, he stops and writes these words in the dust: "Nzambe, Yesu Kristu, Molino Bipuru," — "God, Jesus Christ, Holy Spirit." Then he begins to preach by going through a series of motions. He pantomimes the crucifixion and the resurrection. By motions, he shows two classes of people — those who receive the Saviour, and those who reject Him and are cast into outer darkness. When he pantomimes those who receive the Saviour, his face lights up with radiant smiles, and he points to himself, indicating that he has received Jesus into his heart. He goes through all the motions of washing himself to show that he has been cleansed by the blood of Christ. And he always has a smile. —W. B. K.

* * *

The Witnessing Plumber

Howard E. Butt, Jr., a millionaire grocer, said, "God doesn't issue a special call to pastors and leave everyone else uncalled. Every Christian should think of himself as having a divine call for making Christian witnessing a full-time career."

L. C. Hester of Whitehours, Texas, is a plumber. He packs a New Testament with his tools. He is known as "the witnessing plumber." A minister said of him: "That witnessing plumber has won hundreds to Christ since he became a Christian. Many will listen to a workingman who will not listen to a preacher, you know." —W. B. K.

* * *

Turning Beer Into Food and Furniture

When a coal miner was converted, there was a marked change in his life. He became different from the unbelieving miners with whom he worked, and they took special delight in ridiculing the Bible in his presence. One day they asked him, "You don't really believe that yarn about Jesus turning water into wine, do you?" The converted miner used the hard question as an opportunity to witness for his newly found Saviour. He said, "Fellows, as you know, I am an ignorant man. I know nothing about water and wine. But I know this — Christ has changed my home! Instead of beer, we have food and furniture. That is a good enough

miracle for me, because before Christ came into my life, the corner tavern got a lion's share of my hard-earned wages."
—W. B. K.

* * *

A Queen Testifies

We are commissioned to be witnesses to the truth of the Gospel of our Lord Jesus Christ. A witness is one who speaks of that which he knows about first hand. We need to have a knowledge of our faith that we can be bold in our witness and adventurous in our living. We know that we shall probably be in a minority wherever we are. We know we shall have to face insecurity, opposition, and perhaps danger, for the confession of our faith. But the Christian Church has always prospered in adversity, and we must certainly not be afraid. I think it is comforting to remember those wonderful marching orders, given by Joshua, "Be strong and

of a good courage," and then to think of the other men and women in times past who, through the grace of God, were enabled to go forward into an unknown future with confidence and with resolves. —Queen Elizabeth II, in
The Gospel Witness

* * *

Tell What Christ Means to You

An humble layman was asked by his pastor to give a talk before a large congregation. "I have never spoken in public, and I don't see how I could talk to that large congregation. My knees would shake and I would become paralyzed with fear," he said. "You will do all right," said the pastor. "Just tell the people how Christ saved you and what He means to you." "For Christ's sake, I'll make the effort," replied the man. When he spoke, all fear vanished. The people were deeply blessed and greatly challenged to give their best in service to God. —W. B. K.

WORK

Short Quotes

I venture to say that at the bottom of most fears, both mild and severe, will be found an overactive mind and an underactive body. Hence, I have advised many people, in their quest for happiness, to use their heads less and their arms and legs more — in useful work or play. —Dr. Henry C. Link

* * *

Some laymen just sit back and pay the bills, and some just sit back.
—Dr. Ralph Sockman

* * *

Count your obligations,
  Name them one by one,
And it will surprise you,
  What the Lord wants done!

* * *

On a Friday morning, an eager young man from Stanford University stood before Louis Janin, seeking part-time employment. "All I need right now," said Janin, "is a stenographer." "I'll take the job," said the eager applicant, "but I can't come back until next Tuesday." On

Tuesday he reported for duty. "Why couldn't you come back before Tuesday?" Janin wanted to know. "Because I had to rent a typewriter and learn to use it!" was the unexpected answer. That quickly prepared typist was Herbert Hoover! —W. B. K.

* * *

The most unhappy of all men is the man who cannot tell what he is going to do, that has got no work cut out for him in the world, and does not go into any. For work is the grand cure of all the maladies and miseries that ever beset mankind — honest work which you intend getting done.

* * *

An aged Negro had an excellent garden which was the talk of his neighbors. One of them said to him, "I hear that you asked the Lord to give you a good garden. Is that right?" "Yes, sir, that's right," proudly replied the Negro, whose flourishing garden was his delight, "but I never pray for a good garden unless I have a hoe in my hand. I say, 'Lord, You send the sunshine and the showers, and I'll keep the weeds down!'" —W. B. K.

* * *

There are three kinds of people: those who make things happen, those who watch things happen, and those who have no idea what has happened.

* * *

Even if I knew that tomorrow the world would go to pieces, I would still plant my little apple tree and pay my debts. —Martin Luther

* * *

He who awakes to find himself famous hasn't been asleep.
—Roger Babson

* * *

To stay youthful, keep useful. Busy people have no time to be busybodies.

* * *

Some people fail to recognize opportunity because it so often comes to them in overalls and looks like work.

* * *

The secret of success is to do the common things uncommonly well.
—John D. Rockefeller, Jr.

* * *

No rule will work if you don't.

* * *

The Christian should not differentiate between things secular and things sacred. All that the Christian does should be sacred: "And whatsoever ye do in word or deed, do all in the name of the Lord Jesus" (Col. 3:17). The words, "Holiness unto the Lord," should be emblazoned over everything the Christian does. —W. B. K.

* * *

When the grass looks greener on the other side of the fence, it may be that they take better care of it there.
—Cecil Selig

* * *

A businessman said to his wife: "Three days ago I hired a boy to work in this office. He does his work cheerfully and well. Whenever he finishes a task, he comes to me and says, 'Sir, I have finished all my work! Now what can I do?' Yesterday I gave him a small task to perform. Later he came to me and asked, 'What's next?' He is the only one we have ever had who is willing to do more work than is assigned to him. That boy will make his mark in the world!" —W. B. K.

* * *

Some years ago, many hives of bees were brought from a cold climate to the tropical island of Barbados. Right away the bees went to work, gathering honey for the winter which their instinct taught them to expect. The winter didn't come, however and the bees became lazy. They stopped gathering honey. They spent their time flying about and stinging people. Trouble is usually produced by those who do not produce anything else! —W. B. K.

* * *

Duty makes us do things well, but love makes us do them beautifully.
—Phillips Brooks

* * *

The record of historical achievement cries out in loud condemning tones against laziness. Gibbon spent twenty-six years writing his *The Decline and Fall of the Roman Empire.* Milton used to rise at four o'clock every morning in writing *Paradise Lost.* Bryant rewrote one of his essays ninety-nine times. Webster worked thirty-six years to produce the first edition of the dictionary that bears his name. Cicero practiced speaking before friends every day for thirty years to perfect his elocution.
—*Help and Food*

* * *

There is no limit to what can be accomplished if it doesn't matter who gets the credit. —Emerson

* * *

Life is full of hard knocks, but answer them all. One might be opportunity.

* * *

When the great ships the *Queen Mary* and the *Queen Elizabeth* were launched, much of the work of those momentous events was done by a group of little tugboats — pushing, pulling, puffing and guiding the great ships down the narrow channel, keeping them from the mud banks. All eyes were upon the great ships. Little or no attention was given to the tugboats that did the work.

Never mind if your name is unpraised.
The sky holds many a star men have
not yet seen.
—Rev. John Macbeath, D.D., in
People Without a Name

* * *

Each one of God's commands is designed for the spiritual, physical and
mental well-being of man. Fewer work
days each week and more pay are being
demanded by workmen who labor in the
workingman's paradise — America. One
of God's most helpful provisions for
mankind is work — honest, conscientious
toil: "In the sweat of thy face shalt
thou eat bread" (Gen. 3:19). Whether
our work be physical or mental, let us
give ourselves joyously and wholeheartedly to it: "Whatsoever thy hand find-
eth to do, do it with thy might" (Eccl.
9:10). —W. B. K.

* * *

Everyone can do something to make
the world better — he can at least improve himself.

* * *

John Wesley was a small, tubercular
man. He weighed only one hundred
and twenty pounds. Samuel Johnson
said of him, "His conversation is good,
but he is never at leisure. He always
has to go at a certain hour. This is
very disagreeable to a man who loves
to fold his legs and have his talk out
as I do." Wesley's legs were "unfolded"
most of his ninety years. He had his
Master's passion for souls. He virtually lived in the saddle, riding horseback far and near to tell others of his
Saviour. —W. B. K.

* * *

If you want your dreams to come true,
don't oversleep.

* * *

Luck is waiting for something to turn
up. Labor, with keen eyes and strong
will, will turn up something. Luck lies
in bed, and wishes the postman would
bring him news of a legacy. Labor turns
out at six o'clock and with busy pen or
ringing hammer lays the foundation of
a competence. Luck whines. Labor
whistles. Luck relies on chance. Labor
depends on character. Luck slips down
to indigence. Labor strives upward to
independence. —Gobden in *Link*

A friend said to William Carey one
day, "I want to speak to you very seriously." "Well, what is it?" asked Carey.
"By your going about preaching as you
do, you are neglecting your business.
If you would attend to your business
better, you would get on and prosper.
You are neglecting your business."
Carey exclaimed, "Neglecting my business? Why, my business is to extend
the Kingdom of God. I cobble shoes only
to pay expenses meanwhile!"
—*Christian Herald*

* * *

On Lincoln's birthday an interesting
cartoon appeared in a newspaper. It
showed a small log cabin at the base of
a mountain, and the White House at the
top of the mountain. A ladder connected the two buildings. At the bottom
of the cartoon were these words: "The
ladder is still there!" To climb that
ladder, however, means sweat and toil.
—W. B. K.

* * *

The best place to find a helping hand
is at the end of your own wrist.
—W. B. K.

* * *

As soon as God created man, He gave
him a job to do: "And the Lord God
took the man, and put him into the
garden of Eden to dress it and to keep
it."

* * *

Our hats off to the past — our coats
off to the future! —W. B. K.

* * *

A horse can't pull while kicking,
This fact we merely mention;
And he can't kick while pulling,
Which is our chief contention.
Let's imitate the good horse
And lead a life that's fitting;
Just pull an honest load, and then
There'll be no time for kicking.
—*The Trumpeter*

* * *

Some people remind us of blisters —
they don't show up until the work is
done. —Paul Carruth

* * *

The work is solemn — do not trifle.
The task is difficult — do not relax.
The opportunity is brief — do not de-
lay. The path is narrow — do not

wander. The prize is glorious — do not faint.

* * *

The chief cause of heart disease is simply lack of exercise. Americans get more coronaries than any other race in the world. They also eat less butter than any other, and never use their muscles if they can help it once they can afford an automobile or an apartment with an elevator.
　　　　—Sir William H. Ogilvie, a
　　　　leading British surgeon

* * *

Inspiration is engendered by participation. Participation is sustained by perspiration. —Dr. Clay Risley

* * *

I work with unbroken concentration, but without hurry. However much I am at the mercy of the world, I never let myself get lost by brooding over its misery. I hold firmly to the thought that each one of us can do a little to bring some portion of that misery to an end. —Albert Schweitzer

* * *

Oh, do not pray for easy lives. Pray to be strong men and women. Do not pray for tasks equal to your powers. Pray for powers equal to your tasks. Then the doing of your work will be no miracle; but you shall be a miracle. Every day you shall wonder at yourself, at the richness of life which has come to you by the grace of God.
　　　　—Phillips Brooks

* * *

Blessed is he who has found his work. Let him ask no other blessedness. He has a work, a life purpose.: Labor is life. —Thomas Carlyle

Hard work seldom shortens life. John Wesley was an indefatigable worker, and when he was seventy-three years of age, he felt better and stronger than at twenty-three. He attributed this to his early rising, his activity, his undisturbed sleep, and his even temper. He used to say: "I feel and grieve, but I never fret."

* * *

Make yourself indispensable and you will move up. Act as though you are indispensable and you will move out.

* * *

I am but one,
But I am one.
I cannot do everything,
But I can do something.
What I can do
I ought to do.
And what I ought to do,
With God's help,
I will do.

* * *

At a crossroad in France stood a life-size statue of Christ with arms outstretched to the passers-by. A look of inviting tenderness and compassion shone from His face. His imploring eyes seemed to say, "Come unto me all ye that labour and are heavy laden, and I will give you rest."

One day, during World War I, a fierce battle raged near the statue. Its outstretched arms and hands were blown away by the concussion of shells. Later someone inscribed on the pedestal the words: *Christ has no hands but your hands.*

How true are these words!
　　　　—W. B. K.

Illustrations

Mental Workers — More Sleep

Mental workers who want to avoid "that tired feeling" must realize that the man who works with his brains requires more sleep than the man who earns his living with his muscle. Studies show that while it takes only about four hours sleep to restore our physical energies, it takes twice as long to replenish energy expended in mental efforts. Experiments at Colgate University have shown that while manual workers could accomplish their jobs efficiently on four to five hours sleep a night, mental workers required an additional four hours to turn in a par performance. When a brainworker loses two hours sleep, his efficiency next day not only suffers, but he accumulates twice as much fatigue in the performance of his duties.

—John E. Gibson, *"Think"*

* * *

All V. I. P.'s

All have a share in the beauty
All have a part in the plan;
What does it matter what duty
Falls to the lot of man?

Someone must blend the plaster
And someone must carry the stone;
Neither the man nor the master
Ever has builded alone.

Making a roof from the weather
Or building a house for a king,
Only by working together have men
Ever accomplished a thing.

—*Selected*

* * *

Wreckers and Builders

I watched them tearing a building
down —
A gang of men in a big town.
With a heave ho and a lusty yell
They swung a beam and the sidewalk
fell.
I asked the foreman, "Are these men
skilled?
The kind you would hire if you wanted
to build?"

He laughed and said, "Why, no indeed,
Just labor, common labor, is all I need.
They can easily wreck in a day or two
What builders have taken years to do."
I asked myself as I went my way
Which of these roles have I played to-
day?

As a builder who works with care
Measuring life by ruling square?
Shaping my deeds by the vertical plane,
Or . . . am I the wrecker who lost the
town
Beset with the labor of tearing down?

—*Selected*

* * *

Working Hours of Birds

"Our hours," said a nature student,
"are nothing to the birds." Why, some
birds work in the summer nineteen hours
a day. Indefatigably they clear the
crops of insects.

"The thrush gets up at 2:30 every
morning. He rolls up his sleeves and
falls to work at once, and he never stops
till 9:30 at night. A clear nineteen
hours. During that time he feeds his
voracious young two hundred and six
times.

The blackbird starts work at the same
time as the thrush, but he lays off earlier. His whistle blows at 7:30, and
during his seventeen-hour day he sets
about one hundred meals before his
kiddies.

"The titmouse is up and about at
three in the morning, and his stopping
time is nine at night. A fast worker,
the titmouse is said to feed his young
four hundred and seventeen meals —
meals of caterpillar mainly — in the
long, hard, hot day."

—*Green's Fruit-Grower*

* * *

An Unfailing Remedy

A great physician gave the following
prescription for work: "If your health
is threatened, work. If disappointments
come, work. If you inherit riches, continue to work. If your faith falters and
you become a bundle of nerves, work.
If your dreams are shattered, and the
star of hope begins to darken on your
horizon, work. If sorrow overwhelms
you, or friends prove untrue and desert
you, work. If you are joyous, keep
right on working. Idleness brings doubt
and fear. No matter what ails you,
work. Work as if your life were in
peril, for it is!" —W. B. K.

* * *

This World a Vestibule

This world is but a vestibule of an
immortal life, and every chord of our
life touches some other chord which will
vibrate in eternity. Stern taskmaster's
opportunity is bald behind and must be
seized by the forelock. This world is
full of tragic might-have-beens. We
cannot stick the share into the ground
when we should be wielding the sickle.
No remorse, no regret, no self-accusa-
tion can avail one jot when the time
for sowing is past and unless our
lives are filled each moment with the
tasks apportioned to us we will, throughout eternity, regret lost opportunities!

—*Ivan Maclaren*

Quick! Quick!

As one of the early translators of the Bible was finishing his work, he felt death coming on. "Quick! Quick!" he said to the copyist. "All is done, but a portion of a chapter." He began to dictate rapidly. The penman pushed himself to the limit and the task was completed. The Bible had been translated into the language of the common people. The lips of the translator moved feebly. The faithful scribe, bending low, caught his last words: "Glory be to the Father, and to the Son, and to the Holy Ghost!"

Let us so give ourselves to our apportioned task that when we face life's setting sun we can say, "I have finished the work which Thou gavest me to do!"
—W. B. K.

. . .

Worked by Clock Without Hands

"Work," declared Thomas A. Edison, "is measured not by hours, but by what is accomplished." Edison always kept a clock without hands on his desk. He believed that rewarding toil called for 2 per cent inspiration and 98 per cent perspiration. Those who have wrought most mightily for God and man have usually been short sleepers. Sir Isaac Newton seldom went to bed before 2 A.M. David Livingstone worked in a factory from 6 A.M. until 8 P.M. Then he went to night school for two hours and studied far into the night until his mother took his books from him. "Praying Hyde" was known as "the man who never slept!"

Heights by great men won and kept
 Were not attained by sudden flight,
But they, while their companions slept,
 Were toiling upward in the night.

"I must work the works of him that sent me, while it is day: the night cometh, when no man can work" (John 9:4). —W. B. K.

The Easy Road Crowded

The easy roads are crowded,
 And the level roads are jammed;
The pleasant little rivers
 With the drifting folks are crammed,
But off yonder where it's rocky
 Where you get a better view,
You will find the ranks are thinning
 And the travelers are few.

Where the going's smooth and pleasant
 You will always find the throng,
For the many, more's the pity,
 Seem to like to drift along;
But the steps that call for courage,
 And the task that's hard to do,
In the end results in glory
 For the never-wavering few.
—*Selected*

. . .

The Workman

He was a humble workman
 With the tools with which he wrought.
And he built a common stable,
 Or so it was, he thought!

And he fashioned there a manger
 Where the cattle could be fed,
Never thinking that the Saviour
 Would pillow there His head.

He had only built a stable
 With a manger in the stall,
Yet it cradled there the Christ-child,
 Who is King and Lord of all!

So although our task be humble,
 Let us work each day with care;
For we may not know God's purpose,
 Or why He placed us there.

For the manger that formed the cradle
 Of our Lord and Saviour here,
Was built by a humble workman
 In Bethlehem of Judea.

—Dr. Henry B. Knox

WORLDLINESS

Short Quotes

On one of his seemingly endless marches in Egypt, Napoleon's soldiers were famishing for water. As they trudged onward, a shout was heard from the fore ranks, "Water! Water! Water!" Lifting their weary eyes toward the horizon, they saw what appeared to be a lake. Its waters shimmered and sparkled in the glazing sun. The soldiers ran in the direction of the blue "waters." But as they ran, the lake receded. To their utter dismay and despair, they saw that what seemed to be a lake of refreshing waters was only a mirage in the desert! The illusive, ephemeral delusive sinful pleasures of the world are also only a mirage.

—Told by Dr. George W. Truett

* * *

The "world" is a spirit, and is expressed in things. It defies exact definition because it is a spirit. The closest working definition I have found is that of John Wesley: "Whatever cools my affection toward Christ is the world."

—Dr. V. Raymond Edman

* * *

Opposition! It is a bad sign for the Christianity of this day that it provokes so little opposition. If there were no other evidence of its being wrong, I should know it from that. When the church and the world can go along comfortably together, you may be sure there is something wrong. The world has not altered. Its spirit is exactly the same as it ever was; and if Christians were equally faithful and devoted to the Lord, and separated from the world, living so that their lives were a reproof to all ungodliness, the world would hate them as much as it ever did. It is the church that has altered, not the world.

—Catherine Booth

* * *

"What do you consider a good rule of life?" someone asked Dr. J. Wilbur Chapman. He replied, "This rule governs my life — anything that dims my vision of Christ, or takes away my taste for Bible study, or cramps my prayer life, or makes Christian work more difficult, is wrong for me and I must, as a Christian, turn away from it."

—*Pilgrim Holiness Advocate*

* * *

There was a Scotchman who had a dress shirt which he wore on special occasions. After he had used it several times, he would question its cleanness

and take it to the window for better light. His wife's words were very wise: "If it's doubtful, it's dirty!"

—Dr. V. Raymond Edman

* * *

A boy who wanted to be helpful to his mother would stand by her as she prepared the evening meal. In his eager desire to lighten her work he would ask, "Mother, may I put the bread on the table?" Mother would always reply, "My son, are your hands clean?" Years later he was desirous to give to others God's bread of life and his mother's voice, though long stilled in death, came to him, "My son, are your hands clean?"

"Be ye clean that bear the vessels of the Lord" (Isa. 52:11). —W. B. K.

* * *

A business friend invited Dr. Walter L. Wilson to attend an event which was confessedly not proper for a Christian to attend. "Thank you," said Dr. Wilson, "I'll be there; and may I bring my Friend with me?" "Of course, you may. By the way, who is your friend?" asked the business friend. "He is the Lord Jesus Christ," said Dr. Wilson. "Well," came the reply, "I don't think that He would enjoy the party." Said Dr. Wilson, "If He wouldn't enjoy it, neither would I. I must respectfully decline your invitation." —W. B. K.

* * *

All the water in the world,
However hard it tried,
Could never sink a ship
Unless it got inside.

All the evil in the world,
The wickedness and sin,
Can never sink the soul's craft
Unless it got inside.

* * *

A fine Christian woman once testified: "Shortly after I was married, I lived in a community in which many of the ladies spent much of their time in social affairs, some of which were not necessarily evil but of no lasting value in relation to the judgment seat of Christ. Before I realized it, I found myself enmeshed in an endless round of social functions. I was neglecting my home, prayer, and Bible study. I knew I had to make a choice between the world and giving Christ *first place* in my life. How I praise Him for the decision I made to follow Him!"

—W. B. K.

Illustrations

Why He Sold His Violin

More than once I heard the late Gypsy Smith relate the story of his father's conversion. He heard the message of salvation, and, with penitence, received the Saviour as his own. That evening he returned to his motherless children in the gypsy wagon, and related to them all he knew of the Saviour and of the Scriptures. Then he prayed with them, setting up a family altar the first night of his new life in Christ. The following morning he repeated the whole matter again. Then he went back to town, and took with him the dearest treasure of a gypsy's heart, his violin. On returning home that night, he was without it, for he had sold it. He had sufficient spiritual insight that first day of salvation to realize that the old association with drinking and dancing places, where he had used his violin, would be inconsistent with his stand for Christ, and detrimental to his own conscience. We are glad for those whose background allows them to play the violin for God's glory, but whatever is inconsistent to us and to others must be abandoned.

—Dr. V. Raymond Edman

* * *

I'm That Clown!

"I am suffering from such an overwhelming depression that life has become unbearable," said a patient to a well-known psychiatrist. "Try lively amusement, or try a lively novel. This may take your thoughts from yourself and prove better than any medicine I might prescribe," said the doctor. The patient shook his head gravely, as he stared vacantly and despairingly at the doctor. "Ah," said the medic, "I think I know what will lift you out of your despondency. I want you to go to the circus tonight. There you will see the antics of a world-famed clown. His clowning is the talk of the city, and his merriment is contagious!" Blank despair deepened on the face of the patient as he sadly said, "But doctor, I'm that clown!" —W. B. K.

* * *

I Don't Know Where to Draw the Line

A teen-age girl was converted and filled with love for her Lord. She wanted to please Him in all that she did. "I want to be the best kind of a witness for my Lord, but I don't know where to draw the line," she said to her pastor. "There are certain kinds of worldly pleasures that other Christian young people seem to think are all right. I don't want to go to any place where I cannot take my Lord," she said.

The pastor was understanding and sympathetic. "Elizabeth, Christ is now your Companion. Will your going to questionable places strengthen your daily walk with Him? Can you invite Jesus to accompany you and take part in these things? Should Jesus come when you are in some questionable place, would you be ashamed to be there?" "Thank you, pastor," said Elizabeth. "When I am in doubt about anything, I will give Jesus the benefit of the doubt, and seek to please Him in all that I do." —W. B. K.

* * *

No Half Measures

There is no very great measure of joy in a half-hearted Christian life. Many so-called Christians have just enough religion to make them miserable. They can no longer enjoy the world, and they have not entered into the "joy of the Lord." There they stand, deprived of the "leeks, and the onions, and the garlic" of Egypt, and without the milk and honey and the finest of the wheat of Canaan. That is a wretched place to be in. The way out is simple — absolute surrender to God. Then your joy will be fulfilled. There is but one way to find that fullness of joy — a surrendered life. A will and life completely surrendered to the God of love will bring joy under all circumstances. —R. A. Torrey

WORRY

Short Quotes

Worry is the advance interest you pay on troubles that seldom come.

* * *

"Doctor, I'm all run down," said a patient to a psychiatrist. "No, madam, you are not all run down. You are all wound up!" replied the doctor.

* * *

Worry, like a rocking chair, will give you something to do, but it won't get you anywhere. —Rev. Vance Havner

* * *

To worry means we are mentally normal. The more we worry, the smarter we are likely to be, since worry is trial-and-error thinking about problems. Civilization and all scientific progress are indebted to the worriers of the past. —Dr. George W. Crane, psychologist

* * *

To try to stop worrying completely is a waste of energy. It is perfectly natural and normal to worry about real dangers or threats. It is abnormal not to be concerned about them. —Dr. John E. Gibson

* * *

What does your anxiety do? It does not empty tomorrow of its sorrow, but it empties today of its strength. It does not make you escape the evil — it makes you unfit to cope with it if it comes. —Ian Maclaren

* * *

Blessed is the man who is too busy to worry in the daytime and too sleepy to worry at night. —Phil Marquart, M.D.

* * *

A Negro woman lived to be ninety years old. When asked the secret of her longevity, she said, "When I works, I work hard, when I sits, I sits easy and when I worries, I go to sleep!" —W. B. K.

Never bear more than one trouble at a time. Some people bear three kinds — all they ever had, all they have now, and all they expect to have. —Edward Everett Hale

* * *

Quiet minds cannot be perplexed or frightened, but go on in fortune or misfortune at their own private pace, like a clock during a thunderstorm. —Robert Louis Stevenson

* * *

Most people seem unaware that to be unworried in the face of distressing reality situations may often be a symptom of a serious mental disorder. —Dr. Judd Marmor, psychiatrist

* * *

I complained because I had no shoes until I met a man who had no feet. —An Arab proverb

* * *

"I hear you have a good crop of potatoes this year, Mrs. Higgins. That must cheer your heart," said a neighbor. "Aye, they're good enough, but where's the bad-uns to feed the pigs?"

* * *

"How is it that you are always so cheerful?" a friend asked Bishop William Burt. "The remark of a little child I once heard taught me the uselessness of grumbling and complaining. The child's father was a good man, but a chronic complainer. As I sat with them in their home, the subject of food came up. 'What do I like best?' the father asked his daughter. 'You? Why, Daddy, you like mostly everything we haven't got!'" —W. B. K.

* * *

The beginning of anxiety is the end of faith. The beginning of true faith is the end of anxiety. —George Muller

Illustrations

Don't Forget Past Mercies

There was an old lady who dearly loved her Lord. She delighted to speak of His past mercies and how He had cared for her needs over the years. When her little reserve of money got low, however, she became very fearful. "It will not last long," she sadly said.

A neighbor said to her, "What has happened to your memory? You used to tell me so much about the Lord's goodness to you. Since you have stopped remembering His past goodness, you have become fearful. You had better start remembering the Lord's past mercies!"

Later, the old lady said to her pastor, "What a much-needed rebuke I received from that neighbor! And to think she isn't even a Christian!" —W. B. K.

* * *

Let Not Your Heart Be Troubled

Though all the world be troubled,
  And men's hearts faint with fear
At the danger in the distance
  And dangers drawing near;
Though every help should fail them
  On which their hopes are stayed,
"Let not your heart be troubled,
  Nor let it be afraid."

Though all the earth be troubled,
  And its foundations shake,
Though raging seas shall thunder,
  And mighty mountains quake;
Though lofty walls shall crumble
  And in the dust be laid,
"Let not your heart be troubled,
  Nor let it be afraid."

Though all your way be troubled,
  And bounds and landmarks lost,
Though on the stormy billows
  Your little bark be tossed,
Though all around be changing,
  Here let your mind be stayed,
"Let not your heart be troubled,
  Nor let it be afraid."
      —Annie Johnson Flint

* * *

A Spiritual St. Vitus

Thank God, some dear old things do not change. We work ourselves into a mental and spiritual St. Vitus. We make mountains out of our molehill concerns and think wisdom will die with us. It is refreshing to remember that, long after our stormy issues have been forgotten, plain things like spring and mocking-birds will endure. Why so hot, little man? You are dizzy from modernity's merry-go-round. Your storming and shouting will bring you only high blood pressure. Calm yourself: "the woods are green and the mockingbird is singing" back home!

Let me relax, throw open the windows of my stuffy little soul and let the cooling breezes of a better world sweep through! What will all my petty worries amount to fifty years from now? I will rejoice in the old simplicities which no man can take away — like spring and green woods and mocking-birds. And, better still, I will rest my soul in the goodness of God and His amazing grace, that saves a poor sinner like me.
      —Vance Havner in
       By the Still Waters

* * *

Green Pastures

Last night I started counting sheep
  When I had gone to bed,
For I had worries large and small
  Which drove sleep from my head.
The sheep had many little lambs,
  And these I counted too;
Thus through the flock I went until
  The shepherd came in view.
And then I thought, "Why spend my time
  In simply counting sheep
When I can walk with Him and pray
  For folk who cannot sleep?"
I walked with Him a while, and then
  He smiled and said to me,
"Look back; where are your worries now?"
  But not one could I see!
      —Mildred Allen Jeffery

* * *

Useless Anxiety

A couple started off to ride to a friend. The morning was pleasant, and they enjoyed themselves until they happened to remember a certain bridge which was very old and probably unsafe. "I shall never dare to go over that bridge," exclaimed the wife; "and we can't get across the river any other way!" "Oh," said the man, "I forgot that bridge. It is a bad place; suppose it should break through and we should fall into the water and be drowned!" "Or," said the woman, adding to his complaint, "suppose you should step on a rotten plank and break your leg; what would become of me and the baby?" "I don't know," responded the husband, "what would become of any of us, for I couldn't work, and we should all starve to death!" So the lugubrious talk ran on until they reached the spot where the old bridge had stood — and lo, they discovered that since they had been there it had been replaced with a new one! All their anxiety had been worse than useless.

—*King's Business*

WORSHIP

Illustrations

Deepfreeze Worship

Operation Deepfreeze was the U.S. Navy's expedition to the Antarctic where intrepid men were bedded down at Little America and where the temperature went to ninety degrees below zero. Dr. Paul A. Siple, a scientist, was a member of the exploration group. He radioed a message to the Friendship Bible Class which he taught at the Calvary Baptist Church, Washington, D. C., saying, "We are having regular Sunday services in which Scripture is read and hymns are sung."

A London housewife had the correct idea. Over the sink in the kitchen of her small apartment she hung a motto which read: "Divine worship conducted here three times daily!"

Though we may worship God anywhere, there is no substitute for collective worship in God's house on the Lord's day: "Not forsaking the assembling of ourselves together, as the manner of some is; but exhorting one another" (Heb. 10:25). —W. B. K.

* * *

Heathen and Christian Idols

A missionary became greatly interested in the conversion of a Brahman. The Brahman, however, had seen too much grasping greed among merchants and government officials from so-called Christian nations. He listened with respect to the missionary. At the end of the conversation he placed a little image and a gold coin on a table. He wrote something on a slip of paper and placed it beside the image. Then he wrote on another slip of paper and placed it beside the gold coin. He said to the missionary, "Read these." The note beside the image read: "Heathen idol." The note beside the coin read, "Christian idol." —W. B. K.

What Is Worship?

It is the soul searching for its counterpart.

It is a thirsty land crying out for rain.

It is a man listening through a tornado for the Still Small Voice.

It is a sheep lost in the wilderness pleading for rescue by the Good Shepherd.

It is a soul standing in awe before the mystery of the universe.

It is a poet enthralled by the beauty of sunrise.

It is a workman pausing a moment to listen to a strain of music.

It is a hungry heart seeking for love.

It is a man climbing the altar stairs to God.

—Dwight Jaques Bradley, D.D.

* * *

Why She Was There

An elderly lady was stone-deaf. She was always present at the worship services of her church unless she was ill. "Do give me the secret of your loyalty to God's house," her pastor said to her one day. She answered: "Even though I can't hear one word you say, I love God's house and the fellowship of God's children. When in His house, I feel that I am in direct touch with God. I know the Saviour is meeting with us. It is not enough for me to worship God alone at home. It is my duty and privilege to worship Him publicly in the church service." —W. B. K.

* * *

As God Sees It

A story is told in which a man went to church with an angel as his guide. Every seat in the church was filled, but there was something strange about it all. The organist moved his fingers over the keys, but no music came forth from the pipes. The choir arose to sing, and their lips moved, but not a sound was to be heard. The pastor stepped to the pulpit to read the Scriptures, but not a sound was heard.

The congregation joined in repeating the prayer, but not a single sound was heard. The pastor again stepped to the pulpit, and went through all the motions of preaching, but the man with the angel heard nothing. So he turned to the angel and said,

"What does this mean? I see that a service is being held, but I hear nothing."

The angel replied, "You hear nothing because there is nothing to be heard. You see this service just as God sees it. These are not putting their hearts into it, and so God hears nothing. He hears only that which comes from the heart, and not that which comes from the lips only."

As the angel was speaking, back in the last pew they heard a child saying, "Our Father, which art in heaven, hallowed be thy name," etc. The angel said, "You are hearing the only part of this service that God hears. He hears this little child's prayer because she means what she says, and puts her heart and soul in it." —*The Gospel for Youth*

* * *

What Made the Difference

Many years ago a tourist attended a service in a Scottish church. She greatly enjoyed the sermon and was spiritually blessed. Later she asked who the minister was. "He was Ebenezer Erskine," she was told. "I will surely hear him again next Lord's Day. He is wonderful!" She did this, but she got little out of the sermon. It seemed to lack power. She related her experience to Erskine, who said, "Ah, Madam, last Sunday you came here to worship the Lord Jesus and to hear His voice. Today you came to hear me and exalt me in your heart. That's why you are going away spiritually empty!"
—W. B. K.

* * *

Worship God

A grateful father and mother knelt at the feet of a medical missionary, to worship her as a god, for she had restored their child to health. Hastily the missionary cried out to them, "We are not gods. Worship the true God."

"You must be a god," they said; "no one but a god could have saved our child."

"Suppose," said the missionary, "that I wished to bestow a valuable gift upon you and sent it by the hand of one of my coolies; whom would you thank, the coolie or myself?"

"We would thank you, of course; the coolie is your servant."

"And so I am God's coolie, by whose hand God has been pleased to send you this gift of healing, and it is to Him you must now give thanks."
—*The Sunday School Times*

* * *

A Prescription for Worship

Enter the place of worship a little before the service begins. Enter expectantly. God has promised to meet you there. Whisper a prayer. When the first hymn is announced, open your hymnal to that place. If you cannot sing, follow the words. Bow your head and close your eyes during the prayer. As you give, pray that God will accept the gift. During the special music, be attentive and prayerful. When the minister preaches, pray for him and listen attentively. Be silent except to sing or to say "Amen!"
—*Evangelical Friend*

* * *

Worship God

A visiting minister was substituting for the famed pastor Henry Ward Beecher. A large audience had assembled to hear the popular pastor. At the appointed hour, the visiting minister entered the pulpit. Learning that Beecher was not to preach, several began to move toward the doors. The visiting minister stood and called out, "All who have come here today to worship Henry Ward Beecher may now withdraw from the church! All who have come to worship God, keep your seats!" —W. B. K.

* * *

I Sit Quietly

"What is true worship?" a missionary asked a class of young native Christians. A shy fellow stood and said, "I think I know, but I may not be able to say it so others will understand. Before I knew my Saviour, I used to go late to church. Now I love to go real early, sit quietly, think about Jesus and His great love for me!" Then, with tears running down his face, he said, "Oh, I love Him! Because He loves me, and because I love Him, I want to please Him in all I do and say!" —W. B. K.

* * *

When God Is But a Name

The Jewish rabbis had an interesting tradition concerning the withdrawal of God's glory from the temple. There came a time when the Shekinah, the holy flame in the cloud, having waited for His people to return to their God, departed from the Holy of Holies unto the Mount of Olives, where it waited for three days, if perchance they would repent, and then went "unto his own place." When such a thing had happened, all the outer observances and posturings no longer had any meaning or value. From such a spiritual "recession," what tragic consequences flow!

Ah, dark the shrine whence Light has
    gone!
Cold, cold the altar when the flame
Is quenched, and desolate and lone
My soul when God is but a name!

—Daniel Heitmeyer in
The Watchman-Examiner

YOUTH

Illustrations

Only Abusive, Fault-finding Words

A teen-ager in Muncie, Indiana, was brought into juvenile court. She was in real trouble. A policewoman won the confidence of the girl, who bared her heart to the officer. "My mom and dad live like cats and dogs. They drink and smoke. They never speak encouraging words to me — only abusive, fault-finding words. I tried to go straight, but it was hard to do it with no help from my parents!"

This teen-ager's plight is typical of many others who have godless homes where the name of God is mentioned only in profanity and where strife and confusion reign. How right was J. Edgar Hoover when he said, "Criminals are not born — they are home-grown."

—Rev. J. Claire Peters

* * *

Youth Gangs Not New

Sometimes we talk as if this generation had invented juvenile delinquency, as well as the phrase for it.

A corrective to this view is to be found in the diary of George Templeton Strong, a New York lawyer, whose daily observations from 1835 to 1875 form one of the great documents in American history.

In 1851, one gathers from his notes, delinquency often started even before the "teen-age" was properly under way. Here is what he had to say about the bad girls in New York:

"No one can walk the length of Broadway without meeting some hideous troop of ragged girls, from twelve years old down, brutalized already almost beyond redemption by premature vice, clad in the filthy refuse of the rag-picker's collections, obscene of speech, the stamp of childhood gone from their faces, hurrying along with harsh laughter and foulness on their lips that some of them have learned by rote, yet too young to understand it; with thief written in their cunning eyes. . . . On a rainy day such crews may be seen by dozens. They haunt every other crossing and skulk away together, when the sun comes out and the mud is dry again. And such a group I think the most revolting object that the social diseases of a great city can produce. A gang of black-guard boys is lovely by the side of it."

—*The Chicago Daily News*

* * *

A Diamond in the Rough

One night a boy stood under a street lamp, swearing like a sailor. Dr. Homer

Stuntz, who believed in the limitless possibilities of even bad boys when changed by God's grace, approached the boy and began jollying with him. The friendly approach seemed to cause the boy to swear all the more. Not daunted by the boy's profanity, and seeing beneath his rough exterior great potentialities, the gentleman invited him to become a member of his Sunday-school class. The boy promised to attend, but failed to do so. The faithful teacher did not become discouraged, but continued to invite him to his class.

Finally the boy began to attend the class. He was bullheaded, irreverent, and the "worst boy in the class." He constantly asked questions which nobody could answer. Somehow the faithful and patient teacher saw behind the tricky questions great intelligence. Time passed. Then, one day, Dr. Stuntz said, "My boy, how would you like to go to college?" "The best in the world," replied the boy with a twinkle in his eye. He became a student at Northwestern University, where he made good. Later he became a professional ball player. One Sunday afternoon he heard the gospel preached in Chicago's skid row. He was convicted of sin and converted to the Saviour.

Who was that boy in whom a Sunday-school teacher saw great possibilities and made an investment the dividends of which can never be fully computed this side of the judgment seat of Christ? *Billy Sunday*, the world-famed evangelist, whose faithful preaching and soul-winning ministry brought many to Christ.

Of that faithful Sunday-school teacher, Billy Sunday said after fame came to him, "You are the one who started me in the right direction." —W. B. K.

* * *

The Other Side

Are young people terribly bad nowadays? Some are. Not for one moment would we minimize the seriousness of the juvenile-delinquency problem. The appalling increase of crimes committed by teen-agers is a call to earnest prayer for revival. But there is another side — a brighter one. A front-page news item in a daily newspaper brought the

other side to our attention some time ago. Two short paragraphs told the story of the senior class in an Illinois high school. The twenty-five members of the class voted that the $800 they had saved for a six-day vacation trip to the Ozarks be given to their adviser whose house had been burned down. Given the challenge and opportunity, today's youth will show a spirit of chivalry, unselfishness and heroism equal to the finest presentations of any age. Let's thank God for our young people, and by example and appreciation for them and belief in them inspire them to great things for God and others!

—*The Standard*

* * *

Going to the Dogs

My grandfather in his house of logs
  Said the young folks are going to the dogs,
His grandfather in the Flemish bogs
  Said the young folks are going to the dogs.

And his grandfather in his long, skin togs
  Said the young folks are going to the dogs!
There is but one thing that I have to state:
  The dogs are having a mighty long wait!

—*Selected*

* * *

Give to Christ Your Youthful Years

A Sunday-school teacher became deeply concerned for the conversion of a teen-age girl in her class. Lovingly and earnestly she spoke to the girl on the all-important subject — her soul's salvation. The girl listened respectfully. She decided against Christ, saying that in later years she would give consideration to her relationship to Christ. The teacher went away with a sad heart. On her way home, she thought of a novel plan to impress on the girl the unfairness of giving her youthful years to sin and then turning to Christ for forgiveness. Stopping at a florist's shop she bought a dozen beautiful roses. She kept the roses in the florist's box for several days. Then she sent them to the girl. The girl was elated to receive the gift until she opened the box and saw the faded and wilted flowers. "Some practical joke has been played on me," she said disgustedly.

Shortly thereafter the teacher called on the girl again. The girl told her about the faded roses she had received. "I sent them," said the teacher. "When you chose not to give Christ your youthful years, you decided to present to Him later a life faded and withered like those roses!" The girl answered, "Teacher, I see it. It will not be that way. I will give myself to Christ right now and live for His glory." —W. B. K.